A Companion to the Works of Arthur Schnitzler

Studies in German Literature, Linguistics, and Culture

Edited by James Hardin
(South Carolina)

Camden House Companion Volumes

The Camden House Companions provide well-informed and
up-to-date critical commentary on the most significant aspects
of major works, periods, or literary figures. The Companions
may be read profitably by the reader with a general interest in
the subject. For the benefit of student and scholar, quotations
are provided in the original language.

A Companion to the Works of
Arthur Schnitzler

Edited by
Dagmar C. G. Lorenz

CAMDEN HOUSE

First published 2003
by Camden House

Camden House is an imprint of Boydell & Brewer Inc.
668 Mt. Hope Avenue, Rochester, NY 14620 USA
and of Boydell & Brewer Limited
PO Box 9, Woodbridge, Suffolk IP12 3DF, UK

ISBN: 1–57113–213–9

Library of Congress Cataloging-in-Publication Data

A companion to the works of Arthur Schnitzler / edited by Dagmar C. G.
  Lorenz.
    p. cm. — (Studies in German literature, linguistics, and culturex)
Includes bibliographical references and index.
ISBN 1–57113–213–9 (alk. paper)
    1. Schnitzler, Arthur, 1862–1931—Criticism and interpretation.
I. Series: Studies in German literature, linguistics, and culture (Un-
numbered)

PT2638.N5 Z8176 2003
833'.8 — dc21

                                                          2002153168

A catalogue record for this title is available from the British Library.

This publication is printed on acid-free paper.
Printed in the United States of America.

Contents

The Legacy

Arthur Schnitzler

Principal Works by Year of First Appearance

When available in translation, English title and date of appearance are given.

1885	"Er wartet auf den vazierenden Gott" (short story)
1888	"Das Abenteuer seines Lebens," one-act play; "Paracelsus," one-act play (Paracelsus, 1995)
1889	"Über funktionelle Aporie und ihe Behandlung durch Hypnose und Suggestion"
	"Anatol," one act (Anatol. Prologue, 1986)
	"Amerika," "Mein Freund Ypsilon," "Der Andere" (short narratives; poems)
1890	"Alkandi's Lied" (dramatic poem)
	"Die Frage and das Schicksal," (A Question of Fate, 1986) "Anatols Hochzeitsmorgen" (dramatic scenes, Anatol cycle)
1891	"Das Märchen" (drama)
	"Weihnachtseinkäufe," (Christmas Shopping, 1986)
	"Reichtum" short story (Riches, 1977)
	"Abschiedssouper" (A Farewell Dinner, 1986)
1892	"Der Sohn. Aus den Papieren eines Arztes," novella (The Son, 1977)
1893	*Anatol*, dramatic cycle (engl.: *Anatol*, 1917; 1999)
1894	"Blumen" (Flowers, 1913), "Die drei Elixiere," "Sterben" (Dying, 1977), "Der Witwer" (The Widower, 1986) — short stories
1895	*Sterben* (book edition)
	"Die kleine Komödie," novella (The Little Comedy, 1977)

1896   *Liebelei,* drama (Light-o'-love, 1912; Playing With Love, 1914; Love Games, 1983; Dalliance, 1986; Flirtation, 1999); "Die überspannte Person," drama (The High Strung Woman, 1986)

"Ein Abschied," short story (The Farewell, 1913)

1897   "Die Frau des Weisen" (The Wife of the Wise Man, 1926; The Sage's Wife, 1913), "Der Ehrentag," "Die Toten schweigen" (The Dead Are Silent 1913; 1986, The Dead Don't Tell, 1975) (short stories)

"Halbzwei," drama (One-thirty, 1986)

1898   *Die Frau des Weisen,* short stories ("Die Frau des Weisen," "Ein Abschied," "Der Ehrentag," "Blumen," "Die Toten schweigen")

Freiwild (drama)

1899   "Der grüne Kakadu," drama (The Green Cockatoo, 1914; 1995; 1999; At the Green Cockatoo, 1986), *Das Vermächtnis,* drama (*The Reckoning,* 1907; *The Legacy,* 1911), *Die Gefährtin* (dramas, book editions)

"Um eine Stunde" (narrative)

1900   "Der blinde Geronimo und sein Bruder" (Blind Geronimo and his Brother, 1913; 1929, 1986; The Blind Man and his Brother, 1975), "Leutnant Gustl" (None But the Brave, 1931; Lieutenant Gustl, 1982) — novellas

"Reigen" (drama, 200 copies, Hands Around, 1914; *Merry-go-round,* 1952; The Love Game, 1956; La Ronde, 1954; The Round Dance, 1983, *The Blue Room,* 1999)

1901   "Frau Bertha Garlan," "Lebendige Stunden," narratives (Living Hours, 1977)

"Sylvesternacht. Ein Dialog," drama (New Year's Eve, 1986)

Leutnant Gustl

Der Schleier der Beatrice

Frau Bertha Garlan, novel (*Bertha Garlan. A Novel,* 1914).

1902   "Die Fremde," (The Stranger, 1929), "Andreas Thameyers letzter Brief" (Andreas Thameyer's Last Letter, 1929), "Die griechische Tänzerin," (Greek Dancer, 1924; The Greek Dancing Girl, 1929), "Exzentrik" (narratives)

Lebendige Stunden. Vier Einakter, one-act plays ("Lebendige Stunden" [Living Hours, 1906]; "Die Frau mit dem Dolche" [The Lady With the Dagger, 1904]; "Die letzten Masken"; "Literatur" [Literature, 1914, 1918])

1903   "Der Puppenspieler," one-act play (The Puppeteer, 1966)

        "Die grüne Kravatte" (short story)

        Reigen (book edition)

1904   "Der tapfere Cassian," musical one-act drama (*Gallant Cassian. A Puppet Play in One Act,* 1914)

        "Das Schicksal des Freiherrn von Leisenbohg," novella (The Fate of the Baron, 1929)

        Der einsame Weg, drama (The Lonely Way, 1915; 1924)

1905   "Das neue Lied," novella; "Die Weissagung," novella (The Prophecy, 1929)

        "Zum großen Wurstl" (burlesque)

        Die griechische Tänzerin, novellas, book edition: "Der blinde Geronimo und sein Bruder," "Andreas Thameyers letzter Brief," "Ekzentrik," "Die griechische Tänzerin"

1906   *Zwischenspiel,* comedy (Intermezzo, 1915; 1924); *Der Ruf des Lebens,* drama; *Marionetten,* three one-act plays, "Der Puppenspieler," "Der tapfere Cassian," "Zum großen Wurstl" (Marionettes, The Puppeteer, The Gallant Cassian, The Great Puppet Show, all 1995)

1907   "Die Geschichte eines Genies," novella, "Der tote Gabriel," novella (Dead Gabriel, 1929)

        Dämmerseelen. Novellen ("Das Schicksal des Freiherrn von Leisenbohg," "Die Weissagung," "Das neue Lied," "Die Fremde," "Andreas Thameyers letzter Brief"); "Die Verwandlung des Pierrot," pantomime (The Transformation of Pierrot, 1995)

1908   "Komtesse Mizzi oder Der Familientag," drama (Countess Mizzie, 1915; 1924)

        "Der Tod des Junggesellen," short story (The Death of a Bachelor, 1929; A Confirmed Bachelor, 1974; The Death of the Bachelor, 1975)

1908   *Der Weg ins Freie,* novel (*The Road in the Open,* 1913)

1910   *Der junge Medardus* (drama)

         Der Schleier der Pierrette. Pantomime in drei Bildern, libretto (The Veil of Pierrette, 1995)

1911   "Die dreifache Warnung," novella; "Der Mörder," novella (The Murderer, 1929); "Die Hirtenflöte" (The Shepherd's Pipe, 1922); "Das Tagebuch der Redegonda," novella (Redegonda's Diary, 1915)

         Das weite Land, drama (*The Vast Domain,* 1923; The Undiscovered Country, 1980)

1912   *Professor Bernhardi,* comedy (*The anti-Semites: Professor Bernhardi,* 1920; *Professor Bernhardi. A Play,* 1936; *Professor Bernhardi and Other Plays,* 1995)

         Novellen ("Die Hirtenflöte," "Der Tod des Junggesellen," "Der Mörder," "Der tote Gabriel," "Das Tagebuch der Redegonda," "Die dreifache Warnung")

         Gesammelte Werke in zwei Abteilungen

1913   *Frau Beate und ihr Sohn,* novel (Beatrice, 1926; Mother and Son, 1974)

         Elskovsleg (silent film based on *Liebelei*)

1915   *Komödie der Worte,* three one-act plays (*Comedies of Words,* 1918, 1995: "Stunde des Erkennens" [The Hour of Recognition, 1918, 1995]; "Große Szene" [The Big Scene, 1918; 1995]; "Das Bacchusfest" [The Festival of Bacchus, 1918; The Bachanale, 1995])

1916   "Meine Stellung als Ahnherr der jüdischen Literatur" (debate with Stefan Zweig)

1917   *Doktor Gräsler, Badearzt,* novella (*Dr. Graesler,* 1930)

         Fink und Fliederbusch, comedy (Fink and Fliederbusch, 1995)

1918   *Casanovas Heimfahrt,* novella (*Casanova's Return to Venice,* 1930; *Casanova's Homecoming,* 1959)

1919   *Die Schwestern oder Casanova in Spa* (drama)

         Drei Akte in einem

1921   *The Affairs of Anatol* (silent film, USA)

1923 *Der junge Medardus* (silent film, Vienna)

   Komödie der Verführung, comedy (*Aurelie's Waltz,* 1983)

1924 *Fräulein Else,* novella (*Fräulein Else,* 1930)

1925 *Die Frau des Richters,* novella (The Judge's Wife, 1977)

1926 *Der Gang zum Weiher* (drama)

   Traumnovelle, novella (*Rhapsody; a Dream Novel,* 1927; *Dream Story,* 1999)

1927 *Spiel im Morgengrauen* (novella)

   Der Geist im Wort und der Geist in der Tat (philosophical texts)

1928 *Therese. Chronik eines Frauenlebens,* novel *(Theresa. The Chronicle of a Woman's Life,* 1928)

1929 *Im Spiel der Sommerlüfte,* drama (In the Play of Summer Breezes, 1996)

1931 *Daybreak* (film based on *Spiel im Morgengrauen*); *Flucht in die Finsternis* (novella); *Traum und Schicksal* (novellas)

1932 "Der letzte Brief eines Literaten" (The Last Letter of an Artist, 1986); "Der Sekundant" (The Second, 1986) — narratives

1955 "Anatols Grössenwahn," one-act play (Anatol's Delusions of Grandeur, 1986)

1966 *Das Wort. Tragikomödie in 5 Akten* (The Word, 1996)

1967 *Aphorismen und Betrachtungen*

1968 *Jugend in Wien. Eine Autobiographie (My Youth in Vienna,* 1970)

1969 *Zug der Schatten. Drama in neuen Bildern,* drama fragment (A Procession of Shades, 1996)

1977 *Entworfenes und Verworfenes. Aus dem Nachlaß*

Films

Elskovsleg. Dir. Holger Madsen. Copenhagen: Nordisk Films Kompagni, 1913. (Based on *Liebelei*).

The Affairs of Anatol. Dir. Cecil DeMille, Jeanie MacPherson. Chatsworth, CA: Image Entertainment, 2000 (original Hollywood, Metro Goldwyn Mayer, 1921).

Der junge Medardus. Vienna: Sascha Films, 1923 (silent film).

Liebelei. Vienna: Sascha Films, 1927 (silent film).

Fraulein Else. Vienna: Sascha Films, 1929 (silent film).

Daybreak. Script Arthur Schnitzler. Hollywood: Metro Goldwyn Mayer, 1931. (Based on *Spiel im Morgengrauen*).

Liebelei. Dir. Max Ophüls. New York: Kino International, 1996 (Germany, Janus Films, 1932).

La Ronde. Dir. Max Ophüls. France: Pacific Film Archive Collection, 1950.

La Ronde. Dir. Roger Vadim. Screenplay by Jean Anouilh. France: Paris Film Production, 1980.

Herrera, John. *Romance/Romance.* Cherry County Playhouse and Bristol-Myers Squibb Co. in association with the Arts & Entertainment Network, 1992. (Act I. Based on *The Little Comedy*).

Blind Geronimo and His Brother. New York: Carousel Film & Video, 1992.

Leutnant Gustl. Vier Folgen. Read by Helmut Lohner. Berlin: Deutsche Welle TV, 1997.

Eyes Wide Shut. Dir. Stanley Kubrik. Warner Bros., 1999.

Other Adaptations

LaChiusa, Michael, and Paul McKibbins. *Hello Again: A New Musical.* New York: S. French, 1986.

Hare, David. *The Blue Room.* New York: Grove Publications, 1998. (Drama based on *La Ronde*).

Kanin, Fay and Michael. New York: S. French, 1986. (Based on *The Affairs of Anatol*).

Stoppard, Tom. *Undiscovered Country.* London: Faber and Faber, 1980. (Drama based on *Das weite Land*).

Introduction

Dagmar C. G. Lorenz

ARTHUR SCHNITZLER'S LIFE coincides with a momentous period in Central European history. His own family's ascent took place in the context of Vienna's evolution into a modern metropolis with its unmistakable landmarks: the ostentatious Ringstrasse and the expansive projects of Otto Wagner which included the Stadtbahn; the Karlsplatz; the Secession building; and the progressive hospital developments in the outskirts of the metropolitan area, notably the psychiatric hospital Steinhof. Art Nouveau, epitomized by the paintings of Gustav Klimt — a painter to whom Schnitzler was especially partial — and the designs of the innovative group of painters, architects, and designers known as the Wiener Werkstätte, whose goal it was to make even the functional buildings and interiors of the Habsburg capital aesthetic. Then, during the First World War, Schnitzler witnessed the collapse of the society with which he had closely identified, as had the majority of middle-class Jews.

The images of Schnitzler that emerge from the critical literature are multifaceted. There is the aspiring young author and bon vivant of Vienna's "golden" *fin-de-siècle,* who creates and at the same time makes problematic the existence of playboys and *flâneurs.* There is the physician and scientist of Jewish descent who became known for his experimentation with hypnosis, only to be later discredited. There is the successful dramatist who already in mid-career was receiving awards such as the Grillparzer Prize for Comedy in 1908, and the Vienna Volkstheater proclaimed 1909 the "Schnitzler Year." Schnitzler's fiftieth birthday was celebrated by twenty-six performances of his plays on German-speaking stages. Finally, there is the ladies' man who proudly flaunted his conquests and yet never achieved happiness in his personal life; the ill-fated admirer of a married woman; the deceived lover; the unhappily married man; and finally, the grief-stricken father. The older Schnitzler was plagued by depression and real and imagined ailments.

Schnitzler was born in Vienna's Second District, then a fashionable part of the city, on May 15, 1862, the son of the Jewish laryngologist Johann Schnitzler (1835–1893) and his wife, Louise, née Markbreiter

(1838–1911). In his early childhood years the family moved to the Schottenbastei in the Inner City. After graduating in 1879 from the renowned Vienna *Akademiegymnasium,* among whose students were also Hugo von Hofmannsthal, Richard Beer-Hoffmann, and Peter Altenberg, Schnitzler enrolled at the University of Vienna that same year as a student of medicine. From 1882 to 1883 he served as a volunteer at the military hospital in Vienna. In 1885, at about the time he became acquainted with Sigmund Freud, he completed his doctorate in medicine. Schnitzler's numerous travels to the European cultural centers and resorts throughout his life were characteristic of a man of his class whose life alternated between times of leisure and luxury and his professional career.

Following a journey to Italy in 1885 he became an intern at the *Allgemeines Krankenhaus* in Vienna and, soon thereafter, at the Poliklinik. In that same year he started a correspondence with Theodor Herzl that lasted until Herzl's death in 1904. In 1886 Schnitzler traveled to Meran for health reasons and met Olga Waissnix, the wife of a wealthy hotel owner, whom he courted in the following years. Until 1893 he worked at different Viennese hospitals, including the Poliklinik, and studied several medical specialties: dermatology, sexually transmitted diseases, and diseases of the larynx. He also served as managing editor of the *Internationale medizinische Rundschau,* which his father had founded, and was active writing poems, short stories, and dramatic works that appeared in local papers and journals. In the 1890s, Schnitzler was affiliated with the avant-garde circle *Jung Wien* (Young Vienna), to which Hofmannsthal, Felix Salten, Karl Kraus, Hermann Bahr, and Beer-Hoffmann also belonged. Schnitzler enjoyed the bohemian lifestyle cultivated by the aspiring authors and journalists of the *Jung Wien* circle, and he had several affairs. His relationship with Marie (Mizi) Glümer, the prototype of the "süße Mädel" characters in many of his works, was particularly important for his development as a writer.[1] In 1893, Schnitzler, following the same double standard as his male characters, ended his three-year liaison with Glümer because of her admitted infidelity, and he began a turbulent affair with the actress Adele Sandrock. When in 1893 his father died, Schnitzler resigned his position at the Poliklinik and went into private practice. But his literary career was his primary interest all along, as is evident from his remarkable productivity.

In the late 1880s Schnitzler published several short stories in the Viennese journal *An der schönen blauen Donau,* and the first segments of the *Anatol* cycle, a loosely structured series of one-act plays, began to appear in 1890 in different literary venues. In 1893 the book version of the entire cycle was published in Berlin (*Anatol: Mit einer Einleitung von*

Loris; Anatol, 1911) and established Schnitzler as a major dramatist. The *Anatol* cycle is a document of the directionless and dissolute lifestyle of young leisure-class men in the capital of the Austro-Hungarian Empire. Even in this early work, however, Schnitzler does not merely paint a complacent or idealized portrait of his peer group but reveals also the unspoken despair underlying the luxurious boredom of his privileged protagonists. Sensitive to the issues of his era — psychology, the burden of convention, class conflicts, morality, and the challenge of individualism — Schnitzler was one of the most performed dramatists of the early twentieth century.

Like *Anatol, Liebelei* (1896; *Light-o'-love,* 1912), a drama about class and gender-role expectations, infatuation, attachment, and betrayal, was an instant success. In this work Schnitzler takes issue with the prevailing code of honor and the resultant tragedies: men being called upon to kill or be killed in a duel to safeguard their so-called honor, and young women being encouraged to take their own lives or abort their unborn children to safeguard theirs. Subsequent shorter works include the one-act play *Der grüne Kakadu* (1899; *The Green Cockatoo,* 1913), which is set at the eve of the French Revolution and combines the theme of love and jealousy with political intrigues and social conflicts. *Der grüne Kakadu* examines the implications of revolutionary change and upheaval for the individual, a theme to which Schnitzler returned throughout his career, for example in *Der junge Medardus* (1910; *Young Medardus*). Appearance, play-acting, and life collide in his early experimental drama, which blends class conflict and romantic intrigue.

While in *Liebelei* the female protagonist's lower-middle-class circles are an important aspect of the drama, in *Freiwild* (1898; *Free Game,* 1913) one of the major characters, Karinski, is modeled after Schnitzler's friend, the bon vivant Richard Tausenau, and the play scrutinizes the male environment of officers and "gentlemen." Schnitzler presents a stark portrait of the corruption in the imperial military. He exposes problems associated with the traditional homosocial bonding fostered in all-male institutions, showing that it leads to alienation from civilian life and promotes a predatory attitude toward women. The elitist single lifestyle imposed upon the members of the officer corps is shown to be the breeding ground for addictive behavior, a ruthless kind of competitiveness, alcoholism, and compulsive gambling. Schnitzler also reveals the difficulties women have in a male-dominated society as they try to emancipate themselves, because they are assigned a status of dependency.

In the later part of the twentieth century these and Schnitzler's later controversial dramas such as *Reigen* (1903; *Hands Around,* 1920) and

Professor Bernhardi (1912) are part of the regular fare at German-speaking and international stages. At a time of extraordinary productivity in 1894 Schnitzler met the voice teacher Marie Reinhard and fell immediately in love with her. The result of their liaison was a stillborn child in 1897. The remorse this event seems to have caused Schnitzler is reflected in the novel *Der Weg ins Freie* (1908; *The Road to the Open*, 1932). In this work the relationship between the protagonist, Georg Wergenthin, and his Gentile lover, Anna Rosner, comes to an end after she has a miscarriage,[2] an event that leads to reflection and reorientation on Wergenthin's part. Schnitzler often allowed his own experiences and those of his friends to inform his writing as far as plots and characters were concerned.

Schnitzler found himself at the center of Central European artistic and intellectual life. He repeatedly traveled to the cities that *fin-de-siècle* and early twentieth-century Central Europeans considered gathering places for members of the high society, Prague, Karlsbad, Marienbad, Paris, London, Berlin, Milan, and Copenhagen, and he enjoyed the friendship of important writers such as Salten, Kraus, Max Burckhard, Paul Goldmann, Jakob Wassermann, Georg Brandes, and later Robert Musil, Heinrich Mann, and Ernst von Dohnàny, who composed the score for *Der Schleier der Pierrette* (1910; *The Veil of Pierrette*, 1995). At the height of his career, in 1903, he married the actress Olga Gussmann (1882–1970), although he continued his affairs and encounters with other women. He had known Gussmann since 1899 and had a son with her, Heinrich, who was born in 1902. Lili, their daughter, with whom Schnitzler had a particularly close relationship, was born in 1909.

The controversies involving some of Schnitzler's works did not have an adverse effect on his phenomenal success. In 1896, for example, the then-witty periodical *Simplicissimus* featured the one-act play *Die über-spannte Person* (1896; *The High Strung Woman*, 1986), inspired by Schnitzler's affair with Sandrock; the issue was confiscated because of moral considerations. A much more serious setback involved the dramatic cycle *Reigen*, which portrayed sexual relations between members of all classes and which therefore was condemned by some as pornographic and immoral. In its ten dramatic scenes, each of which ends in the sexual union of the respective couple, *Reigen* exposes the reality beneath the Victorian façade of propriety and decency. In few other works of the time are the links between wealth, social standing, and the luxury of bourgeois morality exposed more succinctly. *Reigen* makes evident that the morality of the upper classes depends on the immorality and corruption of the under-privileged. The play attracted international attention because of its suppos-edly offensive content and was censored in most European countries. The play was outlawed in Germany in 1904. In 1912 a planned performance in Budapest was forbidden. The first production of the entire work took place in 1920 in Berlin, where it immediately became the object of protracted public controversies and legal battles.

Schnitzler's reputation as a prose writer is based on his narrative innovations as well as the boldness of his topics. The novella *Leutnant Gustl* (1900; *None but the Brave*, 1926) is rightfully known as an avantgarde work because of its innovative use of interior monologue as a means of revealing the protagonist's deepest thoughts and feelings. This work also contributed to the author's notoriety because of its allegedly disrespectful and slanderous attitude toward the Austrian military. The scandal cost Schnitzler his rank as an officer of the Austrian imperial military reserves. By making the link between poverty and immoral (if not criminal) behavior transparent, Schnitzler breaks a taboo carefully upheld by the more sentimentally inclined authors of his era such as Rainer Maria Rilke or Hofmannsthal.

Rather than positioning himself at the center of the class whose privileges he enjoys, Schnitzler designs a de-centered narrative point of view and dramatic characters apt to explore the world of the bourgeoisie from the margins. The protagonist of *Leutnant Gustl*, for example, aspires to an upper-middle-class status, but constant worries reveal how far removed he is from actually achieving his ideal. In *Fräulein Else* (1924) the narrative point of view is that of a young woman whose privileged status is jeopardized by her father's financial troubles. Thoroughly familiar with the bourgeois code and at the same time standing apart from it, Schnitzler was both chronicler and critic of his class, one whose illusions, neuroses, and transgressions he reveals masterfully and clinically.

Similar to other writers and intellectuals in *fin-de-siècle* Vienna, which had been governed by a notoriously anti-Semitic mayor, Karl Lueger, since 1895, Schnitzler became increasingly interested in Jewish concerns. In his novel *Der Weg ins Freie* he reviewed the background and aspirations of Viennese Jews at the verge of assimilation and examined the political and existential choices some young Jews make in their search to achieve integration while others try to preserve their distinct identity. Motivated by hostilities and legal problems his father had encountered as a physician and head of the Poliklinik, Schnitzler featured in *Professor Bernhardi* a Jewish doctor who comes into tragic conflict with his anti-Semitic environment as a result of his impeccable professional ethics. Schnitzler's drama, which shows the problems of bigotry and scapegoating in the context of the medical profession, must be considered the precursor of not only Friedrich Wolf's drama *Professor Mamlock* (1935), about the persecution of a professor of medicine by the Nazis, but also the episode in Lion Feuchtwanger's documentary novel *Die Geschwister Oppenheim* (1934; *The Oppermanns,* 1934) about a physician whose career is destroyed after Adolf Hitler's rise to power in 1933.[3] In these works the protagonist is an assimilated Jewish physician, a man committed to his profession and convinced of the benefits of scientific progress. Like Schnitzler's Bernhardi, Mamlock and Gustav Oppenheim are products of the privileged humanistic educational system, Gymnasium and university, and consider themselves first and foremost Germans. Schnitzler's own less than optimistic attitude differed markedly from that of his father's generation. Having experienced the rise of anti-Semitism in Central Europe in the 1880s and 1890s — beginning with the founding of the Anti-Semitic League by Wilhelm Marr in 1879, the mass exodus of Russian Jews to the West after the assassination of Czar Alexander II, the ritual-slaughter trial of Tisza Eszlar in Hungary, the Dreyfus affair that began in 1886 in France, and the manifesto of the anti-Semitic Christian-Social Association against the freedom of Jews and in favor of restricting immigration. Schnitzler was aware of the seriousness of the problem.

Schnitzler's distrust of the social establishment and his skepticism toward heroic causes, patriotism, and military virtues were already apparent in *Der junge Medardus,* a drama set in the Napoleonic era, which reveals how enmeshed personal desire, ideology, ambition, and patriotism can become. The pervasive skepticism in this play expresses Schnitzler's own position at the beginning of the First World War. Partly because of his lack of martial fervor — together with Kraus he was one of the few intellectuals not in support of the war — and partly because his works were not relevant at a time of national mobilization, his popularity suffered considerably. However, in the momentous year of 1913/14 *Liebelei* became Schnitzler's first play to be adapted for motion pictures by a Danish producer, Holger Madsen. Schnitzler's interest in movies began to bear fruit during the war years when he became the target of calumnies, and *Der junge Medardus* was taken off the theater program in Berlin. He provided the scripts for several movie versions of individual works.

Schnitzler's public discussion with Stefan Zweig about Jewish-Austrian literature in 1916 and his preoccupation with his autobiography in the following year reveal the need on the author's part to review his life and revise earlier-held positions. In 1919 Schnitzler voted for the Social-Democratic Party in an attempt to distance himself as far as possible from the extreme right.[4] In 1920 he cast his vote for the Jewish National Party.[5] The rise of extreme nationalism and anti-Semitism in the aftermath of the lost war had made the prominent Schnitzler more vulnerable to attack than ever before. The production of *Reigen* in Berlin in December 1920 was followed by a public outrage. Anti-Semitism clearly played a role in the charges that by having a play with explicit sexual content produced Schnitzler had caused a public disturbance In 1921, when the *Reigen* scandal took up almost all of Schnitzler's energies, his wife divorced him.

In 1921 the silent movie *The Affairs of Anatol* was released by Metro-Goldwyn-Mayer, and in 1923 Austria's leading motion-picture company, Sascha Film, produced a silent movie based on *Der junge Medardus*. In 1927 the silent movie *Liebelei*, on which Schnitzler had collaborated, opened in Berlin, followed in 1929 by the silent *Fräulein Else*, starring Elisabeth Bergner. The same year Schnitzler became president of the Austrian PEN Club, and in 1926 he was honored with the distinguished *Burgtheaterring*, an award for playwrights. Despite these and many other public recognitions he received in the final decade of his life, Schnitzler became increasingly isolated, partly because of physical and psychological ailments, partly because of the increasingly radical political atmosphere in Germany and Austria.

This isolation notwithstanding, he created some of his most profound and complex works in the last ten years of his life, including the novels *Therese: Chronik eines Frauenlebens* (1928, *Therese: The Chronicle of a Woman's Life*, 1928) and *Flucht in die Finsternis* (1931; *Flight into Darkness*, 1931). Some of his best novellas and dramas were written during these years, including *Fräulein Else, Die Frau des Richters* (1925; *The Judge's Wife*, 1977), *Traumnovelle* (1926; *Rhapsody: A Dream Novel*, 1927), and the dramas *Der Gang zum Weiher* (1926; *The Way to the Pond*, 1992), *Komödie der Verführung* (1924; *Aurelie's Waltz*, 1983), and *Im Spiel der Sommerlüfte* (1930; *In the Play of Summer Breezes*, 1996). The perceptions and experiences of women and emotionally fragile men are explored with great insight and sensitivity in these later works. In *Therese*, for example, Schnitzler examines the predicament of a woman struggling to make ends meet. Therese makes a living as a private tutor. Being constantly on call and under the supervision of her employers she has to forego the luxury of a private life. The novel reveals the economic and emotional difficulties Therese faces in a society with only limited career options for women. In *Flucht in die Finsternis* Schnitzler traces the mental illness of a man who gradually loses touch with reality and ends up murdering his brother and killing himself. Schnitzler masterfully describes the murderer's paranoid perceptions and subtly reveals the victim's complicity, which consists of refusal to face up to his brother's actual condition.

Three years before his death, in 1928, Schnitzler was dealt a severe blow by the suicide of his daughter, Lili, who had married the Italian Fascist Arnoldo Cappellini, an officer in Mussolini's army, in June of 1927. Even as a girl, Lili Schnitzler had shown signs of emotional instability, which was exacerbated after her marriage. Following a Mediterranean cruise with her husband and her father in April and May, she committed suicide in Venice in July 1928.

On October 21, 1931 Arthur Schnitzler died in Vienna as the result of a brain hemorrhage. He was buried at the Vienna Zentralfriedhof. A few days earlier Metro-Goldwyn-Mayer had released the motion picture *Daybreak,* based on *Spiel im Morgengrauen* (1927; *Daybreak,* 1927), for which Schnitzler had written the script. Schnitzler was survived by his son, Heinrich, who took refuge in the United States during the Nazi years and played a key role in bringing his father's works back to Austrian stages in the postwar era.

Schnitzler was born fourteen years after the restrictions on Jewish residence in Vienna had been lifted, the son of a Jewish family that had struggled to become fully integrated into Viennese society. In his 2001 study, *Schnitzler's Century,* Peter Gay chose Schnitzler as a witness and representative of European middle-class culture.[6] Gay's choice is as remarkable as it is problematic. In her analysis of late-eighteenth- and nineteenth-century Jewish society, Hannah Arendt would have classified Schnitzler's forebears — the banker Baron Friedrich Schey von Koromla, who left his native Hungary to settle in Vienna; the physician and scholar Philipp Markbreiter, Schnitzler's grandfather; and his father, the Hungarian-born physician Johann Schnitzler — as erstwhile Jewish pariahs who had advanced to the status of parvenus,[7] despite the fact that the values and ambitions of the Schnitzler family were those of the German-speaking Central European elite. Jews realized their aspirations only in terms of economic progress, education, and lifestyle. Otherwise, they remained distinct: "The Jews of Vienna practiced similar professions, lived in the same neighborhoods, attended school together, and married each other," Marsha Rozenblit writes.[8] As a scientist and physician, Johann Schnitzler was excluded from the professional opportunities open to his Gentile colleagues at the university and in the government. As a response to the dilemma he established the Vienna Poliklinik, over which he presided until his death, as an alternative for Jewish doctors. Despite its remarkable successes the clinic was viewed by the anti-Semitic public with suspicion.

Even though Schnitzler's family enjoyed a privileged standard of living, their son's social contacts were mostly confined to his own class, that of the "good Jewish middle-class circles," and did not extend into the Gentile bourgeoisie.[9] Schnitzler attended schools where the majority of students were Jewish or of Jewish descent. Rozenblit explains that studying at a college preparatory school such as the *Akademiegymnasium* from which Schnitzler had graduated provided Jews with access to prestigious careers and "served as a great force for their acculturation and assimilation into the world of European Kultur and Bildung." Furthermore, Rozenblit asserts, "the Viennese Jewish penchant for elite education was part of an empire-wide pattern," and "acquiring secular knowledge" was a "Jewish group activity, and the group nature of this experience modified and attenuated assimilation."[10]

Austrian middle-class Jews stood apart not only in their educational and career preferences but also in the military, where Schnitzler served as a volunteer. The so-called *Mosesdragoner,* the Jewish officers, were a group by themselves. At the same time, Schnitzler was fortunate because Jewish intellectual life flourished in Vienna more so than elsewhere. The names of writers, artists, and thinkers associated with Viennese modernity — Freud, Gustav Mahler, Kraus, Zweig, Herzl, Salten, Ludwig von Wittgenstein, Bertha Pappenheim, and Joseph Roth — are those of Austro-Hungarian Jews with roots in the Eastern European provinces. The vibrant culture with so many nationally and internationally admired Jewish participants in its forefront is evidence of the apparent success of the project of Jewish emancipation and assimilation. At the same time, the pressure exerted upon Jewish individuals by this culture to conform to the Christian mainstream is apparent as well. The virulent self-hatred in Otto Weininger's *Geschlecht und Charakter* (1903; *Sex and Character,* 1906) — a treatise based on the author's dissertation at the University of Vienna, which sets out to prove the constitutional inferiority of women and Jews — the apostasy of Jewish artists and intellectuals such as Mahler and Kraus, and the internalization of values of the Austro-Hungarian monarchy by Zweig and Roth all illustrate the pervasive desire for self-transformation for the sake of equal rights and opportunities.

With the arrival of new Jewish immigrants from Eastern Europe in the 1880s following the pogroms in Russia, the Schnitzlers relocated from the Leopoldstadt, Vienna's Second District, to the Inner City. Many established families felt in the 1880s that the unassimilated newcomers were turning their formerly "genteel and respectable" neighborhood into a Jewish and immigrants' quarter.[11] Young men of Arthur Schnitzler's generation, the descendants of banker and merchant families, chose the arts and liberal professions to avoid the odium of the traditional Jewish trades. Egon Schwarz maintains that precisely because Jews were limited by the larger society to certain trades and commercial occupations "they had an urban middle-class status imposed on upon them."[12] However, the traditional Jewish middle-class status had been associated with the money trade. The aspiring young men and women of the *fin-de-siècle* compensated for the perceived lack of status by taking up aesthetic and cultural pursuits. Schnitzler, with his love of the arts and literature and his predilection for the finer things in life, including his association with women of the world such as the beautiful Olga Waissnix, wife of the owner of a resort hotel, and the actress Adele Sandrock, fits the "Jewish" escape pattern into a half-bohemian, half aristocratic lifestyle.

In his cultural-historical study Gay examines the formation of middle-class culture in the Victorian era, which coincides roughly with Josephinian Austria and Wilhelminian Germany. Gay's title suggests that Schnitzler is a representative, even a paradigm, of the modern bourgeois culture taking shape in the wake of the failed revolution of 1848. "I have used as my guide Arthur Schnitzler, the most interesting Austrian playwright, novelist, and short story writer of this time," Gay writes. Yet, he does not consider Schnitzler, "a man of the nineteenth century," an average or mediocre man by any means, but a "credible and resourceful witness to the middle-class world."[13] Alongside his protagonist's extraordinary traits, including his creativity and his charisma, Gay identifies several other qualities and attitudes that Schnitzler, the famous author and man of the world, shares with the majority of his bourgeois contemporaries. Schnitzler's relative affluence afforded him the lifestyle typical of men of his class. Regular visits to coffee-houses, theaters, and dancehalls, encounters with women of the demimonde, appearances at parties and social functions, gambling, dinners at hotels and restaurants, trips to the nearby mountain resorts and across Europe were all integral parts of a privileged young man's experience, combined, in Schnitzler's case, with social and literary ambition and extraordinary success.[14] Schnitzler's acceptance of the sexual and social double standard and his licentiousness, together with the yearning to conquer a pure woman who would be completely dedicated to him, were part and parcel of the patriarchal ideology of the late nineteenth century.

Gay's study does not account for the years after the collapse of the Danube monarchy during the First World War, notwithstanding the fact that Schnitzler's fame as an author and his literary vision continued to expand in the years of the First Austrian republic. Even though his later works, such as the play *Im Spiel der Sommerlüfte,* are set in the prewar era — or, as *Die Schwestern oder Casanova in Spa* (1919; *The Sisters or Casanova in Spa,* 1992) and *Der Gang zum Weiher,* in an even earlier period — their atmosphere and tone suggest the traumatic transition into a new social and political reality. The awareness of the new social realities and the loss of emotional certainty brought about by the collapse of the familiar value system and fast-changing political and social structures also informs the stark episodes in his later prose works, *Traumnovelle,* and the novels *Therese* and *Flucht in die Finsternis.*

In these texts the traditional class and gender codes have lost their validity entirely. The perceptions of the male protagonists in particular are shown to be so unreliable that, as is the case in *Flucht in die Finsternis,* it becomes impossible to tell friend from foe. Overall, the work seems an especially appropriate contribution to the larger political and social issues of the 1930s, which revolved around loss of direction and uncontrollable fear of political extremism. While other writers such as Feuchtwanger and Alfred Döblin examined these forces in social and political terms, Schnitzler studied the anxieties and fears that drive an individual to extreme actions. The combination of the murder-suicide of two brothers with the theme of paranoia leading to complete insanity can be read in the context of other works of the time as a commentary on the imminent destruction of what was called "German-Jewish symbiosis."[15]

For Jewish intellectuals the demise of the Austro-Hungarian monarchy involved a paradigm shift that affected them directly and ultimately with tragic consequences. In the multination state, Jews had figured among the empire's many nationalities — Bohemians, Hungarians, Romanians, Slovenians, and Germans. In the postwar republic, which many considered a truncated remnant-state without a future, Austrian Jews were relegated to the position of a minority whose status was jeopardized by the ever-increasing arrival of Eastern European immigrants, some of whom considered Vienna a station on their way to Paris or New York, others as their final destination. Schnitzler stayed in Vienna during the 1920s, the sober years when under its Social Democratic leadership the city became a model for social progress despite the postwar economic crisis. Notwithstanding the depression, public housing projects were undertaken, with the Karl-Marx-Hof and the Reumann-Hof as prime examples, and the city sponsored mass education, for example the programs at the Urania in which Hermann Broch and Elias Canetti took part.

Schnitzler, who depicted the pitfalls of the bourgeois dream for men of his background in the Danube monarchy as few other writers had, never felt quite at home in the First Republic, much as he had criticized the culture of the Empire. As time went on, he became increasingly aware of how limited the life choices for Jewish Austrians actually were. They included assimilation, Socialism, and Zionism or Jewish nationalism. Contrary to others who, like Mahler and Kraus, sought a reprieve from their predicament by converting to Christianity, Schnitzler was, in Schwarz's words, "one of those upright Jews."[16] Similar to Freud, he rejected apostasy, but he did not feel drawn to his traditional roots either, as did Martin Buber and Arnold Zweig, inspired in part by the encounters with East European Jewry during the war years. Schnitzler was skeptical of collective solutions to a problem that he, as his protagonists in *Der Weg ins Freie* and *Professor Bernhardi,* experienced as not only social but also psychological.

Schnitzler's writings rarely feature the "new" men and women of the postwar era, proletarians, recent immigrants, and political activists, Socialists, Communists, and Fascists, who feature in the works of Ödön von Horváth and Elias and Veza Canetti. His works continue to examine personal relationships in prewar and even earlier historical settings. The First Republic's housing developments or the working-class neighborhoods of the Leopoldstadt and Floridsdorf are inconceivable as the framework for Schnitzler's writing. Yet, the articles in the volume at hand reveal that Schnitzler was far from closing his eyes to the world around him, even though he writes about the experience of his own class. His point of view is obviously not that of a revolutionary, but rather he calls into question ideologies and doctrines, be they political, philosophical, or scientific.

Early in the First Republic, which ended with the Nazi takeover of Austria in 1938, Jewish integration seemed a *fait accompli,* at least for the bourgeoisie. All professional and legal barriers that had stood in the way of equal access, for military and state offices as well, were removed, preparing the road to complete assimilation. Yet, precisely at that time an unprecedented right-wing radicalism, Austro-Fascism and National Socialism, took shape and became increasingly threatening in the mid-1920s. With its victory the egalitarian social and political programs that had shaped Social Democracy in Vienna came undone. The optimism and liberalism with which the republican era had begun was giving way to a repressive climate, initiated by the burning of the Palace of Justice in 1927. In 1931, the year of Schnitzler's death, the German National Socialists had already celebrated major victories, and the collapse of the stock market led to anti-Semitic violence in major cities.

It has been more than seventy years since Schnitzler's death, time enough to resolve the basic controversies involving the author's rank, the quality of his writing, and his considerable contributions to modern literature and thought. Once a controversial author, praised by some as an innovative prose writer and dramatist and condemned by others as a frivolous sentimentalist with a predilection for pornography, Schnitzler has gained a firmly established significance as a chronicler and analyst of *fin-de-siècle* manners and psychology. Schnitzler is recognized as a key figure of late-nineteenth- and early-twentieth-century Central European culture and as someone influential within the wider spectrum of Western literature. The majority of his works was translated into English, French, and other languages during Schnitzler's lifetime. Multiple English translations exist of his most famous works, notably *Reigen*, and reprints and new editions appear regularly. The extensive critical edition of his diaries undertaken by Werner Welzig in the late 1980s inspired renewed interest in Schnitzler, the man and his writings, on the part of scholars and the general public at the turn of the millennium.[17]

The essays in this volume provide fresh insights into the more complex Schnitzler, who was neither a bourgeois nor a rebel, but an intellectual who recorded the upheavals of his times because he was deeply affected by them.

Gerd Schneider, one of the foremost Schnitzler scholars, chronicles in his essay "The Social and Political Context of Arthur Schnitzler's *Reigen* in Berlin and Vienna: 1900–1933" the many *Reigen* scandals, the surrounding circumstances and the intellectual climate. His study reveals how a literary work can develop a momentum all its own, and finally, with changing times, assume the place in history that it deserves. Schneider traces the fate of this significant work and provides, in his own words, "a window for a better understanding into the time in which Schnitzler lived and wrote, so that one is justified to rewrite the introductory sentences as: *Sua fata libelli habent*."

Evelyn Deutsch-Schreiner, an expert in Austrian *fin-de-siècle* drama history and dramaturgy, examines how different staging techniques and the casting of characters continue to have a profound impact on the reception of Schnitzler. In "'. . . nothing against Arthur Schnitzler himself. . .': Interpreting Schnitzler on Stage in Austria in the 1950s and 1960s" she reveals the ideological factors involved in reintroducing an author banned between 1938 and 1945 to the Austrian public, which had been thoroughly indoctrinated with Nazi ideology. She shows how Schnitzler's work suffered from the desire to dehistoricize it and from being put to use in an attempt to produce politically correct plays. Deutsch-Schreiner credits Schnitzler's son, Heinrich, with the accomplishment of having saved his father's legacy without at the same time being able to prevent him from becoming a cultural icon, a canonical figure, yet possibly preventing him from having the provocative effect he might have had on audiences worldwide.

Clearly, the efforts to denigrate Schnitzler in his own lifetime and during the Nazi era, when his works were forbidden, ultimately came to naught. However, to fully rehabilitate an author whom radicals wanted to eliminate from literary and theater history was not an easy task. Postwar scholars of German literature had lingering uncertainties about Schnitzler, in part because of the legacy of anti-Semitism within the academic establishment, and in part because of the changed circumstances. Schnitzler's career had unfolded during an era that seemed irretrievably past. His works thus seemed incongruous with the concerns of the general public to rebuild society and of the intellectuals who endorsed the literary programs of the immediate postwar era of "Kahlschlag" (*tabula rasa*) and "Nullpunkt" (Point Zero), which proposed that the linguistic and cultural dilemma after the Nazi era required a rejection of tradition and a brand-new start. Even though performing Schnitzler's plays after 1945 would have fit the purpose of de-Nazification, "a public eager to put the Nazi past behind it dismissed him as outdated," Deutsch-Schreiner maintains in her article.

After the Shoah, being Jewish took on a new meaning in the public discourse of German-speaking countries. Even in Austria, where no soul-searching comparable to that in the West German Point-Zero discourse had taken place, there was a widespread awareness that the suffering and the persecution of Jews precluded open anti-Semitism. During the Waldheim affair of the mid 1980s, it even appeared that being Jewish had certain advantages in terms of not being implicated in the Holocaust. Many publications about Jews in Austria, the exile experience, and the Shoah appeared, creating a somewhat mythical image of Jewishness in a country virtually without a Jewish community. Elizabeth Loentz, a scholar of German Jewish and Yiddish literature and culture, goes beyond the myth in her essay "The Problem and Challenge of Jewishness in the City of Schnitzler and Anna O." She provides a detailed account about the larger milieu of Schnitzler's career and uses the renowned social activist and Jewish feminist Bertha Pappenheim as an example of the range of Jewish activities. By comparing Schnitzler's ideas and views on gender roles with those of a prominent woman writer and diarist, Loentz presents a challenging portrait of gendered views in Jewish society and of the rich diversity of Jewish life in Schnitzler's era.

Complementing Loentz's study, Iris Bruce, an expert in late-nineteenth- and early-twentieth-century German Jewish culture, including Kafka and Salten, examines Schnitzler alongside the Zionist Salten in "Which Way Out? Schnitzler's and Salten's Conflicting Responses to Cultural Zionism." Despite the readily apparent differences, she observes a common theme in the work of both authors: the "search for 'a way out,'" which is "a topos in early-twentieth-century Jewish, and especially Zionist, literature." Bruce concludes that neither Schnitzler, the enlightened individualist and author of philosophical-political literature, nor Salten, a Zionist and writer of allegorical didactic children's literature, had the vision that might lead "out of the woods." Both of them, products of the Jewish experience of emancipation, assimilation, and anti-Semitism, failed to realize that reason would not provide an antidote to National Socialism.

Informed by the scholarship of Daniel Boyarin on the construction of Jewish gender roles and Sander Gilman's analysis of Jewish identity, Dagmar C. G. Lorenz, who focuses her research in German and Austrian Jewish topics, examines the sense of self and identity construction in different works by Schnitzler representative of different periods.[18] In "The Self as Process in an Era of Transition: Competing Paradigms of Personality and Character in Schnitzler's Works" she reveals the rational underpinnings of Schnitzler's works. The dilemma the literary characters as well as their creator face calls to mind the problem laid out in Freud's *Das Unbehagen in der Kultur* (1930, *Civilization and Its Discontents*, 1953). Not a disciple of Freud, Schnitzler does not endorse the notion of "dark" insurmountable urges such as the Death Drive. Even though he writes about obstacles frustrating the pursuit and achievement of happiness and even suggests that suffering is predicated by the human condition, aggravated by social institutions, Schnitzler's more successful characters suggest that the continued effort to alleviate suffering and to increase pleasure is the only worthwhile, if not noble, project in the face of certain defeat.

In "Schnitzler's Turn to Prose Fiction: The Depiction of Consciousness in Selected Narratives," Felix Tweraser, a scholar of *fin-de-siècle* Austrian literature, discusses Schnitzler's turn to narrative genres in the course of his career. Maintaining that the *Mittelbewusstsein* (mid-level of consciousness) was a crucial concept in Schnitzler's prose characterizations, Tweraser examines this term to show Schnitzler's responses to Freudian psychoanalysis. Tweraser writes: "While not denying the existence of the unconscious, Schnitzler stresses the importance of the *Mittelbewusstsein* as an area of consciousness where the individual stores the institutional mechanisms that dictate behavior, but which also contains repressed memories."[19] Tweraser takes Schnitzler's battle against the military code as a case in point that the author considered a successful integration into an acquisitive, capitalist, modern society the path to overcoming many of the social and political ills of his time.

Elizabeth Ametsbichler in her comprehensive essay "A Century of Intrigue: The Dramatic Works of Arthur Schnitzler" explores reasons for Schnitzler's enduring popularity on stage and on the screen. In her analysis of the language and plots of his major plays, including *Liebelei, Reigen,* and *Der grüne Kakadu,* as well as works not published during the author's lifetime, such as *Das Wort* (1966; *The Word,* 1995), Ametsbichler concludes that even though Schnitzler's plays are set at the turn of the century, they succeed in shedding light on societal values and perceptions of both the past and present. Ametsbichler asks: "Could Schnitzler hold our imagination still today if he had not somehow established a connection between this and the last fin-de-siècle?" She finds that there is more commonality between nineteenth- and early-twenty-first-century concerns than immediately meets the eye.

The translations of Schnitzler's plays by G. J. Weinberger, a scholar of Elizabethan literature and *fin-de-siècle* Vienna, have played an important role in making the Austrian author accessible to the English-speaking public. This is particularly true for Weinberger's translations and his analyses of Schnitzler's posthumous and lesser known dramas. Weinberger succeeds in revealing the universal message in Schnitzler without compromising cultural and historical specificity. In "Arthur Schnitzler's Puppet Plays" Weinberger examines the tradition of Wurstel, Pierrot and Pierette, a kind of Viennese Punch-and-Judy tradition which Schnitzler re-enlivened and expanded. Weinberger reveals that Schnitzler uses his marionette characters to address transcendental issues in a modern way free of scripture-based morality and traditional religious messages. Schnitzler's agnosticism is obvious in his other works, however, the relationship between the marionettes and the puppeteer allows him to introduce an air of uncertainty that lends these works a particular poignancy. They literally play out the dilemma arising from the question about a possible puppet master who is invisible and unknowable. Unlike the marionettes in Kleist's famous essay, Schnitzler's marionettes do labor under the burden of a modern consciousness. Weinberger emphasizes that if "they stand "widerstandlos" before their puppet-masters, they do so out of hopelessness or helplessness" in the absence of a merciful higher agent.

Hillary Hope Herzog, whose research focus is Schnitzler and his time, brings to the fore a lesser-known genre in "'Medizin ist eine Weltanschauung': On Schnitzler's Medical Writings." Her article reveals intertextualities and thought patterns that connect Schnitzler's literary work and his professional writing as a physician. In certain ways, Herzog suggests, Schnitzler's thoughts on disease, notably mental illness, differ from those of his contemporaries. Rather than depicting a closed case in *Flucht in die Finsternis,* Schnitzler pays attention to the complexities of individual cases. Herzog also discusses Schnitzler's early experiments with hypnosis, which to a contemporary reader appear dated, and the way Schnitzler approached personal encounters in light of the syphilis epidemic. The characters and plots in his novels and dramas reflect his views on medicine and are, for the physician-turned-author, a medium to communicate those views to the public.

Katherine Arens, known for her extensive work on Schnitzler, examines the issue of gender in the context of theories on sex and gender at the turn of the century in Vienna. In "Schnitzler and the Discourse of Gender in *Fin-de-siècle* Vienna" Arens questions earlier-held notions that Schnitzler reproduced gender stereotypes and that he is a fundamentally unpolitical author. She shows that particularly in his "most prickly novellas," *Frau Berta Garlan* (1901; *Bertha Garlan,* 1901), *Dr. Gräsler, Badearzt* (1917; *Dr. Graesler,* 1923), *Frau Beate und ihr Sohn* (1913; *Beatrice,* 1926), *Der Mörder* (1911; *The Murderer,* 1922), and *Therese* Schnitzler emerges as a writer with a much broader vision than he was often given credit for.

John Neubauer, known for his publications on symbolism and *fin-de-siècle* culture, probes the generation gap in upwardly mobile Jewish families in his article "The Overaged Adolescents of Schnitzler's *Der Weg ins Freie.*" Neubauer describes Schnitzler's controversial novel, which has often been maligned for its alleged formlessness, as a deliberate work with a clear formal, ideological, and thematic structure, all of which are interrelated. He pays particular attention to the indirect dialogues in the protagonist's heterosexual love affair complemented by the direct ("mimetic") dialogues in his homosocial fellowship with Jewish intellectuals and writers, and he concludes that Schnitzler painted a comprehensive portrait of a social stratum of overaged adolescents in a historically and culturally unique moment. Neubauer's analysis reveals that the problems faced by Schnitzler's protagonists are not universal middle-class problems but specifically Jewish middle-class problems, an aspect of Schnitzler's writing that moved increasingly to the forefront in his later works. Viennese Jewish culture is part and parcel of the novella *Fräulein Else.* Else's concern as to how Jewish or not Jewish a given character appears (and, by association, will make her appear), calls to mind similar apprehensions described by Ruth Beckermann, journalist and filmmaker who was raised in post-Shoah Vienna. Beckermann wrote about the embarrassment she felt when she was "exposed" as a Jew by being associated with unassimilated members of her community.[20] In other words, the Jewish issues addressed by Schnitzler in *Der Weg ins Freie*, in his autobiography *Jugend in Wien* (1968; *My Youth in Vienna*, 1970), and in his letters and diaries have remained relevant to Jews living in Vienna after the Second World War.[21]

Imke Meyer, an expert in Austrian culture from the *fin-de-siècle* to the postwar era, provides a meticulous close-reading analysis of Schnitzler's novelette *Die Fremde* in "'Thou Shalt Not Make Unto Thee Any Graven Image': Crises of Masculinity in Schnitzler's *Die Fremde*." Meyer focuses on the "crisis of masculinity" which, under different auspices, is also addressed by Neubauer. Her detailed examination of Schnitzler's narrative strategies reveal patterns of turning the familiar object or person into the other, the unfamiliar, that can be applied to other prose works as well.

Finally, a critical look is taken at bourgeois morals and the crises of masculinity at the *fin-de-siècle*. These issues are an integral part of Schnitzler's *Dämmerseelen* collection, and they are connected to the feminist concerns raised in Schnitzler's better-known narratives, such as *Leutnant Gustl, Fräulein Else*, or *Traumnovelle*. *Die Fremde* can thus be read as a text that is paradigmatic for the issues Schnitzler seeks to raise in his prose.

The essay "The Power of the Gaze: Visual Metaphors in Schnitzler's Prose Works and Dramas" by Susan C. Anderson, a scholar of *fin-de-siècle* Austrian and postwar German literature and narrative theory, explores instances of what Andreas Huyssen calls "disturbances of vision," used aesthetically to criticize a persisting hierarchy of "masculine" observer to "feminine" observed and to replace it with a fluid exchange of shifting gazes and positionalities. According to Anderson, the ambiguity, even multivalence, of gender and gender roles, established through the different ways of seeing and being seen, reveals the pervasive bourgeois angst at the *fin-de-siècle*. The blurring of gender roles parallels other challenges to concepts of gender, for example in the work of Mary Cassatt. During the same period, other intellectuals and artists such as Kraus, Weininger, Arthur Strindberg, and Edgar Degas wrote or painted in ways that tried to define masculinity and femininity in terms of opposites. Schnitzler experimented with different ideas of masculinity and femininity and conveyed such ideas by describing ways of looking and being looked at.

Eva Kuttenberg, who has worked extensively on the issue of suicide in Schnitzler, discovers a "hidden agenda" underlying Schnitzler's frequent portrayal of suicide: "Why not live?" In her essay "Suicide as Performance in Dr. Schnitzler's Prose" Kuttenberg maintains that Vienna's coexisting rich aesthetics and atmosphere of crisis did not entice

Schnitzler to aestheticize or trivialize suicide. Rather, as a specialist in the pathology of suicide, Schnitzler described the phenomenon and tried to contribute to its prevention. Schnitzler grants his characters the benefit of the doubt and suggests, "You may as well live!"

Schnitzler's legacy among postmodern Austrian authors, notably Robert Schindel, is the topic of Matthias Konzett's "The Difficult Rebirth of Cosmopolitanism: Schnitzler and Austrian Literature." Konzett, a specialist in contemporary Austrian and German literature, traces Schnitzler's significance for subsequent Jewish writing in Austria. With *Der Weg ins Freie* as a case in point Konzett shows that Schindel models the treatment of his Jewish and non-Jewish characters and character constellations upon Schnitzler's novel. At the same time, Konzett argues, in post-Shoah Vienna, which includes other minorities such as Turks, even Jewish authors, who represented the most visible and critical minority in Schnitzler's times and in the post-Shoah era have shown considerable sensitivity to the minority experience have not yet found ways to represent the multicultural society in their works.

The essays in this volume are representative of the current tendencies in Schnitzler scholarship. By placing the emphasis on texts that were neglected in the past, by examining topics that previously were considered inappropriate to Schnitzler, and by expanding the debates on Schnitzler in new theoretical directions, the volume at hand opens important contemporary perspectives on a canonical author. For example, it is interesting that even those among the contributors who approach literature from a feminist perspective — Meyer, Deutsch-Schreiner, Lorenz, Anderson, and Arens — discuss Schnitzler in remarkably positive terms, despite the fact that he was anything but an early feminist or a proponent of women's rights. However, his writings reveal an unequivocal awareness of the oppressive structures of his native society and his two cultures, that of the Austrian mainstream and Jewish society. These scholars distinguish between Schnitzler the man and his literary production without ignoring that Schnitzler took ample advantage of the opportunities his society offered him, a society that condoned male privilege and the moral double standard. Yet, he recognized the factors that enabled men to become exploiters, and he exposed the fundamentally unjust gender and class structures of Habsburg Austria. Even Schnitzler as he emerges from letters and autobiographical works appears to have been a man far less able to enjoy his position of privilege than an uninformed but widespread image of the carefree, shallow bohemian implies. Schnitzler's star image is incompatible with the documented experience of a man who suffered from bouts of depression and self-doubt, a man far less adroit at juggling his multiple affairs and coping with disappointment than his earlier writings would suggest.

But, most important, it is the insights into the psyche of his female protagonists and their problematic relationships with members of the opposite sex, be they lovers, husbands, fathers, sons, or brothers, that are apt to win Schnitzler the sympathy of female, even feminist, audiences and readers. His female protagonists bear little resemblance to the clichés of femininity so richly represented in *fin-de-siècle*, early-twentieth-century and, later, Nazi and Marxist literature. Similarly, Schnitzler's representation of men deviates considerably from the heroic male stereotypes dominating the nationalist as well as the revolutionary discourse of the time. Schnitzler did not join in the call for the "New Man," whether from a Socialist, a Zionist, or a nationalist perspective. Rather, he revealed the frailties of men and women, their shared goals and wishes, and their suffering because of external as well as emotional or intellectual barriers. There are no constitutional differences between the men and women in his literary works, contrary to Freud's psychology and Weininger's sexology. Schnitzler was thoroughly familiar with these writings, and, without validating them, he alludes to and plays with them. As is the case with his attitudes toward political doctrines, he refuses to subject his literary creation to the psychological doctrines of his time.

The essays in this volume show that the life and thought of Schnitzler, the writer and intellectual, are as paradigmatic of their time and milieu as they are exceptional. Schnitzler's keen insights into the modern condition enabled him to articulate concerns that are still relevant to audiences at the turn of the twenty-first century, as is obvious from Stanley Kubrick's motion picture *Eyes Wide Shut* (1999), which presents many of the same problems addressed by Schnitzler: the erosion of intimacy, trust, and individuality within anonymous urban society, as well as addictions and compulsions ranging from alcoholism to gambling and obsession with sex. Schnitzler's preoccupation with the drive to destroy, manifested in xenophobia, alienated relationships, and a pervasive despair leading to suicide, murder, or both, continues to be a highly controversial topic. So is the problem of mental illness, the individual's detachment from reality leading to neurotic or psychotic states. In Schnitzler the latter are often associated with the impasse created by conflicting imperatives such as the character's ingrained emotional patterns and his or her frustrated desire to take full advantage of the opportunities available to the modern individual. The contemporary media continue to rely on these fundamentally bourgeois issues to attract and entertain millions of spectators and readers, most of whom identify themselves as middle-class in one fashion or another.

Because of political events in Austria in the 1980s and 1990s, which called for renewed attention to the Nazi and Austro-Fascist past, Schnitzler is once again more than a canonical writer represented in university curricula and a solid presence in the programs of the premier German and Austrian theaters. The discussions about his work include issues of morality and quality, aesthetics, and ideological and social issues. Of particular interest are Schnitzler's representation of characters, psychology, his views on gender and class, and the relationships between his own life and his writing as well as between his Jewishness and his professional persona as a physician. His relations with prominent contemporaries and the impact of historical developments on his writing are also important topics in Schnitzler scholarship. The considerable number of innovative close readings of individual works in light of postmodern theory reveals the continued appeal of his writings.

In an era of profound uncertainty in the global political and national arena, morality and ethics remain as contested as ever. Despite their *fin-de-siècle* setting, which seemed nostalgic as early as just after the First World War, Schnitzler's works are radical in the way they expose seemingly private and personal concerns and question concepts of character and the individual as well as psychological and ideological tenets — psychoanalysis, Socialism, and Zionism — of his day. Compared to more radical stylistic innovators, Schnitzler modifies established aesthetic forms only subtly. But his works undermine the traditional value system. His unmasking of outdated social institutions and their fallible representatives has an unsettling effect that suggests the necessary break with the old. The disparity between the decorous language of high culture and the mind-sets of individuals signals a society about to disintegrate. This disparity is especially obvious in his late works, *Therese* and *Flucht in die Finsternis,* which expose the unbearable tension between social form and personal perception.

Schnitzler's Jewishness and his relationship with intellectuals struggling with the issues of emancipation, assimilation, and Jewish distinctiveness has come to the foreground most notably in the wake of the Waldheim election in 1986, at the time when a new Austrian Jewish discourse emerged.[22] For the young intellectuals who had grown up in a Vienna virtually without Jews and who struggled with some of the old issues in a new setting, Schnitzler became an important model. By looking back at the rich Jewish heritage of the *fin-de-siècle* and the interwar period, and by establishing connections with other Jewish texts, authors such as Schindel and Beckermann, who were born at the end of and after the Second World War and members of the following generation, including the scholar Matti Bunzl, the son of the prominent Austrian historian John Bunzl (1945–),[23] were able to shape a Jewish discourse apart from the dominant culture. In her book on Jewish life in contemporary Austria, *Unzugehörig* (1989), Beckermann pays Schnitzler the highest tribute by giving the first chapter of her essay on Jews and Austrians after 1945 the title of his autobiography, *Jugend in Wien*.[24] About Schnitzler's influence on her development as an intellectual Beckermann writes in her essay "Jean Améry and Austria'":

> First came Schnitzler and Zweig. Also, they were secret allies against the daily infamy of the old and young, against the crucifix on the classroom wall and the rod in the bag. No matter how different our chosen writers were, they named the stale atmosphere we felt without being able to express it. Schnitzler discussed everything that mattered to us in his drama *Professor Bernhardi* and particularly in his novel *Der Weg ins Freie*. However that was at a different time.[25]

Bunzl, in turn, recognizes Schnitzler's legacy as well as Beckermann's accomplishment in the title of his own study, "From Kreisky to Waldheim. Another Jewish Youth in Vienna" (1999), an allusion to her chapter "Jugend in Wien" (Youth in Vienna) in *Unzugehörig* and Schnitzler's own autobiography, *Jugend in Wien* (1968, *My Youth in Vienna*, 1970).[26] The "rediscovery" of Schnitzler by the post-Shoah generations, alongside Friedrich Torberg and Joseph Roth as author and witness to a part of Central European culture in danger of being forgotten, as well as the interest sparked by Kubrick's movie, show that even at the beginning of a new millennium, the potential that Schnitzler's texts hold is far from being exhausted. The references of Schnitzler's literary texts follow the standard four-volume *Gesammelte Werke* of 1961–1962.[27] Works not included in this edition — such as *Jugend in Wien*, the *Aphorismen und Betrachtungen*, the *Medizinische Schriften*, Schnitzler's posthumous unpublished works, *Entworfenes und Verworfenes: Aus dem Nachlaß*, and the nine-volume diaries, *Tagebuch* — are cited from their respective Fischer editions. Except for variances in the page numbering, the many hardcover and paperback editions of Schnitzler's writings that appeared from the author's original publisher, S. Fischer, are reprints of the texts authorized by Schnitzler.

Notes

[1] *Arthur Schnitzler. Sein Leben. Sein Werk. Seine Zeit.*, eds. Heinrich Schnitzler, Christian Brandstätter, and Reinhard Urbach (Frankfurt: Fischer, 1981), 50.

[2] *Der Weg ins Freie*, in ES I, 635–958.

[3] Friedrich Wolf, *Professor Mamlock* (Berlin: Volk und Wissen, 1957). The play first appeared in English, translated by Anne Bromberger, as *Professor Mamlock* (New York: Universum Publishers and Distributors, 1935) and had been printed in the Soviet Union. Lion Feuchtwanger's novel *Die Geschwister Oppenheim* was first published in Amsterdam by Querido in 1933. The work became better known as *Die Geschwister Oppermann* in the 1963 edition from the Berlin Aufbau Verlag and the BBC/ZDF television mini-series of 1986, subtitled as *The Oppermanns*. The novel was translated as *The Oppermanns* by James Cleugh (London: Secker, 1934).

[4] *Arthur Schnitzler. Sein Leben. Sein Werk. Seine Zeit.*, 360.

[5] *Arthur Schnitzler. Sein Leben. Sein Werk. Seine Zeit.*, 360.

[6] Peter Gay, *Schnitzler's Century. The Making of Middle-Class Culture 1815–1914* (New York: Norton, 2001).

[7] Hannah Arendt, *Rahel Varnhagen: Lebensgeschichte einer deutschen Jüdin aus der Romantik* (Munich: Piper, 1962), 162. See also: Arendt, *The Jew as Pariah: Jewish Identity and Politics in the Modern Age* (New York: Grove Press, 1978).

[8] Marsha Rozenblit, *The Jews of Vienna 1867–1914. Assimilation and Identity* (Albany: State U of New York P, 1983), 147.

[9] Gay, 4.

[10] Rozenblit, 100, 107. "In short, at the Gymnasium, middle-class Jews absorbed the European cultural legacy in the company of other Jews. They were initiated into secular learning as a group. Despite complete acculturation, Jewish Gymnasium students experienced no compulsion to meet and befriend gentiles." (125).

[11] Gay, 3.

[12] Egon Schwarz, "Jews and Anti-Semitism in Fin-de-Siècle Vienna," in *Insiders and Outsiders. Jewish and Gentile Culture in Germany and Austria*, eds. Dagmar C. G. Lorenz and Gabriele Weinberger (Detroit: Wayne State UP, 1994), 58.

[13] Gay, xix–xx.

[14] Young Schnitzler was fascinated with Vienna's inner city street-walkers and visited some of them. *Arthur Schnitzler. Sein Leben. Sein Werk. Seine Zeit.*, 36–37A discussion with his father about sexually transmitted diseases caused him to use caution in casual encounters but did not discourage him altogether. Gay writes: "Venereal infection was a real menace of the age, and middle-class adolescents, thousands of Arthur Schnitzler's contemporaries, armed with a lighthearted sense of their immortality and given to nocturnal escapades with ladies of dubious reputations, were particularly susceptible to the hazards of gonorrhea and syphilis" (130).

[15] Jakob Wassermann, in *Mein Weg als Deutscher und Jude* (Berlin: S. Fischer, 1921), for example, emphasizes the affinity between Germans and Jews, which exacerbates

German intolerance. Feuchtwanger in *Die Geschwister Oppenheim* (1933), takes up the same theme to explain the outrages of the years 1932–1933, and Wolf's drama *Professor Mamlock*, written in 1933, combines themes familiar from Schnitzler's *Professor Bernhardi* with the tragedy of the all-too-patriotic Jewish doctor who cannot or will not recognize his enemies.

[16] Schwarz, 61.

[17] Arthur Schnitzler, *Tagebuch*, 10 vols., ed. Werner Welzig (Vienna: Verlag der Österreichischen Akademie der Wissenschaften, 1987–2000).

[18] Daniel Boyarin, *Unheroic Conduct. The Rise of Heterosexuality and the Invention of the Jewish Man* (Berkeley: U of California P, 1997); Sander Gilman, *The Jew's Body* (New York: New York UP, 1991).

[19] Horst Thomé, "Kernlosigkeit und Pose: Zur Rekonstruktion von Schnitzlers Psychologie," in *Fin de Siècle*, ed. Klause Bohnen (Copenhagen: Fink, 1984), 62–84.

[20] Ruth Beckermann, *Unzugehörig. Österreicher und Juden nach 1945* (Vienna: Löcker, 1989), 118.

[21] Arthur Schnitzler, *Jugend in Wien. Eine Autobiographie*, ed. Therese Nickl and Heinrich Schnitzler (Vienna, Munich, Zurich: Fritz Molden, 1968). Schwarz writes: "Arthur Schnitzler presented his readers with a gallery of Jewish types, each exemplifying a different aspect of the multiple attitudes available to them in that moment in history" (60).

[22] See for example the interviews in Peter Sichrovsky's *Wir wissen nicht was morgen wird, wir wissen wohl, was gestern war: Junge Juden in Deutschland und Österreich* (Cologne: Kiepenheuer und Witsch, 1985) and Beckermann, *Unzugehörig*.

[23] John Bunzl's publications on Austrian Jewish history were path-breaking in directing attention at a lost tradition, for example *Klassenkampf in der Diaspora: zur Geschichte d. jüdischen Arbeiterbewegung* (Vienna:: Europaverlag, 1975) and John Bunzl and Bernd Marin, *Antisemitismus in Österreich: sozialhistorische und soziologische Studien* (Innsbruck: Inn Verlag, 1983).

[24] Beckermann, *Unzugehörig*, 117–30.

[25] Ruth Beckermann, "Jean Améry and Austria," in *Insiders and Outsiders: Jewish and Gentile Culture in Germany and Austria*, 73–88.

[26] Matti Bunzl, "From Kreisky to Waldheim. Another Jewish Youth in Vienna," in *Contemporary Jewish Writing in Austria*, ed. Dagmar C. G. Lorenz (Lincoln and London: U of Nebraska P, 1999), 346–58. See as an example of the new appreciation for pre-Shoah Jewish authors Ruth Beckermann's volume of photos of Jewish life in the Leopoldstadt and texts by Jewish authors of that era in *Die Mazzesinsel. Juden in der Wiener Leopoldstadt* (Vienna: Löcker, 1984).

[27] *Gesammelte Werke* [*Die Erzählenden Schriften* I and II; *Die Dramatischen Werke* I and II] (Frankfurt am Main: Fischer, 1961–1962). Cited as: DW=*Dramatische Werke*; ES=*Die Erzählenden Schriften*.

The Author and His Audiences

Fig. 1: Lustige Blätter 1904.

The Social and Political Context of Arthur Schnitzler's *Reigen* in Berlin, Vienna, and New York: 1900–1933

Gerd K. Schneider

LIBELLI SUA FATA HABENT — books have their own fate, a saying that is especially true for Arthur Schnitzler's *Reigen*,[1] considered by many to be one of the most scandalous plays written in the German language. Written in the winter of 1896/97, it is a work about people who make love without being in love. It consists of ten dialogues or scenes, in each of which two characters of different social standing engage in a conversation before and after the sexual act, indicated by dashes in the text. In every scene one of the partners is a lover from a previous encounter: The Prostitute and the Soldier, the Soldier and the Housemaid, the Housemaid and the Young Gentleman, the Young Gentleman and the Young Married Woman, the Young Married Woman and her Husband, the Husband and the Sweet Girl, the Sweet Girl and the Poet, the Poet and the Actress, the Actress and the Count. Finally the circle closes with the meeting of the two characters representing the highest and the lowest social rank, the Count and the Prostitute.

Schnitzler's ten dialogues were used by political parties in Austria and Germany to advance their own anti-liberal and anti-Semitic platforms, and they saw in Schnitzler's Jewishness a welcome opportunity to do so. Newspaper reviews and other comments in the media about this play are important because they provide a window on society. It must be remembered that in the beginning of the twentieth century, newspapers were used for political purposes and reached a multitude of people. Their impact cannot be measured only by the numbers of copies sold, because these newspapers were easily obtainable in the coffee houses. Schnitzler also knew what the press wrote about him and his plays, because he employed two newspaper-clipping services, one in Vienna and one in Berlin.

Analysis of the societal and political concerns reflected in responses to this play may be divided into two parts: the reception of *Reigen* in Germany and Austria until 1914, followed by the reception in Germany,

Austria, and the United States after 1918. This division can be justified not only because of the hard times brought upon the Viennese and Austrians as a result of a lost war, but also because *Reigen* was conceived as a work to be read only, which was primarily the case until the end of 1918. After the end of the First World War, *Reigen* was staged in major European cities: In Berlin on December 23, 1920; in Hamburg on December 31, 1920; in Kiel on January 6, 1921; in Munich and Leipzig on January 22, 1921; in Brünn on February 7, 1921; in Vienna on February 1, 1921; in Breslau on May 5, 1921; in Gera on July 1, 1921; in Frankfurt on July 4, 1921; in Köslin on August 31, 1921; in Hannover on September 4, 1921; in Aussig on November 27, 1921; in Königsberg on December 5, 1921; in Eisenach on January 4, 1922; in Dresden on July 28, 1922; in Copenhagen on May 9, 1925; and in Rome on March 9, 1926. Its public staging agitated many more people than reading the ten dialogues.

While few remarks were positive, lauding Schnitzler's artistic expertise to create this work, many reviewers equated Schnitzler's "decadent" portrayal of his "Dance of Lust" with a "Dance of Death." This is also the title of Carl Müller-Rastatt's review, "Totentanz. Zur Uraufführung von Schnitzlers *Reigen* in den Hamburger Kammerspielen":

> Aber die zehn Gespräche, die ohne einen anderen Zusammenhang sind, als daß in jedem mit mathematischer Pünktlichkeit derselbe Akt vollzogen wird, gehören ganz gewiß nicht auf die Bühne. Das war ja bis jetzt so sehr Schnitzlers eigene Meinung, daß er zwanzig Jahre lang jede Aufführung energisch untersagt hat. Er wußte, warum. Wer sich für den *Reigen* als Kunstwerk interessierte, der konnte ihn lesen, denn dafür war er ja geschrieben. Wer diese Dialoge im Rampenlicht von lebendigen Menschen gesprochen haben will, der tut dem Dichter keinen Gefallen und lenkt die Aufmerksamkeit vom Geistigen des Werks auf das grob Stoffliche, grob Sinnliche über. Die Not, die auf Oesterreich lastet, soll Schnitzler jetzt veranlaßt haben, in die Aufführung dieser Dialoge trotz allem einzuwilligen. Die Not, in der sich unsere Theaterkassen befinden, veranlaßt die Theaterleiter, von dieser Einwilligung Gebrauch zu machen. . . . Im Dienst der stittlichen Erneuerung sind die *Reigen*-Aufführungen jedenfalls nicht.[2]

The Period before 1914

The first private printing of *Reigen,* limited to 200 copies, appeared in 1900. The first commercial printing by the Wiener Verlag was published in 1903. By that time Schnitzler had established a reputation as a serious writer, so that *Reigen* could not be easily dismissed as a work of pornography. Schnitzler was courageous enough in writing *Reigen,* because his play took away the proverbial Viennese charm and exposed the psychological and egotistical interplay of sex and social customs, focusing his attention more on the "before" and "after" rather than on the sexual act itself. Schnitzler showed, as Carl Schorske wrote, "that beauty, which his culture had seen merely as an escape from the everyday world, pointed to another world — the ill-defined realm of the irrational."[3] The "irrational" also included political elements, because it showed that the sexual instinct is the same in all social classes, regardless of their special rights and privileges:

> As a Viennese, Schnitzler could readily approach the world of the instinct from the social types disclosed to the literary naturalist. Vienna's playboys and *süsse Mädel,* the debonair sensualists of the age, provided him with the characters of his early works. What he explored in them was the compulsiveness of Eros, its satisfactions, its delusions, its strange affinity to Thanatos and — notably in *La ronde* (*Reigen,* 1896) — its terrible power to dissolve all social hierarchy.[4]

Doing so was not easily accepted in Vienna, of which Renate Wagner observed in her Schnitzler biography that there had rarely been a city as tolerant of sexual license, provided one condition is adhered to: that one never openly discusses the topic.[5]

The first laudatory comments about *Reigen* were written by people who knew Schnitzler either personally or from his works. One example may suffice. On April 18, 1903, Philipp Frey praised Schnitzler's courage in bringing socially taboo subjects into the open, noting that in every scene the author moves resolutely toward a series of hyphens indicating that the level the conversation has reached is far removed from the conceptual plane.[6] Frey, as well as others who commented favorably on *Reigen,* belonged to the Viennese intelligentsia; they were not members of the disadvantaged lower class who saw in *Reigen* a decadent work, dangerous enough to corrupt the moral health of their children. This concern was not unfounded, because *Reigen* appeared at a time when erotic and pornographic literature abounded.

Such explicit works came from Budapest and Munich and were also printed privately in Vienna. The *Oesterreichische Volks-Presse* of June 14, 1903, warned in the section "Moderne Literatur" that these books had a particularly damaging effect on fourteen- to twenty-year-old boys and girls: "Mit glühenden Augen betrachten selbe die dargestellten Szenen, die hier nicht beschrieben werden können." The main point of criticism coming from the Social Democrats was that Schnitzler did not show the dangers inherent in his superficial sexual-partner exchange. The morning edition of the *Arbeiter-Zeitung* of September 10, 1903, accused Schnitzler of a lack of insight into the living conditions of a social class to which he did not belong. *Reigen* lacked, according to the reviewer, psychological and moral depth, and its success could be explained primarily because of its risqué subject matter. Missing was the realistic portrayal of the conditions under which the less fortunate lived: "Wie viel Schrecknisse, wie viel Bitternis in diesem unheimlichen Reigen der Paare, das hatte der mehr zur glatten Liebenswürdigkeit neigende Dichter nicht einmal anzudeuten gewußt." The horrors to which this article referred included venereal diseases found in thirteen- and fourteen-year-old youngsters who lived in asylums similar to the one described in the same edition of the *Arbeiter-Zeitung*:

> [E]ine Wohnung von einem Zimmer, einem Kabinett und Küche, die als Nachtasyl für Kinder dient! Da schlafen drei Kinder in einem Bette, zwei Mädchen und ein Knabe, daneben auf dem Ofen schläft ein vierzehnjähriger Junge und auf dem Boden vor dem Ofen hat sich noch ein fünftes Kind hingestreckt. Entlaufene, obdachlose, verdorbene Kinder liegen da beisammen. Einem der Mädchen hat der Knabe seine Krankheit zu verdanken.

The girl, as the article pointed out, had contracted the disease from a Jewish officer who had an affair with a "verlotterten dreizehnjährigen Mädchen." This side of *fin-de-siècle* Vienna was not shown in Schnitzler's erotic dialogues. As Wolfgang Maderthaner and Lutz Musner point out, Schnitzler did not mention the seedy side of Vienna,

> [d]as dunkle, rauchige, elende und dreckige Wien, bevölkert mit Einwanderern, Proletariern, Hausierern, Dienstbotinnen, Arbeitslosen, Kriminellen und sogenannten Taugenichtsen, welches flächenmäßig das Zentrum bei weitem übertraf. . . . [7]

It may be assumed that the problems facing the homeless were known to the Viennese public because illustrations like this one, published in the magazine *Der liebe Augustin* in 1904, reminded the public of the fate and dilemma of the disadvantaged:

*Fig. 2: "Obdachlos," Der liebe Augustin, 18 (1904), 288.
Published with permission of the Schiller-Nationalmuseum
and the Deutschen Literaturarchiv in Marbach/Neckar.*

As Maderthaner and Musner have shown, the people in the suburbs lived under crowded and unsanitary conditions, with entire families sharing one room. Alcoholism and prostitution, even among children, who often had contracted venereal disease, were common. Schnitzler mentions the suburbs, the "Vorstadt," but primarily as the domicile of the *süße Mädel,* such as the ones represented in *Anatol* (1893), *Liebelei* (1896), and *Reigen*. In Schnitzler's works she is a literary figure, but what was her background and future? Paul Busson's poem appeared in the magazine *Der liebe Augustin* in 1904 underneath a cartoon that highlights the erotic allure of the *süße Mädel*:

Fig. 3: "Das Süße Mädel," Der liebe Augustin, 11 (1904), 169.
Published with permission of the Schiller-Nationalmuseum
and the Deutschen Literaturarchiv in Marbach/Neckar.

Younger children in the suburbs, especially girls, did not fare any better. The fate of some is vividly described by the Slovenian author Ivan Cankar in his novel *Hiša Marije Pomocnice*, published first in Ljubljana in 1904 and translated into German in 1996 as *Haus der Barmherzigkeit*. In this work Cankar describes a hospital in Vienna and its patients, most of them victims of poverty and abuse.[8]

The Social Democrats who were fighting social injustice saw in *Reigen* a danger because the play might contribute to the corruption of young people. The condemnation of *Reigen* did not change in the years to come. When *Reigen* was presented as a public reading in Vienna on February 23, 1905, an anonymous reviewer called reading this particular work during an election meeting of the socialist party an error in judgment. A review titled "Eine unterbrochene Rezitation," published in the *Arbeiter-Zeitung* on February 24, 1905, charged that the play was out of keeping with the Social Democratic cause:

> Durch eine bedauerliche Unvorsichtigkeit der berufenen Funktionäre war für den letzten Vortragsabend des Sozialdemokratischen Wahlvereins Josefstadt die Rezitation von Schnitzlers *Reigen* angekündigt worden. Man mag nun über den Wert dieses Werkes denken, wie man will, zur Rezitation in einem sozialdemokratischen Verein ist die Sache nicht geeignet.

Only a third of *Reigen* was read, upon the request of a member; the overwhelming majority decided to stop the reading. This incident elicited the acclaim of the more conservative forces, as the Viennese edition of the *Deutsche Zeitung* reported on February 26, 1905, in an article that ultimately attributed more decency to the Social Democrats than to the intellectual elite:

> Im sozialdemokratischen Wahlverein des 8. Bezirks wollte dieser Tage ein Herr, [sic] Schnitzlers *Reigen* vorlesen. Das ging selbst den Genossen über die Hutschnur, und ein Genosse stellte den Antrag, daß der Vortrag abgebrochen werden möge, was auch geschah. Dieser Vorfall beweist, daß selbst die Sozialdemokraten mehr Schamgefühl besitzen, als unsere "Intellektuellen."

It is the darker side of the living conditions of Vienna's lower class that lay underneath the beautiful surface. Not only the poor living conditions of the workers contributed to the upheaval caused by the publication of *Reigen* but also the general political climate, which had changed drastically around the turn of the century. Racial anti-Semitism was propagated by Georg Ritter von Schönerer (1842–1921) and Karl Lueger (1844–1910), who served as mayor of Vienna from 1897 to 1910, despite objections by the Emperor Francis Joseph. Schorske describes the period that followed:

The Christian Social demagogues began a decade of rule in Vienna which combined all that was anathema to classical liberalism: anti-Semitism, clericalism, and municipal socialism. On the national level as well, the liberals were broken as a parliamentary political power by 1900, never to revive. They had been crushed by modern mass movements, Christian, anti-Semitic, socialist, and nationalist.[9]

This highly sensitive political situation needed only a precipitating cause to burst out in the open.

Seeds of this outburst were already visible in 1903 after the first publication of *Reigen*. Right-wing parties exploited the fear of families with children, and by coupling pornography with anti-Semitism, fueled already existing anti-Semitic sentiments. Comments expressing moral indignation, such as those written by Friedrich Törnsee and published in the *Neue Bahnen* in 1903, illustrate this strategy:

> Reigen ist nämlich nichts als eine Schweinerei oder, ist das zu deutsch, eine Cochonnerie, die bloß der Esprit eines Parisers oder die Satire eines Künstlers, der moralisch hoch genug steht, um das Lüsterne des Tema's [sic] sachlich verurteilend zu behandeln, aus der Reihe des Pornographischen in das Gebiet der Kunst hätte emporheben können. Über das Buch eingehend zu schreiben, ja es nur inhaltlich zu streifen — hieße ihm Reklame machen.[10]

Ottokar Stauf von der March (Fritz Chalupka) supported his colleague Törnsee in this concerted action by referring to *Reigen* in the morning edition of the *Ostdeutsche Rundschau* on May 17, 1903, as a vulgar and decadent book replete with platitudes, a work without meaning or significance,

> ein ordinäres, sondern auch ein nichtssagendes und plattes Buch, mit dem sich der Verfasser außerhalb des Schrifttums stellt in die Reihen der gewissenlosen Sudler, deren mephitische Erzeugnisse die Spalten der sogenannten Wiener "Witz"-Blätter *ad majorem Veneris vulgivagae gloriam* füllen. Schnitzler hat freilich schon von allem Anfang an starke Neigung zu diesem sauberen Handwerk besessen, für ihn existierte beinahe nichts als das Geschlechtliche, und zwar in seiner grobsinnlichsten Erscheinungsform . . . allenthalben [ist] der bekannte *foetor judaicus* zu spüren . . ., wie bei der "Décadence" überhaupt . . . Dabei ist es [*Reigen*] mit so hündischer Geschlechtsgier geschrieben, daß es einem ekelt.[11]

Some reviews stressed the fact that social truth was superior to a description of reality because showing the truth could prove harmful to young minds. An example is a review published in the *Hamburger Fremdenblatt* on May 2, 1903:

Reigen [zeigt Bilder der Wirklichkeit], aber der sarkastische, häufig spöttische Ton der Wiedergabe grentz an Frivolität. Wir sehen nicht ein, was der Autor damit bezweckt. Der Schaden, den solche "vorurteilslose" Schilderung bei jungen Lesern hervorruft . . . wiegt doch wohl scwerer, als die künstlerische Befriedigung des Autors. In unserem Zeitalter der sozialen Fürsorge hätte ein Schriftsteller wie Schnitzler besser getan, seine Studien im Pulte liefen zu lassen, anstatt die große Bibliothek der "pikanten Lektüre" noch zu vermehren.[12]

The first partial performance of *Reigen,* scenes 4–6, was staged by the *Akademisch Dramatischer Verein* in Munich. The reception was mixed, and many critics agreed that the play ought to be read rather than publicly performed. The students participating in this first production were dismissed from the university by Bavaria's cultural minister, an act with which most newspapers agreed; the *Dresdner Anzeiger* of June 28, 1903, suggested that Schnitzler had written these dialogues for male audiences only, "für *Herrengesellschaften* [bachelor parties] und dort mag man sie aufführen. Einen höheren Wert haben die parfümierten Cochonnerien kaum." More aggressive was the tone of the *Wiener Neues Journal* of July 2, 1903, which depicted the dialogues of "Schnitzlers *Reigen*" as a danger for the purity of family life and the psychological well-being of the sexes. This review also included veiled anti-Semitic sentiments. They are inherent in the clearly stated hostility to modern urban culture and the oblique references to racial stereotypes as expressed in the anti-Semitic press of the time:

Es ist Schnitzlers gutes Recht, die Liebe aufzufassen, wie er will. Aber es ist auch unser gutes Recht, diese Auffassung als unkünstlerisch, als kulturfeindlich, als vom Standpunkt jeder Sittlichkeit aus unsittlich zu empfinden . . . Wir können uns kaum mehr retten vor all dem Schmutz, der von Paris und Berlin, Wien und Budapest her in Deutschland zusammenströmt; es ist geradezu unheimlich, wie tief und rapid der Stand der öffentlichen Anständigkeit in den letzten zehn Jahren gesunken ist, durch Bücher, Bilder, Tingeltangel, Postkarten, Annoncen, Witzblätter, Gassenhauer, Operetten, Possen, reine und pseudowissenschaftliche Pornographie, durch gewisse Redouten und Herrenabende, durch Schaufenster . . . Man mag Katholik oder Protestant, Christ oder Atheist, radikal oder konservativ sein: Reinheit des Familienlebens, Keuschheit der Frau, Treue des Mannes, Reinhaltung der Jugend, Gesundheit der Geschlechter stehen auf dem Spiele! Und da geht einer von den ersten und geachtetsten deutschen Schriftstellern hin und überläßt der Oeffentlichkeit ein solches Buch.[13]

This article was reprinted with only small changes on the first two pages of Munich's morning newspaper *Allgemeine Zeitung* on November 27, 1903. It was quite common for the same article to appear in Vienna and other big German cities, sometimes on the same day, made possible through the advent of wireless telegraphy.

The conservative forces succeeded in having all erotic literature banned. This included *Reigen,* as the *Münchner Nachrichten* of March 18, 1904, announced in its *Vorabend=Blatt* that Schnitzler's *Reigen* was, according to a report from Leipzig, confiscated upon an initiative from Berlin and banned for all of Germany: "Schnitzlers *Reigen* ist, wie aus Leipzig berichtet word, dort auf Veranlassung der Berliner für ganz Deutschland *konfiziert* worden."[14] This edict was used again by the anti-Semitic forces to call for a strike against Jews. On May 13, 1904, Jekelins published a column titled "Arische Literatur" in the morning edition of the *Deutsche Zeitung.* On May 14, 1904, a letter to the editor, signed "Ein arischer Schriftsteller," appeared in response to this column distinguishing between superior Aryan criticism and inferior non-Aryan or Jewish criticism.[15]

The campaign against performance of *Reigen* was continued in Vienna and Germany during the summer of 1905. One of the comments published in the *Allgemeine Rundschau* on May 14, 1905, expressed the harshest criticism against *Reigen* and its "racially foreign" author:

> In den letzten Jahren haben drei land-oder rassenfremde Schriftsteller dem deutschen Volke drei Danaergeschenke angeboten. Schnitzlers *Reigen* war selbst für unsere realistischen Bühnen zu schmutzig. Es grassiert nur in Buchform, im deutschen Volke.

Schnitzler was weary of the complaints lodged against *Reigen,* and also of the personal attacks he had to suffer because of this work. He did not take these aggressive comments in the press lying down; he was a fighter who did not lean toward compromise. His perspective and relativism led him to view a situation from various angles but did not extend toward anti-Semitism. In a comment published posthumously he stated that anti-Semites would never succeed in insulting him, a Jew, notwithstanding the physical violence and verbal attacks they deployed, and he recorded the following prophetic words:

> Keinem Menschen auf der Welt kann es jemals gelingen, mich zu beschimpfen. Man kann mich anschreien. mich verhöhnen, mich — wenn es mehrere sind, und die Antisemiten sind immer mehrere durchprügeln, mich verleumden, mich kreuzigen, mich verbrennen . . . kurz, alles auf der Welt, aber gerade beschimpfen kann man mich nie . . .

beleidigt kann der Schuldlose niemals werden. So kann durch den Antisemitismus der Jude geärgert, geschädigt und vernichtet werden —
aber beschimpft niemals.[16]

In order to escape from the personal vendettas Schnitzler withdrew the
play from public showing, and with the exception of a few unauthorized
performances, it was not offered until after the First World War.

The Period after 1918: Berlin and Vienna

The end of the First World War brought many changes, not only politically but also financially. It seems that financial hardship also motivated
Schnitzler to reconsider his refusal to have *Reigen* staged. He was encouraged to do so by the publisher S. Fischer, who thought that after the
war a more liberal portrayal of sexuality was acceptable. Fischer erred,
however, because the time was not yet ripe for a public performance of
Reigen, as the productions in Berlin and Vienna showed.[17]

There had been a marked rise in anti-Semitism after the war, and
Schnitzler was very much aware of it. New was the "Salzburger-
Programm" of the *Großdeutschen Volkspartei*, which combined many
national parties at the party congress from September 5–7, 1920.[18] The
party platform stressed *Volksgemeinschaft*, or national unity, rather than
liberal individualism, which was associated primarily with Jews. In the
section "Unsere Stellung zur Judenfrage" of the "Salzburger Programm," liberalism, crass materialism, and Jewishness are equated:

> Der Jude betont, seiner Rassenveranlagung entsprechend, stets das Gegen-
> sätzliche, er findet überall das Trennende heraus, nicht das Verbindende.[19]

Interesting in this article is also the vocabulary taken from the world of
business — *Geldverdienen, Marktgegenstand, Saisongeschäft, Reklametrommel*. This commercial attitude is also part of Schnitzler's time and
society. He himself showed the tragic consequences of this capitalistic
thinking in the interior-monologue novella *Fräulein Else* (1924), in
which an art dealer offers to "buy" a favor from the female protagonist.

The "Salzburger Programm" was far more radical than point 12 of
the "Linzer Programm der Deutschnationalen"(1882), which called for
eliminating Jewish influences in all sectors of public life and was actually
added after 1885: "Zur Durchführung der angestrebten Reformen ist die
Beseitigung des jüdischen Einflusses auf allen Gebieten des öffentlichen
Lebens unerläßlich."[20] In addition, Otto Weininger's anti-feminist and
anti-Judaic book *Geschlecht und Charakter*, which was first published in

1903, had until 1918 gone through seventeen printings and was republished from 1920 on. Weininger complained about "[u]nsere Zeit, die nicht nur die jüdischeste, sondern auch die weibischeste aller Zeiten ist."[21] The polarities he establishes are quite evident when he writes that humanity is called upon to choose between Judaism and Christianity, business and culture, woman and man:

> Zwischen Judentum und Christentum, zwischen Geschäft und Kultur, zwischen Weib und Mann, zwischen Gattung und Persönlichkeit, zwischen Unwert und Wert, zwischen irdischem und höherem Leben, zwischen dem Nichts und der Gottheit hat abermals die Menschheit die Wahl. Das sind die beiden Pole: es gibt kein drittes Reich.[22]

The "Third Reich" as a compromise did not exist in Weininger's time, but in the 1920s it was already in the making, although in a different way than Weininger anticipated in his terminology. The reception of *Reigen* in Berlin may serve as an example of how the forces that shaped the Third Reich operated. Again, a literary work was used for political purposes, only this time the anti-liberal forces had gained in strength compared to the period around 1900.

The Berlin Scandal

Schnitzler, after much deliberation, authorized a public performance of *Reigen* in 1920. Since Max Reinhardt had given up the directorship of his theaters in the summer of 1920, Felix Holländer, the new director, arranged for the production of *Reigen* as "Ensemblegastspiel des Deutschen Theaters" in the Kleines Schauspielhaus, which was part of the Hochschule für Musik. This factor was important since the theater fell under the authority and jurisdiction of the Prussian Ministry of Arts, Sciences, and Education, which could intervene if it felt that the performance did not meet the moral standard it had set. The producers, Gertrud Eysoldt and Maximilian Sladek, were aware of that, and they discussed with Schnitzler every aspect of the staging, making forty-one textual changes and omitting everything that could be inflammatory. *Reigen,* under the direction of Hubert Reusch, premiered on December 23, 1920, in the Berliner Kleines Schauspielhaus, despite an injunction by the Hochschule für Musik two hours before the performance. The producers ignored this detail and went ahead with the performance after Eysoldt had stepped in front of the curtain and informed the audience of the injunction. The 6. Zivilkammer des Landgerichts III legally withdrew the injunction on January 3, 1921.

In order to understand the events that followed from the performance of *Reigen* in Berlin, one has to recall the overall social-political context of the period after 1918. The shaky start of the Weimar Republic in Germany provided a fertile ground for anti-Semitism. Although the Jews in the Weimar period numbered only 600,000 of a total population of 65,000,000 — only 0.9% of the German population — Jews held approximately 3.5% of the positions in trade, commerce, banking, and especially the professions of medicine and law.[23] Jews, then, although a minority, "presented a physical target on which frustrations and hatreds of a society in crisis could be most easily focused. The Jews were the lightning conductor which such institutions as the Labour movement and the Church could not provide."[24] The term Jews, as used in the publications dealing with this period, included all strata, ranging from the wealthy, highly cultured intelligentsia and the economically successful professionals, such as lawyers, doctors, and journalists, to the small urban businessmen and traveling salesmen. These groups varied in wealth, but the prosperous business people and professionals raised the average income of Jews in Weimar Germany to 3.2 times the average income of the total population.[25] The living standard of these groups was also considerably higher than that of average German middle-class citizens, who lost most of their financial resources after the war because of rampant inflation. This economic disparity caused envy that manifested itself in anti-Semitic attitudes and aggressive behavior.

In addition to the economic factor, another root of anti-Semitism that existed at the beginning of and during the Weimar Republic was the frustration about the lost war. The demoralization resulting from the national defeat, which for many was a personal defeat as well, was exacerbated by the *Dolchstoßlegende*. The latter provided the basis for the widespread consensus that the war could have been won if the traitors on the home front, the enemy within, had not prevented the victory. And the enemy within was, in the minds of many, the Jews or groups under the influence of Jews. Aggression on the battlefields was now replaced by increasing hostility against the Jews. This hostility was fueled by the return to community life, as advocated by Ferdinand Toennies in his popularized work *Gemeinschaft und Gesellschaft* (1887).[26]

Another important factor reinforcing anti-Semitism at this time was the fear that the Jews contributed to the many publications of erotic literature that were thrown onto the market, often under the guise of scientific investigation into sexual behavior. A decline of morals was anticipated, especially in large cities when obscene works were made available to minors. The larger cities, especially Berlin and Munich, did show an increased development of gambling, erotic scandals, and homosexuality, nudism, jazz mania, and various forms of the occult, astrology, and magical hocus-pocus. A class of society came into being that made its living by providing for these experiences, and another class that found its highest satisfaction in their enjoyment.[27] Suggestive titles of publications bordering on pornography included *Fräulein Sünde; Sylvias Liebesleben; Das Liebesnest am Gänsemarkte; Bücher der Leidenschaft; Die Bücher der Venus; Schamlose Seelen; Der Weg zum Laster; Der heimliche Wollüstling; Chaiselongue-Geschichten; Pst; Was man sich nicht laut erzählt;* and *Aus dem Leben eines Hotelkellners.*[28] Most of these titles were privately printed in relatively small editions, but others were readily available, sometimes under the disguise of fairy tales, such as *Erotische Märchen. Mit 27 Bildern in Dreifarbenätzung.* Paul Englisch counts Schnitzler's *Reigen* among the morally questionable products and he considers the possibility, "daß der Leser, durch das Denken in Hitze geraten — wenn gerade ein geeignetes Objekt bei der Hand ist —, auf die weitere Lektüre ein Viertelstündchen lang verzichtet."[29]

Additionally, there was the medium of motion pictures, which after 1918 became an important form of entertainment. Erotic and pornographic movies flooded the market after the First World War and were a commercial success. Viewers were not only soldiers returning home after the many years at the front, where they had been deprived of female companionship, but also teenagers who saw these explicit films under the pretext of sexual enlightenment. These *Aufklärungsfilme,* which the producers marketed as having scientific and educational value, "reinforced low cultural and artistic standards."[30] Since censorship was abolished in 1918, there was no danger of government interference in the portrayal of sensual debaucheries. Titles included *Vom Rande des Sumpfes; Frauen, die der Abgrund verschlingt; Hyänen der Lust;* and *Verlorene Töchter.* Homosexual love was also represented, with suggestive titles such as *Aus eines Mannes Mädchenjahren* and *Anders als die Andern.* Siegfried Kracauer points out that there still was a stigma attached to seeing these movies: "Of course, one avoided being seen on such occasions."[31] There was widespread moral indignation over these movies, labeled *Schundfilme,* or trashy films, because "[d]ie Gefahren, die durch solche Piraten der Aufklärungsliteratur entstehen, sind tausendmal schlimmer als die Wirkungen des zotigen Erotikums."[32] State censorship was re-introduced in 1920. These products continued to be sold in private clubs and through underground channels, which continued to contribute to anti-Semitism, because the Jews were held responsible for the production of sex movies.[33]

This background should help to shed some light on the reception of *Reigen* in 1921, when the race of an author played a greater role than the artistic quality of his or her works. This factor is especially true for Schnitzler and his ten so-called suggestive dialogues.

One of the most ardent and visible fighters against performance of *Reigen* was the privy councilor Professor Dr. Karl Brunner, referred to by Ignaz Wrobel (Kurt Tucholsky) in his weekly *Die Weltbühne* as a "Kamillentee-August" — a chamomile-tea-drinking clown.[34] Working for the government as an expert adviser, who was attached to the "Zentralstelle zur Bekämpfung unzüchtiger Darstellungen und Schriften," Brunner succeeded in his attempt to bring together patriotic, nationalistic, and anti-Semitic groups. The mood was against *Reigen,* and the scandal took place on February 22, 1921, when during the fourth scene someone yelled "Schweinerei." Although the performance continued, the prosecutor leveled charges of indecency against the directors and the actors, resulting in the infamous trial, which took place November 5–12, 1921. Right-wing groups used the trial to further their own agenda, which consisted mainly of attacking the Jews. Inflammatory statements against the Jews were common; for example: "Das verdanken wir diesem Judenpack! Das wäre noch schöner, wenn wir uns das gefallen ließen, wenn wir auf diese Weise das deutsche Volk vergiften ließen."[35] The anti-Semitic invectives came not only from organized Nazi-groups, such as the *Hakenkreuzler,* but also from other right-wing associations that saw an opportunity during the trial to publicize their anti-Semitic bias. Repeatedly it was said that there had to be an end to Jewish influence in the public sphere, even to Jewish life in Germany: "Mit diesen Juden muß Schluß gemacht werden! Wir sind doch schließlich Deutsche! . . . diese Saujuden . . . diese Bande . . . dieser jüdische Direktor . . . die Juden muß man alle ausräuchern . . . dieses Gesindel . . . die Juden sollen nach Palästina gehen."[36]

Moreover, *Reigen* became a propaganda tool in order to attract people to the meetings of the National Socialists. The leaflet below, distributed by the Nazis in 1921, is interesting because it was directed to the workers and the proletariat. The place where the meeting was held was Haverlands Festsäle in the Neue Friedrichstraße, a section of Berlin located in a working-class neighborhood — the proletariat resided primarily in Berlin-Wedding. The leaflet addressed the women of the proletariat, contrasting their poor living conditions with those of the rich residing at the Kurfürstendamm:

Nationaldemokratische Partei

Berlin C. 2, Breite Straße 4

Am **Mittwoch**, den 16. November 1921, abends ¹/₂8 Uhr, in **Haverlands Festsälen** (Luisensaal), Neue Friedrichstr. 35 (Bahnhof Börse)

Versammlung.

Vortrag: 1. Die Pazifisten als Vorkämpfer für die Versklavung Deutschlands.

2. Schnitzlers „Reigen" und die freie Liebe.

Gäste willkommen.

Bürger, Arbeiter, Frauen! Die Gerichtsverhandlung in Moabit gegen die „Reigen"-Vorführung ist ein wenig erbauliches Schauspiel. Freie Liebe ist Herren- und Männerrecht. Die Frau ist der leidtragende Teil. Der Herr hat nur das Vergnügen. Die Frau hat das uneheliche Kind zu ernähren. Der uneheliche Vater drückt sich gewöhnlich von den Vaterpflichten und Kosten. Genosse Heine als Vorkämpfer für die Wüstlinge vom Kurfürstendamm und als Vernichter der Menschenrechte der Proletarierfrauen: Welch ein Schauspiel!

Die Pazifisten wiederum gebärden sich wie Organe des französischen Militarismus. Sie fordern die einseitige Entwaffnung Deutschlands. Sie behaupten, wie es die französische Militärpartei wünscht, daß Deutschland allein Schuld am Kriegsausbruch ist. Sie befürworten die Losung „Nie wieder Krieg", d. h. bis in die Ewigkeit sollen bleiben die Franzosen die Herren, die Deutschen die Sklaven. Glaubt ihr, daß wir die Franzosen jemals wieder loswerden?

Schlno-Druckerei, Berlin C. 2, Kryßstr. 4

Fig. 4: "Nationaldemokratische Partei."
From the collection of Gerd K. Schneider.

Reigen was again no longer a literary work but a political tool used to advance sentiments against Jews and for the upcoming Nazi regime. Dr. Rosenberger, an attorney for the defense at the Berlin trial, recognized this fact and concluded that it was necessary to establish that the controversy was actually not about *Reigen* but rather about anti-Semitism:

> Für die Verteidigung kommt es darauf an, festzustellen, daß es sich gar nicht um einen Kampf gegen den *Reigen* handelt, sondern um einen Kampf gegen die Juden, daß man den *Reigen* nur benutzt hat, um in dieser Form eine anti-semitische Aktion ins Werk zu setzen.[37]

The trial ended with the acquittal of the accused on November 18, 1921. Looking at the trial from a present perspective, one probably will agree with Ludwig Marcuse's conclusion that the indignation, apt to incite the public in 1921, was the first rehearsal prior to the great premiere of 1933.[38] The importance of the trial today is that it showed the antidemocratic forces at work. Most of the witnesses for the prosecution belonged to anti-Semitic organizations. Groups involved in the action included the Deutsch-Völkische Schutz und Trutzbund, the Deutsche Offiziersbund, the Deutsch-Völkischer Geselligkeitsverein, the Bund der Wandervögel, the Deutsch-Christliche Vereinigung, and the Verein Berliner Lehrerinnen. As Annette Delius has pointed out, for many members of these associations Schnitzler's *Reigen* was merely an occasion to defend their chauvinistic or reactionary views against a perceived liberal threat.[39]

It should not be overlooked, however, that some witnesses were serious in considering *Reigen* a danger for young people whose attitudes toward women and sex might be shaped by what they saw and heard. The trial transcript shows occasionally real concern to protect young and still immature people. Some critics agreed that *Reigen* was meant to be read and not seen on stage. An influential and well-known writer, Josef Roth, was among them, and in his "Epilog zum Reigenprozeß" he distances himself from Schnitzler with these comments:

> Pathetische Menschen empfinden Schnitzlers Lächeln arrogant. Der *Reigen* ist ihnen eine Naturlästerung. Den Sensiblen kann die Aufführung eine Preisgabe keuscher Verschwiegenheit bedeuten. Alles Geschlechtliche ist zwar nicht Geheimnis, aber Verschwiegenheit. Es auf die Bühne bringen, heißt es an die Öffentlichkeit zerren und entweihen.[40]

Most of the reviews were complimentary, but a few papers with a more right-wing orientation objected to a performance on ethical grounds:

> Das Kleine Schauspielhaus hat um Arthur Schnitzlers willen eine Widerspenstigkeit gegen die Staatsgewalt gewagt. Er hat der Kritik und einem

fast gefüllten Parkett den *Reigen* vorgeführt, den die Gerichtsverfügung als
unzüchtig verbot . . . Ist es ein unsittliches Stück? Kaum . . . Die Frage ist
nun: gehören so freie erotische Dinge auf die Schaubühne? Frau Eysoldt
mein[t]: "Ja!" Schnitzler selbst hielt sein Stück ein Vierteljahrhundert von
jedem Theater fern. Wer Gesundung und ethische Säuberung will, wird er-
klären: Fort mit all diesen Kitzlichkeiten . . . die im Scheinwerfer der Ram-
pen wirklich nichts anderes bewirken als Schönheitstänze in
Animierkneipen . . . Den Zensor rufen wir nicht. Auch vor sittlichem Niedergang braucht man nicht gleich zu sprechen. Etwas mehr Reinlichkeit
aber ist dringend vonnöten in unseren "moralischen Anstalten." Mit den
erotischen Reigentänzen mag endlich Schluß gemacht werden.[41]

Although the legal proceedings against *Reigen* ended in 1921, the controversy over selling the text continued, as the flyer (see figure 5) indicates. Schnitzler did not believe that objections to *Reigen* would last for
long. In a letter of February 17, 1921, to Stefan Grossmann[42] he wrote:

Nach einigen Jahren bleibt von all dem Lärm nichts weiter übrig als die
Bücher, die ich geschrieben, und eine dunkle Erinnerung an die Bla-
mage meiner Gegner. In diesem Falle wird es nicht anders sein.[43]

The Scandal in Vienna

The disturbances in Berlin are closely linked to the Viennese reaction to
this play. One has to keep in mind that the media played a major role in
influencing attitudes toward *Reigen*. Advances made in technology allowed the transmission of news items across national borders without any
great loss of time, and sometimes the same journalists wrote for papers
in Austria as well as Germany. Since there was no television to propagate
the political platform and agenda, newspapers had a strong impact on
reporting events, and at the same time, publicizing their political stand.

It was, therefore, not surprising that the Viennese followed the
events in Germany quite closely, just as the German newspaper-reading
public was well informed about the sequence of events in Austria. The
Viennese did not want to appear too parochial, and the censure of *Reigen* was dropped, as the evening edition of the *Illustrirtes Wiener Extrablatt* reported in "Schnitzlers *Reigen* freigegeben" on January 9, 1921,
adding that the rehearsals had started on January 4. The premiere then
was set for February 1.

On February 7, *Reigen* was performed in Vienna as a benefit for
children, and the right-wing press considered this community service a
Jewish trick to promote business, as the *Neue Montagsblatt* of February

FRISCH & Co. VERLAG
WIEN-LEIPZIG
WIEN III. ERDBERGSTR. 3
TELEPHON 46-2-13

Verehrliche Schriftleitung!

Der in unserem Verlage erschienene Luxusdruck „Schnitzler: Reigen, mit 10 Radierungen von Stefan Eggeler" wurde von einem Zollbeamten in Hof (Oberbayern), **der sich für zensurberechtigt hielt, als unzüchtig beschlagnahmt** und dem Landgericht Hof zur weiteren Amtshandlung übergeben. Das Amtsgericht Hof hat demgemäß die Beschlagnahme ausgesprochen und das Strafverfahren gegen uns eingeleitet. Auf den von uns eingebrachten Rekurs erhielten wir von der Strafkammer, Landgericht Hof, die Mitteilung, daß die Beschlagnahme aufgehoben wurde, unter Angabe der nachstehend angeführten Gründe. Da diese Entscheidung auch für die Öffentlichkeit von Interesse ist, stellen wir es Ihnen anheim, das unten angeführte Gutachten in Ihrem geschätzten Blatte zu veröffentlichen.

Hochachtungsvoll

FRISCH & Co. VERLAG

Begl. Abschrift.

Hof, den 14. Januar 1922.

B e s c h l u ß
der Strafkammer des Landgerichts Hof.
Der Beschluß des Amtsgerichts Hof vom 17. November 1921 wird aufgehoben.

G r ü n d e :

Das Amtsgericht Hof hat mit vorbezeichnetem Beschluß die Beschlagnahme eines Exemplars Nr. 224 des im Verlag von Frisch & Co. in Wien—Leipzig erschienen Buches: „Reigen", von Arthur Schnitzler, ausgesprochen, da Inhalt und Abbildungen desselben unzüchtig seien, und das Buch als Beweismittel für die Untersuchung von Bedeutung sei und der Einziehung unterliege. §§ 184, Z. 1, 41, 42, St.-G.-B., §§ 94, 98, St.-P.-O.

Die von der Verlagsbuchhandlung wirksam dagegen eingelegte Beschwerde ist begründet. **Weder der Inhalt der den „Reigen" bildenden 10 Dialoge, noch die 10 Illustrationen hiezu nach Radierungen von Stefan Eggeler sind unzüchtig** im Sinne des § 184, Z. 1, St.-G.-B. Das geht schon aus der künstlerischen Form der Darstellung hervor. **Aber auch vom Inhalt kann nicht gesagt werden, daß er geeignet sei, das Scham- und Sittlichkeitsgefühl des normal empfindenden Menschen in geschlechtlicher Beziehung zu verletzen.** In den Dialogen treten verschiedene Typen des Wiener Volkslebens auf. Deren in sittlicher Hinsicht allerdings zum Teil sehr tiefstehende Anschauungen über geschlechtliche Dinge darzustellen, ist der wahre Zweck der Schrift. Zu berücksichtigen ist auch, daß das Buch in einer kleinen, numerierten, sehr teueren Ausgabe hergestellt ist.

Trotzdem der Text des Buches schon seit zirka 20 Jahren im Buchhandel erschienen ist, ist nach Mitteilung der Polizeidirektion München bis jetzt nicht bekannt geworden, daß bayerische Gerichte das Buch als unzüchtig im Sinne des § 184, St.-G.-B., erklärt haben.

gez. Walber

Dr. Thomas
Zur Beglaubigung.
Hof, den 16. Januar 1922.
Gerichtsschreiberei des Landgerichts.
Hallmeier, O.-Sekr.

Leupoldt

L. S.

Fig. 5: "Verehrliche Schriftleitung!"
From the collection of Gerd K. Schneider.

7, 1921, reported. An article titled "Kohnnationales Reigenspiel" reflected the familiar stereotype of the Jew by emphasizing the author's supposed predilection for bordello themes, which, in turn, were interpreted as evidence of an uncanny business sense.[44]

The anti-Semitic sentiment grew rapidly, fueled by press reports of the audience reaction to *Reigen* in Munich and Berlin. For instance, the Viennese paper *Neuigkeits Welt=Blatt* of February 9, 1921, described a *Reigen* performance in Munich, informing the Viennese that the Germans did not put up with the implications of this scandalous play:

> Auch in München entfesselte Sonntag, die Aufführung des Schnitzlerschen Stückes einen großen Theaterskandal im Schauspielhaus. Eine Besucherin rief vom ersten Rang im dritten Bilde nach Verdunkelung in den Saal: *"Das ist ja eine Schweinerei! So 'was wagt man den deutschen Frauen zuzumuten!"* Nunmehr tönte es von allen Seiten: *"Saustall! Gemeinheit! Unverschämtheit! Frechheit!* und dabei wurde gezischt und gepfiffen.

Some radical groups, especially the anti-Semitic Deutsche Volkspartei (Orel-Partei), decided that now was the time to move in. The first major disturbance occurred during the Monday performance on February 7, 1921, when fifteen to twenty young people caused a riot during the performance that was, however, brought under control. The dispute spilled over into the parliament, where a discussion of *Reigen*, a literary work, became the vehicle to voice political differences. The verbal fight between the Social Democrats and the Christian Socials escalated into a fist fight after the Christian Socials used invectives such as "Juden, Saujuden, Judenbagage" against the Social Democrats. Prophetic was the reference to Germany and the "Anschluß," made in the *Kleine Volks=Zeitung* of February 12, 1921, by deputy Leopold Kunschak, who stated that even if the peace treatise forbade the unification of Austrian and the German Empire, it was not forbidden to have Austria join Germany as far as morality and culture were concerned.[45]

Public opinion became more intolerant, and the media escalated the tense situation by reporting that the book edition of *Reigen* had been banned in Berlin. It did not help much to defuse the politically explosive situation that *Reigen* premiered in Leipzig in the Kleine Theater under the direction of Fritz Viehweg on February 15. The review "Ueber Schnitzlers *Reigen*," written by Dr. Johannes Volkelt, professor of philosophy at the University of Leipzig and an ardent nationalist and Friedrich Nietzsche admirer, was published on the first two pages of the *Voralberger Tagblatt* (Bregenz) on February 15, 1921.[46] In it Volkelt accused the board of directors of the Kleine Theater, "sich am Tage seiner Eröffnung durch Schnitzlers pornographische Skizzen die Weihe zu geben." The article ended with a virulently anti-Semitic statement according to which *Reigen* was nothing but an indecency, written — of course — by a Jewish author. Volkelt went on to deplore that the German people will put up with "something like that." The major attack on *Reigen* came on the same day, February 16, 1921, when a mob of approximately 600 invaded the theater during the fifth scene. Schnitzler, who was also present during this showing, recorded his experiences of the riot-like conditions in a diary entry of February 16, 1921:

> Lärm . . . Garderobiere stürzt herein, weinend . . . [Schauspielerin] Carlsen von der Bühne fluchtartig, Geschrei, Toben, Brüllen; — Leute aus dem Zuschauerraum — ein paar hundert sind eingedrungen, — attakiren die Besucher, Publikum flieht, wird insultirt; — ich auf die Bühne, ungeheure Erregung, eiserner Vorhang vor, Spritzen in Thätigkeit, Publikum flieht auf die Bühne, Requisitenkammer, — das Gesindel tobt, schmeißt Sachen an den Vorhang, will die Thüren einbrechen; — Wasser fließt in die Garderoben . . . wir [A.S. und Heinrich Schnitzler] gehen in den Zuschauerraum; — Bänke und Sessel aus den Logen heruntergeworfen . . . Polizei verbietet die 10 Uhr Vorstellung . . . Der ganze Abend ein Unicum in der Theatergeschichte.[47]

Schnitzler did not exaggerate, as the cartoon published in the *Illustriertes Wiener Extrablatt* of February 18, 1921 shows (see figure 6). This scandal made headline news in almost all Austrian papers, where it was reported under headings similar to the ones of the *Neue Freie Presse* of February 17, 1921 (morning edition), which described in detail the unrest:

> Die Frauen bei den Demonstranten. — Der Sturm gegen die Kammerspiele. — Stinkbomben im Theater. — Wilde Demonstrationen auf der Straße. — Der Sturmangriff gegen die Theaterbesucher. — Die Panik im Publikum. — Mißhandlung weiblicher Theaterbesucher — Das Eingreifen der Sicherheitswache. — Sieben Arretierungen. — Lärmszenen nach der Saalräumung. — Die Verwüstung in den Kammerspielen. — Verbot der Nachtvorstellung. — Die Frage weiterer Reigen-Aufführungen. — Mitteilungen der Schauspieler.

The stagehands, as the article continued, came to the rescue of the audience by dousing the attackers with water from the hydrants. That people got "soaked" in another manner was sarcastically mentioned in "Der Reigen-Skandal," published in the evening edition of the *Deutsches Volksblatt* of February 17, 1921, which revealed how anti-Semitism colors criticism in an atmosphere calling to mind the Nazi witch-hunts:

Die Namen der Frauenzimmer, die so schamlos waren, dorthin zu gehen, sollten öffentlich bekanntgegeben werden. Gestern sind diese Leute einmal nicht auf ihre Rechnung gekommen, und durch die Unvorsichtigkeit übereifriger Organe, die die Hydranten gegen die Demonstranten in Anwendung brachten, kamen sie auch noch, da die Demonstranten, über deren vergebliches Bemühen die Judenpresse in den letzten Tagen in der frechsten Weise spottet, sich als die stärkeren erwiesen, zu einem unerfreulichen Bade . . . [Schnitzler] blieb glücklicherweise davon verschont; seine "Gemeinde" atmet wieder auf. Trokkenen Fußes, wie seine Vorfahren beim Marsche durch das Rote Meer, konnte er das Theater verlassen, das dieser Schweinerei Obdach bot, bis es nun von der gerechten Empörung des bodenständigen Wien und einem orkanartigen Volkssturm mit begreiflicher Entrüstung etwas unsanft daran gemahnt wurde, daß es in Wien auch noch andere Leute gibt wie die Juden, auf die die Direktion des Volkstheaters, wie es scheint, allein glaubte, Rücksicht nehmen zu müssen, weil ja die Mehrzahl der Stammgäste des Volkstheaters und der Kammerspiele Juden sind . . . [die] im Schleichhandel bis zu 1000 K. [für die Karten zahlen].[48]

On February 18, 1921, the morning edition of the *Reichspost* reported that there would be no further performance of the play in order to safeguard public peace and order. Most publications referring to the scandal voiced the view that it was staged by anti-Semitic elements. The *Wiener Morgenzeitung* of February 18 mentioned in its article "Der *Reigen*-Krawall" an idea that proved true a few years later: *Reigen* had fallen victim to anti-Semitism and reactionary politics. The protest was never about literary and artistic matters:

Aber die Vorgänge von vorgestern wollen nicht leichtsinnig gewertet werden. Es ist natürlich kein Protest gegen die Aufführung des *Reigen* und es handelt sich nicht um eine literarisch-künstlerische Frage, die durch einen Theaterkrawall gelöst werden soll. Es ist ein Rekognoszierungsgefecht der antisemitisch-reaktionären Elemente, die sich überzeugen wollen, ob die Morgenröte schon da ist.

After the scandals in Berlin and Vienna, *Reigen* was again performed in German cities as well as in Vienna, where police protection ensured the safety of the audience.

The last Viennese theater performance of *Reigen* took place on June 30, 1922. After that, the forces that had fought against *Reigen* and its Jewish author were on their "Flight into Darkness" — the title of Schnitzler's last novella, published shortly before he died (*Flucht in die Finsternis*, 1931). Schnitzler had previously titled this work "Der

Verfolgte," the persecuted, and later "Der Wahn," madness or mania. The attacks on *Reigen* signaled the path into an era of national darkness and madness. Only an audio play was performed in February 1933. *Reigen* was no longer produced on the European stages, with the exception of France, until January 1, 1982, when Heinrich Schnitzler, the playwright's son, lifted the ban on public performances. This legal ban, however, did not apply to the United States.

Fig. 6: "Das Verbot der Reigen-Aufführungen."
Illustriertes Wiener Extrablatt, 18 February 1921.
From the collection of Gerd K. Schneider.

Reigen in the Literary, Social, and Political Context of New York in the Twenties

Modern Austrian literature was not highly regarded in the United States after the First World War, as Emil Lengyel noted in his lengthy essay "Modern Austrian Theater is Reflection of Rome's Last Days," published in the *New York Tribune* of March 11, 1923. According to him, "pre-misery" dramas (before 1918) were renowned for their "purity," while present Austrian productions "specialized in the most vivid depiction of the sexual life." The European scandals surrounding *Reigen*, translated into English in 1920 as *Hands Around*, were well-known in the United States because of the press coverage. An example is the feuilleton by William G. Shepherd in the *World* of June 12, 1921, which includes an interview with Gertrude Eysoldt, the co-director of the Berlin performance of *Reigen*:

> Berlin's "wickedest" play is *Reigen*. There have been risqué plays this season, and playlets; shady plays and downright naughty plays. These pieces have run the gamut. But *Reigen* tops them all. *Reigen* would either fill Madison Square Garden nightly for ten successive years, or the would-be producer would spend his life in Sing Sing, if he was not led to the electric chair. As a matter of fact, the play could not be given in New York. It has been mobbed in Vienna, but at this writing is still running there; it has been mobbed in Munich, but the end of the Munich run is not in sight; it was mobbed, in a half-hearted way, in Berlin, a few nights ago . . . [but] the public thinks the Berlin raid was a press-agent stunt.

Shepherd concludes that a performance of *Reigen* in New York City would be in bad taste; moreover, "from the American viewpoint, the thing is absolutely impossible. It would not even be decent for an American reviewer to try to tell the story."

This attitude was not surprising if one looked at the public reactions to Yiddish theater offerings in this period. After the death of Jacob Gordin, the pioneer of the Yiddish theater, in 1909, theaters performed more and more "risqué plays." According to David Lifson:

> Sex had its vogue after the Gordin era, when a plethora of sex-oriented dramas appeared. Just prior to the U.S. entry into World War I, despite efforts to present better plays and plays of nationalistic content, lurid melodramas of sex were very popular. A sampling of the year 1915– 1916 offers revealing titles: *White Slaves*, by Isadore Zolatorevsky; *Red Light* and *Red District*, by Itzhok Lash; *Slave Dealer* and *Her Awakening*, by Moishe Richter; and *The Pure Conscience*, by Max Gabel.[49]

Public opinion was against these sexually liberal plays, just as public opinion had turned against them in the metropolis of Berlin and Vienna. New Yorkers also found Sholem Asch's *God of Vengeance* (1918) highly objectionable because of its lesbian content. This "scandalous play" was staged the same year as the planned performance of *Reigen*. The play was banned, and the producer of *God of Vengeance* as well as the male lead actor were fined $300.00 each, despite the public support by well-known writers such as Eugene O'Neill and Elmer Rice. The puritan American was clearly not yet ready for such sexual liberalism.

Another reason plays coming from Europe received a lukewarm reception was the reporting of the German reaction to losing the First World War and to the conditions imposed on the German population by the Versailles Treaty. The *New York Tribune* of March 18, 1923, published a front-page article titled "Hate Taught in Germany's Schoolrooms," informing the New York public that German textbooks for teenagers urged them to plan revenge, that the Versailles Treaty was brutal, and that Americans were arch-hypocrites. Young Germans were reminded what they had lost and what was their duty to reclaim, as in a quoted excerpt:

> You must engrave in your heart as on the stone these words: What we have lost must not be lost forever, for the land is sacred over which, during thousands of years, the soft and harmonious German language has re-echoed. Contemplate the forests which rise majestically in the blue air of the Vosges, look at the rich country lands of Sleswig, which bound Koenigsau; look at the beautiful country of the Sarre, which bears the precious coal in its bosom; see the pier of Danzig bathed by the waves of the Vistula . . . Awaken! Shake off thy shame, think of the day of vengeance! Let not the fire be extinguished whose flames rise up unto the heavens; you and your heirs have a sacred duty to fulfill. Engrave these words deeply in the heart of your son, "that which we have lost shall be returned unto us once more."[50]

Because public sentiment and the press were against endorsing a public staging of *Reigen,* a performance originally scheduled at the Belasco Theater for March 1923 had to be changed to a reading in the Green Room Club. This alteration of plans was the result of objections voiced by the Lord's Day Alliance and a letter written by John S. Sumner, secretary of the New York Society for the Suppression of Vice, in which "[he] threatened to prosecute on the ground that the play was 'obscene.'"[51] Sumner threatened to use police force to prevent this play from being shown, and he based the legality of this interference on a precedent, as the *World* of March 12, 1923, reported:

> He [Sumner] alleged it violates section 1140-AQ of the Penal Laws, under which the producers and cast of *The God of Vengeance,* playing at the Apollo Theatre, were indicted last Tuesday and held in $300 bail each the next day, by Judge Crain in Special Sessions.

Because of the political implications, the guest of honor for the performance, the successful German-born banker and board member of many cultural organizations Otto Hermann Kahn, decided to attend only the dinner, but not the reading. Kahn's statement was printed in various papers, including the *New York Tribune* of March 9, 1923:

> I do not desire to participate in any function which runs counter to the susceptibilities and the moral sentiments of any substantial body in the community, whose motives are entitled to respect, and, without wishing to be misunderstood as passing upon the merits of the case, I purpose [sic] to act accordingly in the present instance.

Because of the negative publicity, only fifty male club members and their male guests (women were not allowed) attended the reading. Rollo Lloyd, vice-president of the club, announced after the reading that they had not expected more than a handful of "intelligent adults" to attend. As reported by the *New York Tribune* on March 12, 1923, it was never the intention of the club to present the play to the general public, "not so much to protect the public from Arthur Schnitzler, but to protect Arthur Schnitzler from the public, which would debauch him." This fear did not extend to the Jewish population of New York City, which considered Schnitzler one of the most outstanding writers, as Schnitzler's letter to Hermann Bernstein on October 8, 1923, indicates: "Vielen Dank für die freundliche Übersendung der *Jewish Tribune;* daß ich nach Ansicht Ihrer Leser den 'twelve foremost Jews in the world' beizuzählen bin, hat mich sehr gefreut."[52]

The first stage performance of *Reigen* in New York City took place on October 23, 1926, in the Triangle Theatre under the direction of Kathleen Kirkwood, who had also translated the play. No disturbances were reported, and only male subscribers were allowed. The precaution of a subscription theater was well taken, because the sale of Schnitzler's *Reigen* had been banned. In 1929, when a copy of the book was found in a bookstore, its owner was charged with violating Section 1141 of the Penal Law. The presiding judge, however, dismissed the charges:

> Although the theme of the book is admittedly the quite universal literary theme of men and women, the author here deals with it in a cold and analytical, one might even say scientific, manner that precludes any salacious interpretation. A careful scrutiny of the text reveals not a single line, not a single word, that might be regarded as obscene, lewd, lascivious, filthy, indecent, or disgusting within the meaning of the statute.[53]

The controversy about *Reigen* continued until the Appellate Division of the Supreme Court of New York and the Court of Appeals of the State of New York lifted the ban against the book in 1930.

Reigen, however, was not yet fully accepted into the American repertoire, as the reaction to the French movie version *La Ronde* by Max

Ophüls showed. Directed in 1950 and shown in America in 1951, it was opposed in New York State as immoral and banned by the Division of Motion Pictures of the State Education Bureau and the National Legion of Decency. The Supreme Court overruled the State Court in 1954, citing that the State had violated the constitutional right to freedom of expression. That decision meant that *Reigen* could be staged in the United States without difficulties.[54]

Since then, this disputed work has been shown all over Europe and also in the United States, and it has inspired many writers and other artists to create their own *Reigen* based on Schnitzler's work. *Reigen* experienced a metamorphosis, coming alive in more than half a dozen movies, many ballets, and also operas. Although it has lost some of its punch in our time, which tends to be more liberal toward sexual displays on the stage, it still offers great entertainment. Proof of this appeal is David Hare's 1998 New York performance of *The Blue Room* with Nicole Kidman and Iain Glen. *Reigen* is also thought-provoking because it contains certain truths that are as valid today as they were in Schnitzler's time. But since the social and political contexts have changed in the last one hundred years, *Reigen* is now judged on its artistic merit and not on the race of its author. Surprising, though, is the fact that society in Schnitzler's time took literature seriously and used it for personal edification as well as entertainment, but organizations and the media in Austria and Germany also misused it to advance their political antiliberal and anti-Semitic agenda. The fate of this work, therefore, provides a window for a better understanding into the time in which Schnitzler lived and wrote, so that one is justified to rewrite the saying as: *Sua fata libelli habent.*

Notes

[1] Arthur Schnitzler, "Reigen," in DW I (Frankfurt: Fischer, 1962), 327–90.

[2] Carl Müller-Rastatt, "Totentanz. Zur Uraufführung von Schnitzlers Reigen in den Hamburger Kammersplielen," in *Hamburger Correspondent* (January 8, 1921): n.p.

[3] Carl E. Schorske, "Politics and the Psyche," in his *Fin-de-Siècle Vienna. Politics and Culture* (New York: Vintage Books, 1981), 19.

[4] Carl E. Schorske, "Politics and the Psyche: Schnitzler and Hofmannsthal," in his *Fin-de-Siècle Vienna. Politics and Culture* (New York: Vintage Books, 1981), 11.

[5] "Es gibt kaum eine andere Stadt, die sexuelle Freizügigkeit so anstandslos toleriert wie Wien — wenn nur eine Bedingung erfüllt wird: daß man nie darüber redet," Renate Wagner, *Arthur Schnitzler. Eine Biographie* (Vienna: Fritz Molden, 1981), 338.

[6] "Herr Schnitzler geht in jeder Szene resolut auf eine Zeile Gedankenstriche los, die jeweilig den Stand der Unterhaltung andeuten, in dem sie vom Gedanklichsten am weitesten entfernt sind. . . . [Der leitende Einfall ist es], das erotische Treiben von Großstadttypen in sozialer Skala zu verfolgen und die leicht Entbrannten und rasch Gestillten in doppeltem *tour de main* auftreten zu lassen," Philipp Frey, "Schnitzlers *Reigen*," *Die Wage* 6/17 (1903), 533.

[7] Wolfgang Maderthaner and Lutz Musner, *Die Anarchie der Vorstadt. Das andere Wien um 1900* (Frankfurt and New York: Campus Verlag, 1999), 69.

[8] Cankar describes, as Katja Sturm Schnabl notes, "das Haus der Barmherzigkeit, ein Krankenhaus im 17. Wiener Gemeindebezirk. In diesem Krankenhaus ist es die Abteilung für Haut — und Geschlechtskrankheiten. Hier liegen in einem Zimmer im 2. Stock 14 Kinder, Mädchen, die alle durch die Lebensumstände, in denen sie leben mußten, krank geworden waren, mit unheilbaren Krankheiten angesteckt wurden. . . . An Hand der Einzelschicksale zeigt Cankar die verschiedensten sozialen Zustände in Wiener Familien, wie Armut, Wohlstandsverwahrlosung, sexueller Mißbrauch, Brutalität, Vergewaltigung, die letztlich die Ursache der Erkrankung waren." Katja Sturm Schnabl, "Soziales Engagement und symbolistische Stilmittel bei Ivan Cankar. Das Wien der Jahrhundertwende aus dem Jahrhundertwende eines europäisch-slowenischen Autors," *Trans: Internet-Zeitschrift für Kulturwissenschaften* 7 (September 1999): 3.

[9] Schorske, 6.

[10] Fr[iedrich] Törnsee, "Bücherschau: Arthur Schnitzlers *Reigen*," *Neue Bahnen* 3/9 (May 1, 1903): 245.

[11] Friedrich Törnsee, "Reigen," in *Ostdeutsche Rundschau* (May 17, 1903): 15.

[12] "Bilder der Wirklichkeit," in *Hamburger Fremdenblatt* (May 2, 1903): n.p.

[13] "Schnitzlers *Reigen*," in *Neues Wiener Journal* (July 2, 1903): n.p.

[14] "Literatur und Wissenschaft," *Münchner Nachrichten* (March 18, 1904): 3.

[15] "Die arische Presse hat die Pflicht, die traurigen Ausgeburten der Spekulation zu charakterisieren und vor ihnen zu warnen. Das lateinische Sprichwort: Wer schweigt, scheint zuzustimmen, gilt auch hier. Und vor allem wäre zu wünschen, daß jeder, der sich Selbstgefühl gewahrt hat, nur arische Kritik brächte und sich sein gesundes Urteil nicht von nichtarischen Stimmen trüben lasse."

[16] Friend, "Arthur Schnitzler: 'Ich habe Heimatgefühl, aber keinen Patriotismus,'" *Literatur und Kritik* 269/270 (1992): 59.

[17] Fischer's letter, dated April 8, 1919, encouraged Schnitzler to have *Reigen* produced on stage: "Vielleicht sollten Sie sich gegen die Aufführung des *Reigen* nicht mehr so spröde verhalten. In unserer entfesselten Zeite wiegen Zweifel und Bedenken nicht mehr so schwer wie sonst und da Sie den Reigen ja geschrieben haben, werden Sie sich auch zu ihm auf der Bühne bekennen. Ich bin aber dann in erster Linie für Reinhardt." Peter de Mendelssohn, "Zur Geschichte des *Reigen*. Aus dem Briefwechsel zwischen Arthur Schnitzler und S. Fischer," *Almanach. Das sechsundsiebzigste Jahr* (Frankfurt am Main: S. Fischer, 1962), 28-29.

[18] Klaus Berchtold, ed. "Das Salzburger Programm der Großdeutschen Volkspartei, 1920," in *Österreichische Parteiprogramme 1868–1966* (Munich: R. Oldenbourg, 1967), 439–82.

[19] The article continues: "Auch im deutschen Kunstleben hat sich jüdischer Geschäftsgeist breitgemacht. Nach dieser Auffassung ist die künstlerische Leistung nicht Selbstzweck, sondern Mittel zum Geldverdienen. Das Kunstwerk wird Marktgegenstand, der im Saisongeschäft verhandelt wird. Daher die Spekulation auf Tagesstimmungen, mitunter auf die niedrigsten Instinkte, die Originalitätshascherei, die künstlerische Eigenart vortäuschen will, und der alles übertäubende Lärm der Reklametrommel."

[20] Berchtold, "Das Linzer Programm der Deutschnationalen, 1882," in *Österreichische Parteiprogramme 1868–1966* (Munich: R. Oldenbourg, 1967), 203.

[21] Otto Weininger, *Geschlecht und Charakter* (Vienna and Leipzig: Braumüller, 1903), 441.

[22] Weininger, 441.

[23] Donald L. Niewyk, *The Jews in Weimar Germany* (Baton Rouge and London: Louisiana State UP, 1980), 13.

[24] Richard Grunberger, *Germany 1918–1945* (Philadelphia: Dufour Editions, 1964), 99.

[25] Niewyk, 16.

[26] "[C]ountless ideologists wanted to turn mass society back into organic communities, depopulate the cities, and make the rural and federative forms of communal living the sole standard in politics. The idea of a national or German socialism was, in the final analysis, the idea of an ethnic community (*Volksgemeinschaft*), which was the ultimate goal of the movement for renewal. For the anti-democrats, too, the order of the day was to 'think in folk terms.' For many people, this meant to 'think as a German,' and 'German,' for the so-called 'folk-minded,' meant first and foremost 'non-Jewish.'" Kurt Sontheimer, *Antidemokratisches Denken in der Weimarer Republik* (Munich: dtv, 1992), 42–43.

[27] Koppel S. Pinson, *Modern Germany. Its History and Civilization* (New York: Macmillan, 1954), 457. For a more detailed and descriptive analysis of the sexual atmosphere and sexual practices in Berlin between the two world wars, see Mel Gordon, *Voluptuous Panic. The Erotic World of Weimar and Berlin* (Los Angeles: Feral House, 2000).

[28] Paul Englisch, *Geschichte der erotischen Literatur* (Stuttgart: Julius Püttmann, 1927), 273.

[29] Englisch, 269.

[30] Bruce Murray, *Film and the German Left in the Weimar Republic. From* Caligari *to* Kuhle Wampe (Austin: U of Texas P, 1990), 30.

[31] Siegfried Kracauer, *From Caligari to Hitler. A Psychological History of the German Film* (Princeton, NJ: Princeton UP, 1947), 45.

[32] Englisch, 306.

[33] Kracauer, 47. For a more detailed description see Gerd K. Schneider, *Die Rezeption von Arthur Schnitzlers* Reigen *1897–1994. Text, Aufführungen, Verfilmungen; Pres-*

sespiegel und andere zeitgenössische Kommentare (Riverside: Ariadne Press, 1995), 183–90.

[34] Ignaz Wrobel [Kurt Tucholsky], "Brunner im Amt," *Die Weltbühne* 18/36 (September 1922), 267.

[35] Wolfgang Heine, ed., *Der Kampf um den Reigen. Vollständiger Bericht über die sechstägige Verhandlung gegen Direktion und Darsteller des Kleinen Schauspielhauses* (Berlin: Rowohlt, 1922), 95.

[36] Wolfgang Heine, 161, 165.

[37] Wolfgang Heine, 164.

[38] "Das aufhetzende Anstoßnehmen 1921 war eine erste Probe vor der großen Premiere 1933," says Ludwig Marcuse, "Berlin 1920: Sex, Politik und Kunst im *Reigen*," in *Obszön. Geschichte einer Entrüstung* (Munich: Paul List, 1962), 214.

[39] Annette Delius, "[Arthur] Schnitzlers *Reigen* und der *Reigen*-Prozeß. Verständliche und manipulierbare Mißverständnisse in der Rezeption," *Der Deutschunterricht* 28/2 (1976): 101.

[40] *Börsen Courier*, November 16, 1921, Nr. 537. Rpt. in Anton Kaes, ed. and com., *Weimarer Republik. Manifeste und Dokumente zur deutschen Literatur 1918–1933* (Stuttgart: Metzler, 1983), Dokument 45.

[41] J. L., "Der verbotene *Reigen*," 1. Beilage der *Deutschen Warte,* Nr, 320 (December 25, 1920): 7.

[42] Stefan Grossman's real name was Thomas Wehrlin (1875 Vienna–1935 Vienna). Publicist, dramatist, essayist, and story writer; known as the feuilleton-director of the *Arbeiter-Zeitung* (Vienna). He founded and wrote for the weekly *Das Tagebuch* (1920–1933).

[43] Arthur Schnitzler, *Briefe 1913–1931,* ed. Peter Michael Braunwarth, Richard Miklin, Susanne Pertlik and Heinrich Schnitzler (Frankfurt: Fischer, 1984), 235.

[44] "Der nicht alltägliche Skandal, daß man es gewagt hat, die bisher verpönt gewesene Vorführung der dramatisierten, unter dem Namen *Reigen* an die Öeffentlichkeit gebrachten Bordellprologe des Juden Schnitzler durch Anlehnung an eine allgemeine Fürsorgeaktion für die darbenden Kinder zu ermöglichen . . . war von einem Reigen nicht ganz wertloser Selbstentlarvungen und Enthüllungen begleitet . . . typische[r] jüdische[r] Schiebereinfall, sogar mit der Wohltätigkeit unsaubere Geschäfte zu versuchen und hungernden Kindern Brosamen vom Tische der Geilheit zu offerieren, um dadurch desto eher die Duldung für die Vorführung zu erlangen . . . von alldem sei nicht die Rede, denn wer, um jüdischen Geschäftsgeist, Judenkunst und Judenpresse zu durchschauen, erst auf die allerdings unmöglich mißzuverstehenden Offenbarungen dieser *Reigen*-Tage hat warten müssen, der wird wohl auch weiterhin unbelehrt bleiben" (*Das Neue Montagsblatt* [February 7, 1921]: 3).

[45] "Wenn schon der Friedensvertrag den Anschluß Oesterreichs an das Deutsche Reich untersage, so sei doch nicht verboten, daß sich Oesterreich *in sittlicher und kultureller Beziehung* an das Deutsche Reich anschließe" (*Kleine Volks=Zeitung* [February 12, 1921]: 3).

[46] "Das auf gut Deutsch als Schweinerei zu bezeichnende Stück hat natürlich einen Juden zum Verfasser. Es ist ein trauriges Zeichen der Zeit, daß sich das deutsche

Volk so etwas bieten läßt." Johannes Volkelt, "Ueber Schnitzlers *Reigen*" (*Voralberger Tagblatt* [February 15, 1921]: 2).

[47] Arthur Schnitzler, *Tagebuch 1920–1922*, ed. Werner Welzig with Peter Michael Braunwarth, Susanne Pertlick, and Reinhard Urbach (Vienna: Verlag der Österreichischen Akademie der Wissenschaften, 1993), 145.

[48] "Der *Reigen*-Skandal," in the evening edition of *Deutsches Volksblatt* (February 17, 1921): 2.

[49] David S. Lifson, "Yiddish Theatre," in Maxine Schwartz Seller, *Ethnic Theatre in the United States* (Greenwood, CT and London: Greenwood Press, 1983), S. 567.

[50] Stephane Lauzanne, "Hate Taught in Germany's Schoolrooms," in *The New York Tribune* (March 18, 1923, Sunday edition): 1.

[51] "Kahn Missing When 'Reigen' Finally Is Read," *New York Tribune* (March 12, 1923): 8.

[52] Schnitzler, *Briefe 1913–1931,* ed. Peter Michael Braunwarth, Richard Miklin, Susanne Pertlik, and Heinrich Schnitzler (Frankfurt am Main: S. Fischer, 1984), 327–28.

[53] "When Judges Disagree," *Publisher's Weekly* 116 (December 14, 1929): 2759.

[54] For specific performances in the United States see Schneider, *Die Rezeption von Arthur Schnitzlers* Reigen *1897–1994,* 477–529, and Schneider, "The Reception of Arthur Schnitzler's *Reigen* in the Old Country and the New World: A Study in Cultural Differences," *Modern Austrian Literature* 19/3–4 (1986): 75–89.

" . . . nothing against Arthur Schnitzler himself . . .": Interpreting Schnitzler on Stage in Austria in the 1950s and 1960s

Evelyn Deutsch-Schreiner

THE HIGHLIGHTS OF Arthur Schnitzler's work that continue to be widely appreciated today were already addressed back in 1922 by Sigmund Freud in his celebrated birthday greeting to Schnitzler:

> Ihr Determinismus wie Ihre Skepsis, Ihr Ergriffensein von den Wahrheiten des Unbewußten, von der Triebnatur des Menschen, Ihre Zersetzung der kulturell-konventionellen Sicherheiten, das Haften Ihrer Gedanken an der Polarität von Lieben und Sterben, das alles berührt mich mit einer unheimlichen Vertrautheit.[1]

In these well-known words Freud rediscovered the basic propositions of his own work in the literature of a doppelgänger named Arthur Schnitzler. But these words can also help to reveal the major reasons why Schnitzler's plays had problems on stage in the Austrian postwar period after 1945: they dealt with topics such as determinism, skepticism, the unconscious, human sexual drives, and an undermining of securities — topics that postwar society did not want to face. The delayed acceptance of Schnitzler's work is to a considerable extent the legacy of National Socialism and the Catholic Austrian fascism of the years 1934 to 1938. Indeed, the postwar elite dismissed both Schnitzler's work and Freud's psychoanalysis as being passé, created by men whose work was over and shunned. When Freud's reputation began to flourish internationally, *Die Furche,* the main Catholic newspaper, wrote: "für die Wiener von 1953 ist Freud bereits Literatur."[2] Even the slightest trace of a psychoanalytical approach on stage was considered pathological and put down as "Kombinationen von Freud."[3] When texts called for the exact characterization of mental states and emotions — as in, for instance, *Beyond the Horizon* by Eugene O`Neill in the USIS-Theater in Vienna in 1950 — this depiction was referred to as "komplizierte Seelenverklemmung."[4] The defamation of psychology and psychoanalysis by Austrofacism and National Socialism continued in the Second Republic for more than a dec-

ade and was evident in the way critics wrote. Practically all important
newspapers and journals shared the same hostility. First of all it showed
up in the press of the three large political parties (Christian Democrats,
Social Democrats, and Communists). While the *Wiener Kurier,* under
the influence of America, did somewhat abstain from that bias, other
newspapers under control of the allies raised similar voices, including the
Weltpresse (British), *Welt am Abend* (French) and *Österreichische Zeitung,*
Volksstimme, and *Der Abend* (under the influence of the Soviets).

Oddly enough, even the daily *Wiener Zeitung,* which still serves as
an official forum for public announcements and notices, saw in
Schnitzler's *Reigen* (1903) a kind of aberrant mental erotic, "Gehirn-
erotik."[5] The *Weltpresse* called Anatol a "neurotischer Erotiker."[6] Hugo
Huppert, chief editor of the *Österreichische Zeitung* and Soviet cultural
officer, put considerable effort into deriding *Der Ruf des Lebens* (1906)
as a "psychoanalytische Studie vom Leben der Gespenster unter sich."[7]
This journal and others went so far as to use the word "abseitig," which
formed a core propaganda term under the Nazis whenever they agitated
against "perverse" art. Beyond its proximity to Freud, Schnitzler's work
was rejected for reasons of its subjects and its presumed immorality. The
critics perceived only fatuous stories of adultery and permissiveness. Thus
only a certain number of Schnitzler's plays were performed on Austrian
stages, and it is revealing to look at which ones were performed by
whom, in which theater, when, and in which way.

To understand the political background it is worth noting that after
the Second World War Austrian society remained divided and even
controlled by party politics.[8] The three major parties — the Social
Democratic (Sozialdemokratische Partei Österreichs, SPÖ); the Christ-
Democratic (Österreichische Volkspartei, ÖVP), with its adherence to
the Catholic Church; and for a certain period also the Communist party
(Kommunistische Partei Österreichs, KPÖ) — struggled for dominance
in virtually all domains of society. The theaters were equally divided into
political spheres of influence. The Volkstheater was controlled by the
trade unions, where the Social Democratic faction held the absolute
majority in decision-making; the Burgtheater adhered to the sphere of
the ÖVP, not least because it nominated the cultural minister from 1945
to 1970; and finally, the KPÖ sponsored its own theater, Neues Theater
in der Scala. During these years that system of political influence must be
taken into account to see how all parties strove to propagate their ideals
of man and history. The manner in which plays were performed and
received by the audience reflects both the political situation and the
arduous construction of an Austrian identity after Austria's disastrous

experiences with war and fascism, an identity based on defending, oppressing, and forgetting. The theater sheds light on the emotional and psychological state prevalent in Austria at the time. Or stated the other way around, the emotional and intellectual experiences in Austria at the time impinged on the performances and controlled their reception. A closer analysis of the programs of Austrian theaters in the three decades after 1945 shows three rather different phases of the Schnitzler reception: the first, from 1945 to 1948, can be called the phase of reinstatement; the second, from the 1950s to 1960, is the phase of misjudgment; and finally, the third, from about 1960 to 1970, is the phase of rediscovery and utilization.

First Phase — Reinstatement

In the years immediately following the war, 1945 to 1948, plays that had been banned by the Nazis figured prominently in many theaters. Authors whose works were forbidden during the Third Reich were supposed to demonstrate a new beginning and to create distance from the Nazi dictatorship. That is also why Schnitzler is found often on the theater programs in these early years. The Tyrolian Landestheater in Innsbruck performed *Liebelei* (1896) in August of 1945. The Vienna Burgtheater put *Weihnachtseinkäufe* (1891) and *Liebelei* on the program in its first season; *Die Frage an das Schicksal* (1890) was performed on its second stage Akademietheater just a few months later. On the occasion of Austria's 950th anniversary in 1946, the Volkstheater in Vienna added *Zwischenspiel* (1906) to its repertoire. One year later *Professor Bernhardi* (1912) appeared at the Renaissancetheater. *Die Gefährtin* (1899) was staged at the small Viennese theater Die Insel in 1947/48, *Das weite Land* (1911) was produced by the same company in 1949.[9]

Professor Bernhardi took on a special role among these productions. Under Social Democratic sponsorship, Vienna's Renaissancetheater performed it in 1947. The fact that it remained a Social Democratic initiative did not prevent the other sides of the Austrian political spectrum from welcoming the play, mostly because it signaled political correctness. *Professor Bernhardi* served the educational purpose of de-Nazification, much as Gotthold Ephraim Lessing's *Nathan der Weise* (1779) did.[10] Staging these two dramas was a reaction to the Shoah. In both of them, the main characters are Jews who call for greater tolerance and reason in their effort to overcome anti-Semitic prejudices rather than accusing anyone or demanding revenge. Lessing's Enlightenment drama as well as Schnitzler's work were welcome because they were written before the Shoah. Both plays conveniently end in reconciliation, the first one as a landmark for enlightened temperament, the latter one symbolizing a utopian German-Jewish cultural symbiosis.

One important aspect of the postwar success of these plays was that for almost two decades both title roles, that of Nathan and that of Bernhardi, were played by the famous Jewish actor Ernst Deutsch (1890–1969). He had returned from his exile in the United States, and these roles became his trademark. Deutsch's performance style influenced the way these characters were perceived in the entire German-speaking world for years to come. His interpretations created a new, post-Shoah image of Jews. Revealingly, a newspaper critic wrote in 1947 that through the interpretation of his role as Bernhardi Deutsch had successfully conveyed the perception becoming characteristic of his era, namely that of the Jew as intellectual "der alles sieht, was um ihn herum vorgeht, aber trotzdem so tut, als hätte er nichts gesehen. Einer, der verzeiht, obgleich er seine Mörder kennt."[11] It might be hard to find a clearer statement about what in fact was expected from Jews after 1945. By following that rule Deutsch became the most successful Jewish actor in the postwar era. He aimed at presenting Nathan and Bernhardi in a consciously "non-Jewish" manner, avoiding the slightest trace of peculiar intonation or body language traditionally construed as Jewish. He reversed the codes and played a noble, enlightened gentleman surrounded by "dunklem Glanz," "vornehmer Güte,"[12] and a kind of "Traum-Befangenheit."[13] Of the utmost importance was the "durch Leid gewonnener, verklärter Humor"[14] by which Deutsch honored Professor Bernhardi's character. His performance amounted to a gentle de-Nazification that did not burden the conscience of the perpetrator generation and reassured them that everything was now over and done with, forgiven. In a rather sharp manner the contemporary Swiss critic Elisabeth Brook-Sulzer commented on this way of dealing with Jewish figures as a "selbstveranstalteter Entnazifizierungsprozess."[15]

This view of *Professor Bernhardi* not only started right after the Second World War but remained the dominant and only image for years. Deutsch played Bernhardi in 1955 in Berlin's Theater am Kurfürstendamm and in 1965 in the Vienna Burgtheater. These productions assisted postwar society in showing off its insight and good will, particularly the Burgtheater production, which toured in 1967 and 1968 in the United States, France, Holland, and Germany and served to represent the best of great Austrian literature. However, the Austrian public of the 1950s and 1960s was still far from coming to terms with the Shoah and anti-Semitism. Indeed, the inherent danger of Deutsch's noble way to produce *Professor Bernhardi* was to mislead the public into believing that the basic issues addressed in that play had already been brought into the forefront.

Second Phase — Misjudgment

In the second phase, the decade from 1950 to 1960, Schnitzler's dramas were misjudged as "outdated" and were rarely performed. His plays were completely ignored by the Theater in der Josefstadt and not performed at all at the Burgtheater in the years 1954 to 1959. Only the Volkstheater produced *Der junge Medardus* (1910) in 1950 and *Liebelei* in 1958.[16] This neglect led Felix Kreissler rightfully to describe Schnitzler not only as a pre-exile and exile author but also as a post-exile author.[17] Although Schnitzler was clearly not forbidden, postwar society was not able to appreciate his qualities, neither for the subject nor from an aesthetic point of view: "Immer wieder erweist es sich von neuem: für unsere Gegenwart ist die Schnitzler-Welt und ihre Atmosphäre [. . .] versunken und dahin."[18] This statement appeared in a review of a performance of *Das weite Land* in the theater Die Insel in 1948. *Die Presse* had seen some "ziemlich verworrene Eheproblematik,"[19] and the women's magazine *Die Österreicherin* noted: "Haltlose Menschen in wirren Verkettungen von Schuld treiben durch ein Leben, das keine Zusammenhänge mit dem Alltag und dem Leben hat."[20] The plays were judged in a similarly negative fashion. As it is traditional in Vienna to spare the actors, the reproach of being old-fashioned was not directed at them but at the dramatist and his plays. The well-known leftist journalist Otto Basil postulated that Schnitzler had become incomprehensible to the people of the postwar generation,[21] a claim that caused worried reactions among exiles in the United States, especially in the Los Angeles circle around Ernst Lubitsch, Gottfried Reinhard, Billy Wilder, Marlene Dietrich, Josef von Sternberg, Hans Jaray, Rose Stradner, and Salka Viertel. A letter addressed to the editor Basil and published in the *Plan* stressed the indignation of German and Austrian emigrants on the West Coast, pointing out that they kept Schnitzler and his plays fresh in their minds.[22]

In the 1950s the political movements as well as the Catholic Church were skeptical of Schnitzler's works, with *Professor Bernhardi* being the only exception. The main argument was that in Schnitzler's dramas the view on life and society was barren. The conservatives and the Church abhorred the idea of an ambiguous bourgeoisie and dismissed the plays as "eine Art kulturhistorisches Museum der Jahrhundertwende,"[23] as Heinz Kindermann wrote in the *Neue Wiener Tageszeitung* on the occasion of the twentieth anniversary of Schnitzler's death. The conservatives demanded a theater to counteract the widespread perception of the 1950s as a nihilistic period, full of crises and chaos, by installing instead a sense of unity and Catholic order. They wanted a revival of the Catholic drama in the tradition of baroque *theatrum mundi* and espoused concepts of "Welttheater."[24] In contrast to Hugo von Hofmannsthal, however, Schnitzler perceived the world as a game. He referred neither to God nor to a purely materialistic ideology — he simply resisted being pinned down. He himself stated: "Alles hat seinen Grund, aber nicht alles hat seinen Sinn, zumindest einen uns faßbaren."[25] This point of view was unacceptable to people who were searching eagerly for "sense" and "values."

The other political party, the Communists, thought that Schnitzler's social criticism was not aggressive enough, but they noticed negativism in Schnitzler's plays: "sie vermitteln den Eindruck, daß gegen die sozialen Übel keinerlei Remedur möglich ist."[26] The Social Democrats, who had stood up for Schnitzler during the scandal surrounding *Reigen* in the First Republic,[27] were now on the lookout for an Austrian historical piece, a popular drama or "Volksstück." They tried to express their views by promoting *Der junge Medardus* as an historical play and *Liebelei* as a "Volksstück." But they were disappointed, since Schnitzler's works did not accommodate a perspective coming solely "from below," nor did they conform to the concept of "Volk" established by a sort of social realism. Consequently the Social Democratic *Mitteilungsblatt* informed their public, in an edition of 19,000 copies, that "das historische Schauspiel abgebogen wird zu einer Liebestragödie im gewohnten Stil Schnitzlers. [. . .] So geistvoll und interessant auch die historische Szenerie dieses Dramas gestaltet ist, es wird auch hier wieder das Hauptaugenmerk dem erotischen Problem zugewandt."[28] So the Left was still asking for moralizing messages. Schnitzler instead is ill-suited for such strategies, because he knew too much about humankind. His unflinching look, which Ulrich Weinzierl called "Durchschauerblick,"[29] his penetrating eye, insisted on examining issues about which the postwar generation wanted no part — questions concerning the conscious mind and the subconscious, sexuality, reality and illusion, vanity, truth, lies, and a panoply of masks that people wear.

The effort in the 1950s to banish what was usually seen as sort of chaotic disorder was closely associated with an insistence on an artistically valid form. Schnitzler's dramaturgy and his way of presenting "zwischen dem Typischen und dem Individuellen"[30] was not understood at all. When *Zwischenspiel* was performed at the Volkstheater in 1946,

Schnitzler received devastating reviews. Hans Weigel wrote: "er zerredet, er horcht allzu begierig nach psychologischen Nuancen; so entsteht wirklich nur ein Spiel statt eines Dramas und das Lebendige-Gültige kommt zu kurz."[31] The constantly reiterated reproach that there is "wenig gesagt und viel zerredet"[32] shows that postwar society overlooked the fact that psychological depths were being revealed in Schnitzler's seemingly trivial dialogues. The very quality that made Schnitzler a writer of the modern era was not recognized.

People also had trouble with the dramatic short form of the one-act plays and especially with the dramaturgy of the cycle of *Anatol* (1893).[33] The *Neues Wiener Tagblatt* characterized *Anatol* as a "Sammlung von Komödiensplittern [. . .] Sie geben nicht die Essenz, sondern nur einen Widerschein des Wesentlichen."[34] In order to counteract the accusation that it was fragmentary, the director and prominent actor Curd Jürgens created a revue type of story in his production at the Burgtheater in 1952. He linked the individual episodes together by his use of musical accompaniment and pantomime as well as by interpolating a master of ceremonies. Incapable of deciphering the psychological depth of the characters, the director resorted to superficialities. Hans Holt, who played Anatol, was made up to look like a young Arthur Schnitzler; Albin Skoda, who played Max, was made up to resemble Hofmannsthal and, as the master of ceremonies, he spoke the prologue. Although the scenic trick of linking the episodes received praise, it "rettet nicht den Gesamteindruck von Szenen zwischen uns fremden, ganz fremden Menschen."[35] The Landestheater Linz was also unable to do much with this loosely interconnected series of episodes. In 1957 *Anatol* was put on stage as a popular production. The scenes were linked by popular hits sung in the "Heurigen," the suburban Viennese wine and cheese restaurants, and the characters were reduced to rough caricatures.[36] What made it so difficult to handle the dramaturgy was no doubt the basic rejection of Schnitzler's method of beginning with situations "die ihrer Struktur nach einen fast überdeutlichen Mechanismus darstellen,"[37] as Peter von Matt asserts.

The unqualified defamation Schnitzler had to endure in the 1920s during the controversy surrounding *Reigen* was not repeated after 1945, although the scandal was still bubbling beneath the surface. Before *La Ronde,* a French motion picture based on *Reigen* and directed by Max Ophüls, could open in Austrian cinemas in 1950, a month-long tug-of-war had taken place in the ministries.[38] The Ministry of Education, which supported the socialization claims of the Catholic Church, feared the movie would lead to a loosening of public morals. The *Arbeiterzeitung* ridiculed the Ministry's position by quoting: "Nichts gegen die künstlerischen Qualitäten der Darsteller oder des Regisseurs Max Ophüls, nichts gegen Arthur Schnitzler an sich, aber es mußte doch nicht gerade dieser gewagte *Reigen* sein."[39] The Ministry was in trouble, since censorship had been constitutionally outlawed in Austria. As a solution, the Ministry of Trade and Commerce tried to find economic reasons to ban the movie and claimed the Austrian National Bank had to save its foreign exchange resources. The politicians were careful not to let the problem become a "case," however, since the memory of the 1920s, when the *Reigen* scandal degenerated into a dangerous political mudslinging, was still vivid. Moreover, the government was wary of aggravating the French occupation forces. Finally the movie was shown in Austrian cinemas starting in the autumn of 1951, even though it was dismissed by the press as "eine antiquierte kleine Cochonerie,"[40] as expressed by the *Wiener Zeitung.* The Communist newspapers did not hesitate to join the hostile climate, publishing letters to the editor from so-called respectable female workers; one of them ended with the note: "Das war und das ist nicht unsere Welt, das ist eure Welt, das ist die Welt, die wir bekämpfen und beseitigen werden."[41]

In spite of the negative press, the movie did have considerable impact on the theater. First introduced by Ophüls, the device of a master of ceremonies turns up in various subsequent productions of Schnitzler, including the 1952 production of *Anatol* in the Burgtheater. In 1951 a progressive theater, the Studio der Hochschulen, ran 125 performances of *Reigen 51, Variationen über ein Thema von Schnitzler,* which became one of the most successful box-office hits in the postwar years. Helmut Qualtinger, Carl Merz, and Michael Kehlmann wrote the lyrics, and the cabaretist Gerhard Bronner provided the music. The fact that Schnitzler's son Heinrich and the publishing house of S. Fischer sued the artists for plagiarism promoted effective advertising. In this freely adapted piece, there are ten characters: whore, wrestler, lady, deputy to the National Assembly, fashion model, Beatnik, secretary, poet, actress, and bearer of the Iron Cross. Cabaret-style, they provide an insightful glimpse into postwar Viennese society. Qualtinger played the wrestler, and Bronner played a bar pianist to link the scenes. Somewhat in contrast to Schnitzler's original, the piece lacked poetic dimensions. Worse yet, the authors made it kitschy by adding an eleventh sentimental scene. They introduced a young couple, happily in love, looking to the future with confidence, equipped with the stage direction to give "den vorhergegangenen 10 Szenen Richtung, Sinn und den Schuß Optimismus."[42] The piano player offers the final song in a sober and heartfelt way. In short, it was a trivialized version intended to titillate the audience. It diluted the major theme, the ironic depiction of the sex drive. Evidently these were desires people were still afraid to admit, to the point that even creative young Austrian artists of the early 1950s had to circumvent the motif of casual sex and to invent a happy ending. The hesitation to come face to face with the unresolved conflicts is especially significant since ten years later Qualtinger and Merz wrote an epoch-making piece exposing the mentality of "the Austrian": *Der Herr Karl*.

Third Phase — Rediscovery and Utilization

The third phase in Schnitzler's stage reception started when his son Heinrich returned to Europe from his exile in California and took a position as a director and co-manager of the Theater in der Josefstadt in 1958. His return brought far-reaching consequences as he staged his father's plays frequently.[43] As Renate Wagner noted in *Wiener Schnitzler-Aufführungen 1891–1970,* the younger Schnitzler developed "einen für die Josefstadt charakteristischen Schnitzler-Stil, der heute [1970] vielfach als verbindlich für Inszenierungen der Werke des Dichters angesehen wird."[44] In fact, Schnitzler's reception mounted step by step: Heinrich Schnitzler's first production, *Der grüne Kakadu* (1899) in 1960, was not yet accepted.[45] This pessimistic parable of the French Revolution and of life as a game met with reticence. But *Literatur* (1904), a much more amusing one-act play performed the same evening, was met with enthusiasm. With the cycle of *Komödie der Worte* (1915) in 1960, according to one newspaper, the theater had found its "Säulenheiliger."[46] The subsequent productions were immensely successful with both theatergoers and critics and went down in Vienna theater history. Parallel to the success of the Theater in der Josefstadt, the Burgtheater started performing Schnitzler in 1959. Largely because of the fact that they were filmed for television, two productions directed by Ernst Lothar[47] became legendary: *Das weite Land* (1959) and *Anatol* (1960).

The question then arises why a work that had already been dismissed as being entirely old-fashioned had suddenly become so popular and celebrated as a classically Austrian piece. "In Arthur Schnitzlers Lager ist Österreich," the *Arbeiterzeitung* enthusiastically claimed in 1965.[48] Despite the lingering reservations toward Schnitzler's plays, Austrians became increasingly attracted by the exclusively Viennese atmosphere in them and the acting ability of the casts. Burgtheater and Theater in der Josefstadt were careful to cast the public's favorite actors and actresses, such as: Paula Wessely, Alma Seidler, Robert Lindner, Attila Hörbiger, and Wolf Albach-Retty (Burgtheater); and Vilma Degischer, Susi

Nicoletti, Leopold Rudolf, and Hans Thimig (Josefstadt). It is worth noting that the directors Ernst Lothar and Heinrich Schnitzler approached the productions in such a way as to steer clear of making statements that might have seemed too profound. Making use of the same genre, the conversation comedy, both directors kept the pieces set at the turn of the century and celebrated the era with vintage costumes, beautiful sets, and elegiac music. The distance from the characters was now felt to be a positive element. The identification happened by way of an aesthetic appropriation of the atmosphere, which was interpreted as genuinely Austrian. The newfound appreciation of turn-of-the-century Vienna that gained ground at the end of the 1950s was part of the larger Austria ideology agenda doggedly pursued by the conservative party (ÖVP) and the Catholic Church since 1945. They utilized Austrian identity and the label of Austrianness as a strategy to swindle their way out of sharing the responsibility for the Nazi past. Being Austrian meant not being German, and therefore not being involved in the crimes of the Nazi regime.

In the course of the 1950s the emphasis on Austrianness turned into a self-indulgent tourism marketing tool and became a part of Austria's national identity. When this Austrian ideology based on clichés and untenable historical content reached the theater, it is not surprising that *fin-de-siècle* plays were so popular. It was on this level, the level of Austrian clichés, that Schnitzler's work finally achieved success. Remarkably enough, Ernst Lothar and Heinrich Schnitzler, both profound connoisseurs of Schnitzler's work and both exiles during the Nazi-dictatorship era, succeeded only because they heavily appealed to the self-esteem of the Austrian public at the time. In this way they accepted the mainstream. Exiles who attempted to resist this ideology were not offered similar opportunities. This exclusion happened for instance with Fritz Kortner. A famous actor and director who was unwilling to make any concession, he was invited to direct on stage in his native city, Vienna, only a few times and late in his career. He was, as he said about himself, "Jude und Rebell gegen das privilegierte Konventionelle."[49]

Schnitzler's interpretation in the spirit of Austrian ideology was not shared unanimously. Critical voices mounted, this time not against Schnitzler's work as such, but against the style in which his plays were scenically produced. In 1962 a critic for the Communist newspaper *Volksstimme*, writing about the performance of *Der junge Medardus* at the Burgtheater, asked provocatively: "Ist es der bestellte schwarzgelbe Patriotismus, der vergoldete Lorbeerkranz mit der Kaiserkrone, der den Urösterreicher Arthur Schnitzler, dessen geistige Heimat der Zweifel war, mundtot macht ?"[50] Other critics such as Otto Basil, Edwin Rollett, and Hans Weigel also fought against the move to lay claim to Schnitzler at first. Furious, Weigel called Lothar "the false prophet" after a performance of *Das weite Land* in 1959, writing that "das Akademietheater präsentiert einen neuen Exzeß inkompetenter, unverzeihlicher, bewußter Entstellung."[51] He claimed that the acting was not serious enough and the actors' posing was *in jest*. He was the only one to dare to criticize the popular actress Paula Wessely, who played Gabriele.

Yet, the massive wake of Austrian ideology had prepared the way for Schnitzler as well. Phrases such as Viennese charm, quiet noblesse, dreamy graciousness, soaring sounds, lighthearted sarcasm, butterfly colors, and sweet agonies of love were used to describe the productions. The language made a lasting impact on the way people viewed Schnitzler in the 1960s. The following sentence from a review of *Anatol* in 1960 was symptomatic: "Robert Lindner verleiht Anatol eine melancholische Liebenswürdigkeit voll des Schwebenden in der Tonlage und eben dadurch etwas ausgesprochen Schnitzlerisches."[52] The Schnitzlerian atmosphere had to be Viennese, or at least what people in the 1960s imagined what Vienna was like around 1900, namely tasteful and precious. On the occasion of an evening of one-act plays at the Theater in der Josefstadt in 1964, a critic for the *Volksstimme* wrote, "Lucullus speist mit Lucullus, wenn Schnitzler (Heinrich) Schnitzler (Arthur) serviert."[53] "Schnitzler im Goldschnitt,"[54] declared the *Express*. In the provinces too, where people remained more reluctant for a longer period of time, the process of accepting Schnitzler's works was accomplished by emphasizing their distinctly Viennese atmosphere. For its production of *Das weite Land* in 1964, the Schauspielhaus in Graz purchased Otto Niedermoser's set and Erni Kniepert's costumes from the Akademietheater in Vienna, saying that the most important aspect was the atmospheric element.[55]

In 1962 Paul Blaha, a critic who stood behind both Schnitzler's canon and Heinrich Schnitzler's work as a director, was already aware of the director's balancing act between psychological analysis and concessions to the audience. In his essay "Heinrich Schnitzler — oder Die Arbeit mit dem Schauspieler" he states: "Ich sehe die Gefahr einer verhängnisvollen Begrenzung: Milieu und Atmosphäre — wer dies in dieser Theaterstadt auf der Bühne herzustellen vermag, dem mag es passieren, daß man ihn lobpreist und bagatellisiert in einem."[56] That is exactly what happened: the precious ambience, sophisticated Austrian acting, and last but not least, the dramatic plots, which were not seen as political, made Schnitzler's work predestined to serve as the representative theater of high culture, "Hochkultur," and prone to being treated as museum pieces in which the content had become obsolete. The productions of the 1960s reveal a great deal about the feelings people had during the years of the economic miracle. The "poetics of memory" in Schnitzler's works, analyzed by Konstanze Fliedl in 1997, was far removed from their perception.[57] Friendly self-glorification was the call of the day, and not Schnitzler's penetrating insights. The public did not want to be confronted with the masks people wear all their lives and the anxieties and drives that lie underneath the surface. The erotic and sexual atmosphere threatened by death and destruction was made less threatening in the cleansing spirit of the 1960s, which converted them into an elegant "Jugendstil" ambience. After all, many thought the basic mood in the theater should be *con sordino*. In other words, the theater should be a place where one can escape the increasingly hectic outside world for a few hours. Gracious, melancholy, elegant Austrian-speaking characters on stage showed a longing for a world where everything was still in order, a world projected on *fin-de-siècle* Vienna. Thus Anatol was not someone who was caught in an illusion but someone who was swaying comfortably in the illusion. Thus the story took on an entirely different dimension.

Schnitzler's image of females was dominated on stage by the conventional erotic yet sanitized perception of women in the 1960s. Female characters were played just in the way that women were expected to behave. Although Schnitzler shared a traditional male's perspective, he nevertheless created the "süße Mädel" as a self-confident figure who has both feet on the ground and is in control of her sexuality. She realizes the consequences an affair with the "young gentleman" may have, but at the same time she knows what is in it for her too: gratification, excitement, and material advantages. From a small-minded androcentric point of view this complex character was de-eroticized in the productions of the postwar era and the years that followed. The "sweet girl" was transformed into a submissive and quietly suffering type. (One exception was Inge Konradi's Christine in a 1954 production of *Liebelei* at the Burgtheater.) In Heinrich Schnitzler's production of *Liebelei* in 1968 Marianne Nentwich still portrayed Christine as a sweet, innocent girl who was clingy and a bit whiny, not exactly someone who could be trusted when saying she had given Fritz "everything." Critic Hugo Huppert felt that Nentwich played "fälschlich ganz auf Unterwerfung, weshalb das Aufbäumen in der verzweifelten Schlußszene unglaubhaft wird."[58] Gertraud Jesserer, who played Schlager Mizi, came across as a silly goose whose constant laughing and giggling were supposed to suggest childish lightheartedness. The audience laughed right along with her, as can be heard clearly on the recording of the performance made for television in 1969. Only occasionally was the actress allowed to put seriousness as well as clarity and directness into her role in order to portray Schlager Mizi as an intelligent young woman who knows what is going on in life. In addition, the overall picture of women in this production was completely off the mark as a result of the way Fritz's character was interpreted. Since Michael Heltau played a man who was really in love, he considered his figure a victim. The actor played a hero steeped in tragedy and innocence rather than a weakling whose sexual practices took place in the context of a bourgeois system of double standards. It is odd that in 1968, the year of the international student protests that caused the conservative image of women to fall, a schmaltzy bourgeois love story was produced that cast women as being far less self-confident and complex than Schnitzler himself had drawn them several decades earlier.

Clearly, the "Durchschauerblick" was still not in demand. Schnitzler productions were done in the tradition of the conversation play and the audience kept to the witty parts. As Wolfgang Sabler observed, Schnitzler's plays emerge from a tradition of conversation theater, and the roles are imbued with a marked comic quality.[59] While indeed employing the means of boulevard drama, Schnitzler went beyond this tradition: he invented a contrary dramaturgy, and that is what marks him as a modern dramatist. His texts are for actors and actresses rather than readers. They always begin with a specific situation that leaves a lot of room for the performers. Pauses, shifts in intonation, and nonverbal language can strengthen the comic aspects of the roles. Comedy and conversational tone can also be used to highlight the discrepancy between the surface and what is actually meant, which is usually deadly serious. "Die Brutalität trägt bei Schnitzler oft Glacéhandschuhe," remarked Weinzierl.[60]

Although he stayed in the tradition of the conversation play, it is fair to say that Heinrich Schnitzler sometimes succeeded in breaking away from that tradition. He attempted to free the characters from stubborn stage clichés. He left nearly the entire text intact and, in contrast to Lothar, made his actors use the author's exact syntax. He also took the characters seriously, which was increasingly appreciated. With regard to the stage set, however, he stuck to traditional illusionism. The opulent sets filling the entire stage made it impossible for the space to take on any significance of its own, which might have made the relationships between the characters more transparent. He also let his actors use conventional postures, gestures, and facial expressions. He did not dare to employ any physicality by which the genre of the social comedy would have been overcome. His theater remained attached to the word. That is why it appeared so unusually old-fashioned and devoid of tension and excitement, scenically speaking. Instead, on the international scene, theater was developing a new sense of space and body. Nevertheless, Heinrich Schnitzler deserves the credit for initiating a renaissance of his father's works in Austria, even if his efforts were not yet appreciated internationally.

It was not until the 1980s that the plays were finally freed of their Viennese color and Arthur Schnitzler came to be seen as a modern European writer. International Schnitzler research has contributed immensely toward this end, as has the criticism since Carl Schorske's[61] effort to re-assess the entire period ranging from the decadent *fin-de-siècle* to the *Wiener Moderne* in his path-breaking work *Fin-de-Siècle Vienna*. Little stood in the way of understanding Schnitzler's precise analysis of isolation, alienation and addiction to illusion, nothing to block his dramaturgy. In the last two decades of the twentieth century, his work conquered the international and Austrian stages.

Translated by Frank Newman, Karl-Franzens-Universität, Graz

Notes

[1] Sigmund Freud, quoted in Ulrich Weinzierl, *Arthur Schnitzler. Lieben Träumen Sterben* (Frankfurt: Fischer, 1994), 9.

[2] *Die Furche* (Vienna), March 10, 1953.

[3] *Neues Wiener Tagblatt*, February 14, 1951.

[4] *Weltpresse* (Vienna), October 24, 1950.

[5] *Wiener Zeitung*, September 2, 1951; *Reigen* in DW I, 327–90.

[6] *Weltpresse* (Vienna), June 14, 1952.

[7] *Österreichische Zeitung*, January 27, 1949. *Der Ruf des Lebens* in DW I, 963–1028.

[8] See Evelyn Deutsch-Schreiner, *Theater im Wiederaufbau. Zur Kulturpolitik im österreichischen Parteien-und Verbändestaat* (Vienna: Sonderzahl, 2001).

[9] *Liebelei* in DW I, 215–64; *Weihnachtseinkäufe* in DW I, 41–49; *Die Frage an das Schicksal* in DW I, 30–40; *Zwischenspiel* in DW I, 895–902; *Professor Bernhardi* in DW II, 337–464; *Die Gefährtin* in DW I, 499–514; *Das weite Land* in DW II, 217–320.

[10] Evelyn Deutsch-Schreiner, "Die Opfer schützen die Täter. Jüdische Figuren in der österreichischen Bühnenpraxis nach dem Holocaust," in *Theatralia Judaica 2: Nach der Shoah. Israelisch-deutsche Theaterbeziehungen seit 1949*, ed. Hans-Peter Bayerdörfer (Tübingen: Niemeyer, 1996), 100–114.

[11] *Wiener Wochenausgabe*, October 11, 1947.

[12] *Weltpresse* (Vienna), September 26, 1947.

[13] *Plan* 2/5 (1947): 328.

[14] *Welt am Abend* (Vienna), September 5, 1947.

[15] Brook-Sulzer quoted in Bettina Dessau, *Nathans Rückkehr. Studien zur Rezeptionsgeschichte seit 1945* (Frankfurt: Lang, 1986), 243.

[16] *Der junge Medardus* in DW II, 27–216.

[17] Felix Kreissler, "Österreichische Nation und Kultur im Theater des Exils. Ein fragmentarischer Essay," in *Zeit der Befreiung. Wiener Theater nach 1945*, eds. Hilde Haider-Pregler and Peter Roessler (Vienna: Picus, 1997), 21.

[18] *Die Zeit* (Vienna), December 1, 1948.

[19] *Die Presse*, November 10, 1948.

[20] *Die Österreicherin* (Vienna), Vol. 1 (1948).

[21] Otto Basil, "Schnitzler und die Nachwelt," in *Neues Österreich*, May 15, 1947. At the same time, it is interesting to note that Basil also had misgivings about publishing Paul Celan's poem about the death camps, "Todesfuge" ("Death Fugue").

[22] *Plan* 2/5 (1947): 358. Letter to the editor by Walter Reisch from Los Angeles: "Sehr verehrter Herr Basil! [. . .] hier an der Westküste Amerikas, sechstausend Meilen von Schnitzlers geliebtem achtzehnten Bezirk, vergeht kaum eine Woche, niemals aber ein Sonntagnachmittag, daß wir nicht über ihn debattieren. Ernst Lubitsch kann ganze Seiten aus Schnitzlers Dramen zitieren, der "Weg ins Freie" gehört zu Lubitsch' Lieblingsbüchern, und immer wieder kommt er auf des Dichters Dramentechnik und Tiefe des Dialogs zu sprechen. Billy Wilder hat immer ein Schnitzlerbuch auf seinem Nachttisch liegen, und unlängst erst wurden Gottfried Reinhardt und ich von einigen Amerikanern dabei ertappt, wie wir über "Casanovas Heimkehr" plauderten, und Sie würden erstaunt gewesen sein, wie genau die Amerikaner Schnitzlers schönste Novelle kannten. Wenn ich Ihnen andere aufzählen wollte, die immer wieder an Schnitzler denken, von ihm träumen, ihn lieben und lesen, würden Sie sicherlich erfreut sein. Marlene Dietrich und Josef von Sternberg, Rose Stradner und Hans Jaray und alle, die zu unserem Kreis gehören, haben ihn nicht vergessen, können ihn nicht vergessen."

[23] *Neue Wiener Tageszeitung*, October 21, 1951. The author of the article is Heinz Kindermann, whom the Nazis appointed the chair of Theaterwissenschaft at the Universität Wien in 1943. He lost the chair in 1945 but was reinstalled therein in 1954. For many years he was also theater critic for the *Neue Wiener Tageszeitung*, an ÖVP-dominated daily.

[24] See Judith Beniston, *"Welttheater": Hofmannsthal, Richard von Kralik and the Revival of Catholic Drama in Austria 1890–1934* (London: W.S. Manley & Son, 1998).

[25] Arthur Schnitzler, "Aphorismen und Betrachtungen," in his *Über Kunst und Kritik*, vol. 3 (Frankfurt: Fischer, 1993), 15.

[26] *Volksstimme*, October 21, 1951.

[27] See Alfred Pfoser, Kristina Pfoser-Schweig, and Gerhard Renner, eds., *Schnitzlers "Reigen." Zehn Dialoge und ihre Skandalgeschichte*, vol. I: *Der Skandal: Analysen und Dokumente* (Frankfurt: Fischer, 1993).

[28] *Volkstheaterfreunde* (Vienna*)*, *Mitteilungsblatt* 1 (1950).

[29] Weinzierl, 10.

[30] Reinhard Urbach, *Arthur Schnitzler* (Velber bei Hannover: Friedrich, 1968), 25.

[31] Hans Weigel, "Gruß von gestern," *Turm* 2/3–4 (1946): 160.

[32] *Salzburger Nachrichten,* February 18, 1955.

[33] *Anatol* in DW I, 28–79.

[34] *Neues Wiener Tagblatt,* June 15, 1952.

[35] *Kunst & Film,* May 14, 1952.

[36] *Neue Zeit* (Linz), December 24, 1957.

[37] Peter von Matt, *Liebesverrat. Die Treulosen in der Literatur* (Munich: Deutscher Taschenbuchverlag, 1991), 284.

[38] *La Ronde* [Reigen], dir. Max Ophüls, Janus Films, 1950. VHS: Irvington, NY: The Voyager Company, 1995.

[39] *Arbeiterzeitung,* May 1, 1951.

[40] *Wiener Zeitung,* February 2, 1951.

[41] *Österreichische Zeitung,* September 20, 1951.

[42] Carl Merz and Helmut Qualtinger, "Reigen 51," in *Der Herr Karl und andere Texte fürs Theater,* vol. I, ed. Traugott Krischke (Vienna: Deuticke, 1995), 160.

[43] *Der grüne Kakadu* and *Literatur* (1960), *Komödie der Worte (1960), Der einsame Weg* (1962), *Die letzten Masken* (1962), *Lebendige Stunden, Die Gefährtin,* and *Komtesse Mizzi* (1964), *Liebelei* (1968).

[44] Renate Wagner and Brigitte Vacha, *Wiener Schnitzler-Aufführungen 1891–1970* (Munich: Prestel, 1971), 144.

[45] *Der grüne Kakadu* in DW I, 515–52.

[46] Wagner and Vacha, 146. *Komödie der Worte* in DW II, 465–528; *Literatur* in DW I, 735–58.

[47] It is worth mentioning that Ernst Lothar (1890–1974), director of the Theater in der Josefstadt from 1935–1938, was a prominent exile artist in the United States and came back to Austria as a theater officer of the U.S. Army.

[48] *Arbeiterzeitung,* May 4, 1965.

[49] Fritz Kortner quoted in Klaus Völker, *Fritz Kortner. Schauspieler und Regisseur* (Berlin: Hentrich, 1987), 223.

[50] *Volksstimme,* December 25, 1962.

[51] *Illustrierte Kronenzeitung,* June 14, 1960.

[52] *Österreichische Tageszeitung,* June 14, 1960.

[53] *Volksstimme,* June 5, 1964.

[54] *Express,* June 19, 1964.

[55] *Neue Zeit* (Graz), September 25, 1964.

[56] Paul Blaha, "Heinrich Schnitzler oder Die Arbeit mit dem Schauspieler," in *Maske und Kothurn, Vierteljahresschrift für Theaterwissenschaft* 8 (1962), 182.

[57] Konstanze Fliedl, *Arthur Schnitzler: Poetik der Erinnerung* (Vienna: Böhlau, 1997).

[58] *Volksstimme* (Vienna), September 14, 1968.

[59] Wolfgang Sabler, "Moderne und Boulvardtheater," *Text + Kritik* 4 (1998): 89–101.

[60] Weinzierl, 186.

[61] Carl E. Schorske, *Fin-de-Siècle Vienna. Politics and Culture* (New York: Random House, 1961).

Contexts

The Problem and Challenge of Jewishness in the City of Schnitzler and Anna O.

Elizabeth Loentz

SIGMUND FREUD recognized in Arthur Schnitzler his doppelgänger. Freud wrote to Schnitzler on May 14, 1922 that he felt as though Schnitzler knew through intuition what he himself had discovered only through painstaking clinical study: the principles of psychoanalysis.[1] Although Freud and Schnitzler shared common interests (medicine and literature), their courses ran parallel, rarely intersecting. They did cross in the person of Bertha Pappenheim, better known as Anna O. (the first case study in Freud and Josef Breuer's *Studien über Hysterie*, 1895), who is now frequently credited as the true inventor of the "talking cure" or the mother of psychoanalysis.[2] In 1880, Anna O. became ill while nursing her dying father and exhibited an arsenal of symptoms (a nervous cough, partial paralysis, severe neuralgia, anorexia, partial blindness and deafness, frightening hallucinations, alternation between two distinct states of consciousness, violent outbursts, and the inability to speak in her native tongue). According to Breuer's published case study, the patient herself led him to her therapy, which she called the "talking cure" or "chimney sweeping." Her symptoms were eliminated one by one as she recounted to her doctor (while in a state of hypnosis) her hallucinations and the genesis of individual symptoms.

However, Pappenheim's recovery was not as miraculous and straightforward as Breuer portrayed it. Pappenheim was not relieved by her talking cure. Indeed, according to Freud's later accounts, Breuer deserted his patient, who was anything but cured, when he was summoned to her bedside and found Pappenheim in the throes of false labor, announcing, "Dr. B.'s baby is coming!" According to medical records discovered by Albrecht Hirschmüller[3] and others, Pappenheim, who by the end of her treatment by Breuer in June 1882 was also addicted to chloral and morphine, spent another six years in and out of sanatoria.

While Pappenheim is far better known today as Anna O., the patient whose story is widely held to be the keystone of the founding myth of psychoanalysis, Bertha Pappenheim was one of the most famous and influential German Jewish women of her time. During her lifetime her fame was based not on her illness and supposed cure but on her outstanding achievements as a leading Jewish social worker, a feminist leader, and an influential social activist. After her recovery, Pappenheim founded the Jüdischer Frauenbund (German Jewish Women's League, to which approximately one in five German Jewish women belonged) and served as its president; she co-founded the International Jewish Women's League and was elected co-chairperson; she founded the Frankfurt organization Weibliche Fürsorge (Care by Women, which provided aid for Eastern European Jewish immigrants and refugees, job referrals, legal aid, assistance for nursing mothers, and a dormitory and club for single girls); she founded a home for unwed mothers and endangered girls; she was a leading figure in the international crusade against white slavery and prostitution; and she was a gifted translator, a charismatic public speaker, and a prolific author of both literary and polemical works.

Freud knew Bertha Pappenheim personally. His wife, Martha Bernays, was a close relative and friend of the Pappenheim family.[4] Although Schnitzler did not know Pappenheim personally, he knew her doctor, Breuer, to whom he was related by marriage. Given Schnitzler's strong interest in hysteria and hypnosis (he read the *Studien über Hysterie,* wrote a review of Freud's translations of Jean-Martin Charcot's lectures on hysteria, and even conducted experiments in hypnosis himself in the late 1880s), he likely knew that Anna O., arguably Vienna's most famous hysteric and hypnotic, was Bertha Pappenheim. In addition, several works written by Schnitzler's friends or acquaintances were influenced by the case study: Hugo von Hofmannsthal's *Elektra* (1903), Stefan Zweig's *Heilung durch den Geist* (1931), and Frank Wedekind's *Tod und Teufel* (1905).[5]

Pappenheim was, of course, familiar with Schnitzler's work. In 1911 she attended a performance of *Der junge Medardus* (1910) on a visit to Vienna from Frankfurt, where she was then living.[6] She appears, however, to have been less impressed by Schnitzler's "traurigen, willenlosen und unheldigen Helden" than by the lavish costuming, the nostalgic portrayal of "Old Vienna," and the fact that the Burgtheater offered ham sandwiches and beer during intermission.[7] No other references to Schnitzler are extant. However, Pappenheim, who campaigned vigorously against prostitution, devoted years to redeeming unwed mothers and illegitimate children, and espoused early marriage as a remedy to venereal disease, would surely have had at best an ambivalent relationship to Schnitzler's works.

Despite their obvious differences, Schnitzler and Pappenheim came from similar backgrounds. Their fathers both immigrated to Vienna from Hungary as adults (from Gross-Kanisza and Pressburg, today's Bratislava, respectively). Although both were members of the upper-middle class, their social and economic status was of relatively recent vintage. Johann Schnitzler worked his way through medical school as a private tutor and later became a famous laryngologist and founder of the Vienna Poliklinik. Siegmund Pappenheim's grandfather, a modest grain merchant, had inherited a fortune from an estranged brother-in-law. The authors' mothers, however, had more auspicious origins. Schnitzler's mother was from an established Viennese family. The Markbreiters had been court jewelers and academics, and some of the Scheys had been ennobled. Recha Pappenheim came from the Frankfurt Goldschmidt family, a merchant and banker dynasty related to members of the *haute bourgeoisie* throughout Europe.

Pappenheim and Schnitzler were born only three years apart (1859 and 1862) in the same street, the Praterstrasse in the Leopoldstadt. As the Leopoldstadt gradually became home to newer and poorer Jewish immigrants from the East, both families left for more prestigious addresses. Schnitzler's family relocated to the first district (from the Schottenbastei, to the Giselastraße, and then to Burgring 1 opposite the Kaisergarten), and Pappenheim's family to the ninth district (Lichtensteinstraße 2) and after her father's death to the first district (Neuer Markt 7).

Like Pappenheim's brother Wilhelm (born 1860), Schnitzler attended Gymnasium and pursued university studies leading to one of the "free professions" (medicine for Schnitzler, law for Wilhelm Pappenheim). Bertha Pappenheim, however, received an education similar to Schnitzler's first flame, Fännchen (Franziska Reich); Schnitzler wrote in his posthumously published *Jugend in Wien* (1968; *My Youth in Vienna*, 1970) that Fännchen "besaß gerade so viel Bildung, als man in jener Zeit den Töchtern mittlerer jüdischer Hausstände zu geben für nötig fand."[8] This education was, according to Pappenheim's doctor Breuer, wholly inadequate for Pappenheim, who possessed "einen kräftigen Intellekt, der auch solide geistige Nahrung verdaut hätte, nach Verlassen der Schule aber nicht erhielt."[9] She had a governess and attended Catholic girls' school until age sixteen. She was talented at languages and the piano, was a passionate horsewoman, and in general led the leisurely and, according to her, pointless life of a "höherer Tochter," biding her time until an arranged marriage.[10] In her case the wedding never took place. She left Vienna with her mother in 1888 to escape the stigma of her illness, settling in Frankfurt, where she embarked on a new life as social worker, activist, feminist leader, and writer.

Although she spent the remainder of her life in Frankfurt and its suburb Isenburg, Pappenheim never relinquished her Austrian passport, and her colleagues insisted that she never ceased being a Wienerin:

> Bertha Pappenheim war Wienerin und ist es in ihrer innersten Wesensart immer geblieben [. . .] der Geist ihrer alten Heimat, das Wienertum in seiner Lebendigkeit, mit seinem Humor, seiner Grazie, ja auch seiner beschwingten Lebendigkeit, waren in ihr verkörpert und kamen in ihrem Wesen, in so manchen Zügen ihrer Lebensführung, immer wieder zum Durchbruch [. . .] In ihrem Herzen lebte die Liebe zu Wien und den Wienern, aus dieser Stadt kamen die Wurzeln ihres Daseins.[11]

The Jewish community of Vienna likewise showed a continued interest in Pappenheim's achievements. *Dr. Bloch's Österreichische Wochenschrift* published several articles on Pappenheim's activities as founding president of the Jüdischer Frauenbund Deutschlands; her role in founding the Vienna Weibliche Fürsorge; her speeches on white slavery, Jewish social work, and women's issues; her travels; and her literary works. These articles never failed to include a proud mention of her Viennese heritage.

Despite their common origins, the Schnitzler and Pappenheim families parted ways in a matter of highest significance, one that ultimately shaped Schnitzler's and Pappenheim's divergent approaches to the so-called "Jewish Question," namely in their relationship to the Jewish religion. The Pappenheim family came from the tradition of strict Hungarian Orthodox Judaism. Bertha's uncles Kalman, Samuel, and Hermann were *Gemeindevorsteher* in Pressburg. Her cousin Wolf was the leader of the Agudat Israel (an Orthodox organization) in Vienna. Her cousin Isidor served as head of the Jewish community in Pressburg and as head of the National Organization of the Orthodox Communities in Czechoslovakia. Upon immigrating to Vienna, her father became one of the founders of the Bethaus in the Ankergasse, and in 1864 he was a founder of the Orthodox Schiffschul. Pappenheim's brother served as the *geschäftsführender Vicepräsident der Isrealitischen Kultusgemeinde* of Vienna.[12]

Schnitzler's father, Johann, on the other hand, traded Jewish religion for the universal humanitarian "religion" of medicine. His 1884 "Bekenntnis zum Arztberuf" reads:

> Die Religion des Arztes ist die Humanität, d.h. die Liebe zur Menschheit, ohne Rücksicht auf Reichthum und Armuth, ohne Unterschied der Nationalität u. der Konfession. Er soll u. muss daher immer u. überall, wo Kampf der Klassen u. Rassen, wo nationaler Chauvinismus u. religiöser Fanatismus herrschen, als Apostel der Humanität für Völ-

kerfrieden und Menschenverbrüderung eintreten und wirken. Wer nicht so denkt, nicht so fühlt, ist kein wahrer, kein echter Arzt.[13]

The Schnitzler family maintained only the barest vestige of Jewish religious practice. Schnitzler's bar mitzvah was celebrated "ohne jedes rituelle Gepränge, aber durch besonders zahlreiche und schöne Geschenke."[14] His family observed the high holy days merely out of respect for his maternal grandmother, whom he describes as the only truly pious member of the family. Even she, however, did not practice kashrut, celebrate the lesser holidays, or keep the Sabbath. According to Schnitzler, his parents' generation, despite their stubborn insistence on their Jewish ethnic solidarity (Stammeszugehörigigkeit), were indifferent to the precepts of Jewish religion and opposed or even derided its formalities.[15]

Because Orthodox religious practice is all-encompassing, defining virtually every aspect of lifestyle and daily activity, the two families' religious habits would necessarily have defined which Vienna, especially which "Jewish Vienna," Pappenheim and Schnitzler would have been exposed to or identified with, and accordingly shaped their understanding of the "Jewish question" and how best to negotiate it. Johann Schnitzler, like the majority of Hungarian, Bohemian, and Moravian Jewish immigrants to Vienna, was what Berkley and Rozenblit term "integrationist" or "Germanized," German-speaking and with a strong affinity to German culture. Siegmund Pappenheim, however, was an Orthodox Hungarian Jew and founding member of the Schiffschul.[16] Berkley asserts that the Hungarian members of the Schiffschul must be viewed as an entity separate from their integrationist countrymen. Because they were united with the Galicians in their congregation in the common struggle against Liberal and Reform Judaism and against the assimilationism and secularization of the Viennese Jewish mainstream, they identified to a greater degree with Eastern European Jews, from whom Viennese Jews of Schnitzler's background and class generally sought to distance themselves. While Pappenheim's circle of acquaintances was defined at least in part by her father's position in the Schiffschul, and thus would have included very Orthodox Jews, including unassimilated Eastern European Jews, the social circle of Schnitzler's definitive years was determined by his father's position as a famous physician, and therefore included other doctors, as well as singers, actors, and other socially prominent patients. Schnitzler writes that his father had become fixated on appearances and preferred to forget his own origins. He opposed, for example, his daughter's union with his protégé Hajek, the "ungarischer Judenbub, [. . .] dessen Umgangsformen [. . .] mancherlei zu wünschen übrigließen" (that is, he was presumably not unlike Johann Schnitzler in his youth).[17] Certainly, there was overlap between the families' circles. Schnitzler, particularly in his life as a writer, associated with a vast variety of individuals, including religious Jews and more recent Jewish immigrants from Eastern Europe; and Pappenheim's socioeconomic class determined that her circle of acquaintances would include Viennese intellectuals and artists. However, their primary identifications were different, and this difference, coupled with their chosen professions, defines their understanding of the "Jewish question" and its solutions.

Pappenheim, as a social worker and professing member of the Jewish religious community, favored wide-reaching communal and societal solutions to the so-called Jewish Question, anti-Semitism, women's rights, and the "Sittlichkeitsfrage" (which encompassed premarital and extramarital sex, prostitution, white slavery, and related issues).[18] Schnitzler, on the other hand, tended to distance himself from politics, mass movements, and communal or organizational efforts aimed at solving the Jewish problem; he favored individual, psychological solutions.[19]

In the "Autobiographische Notizen" to *Jugend in Wien* Schnitzler recalls having experienced little anti-Semitism until his university years. Although he reports that there were "kaum Spuren" of anti-Semitism in his Gymnasium, which he attended from 1871 to 1879, Viennese anti-Semitism was well into its formative years in the 1870s. Jews became ready scapegoats for the stock market crash of 1873 and the ensuing depression, despite the fact that many prominent Jewish financiers had warned against speculation. In 1876 Theodor Billroth, now considered internationally the founder of modern abdominal surgery, published *Über das Lehren und Lernen der medicinischen Wissenschaften an den Universitäten der deutschen Nation nebst allgemeinen Bemerkungen über Universitäten,* in which he asserted that Jews were a distinct nation who could never become Germans.[20] Having seen impoverished Eastern European Jewish medical students peddle firewood in the streets, Billroth concluded that the compulsion to make money was a Jewish racial trait. Billroth's authority as one of Vienna's foremost physicians lent credibility to this "racial" anti-Semitism, as distinguished from religiously or economically based anti-Semitism. Racial anti-Semitism was burgeoning throughout Europe in the wake of Charles Darwin's theory of evolution and increased fascination with anthropology and the "racial sciences."[21]

Before Schnitzler graduated from Gymnasium in 1879, both Georg Ritter von Schönerer and Karl Lueger, who became Vienna's most notorious anti-Semitic politicians, had been elected to political office. At that point in their careers, neither publicly supported anti-Semitism. Von

Schönerer was elected as a left-wing liberal to the Reichsrat in 1873 and Lueger as a liberal to Vienna's municipal council in 1875. By 1879, however, von Schönerer was campaigning on an anti-Semitic platform, and in 1885 he founded the Pan-German party, which was immensely popular among Vienna's German nationalist fraternities; its pro-German and anti-Habsburg stance went hand in hand with racial anti-Semitism. In 1888 von Schönerer was stripped of his right to hold office for five years after inciting an anti-Semitic riot and attack on a publishing house. He was re-elected in 1897, and the party reached its high point in 1901, when twenty-one Pan-Germans sat on the Reichsrat.

Schnitzler took a more personal interest in Vienna's future mayor Lueger, whose mentor early in his political career had been the Jewish physician and politician Ignaz Mandl, Schnitzler's relative. Both before and after Lueger assumed leadership of the Christian Social Union (CSU) in 1890, his public stance toward Jews was strikingly inconsistent. Lueger offered, for example, his services as a defense attorney to Dr. Rabbi Samuel Bloch in the Rohling libel suit. In the early 1880s August Rohling, whose popular tract *Der Talmudjude* (1871) charged that the Talmud contained derogatory remarks about Christians, testified in the notorious Tisza Eszla case, in which a group of Jews in a Hungarian village were charged with the ritual murder of a teenage girl.[22] When Bloch publicly denounced as a vicious lie Rohling's testimony concerning the veracity of the blood libel myth,[23] Rohling threatened to sue him for libel. Although Lueger's embrace of anti-Semitism for political gain was dismissed as disingenuous pragmatism, Schnitzler was particularly critical of Lueger's opportunism. He comments in *Jugend in Wien*:

> So unbedenklich er die niedrigsten Instinkte der Menge und die allge-
> meine politische Atmosphäre für seine Zwecke zu nützen wußte, im
> Herzen war er, auch auf der Höhe seiner Popularität, sowenig Antise-
> mit als zu der Zeit, da er im Hause des Dr. Ferdinand Mandl mit des-
> sen Bruder Ignaz und anderen Juden Tarock spielte. Es gab und gibt
> Leute, die es ihm als Vorzug anrechnen, daß er auch in seiner stärksten
> Antisemitenzeit persönlich für viele Juden eine gewisse Vorliebe beibe-
> halten und daraus kein Hehl gemacht hatte: Mir galt gerade das immer
> als der stärkste Beweis seiner moralischen Fragwürdigkeit.[24]

In 1895 the CSU won 92 of 138 seats in the Vienna Municipal Council, and Lueger was elected mayor of Vienna, but Emperor Franz Joseph refused to endorse his appointment until 1897. Lueger held the post until his death in 1910. Vienna became the schoolroom for Adolf Hitler's anti-Semitic politics, in no small part because of von Schönerer and Lueger — Hitler had been in Vienna just prior to the First World War. While Pan-Germanism's anti-Habsburg stance and principles of racial anti-Semitism were more in keeping with Hitler's worldview as expressed in *Mein Kampf* (Vol. 1, 1925; Vol. 2, 1927) (for the CSU, whose anti-Semitism was, at least in theory, religiously founded, baptism could redeem Jews), Hitler was a great admirer of Lueger's political acumen (namely his ability to read the pulse of his constituency and devise a blend of anti-Semitism, socialism, and Catholicism that appealed to Vienna's lower-middle class) and patterned his own political persona after Lueger.[25]

Schnitzler remarks in his "Autobiographische Notizen" that his experience with anti-Semitism began in earnest at the university. In *Jugend in Wien* Schnitzler focuses especially on the growth of "deutschnationalen Verbindungen," which since 1878 (the fraternity Libertas was the first) had begun to ban Jews from their ranks. Schnitzler reports that, because provocations and physical altercations between anti-Semitic and "freisinnigen" ("free-thinking") fraternities (which were often largely Jewish in membership) as well as between individual students had become frequent, Jewish students had become expert and "dangerous" swordsmen. Schnitzler attributes the "Waidhofener Beschluß," which declared Jews "satisfaktionsunfähig," to anti-Semitic students' fear of embarrassing themselves by losing duels to Jews. Although the "Waidhofener Beschluß" was not officially decreed until 1896, Schnitzler writes that its principles were already deeply ingrained by the early 1880s.[26] He conjectures that the expulsion of Jews from Theodor Herzl's German nationalist fraternity, Albia, was the first episode in Herzl's transformation from German nationalist to Zionist.[27]

In *Jugend in Wien* Schnitzler reports having experienced far less anti-Semitism in the military than at the university, which can perhaps be attributed to his service in the predominantly Jewish corps of medical students, who were nicknamed the *Mosesdragoner*. According to Schnitzler, although the head doctors were mostly anti-Semites, the Jewish cadets suffered few repercussions. There was, however, especially in social interactions, a "'reinliche Scheidung' [. . .] zwischen arischen und semitischen Elementen."[28] Other branches of the military were less accommodating to Jews, especially those aspiring to the higher ranks. A baptized Jewish baron and lieutenant advised Schnitzler's friend Rudi Pick against embarking on a military career, "Im Offiziersstand, besonders bei Kavallerieregimentern, wäre es schwer (— als Jude, auch als getaufter, denn ungetauft hätte man ja überhaupt keine Aussicht —) Konflikten mit den Kameraden auszuweichen," and he had the dueling scars to prove it.[29] Only later did Schnitzler himself experience the latent anti-Semitism of the military, when he was stripped of his reserve officer's commission for damaging the "Ehre und Ansehen der österr. u. ung. k.u.k. Armee" through the publication of *Leutnant Gustl* (1900) and for failing to defend his honor against subsequent personal attacks rendered by the paper *Reichswehr*.[30] Schnitzler's literary career was, in general, plagued by negative criticism and scandal, which he attributed in large part to his Jewishness.[31] Several years before the *Reigen* (1903) scandal and hearings, Schnitzler wrote in his diaries: "Daß ich — schon durch das ewige Gekläff des Antisemitengesindels — seit der Erfindung der Buchdruckerkunst, der am meisten beschimpfte Dichter deutscher Sprache bin, halt ich für zweifellos."[32]

In letters to his critics, Schnitzler insists that he had no intention to write tendentious literature or propaganda, even in the two works that explicitly address the Jewish Question, *Professor Bernhardi* (1912) and *Der Weg ins Freie* (1908).[33] In the case of *Der Weg ins Freie* Schnitzler was compelled to defend himself against two diametrically opposed critiques. One faction of critics complained that he had failed to address the Jewish Question with enough courage, and the other charged that he had failed to connect the two thematic threads of the novel, Georg's personal and artistic crises and the "Jewish question."[34] In other words, the book was actually two novels. To the former accusation Schnitzler replied, "Bisher hätte ich nur das Gegenteil gehört — im übrigen sei ich nicht dazu da 'Fragen' anzupacken, sondern Gestalten darzustellen, die sich so oder so zu Fragen stellen."[35] To the latter, Schnitzler replied that there may seem to be no "absolut notwendige" connection between the two themes artistically, but that,

> sie flossen ineinander, ganz ohne mein Zuthun — sodaß ich unmöglich daran hätte etwas ändern können. Ich habe nichts hineingestopft, weil ich eben Gelegenheit suchte, gewisse Ansichten oder Aphorismen anzubringen — sondern im Laufe der Erzählung [. . .] war jede Gestalt mit ihren Anschauungen dahingerückt, wie sie nun stehen geblieben ist. Mir war das Verhältnis Georgs zu seiner Geliebten immer geradeso wichtig wie seine Beziehung zu den verschiedentlichen Juden des Romans — ich habe eben ein Lebensjahr des Freiherrn von Wergenthin geschildert, in dem er über allerlei Menschen und Probleme und über sich selbst ins Klare kommt [. . .] Ich wollte, ohne Tendenz, Menschen und Beziehungen darstellen — die ich gesehen habe.[36]

Schnitzler describes his approach to *Professor Bernhardi* in similar terms:

> Ich habe eine Charakterkomödie geschrieben, die in ärztlichen und zum Teil in politischen Kreisen spielt, kein Tendenzstück, das den Konflikt

zwischen Wissenschaft und Kirche oder gar, wie Sie meinen, den Streit zwischen zwei Religionen darzustellen oder am Ende in irgend einer Richtung zu entscheiden sucht. Es war nicht meine Absicht [. . .] eine Frage zu lösen [. . .] Ich empfinde es als meinen Beruf Menschen zu gestalten und habe nichts zu beweisen als die Vielfältigkeit der Welt.[37]

Schnitzler's professed intent was to create and portray individuals and their relationships in the full spectrum in which they appear in the world (or more precisely, in his world — Jewish Vienna). It was not to portray, much less to solve, any political or societal "question."[38] In regard to *Professor Bernhardi* Schnitzler writes, "ein Stück wie das meine, das von den einmal bestehenden Verhältnissen zwischen Juden und Christen, zwischen Juden und Germanen in Österreich absehen zu können glaubte, wäre kein wahres Stück geworden und gewiß kein aufrichtiges — zumindest, wenn ich es geschrieben hätte." Schnitzler continues, "Und eine österreichische Komödie habe ich geschrieben. Eine . . ., nicht die." As a Jew, he could not portray the political machinations that infiltrate a clinic such as the Elisabethinum (or his father's own Poliklinik, on which it was patterned) with a character named "Wahrmund," because the Wahrmund affair would not allow him to portray "höchstwichtige uns allen nicht unbekannte Bestandteile der österreichischen Atmosphäre" that are an indomitable aspect of his Vienna.[39] Schnitzler could not portray his Austria/Vienna without combining in one character elements of both Wahrmund and Johann Schnitzler. The *Professor Bernhardi* plot combines two "affairs": the public political struggle between the Catholic church and medical science,[40] which invokes the Wahrmund affair but is further complicated by Bernhardi's Jewishness; and the internal politics (the hiring of a Catholic candidate over a better-qualified Jewish one) of a clinic founded and funded in large part by Jews but increasingly dominated by an emergent anti-Semitic faction. The two affairs become intertwined when Ebenwald suggests that naming a Catholic candidate as Tugendvetter's successor would prove that Bernhardi is not anti-Catholic. Just as Schnitzler's Viennese "Ärztestück" inevitably develops into a piece addressing the "Jewish question," so must his "Wiener Roman" *Der Weg ins Freie,* which Schnitzler had originally conceived as a play about a man who confronts his sister's seducer, likewise become a story about the "Jewish question." The Catholic nobleman Georg von Wergenthin would, as an aspiring composer, socialize within the Viennese art world and with its consumers and patrons, the majority of whom were middle-class and Jewish. As Schnitzler explains in his "Autobiographische Notizen" to *Jugend in Wien,* it was impossible for Viennese Jews to elude the Jewish Question:

Es war nicht möglich, insbesondere für einen Juden, der in der Öffentlichkeit stand, davon abzusehen, daß er Jude war, da die andern es
nicht taten, die Christen nicht und die Juden noch weniger. Man hatte
die Wahl, für unempfindlich, zudringlich, frech oder für empfindlich,
schüchtern, verfolgungswahnsinnig zu gelten. Und auch wenn man
seine innere und äußere Haltung so weit bewahrte, daß man weder das
eine noch das andere zeigte, ganz unberührt zu bleiben war so unmöglich, als etwa ein Mensch gleichgültig bleiben könnte, der sich zwar die
Haut anaesthesieren ließ, aber mit wachen und offenen Augen zusehen
muß, wie unreine Messer sie ritzen, ja schneiden, bis das Blut kommt.

In *Der Weg ins Freie* and *Professor Bernhardi* various modes for negotiating Jewishness in Vienna are explored via a menagerie of characters.
Schnitzler also portrays their corollaries, the various incarnations of Viennese anti-Semitism. These range from the blatant, such as the racially anti-
Semitic Pan-Germanism propagated by von Schönerer, or Lueger's
Christian Socialist anti-Semitism, to the more subtle, such as claiming
"alibi-Jews" (whereby a single Jewish friend serves as evidence of absolute
tolerance), or the deep-rooted, yet outwardly imperceptible, anti-
Semitism of even the most well-intentioned individuals, such as Georg.[41]

The strategies for negotiating Viennese anti-Semitism range in *Der
Weg ins Freie* and *Professor Bernhardi* from fervent Zionism to over-
assimilation nearing the point of total internalization of clerical and/or
racial anti-Semitism. The Zionist strategy is demonstrated in *Der Weg ins
Freie* by Leo Golowski, who views Viennese "Germans'" belief that Jews
are unassimilable foreigners not as bias but as an expression of their unerring instinctual perception of "anthropological and historical" fact. This
conviction does not, however, prevent him from challenging an anti-
Semitic lieutenant, who subjected him to a series of humiliations during
his military service, to a duel. Golowski emerges the victor but faces criminal charges, a fate that a Gentile would likely have been spared. Golowski
finds a sympathizer in the wealthy, aging businessman Salomon Ehrenberg, whom experience has convinced that Zionism is the only viable
alternative for Viennese Jews and who plans to visit Jerusalem before his
death. Having watched the Jews who created the Liberal movement (in
the novel Dr. Stauber Sr. and Heinrich Bermann's father) and those who
supported the German Nationalist movement deserted and betrayed by
their parvenu Gentile compatriots, he predicts that the same will happen
to the next generation, to Leo's sister Therese Golowski and other Austrian Jewish Social Democrats and Communists who believe that the
"Jewish problem" will disappear with the solution of the class problem:

Wer hat die liberale Bewegung in Österreich geschaffen? . . . Die Juden! . . . Von wem sind die Juden verlassen und verraten worden? Von
den Liberalen. Wer hat die deutschnationale Bewegung in Österreich
geschaffen? Die Juden. Von wem sind die Juden im Stich gelassen . . .
was sage ich im Stich gelassen . . . bespuckt worden wie die Hund'! . . .
Von den Deutschen! Und gerade so wird's ihnen jetzt ergehen mit
dem Sozialismus und dem Kommunismus. Wenn die Suppe erst aufge-
tragen ist, so jagen sie euch vom Tisch. Das war immer so und wird
immer so sein.[42]

Schnitzler had witnessed a similar betrayal in his own family. In *Jugend
in Wien* he describes how Lueger betrayed his mentor, Mandl, who had
formed with him an "anticorruptionist-democratic" faction in the city
government, as it became politically expedient to target an easily defined
enemy, the Jews.[43] To spite his assimilationist, appearance-minded wife and
children, Ehrenberg delights in publicly exhibiting stereotypically "Semitic" characteristics, namely the use of a Yiddish accent and an unkempt
appearance. According to an acquaintance, he would like best to appear in
public wearing caftan and peyes. His wife and children deride his "idée
fixe" of anti-Semitic persecution, yet tacitly validate it by shrinking in
embarrassment at his public display of supposedly Jewish traits.

Ehrenberg's son Oskar, a reserve lieutenant with Catholic feudal aspirations who remains unbaptized only because of a stipulation in his father's
will, represents the opposite pole. Oscar is, in Heinrich Bermann's assessment, a "tragic-comic figure."[44] He attempts suicide after his father slaps
him when he sees him lift his hat upon passing St. Michael's, mimicking
Catholic piety. Ironically, both father and son face the criminal charge of
disruption of religion (Religionsstörung), the same charge raised against
Bernhardi. The cast of *Professor Bernhardi* also includes two converted, yet
still over-compensating Jews: the German-Nationalist Schreimann, who
flaunts a *Schmiß* (dueling scar) and affects an exaggerated Austrian accent
(albeit tainted with an occasional hint of *Jargon* — Yiddish or Yiddish-
accented German), and the defense lawyer Goldenthal, whose wife wears
a cross and whose son goes to Kalksberg, a prestigious Catholic school.

Between these two extremes, Schnitzler portrays individuals who do
not convert but either make light of anti-Semitism, such as the "born
cavalier" Willy Eissler, or pretend not to notice or at least not to be affected
by it, such as Nürnberger. Unlike Nürnberger, Eissler does not deny the
existence of Viennese anti-Semitism. He is an astute critic of its various
manifestations, for example the hypocrisy of opportunistic anti-Semites who
associate with Jews when it is to their advantage, or the double standard by
which a Catholic who declines a duel is pious but a Jew who does the same

is cowardly. Nürnberger, on the other hand, denies the existence of racial anti-Semitism, clinging to the belief that he is not a "Jew," because he has renounced Jewish religion by declaring himself "konfessionslos"[45] and has never felt like a Jew. He calls Zionism the "neueste Nationalkrankheit der Juden," claiming that anti-Semitism did not affect Jews of his class and that the only real anti-Semite he ever encountered was a Jew.[46] In *Professor Bernhardi* Cyprian objects to his less optimistic and vocally resistant colleague Löwenstein's "idée fixe" and "Verfolgungswahn," and pragmatically, naively believes that anti-Semitic intrigue can be combated with a bit of diplomacy.[47] In a letter of January 4, 1913 to Richard Charmatz,[48] Schnitzler voiced his low opinion of such evasive tactics:

> Als die peinlichsten Zeitgenossen freilich empfinde ich diejenigen Juden, die vom Antisemitismus nichts spüren oder nichts zu spüren vorgeben, sei es nun aus Mangel an Feingefühl, aus Bequemlichkeit, aus Saturiertheit, aus Snobismus oder aus Kriecherei. In Hinsicht auf diese Sorte Juden bin ich sogar Antisemit wie nur irgend einer, und mein Antisemitismus hat den Vorzug, den Richtigen zu treffen. . . .[49]

Schnitzler clearly identifies most strongly with the strategy espoused by Heinrich Bermann, who echoes the views expressed in Schnitzler's diaries and letters. Bermann asserts:

> Mein Instinkt [. . .] sagt mir untrüglich, daß hier, gerade hier meine Heimat ist und nicht in irgendeinem Land, das ich nicht kenne, das mir nach den Schilderungen nicht im geringsten zusagt und das mir gewisse Leute jetzt als Vaterland einreden wollen, mit der Begründung, daß meine Urahnen vor einigen tausend Jahren gerade von dort aus in die Welt verstreut worden sind.[50]

In *Jugend in Wien* Schnitzler writes that his feeling of alienation in his grandfather's hometown in Hungary led him to find suspect the view,

> nach der jemand, der in einem bestimmten Land geboren, dort aufgewachsen, dort dauernd tätig ist, ein anderes Land — nicht etwa eines, in dem vor Jahrzehnten seine Eltern und Großeltern, sondern eines, wo seine Urahnen vor Jahrtausenden zu Hause waren — nicht allein aus politischen, sozialen, ökonomischen Gründen (worüber sich immerhin diskutieren ließe) sondern auch gefühlsmäßig als seine eigentliche Heimat zu betrachten habe.[51]

Like Schnitzler's, Bermann's concept of Heimat is an apolitical one, in which sentiment, the feeling of belonging, and not the abstract concept of Fatherland determines right of settlement. Both Schnitzler and his double Bermann likewise deny the necessity of feelings of belonging or solidarity grounded in the arbitrary abstract concepts of nation, class, or race. Schnitzler's "Bekenntnis" reads:

> Ich fühle mich mit niemandem solidarisch, weil er zufällig derselben Nation, demselben Stand, derselben Rasse, derselben Familie angehört wie ich. Es ist ausschließlich meine Sache, mit wem ich mich verwandt zu fühlen wünsche; ich anerkenne keine angeborene Verpflichtung in dieser Frage.[52]

Bermann mirrors these sentiments:

> zusammengehörig fühlte er sich mit niemandem, nein mit niemandem auf der Welt. Mit den weinenden Juden in Basel gerade so wenig als mit den grölenden Alldeutschen im österreichischen Parlament; mit den jüdischen Wucherern so wenig als mit den hochadligen Raubrittern; mit einem zionistischen Branntweinschänker so wenig als mit einem christlich-sozialen Greisler. Und am wenigsten würde ihn je das Bewußtsein gemeinsam erlittener Verfolgung, gemeinsam lastenden Hasses mit Menschen verbinden, denen er sich innerlich fern fühlte.[53]

In an unmailed, undated letter to the Jewish National Fund, Schnitzler writes that he does not oppose Zionism in its role in developing Jewish self-esteem or as a "Wohlfahrtsaktion," but rejects the notion of a Jewish homeland in Palestine:

> Ich werde erst dann an ein solches eingeborenes Heimatsgefühl der Juden in Palästina glauben, wenn man mir einen Menschen zeigt, der in Unkenntnis seines Judentums, ohne persönlich je unter der Tatsache dieses Judentums subjectiv oder objektiv gelitten zu haben, in einem andern Lande und in einer andern Sprache als dem Hebräischen aufgewachsen und einmal zufällig in Palästina landend, mystisch in sich zu fühlen beginnt, daß er eigentlich nicht in Deutschland, in Frankreich, in England usw., sondern in Palästina zuhause sei.[54]

Bermann echoes Schnitzler's rejection of Zionist ideology, expressing sympathy with the Zionist project only in terms of a social welfare project:

> Als moralisches Prinzip und als Wohlfahrtsaktion wollte er den Zionismus gelten lassen, wenn er sich aufrichtig so zu erkennen gäbe; die Idee einer Errichtung des Judenstaates auf religiöser und nationaler Grundlage erschiene ihm wie eine unsinnige Auflehnung gegen den Geist aller geschichtlichen Entwicklung.[55]

In *Jugend in Wien* Schnitzler states that the Jewish Question was of interest to him not as a religious or political but as a psychological problem (96). It follows that Schnitzler's solution to the Jewish problem would be not a political or religious one but an individual solution in the manner outlined by Heinrich Bermann:

> Für unsere Zeit gibt es keine Lösung . . . Keine allgemeine wenigstens, Eher gibt es hunderttausend verschiedene Lösungen, weil es eben eine Angelegenheit ist, die bis auf weiteres jeder mit sich selbst abmachen muß, wie er kann. Jeder muß selber dazusehen, wie er herausfindet aus seinem Ärger, oder aus seiner Verzweiflung, oder aus seinem Ekel, irgendwohin, wo er frei aufatmen kann. Vielleicht gibt es wirklich Leute, die dazu bis nach Jerusalem spazieren müssen . . . Ich fürchte nur, daß manche, an diesem vermeintlichen Ziel angelangt, sich erst recht verirrt vorkommen würden. Ich glaube überhaupt nicht, daß solche Wanderungen ins Freie sich gemeinsam unternehmen lassen . . . denn die Straßen dorthin laufen ja nicht im Lande draußen, sondern in sich selbst. Es kommt nur für jeden darauf an, seinen inneren Weg zu finden. Dazu ist natürlich notwendig, möglichst klar in sich zu sehen, in seine verborgensten Winkel hineinzuleuchten![56]

Whereas Schnitzler espoused an individual, interior solution to the Jewish problem, Pappenheim eschewed individual solutions in favor of broad societal reforms. Pappenheim rejected what she believed to be opportunistic individual responses to anti-Semitism. She was highly critical, for example, of the conversion of middle-class Jews for the sake of social advancement, and she vehemently opposed individual emigration, even after 1933. Nuanced psychological explorations of Jewish reactions to anti-Semitism in the vein of Schnitzler are absent from her writings. There are several reasons for this difference. First, Pappenheim identified strongly with the Jewish religion. Therefore, she felt a sense of community and solidarity with all Jews, even with those who no longer believed, as she hoped to bring them back into the fold. She believed, in fact, that institutionalized Nazi anti-Semitism had its merits: for one thing, it would return those who had denied their origins (such as converts) to the community, where they could embrace their religion anew; moreover, banishment from the public sphere would return Jews to their homes and families and promote a renewal of Jewish religious life.[57] Although Pappenheim's opinions were no anomaly, they were not shared by Schnitzler. In 1931 he wrote a letter to the editor of the *Neue Jüdische Monatsschau,* which had attributed to him an essay, "Das Gute am Antisemitismus," denying authorship and expressing his disagreement with the arguments of the article.[58]

Second, as a social worker Pappenheim believed that curing the social ills that plagued less fortunate Jews (especially Eastern European Jews and Jewish women) would bring about the end of anti-Semitism. This reasoning, of course, presupposed that certain traits and behaviors of Jews, especially unassimilated Eastern European Jews, caused anti-Semitism, that Jews themselves were at fault for anti-Semitism.

The third reason for the major differences between Pappenheim and Schnitzler is Pappenheim's identification, via her father's position in the Schiffschul, with Vienna's less assimilated Eastern European Jewish immigrants, who began arriving to Vienna in great numbers in the late nineteenth century. In her 1903 essay *Zur Lage der jüdischen Bevölkerung in Galizien,* in which she describes the abysmal living conditions of Galician Jewry and outlines proposals for relief and reform efforts, she credits her expertise in matters concerning Eastern European Jews to her dual Austrian and Orthodox Jewish heritage and her knowledge of Yiddish.[59] It is important to note that this milieu, which was hardly invisible in Vienna and certainly played a large role in the development of Viennese anti-Semitism, is virtually absent from Schnitzler's literary work, even in *Der Weg ins Freie* and *Professor Bernhardi.* Poor Eastern European Jews, living both in Eastern Europe and in Vienna and other Central and Western European cities, however, are the chief players in Pappenheim's most extensive literary work, a collection of short stories, *Kämpfe* (1916).[60] Unlike Schnitzler, who believed that his chief role as an author was to create and portray individuals, Pappenheim did not separate her literary endeavors from her social work. Therefore, while Schnitzler offers psychologically nuanced portrayals of individuals' interior negotiations of the Jewish problem, Pappenheim utilizes "types" to illustrate the common woes of entire classes and groups of people in order to generate interest in her social-work projects, her "Kämpfe" with the "Jewish question."

In "Der Erlöser" Pappenheim portrays the attempted proselytization of two pogrom orphans by Catholic missionaries, and the female orphan's (Reisle's) fall into white slavery and prostitution (in the employ of an Eastern European Jewish bordello mistress, Muhme Rifke). This unapologetically tendentious work agitates for Jewish social services for pogrom orphans, for better religious and vocational education for Jewish women, and for the Jüdischer Frauenbund home for unwed Jewish mothers and endangered girls. In this story Pappenheim even refers to Reisle and Muhme Rifke as two "Typen der osteuropäischen Jüdin."[61]

In "Freitag Abend" Pappenheim portrays the plight of a young Galician girl sent by her parents to the big city, Frankfurt am Main, in order to earn money to support her brother's university education. She earns little because of her lack of education and unwillingness to work on Saturday; she has no safe place to spend leisure hours, especially the Sabbath; and she can find no secure, affordable housing. Pappenheim wrote this short story in support of the Mädchenklub and its dormitories, projects of the Frankfurt Weibliche Fürsorge, which she founded. At the Mädchenklub and dormitories single girls (mostly Eastern European immigrants) could find safe, affordable lodging, kosher food, wholesome leisure-time activities, the company of other Jewish girls, and courses in vocational skills and German language and diction.

In "Der Schwächling" Pappenheim agitates for secular education and openness to secular culture in the Ultra-Orthodox Eastern European Jewish community by portraying the flight from Pressburg to Vienna and conversion to Catholicism of a young man whose father, a Rabbi, forbids him to draw and paint. In "Ungarische Dorfgeschichte" she portrays the positive alternative. A young boy is suffering from the early signs of tuberculosis, brought on by the stress of hiding his nocturnal forays into German literature from his Wunderrabbi father; but his father rescues him by sending him to Vienna to study literature.

Notably, many of Pappenheim's social-work projects were aimed at eliminating certain traits and behaviors commonly attributed to Eastern European Jews (such as the use of Yiddish and *Jargon;* involvement in prostitution and the white slave trade, which supported the stereotypes of Jewish men as degenerate sexual predators and Jewish women as "hot-blooded Jewesses"; and the supposedly non-European dress and behavior of Hassidic "caftan and peyes Jews"), which she and others believed caused anti-Semitism, which was in turn indiscriminately directed also at assimilated Western Jews. Secondarily, she sought to improve conditions in Eastern Europe in order to prevent Eastern European Jews from emigrating in the first place. Pappenheim's strategy for negotiating the Jewish problem allowed Western Jews, through their status as teachers and social workers, to distance themselves from their supposedly backward Eastern European beneficiaries; but this approach required a delicate balancing act. If the separation was perceived as too great, then a sense of identification and solidarity sufficient to move assimilated Western Jews to help Eastern Jews would dissipate.

Although she advocated communal solutions to the Jewish problem, Zionism was for Pappenheim, as for Schnitzler, not an option, albeit for different reasons. She believed: (1) that emigration to Israel was prohibitively expensive, and that only wealthy Jews would be able to escape in this fashion; (2) Zionism would reintroduce Jewish ghettoization; (3) Zionists were blind to social and women's issues, such as the care and rearing of children (which she believed should happen at home and not collectively as in some Kibbutzim), and white slavery and prostitution; (4) Zionism was anti-religious; (5) Zionist rhetoric supported the claims of anti-Semites that Jews did not belong in Europe; (6) Zionist agitation caused divisions within the Jewish community; and (7) Zionism was philosophically at odds with her staunch belief in a (cultural) German-Jewish symbiosis.

In her 1936 essay "Die jüdische Frau"[62] Pappenheim described the Jüdischen Frauenbund (which she founded and led according to her own personal philosophy) as "jüdisch-religiös und deutsch-kulturell"[63] and insisted that, even in 1936, it would be "Dummheit und Undank" to desert "Deutschland, dessen deutscher Kultur 'Tarbut Germania' wir [German Jews] so unendlich viel verdanken."[64] Pappenheim's understanding of the German-Jewish symbiosis was, however, a two-way street, whereby Christian German culture was also indebted to its precursor, Judaism. Pappenheim attributes some anti-Semitism to the envy of Christians and Muslims, who resent being a derivative faith. In her poem "Jüdische Mütter: Pogrom 1905" Pappenheim writes, "Voll Neid sind sie, weil Ihr vom Stamme derer, die schon glaubten an einen Gott, da sie nur Götzen kannten; die unsere Weisheit raubten, und uns dann Räuber nannten."[65] In "Der echte Ring" (1936), her rendition of Gotthold Ephraim Lessing's "Ringparabel," from his play *Nathan der Weise* (1779), the artisan commissioned to duplicate the original ring (Judaism) is unable to simulate its singular beauty.[66] Enraged, he destroys its setting and hurls the pieces into space, where the stone continues to shine down on believers as the Shekhinah.

Schnitzler shared a similar understanding of an Austro-German-Jewish symbiosis. In his January 4, 1913 letter to Charmatz he writes:

> Nicht weniger stark als Sie glaube ich zu empfinden, was ich dem deutschen Volke danke. Aber selbst wenn ich, unter völliger Vernachlässigung meiner Rassenzugehörigkeit, (was mir anfechtbar erschiene) alles, was ich besitze, dem Deutschtum zu danken glaubte, so drängte sich mir doch manchmal die Überlegung auf, wie vieles das Deutschtum selbst den kulturellen und ethischen Leistungen des Judentums, so weit seine Geschichte zurückreicht, zu verdanken hat, und würde mich immerhin auch einigermaßen in der Schuld meiner Ahnen fühlen.[67]

Pappenheim never altered her position on Zionism. As late as 1935 she accused Henriette Szold, who orchestrated mass emigrations of children to Palestine, of leading children's crusades; and in 1936 (the year of her death) she referred to Zionism as one of three major "Kerben" endangering the Jewish community in Germany. Schnitzler, on the other hand, had he lived to witness the Anschluß in 1938 (or even post-1933 National Socialist Germany), might have become a reluctant Zionist, that is, the proponent of a political solution to the "Jewish problem," just as his double Bermann admitted that he would do, "wenn die Scheiterhaufen wieder angezündet werden."[68]

Notes

[1] Sigmund Freud, *Briefe, 1879–1939,* eds. Ernst and Lucie Freud (Frankfurt: Fischer, 1960), 357.

[2] Josef Breuer and Sigmund Freud, *Studien über Hysterie* (Frankfurt: Fischer, 1996).

[3] Albrecht Hirschmüller, *The Life and Work of Josef Breuer: Physiology and Psychoanalysis* (New York: New York UP, 1978).

[4] After Martha Bernay's father's death, Siegmund Pappenheim, Bertha Pappenheim's father, served together with Emma Bernays, the widowed mother, as Martha and her siblings' legal guardians.

[5] Several scholars have investigated the affinity between Schnitzler and Freud, Schnitzler's interest in psychoanalysis, and the influence of psychoanalytical thought on his literary work. These include, among many others: Kenneth Segar, "Determinism and Character: Arthur Schnitzler's *Traumnovelle* and his Unpublished Critique of Psychoanalysis," *Oxford Germanic Studies* 8 (1973): 114–27; Michael Rohrwasser, "Arthur Schnitzler's Erzählung 'Die Weissagung': Asthetizismus, Antisemitismus und Psychoanalyse," *Zeitschrift für deutsche Philologie* 118 (1999 Supplement): 60–79; Bernd Urban, John Menzies, and Peter Nutting, "Schnitzler and Freud as Doubles: Poetic Intuition and Early Research on Hysteria," *Psychoanalytic Review* 65 (1978): 131–65; Bernd Urban, "Arthur Schnitzler und Sigmund Freud: Aus den Anfängen des Doppelgängers. Zur Differenzierung dichterischer Intuition und Umgebung der frühen Hysterieforschung," *Germanisch-Romanische Monatsschrift* 24 (1974): 193–223; Henry H. Hausner, "Die Beziehungen zwischen Arthur Schnitzler und Sigmund Freud," *Modern Austrian Literature* 3/2 (1970): 48–61; and Michael Worbs, *Nervenkunst: Literatur und Psychoanalyse in Wien der Jahrhundertwende* (Frankfurt am Main: Athenäum, 1983).

[6] *Der junge Medardus* in DW II, 27–216.

[7] Bertha Pappenheim, *Sisyphus-Arbeit: Reiseberichte aus den Jahren 1911–1912* (Leipzig: Paul Linder, 1924), 9.

[8] Arthur Schnitzler, *Jugend in Wien* (Frankfurt: Fischer, 1968), 83.

[9] *Jugend in Wien,* 42.

[10] *Bertha Pappenheim zum Gedächtnis, Blätter des Jüdischen Frauenbundes* 12 (1936): 11.

[11] Stephanie Forchheimer, "Wiener Erinnerungen," *Bertha Pappenheim zum Gedächtnis, Blätter des Jüdischen Frauenbundes* 12 (1936): 27–28.

[12] Ellen M. Jensen, *Streifzüge durch das Leben von Anna O./Bertha Pappenheim: Ein Fall für die Psychiatrie-Ein Leben für die Philanthropie* (Frankfurt: ztv, 1984), 15, 21.

[13] Quoted from Hans-Ulrich Lindken, *Arthur Schnitzler Aspekte und Akzente: Materialien zu Leben und Werk* (Frankfurt: Peter Lang, 1984), 3–4.

[14] *Jugend in Wien,* 59.

[15] *Jugend in Wien,* 19.

[16] Marsha L. Rozenblit, *The Jews of Vienna, 1867–1914: Assimilation and Identity*, SUNY Series in Modern Jewish History (Albany: State U of New York P, 1983); George E. Berkley, *Vienna and Its Jews: The Tragedy of Success, 1880s–1980s* (Cambridge, MA: Abt, 1988).

[17] *Jugend in Wien*, 312–13.

[18] For Pappenheim's understanding of the so-called "Sittlichkeitsfrage" see her essay "Die sozialen Grundlagen der Sittlichkeitsfrage," *Die Frau* 9/3 (Dec. 1901): 129–38, and her speech "Zur Sittlichkeitsfrage," 2. Delegiertentage des Jüdischen Frauenbundes, Frankfurt a. M., October 2–3, 1907.

[19] Schnitzler was by no means apolitical or disinterested in Jewish social issues. His diaries attest to frequent discussions of Viennese and Austrian politics, anti-Semitism, Zionism, and the plight of Eastern European Jewish pogrom and war refugees. Schnitzler was not, however, an organizer, activist, or "joiner." Highly skeptical of the efficacy of such groups, he never became a member of one of Vienna's many organizations devoted to Jewish social welfare or combating anti-Semitism, such as the Austrian Israelite Union or the B'nai B'rith, of which Freud was a member. After discussing anti-Semitism with Rabbi Dr. Feuchtwang in 1917, Schnitzler wrote in his diary, "Er wünscht einen 'Zusammenschluß' der Juden; — worin ich nicht das Heil sähe, auch wenn es durchführbar wäre" (*Tagebuch, 1917–1919*, 34; April 10, 1917). For detailed accounts of the social and political landscape of Vienna's Jewish community and of Viennese anti-Semitism see Walter R. Weitzmann, "The Politics of the Viennese Jewish Community, 1890–1914," *Jews, Antisemitism and Culture in Vienna*, eds. Ivar Oxaal et al. (London and New York: Routledge/Kegan Paul, 1987), 121–51; Robert S. Wistrich, *The Jews of Vienna in the Age of Franz Joseph* (Oxford: Oxford UP, 1989); and Berkley, *Vienna and Its Jews*.

[20] Theodor Billroth, *Über das Lehren und Lernen der medicinischen Wissenschaften an den Universitäten der deutschen Nation nebst allgemeinen Bemerkungen über Universitäten. Eine culturhistorische Studie* (Vienna: Carl Gerold's Sohn, 1876).

[21] Billroth eventually revised his views, became one of the few university professors to support the founding of the Poliklinik by younger, mostly Jewish colleagues, and was a founding member of the Society to Combat Anti-Semitism. While studying medicine, Schnitzler attended Billroth's lectures.

[22] August Rohling, *Der Talmudjude: zur Beherzigung für Juden und Christen aller Stände* (Münster: Adolph Russell's Verlag, 1872).

[23] Blood libel is the accusation originating in medieval Europe, that Jews killed Christians to obtain their blood for use in ritual practice.

[24] *Jugend in Wien*, 146.

[25] See Adolf Hitler, *Mein Kampf*, trans. Ralph Manheim (Boston and New York: Houghton Mifflin, 1943), first edition, chapters 2 and 3 ("Years of Study and Suffering in Vienna" and "General Political Considerations Based on my Vienna Period"); *Mein Kampf* (Munich: F. Eher nachf., 1935).

[26] Schnitzler quotes the "Waidhofener Beschluß" as follows: "Jeder Sohn einer jüdischer Mutter, jeder Mensch, in dessen Adern jüdisches Blut rollt, ist von Geburt aus ehrlos, jeder feineren Regung bar. Er kann nicht unterscheiden zwischen Schmutzigem und Reinem. Er ist ein ethisch tiefstehendes Subjekt. Der Verkehr mit

einem Juden ist daher entehrend; man muß jede Gemeinschaft mit Juden vermeiden. Einen Juden kann man nicht beleidigen, ein Jude kann daher keine Genugtuung für erlittene Beleidungen verlangen" (156). The actual final wording of the "Beschluß" was somewhat different (360).

[27] *Jugend in Wien*, 156.

[28] *Jugend in Wien*, 158.

[29] *Jugend in Wien*, 251.

[30] *Leutnant Gustl* in ES I, 337–66. For Schnitzler's account of the affair see "Die Wahrheit über 'Leutnant Gustl,' Eine Novelle, die einst zu einer Affäre wurde," published posthumously in *Die Presse* and reprinted in Lindken, *Arthur Schnitzler Aspekte und Akzente: Materialien zu Leben und Werk.*

[31] *Tagebuch*, 10 vols. Vienna: Verlag der Österreichischen Akademie der Wissenschaften, 1987 ff. *1909–1912,* ed. Werner Welzig, 1995; *1917–1919,* 225 (January 29, 1919).

[32] *Tagebuch, 1917–1919,* 97 (December 13, 1917). The work suffering the most strenuous anti-Semitic attacks was *Der Reigen,* which Austrian Prime Minister Ignaz Seipel called a "Schmutzstück aus der Feder eines jüdischen Autors" (quoted in Alfred Pfoser, Kristina Pfoser-Schewig, and Gerhard Renner, eds., *Schnitzler's Reigen: Zehn Dialoge und ihre Skandalgeschichte,* vol. 2 [Frankfurt: Fischer, 1993], 35). For the most complete documentation of the *Reigen* scandal see Pfoser et al. For documentation of the censorship and reception of *Professor Bernhardi* see W. E. Yates, "The Tendentious Reception of Professor Bernhardi: Documentation in Schnitzler's Collection of Press-Cuttings," in *Vienna 1900: From Altenberg to Wittgenstein,* Austrian Studies 1, eds. Edward Timms and Ritchie Robertson (Edinburgh: Edinburgh UP, 1990), 108–25; and Werner Wilhelm Schnabel, *"Professor Bernhardi* und die Wiener Zensur: Zur Rezeptionsgeschichte der Schnitzlerschen Komödie," *Jahrbuch der Deutschen Schillergesellschaft* 28 (1984): 349–83.

[33] *Professor Bernhardi* in DW II, 337–464, and *Der Weg ins Freie* in ES I, 635–958.

[34] Clearly, Schnitzler connected the two narratives at least in part to demonstrate, by presenting the bulk of the discussion of the Jewish Question from Georg's perspective, the latent anti-Semitism of even the most well-meaning Gentiles and the unbridgeable gap between Viennese Gentiles and Jews. After more or less silently observing Leo and Heinrich's discussion of anti-Semitism, Zionism, and Jewish identity, the narrator describes Georg's thoughts, "in diesem Augenblick wußte er, daß er mit keinem von den beiden bei aller Sympathie jemals zu einer unbefangenen Vertrautheit gelangen werde [. . .] Er dachte darüber nach, ob das vielleicht wirklich in dem Rassenunterschied zwischen ihm und jenen begründet sein mochte [. . .] Er zweifelte daran. Fühlte er sich nicht gerade diesen beiden und manchen andern ihres Volkes näher, ja verwandter als vielen Menschen, die mit ihm vom gleichen Stamme waren? [. . .] Aber wenn es so war, hätte er das nicht diesen beiden Menschen heute nachmittag in irgendeinem Augenblick sagen müssen? [. . .] Und als er sich fragte, warum er das nicht getan und an ihrem Gespräch nicht teilgenommen hatte, da ward er mit Verwunderung inne, daß er während dessen ganzen Dauer eine Art von Schuldbewußtsein nicht los geworden war, gerade so, als wäre auch er sein Leben lang von einer gewissen leichtfertigen und durch persönliche Erfahrung gar nicht

gerechtfertigten Feindseligkeit gegen die 'Fremden' [. . .] nicht frei gewesen" (*Der Weg ins Freie*, 730).

[35] *Tagebuch, 1903–1908,* 371 (December 2, 1908).

[36] Arthur Schnitzler, *Briefe.* 2 Vols. (Frankfurt: Fischer, 1981, 1984). *Briefe* I, 579–80 (Letter to Georg Brandes, July 4, 1908).

[37] *Briefe* II, 1–2 (Letter to Richard Charmatz, January 4, 1913).

[38] There is, however, evidence that writing *Professor Bernhardi* was a self-therapy of sorts. After finishing the first act, Schnitzler wrote in his diary, "Man könnte viel Ekel hinein dichten und aus sich heraus dichten" (*Tagebuch,* vol. 4 (September 15, 1909), 90.

[39] *Briefe* II, 3 (Letter to Richard Charmatz, January 4, 1913). Ludwig Wahrmund was a Catholic professor who was transferred amid heated debates and sometimes violent demonstrations from Innsbruck to Prague following his controversial publication, "Katholische Weltanschauung und freie Wissenschaft." Schnitzler knew Wahrmund personally (see *Tagebuch, 1909–1912,* December 25, 1904 and February 22, 1905).

[40] Wishing not to deprive a dying patient of her state of hallucinatory euphoria, Bernhardi denies entrance to a priest wishing to administer the last rites.

[41] Although Schnitzler resisted claims that *Der Weg ins Freie* was a *roman à clef* and *Professor Bernhardi* a *Schlüsselstück,* he acknowledged in his diaries, letters, and autobiography that various characters were influenced by acquaintances or public figures. For example, Schnitzler patterned Willy Eissler of *Der Weg ins Freie* after his friend Rudi Pick and Eissler's father after Pick's father, the composer of the beloved "Fiacrelied" (JW, 238). Georg Wergenthin was inspired by Bubi Franckenstein (*Tagebuch, 1903–1908,* 196, 223, 207), Heinrich Bermann by author Jakob Wassermann (*Tagebuch, 1903–1908,* 313, 334), Else Ehrenberg by Minnie Benedict (*Tagebuch, 1903–1908,* 334), and Nürnberger by Gustav Schwarzkopf (*Tagebuch, 1903–1908,* 339). The student Hochroitzpointer in *Professor Bernhardi* is a combination of a student called Mäusetschläger (Schnitzler's anti-Semitic successor in the medizinischen Unterstützungsvereins, a university club that aided needy, mostly Jewish, medical students) and of a fellow doctor, whom he treated at the Standhartner'schen Klinik, who while convalescing refused to greet him in public (JW, 158). Minister Flint was inspired by Minister Hartl, and the conflicts between Johann Schnitzler and Dr. Hochenegg of the Poliklinik provided the raw material for Bernhardi and Ebenwald (*Briefe* II, 90, 156). Stadtrat Jalaudek is believed to be based on Hermann Bielohlawek.

[42] *Der Weg ins Freie,* 697.

[43] *Jugend in Wien,* 146.

[44] *Der Weg ins Freie,* 843.

[45] "Konfessionslos" is generally translated "non-denominational," but in this context, means "without religious affiliation." By declaring himself "konfessionslos," Nürnberger is able to renounce Jewish religion without converting (accepting another religion). He is thus able to reject the Jewish religion while maintaining a vestige of non-religious Jewish identity.

[46] *Der Weg ins Freie*, 689.

[47] *Professor Bernhardi*, 419–20.

[48] Richard Charmatz (1879–1963) was an Austrian historian.

[49] In this letter Schnitzler states that he identifies with misanthrope Kurt Pflugfelder in *Professor Bernhardi*, who declares that he is both "Antisemit" and "Antiarier" because, "die Menschen sind im allgemeinen eine recht mangelhafte Gesellschaft" (352). Heinrich Bermann likewise admits to being both anti-Semite and anti-Aryan, finding each race, as such, "widerwärtig." He explains his anti-Semitism, "Wahrscheinlich liegt es daran, daß ich, wir alle, auch wir Juden mein' ich, zu dieser Empfindlichkeit systematisch herangezogen worden sind. Von Jugend auf werden wir darauf hingehetzt, gerade jüdische Eigenschaften als besonders lächerlich oder widerwärtig zu empfinden, was hinsichtlich der ebenso lächerlichen und widerwärtigen Eigenheiten der andern eben nicht der Fall ist" (756).

[50] *Der Weg ins Freie*, 720.

[51] *Jugend in Wien*, 15.

[52] Arthur Schnitzler, *Aphorismen und Betrachtungen*, ed. Robert O. Weiss (Frankfurt: Fischer, 1967), 231.

[53] *Der Weg ins Freie*, 721.

[54] Quoted from Lindken, 86.

[55] *Der Weg ins Freie*, 721.

[56] *Der Weg ins Freie*, 833.

[57] See Pappenheim's short story "Die Erbschaft," *Frankfurter Israelitisches Gemeindeblatt* 11 (1933): 277–78, and her essay "Der Einzelne und die Gesellschaft," *Blätter des jüdischen Frauenbundes* 9/6 (1933): 1. In "Die Erbschaft" a baptized Jewish professor who loses his position in the *Gleichschaltung* of 1933 receives from American relatives who had heard of the family's misfortune a valuable "inheritance," a yellowed piece of paper with the Shema and the words "Love your neighbor as yourself" in Hebrew. The rediscovery of Jewish religion would presumably compensate for loss of livelihood and social status.

[58] *Briefe* II, 809–12.

[59] Bertha Pappenheim, *Zur Lage der jüdischen Bevölkerung in Galizien: Reise-Eindrücke und Vorschläge zur Besserung der Verhältnisse* (Frankfurt: Neuer Frankfurter Verlag, 1903).

[60] Bertha Pappenheim, *Kämpfe: Sechs Erzählungen* (Frankfurt: J. Kauffmann, 1916).

[61] Interestingly, Schnitzler donated money and did a reading to benefit pogrom orphans (*Tagebuch, 1903–1908*, January 24, 1906, and February 10, 1907).

[62] Bertha Pappenheim, "Die jüdische Frau," in *Bertha Pappenheim: Leben und Schriften*, ed. Dora Edinger (Frankfurt: Ner Tamid Verlag, 1963).

[63] "Die jüdische Frau," 111.

[64] "Die jüdische Frau," 117.

[65] Bertha Pappenheim, "Jüdische Mütter: Pogrom 1905." Ms. Leo Baeck Institute Archives, New York.

[66] Bertha Pappenheim, "Der echte Ring," *Frankfurter Israelitisches Gemeindeblatt* 14/10 (1936): 393–94.

[67] Schnitzler, *Briefe* II, 4. Despite his belief in a German-Jewish symbiosis, Schnitzler insisted on designating himself a "German" rather than a "Jewish" author. He writes: "Ich betrachte mich nämlich keineswegs als einen jüdischen Dichter, sondern als einen deutschen Dichter, der, soweit sich so etwas überhaupt nachweisen lässt, der jüdischen Rasse angehört, dessen Blut jedenfalls vorwiegend jüdisch ist und der auch in manchen seiner Eigenschaften vieles findet, das als charakteristisch jüdisch angesprochen werden darf. Ich schreibe in deutscher Sprache, lebe innerhalb eines deutschen Kulturkreises, verdanke gewiss von allen Kulturen der deutschen weitaus am meisten, wenn ich auch ganz genau weiss, was ich der hebräischen, der hellenischen und der römischen schuldig geworden bin, von der romanischen ganz zu schweigen. Daran, dass ich ein deutscher Dichter bin, wird mich weder jüdisch-zionistisches Ressentiment, noch die Albernheit und Unverschämtheit deutscher Nationalisten, im geringsten irre machen; nicht einmal der Verdacht, dass ich mich beim Deutschtum oder gerade bei seinen kläglichsten Vertretern anbiedern möchte, wird mich daran hindern zu fühlen, zu wissen, oder auszusprechen, was ich fühle und weiss." ("Nicht abgesandter Brief an den Jüdischen National Fonds," quoted in Lindken, 86). In general, Schnitzler resisted the notion that "German," "Austrian," and "Jewish" identities were mutually exclusive. During the First World War, he wrote in a letter to Elisabeth Steinrück, "Ich bin Jude, Oesterreicher, Deutscher. Es muss wohl so sein — denn beleidigt fühle ich mich im Namen des Judentums, des Oesterreichertums u. Deutschland, wenn man einem von den Dreien etwas Schlimmes nachsagt" (*Briefe* II, 69 [December 22, 1914]).

[68] *Der Weg ins Freie*, 724.

Which Way Out? Schnitzler's and Salten's Conflicting Responses to Cultural Zionism

Iris Bruce

> *Ich hatte keinen Ausweg, mußte mir ihn aber verschaffen, denn ohne ihn konnte ich nicht leben. . . . Nur einen Ausweg; rechts, links, wohin immer; . . .*
>
> Franz Kafka, *Ein Bericht für eine Akademie*

THE SEARCH FOR "a way out" is a topos in early twentieth-century Jewish, and especially Zionist, literature. From Arthur Schnitzler's *Der Weg ins Freie* (1908) to Franz Kafka's *Ein Bericht für eine Akademie* (1917; *A Report to an Academy*, 1948) to Felix Salten's *Bambi* (1923; tr. 1928), *Freunde aus aller Welt* (1931; *The City Jungle*, 1932) and *Bambis Kinder* (1940; *Bambi's Children: The Story of a Forest Family*, 1939), themes of assimilation and self-assertion, of bondage and freedom from bondage, abound.[1] These themes appear in political writings as well as in literary texts. Cultural Zionism, emerging as *the* prominent Jewish national movement, became a reality to be reckoned with, and Jewish authors took different sides in the ideological debates. Two writers, one of whom is more well-known and canonical than the other, serve as a case in point: Arthur Schnitzler (1862–1931), who kept his distance from the Zionist movement, and Felix Salten (Siegmund Salzmann, 1869–1945), novelist, journalist, and theater critic in Vienna, who became an active Zionist. Ironically, Schnitzler's *Der Weg ins Freie* was immediately perceived as a "Jewish" novel and appropriated for the Zionist cause, while Salten's *Bambi* and his other animal tales have never been seen as much more than children's literature.[2] Yet Schnitzler's novel is less radical than many Zionists wanted it to be, whereas Salten's political commitments translate into an innovative literary production, contributing to the newly emerging genre of Zionist children's literature.

Metaphorically speaking, both authors attempt to show Jews a way out of the woods. Schnitzler's opting for individualism as a road to freedom may seem politically naïve for readers today in view of the Final Solution thirty years later. Salten's representation of the coming danger is more astute: his deer in *Bambi* want to be separate and learn to develop caution as well as national pride in the woods. However, their way out is blocked as well by the turn of historical events. In the sequel, *Bambis Kinder,* escaping into the forest becomes their only way out.

Zionism

When first published in 1908, Arthur Schnitzler's *Der Weg ins Freie* was hailed by Zionists as an important novel, and the author was invited to give readings in Zionist circles and asked to publish excerpts in a Zionist publication. Felix Salten, already a strong Zionist, was the first of Schnitzler's close friends to congratulate him, and Schnitzler's response was enthusiastic:

> Mein lieber, ich kann Ihnen gar nicht sagen, *wie* ich mich gefreut habe. Aber Sie können sichs ja denken. Daß Sie der Erste sind, der sich vernehmen ließ, und so, gerade so, bedeutet mir viel — vielleicht mehr als Sie vermuthen. An gewissen Stellen sind mir Thränen gekommen. "Naja . . . weil's wahr is."[3]

At times there were rumors that Schnitzler was as dedicated a Zionist as Salten. In September 1911, Schnitzler recorded in his diary how the nationalist Social Democrat Engelbert Pernerstorfer, a journalist and political activist, had informed the director of the Burgtheater, Alfred Freiherr von Berger, "über Salten — er sei Zionist, hasse alles nicht jüdische, besonders alles germanische . . . 'Und Schn. ist geradeso.'" The director panicked and needed to be reassured that this was not the case. Alfred von Berger did not want publicity of this kind: as it was, he received numerous slanderous letters about Schnitzler. Since the director was so easily influenced and this negative response had repercussions for Schnitzler, the administrators of the Burgtheater would sometimes withhold potentially upsetting letters from Berger, such as one letter that criticized Berger for performing plays by the "Jew" Schnitzler.[4]

Though no Zionist, Schnitzler agreed with Zionist criticism of the anti-Semitic culture around him — a commonplace in Zionist discourse and the driving force behind Zionism as a political movement. In 1897 he wrote to a friend:

> in der letzten Zeit verstimmt mich auch der Antisemitismus sehr stark — man sieht doch eigentlich mit merkwürdiger Ruhe zu, wie man

einfach aus dem Geburtsgrunde von Millionen Menschen nicht für voll genommen wird. Ich habe ein so starkes Rachegefühl gegenüber diesem Gesindel, daß ich sie mit Ruhe persönlich hängen würde. Es wird bald wieder Zeit, die Tragödie der Juden zu schreiben.[5]

This personal comment in a private letter identifies contemporary anti-Semitism as a catalyst for the conception of *Der Weg ins Freie,* a novel (as yet unnamed) that Schnitzler said he could write only in a few years.[6] Yet later, when most Jewish readers of *Der Weg ins Freie* immediately identified the "Jewish Question" as the central issue, Schnitzler repeatedly stressed that this emphasis had not been his intention.[7] Nonetheless, despite the author's many protestations to the contrary, the reputation of the novel was established by its critics as well as by its admirers in the context of the debates around the Jewish Question. The playwright and poet Hugo von Hofmannsthal (1874–1929), for instance, pointedly informed Schnitzler that he had left his copy of the novel, which was personally dedicated to him, on the train, "halb zufällig halb absichtlich." Schnitzler did not think this comment was humorous:[8] unlike Hofmannsthal, who was raised a Catholic and paid little attention to his Jewish ancestry, Schnitzler identified with his Jewishness. His Zionist reputation, though, seems to have come about largely through his association with Salten, for his friend was known publicly as a Zionist.

Salten is renowned mostly as a children's author for his animal tales; next to nothing is known today of his Zionist sympathies and activities,[9] for which he was loved by many and hated by others, most notably by his Viennese contemporary Karl Kraus (1874–1936) who said about him, in 1901: "er kann empfindsam sein und Herrn Herzl [Theodor Herzl, 1860–1904, founder of national Zionism, a much admired Zionist leader] . . . zuliebe den tausendjährigen Schmerz des Judenthums für ein zionistisches Wochenblatt übernehmen. Herr Salten *kann* manches, aber er *ist* nichts."[10] Salten greatly admired Herzl and records in *Neue Menschen auf alter Erde: Eine Palästinafahrt* (1925), an account of his travels to Palestine in 1924, the deep impact Herzl made on him.[11] As a Zionist, Salten enjoyed a reputation much beyond Vienna. In Prague, his speeches were more popular than those of the philosopher Martin Buber (1878–1965).

When Buber came to Prague on the evening of January 20, 1909, Salten was the other speaker at this gathering for the Prague Zionist *Bar Kochba* association. The critic Hartmut Binder describes the evening as follows: "Zuerst sprach Felix Salten über das Thema 'Der Abfall vom Judentum.' . . . Dann war Martin Buber an der Reihe. Er hielt die erste seiner *Drei Reden über das Judentum*. . . . Er trug mit solchem Enthusiasmus vor, daß die Zuhörer nachher wie betrunken waren."[12] The articles in the Prague Zionist newspaper *Selbstwehr*, however, tell a slightly different story. Before the event a journalist already predicted "Ironie und Pathos," with "Pathos" referring to Buber's yearning for the impossible, the unreachable ideal.[13] After the occasion, another reviewer observed that the audience responded more to Salten than to Buber and considered the two speeches "Extreme in beiden Themen" which were nonetheless "wohltuend": "Salten plauderte über Juden und Judentum, deshalb gewann er sich rasch sein Auditorium, Buber dagegen kämpfte mit Juden und betonte weniger ihre Leiden und Kämpfe mit Nichtjuden, als die Eigenart ihrer Innenwelt und ihre Zukunft. — Dem konnten natürlich nicht alle folgen; aber die es taten empfanden ein 'geistiges Mittönen.'"[14]

In his speech, "Der Abfall vom Judentum," Salten argued against those who seem to think that an "enlightened" Jew would not care about being Jewish. On the contrary, he insisted, an enlightened thinker would choose to be Jewish in full awareness of the contributions of Jewish culture to Western civilization. He singled out the Bible, in particular, as the foundation of Western culture, and stressed that there was no need to feel thankful for being tolerated and accepted by "enlightened" Gentiles. The bill is paid. Jews have survived for centuries, which is a sign of their strength, and they will now launch a new future. The evening, then, was successful not so much because of Buber but mostly because of Salten's charismatic performance.

Schnitzler mentions Salten's "Zionismus" explicitly in his diary during this period. Generally, he shared Salten's main argument, but unlike Salten, who polemically asserts that "the bill is paid," Schnitzler more modestly concludes: "Der jüdischen Kulturarbeit höheren Wert zuzugestehen oder sie im ganzen als eine mir sympathischere einzuschätzen, als die irgend eines andern Kulturvolkes . . . versuche ich keineswegs."[15] While Salten loved standing in the limelight, Schnitzler was more reserved and declined invitations to Zionist gatherings. A month after Salten's enthusiastic reception in Prague, the Prague Zionist Leo Herrmann visited Schnitzler in Vienna. The previous summer, he had sent Schnitzler his review of *Der Weg ins Freie*, and he now invited the author to give a talk for the same *Bar Kochba* organization that had greeted Salten so approvingly. Schnitzler noted in his diary that he declined.[16]

In January 1911 Salten was again the main attraction at a "Bibelabend" in Prague. The newspaper reports: "Ein Beifallssturm durchbraust den Saal, als Felix Salten aufs Podium tritt. Nach wenigen Worten stehen alle im Banne seiner Worte. Salten spricht über die Bedeutung der Bibel für uns Juden."[17] Salten's speeches were passionate, down to earth, and filled with humor. He was so popular that he was invited to Prague several times. Franz Kafka (1883–1924) attended a further Salten lecture in 1914, on the occasion of the sixth anniversary of *Bar Kochba*.[18] According to *Selbstwehr* the "Hotel Zentral" was entirely booked, and about 300 people were unable to obtain seats. Salten talked about the future language of "Die jüdische Moderne," took issue with the "Sprachkampf" then raging in Palestine, and favored Hebrew as a first language, joking: "Wenn man bisher die Juden in den europäischen Sprachen nicht verstanden habe, so werde man sie vielleicht in der hebräischen verstehen."[19] He also spoke about modern Jewish art and the problem of defining the "Jewish" artist.

In contrast to Salten, Schnitzler was not interested in defining anyone — least of all himself — as a "Jewish" artist. In 1907 he declined participating in a Jewish authors' reading, rejecting the very idea of a "Jewish author" — since what is meant is "offenbar ein Abend deutscher Autoren jüdischer Abkunft." This remark shows Schnitzler's assimilationist leanings. He further made a distinction between ideologically inspired ethnic typing and his own concern for real, contemporary Jewish problems, stressing that although he hardly ever gave readings in Vienna, he had recently made an exception "anläßlich eines wohltägigen Zwecks (zugunsten der nach den ermordeten russischen Juden hinterbliebenen Waisen)."[20]

Der Weg ins Freie

The Prague Zionists continued to invite Schnitzler. When he finally came to lecture in November 1911, *Der Weg ins Freie* was admired as a Zionist novel. *Selbstwehr* highlights how Schnitzler read from the "Zionist dialogue" between Leo Golowski and Heinrich Bermann:

> Es war ganz reizvoll, Schnitzler selbst von den Basler Kongreß-Erinnerungen seines zionistischen Studenten — Typus: 7. Kongreß — und dem verzweifelten Assimilationsfieber des Wiener Schriftstellers sprechen zu hören. Nicht ganz ohne Schadenfreude soll angemerkt werden, daß ein Teil des Publikums nervös wurde, als Schnitzler im Deutschen Haus aus dem 'Weg ins Freie' zu lesen begann. Schade, daß Geiger nicht in Prag lebt: wir hätten wahrscheinlich eine Protestresolution gegen die Entweihung der deutschen Kultur zu lesen bekommen, die doch bedroht ist, wenn jemand das Judentum nicht ausschließlich als 'Konfession' auffassen will.[21]

The reviewer ignores the central place that Heinrich Bermann's assimilationist position has in the novel (a stance shared by the author) and reduces Bermann's assimilationist convictions to a "verzweifeltes Assimi-lationsfieber," as if this belief were a disease. The ideological battle was more important than understanding Schnitzler's position. Thus, the Zionists were delighted when they sensed an increasing nervousness among those in the audience who believed in German culture and as-similation, that is, those who shared the views of Ludwig Geiger, the editor of the *Allgemeine Zeitung des Judentums*. Geiger was an easy and frequent target.[22] Schnitzler's outlook was actually close to the views expressed in the *Allgemeine Zeitung*. When the journalist Victor Klem-perer had sent his review of Schnitzler, which had appeared in the *Allge-meine Zeitung*, to Schnitzler himself, the latter had thought highly of it.[23] In contrast, when *Selbstwehr* published sections from this same review, the editor Hugo Herrmann included a preface to distance himself from Klemperer, whom he considered too Germanophile.[24] Though Herrmann admits "ein vom Deutschtum völlig losgelöstes Leben ist auch mir undenkbar," he insists "daß eine klare und schärfere Erkennung und Sonderung des Jüdischen und des Nicht-Jüdischen möglich sein wird." At this moment in history, Herrmann believes, it is a "geschichtli-che[] Notwendigkeit, daß wir jetzt einmal *Juden* sein müssen; Deutsche, Tschechen, Franzosen waren wir lange genug, das Deutschtum kann uns entbehren, aber das Judentum *braucht* uns."[25] Nonetheless, Schnitzler's own regard for Klemperer's review article reveals the great distance between his views and Herrmann's monological, Zionist discourse.

In this tense environment of national self-assertion, writings by Jew-ish authors were scrutinized to ensure that they were "politically cor-rect," and if they were, as Schnitzler's example shows, they were appropriated to further the Zionist cause. It was not hard to give a Zi-onist slant to Schnitzler's novel. The structure of *Der Weg ins Freie* conformed to contemporary Zionist taste. In May 1911 a sensational controversy arose in Prague Zionist circles. The subject was "what makes a 'Jewish' novel." The debate began when the Zionist Hugo Herrmann challenged Kafka's friend, the writer and journalist Max Brod (1884–1968) on the front page of *Selbstwehr* and insisted that Brod's recent novel *Jüdinnen* (1911) was not a "Jewish" novel, not even a "novel" but a "Darstellung" of the most typical, the most common and ordinary Jews.[26] The main character was no fighter for a cause (that is, a Zionist), and there were hardly any conflicts and no tragic end; instead, the author simply wished his protagonist good luck at the end of the book, which was considered poor construction. The greatest flaw, though, was that Brod never took a stance vis-à-vis his characters. For this reason Brod's work was definitely "nie der jüdische Roman."[27]

Herrmann's criticism of Brod sheds light on what the Zionists expected of a Jewish novel and why Schnitzler was more acceptable to them than Brod. Kafka, with great irony, rephrased Herrmann's objections to Brod's novel in the form of guidelines for a contemporary Jewish novelist:

> Den Jüdinnen fehlen die nichtjüdischen Zuschauer, die angesehenen gegensätzlichen Menschen, die in andern Erzählungen das Jüdische herauslocken, daß es gegen sie vordringt in Verwunderung, Zweifel, Neid Schrecken und endlich, endlich in Selbstvertrauen versetzt wird, jedenfalls sich aber erst ihnen gegenüber in seiner ganzen Länge aufrichten kann.[28]

In this regard, Schnitzler's novel is indeed a model Jewish novel. There are many non-Jewish characters, who reveal various shades of anti- and philo-Semitism. The non-Jewish protagonist, Georg von Wergenthin, has precisely the function of bringing out the Jewish element, placed as he is as a "neutral" observer at the center of the main Jewish debates. Klemperer had already seen Georg's mediator position as a conscious narrative device, and later Schnitzler scholars have made the same point.[29] Moreover, much of what the Jews talk about in Wergenthin's company reflects contemporary Zionist concerns. Thus Schnitzler thematizes the Zionist critique of the earlier generation of assimilated Jews in Heinrich Bermann's father: "Wie hat der Mann sein Vaterland geliebt! Und wie hat man ihm's gedankt."[30] He also addresses the psychological consequences of assimilation, such as self-hatred (exemplified in Oskar Ehrenberg), and employs contemporary medical/racial stereotypes: the Jew as diseased, sick, insane (Heinrich Bermann's father), and charges against "Sentimentalität" as a Jewish "Nationalkrankheit,"[31] all common elements in Zionist rhetoric. Moreover, the repugnance felt for those who convert or are ashamed of their Jewishness, which shows in old Mr. Ehrenberg,[32] was also shared by the Zionists. In his personal correspondence, Schnitzler confirms many of these views as his own.[33]

Schnitzler's Jewish characters also cannot be called nondistinct and nothing out of the ordinary. In Leo Golowski readers have the ideal "tough Jew," who is also a Zionist. Schnitzler thereby fulfills the most significant requirement for modern Zionist taste. As early as 1894, in his critique of Theodor Herzl's play *Ghetto,* Schnitzler had objected to Herzl's depiction of the Jews as weak: "die Figur des *Kraftjuden* fehlt mir geradezu in Ihrem Stück. Es ist gar nicht wahr, daß in dem Ghetto, das Sie meinen, alle Juden gedrückt oder innerlich schäbig herumlaufen. Es *gibt* andre — und gerade die werden von den Antisemiten am tiefsten gehaßt."[34] Leo Golowski is an exemplary Zionist "Kraftjude" when he kills his anti-Semitic military superior in a duel. Herrmann immediately identified Golowski as "Typus: 7. Kongress," even though the historical setting of the novel was meant to be a few years earlier.[35] At the seventh Zionist Congress in Basel in 1905 Max Nordau (Simon Maximilian Südfeld, 1849–1923) became president of the Zionist organization. Nordau (the originally assimilated doctor who became ideologue, famous for his work *Entartung* [1901]) championed the concept of the "muscle Jew." However, Nordau's ideology does not present a solution for Schnitzler. Turning the "Kraftjude Golowski" into a Zionist hero works only when one ignores that he is not the main character in the novel and that his ideological views are juxtaposed with Heinrich Bermann's, who firmly asserts his assimilationist position. Another Nordau type is represented critically as well: Nordau's biological-racial views are caricatured in the young doctor who turns politician, Bertold Stauber.[36] Moreover, the Zionists and anti-Semites are criticized equally because they agree on fundamental issues. When Bermann is upset at Anna's brother, Josef Rosner, for denying the Jews the right to call Austria their home, the Zionist Golowski agrees: "da werden sie wohl nicht so unrecht haben, diese Kerle."[37] Golowski feels comfortable with the growing nationalism in his time. Bermann's position is not represented as an alternative, either: he is not satisfied with his personal life. And although Golowski has found a direction for himself once he decides to fight for a cause, even "Leos Leben ging nach keinem sicheren Ziel."[38] Schnitzler thus presents personal choices and solutions for different individuals in various circumstances, favoring psychological analysis over ideological typing. There is no hero and therefore no role model who can show a "way out" of this unanchored diaspora existence. Schnitzler also made sure none of these characters could be perceived as heroes by presenting them as morally flawed: "fiel es Ihnen nicht auch auf, wie sowohl Georg als Heinrich Bermann als Leo Golowski jeder ein Menschenleben auf dem Gewissen haben?"[39]

Brod had defended his novel *Jüdinnen* to the Zionists by referring to Homer, William Shakespeare, and Gustave Flaubert, none of whom created unambiguous one-dimensional characters, monological in the extreme. Schnitzler, too, though sympathetic to many Zionist concerns, does not present a one-dimensional ideological message and is more interested in the grey zones where psychologies and ideologies overlap. In his critique of Herzl's play *Ghetto* Schnitzler had already missed the "Gegenspieler," such as those who are excluded from duels because they are Jewish, or the Jew who belongs to the Catholic hiking club and cannot duel because of his "catholicism," and especially the presence of a sweet girl or sympathetic woman.[40] *Der Weg ins Freie* includes these

"Gegenspieler," and Klemperer in his review describes the effect of Schnitzler's character juxtapositions:

> was schließlich bleibt, ist nur ein dickes Bündel betrachtender und charakterisierender Gespräche über jüdische Probleme und jüdische Menschen. Aber freilich — "nur." . . . So ergreifend tief und mit so starker seelischer Anteilnahme hat Schnitzler in diesen Gesprächen . . . das jüdische Wesen, die jüdische Seelennot gezeichnet. Männer und Frauen, Junge und Alte, Sittliche und Unsittliche, leidenschaftliche Zionisten und ebenso leidenschaftliche Anhänger des Assimilationsgedankens enthüllen sich in diesen Gesprächen . . . in allen fühlt er dasselbe Schwanken der entwurzelten Persönlichkeit, dasselbe Wühlen des zerrissenen Wesens, das ihm selber im Blute liegt.[41]

Klemperer highlights what the Zionist Herrmann ignored: Schnitzler's dialogical technique, which represents many voices. His continual narrative juxtapositions bring out the complexity of the Jewish Question, the different shades, a panorama of Jewishness.

Schnitzler presents, quite deliberately, no solution to the Jewish Question outside of a personal, private one. As Bermann puts it: "Ich glaube überhaupt nicht, daß solche Wanderungen ins Freie sich gemeinsam unternehmen lassen . . . denn die Straßen dorthin laufen ja nicht im Lande draußen, sondern in uns selbst. Es kommt nur für jeden darauf an, seinen eigenen inneren Weg zu finden."[42] This individualistic private solution is Schnitzler's way of opposing contemporary nationalisms, as if it were possible for anyone to remain neutral. Juxtaposing various positions, he chooses to remain in between, since no character's views are ultimately more convincing than another's.[43] Thus, he disliked it when readers stressed the Jewish Question too much, but on the other hand he was also unhappy when they did not mention it at all, because that meant "also auch keine Judenantwort, keinen Judendialog."[44] Then again he generally sympathized with Zionist concerns, but when he was asked to commit himself a little he would withdraw this sympathy altogether.[45]

Der Weg ins Freie provokes and challenges ideologies *per se,* but Schnitzler's philosophy of liberal individualism can only be realized within the framework of a comfortable, well-to-do social class like the one he belonged to. His novel depicts the end of liberalism and the psychological compromises that individuals are required to make, yet suggests no solutions and no alternatives to the danger of growing nationalism with its new ideological formations. We have reached the end of the road; only Schnitzler is not willing to acknowledge, as the Zionists do, that this road was ultimately a dead end. Given his noncommittal stance, the Zionists drew their own political conclusions from the narratives he constructed. In 1917, in a review of Schnitzler's *Doktor Gräsler, Badearzt,* the Zionist reviewer in *Selbstwehr* asks a typical question: "Die Frage drängt sich auf: Ist er ein Jude, der Badearzt Doktor Emil Gräsler? Der Dichter verrät es nicht. Doch so ist sein 'Held': Er ist einsam." In the end the reviewer decides that Schnitzler is giving readers a "Seelenschilderung" that cannot be reduced to essentialist judgment.[46] The Zionist attempts to appropriate Schnitzler were obviously ideologically motivated, but they were almost invited to do so because of the ambiguity of his texts. They were dealing with a writer who pushed so far in rendering a "Seelenschilderung" of his time but in the end refused to draw the logical conclusions or name possible solutions. Preferring not to remain in limbo, the Zionists drew these conclusions for him.

Into the Forest

There was no need to appropriate Felix Salten in this fashion, because his Zionist sympathies were openly stated. Yet, for all of his Zionist fervor, Salten in his fictional work seems much less explicit about the Jewish Question than Schnitzler. *Bambi* is a children's book with a universal appeal, famous worldwide because of the phenomenal success of the Walt Disney motion picture (1942).[47] Salten was not appropriated by the Zionists but by Disney, because the universal message of the movie made *Bambi* lose all historical specificity. In fact, modern audiences only know this ahistorical Disney *Bambi*. It may come as a surprise, therefore, that the original is a children's book that includes the major Zionist concerns of its day.[48] Disney's dehistoricization of Salten's text is an example of how modern mass media can take a story and transform it; yet at the same time, ideological reasons may well have played a role in the omission of the Jewish subject matter, too. Given Disney's latent anti-Semitism, he was not likely to highlight a Jewish theme during the Second World War.[49]

Bambi differs both in its literary form — as children's literature — and in the treatment of the Zionist subject matter from other Zionist discourses of this period. When the novel was written there was no Jewish children's literature to speak of, and certainly no Zionist children's literature, which developed as a genre largely in the 1930s. However, many Zionists were already concerned with providing a Jewish education for Jewish children and preoccupied with producing and collecting suitable literature. With *Bambi* Salten lent a new voice to Zionist literature by engaging in the creation of this new genre of Zionist children's literature.

Salten's choice of animal to represent the Jews is exceptional and uncharacteristic, because generally Zionist writers drew on ferocious animals or even on common anti-Semitic metaphors (jackals, vermin, goats, mice, lizards) for polemical purposes. Considering the young audience for this book, however, ugly subject matter does not translate into ugly animals: the deer are beautiful, elegant, and gracious, although the main link between the Jews and the gentle deer is their shared history of persecution. The cultural historian Eduard Fuchs, in his 1921 study *Die Juden in der Karikatur,* remarks "daß diese ganze Volksschicht [that is, the Jews] für jedermann . . . als Freiwild galt."[50] In *Bambi* the deer discuss their fate in these terms[51] and pass on their history to the new generation so that it will not be forgotten: "Begierig lauschten sie den vielen Erzählungen, die immer voll von Schrecknissen waren, voll Blut und Jammer."[52]

The experience of exclusion and discrimination, a reality of life in the Diaspora, similarly does not find expression in the typical Zionist representation of Jews as hunted, wild animals, filled with anger and frustration. In *Bambi* there are beautiful butterflies that look like

> wandernde Blumen . . ., lustige Blumen, die auf ihrem Stengel nicht still-halten wollten und sich aufgemacht hatten, um ein wenig zu tanzen. Oder Blumen, die mit der Sonne herniederkamen, noch keinen Platz hatten und wählerisch umhersuchten, sich herabsenkten, verschwanden, als seien sie schon irgendwo untergekommen, aber gleich wieder empor-gestiegen, bald nur ein wenig, bald höher, um weiter zu suchen, immer weiter, weil die besten Plätze eben schon besetzt waren.[53]

The myth of the Wandering Jew is humorously alluded to in "wandernde Blumen," while the frustrating search for a permanent home, a landing place or base, is mitigated by the metaphor of the colorful butterflies, which resemble floating flowers that rise and rest and dance in the circle of life. The social critique, which is implied by their endless search — "um weiter zu suchen, immer weiter, weil die besten Plätze eben schon besetzt waren" — is aimed against forms of discrimination. The critique is no less effective for being clothed in poetic language: the butterflies become "beautiful losers."

Salten juxtaposes this political reality with the dream of an ideal universe. As one critic remarks: "Salten's depiction of nature serves, among other things, to convey the idea of a basic equality of all creatures over and above the affirmation of their diversity, a message that can be heard on the level of cultural differences and criticism of assimilation."[54] This message of tolerance, which is now perceived as a universal message, was in its time and by Jewish readers in particular also perceived as a "Jewish" message. Karl Kraus even identified the very language used by the hare as Jewish.[55] Kraus resented the sentimental humanitarian appeal in many of Salten's works and frequently ridiculed him for it in his journal *Die Fackel.*

However, Salten is more subtle than Kraus gives him credit for, especially in his treatment of alterity and the way it is tailored to young readers.

Bambi shows how Difference can often be overcome through communication. Readers see this point in Bambi's encounter with the elk, who is a very significant Other. Whenever the deer meet these imposing relatives they always become scared and agitated. As Bambi grows older, he begins to feel ashamed of the deer's meekness and boldly approaches an elk one day, telling himself all the time that he is his equal. But soon readers are told: "Es half nichts. Bambi blieb eingeschüchtert und spürte es im Grunde seines Wesens, daß er doch nicht gerade so viel sei. Lange nicht."[56] What Bambi does not know, though, is that his perception is all wrong: when he misinterprets the elk's helpless glance as, "Dieser hochmütige Blick!," ironically the elk thinks to himself "ich möchte gerne mit ihm sprechen . . . er ist so sympathisch . . . wie dumm, daß man nie miteinander redet!"[57] Such ironic narrative juxtapositions make young readers see that Bambi's prejudices about the elk, which are shared by all deer, are the result of preconceived notions about the Other, which any communication might do away with. The utopian encounter between Bambi and the elk, framed by a pastoral setting, suggests the possibility of an ideal world. By rendering the complex question of alterity as a humorous anecdote about cultural misunderstandings, Salten, unlike Schnitzler, opens a fairy-tale door and creates a road into the open.

Bambi also represents alterity in a less optimistic and historically more specific context: the Zionist response to anti-Semitism and assimilation. There is one Other who must be feared at all costs: "MAN," "HE," "Er," as he is called. The animals hold conflicting views as to how HE should be perceived. They all agree that when a third hand, the gun, is attached to his body then HE is evil because HE brings death and destruction. But some believe, and Bambi's mother is one of them, that not every human is equally dangerous. Old Nettla asks ironically if that is the reason why she usually stays behind to greet them, and Bambi's mother replies that of course she runs away like everyone else. A young female deer, though, sighs longingly: "Es heißt, eines Tages wird Er unter uns treten und sanft sein wie wir. Er wird mit uns spielen, der ganze Wald wird glücklich sein und wir werden uns versöhnen."[58] For Old Nettla such wishful thinking is utterly dangerous; she is openly sarcastic about this foolish hope for reconciliation: "Versöhnen! Seit wir denken können, ermordet Er uns, uns alle, unsere Schwestern, unsere Mütter, unsere Brüder! Seit wir auf der Welt sind, läßt Er uns keinen Frieden, tötet Er uns, wo wir uns zeigen . . . und dann sollen wir uns mit Ihm versöhnen? Was für eine Dummheit!"[59] *Bambi* illustrates how right

Nettla is through the fate of Gobo, brother of Faline (who becomes Bambi's wife). Gobo's fate also shows how differently Schnitzler and Salten treat the question of cultural assimilation.

Gobo becomes an assimilated deer. He is a weak deer from birth, delicate and fragile, and can barely survive his first winter. During a hunt he collapses and is left behind. Everyone thinks he is dead, but he reappears months later and tells his story: how he was rescued by a good human, accepted by the whole family, and welcomed as a playmate by the children and even the dogs; then when the weather got better the humans set him free again. Gobo has had a wonderful experience that seems to counter all preconceptions about the evil nature of Man.

Most deer admire Gobo and believe he has become "was Besonderes" because he has achieved the unbelievable.[60] But Gobo's life is of short duration. When the next hunt comes he insists on greeting the first human he sees, fully convinced it will be a friendly encounter; but as soon as he steps into the open field he is shot. His last words to his friends are: "Er hat mich nicht erkannt."[61] This phrase echoes through much Zionist writing. Kafka's ape in *Ein Bericht für eine Akademie* knows that ultimately humans will never make a distinction between him and any other ape; but Gobo is taken in by the dream, the illusion, that reconciliation and existence in harmony are attainable. His reward is to have his throat cut by the approaching hunter: "Dann hörten sie Gobos klagenden Todesschrei."[62]

Salten is much more skeptical about the possibility of assimilation than is Schnitzler. Gobo's death is a rude awakening from the "Angleichungstraum, den seit den Tagen der Henriette Herz und der Rahel Varnhagen so viele edle und gutgesinnte Juden geträumt haben."[63] For Salten, Herzl was the first to wake up from this dream and to recognize "daß Versöhnung nur werden könne, wenn die Juden sich zu ihrem eigenen Volkstum bekannten, zu ihren uralten Überlieferungen und zu ihrem uralten Lande."[64] Gobo's fate in *Bambi* illustrates that friendship with Man is possible only on an individual basis; it is a misplaced and ill-conceived hope to believe that one day there will be tolerance and acceptance between animals and humans. Annegret Völpel rightly argues that a "Jewish" reading of *Bambi* "contains a skeptical warning against a Jewish readiness to assimilate that was going too far, that would lead to the loss of identity and that was a threat to the Jews' very existence."[65]

In contrast to Schnitzler, Salten likens assimilation to a life in bondage. When Gobo tells the story of his miraculous rescue, the old Prince of the Forest appears — the King of the deer, who shows himself only on rare occasions. The old deer asks one crucial question, pointing to the mark around Gobo's neck: "Was hast du da für einen Streifen am Halse?"[66] And Gobo admits — not proudly this time, as the text says "unsicher": "'Das . . .? Das ist von dem Bande, das ich getragen habe . . . es ist Sein Band . . . und . . . ja . . . und es ist die größte Ehre, Sein Band zu tragen . . . es ist . . .' Er wurde verwirrt und schwieg"[67] Thus, it is bondage that makes him so endearing to Man: they treat him well, but he is not free. He has become property, a pet, a dog, their plaything, dependent on Man for everything, for his food, keep, protection. This is no road into the open. It is reconciliation at a high price, at the cost of freedom and the loss of personal identity and self-esteem. The King says only one word, "Unglücklicher," and disappears.[68] This rejection of bondage is a strong Zionist message. It is crucial to point out that in Zionist discourses of the period, Herzl (the idolized Zionist leader) is often referred to as "the King," or "the Prince."[69] The old Prince of the Forest, then, can be said to represent Herzl. This link underscores the political significance of the King's intervention at this point in the narrative, which marks the turning point for Bambi: the King from now on becomes a model to be emulated, not only for Bambi but also (perhaps) for a new generation of young readers who learn from Gobo's fate that the King's warning was right.

All deer have internalized the belief that Man is omnipotent, and they are paralyzed by their mind-forged manacles. They do not see that a true Leader exists, one of their own kind: the King of the Forest. This enigmatic Herzl-Messiah figure has been seen by only a few, disappears altogether for long stretches of time, and reappears in times of need when no one expects him.

Written many years after Herzl's death, *Bambi* is a novel of abandonment.[70] But here the deer King returns and prepares his "people" for the time when he can no longer be with them. Bambi is not only the King's son but also his Chosen Deer, worthy of becoming his successor. He is the only one the King takes the trouble to teach and the only one he takes the trouble to save. The young prince Bambi is a protagonist that young readers can identify with, one who will show them a road into the open.

From the beginning the King teaches Bambi to learn to be alone. When Bambi is little, crying for his mother, the King reprimands him with: "Kannst du nicht allein sein? . . . Schäme dich!"[71] Bambi never forgets this chastisement. He learns self-control and independent thinking, which explains why he is the only deer who feels ashamed for Gobo.[72] Bambi also intuitively knows what is right: without being able to conceptualize yet, he knows to reject the promises associated with assimilation. Similarly, when he begins searching for answers to his many questions, he knows to isolate himself from the community, and sets out to find his own way — alone — which eventually leads him back to the old King of the Forest. Bambi's quest strengthens his self-endurance and self-reliance, and he also learns to form an emotional bond with the King. Like all children, he is searching for a mentor, and when he does find him, the old deer remarks: "Du suchst mich nicht erst seit heute."[73] This phrase echoes the continual quest for a Messiah figure, a topos in Zionist literature and in Judaism in general. To this end it was necessary for Bambi to develop the emotional side of his character as well, rather than the purely rational part alone: recognizing the messiah or new leader must be based on "feeling" first and not "begreifen," which will come later.[74] This understanding is the base for a new kind of faith in the future of the deer.

The novel ends on an optimistic and comforting note, with a message of continuity, as Bambi passes on the King's wisdom to a little deer, who — it is intimated — is Bambi's own son. Bambi uses the same words his own father had used with him: "Eure Mutter hat jetzt keine Zeit. . . . Kannst du nicht allein sein?"[75] Thus Bambi, too, like his father before him, will have a worthy successor in the new generation, and the circle of life continues.

Bambi, with its talking animals, not only reads like a fairy tale but also can be understood as a political allegory for children that retells the story of the Jewish people in exile waiting for a Messiah who will redeem them. *Bambi* has Zionist overtones because the critique of assimilation and the longing for a new Herzl figure are prominent themes. However, there is no Zionist gathering of deer who rebel against their lot. By the 1920s Salten had become more critical of Zionist discourse and Zionist politics. When he visited Palestine, for instance, Salten admired some of the young colonies because they existed "ohne lautes Parteiprogramm, ohne den starren Eigensinn des Parteigeistes."[76] As a children's parable, *Bambi* is quite consciously cast in a broader light and stresses the development of self-confidence, self-control, and faith in oneself as well as in a superior benevolent being for whom everyone is equal. *Bambi* offers a fairy-tale solution, and Herzl's famous slogans, "Wenn du nur willst, ist es kein Märchen," or "Wir sind ein Volk, EIN Volk!" come to mind. These slogans are accompanied by the faith that a new education will create new leaders and a strong independent community in the future.

In later years Salten's writings regained a polemical edge. The theme of bondage and imprisonment is prominent in *Freunde aus aller Welt,* published in the year of Schnitzler's death. In this work, animals in a zoo are looking in vain for a "way out" — an obvious allusion to Schnitzler's *Der Weg ins Freie,* and a much more extreme representation of political despair. The animals behind bars are in a hopeless situation: they either go insane in their confinement or grow physically ill and die at a young age. Consequently, the criticism of Man is uncompromising: slogans such as "Der Tag wird kommen"[77] and "Vergeltung für alles und für alle!"[78] reverberate throughout the novel and reveal that Salten's Zionist convictions were never abandoned. The novel ends with all the imprisoned animals joining in a chorus, making their voices heard, a chorus similar to that of the prisoners in Ludwig van Beethoven's *Fidelio* (1814) — voices united, yearning and struggling for freedom from bondage.

Salten continued to comment on contemporary reality in *Bambis Kinder* (1940), which brings readers close to the Holocaust. In this novel there is a similar instantiation in narrative (again, an allegorical children's story) of tropes and thematics pertaining to the Jewish Question in general and to Zionism specifically, as well as to larger political-philosophical issues. Read against its historical background, however, the novel seems more subdued. Unlike George Orwell's *Animal Farm* (1945), which utilizes the same genre for overt political commentary (a satire on Stalinism), Salten's novel is less explicit. However, given Salten's personal circumstances and the political climate at the end of the 1930s (he had lost the copyright for his novel *Bambi,* was forced to leave Austria, found exile in Switzerland, and was unable to publish anything but "harmless" animal stories), any historical and political subtext had to be hidden, if he wanted to get published at all.[79]

The novel begins in desperate times, a period of drought in the forest. Even the trees are worried: "Niemand kommt um! Niemand darf verzagen! Es ist eine Zeit der Not, da muss man aushalten und den Mut nicht sinken lassen. Erinnert euch doch, welche Stürme, welche bitteren Entbehrungen wir durchgemacht haben, und wie wir trotzdem gewachsen, trotzdem stark geworden sind."[80] As in the previous *Bambi,* the animals fear the hunting season, which they refer to as "der große Schrecken." Bambi — who is now the King of the Forest as his father had been before him — states that all animals in the forest are refugees in times like these: "Wir alle hier sind Flüchtlinge, wenn Er kommt."[81] But there is a difference between the animals' perception of the hunt in this novel compared to the *Bambi* of 1923. In *Bambis Kinder* there is a new violence that makes the regular hunting season, in hindsight, appear almost a part of the natural cycle. Contrasting human (historical) time with animal (seasonal) time, Salten is playing human and animal perception against each other for the ironic effect. Readers are told that in the past the animals had learned to deal with the regular hunting season, because they knew it would not last forever and was always followed by a "Schonzeit," the close season, when peace returned to the forest. This violence was tolerable because one knew what to expect: it had structure and was predictable. The new violence that has entered into their lives during the recent historical developments, however, is unpredictable. With this turn of events the earlier natural catastrophe turns into a political catastrophe, when base instincts in human nature are allowed to run their natural course, unchecked by social structures or laws of morality. Once the layers of civilization disappear, animals and humans are alike. For instance, the dog Nero, who is so civilized, trained, and obedient until his master falls ill, begins to roam around and discovers his wolf-like nature, his taste for hunting. As long as he is not punished, he keeps going back for more, for the excitement of killing. Readers encounter the same "Wolfstrieb" and "Blutrausch,"[82] in a young man who is given his first gun and who shoots for the thrill of it. He is ultimately admonished by an adult but kills indiscriminately until he is caught. The analogy to the abuse of power by young Nazi brutes in the late 1930s is obvious.

During these times, the animals of the forest live in great discord and distrust of one another. Fatalism pervades the novel, especially when those who are persecuted turn against each other.[83] Selfishness and self-preservation win the day. This development is the worst that can happen, because a community that is divided will have no power to resist and fight. The greatest struggle is to establish a feeling of solidarity. Bambi's daughter, Gurri, stubbornly and firmly insists: "Ich wünsche allen Rettung, allen! Ohne Ausnahme!"[84] The Bambi family adopts two orphan deer who have lost their parents during the last hunt, and they also begin to break down cultural and social hierarchies by calling their friend Perri, the squirrel, by the familiar form "du."[85] Gurri's brother Geno joins her peace-making efforts, and sets an example by teaching other deer when to run and hide and when to fight. Bambi himself fights the young human who is known for his senseless killing, thereby showing that resistance is possible. The news of this battle, and the fact that a deer has been stronger than a human, spreads like wildfire through the forest. Bambi's act of resistance leads to renewed self-respect among all animals, since even previous enemies now admire him for his courage.

Like many Jews who supported the political power structures, several animals in the forest were indecisive and even supportive of Man until they realized that they themselves were threatened. Some had even profited from the hunting season because Man killed animals such as the marten, who endangered the lives of the squirrels, for instance. For many victims, therefore, Man was both "der grausamste Feind . . . und das andere Mal der Retter,"[86] something that, according to Perri, goes beyond anyone's comprehension: "Nachdenken hat keinen Sinn! Versucht man's, wird man wahnsinnig!"[87] Perri himself is a sweet friend, but he has no backbone. His insight and feeling of solidarity develop only because he feels himself suddenly in danger: he admits that if the young man had not shot at him indiscriminately, he would have supported Man as before: "Oh! . . . hätte er mich in Ruhe gelassen, ich würde wie früher zu ihm stehen!"[88]

Similarly, in Schnitzler's *Der Weg ins Freie,* the assimilated Heinrich Bermann acknowledges that there is one condition upon which he would become a Zionist without hesitation, if things were to get bad again:

> "Hm," sagte Leo, "aber wenn die Scheiterhaufen wieder angezündet werden . . .?" "Für diesen Fall," entgegnete Heinrich, "dazu verpflichte ich mich hiermit feierlich, werde ich mich vollkommen nach Ihnen richten." "O," wandte Georg ein, "diese Zeiten kommen nicht mehr wieder." Die andern mußten lachen, daß Georg sie durch diese Worte, wie Heinrich bemerkte, im Namen der gesamten Christenheit über ihre Zukunft zu beruhigen so liebenswürdig wäre.[89]

Call it irony, premonition, political naiveté or blindness. Support for political Zionism at that point would, of course, be much too late. But Zionism or no Zionism, Salten or Schnitzler, in the end neither position would have made any difference since no ideological stance in the Jewish political spectrum would have prevented the "Final Solution." Both writers put into narrative political ideas of their time, writing history into fiction, adapting the story to contemporary historical circumstances, and using recognizable genres for their political commentary: the philosophical-intellectual novel (Schnitzler) and allegorical children's literature (Salten). Neither reason nor an emotional call for action represented a road into the open. No matter how much they tried to escape or hide in the forest, they could never get out of the woods.[90]

Notes

[1] Felix Salten, *Bambi. Eine Lebensgeschichte aus dem Walde* (Berlin/Vienna/Leipzig: Paul Zsolnay Verlag, 1928); *Freunde aus aller Welt. Roman eines zoologischen Gartens* (Berlin/Vienna/Leipzig: Paul Zsolnay Verlag, 1931); *Neue Menschen auf alter Erde. Eine Palästinareise* (Berlin/Vienna/Leipzig: Paul Zsolnay Verlag, 1925); *Bambis Kinder. Eine Familie im Walde* (Zurich: Albert Müller Verlag, 1940).

[2] *Der Weg ins Freie* in ES I, 635–958.

[3] Arthur Schnitzler, *Briefe.* 2 vols. (Frankfurt: Fischer, 1981–1984). [Vol I: *Briefe 1875–1912.* Eds. Therese Nickl & Heinrich Schnitzler. Frankfurt: Fischer, 1981; Vol. II: *Briefe 1913–1931.* Eds. P. M. Braunwarth, R. Miklin, S. Pertlik & H. Schnitzler.

Frankfurt: Fischer, 1984.] Cited as *Briefe* I and II. *Briefe* I, 578 (May 30, 1908)].
Schnitzler mentions only one criticism: a recent visitor to Palestine took offense at
the fact that old Mr. Ehrenberg, a figure in the novel, returns from his visit to Palestine disillusioned because he had not seen any Zionist settlements (*Der Weg ins Freie*,
741). Schnitzler replied politely: "Was die Äußerung des alten Ehrenberg anbelangt,
so müssen Sie bedenken, daß der Roman nicht heute, sondern Ende der Neunziger-
jahre spielt, zu einer Zeit also, da die Kolonisationen in Palästina noch sehr weit von
der Ausbildung entfernt waren, in der Sie und Ihr Vater diese Kolonisationen anläßlich Ihrer eben abgelaufenen Reise vorgefunden haben. Überdies ist es fraglich, ob
der alte Ehrenberg als ein absolut verläßlicher Beobachter oder gar Berichterstatter
zu betrachten wäre. Etwas besser, als er die Zustände in seiner skeptischen Art
gesehen haben will, mag es ja schon damals gewesen sein" *(Briefe* I, 647–48 [January
10, 1911]).

⁴ *Tagebuch.* 10 vols. (Vienna: Verlag der Österreichischen Akademie der Wissenschaften, 1987 ff.). *1909–1912,* 264–65 (September 20, 1911).

⁵ *Briefe* I, 316 (letter to his friend Olga Waissnix, March 29, 1897).

⁶ *Briefe* I, 314 (March 26, 1897).

⁷ After it was published, Schnitzler was quick to remark: "Mir war das Verhältnis
Georgs zu seiner Geliebten immer geradeso wichtig wie seine Beziehung zu den
verschiedenen Juden des Romans" (*Briefe* I, 579 [July 4, 1908]). He also knew that
some readers thought a Jewish lover for Georg more appropriate; but he argued: "ob
es nicht klüger gewesen wäre, Georg zum Liebhaber einer Jüdin zu machen. Ich
konnte nicht. Die Gestalt der Anna stand von Anfang an eben so unwidersprechlich
also katholisch da. Und es kam mir ja schließlich nicht darauf an, irgendwas nachzu-
weisen: weder daß Christ und Jude sich nicht vertragen — oder daß sie sich doch
vertragen können — sondern ich wollte, ohne Tendenz, Menschen und Beziehungen
darstellen — die ich gesehn habe (ob in der Welt draußen oder in der Phantasie
bliebe sich gleich)" (*Briefe* I, 580 [July 4, 1908]).

⁸ See *Briefe* I, 631–32 (November 2, 1910).

⁹ There is no scholarship on Salten's Zionism, only a brief commentary on his book
Neue Menschen auf alter Erde and on his admiration for Herzl in the only, and so far
most up-to-date, article on his life and work: Lore Muerdel Dormer, "Felix Salten,"
in *Major Figures of Turn-Of-The-Century Austrian Literature,* ed. Donald G. Daviau
(Riverside: Ariadne Press, 1991), 421–22 and 435 n. 31.

¹⁰ *Die Fackel* 87 (December 7, 1901): 23. For Kraus's dislike of Salten see Kari
Grimstad, *Masks of the Prophet. The Theatrical World of Karl Kraus* (Toronto: U of
Toronto P, 1982), 69, 72–73, 156, 162, 206, 278 n. 18, and Wilma Abeles Iggers,
Karl Kraus. A Viennese Critic of the Twentieth Century (The Hague: Martinus
Nijhoff, 1967), 33, 68, 107.

¹¹ Felix Salten, *Neue Menschen auf alter Erde; eine Palästinafahrt* (Berlin: P. Zsolnay,
1925). "Dann aber, als Theodor Herzl auftrat und ich mich an ihm bestätigt fand,
als mich seine Gestalt, seine Menschlichkeit, der Umgang mit ihm entflammte, als
sein opferbereites, mutiges Bekennertum mir und jedem ehrlich Empfindenden die
Pflicht vorschrieb, bei ihm zu stehen und Israel zu bekennen" (103).

[12] Hartmut Binder, ed. *Kafka Handbuch. Bd. 1: Der Mensch und seine Zeit* (Stuttgart: Alfred Kröner Verlag, 1979), 374. Cf. Martin Buber, "Das Judentum und die Juden," *Der Jude und sein Judentum: Gesammelte Aufsätze und Reden* (Köln: Joseph Melzer Verlag, 1963), 9–18. Cf. Felix Salten, "Der Abfall vom Judentum," *Selbstwehr* (January 22, 1910): 1–2.

[13] "Martin Buber und Felix Salten," *Selbstwehr* (January 15, 1909): 2.

[14] Felix Salten, "Festabend der Bar Kochba," *Selbstwehr* (January 22, 1909): 3.

[15] *Briefe* II, 4 (January 4, 1913). What Schnitzler shares with Salten is his pride in Jewish contributions to German culture: "so drängte sich mir doch manchmal die Überlegung auf, wie vieles das Deutschtum selbst den kulturellen und ethischen Leistungen des Judentums, so weit seine Geschichte zurückreicht, zu verdanken hat."

[16] *Tagebuch 1909–1912,* 51 (February 26, 1909).

[17] Felix Salten, "Der Bibelabend Bar Kochbas," *Selbstwehr* (January 27, 1911): 5.

[18] Kafka, who was accompanied by his sister Ottla, recollects how much Ottla and her girlfriends enjoyed Salten's talk. Franz Kafka, *Tagebücher in der Fassung der Handschrif,* eds. Hans-Gerd Koch, Michael Müller, and Malcolm Pasley (Frankfurt: Fischer, 1990), 626.

[19] Felix Salten, "Festabend Bar Kochba," *Selbstwehr* (February 6, 1914): 1.

[20] *Briefe* I, 555 (April 17, 1907).

[21] "Artur [sic] Schnitzler," *Selbstwehr* (November 3, 1911): 2.

[22] Hugo Herrmann, in the same issue of *Selbstwehr,* ridicules Geiger's assimilationist views, singling out the following quotation from Geiger on the assimilation question: "Eine Assimilation wird und kann meiner Überzeugung nach erfolgen ohne Taufe und ohne Mischehe. Die Folgen dieser immer stärker werdenden Assimilation, das heißt des vollkommenen Aufgehens der Juden in Kultur und Gesittung der Länder, in denen sie wohnen, wird sich im Laufe der Zeit durch Veredelung und Vervollkommnung der Juden vollziehen." Herrmann's sarcastic comment on this: "Ich bewundere die Geduld des Papiers, das sich diesen Satz gefallen läßt." ("Ludwig Geiger über uns!," *Selbstwehr* [November 3, 1911]: 4).

[23] "Victor Klemperer übersendet mir Separat Abdruck *Allg. Ztg. des Judentums* Artikel über mich; so ziemlich das tiefstgehende, was bisher über mich geschrieben, wenn auch nicht in den Einzelurtheilen durchwegs zutreffend; Unter-und Überschätzungen" (*Tagebuch 1909–1912,* 215–16 [February 1, 1911]).

[24] "Viktor Klemperer sieht in Schnitzler einen deutschen Dichter jüdischen Gepräges, aber doch eben einen *deutschen* Dichter, der nicht etwa nur jüdischen, sondern auch in hohem Grade deutschen, deutschsprachlichen, deutschkulturellen Einflüssen unterworfen ist. Überhaupt ist, wie Klemperer an anderer Stelle ausgeführt hat, die Grenze des Jüdischen in der deutschen Literatur nicht scharf zu bestimmen" ("Victor Klemperer, 'Schnitzler und das Judentum,'" *Selbstwehr* [March 10, 1911]: 1).

[25] "Victor Klemperer, 'Schnitzler und das Judentum,'" *Selbstwehr* (March 10, 1911): 1.

[26] Max Brod, *Jüdinnen* (Berlin: A. Juncker, 1911).

[27] Hugo Herrmann, "Jüdinnen," *Selbstwehr* (May 19, 1911): 3.

[28] Kafka, *Tagebücher in der Fassung der Handschrift,* 160.

[29] Klemperer remarks: "Georg kommt viel mit Juden zusammen, und sie sprechen immer über ihr Judentum." ("Schnitzler und das Judentum," 1). Detlev Arens, in *Untersuchungen zu Arthur Schnitzlers Roman "Der Weg ins Freie"* (Frankfurt am Main: Peter Lang, 1981), also sees in the dominating perspective of Wergenthin the "spezifische Konfrontation zweier gegensätzlicher Standpunkte" and argues that this technique enables Schnitzler to juxtapose "die Dialektik von fremdem Blick und eigener Sache zu deren eindringlicheren Darstellung" (25–26). Cf. also Heidi Gidion," "Haupt-und Nebensache in Arthur Schnitzlers Roman *Der Weg ins Freie.*" *Text + Kritik* 138/139, special volume on Schnitzler, ed. H. L. Arnold (1998): 48.

[30] *Der Weg ins Freie*, 830.

[31] *Der Weg ins Freie*, 789.

[32] *Der Weg ins Freie*, 807.

[33] Responding to a reader who found it sad that Schnitzler seemed to be suffering from his Jewishness, Schnitzler replied: "Ich leide nicht im geringsten unter meiner jüdischen Abstammung. . . . Wenn ich unter etwas leide, so ist es höchstens das Judentum mancher andern Leute, oder richtiger die klägliche Art, in der sich so viele Juden gerade innerhalb unserer Kultur zu der Tatsache ihrer Abstammung verhalten. Der Widerwille gegen diese Leute mag in meinem Roman da und dort sehr lebhaft durchleuchten" (*Briefe* I, 589–90 [March 15, 1909]). A group whom Schnitzler found especially "zuwider" were "Getaufte Juden mit clericalen, sportlichen und snobischen Anwandlungen" (*Briefe* I, 362 [October 11, 1898]). Though not baptized, Oskar Ehrenberg is well on his way to becoming such a grotesque figure, and his failed suicide attempt in the end is presented as a tragicomic farce.

[34] *Briefe* I, 239 (November 17, 1894).

[35] Several critics have pointed out that the novel begins after the first Zionist congress in Basel in 1898: Andrea Willi, *Arthur Schnitzlers Roman "Der Weg ins Freie." Eine Untersuchung zur Tageskritik und ihren zeitgenössischen Bezügen* (Heidelberg: Carl Winter, 1989), 176, and Wolfram Kiwit, *"Sehnsucht nach meinem Roman." Arthur Schnitzler als Romancier* (Bochum: Verlag Dr. Dieter Winkler, 1991), 23 n. 56. They therefore assume that Golowski's attendance at the Zionist congress must refer to this first congress. But Schnitzler does not seem to have stuck inflexibly to the time line of his novel and may also have incorporated further developments from the history of the Zionist movement at this point in the narrative: "Obwohl der Roman im Jahr 1898 angesiedelt ist, im Jahr nach dem 1. Zionistenkongress, scheint Schnitzler, der in den Jahren 1902–1907 an ihm arbeitet, zeitgenössische Entwicklungen und Veränderungen zum Zionismus berücksichtigt oder gar vorgeahnt zu haben" (Willi, 176).

[36] *Der Weg ins Freie*, 903. Though he does not mention Max Nordau, Bruce Thompson's description of Stauber corresponds not only with later Nazi ideology but also with Nordau's beliefs: "his programme appears to condone the sacrifice of the weak and sick to prevent the spread of infection. . . . Stauber is a Jew, and a professed socialist, but his words, taken out of context, provide a chilling anticipation of the selective removal of those designated as the 'subhumans' in Nazi Germany. And more pointedly, they reflect the disregard for the individual on the part of the mass political movements of the time, that were to play such a dominant role in the twentieth century to come" (Willi, 176).

[37] *Der Weg ins Freie,* 719.

[38] *Der Weg ins Freie,* 725.

[39] *Briefe* I, 579 [July 4, 1908].

[40] *Briefe* I, 237–38 [November 17, 1894].

[41] "Victor Klemperer, 'Schnitzler und das Judentum,'" *Selbstwehr* (March 10, 1911): 2.

[42] *Der Weg ins Freie,* 833.

[43] Thus he grants the great importance of the Jewish Question in contemporary life but at the same time is unwilling to give it an important status in *Der Weg ins Freie,* stating that the reason for the "Jewish/Zionist appropriation" of his novel lies "wohl mehr in der großen Bedeutung der Judenfrage an sich begründet, als in dem Ausmaß, das der Frage innerhalb meines Romans eingeräumt ist" (*Briefe* I, 583 [December 7, 1908]).

[44] Kiwit, 80–81. Schnitzler is responding here to Raoul Auernheimer's review of June 3, 1908. For the review see Willi, 250–54.

[45] Writing to his aunt in 1912 he remarks ironically: "Was den Wunsch des Zionisten-Vereines anbelangt, so würde ich ihn am liebsten erfüllen, indem ich für das projektierte Buch diejenigen Stellen aus dem 'Weg ins Freie' zum Abdruck gestatte, in welchen über den Zionismus geredet wird. Allerdings in einem Sinne, der dem der Zionisten nicht ganz entsprechen dürfte" *(Briefe* I, 690 [February 3, 1912]).

[46] "Arthur Schnitzler, Doktor Gräsler, Badearzt," *Selbstwehr* (September 21, 1917): 6–7.

[47] *Bambi,* Walt Disney Home Video, distributed by Buena Vista Home Video, Burbank, CA, 1997, videocassette.

[48] In the scarce literature on *Bambi,* the novel is placed in the context of "the world-wide 'back to nature' movement" (Dormer, 413) and is said to owe its success to the fact that "its author shared a popular movement of the 1920s when a childlike view of nature was still possible for the average reader" (Dormer, 430). Only one scholar, Annegret Völpel, has briefly commented on *Bambi* from a Jewish-nationalist perspective (Völpel, "1928," in *Yale Companion to Jewish Writing and Thought in German Culture 1096–1996,* eds. Sander L. Gilman and Jack Zipes [New Haven and London: Yale UP, 1997]: 490).

[49] Salten did not get a penny for the movie: "He had sold the motion picture rights in 1933 to the producer Sidney Franklin, who passed them on to Disney" (Dormer, 417). When Thomas Mann, from his exile in the United States, approached Disney to help out the destitute Salten in Switzerland, Disney ignored the appeal. Thomas Mann, *Die Briefe Thomas Manns. Regesten und Register. Band II. Die Briefe von 1934 bis 1943,* eds. Hans Bürgin and Hans-Otto Mayer (Frankfurt: Fischer, 1980), 39/84, 1939, 283.

[50] Eduard Fuchs, *Die Juden in der Karikatur* (Munich: Verlag Albert Langen, 1921), 129–30.

[51] *Bambi,* 92: "Wird Er niemals aufhören, uns zu verfolgen?"

[52] *Bambi,* 90.

[53] *Bambi,* 23.

[54] Völpel, 490.

[55] Sensitive to any trace of *Mauscheln* in German (speaking German with a Jewish accent), he "thought he found it even in Felix Salten's *Bambi* and wrote about it one of his most amusing satires: *Jüdelnde Hasen*" (Iggers, 33).

[56] *Bambi*, 132.

[57] *Bambi*, 133.

[58] *Bambi*, 92.

[59] *Bambi*, 92.

[60] *Bambi*, 163.

[61] *Bambi*, 168.

[62] *Bambi*, 168.

[63] *Neue Menschen*, 171.

[64] *Neue Menschen*, 171–72.

[65] Völpel, 490.

[66] *Bambi*, 153.

[67] *Bambi*, 153.

[68] *Bambi*, 153.

[69] For the religious mystical aura staged around Herzl, see Michael Berkowitz, *Zionist Culture and West European Jewry Before the First World War* (Cambridge: Cambridge UP, 1993), 27–30, 136.

[70] I would like to thank Sander Gilman for suggesting this term.

[71] *Bambi*, 61.

[72] *Bambi*, 157.

[73] *Bambi*, 161.

[74] *Bambi*, 161.

[75] *Bambi*, 161.

[76] Salten, *Neue Menschen*, 68.

[77] Salten, *Freunde*, 202.

[78] Salten, *Freunde*, 144.

[79] The English translation of *Bambis Kinder* was published in 1939, a year before the German publication (Dormer, 438 and 439).

[80] *Bambis Kinder*, 33.

[81] *Bambis Kinder*, 245.

[82] *Bambis Kinder*, 163, 175.

[83] Aunt Rolla, hunted by the wolf-dog Nero, runs for her life and by chance leads the beast to Bambi's family, endangering their lives. The dog leaves her alone and instead pursues Bambi's son Geno, whom everyone except Gurri, his sister, expects to get killed. His mother, Faline, unjustly accuses Rolla of selfishness in endangering her family, and they do not see each other for a long time. Other deer argue and even fight over who has suffered most, which also ends their friendship.

[84] *Bambis Kinder*, 256.

[85] *Bambis Kinder*, 218.
[86] *Bambis Kinder*, 219.
[87] *Bambis Kinder*, 220.
[88] *Bambis Kinder*, 237.
[89] *Der Weg ins Freie*, 724.
[90] Many thanks to Katherine Arens for searching out and sending me a copy of *Bambis Kinder*. I also wish to thank Hillary Herzog, Don Bruce, and Michael Greenstein for their helpful comments.

The Writings

The Self as Process in an Era of Transition: Competing Paradigms of Personality and Character in Schnitzler's Works

Dagmar C. G. Lorenz

SCHNITZLER'S WORKS ARE considered paradigmatic of Austrian *fin-de-siècle* culture, and in his 2001 study *Schnitzler's Century: The Making of Middle-Class Culture, 1815–1914* Peter Gay uses Schnitzler as an example of nineteenth-century thought and behavior.[1] Implied in Gay's title is that Schnitzler's career as an author and intellectual peaked before the First World War. While much about Schnitzler's dramatic settings and some of the episodes in his own life fit the general climate of the Victorian age, for example his pining for a married woman, Olga Waissnix, and his unabashed endorsement of the sexual double standard, there is something breathtakingly revolutionary about his insights into the arbitrariness of character formation and gender role expectations. Schnitzler dealt with class, race, ethnicity, and gender, the most explosive issues of his time, in an innovative, and as the scandals involving some of his works show, unheard-of and transgressive manner. Like few other authors of the early twentieth century, he reveals in his narratives and dramas new ways of perceiving and describing relationships and the role of the individual, male and female.

Eike Middell notes that Schnitzler's work is characteristic of a particularly Viennese strain of European modernity that combined ideological conservatism with modern aesthetics.[2] In addition, Schnitzler brought to his writings special insights into the relativity of cultural modes and ideological tenets. His bicultural Jewish-Austrian perspective enabled him to develop a dynamic anti-essentialism in matters of gender, ethnicity, and character. Time, age, and aging as they affect individuals and civilizations are prominent themes in Schnitzler's works. Despite his innovative approach to these topics, Friedrich Nietzsche's call for a new man found little agreement in Schnitzler's writing. It is true that Schnitzler perceives a liberating potential in the cultural decline to which authors more firmly imbedded in the classical German tradition attributed catastrophic or tragic dimensions, implied in the notions of decadence, *Wertzerfall,* the disintegration of values, or apocalypse. Schnitzler moves away from the classical humanist concept of the self as implied in the individual's striving for ever greater knowledge and realization in Johann Wolfgang von Goethe's *Faust* (1808, 1832) and *Wilhelm Meister* novels or in Gustav Freytag's *Soll und Haben* (1855). Schnitzler does not envision a revitalization of humanity as did the Expressionists inspired by Nietzsche, and he does not fill the void left by outdated concepts and conventions with revolutionary ideas. Contrary to those of his contemporaries who embraced social utopias such as Socialism or Zionism, Schnitzler was one of the few authors of his time capable of tolerating and sustaining ambivalence. Schnitzler's sober assessments of late-nineteenth- and early-twentieth-century society and his openness to new technologies such as motion pictures call to mind his professional background as a physician. His literary approach to writing is empirical — he portrays the segments of Viennese society with which he is most familiar, the bourgeoisie and the bohème, and he does so without condemnation or glorification.

Schnitzler shared his contemporaries' fascination with the dark underside of Viennese culture, described by Hilde Spiel as insecurity, hectic sensuality, promiscuity, crime, and perversion lying right beneath the surface of ostentatious bourgeois luxury.[3] Curious and hypersensitive, Schnitzler was cognizant of the brittle underpinnings of social make-believe on which he and his peers based their lives of privilege and relative leisure.[4] He combined profound pessimism with the ironic mastery of social form and revealed the superficiality as well as the indispensability of convention. At times a semblance of happiness emerges in his works as the result of the successful negotiation of social rules, personal desires, and proper timing. An example is *Komtesse Mizzi oder der Familientag* (1908), in which after decades of sublimation and substitute pleasures, a renewed relationship between two lovers becomes possible, this time under the right conditions.[5] Schnitzler's autobiography, *Jugend in Wien* (1968), conveys a similar outlook.[6] Despite his unrequited love for Waissnix, Schnitzler engaged in affairs and erotic encounters, suspecting that his true love might be doing the same with men other than himself. Overall, Schnitzler presents himself as a somewhat detached, albeit not disinterested young dandy, an observer of his contemporaries. Socialized in a culture obsessed with its own impending demise, he also explores social forces that were fully revealed as insidious in the decades to come.

Schnitzler's representation of what Peter Heller calls the "dual presence of the upper and under-world" differs from Robert Musil's or

Hugo von Hofmannsthal's point of view. Schnitzler does not shroud the unfamiliar in mystery or cast it as the impenetrable other.[7] Instead, he examines the effects and function of dogmatic notions such as the ones underlying Otto Weininger's and Houston Stewart Chamberlain's racist and sexist theories. The drama *Das Märchen* (1894), for example, illuminates the coexistence of widely disparate elements in the individual psyche.[8] Fedor Denner, the most enlightened character, is incapable of putting his progressive views into practice. Not his intellect but his nineteenth-century middle-class morality dominates his love life. Fedor's commitment to the actress Fanny Theren fails because he cannot come to terms with the fact that she was involved with other men before him. Bewildered and frustrated, he asks himself if it is only the traditional bias against "fallen women" or something more deeply ingrained that prompts him to torment his fiancée with fits of jealousy.[9] *Das Märchen* shows how a spokesman for egalitarianism and women's rights can be as possessive as the patriarchs of old. Fedor wants his future wife to sever all ties to her past, knowing that she can do so as he can.[10] It is obvious to the viewer that Fedor's jealousy stems from his self-awareness. Like Fridolin in *Traumnovelle* (1926), he distrusts his partner because he knows how little he can be trusted.[11]

Schnitzler steered clear of the rhetoric of high drama or melodrama. His secular settings preclude the element of mystery, at least in the sense of the gothic thriller. The uncanny element is present, though, and emerges from within mundane everyday reality. The interactions and encounters in a world without discernible meaning are the ultimate mystery — hence the recurrent theme of the inability of one person to understand another's feelings or actions. In the one-act play *Die Gefährtin* (1899), for example, the self-deception of Robert Pilgram, an aging professor married to a younger woman, comes to light.[12] After the death of his wife, other people open his eyes to her indiscretions and the way she in turn was trifled with by her lover. Though belated, the new awareness that his wife had had a superficial affair rather than a major romance comes to Pilgram as a liberation.

In all of Schnitzler's works there is at least one character who, like the finally enlightened Pilgram, provides a realistic dimension and an awareness of the connectedness of all human concerns. Max in *Anatol* (1893), Theodor in *Liebelei* (1896), and Mizzi in *Komtesse Mizzi* have this function.[13] In Schnitzler's prose a realistic basis is established by a narrator or narrative point of view that allows for dispassionate observation. Thus alternatives to the protagonists' decisions become apparent, undermining the tragic potential of the text and leaving the reader with the realization that the narrated events are well within the ordinary. Characters who follow their flair for the heroic or melodramatic deprive themselves of the freedom of choice, for example the title character in *Fräulein Else* (1924), Christine in *Liebelei,* or Karinski in *Freiwild* (1898).[14]

The avoidance of Nietzsche's proverbial "Geist der Schwere" earned Schnitzler the reputation of being a frivolous, if not trivial author. His early critics tended to overlook the ramifications of his work. Even Sol Liptzin, who praised Schnitzler's casual conversational mode and the "charming wit and delicate humor, the graceful philandering of his frivolous and melancholy hero [Anatol]," underestimated the author overall.[15] So did the critic Josef Körner, who maintained Schnitzler's greatest skill was his ability to create impressionistic ambiences.[16] Although the romancing, loafing, and gambling that Schnitzler's male protagonists engage in is undoubtedly pleasurable, the fleeting enjoyment they derive from their idle lives does not cure their underlying melancholy. Anatol, like Schnitzler and his friends in *Jugend in Wien,* are busy pursuing pastimes with little hope of overcoming their passivity and lethargy, or in modern terms, their depression.[17] The latter is indicative of a profound personal malaise and a major cultural crisis.

Symptomatic of this crisis are the wasteful and wasted lives and senseless deaths of many of Schnitzler's characters, deaths that a different author might have cast as tragic or heroic. Instead, Schnitzler stresses the failure to negotiate the mutually exclusive paradigms of convention and free choice, the old and the modern, which collided also in his plays. He shows that, more often than not, the violent, unrefined paradigms prevail — as they do in *Freiwild* and *Liebelei.* Dr. Albert Wellner in *Freiwild* aptly corrects his friend Paul Rönning, who surmises that Lieutenant Karinski, whom he refuses to confront in a duel, has nothing to gain in this matter. On the contrary, deprived of his traditional prerogative as an officer and a gentleman, Rönning's opponent is dishonored and has nothing left to lose, as Wellner points out. Shamed and bankrupt, Karinski faces exclusion from the social order to which he aspires, and he resorts to murder.[18] From a rational point of view, neither the duel nor the murder seems necessary except that they are predicated by convention. Karinski's predicament reveals that Schnitzler regarded identity as not merely a matter of character and choice but as a function in a mosaic of variables.

Like Karinski, many other characters consider the exclusion from the urban bourgeoisie as worse than death, as the destruction of their identity. *Leutnant Gustl* (1900) features an officer who in his heart of hearts is neither a man of honor nor a hero.[19] Yet he contemplates suicide after being insulted by a baker who cannot grant him satisfaction because of his social standing. In his inner monologue Gustl, an altogether mediocre intellect, exposes the superficiality of a code based on appearances, as well as the homicidal and suicidal collective mentality that produced it. Reason alone, however, cannot put an end to these deadly conventions and the ideology they reflect. In contrast to Karinski in *Freiwild,* Gustl is lucky: the incident went unobserved, and the baker died unexpectedly. Since there is no need for him to kill himself, Gustl gets ready for his next duel.

From a rational point of view the suicide of Christine Weiring in *Liebelei* is as uncalled-for as the duels and murders. In light of the relaxed sexual mores of her environment and her father's liberal views, there is no need for her to become a tragic heroine. Hans Weiring, aware of the hardships awaiting adult women of his class, wants his daughter to enjoy herself and does not oppose her flirtation and eventual affair with an attractive gentleman. She, on the other hand, has thoroughly internalized the Victorian moral code. Considering that the cause of her despair is an insincere young man without distinction, Christine's suicide would seem grotesque were it not in keeping with a code alive on Vienna's stages. The daughter of a musician at the Theater in der Josefstadt, Christine is steeped in the discourse of female virtue, chastity, and the one and only love. Her suicide, rather than being the autonomous act Renate Möhrmann makes it out to be, emulates the uncompromising responses characteristic of German stage heroes. In the later novella *Fräulein Else,* which Schnitzler began to write in 1921, the inappropriateness of the melodramatic suicidal impulse is expressed in the dying protagonist's regrets over having taken a fatal overdose.[20]

Christine is out of step with the society represented in Schnitzler's dramatic works. Modernity has many different options available and does not sustain tragedy. Rather than tragic, Christine's demise is misguided and unfortunate. Through characters such as Christine, Schnitzler reveals the problems inherent in melodramatic representations of personal relationships and society on stage and in literature and criticizes the effects such representations may have on impressionable minds. *Liebelei* suggests that different models of solving relationship problems are available at the *fin-de-siècle,* which makes the lover's death appear dated and contrite. In the absence of a binding transcendental framework or higher authority, suicide too is a matter of personal choice and far less glamorous than it may appear to the given character. Goethe had already touched upon this notion in *Die Leiden des jungen Werthers* (1774). Werther believes that killing himself is like stepping from one room into another, but in fact he dies a slow and painful death. Schnitzler's criticism of the heroic mode, also apparent from his pacifist stance during the First World War, is part of a political oppositional Jewish discourse manifest also in the writings of Heinrich Heine.[21]

Throughout his career Schnitzler depicted the confusion created by conflicting cultural paradigms and the individuals' desires. Stanley Kubrick's motion picture *Eyes Wide Shut* (1999), based on *Traumnovelle*, draws attention to some of the parallels and differences between Vienna of the last and New York of the most recent turn of the century.[22] The fact that Schnitzler's story has lost its earlier ability to shock demonstrates that notions of morality and authority have undergone radical changes in the last seventy-five years. At the same time, the lack of acclaim for the movie may be the result not only of Schnitzler's historic specificity but also of discomfort about the way in which relationships and the self are configured. A movie that undermines the potential for heterosexual coupled bliss and draws into question the viability of the nuclear family would still today be problematic. Some of the issues raised by Schnitzler and Kubrick remain unresolved in the postmodern era and are by and large taboo in popular culture.

More provocative than the orgy scenes in *Eyes Wide Shut* is the theme of complicity. Both in Kubrick's movie and Schnitzler's novella, upstanding citizens are implicated in the world of drugs, illicit sex, violence, and crime. The cross-connections imply that it is impossible for Western culture to sustain its values of propriety and family and to prosper in isolation from the social realms where these norms do not and cannot apply. Moreover, both works show the dividing lines between the different spheres to be imperceptible. The bourgeois world and the so-called dark underside are one and the same. The conclusion that ignorance, deliberately chosen over awareness, is the only way for the bourgeois dream to continue is no less upsetting now than it was in the early twentieth century. Schnitzler's play implies that in spite of their verbal, emotional, and legal commitments, the partners in a relationship are alone and live as strangers to the person with whom they share their house and their bed. Maintaining their idyllic family life and the illusion of exclusivity requires of Fridolin and Albertine role-playing and self-imposed ignorance. *Traumnovelle* is an excellent example of the multilayered identity construction in Schnitzler. A person's social role and function and his or her existential isolation present an unresolvable, even tragic dilemma.

Schnitzler's work is part of the ubiquitous *fin-de-siècle* project of developing expressions appropriate to modern reality.[23] In an earlier transitional era Goethe had designed Werther, a character as pathbreaking as Anatol and Lieutenant Gustl. As with Werther, the struggle of Schnitzler's protagonists with new modalities and levels of consciousness takes place in isolation from the world of work and careers, as if in defiance of the bourgeois work ethic. Unable and unwilling to assume the roles their respective societies have in store for them, and for the most part mildly bored, Schnitzler's young men, like Werther, seek authentic experiences through their emotions and senses.[24] Their encounters with women and their interactions with one another provide them with a sense of self. However, in contrast to Werther, who is taken in by the sentimental drama of which he is the producer and the director, Schnitzler's Anatol and Fritz Lobheimer (*Liebelei*) are beyond deceiving themselves. Like Schnitzler, the diarist and autobiographer, they take part in and at the same time stand apart from their culture of feeling.[25]

The emotional detachment of Anatol, Fritz Lobheimer, the couple in *Halbzwei* (1894), or Stephan von Sala in *Der einsame Weg* (1904) is a reflection of Schnitzler's experience as a Jewish man in Vienna. Schnitzler was alienated from the political arena dominated by anti-Semitism. Basic to his aesthetics is a sense of belonging and being excluded, expressed also in his distinction between *Heimatliebe* and *Patriotismus*.[26] Thoroughly imbued with German literature, art, and music, with the sentimental, mystical, heroic, and tragic modes of which Richard Wagner, Makart, Gustav Klimt, Hofmannsthal, and Rainer Maria Rilke freely availed themselves, Schnitzler admits sentimentality and high drama into his works only to be satirized. Especially when issues of existential importance are at stake he avoids the kind of grandiosity associated with, for example, Wagner. Like Heine, he scrutinizes literary conventions as well as his characters, many of whom were reflections of people he knew.[27] In his diaries and autobiography a Schnitzler emerges to whom sentimentality is basically foreign. Even the dramatic intrigues in *Der einsame Weg* involving paternity, the protagonist's impending death, and the suicide of the female heroine evolve among *causeries* and casual encounters. Though ill-fated like a Byronic hero, Sala makes his final arrangements deliberately and rationally.

Schnitzler explores the concepts through which his social class and generation defined themselves without validating reality constructs of earlier epochs or the fashionable ideologies of his time.[28] From a distance he reveals the inner workings of Viennese society, but he does not hold his characters up to ridicule.[29] *Reigen* (1903) and *Traumnovelle* are among those works that expose the relativity of social norms without losing sight of the fact that they determine an individual's status and social range. Fridolin and Albertine are perfectly well suited to their station in life — they would be incapable of functioning in a setting that defies the moral double standard on which their relationship is based.[30]

Similarly, in *Reigen* encounters between unequal partners such as a count and a prostitute are possible only on a physical level and in a state of drunkenness. The prostitute does not allow herself to be used as a canvas for the count's sentimental projections. She has no notion of or respect for his status, nor is she interested in small talk. Schnitzler portrays the entanglements across class boundaries as being devoid of intimacy or compassion — they certainly do not pave the way toward a fairer society.

At the same time Schnitzler shows status, gender, and ethnicity to be in flux in Vienna's transitional society. The presence of diverse cultures challenges individuals to find their own values and meaning in life. The protagonists cast and recast themselves in each new context. Anatol, for example, displays chameleon-like traits in his conversations with different partners. Around Max, whom he considers his equal, he appears moody, pensive, and unsure of himself. In the company of women he assumes various roles. He treats his lover Cora with ironic condescension, yet is possessive and always eager to charm her. He approaches Gabriele, a married woman of his own class, with a gallantry that borders on servility were it not for Anatol's obtrusiveness. He acts the passionate romantic lover with Else, who has just returned from her honeymoon and, no less flirtatious than Anatol, plans on adventures to come. Failing to conceal from Ilona, yet another lover, his impending marriage, he convinces her nonetheless to continue their affair in the near future.

The prose works uncover through inner monologues a character's maneuvering through the sophisticated urban landscape, where anonymity offers an unprecedented mobility but also threatens one's sense of self, because the benefits of modern society are available to everyone. Mass events such as public balls, strolls in the parks, shopping sprees the city, and the coffeehouse culture facilitate the dates and chance encounters around which Schnitzler's writing revolves. The city is an arena for social games. The concept of play is applicable not only to gambling and formal acting, but to identity formation through relationships, language, manners, and customs. It involves, as in Johan Huizinga's *Homo ludens* (1955), death itself.[31] Andreas Huyssen has argued that the crisis of language manifest in the works of Schnitzler, Hofmannsthal, Mach, Karl Kraus, Mauthner, Sigmund Freud, and Wittgenstein is "more than a trigger of a 'crisis of identity and its overcoming'" and that "notions of the split or decentered subject permit us to go beyond the traditional codings of the modernist identity crisis as a binary opposition between a stable ego or self versus ego loss or deindividualization."[32] Huyssen's approach seems particularly productive for authors of Jewish descent who represent in the dominant discourse the demonic other and are stereotyped through anti-

Jewish iconography. At the same time they are self-defined in terms of their Jewish experience and Central European Jewish society. Not unlike Franz Kafka, Freud, and Weininger, Schnitzler is conversant with competing paradigms, Jewish and Gentile, from which his writing emerges.

Born into a group of Austro-Hungarian Jews striving for integration, Schnitzler had no unequivocally positive concept of Jewishness and was painfully aware of the exclusion of Jews in Austrian society. The son and grandson of physicians and journalists, himself a successful author and medical doctor, he belonged to the privileged class. As a Jew, however, he was an outsider and, to use Hannah Arendt's terminology, the descendent of pariahs and parvenus. Like most Austrian Jews he moved primarily in the circles of emancipated or assimilated Viennese Jewry.[33] Cognizant of his father's humble origins in small-town Hungary, Schnitzler's attitude toward unassimilated Jews is ambivalent at best.[34] He did not share the nostalgia for his Eastern European roots that emerged among Jews of the generation of Martin Buber and Arnold Zweig. In *Jugend in Wien* Schnitzler notes that he was never tempted to visit his father's hometown of Groß-Kanizsa, where he had spent some time as a boy. In many comments he expresses dislike of Yiddish and Jewish speech and the shtetl culture. Despite his keen intuitive understanding of their plight, he keeps an emotional distance from the "sehr begabte Jungen oder Jüngelchen" from Hungary, Bohemia, and Moravia who come to study in Vienna. The terms "Judenjunge" and "Judenmädel" denote in the context of his autobiography a group he does not consider his own. Yet he was disturbed by the self-hatred of his friend Louis Friedmann, who decided to remain childless because he was a Jew.

Contrary to the assumption that Jews in Schnitzler's position were already assimilated, the fact is that they faced serious obstacles in the dominant culture and carried their own, distinct cultural memories. *Jugend in Wien* opens with a review of Schnitzler's family history. Structured like a Bildungsroman, the narrative begins with Schnitzler's birth in the Leopoldstadt before it became the center of Jewish immigration for which it was later known. Schnitzler writes at some length about Jewish holidays at his grandmother's house, in a nostalgic tone reminiscent of Heine's portrayal of the Seder in *Der Rabbi von Bacharach,* as well as about Jewish traditions, foods, and attitudes in his extended family. To fully appreciate Schnitzler's closeness to Jewish culture one needs to remember that one of his earliest dramatic attempts was devoted to the topic of the Eternal Jew. In his openness Schnitzler comes across as an "upright Jew" who "acknowledged the socio-psychological fact of anti-Semitism but lived his life as a Jew."[35] His description of the years he spent as a student in a secular Viennese Gymnasium attended predominantly by Jews, and the passages about his emerging love of German literature and his development as a writer, reveal that Schnitzler was caught in a double bind. Like most Viennese Jews, he had to negotiate mutually exclusive paradigms.

The issue of gender is no less complex. Contrary to critics who viewed Schnitzler's preoccupation with gender relations as indicative of a "politically dead era"[36] or dismissed them, as did Kraus, as the trivial pursuit of a dandy, Schnitzler's analysis of love and sexuality goes to the core of Gentile middle-class ideology. Gender role expectations and sexual mores are the cornerstones of bourgeois identity.[37] As far as male and female characters are concerned, Schnitzler lacks the conviction through which generations of Gentile males had rationalized the double standard and produced an iconography that also justified the subjugation of the underprivileged as well as of other nations and races.

The subversive configuration of gender among the often trivial characters in anything but trivial texts has evoked the wrath of critics who missed the glamour traditionally associated with love and sexuality. Schnitzler exposes the culturally predicated alienation from the body and the function of the sentimental trappings of love-making within a capitalist environment, namely to provide gratification without guilt.[38] The cultural code Schnitzler holds up to criticism is, of course, that of the Gentile majority.

Jewish and Christian cultures are both patriarchal. They have, however, distinct methods of assessing status and regulating the access men and women have to the goods their respective societies offer. Traditional Judaism excluded women from religious learning and participation in the synagogue. Yet women did take part in family businesses and had exposure to secular public life and matters of finance. Jewish daughters of the middle class were free to pursue a secular education.[39] The greater mobility of Jewish women was not an indication that they occupied male roles. The interchange between German and Jewish culture contributed to the destabilization and the modification of identity and gender roles in both. Schnitzler reveals the discrepancy between gender stereotypes and the actual behavior of men and women, calling into question a static gender identity. He presents the concept of a dynamic self susceptible to moods and adapting to its environment.

In *Jugend in Wien* Schnitzler is preoccupied with Jewish issues. Naturally, he writes of the discrimination he and his family had to face. His outlook on politics is clearly affected by the prevailing anti-Semitic climate. He notes for example that he was interested in the issue of Austrian and German nationality only inasmuch as it related to anti-

Semitism, by which he was concerned and enraged. His aversion to student dueling societies and the military also involves the manifestations of Jew-hatred in academic and public life, such as the brutal attacks on Jewish students at the university and the segregation between Jewish and non-Jewish military units. Schnitzler also discusses the anti-Semitic dimensions of the problems his father encountered as a physician and founder of the Viennese Poliklinik. Moreover, Schnitzler describes some of the strategies through which his friends tried to compensate for their Jewish background. Richard Tausenau joined a German nationalist fraternity, and Louis Friedmann decided to remain childless so as to prevent the propagation of Jewish blood. The linguistic and cultural ambiguities in Schnitzler's Vienna, so decidedly shaped by its Jewish citizens and so clearly anti-Jewish, emerge also in his correspondence with Olga Waissnix, née Schneider (1862–1897), the daughter of a Viennese hotel owner, wife of the owner of the resort hotel Thalhof, and the object of Schnitzler's unrequited love for many years. Hans Weigel explains Waissnix's anything-but-flawless German and her use of Yiddish terms such as "broiges," "nebbich," "mies," and "meschugge" in the context of Jewish migration to the imperial capital and the ascent of Jews into the upper middle class and lower nobility. Waissnix's letters reveal the influence of Yiddish on Viennese German and the multiple layers of personal and cultural connection between the two groups.[40]

Weigel observes the eccentricity of Schnitzler's first major protagonist, Anatol, whose adventures in many ways reflect those of Schnitzler and his friends. Through the Russian-sounding name, uncommon in *fin-de-siècle* Vienna, his gender coding, and several subtle hints throughout the play, Anatol is associated with the stratum of social climbers of Jewish extraction who, like the recently ennobled Scheys, Thorschs, and Hofmannsthals, played a leading role in late Habsburg society.[41] Protected by a layer of wealth and luxury, Anatol is excluded from the world of work and commerce. Basically unproductive, his lifestyle resembles that of women of the privileged classes: he sleeps late, socializes, goes shopping, and dabbles in the arts. With the exception of his intimate, Max, he is shown in the company of women whose preoccupation with social detail, elegant objects, emotions, relationships, and intrigues he and Max share. Yet also in the women's sphere Anatol is a mere onlooker, almost a voyeur. He is the outsider *par excellence* in Gentile Viennese and traditional Jewish culture. Jost Hermand's description of Heine's predicament comes to mind as an earlier but nonetheless parallel experience to that of Schnitzler's Anatol. In the latter case the predicament of the literary character mirrors the situation of the author: "Only the so-called fast girls, the ones who can be bought, open their doors and their bodies to him, while all the so-called better girls and women turn away from him. As a Jew, he could not 'win' them even by promising them to marry them."[42] Anatol's somewhat naive statement that contrary to most men who seek the courtesan in every woman he seeks the woman in every courtesan confirms the notion that his access to chic women is limited.

Anatol's nonparticipation in the male domain is part and parcel of his eccentricity and foreignness, his elusive Jewishness. Like Goethe's Werther, Anatol exists in a social vacuum. Werther faces the dilemma of being an educated and ambitious but poor middle-class male in a society that offers him no real advancement. His isolation is in part the result of the social inferiority he attributes to the middle class to which he belongs and the unattainability of a higher status. Anatol is in a similar position. Neither to Goethe's nor to Schnitzler's character is ascending into the elite an option, nor is taking up a business or trade. Similarly for Schnitzler in Lueger's Vienna the political and social service hierarchy was closed, just as it was to Heine in pre- and post-1848 Germany. Even as a physician, Schnitzler faced serious difficulties: his initial successes with hypnosis were so ridiculed that they compromised the reputation of the Poliklinik. Finally, his literary career was overshadowed by scandal and controversy fueled, as Gerd Schneider has shown, not merely by moral indignation but anti-Semitism. These experiences of exclusion constitute the background against which Schnitzler created his idle dandies and wealthy loafers.

Most of Schnitzler's protagonists have no foundation for a stable sense of self. This difficulty is as true for blond-haired Jewesses such as Else, who are glad that their Jewishness does not show, as it is for Lieutenant Gustl, bent on acting like a hero.[43] Else's dislike of von Dorsday derives from anti-Semitic as well as age-related antipathies.[44] She is repulsed by his aging body, but she also speculates that he may have changed his name to avoid the odium of Jewishness and considers it mere chance that he can deal in art rather than old clothes.[45] Similarly, Gustl's unerring eye for Jewish traits in others around him calls into question his own identity. One may wonder if his defensiveness regarding his honor as an officer and his prowess as a lover stems from insecurity regarding his background. There is something personal about his horror of living in Galicia, where he was stationed briefly prior to his assignment in Vienna. Gustl's ambivalent identity calls to mind Lieutenant Karinski in *Freiwild*, a man described as being of dark complexion with black hair and dark eyes. Karinski considers the prospect of returning to his earlier rural life worse than death.

To a Jew seeking assimilation through a military career, losing his uniform would equal social death. Many citizens of the Danube monarchy fled from their Jewish or otherwise obscure origins into the uniform of a dueling society or that of the k. and k. military, as was the case with the Austro-Hungarian colonel Alfred Redl (1864–1913), who was accused of espionage in a case as notorious as the Dreyfus affair; Kafka's father, Hermann Kafka (1852–1931); and the writer Joseph Roth (1894–1939), a native of the Galician shtetl of Brody, who owed his social graces to his years in the military as an Einjährig-Freiwilliger.[46] Schnitzler also welcomed the uniform and used it as a prop for adventures with women apt to be impressed by an officer no matter his background, notably simple suburban girls, the prototype of Schnitzler's accessible but not marriageable "sweet" girls.

The exploits of Schnitzler's young men have clearly Jewish dimensions. Anatol, like Fritz Lobheimer and Theodor Kaiser in *Liebelei* — the names of both young men can be considered Jewish-defined — are engaged in self-finding missions mediated through sexual conquests. Public and professional life, social status, and politics are conspicuous by virtue of their exclusion. For some of the female characters, on the other hand — shop girls, actresses, and prostitutes — work does play a role, a situation reminiscent of traditional Jewish gender roles. Since individualism is central to the German Humanist ideal, Schnitzler's focus on the private sphere must be read as a cultural issue. Jewish intellectuals on their way toward assimilation had to wrestle with the extreme validation of emotional and personal matters within bourgeois society.

Identification through another, a partner of the opposite sex, presupposes predictable gender roles and an emotional synchronization supported by the larger cultural and social framework. The literary discourse of nineteenth-century Central European Christian and secular society associated the experience of one's self with love and sexuality. Feeling and being felt were considered essential to a person's ability to define himself, and less so, herself. Observing one's effect on another human being was the prerequisite for feeling validated. Proof of their own importance, even their existence, is what Anatol and characters search for in the arms of their female partners.

Anatol portrays the protagonist in amorous constellations that are familiar from the literary canon. He appears with his lover Cora, an unmarried woman; with Gabriele, married and inaccessible; with Bianca, a former lover, now Max's girlfriend, who, much to Anatol's dismay, does not recall their earlier encounter; with the elegant Emilie, whom he seems ready to marry if she were willing or able to erase her past; with

Annie, a sweet Viennese girl such as the ones men met at public dance halls, who leaves Anatol for a man she prefers to him; with Else, a married woman in search of an affair; and with Ilona on the morning of his wedding. His lack of commitment prevents Anatol from establishing a relationship that might provide him with a sense of identity. However, rejecting the consolations of self-deception, he prefers to deal with infatuations that pass and a fluctuating sense of self. Anatol plays along with Gentile typecasting, knowing that it is only make-believe. Schnitzler, who is familiar with Jewish and Gentile gender role expectations, is at liberty to experiment with both models. For instance, he has Anatol articulate that women and men are similar in their desires and acknowledge that a woman's propensity for monogamy is a myth. Aware that female virtue is the result of oppression, Anatol opts for the prevailing double standard.[47] His choice brings him closer to the privileged cultural paradigm. However, assimilation has its pitfalls. As Schnitzler's protagonists adapt to the dominant model, they feel the urge to escape it as well. Anatol flirts with lower-class Gentile girls because of their social inferiority and supposed simplicity. Gabriele pokes fun at his adventures in the "small world" of Hernals.[48] Other characters escape into death, as did Schnitzler's friend Tausenau in 1893, or they follow their self-destructive bent by fighting duels they cannot win.[49]

Mark Luprecht maintains that Schnitzler's pessimism is less pervasive than Freud's because Schnitzler is not a determinist.[50] Schnitzler may consider gender and ethnic models a matter of convention and choice, but his position does not entail an optimistic outlook. His awareness of the ravages of time, the volatility of emotions, the fallibility of the mind, the fragility of situations, and the elusiveness of the self prove rather the opposite. There is little hope in Schnitzler's relativism derived from his dual perspective. He designed romantic and erotic plots in the German tradition and deconstructed them from a Jewish point of view. He exposed the self-deception required to make the traditional plots work and uncovered the exploitation and seediness inherent in the concept of romantic love in a hierarchical system. The results are disquieting and disillusioning. *Anatol* ends by showing the institution of marriage as an emotional buffoonery that stresses the opportunism and the economic dimensions that traditional literature tends to conceal. *Anatol* also exposes the predatory behavior of men who associate with low-status women. *Anatol's Größenwahn* (1932) deals with the tragicomic existence of an aging philanderer and the protagonist's failure to achieve the attention he has longed for so desperately.[51] Anatol's yearning to make a difference in a woman's life or at least to be remembered by her meets with indifference on the part of women. Anatol, who in his prime may have been amusing, appears pathetic as a middle-aged man. The senselessness of Christine's death in *Liebelei* is another example, a death as senseless as that of her lover Fritz, who is killed in a duel by a jealous husband.

Komtesse Mizzi, on the other hand, shows examples of the successful management of feelings and conventions, showcasing the amicable termination of affairs that have run their course and the resumption of an erstwhile thwarted love affair. Mizzi dismisses her lover, a younger professor, while her father separates from his mistress of long standing who is about to marry a man of her own class. Mizzi is likely to enter a union with a prince who has finally adopted the illegitimate adult son Mizzi secretly had with him when he was still married. There is no sign of moral misgiving on the author's part when the rich in *Komtesse Mizzi* turn the legal code to their advantage and leave moral scruples to the ignorant and underprivileged.

The attitude toward social structures, desire, and relationships in Schnitzler reveals a pragmatic and eminently liberal stance. It is up to the individuals to make the most of the circumstances they are presented with in their lives and to carefully weigh the advantages and disadvantages in every situation. In the case of Mizzi, timing, coincidence, convention and desire need to be negotiated to prevent scandal and disaster from happening and to ensure the greatest benefit for all concerned. The abilities to compromise and to take charge of one's life are equally important. Renunciation, delaying gratification, and self-discipline are balanced with substitute pleasures and sublimation through art and nature as strategies available to a person unable to find immediate fulfillment of his or her passion. Rather than falling into depression, Mizzi seeks consolation in affairs with other men and through painting.

From Schnitzler's work emerges a plea for rationality and enlightened free choice, for the right to make autonomous decisions and to select identity roles according to the possibilities of the moment. On the other hand, Schnitzler creates in his works a profoundly pessimistic dimension with the portrayal of external and psychological obstacles to free association and personal development. Desire and potential for progress are balanced against the physiological, psychological, and cultural restrictions to freedom and happiness. The dilemma the literary characters as well as their creator face call to mind the problem laid out in Freud's *Das Unbehagen in der Kultur* (1930). Even in his earliest writings Schnitzler examined the insurmountable obstacles frustrating the pursuit and the achievement of happiness, leading up to the conclusion that suffering is predicated by basic human conditions and aggravated by social institutions. Yet, as Schnitzler's more successful characters suggest, the continued effort to alleviate suffering and to increase pleasure is the only worthwhile, if not noble, project in the face of certain defeat.

Notes

[1] Peter Gay, *Schnitzler's Century: The Making of Middle-Class Culture, 1815–1914* (New York: Norton, 2001).

[2] Eike Middell, *Literatur zweier Kaiserreiche. Deutsche und österreichische Literatur der Jahrhundertwende* (Salzburg: Akademie, 1993), 48, 61. Middell observes that Viennese modernism flirted with the notions of decay and decadence and cultivated an aura of classicism. Schnitzler was part of this discourse and distinct from avantgarde writing in Germany.

[3] Hilde Spiel, "Im Abgrund der Triebwelt oder Kein Zugang zum Fest. Zu Schnitzlers 'Traumnovelle,'" in *Akten des Internationalen Symposions 'Arthur Schnitzler und seine Zeit,'* ed. Guiseppe Farese (Bern: Peter Lang, 1985), 166. Alfred Doppler, in "Der Wandel der Darstellungsperspektive in den Dichtungen Arthur Schnitzlers. Mann und Frau als sozialpsychologisches Problem" (41), emphasizes the experience of the "Fassadenhaftigkeit des Lebens" that Schnitzler had early in life when, used to an upscale, aestheticized lifestyle, his father lost his entire fortune in the stock market collapse of 1873.

[4] Ulrich Weinzierl, *Arthur Schnitzler. Lieben, Träumen, Sterben* (Frankfurt: Fischer, 1994), 12.

[5] *Komtesse Mizzi oder der Familientag,* in DW I, 1029–1062.

[6] Arthur Schnitzler, *Jugend in Wien. Eine Autobiographie,* ed. Therese Nickl and Heinrich Schnitzler (Frankfurt am Main: Fischer, 1968).

[7] Peter Heller, "Freud as a Phenomenon in the *Fin de Siècle*," in *Arthur Schnitzler and his Age. Intellectual and Artistic Currents,* eds. Petrus W. Tax and Richard H. Lawson (Bonn: Bouvier, 1984), 3.

[8] *Das Märchen* in DW I, 125–200.

[9] *Das Märchen* in DW I, 162.

[10] *Das Märchen* in DW I, 198.

[11] *Traumnovelle* in ES II, 434–504.

[12] *Die Gefährtin* in DW I, 499–514).

[13] *Anatol* in DW I, 28–88; *Liebelei* in DW I, 215–64.

[14] *Freiwild* in DW I, 265–326; *Fräulein Else* in ES II, 324–81.

[15] Sol Liptzin, *Arthur Schnitzler* (New York: Prentice Hall, 1931), 26, 29. Also: Josef Körner, *Arthur Schnitzlers Gestalten und Probleme* (Zurich: Amalthea, 1921), 221.

[16] Körner, 221.

[17] Alfred Doppler, "Der Wandel der Darstellungsperspektive in den Dichtungen Arthur Schnitzlers. Mann und Frau als sozialpsychologisches Problem," in *Akten des*

Internationalen Symposions "Arthur Schnitzler und seine Zeit," ed. Guiseppe Farese (Bern: Peter Lang, 1985), 41.

[18] *Freiwild,* 311–12.

[19] *Leutnant Gustl* in ES I, 337–66.

[20] *Fräulein Else,* 380. The concept for the novella "wurde deutlich" for Schnitzler in 1921. See "Vergleichende Zeittafel," in *Arthur Schnitzler. Sein Leben. Sein Werk. Seine Zeit.,* eds. Heinrich Schnitzler, Christian Brandstätter, Reinhard Urbach (Frankfurt: Fischer, 1981), 349–66.

[21] Jost Hermand, "The Wandering Jew's Rhine Journey: Heine's *Lorelei,*" in *Insiders and Outsiders. Jewish and Gentile Culture in Germany and Austria,* eds. Dagmar C. G. Lorenz and Gabriele Weinberger (Detroit: Wayne State UP, 1994), 44.

[22] *Eyes Wide Shut,* dir. Stanley Kubrick, Warner Brothers, 1999.

[23] Carl E. Schorske writes in *Thinking with History. Explorations in the Passage to Modernism* (Princeton: Princeton UP, 1999): "What remained was for modern man to find his own voice, to learn how to state his own truth, independent of the dead hand of the past" (147).

[24] "The Jung-Wien writers explored the sensuous life, now artistic, now erotic. Their characters, like themselves, suffered from a seismographic consciousness, assailed now by the forces of instinct within, now by the inchoate powers of the world without" (Schorske, 132).

[25] Schorske, 133.

[26] *Halbzwei* in DW I, 207–14; *Der einsame Weg* in DW I, 759–837. Richard Miklin, "Heimatliebe und Patriotismus: Arthur Schnitzlers Einstellung zu Österreich-Ungarn im Ersten Weltkrieg." *Modern Austrian Literature* 19/3–4 (1986): 198, 205, 209; Lorenz/Weinberger, 8–9.

[27] Renate Möhrmann, "Schnitzlers Frauen und Mädchen. Zwischen Sachlickeit und Sentiment," in *Akten des Internationalen Symposions "Arthur Schnitzler und seine Zeit"* (Bern: Peter Lang, 1985), 93–107. Möhrmann correctly observes the unconventionality of Schnitzler's view of women, noting the absence of the *fin-de-siècle* stereotypes of the virtuous housewife, femme fatale, and femme fragile (93). However, her assessment of the petty bourgeoise Christine, who transforms a love affair into love, as a model character (101) appears out of keeping with the overall tenor of Schnitzler's work.

[28] Weinzierl, 11–12. Schorske writes: "Schnitzler treats the Oedipal tension, despite its omnipresence, in terms of cultural difference between generations, not as an eternal verity" (147). Mark Luprecht, in *"What People Call Pessimism": Sigmund Freud, Arthur Schnitzler, and Nineteenth-Century Controversy at the University of Vienna Medical School* (Riverside: Ariadne, 1991), writes that Schnitzler's skepticism vanquished *all* systems (142).

[29] Gottfried Just, *Ironie und Sentimentalität in den erzählenden Dichtungen Arthur Schnitzlers* (Berlin: Erich Schmidt, 1968). Just maintains that Schnitzler regarded it in bad taste to empathize with his own literary creations or to make fun of them (39).

[30] Eric Santner, "Of Masters, Slaves, and Other Seducers: Arthur Schnitzler's *Traumnovelle,*" *Modern Austrian Literature* 19/3–4 (1986): 33–48. Santner terms Fridolin's behavior "misogynous" (34).

[31] Johan Huizinga, *Homo ludens* (Boston: Beacon Press, 1955), ii. See also Susan Anderson's views on the gambler Willi Kasda: "Profile of a Gambler: Willi Kasda in *Spiel im Morgengrauen*," in *Arthur Schnitzler and his Age. Intellectual and Artistic Currents*, 90–102.

[32] Andreas Huyssen, "The Disturbance of Vision in Vienna Modernism," *Modernisms/Modernity* 5/3 (1998): 34.

[33] "Arthur Schnitzler moved 'in the solid Jewish bourgeois circles,' and Sigmund Freud also associated almost entirely with other Jews," Marsha L. Rozenblit writes in *The Jews of Vienna, 1867–1914: Assimilation and Identity* (Albany: State U of New York P, 1983), 8. She suggests that the hostile environment of Vienna prevented complete assimilation, and refers to Schnitzler's observation from *Jugend in Wien* that it was impossible for a Jew in public life to ignore the fact that he was a Jew (9).

[34] See *Arthur Schnitzler. Sein Leben. Sein Werk. Seine Zeit.*, 13.

[35] Egon Schwarz, "Jews and Anti-Semitism in Fin-de-Siècle Vienna," in *Insiders and Outsiders*, eds. Lorenz and Weinberger, 61.

[36] Körner, 13.

[37] In *Jugend in Wien* Schnitzler confesses that his "Mißtrauen in Liebesdingen war universell. Treue zwischen zwei Liebes-oder gar Eheleuten vermochte ich bestenfalls als einen glücklichen Zufall aufzufassen, von dem ich freilich immer gerne annahm, daß er sich gerade mir auch unter den unwahrscheinlichsten Umständen als günstig erweisen würde" (295).

[38] Claudia Benthien, "Masken der Verführung — Intimität und Anonymität in Schnitzlers *Reigen*," *Germanic Review* 72/2 (1997), 132. Benthien notes that through his use of formulaic phrases, Schnitzler unmasks the discourse of love as a discourse of love-making (132).

[39] Daniel Boyarin, *Unheroic Conduct. The Rise of Heterosexuality and the Invention of the Jewish Man* (Berkeley: U of California P, 1997). Boyarin cautions not to mistake these patterns for a "kinder, gentler" patriarchy (157) and underscores that "male domination was firmly in place" (160).

[40] Hans Weigel, ed., *Olga Waissnix. Liebe, die starb vor der Zeit. Ein Briefwechsel* (Vienna: Fritz Molden, 1970), 16–17.

[41] *Anatol*, 16–17. For example, in the scene "Weihnachtseinkäufe" (Christmas Shopping) Gabriele, a "respectable" married woman, expresses her surprise at the notion that Anatol is buying Christmas presents. He does so for a Gentile "sweet girl" ("süßes Mädl") of the lower classes who is accessible to him (*Anatol*, 43).

[42] Hermand, 44.

[43] *Leutnant Gustl*, 333.

[44] *Leutnant Gustl*, 326.

[45] *Fräulein Else*, 333.

[46] Despite indisputable inequities the Austro-Hungarian military was the place where differences of language, education, and ethnicity were curbed in the name of imperial unity. On Schnitzler, who enlisted for a year in the military medical corps in Vienna (jokingly referred to as "Mosesdragoner," dragoons of Moses) — during 1882–

1883, military life had no such profound effect. He considered the uniform something like a costume that provided him with a new identity after he had exhausted the possibilities of his earlier artistic wardrobe (*Jugend in Wien*, 137–38).

[47] *Anatol*, 32, "Die Frage an das Schicksal."

[48] *Anatol*, 44, "Weihnachtseinkäufe."

[49] Weinzierl, 200.

[50] Luprecht, 142–44.

[51] *Anatols Größenwahn* in DW I, 105–124.

Schnitzler's Turn to Prose Fiction: The Depiction of Consciousness in Selected Narratives

Felix Tweraser

Taking into account the whole arc of Arthur Schnitzler's literary career, one notes an increasing emphasis on epic forms, to some degree at the expense of dramatic forms. Whereas his early literary success was often tied to performance in the leading theaters (particularly the Burgtheater in Vienna) and fruitful personal relationships with prominent directors and actors (Otto Brahm, Joseph Kainz, and Adele Sandrock, for example), in the last two decades of his life, around 1905, Schnitzler increasingly turned to narrative. Consistent with this notion is Schnitzler's assessment committed to his diary on October 1, 1911, at the height of his literary fame: "Als Erzähler behaupte ich mich besser wie als Dramatiker."[1] A key to understanding this turn to narrative production is the author's conception of the personality. The narrative medium in many ways best approximated his interest in individual psychology and the linguistic aspects of identity formation.

Schnitzler's prose works encompass the shortest of short stories, novellas of varying lengths, and two novels, *Der Weg ins Freie* (1908) and *Therese: Chronik eines Frauenlebens* (1928); he was working on a third, "Theaterroman," when he died. This work has never been published. The vast majority of his narratives was published by S. Fischer, one of the leading houses promoting modernism, beginning with the story *Sterben* (1895).[2] Within Schnitzler's short stories, novellas, and novels, some particular techniques stick out: the diary, letter, and chronicle; and there are many first-person and third-person accounts. The novellas *Leutnant Gustl* (1900) and *Fräulein Else* (1924) represent two of the most successful examples of interior monologue in the German canon. Perhaps surprisingly, given the strong critical interest in his works, there have been few attempts in the secondary literature to come to terms with Schnitzler's prose in a synthetic or comprehensive way. By far the most successful comprehensive accounts of Schnitzler's narratives come from the ranks of

Austrian and German specialists (in spite of a substantial academic infra-structure in the United States promoting Schnitzler studies).[3]

Schnitzler's turn to narrative is characterized by increased attention to nuance in the depiction of the individual psyche and a greater precision of expression. The topics that Schnitzler develops in his narratives, including fealty to the military honor code, marital relationships, and the doctor-patient relationship, remain relatively constant, but changes in the per-spective used to describe the workings of the mind tend to become more sophisticated; this figural perspective becomes the prism through which social reality is refracted. It is in the inherent tension between such a fig-ural narrative perspective — with its attendant depiction of self-stylization and ego survival — and the broader political and social reality depicted in the texts that Schnitzler's most compelling work lies.[4] While the gallery of characters in Schnitzler's prose work also remains constant over time — upper-middle-class professionals, army officers, and artists — so do the general themes, including crises of interpersonal relationships, role-playing, and professional ethics. The development of Schnitzler's formal narrative technique reflects an increased precision in the description of complex influences on the development of consciousness.

Schnitzler's path to becoming a narrative stylist was circuitous. Dur-ing the period between taking his medical degree in Vienna in 1885 and his father's death in 1893 — also the year of his artistic breakthrough, the production of *Liebelei* (1896) at the *Burgtheater* — Schnitzler was torn between the career that familial expectation dictated, medicine, and his own growing inclination to use his medical knowledge to inform his artistic pursuits. Schnitzler displayed ambivalence about both directions, and his diaries from this period, as well as his autobiography *Jugend in Wien* (1968), attest to this identity crisis.[5]

Schnitzler's father attempted to appease his son's belletristic inclina-tions by allowing him to work as a medical journalist: his first published works appeared in his father's journal, the *Internationale Klinische Rundschau*, for which he wrote essays on developments in the medical arts and more generally on Austrian society; these writings appealed to the educated reader but were far from original. Nevertheless, Schnitzler did read and review the works of many of the leading thinkers in modern psychiatry, including Theodor Meynert (1833–1892) and Richard von Krafft-Ebing (1840–1902), and particularly the latter's insights into the nature and care of mental illness increasingly informed Schnitzler's nar-rative characterizations.

Like many authors of his time, Schnitzler published his narrative works in various periodicals before they appeared in book editions. Many of his works were first serialized in the organs of political liberalism such as the *Neue deutsche Rundschau, An der schönen blauen Donau, Die Zeit,* and perhaps most importantly for reaching a wide audience, *Die Neue Freie Presse.* In the 1890s, Schnitzler enjoyed success as a dramatist but did not really break through as a prose stylist until the publication of *Leutnant Gustl* in 1900 in the *Neue Freie Presse,* followed shortly thereafter by its publication in book form. Over the course of his career, Schnitzler's narrative production took on greater financial importance, particularly after his dramatic star waned in the 1920s.

The themes that inhabited Schnitzler's prose works include fealty to the military honor code and other outmoded systems of social and political organization that inhibited the democratization of Austrian society; the obstacles for women in emancipating themselves from this social order; and the transitory nature of human relationships. Most of these concerns come together in *Der Weg ins Freie* and *Therese,* the narrative protagonists of which do not transcend the limitations of their point of view; yet it is the paradox of this limited perspective that allows Schnitzler to present a broad indictment of the society that holds Georg to a less exacting standard, because he so embodies the dominant culture, while Therese is marginalized at every turn. While it is true that Schnitzler set most of his narratives in turn-of-the-century Vienna, it is also true that many representative works are set in the period of European Enlightenment, such as *Casanovas Heimfahrt* (1918) and *Die Frau des Richters* (1925).[6] Such a turn to more historical settings coincided with a turn to more overtly political themes — if well disguised — that may be read as commentary on democratic identity formation in Austrian society.

Three works in particular are representative of different phases of Schnitzler's career as prose stylist. The early phase of technical experimentation culminates in *Leutnant Gustl,* with its employment of the interior monologue, in which the protagonist's thoughts and experiences are rendered in a stream of consciousness; *Casanovas Heimfahrt* is typical of a turn to specifically intergenerational themes brought into focus by Schnitzler's reaction to the First World War; and *Spiel im Morgengrauen* (1927) was received in its time as representative of Schnitzler's increasing anachronism, a putative inability to come to terms with contemporary Austria by a flight into the Habsburg world. The close reading of these works suggests that they really have more in common than might first meet the eye: all relentlessly explore the formation of human personality, its indebtedness to received wisdom, its fealty to acquisitive imperatives, and its propensity for denial in the face of, respectively, professional embarrassment, aging, and lost honor.[7]

A crucial concept that informed Schnitzler's prose characterizations was the *Mittelbewusstsein* (mid-level of consciousness), a term that Schnitzler developed with varying degrees of theoretical precision in his own responses to Freudian psychoanalysis. While not denying the existence of the unconscious, Schnitzler stresses the importance of the *Mittelbewusstsein* as an area of consciousness where the individual stores the institutional mechanisms that dictate behavior, but which also contains repressed memories.[8] Of primary importance is that this area of the psyche is accessible through introspection, but also subtly influences conscious decision-making. In other words, it is the part of the individual personality subject to denial and self-deception, where self-image is stored and self-stylization occurs, and where the key to responsible, autonomous action lies. Schnitzler did not think that Freudian psychoanalysis, at least as he understood it, accounted for this middle range of the psyche:

> Das Mittelbewusstsein wird überhaupt im Ganzen zu wenig beachtet. Es ist das ungeheuerste Gebiet des Seelen-und Geisteslebens; von da aus steigen die Elemente ununterbrochen ins Bewußte auf oder sinken ins Unbewußte hinab. Das Mittelbewusstsein steht ununterbrochen zur Verfügung. Auf seine Fülle, seine Reaktionsfähigkeit kommt es vor allem an.[9]

Schnitzler's notion of this region of the psyche is significant to an understanding of the way social criticism is generated in his works. As the principal figures experience psychic crisis, their recourse is most often to an unacknowledged allegiance to institutionally conditioned modes of behavior, such as the military honor code or the morality of patriarchy; such allegiance is present in the forms of speech used to describe the individual's experience of social relations.[10]

Schnitzler's formal approach to narrative composition complements the social criticism that his works manifest thematically. He achieves this goal by employing strategies that render the workings of the individual's conscious mind transparent; he shows the assumptions, rationalizations, and denial that constitute the personality.[11] Schnitzler simultaneously evokes the protagonist's inability to contextualize experience within a broader framework of institutional or professional activity. He remains notably disciplined in this compositional technique: the narrators possess intimate knowledge of the inner workings of only one character's mind, while peripheral characters' inner lives can only be deduced by the reader in the interpretation of direct quotations, gestures, or other outward physical manifestations.[12] Thus a consistent feature of Schnitzler's narratives is the resistance to global pronouncements that might go beyond those generated by the figural narrative perspective, even in third-person works.[13]

In many of Schnitzler's narratives, one finds treatments of the often nebulous boundary between domestic and public relationships; such relationships are characterized by power and exploitation in both the domestic and public spheres, and while the characters tend to draw an arbitrary line between these spheres, Schnitzler shows that any attempt to separate them is illusory.[14] The fact that he set most of these narratives in the age of the monarchy does not mean that they nostalgically depict this era, quite the contrary: the monarchy had functioned so smoothly in part because of the subservient coterie of officials that executed its policies and permeated all aspects of daily life. It was in its interest to perpetuate the division between private and public life, allowing the oppressed individual at least the fiction that he retained autonomy in the private sphere.

For Schnitzler, the fracture of the ego and the consequential inability of the individual to engage in socially responsible activity are functions of a fundamental imbalance in the *Mittelbewusstsein,* for it is here that the particular items of social convention and normative language are processed. The recourse to the only dimly reflected behavioral and linguistic clichés of such convention is easy when there is no acknowledgment of the implications of one's actions. While insight into the operation of these mechanisms is possible, it may be achieved only by the recognition of these competing influences and their harmonizing with actual experience. One prominent thread in the secondary literature on Schnitzler is his diagnosis of a so-called impressionist personality, one that is carried from moment to moment without any insight into its indebtedness to external influences.[15] Schnitzler achieves this diagnosis through a narrative distance from the principal characters, whereby their false consciousness is exposed to the reader without them gaining any insight into its mechanisms. Horst Thomé has aptly captured the nature of this narrative strategy: the principal characters do not comprehend the mechanisms of their crises, so they ascribe their catastrophic experiences to the whims of fate and thereby absolve themselves of responsibility. The narrative presence, on the other hand, implies, in the sense of an ethic of personal responsibility in concrete situations, that they are capable of recognition of their crises' and appropriate action, without postulating materially generalized conclusions.[16] To take Thomé's point a step further, the point of social criticism is reached in Schnitzler's works when individuals experience psychic crisis. The social conventions and mediated experience prove morally bankrupt for the individual, yet the society is only seen through the figural perspective of those who cannot transcend its mores. Since the social criticism is generated in this way, the narrative voice necessarily retreats to the background, so there are no objective pronouncements (that is, stated, but not attributed to a particular figure) about social reality. It is the task of the *reader* to apply the analogy by inference to the contemporary situation.

Schnitzler was a consistent critic, for instance, of the influence that martial values had on many aspects of social relations in Austria. Such criticism emerges most forcefully at the micro-level of individual pathology, since that is where received institutional language and traditions are processed. It is the individual who receives and transports martial values; the degree to which such fealty to received wisdom becomes the chosen model to understand the world is directly proportional to the strength of the institutional framework that allows it to thrive. In Schnitzler's narratives the military honor code, and by extension the compulsion to duel, plays a prominent role in the self-understanding of the primary characters. One of Schnitzler's earliest treatments of Imperial officers, *Leutnant Gustl,* exposed the hypocrisy of a representative member of the officers' corps.[17] Told entirely in interior monologue and compressed to action within an eight-hour period, the novella provides a picture of the title character's thought processes in casual moments and times of crisis, not as easily distinguishable as might be assumed. After he attends an oratorio, where he has not paid attention to the contents of the music but has taken inventory of others in attendance, Gustl's honor is compromised by a baker, who grabs Gustl's sword and calls him a "dummer Bub"; since the baker is not *satisfaktionsfähig,* or worthy of challenging to a duel, the honor code dictates that Gustl either resign his commission or take his own life to restore his honor (there is also a parallel plot-line of an unrelated duel in which Gustl is involved). Gustl, faced with the ultimate questions of life, death, and honor, reveals himself as an individual incapable of transcending the boundaries of his conventional existence. Instead, because he has not developed any independent critical judgment and accepts the dictates of the honor code at face value, his final moments are not given to honest introspection but to a continuation of his devotion to the code by way of uncritically adopted platitudes. Characteristically, he is more concerned with how he will appear in others' memories than with actually drawing anyone into his confidence or sharing his experience. When the baker dies before the incident becomes public knowledge, Gustl may be considered off the hook in everyone else's eyes, but not according to the terms of the very honor code that he selectively invokes. That he has not learned anything from the process is clear when he enthusiastically reaffirms his desire to duel at the end of the novella.

When the novella was published on December 25, 1900 in the *Neue Freie Presse*, there was an immediate and negative reaction within military circles. At that time Schnitzler was a reserve officer in the Imperial army, so his superiors argued that his publications were within the army's jurisdiction and thus subject to its code of honor. Schnitzler disputed the notion that his artistic works had any bearing on the military itself or on his ability to discharge his duties as an officer. When the military tribunal handed down its decision to strip Schnitzler of his officer's commission, they gave two reasons: first, that the contents of the novella constituted an insult to the honor of the army; and second, that by not responding to a particularly libelous article in the press with a challenge to duel, Schnitzler had brought dishonor upon himself and the uniform.[18]

The element of the novella that likely gave the most offense to military authorities was the way Gustl opportunistically uses the honor code to cover up his social resentment, anti-Semitism, and personal weakness. Thus, when Gustl scans the crowd at the oratorio, his thoughts turn to a Jewish reserve officer (perhaps an identification figure for Schnitzler himself): "Muß übrigens ein Jud' sein! Freilich in einer Bank ist er, und der schwarze Schnurrbart . . . Reserveleutnant soll er auch sein! Na, in mein Regiment sollt' er nicht zur Waffenübung kommen! Überhaupt, daß sie noch immer so viel Juden zu Offizieren machen — da pfeif' ich auf'n ganzen Antisemitismus!"[19] Gustl's thought process shows that he is not averse to employing stereotypes in his assessment of others. This trait prevents him from acknowledging his own financial dependence and the nature of economic relations in the society, which tolerated the new reserve officer corps as recognition of the rise of a powerful middle class; the potential of common ground among officers based on shared economic status runs aground on the facile stereotype that Gustl applies to another individual.

Gustl's resentment broadens to one against all civilians, whom he accuses of not appreciating the strictures of living by the honor code. In this way Gustl rationalizes away his self-pity and economic impotence: "Ganz wehrlos sind wir gegen die Zivilisten. Da meinen die Leut', wir sind besser dran, weil wir einen Säbel haben . . . und wenn schon einmal einer von der Waffe Gebrauch macht, geht's über uns her, als wenn wir alle die geborenen Mörder wären."[20] Yet Gustl's adherence to the honor code is selective at best: at the end of the novella, he reaffirms his desire to duel with a civilian, thus upholding one of the traditions of the code; but he does not kill himself after the baker's affront simply because no one else witnessed their exchange, which constitutes a violation of the spirit of the code.

A significant aspect of *Leutnant Gustl* is the collision between the honor code and materialism. To Gustl, the military provides escape from a confrontation with his own grim financial reality.[21] The officers' inability to come fully to terms with their changed economic status leaves them extremely vulnerable to figures who act not out of prejudice but with shrewd honesty (the ends notwithstanding). In Schnitzler's ethical system, honesty in word, deed, thought, and action was better suited to survival in a changing world than deference to the conventions of an institution: "Die reinigende Kraft der Wahrheit ist so groß, daß schon das Streben nach ihr ringsum eine bessere Luft verbreitet; die zerstörende Macht der Lüge ist so furchtbar, daß schon die Neigung zu ihr die Atmosphäre verdunkelt."[22] The key to ultimately changing such a state of affairs would be to unmask the social institutions that sanction such lies.

Schnitzler's prose works often emphasize the triumph of reactionary forces over liberating or emancipatory potential. By focusing on crucial moments in the fate of individuals, he gives the reader a glimpse of the micro-tragedies of history, that is, points in time where those who transcend social and political expectation pay the price for their vision. It is characteristic of these works that the reader is not given an unequivocal model of liberation but is asked to reflect on how and why authority, repression, and reaction perpetuate themselves in a given context. It is a complex matrix of linguistic, psychological, and social factors that denies or co-opts emancipatory potential. While the protagonists remain unaware of their indebtedness to such factors, Schnitzler is at pains to show the reader the specific mechanisms that allow, perhaps even encourage, the individual to forfeit moral responsibility.

Casanovas Heimfahrt is particularly relevant in this regard, for it describes the events immediately preceding Casanova's return to his native Venice, from which he had been banished twenty-five years before by the city authorities — not because of his sexual escapades, but because of his political activities.[23] The action begins when Casanova, occupied simultaneously by his missives to Venice and a treatise against Voltaire, encounters Olivo, an acquaintance from fifteen years before, whom Casanova had helped to marry Amalia. Olivo is now a wealthy landowner, whose bourgeois sensibilities are well-reflected in his fertile soil and the three daughters he has raised with Amalia. Casanova consents to spend a few days on Olivo's estate, where he meets the people who come to play cards and encounters Olivo's niece Marcolina and her lover, a soldier named Lorenzi. Casanova's desire for Marcolina grows, especially when she politely but firmly declines his advances and proves to be his superior in philosophical argument. Meanwhile, Casanova receives word from his benefactor on the Venetian city council, Bragadino, that his return will only be possible if he consents to spy on certain freethinking citizens that the council considers politically dangerous. Consumed by ambivalence and cynicism, Casanova proceeds to win a great deal of money at cards, use his winnings to extort the debtor Lorenzi in order to sleep with Marcolina, kill Lorenzi in a subsequent duel, and flee the scene to his homecoming in Venice, as he has long since overcome the initial indignation over the terms of his return to do the bidding of the city authorities.

The aging hero thus betrays himself and those who would continue his libertarian project; captured by a nostalgic longing to return to his native city — "Die Stadt seiner Jugend stieg vor ihm auf, umflossen von allem Zauber der Erinnerung, und das Herz schwoll ihm in einer Sehnsucht, so qualvoll und über alles Maß, wie er sich noch nie empfunden zu haben glaubte"[24] — Casanova is willing to destroy the lives (and revolutionary potential) of the representatives of a younger generation and becomes a spy in the service of the same state authority that had exiled him from Venice. His seduction of Marcolina and killing of Lorenzi are not only the last gasps of the hero; they function as metaphors for the way in which the representatives of the established order (Casanova as the ironic instrument of its will) destroy or co-opt the aspirations of those who wish to reform it.

This destruction is exemplified by the way Casanova approaches the learned (in mathematics) and ambitious Marcolina: in their philosophical argument, he takes an antiquated position; and when his direct attempts to seduce her fail, he must resort to deception in the manner of Don Juan. When Marcolina expresses political opinions, particularly when she defends Voltaire, Casanova is quick to point out the potential danger of her views:

> So rettete er [Casanova] sich in die allgemein gehaltene Betrachtung, daß Ansichten, wie Marcolina sie eben ausgesprochen, nicht nur die Ordnung im Bereich der Kirche, sondern daß sie auch die Grundlagen des Staates in hohem Grade zu gefährden geeignet seien, und sprang von hier aus gewandt auf das Gebiet der Politik über.[25]

Marcolina, for her part, is not impressed by such argument, and proceeds to offer an acute analysis of the way authoritarianism perpetuates itself within a society:

> [A]us ihren [Marcolina] Bemerkungen ging unwidersprechlich für ihn hervor, daß die weder vor den Fürsten dieser Erde, noch von den Staatsgebilden als solchen sonderliche Achtung hegte und der Über-zeugung war, daß die Welt im Kleinen wie im Großen von Eigennutz und Herrschsucht nicht so sehr regiert, als vielmehr in Verwirrung ge-bracht werde.[26]

Casanova is not able to draw the inference from what Marcolina says and apply it to his own situation, in which his return to Venice is contingent upon betraying erstwhile kindred spirits. Instead, he is prone to a certain sentimentality in the manner in which he glories in his own past political exploits while at the same time upholding the interests of a reactionary regime. Thus, his thoughts upon hearing Marcolina's condemnation of absolute rule:

> [U]nd nicht ohne Wehmut erinnerte er sich, daß sein eigner Geist in vergangenen Tagen, die schöner waren als die gegenwärtigen, mit einer bewußten und etwas selbstzufriedenen Kühnheit die gleichen Wege gegangen war, die er nun Marcolina beschreiten sah, ohne daß diese sich ihrer Kühnheit überhaupt bewußt zu werden schien.[27]

In spite of such apparently shared views, Casanova continues to objectify Marcolina — her ability to think clearly and without sentimentality becomes the object of Casanova's increasingly corrosive cynicism, ultimately culminating in his betrayal of her trust.

Similarly, Casanova murders Lorenzi, the one character who has the potential to put Casanova's own revolutionary rhetoric into practice. Casanova recognizes the younger man as his doppelgänger, but this awareness does not prevent him from removing Lorenzi from the scene. Schnitzler subtly emphasizes the degree to which sentimental attachment to things past, things never achieved, and images of one's self allows the individual to forfeit moral responsibility, even to the extent of abandoning political positions that served to define the self in a different context.[28] Schnitzler thus intimates that authoritarian institutional structures (regardless of their purported ideals) only survive because of the individual subjects' abandonment of moral responsibility. Rather than focus on the tyranny of state authority as personified in the evil of those at the top of the social and political pyramid (Bragadino, for instance, could hardly be a less imposing figure), Schnitzler emphasizes the responsibility of each citizen, no matter what his or her position, to build a democratic order from the ground up.[29]

Casanova adopts the ideology of his Venetian patrons through his actions, while the rhetoric he employs to survive from situation to situation becomes increasingly meaningless. The individual's adoption of ideology does not necessarily correspond to the language he uses, but is necessarily betrayed in his relationship to power. To Schnitzler, the clearer one perceived the political reality in each social situation, the less prone one was to act out a socially conditioned, thereby ideological, role. The act of role-playing itself connotes a forfeiture of social utility and revolutionary potential, because it adapts to a given state of affairs rather than changing it.

Schnitzler's social criticism in *Casanovas Heimfahrt* takes on a particularly generational dimension. The hero's last acts of complicity with the Venetian state authority are only separated by degree from his rationalizations of rape and murder, in which he violates the potential and trust of a younger generation as well as the ideals by which he had previously defined himself. The institutional dimension of Schnitzler's analysis emerges in Casanova's tendencies to self-stylization, role-playing, and self-deception, all of which obscure his ability to recognize the nature of power in the society; the overwhelming nostalgic longing to return to an idealized home becomes the justification for abandoning his ideals and serving reactionary forces:

> [A]ber klüger war er noch immer als alle! Und wenn er nur einmal in Venedig war, so konnte er dort treiben und lassen, was ihm beliebte; es kam nur darauf an, endlich dort zu sein! Dann war es vielleicht gar nicht nötig, irgendwen umzubringen.[30]

Thus, Casanova is revealed to be a key cog in the maintenance of institutional continuity; by deserting his libertarian ethos he forfeits his ability and responsibility to change the social order.

In *Casanovas Heimfahrt* Schnitzler also employs the topos of *Heimat* to telling effect. When Casanova returns to Venice, the image of his homeland that has sustained him reveals itself to be a considerably less enchanting reality; "Er fand das Haus verfallener, oder mindestens vernachlässigter, als er es im Gedächtnis bewahrt hatte."[31] The cynicism of Bragadino and the other Venetian overlords is measured by the extent to which they use such sentimental appeals to lure Casanova back into their service — "Vor allem aber bedenken Sie, daß die Erfüllung Ihres sehnlichsten Wunsches — Ihre Rückkehr in die Vaterstadt — wenn Sie den gnädigen Vorschlag des Hohen Rats ablehnen sollten, auf lange, ja wie ich fürchte, auf unabsehbare Frist hinausgeschoben wäre"[32] — and the extent to which he is susceptible to such tactics. The overlords take advantage of Casanova's sentimental attachment to Venice in hiring him to do their bidding. Casanova is far from an unwilling participant in this transaction; Venice appears in his dreams as a kind of mythical city, and his actions are based on this dream-image.[33] This ultimately hollow goal of returning to an idealized homeland is invoked by Casanova to justify all manner of role-playing, lies, and the psychic abandonment of others. At various points in the novella, Casanova envisions himself as a figure of revolution alongside Marcolina and Lorenzi, themselves embodiments of youthful emancipation from social roles — "Denn auch sie [Marcolina] ist Philosophin und daher so frei von Vorurteilen wie wir beide [Casanova and Lorenzi]."[34] Yet Casanova easily abandons any feelings of solidarity with this younger generation by projecting his own psychic emptiness and cynicism onto them; it is precisely this willful abandonment of ideals that allows him to justify his violation of their potential. Following his night with Marcolina, Casanova begins to acknowledge the depths to which he has sunk:

> Etwas andres verhieß vielleicht eher Genugtuung: Marcolina mit an-spielungsreicher, mit höhnisch-lüsterner Rede zu erniedrigen: — doch auch dieser tückische Einfall schwand dahin vor einem Blick, dessen entsetzensvoller Ausdruck sich allmählich in eine unendliche Traurig-keit gewandelt hatte, als wäre es nicht nur Marcolinens Weiblichkeit, die Casanova geschändet — nein, als hätte in dieser Nacht List gegen Vertrauen, Lust gegen Liebe, Alter gegen Jugend sich namenlos und unsühnbar vergangen.[35]

This momentary recognition of his own depravity does not translate into forgiveness or redemption; rather, the hero systematically eliminates those who might expose him and returns to Venice to serve the state.

Schnitzler depicts once again the triumph of reaction over reform. The institutional basis of reaction is maintained not so much by the holders of power as by a cynical citizenry that resigns itself to the order of things. By adopting an authoritarian ideology in practice, such citizens (Casanova is the prime example) give the lie to their own pronounce-ments of liberation from an unacceptable state of affairs. It is instructive that the language of state authority — and here one might see a direct correlation to the reception of the First World War in Austria, the time in which the novella was finished and published — increasingly becomes a metalanguage invoking myth to supplant historical or contemporary reality. The general tendency to abstraction among individuals from the concrete consequences of authoritarian rule or war becomes, almost stealthily in Casanova's case, the actual maintenance of the old order by its citizens. Thus, when he receives the letter offering him the post in Venice, indignation almost seamlessly blends into resignation, rationali-zation, and ultimate cooperation with the state:

> Und mit fliegender Hand entwarf er einen Brief an den alten Dumm-kopf Bragadino, einen Brief voll geheuchelter Demut und verlogenen Entzückens: er nehme die Gnade des Hohen Rats mit freudiger Dank-barkeit an und erwarte den Wechsel mit wendender Post, um sich sei-nen Gönnern, vor allem seinem hochverehrten väterlichen Freunde Bragadino sobald als möglich zu Füßen legen zu dürfen.[36]

Casanova's ultimate fulfillment of such promises invalidates his smug indifference to the broader implications of his behavior. A more accurate gauge of Casanova's moral state is rendered right after he writes the letter: he rapes one of Olivo's daughters.

Casanova's lack of accountability and abandonment of ideals are rendered most aptly in the narrative techniques employed by Schnitzler. The narrative is generated by Casanova's *Mittelbewusstsein,* the storehouse of denial, self-stylization, and rationalization that he invokes when justifying his own cruelty. Casanova's self-loathing emerges most clearly in his objectification of women. The speed with which he changes partners and the way in which he flaunts his reputation in order to accomplish his goals are testament to this lack of empathy and respect for others. His libertarian project of earlier years, in which political emancipation blended seamlessly with sexual liberation, has now become a caricature. It is in this context that his attempted conquest of Marcolina takes place. In Marcolina, Casanova is confronted with a new type of woman who is independently learned and sexually opportunistic; she proves his superior on both counts by defending Voltaire and the Enlightenment against Casanova's antiquated position in a philosophical argument and by freely choosing a liaison with Lorenzi without intention of marriage. Casanova is only able to seduce Marcolina by means of deception; after winning money from Lorenzi in a card game, he extorts Lorenzi's cloak from him in order to appear as the younger man to Marcolina. Thus, Casanova can only reach his goal by objectifying himself; in the process he inflicts grievous psychic damage upon Marcolina and reinforces his rampant cynicism with respect to social renewal. Even more egregious is Casanova's rape of the innocent Teresina under her father's own roof. Casanova's descent from spontaneous seducer to cynical schemer has its corollary in the assessment of his own role in public affairs.

Schnitzler is careful to suggest the connection between libidinous conquest in the private sphere and the suppression of democratic impulses in the public sphere. Casanova acts out the rage, self-loathing, and resentment that accompany his diminishing powers in the public arena by undermining the freethinking elements in the society. This sort of backlash upholds authoritarian rulers, since it allows them to impose their political will on the society by means of surrogates and deception rather than the overt use of power by physical means. Thus, continuity in state institutions is supported above all by ideology, in this case one of authoritarianism that Casanova never explicitly recognizes even as he enacts it in his private relationships and functions as its instrument in public life.

The chief example of his public persona is occasioned by his treatise against Voltaire, which occupies him through most of the novella. In this venture, as with others, his intentions are cynical; he hopes that by refuting the famous religious skeptic's argument he will curry favor with the Venetian city council, since this refutation would prove once and for all that he had abandoned the libertarian ideas that prompted his original imprisonment in Venice. He also uses the treatise as a means to confront Marcolina in their philosophical debate (he believes that such a demonstration of his learning is the only way to seduce her), but she proves him to be inadequate to the task. In both cases, Casanova uses a public forum to advance purely private and personal interests. In so doing he acts without responsibility or accountability, the two traits that Schnitzler emphasizes as being essential to the establishment of a democratic political order. This aspect of Schnitzler's characterization of Casanova implicitly criticizes the use and abuse of public forums during the First World War. As Schnitzler saw it, many private figures, including more than a few authors, lent the prestige of their names to furthering the war effort, thereby overwhelming the voices of dissent or, the most appropriate response in his opinion, silence. In fact, the enactment of filicide in the novella works quite well as a commentary on the war, in which the holders of power sacrificed a younger generation in the public interest. In this sense, Casanova functions as a cipher for the hypocrisy inherent in the dilution of the integrity of the public and private spheres. His opportunism, cynicism, and denial all influence his relationships with others, so each is undermined by lies and deception.

In the novella Casanova plays many roles, evident in the frequent changes of costume, the disguise to betray Marcolina, and the versions of himself that he disseminates in accounts of his own exploits in various European courts. Such role-playing is subtly influenced by social expectation, political intrigue, and class difference; what Schnitzler's narrative technique underscores is the degree to which such roles come to dominate the individual personality at the expense of a moral core and any accompanying impulses toward social utility, expansion of political opportunity, and class or gender equity. The individual, in the case of Casanova, assumes each role with but dim awareness of the alienation from himself and from others that this act entails. The one instance in which Casanova dispenses with such pretense, his naked duel with Lorenzi, represents the most basic struggle for survival; yet as Casanova admits, he has transgressed not just in the act of killing another so like what he used to be, but in extinguishing the ideals that he once believed himself to embody.

The abandonment of responsibility to create a more just social order emerges for Schnitzler most clearly in individual transgression against one's own better judgment. Even in isolation, such individual acts of complicity with state authority can have far-reaching deleterious effects on the society — witness Casanova's destruction of others in the interest of realizing a nostalgic dream. In his writings on politics and ethics Schnitzler stressed that the creation of a just society would only occur when its individual members adopted an ethic of personal responsibility: "Es gibt nur drei absolute Tugenden: Sachlichkeit, Mut, und Verant-wortungsgefühl; diese drei schließen nicht nur alle anderen gewisserma-ßen in sich ein, sondern ihr Dasein paralysiert sogar manche Untugenden und Schwächen, die gleichzeitig in derselben Seele vorhanden sein mö-gen."[37] It is indeed rare in Schnitzler's narrative production to find pri-mary characters that possess any of these "absolute virtues" in great measure. Gustl, Casanova, and Willi Kasda, the protagonist of *Spiel im Morgengrauen,* do not develop these virtues independently, yet all are beholden to codes of conduct that, at least on the surface, operate to uphold them in social relations.

Spiel im Morgengrauen represents a particularly engaging treatment of the relevance of the honor code and individual responsibility.[38] The protagonist, the imperial and royal Austrian Lieutenant Willi Kasda, is unable to confront the manifestations of his economically deteriorating status, including increasing financial dependence and endangered pres-tige, because the honor code to which he subscribes prevents him from comprehending this changing reality. Kasda's sporadic moments of insight into the causes of these changes are quickly trumped by paranoia, jealousy, self-pity, and, ultimately, aggression toward himself and those around him. The origins of these emotions lie in the disconnectedness between the representation of reality which he has adopted, that is, the honor code, and the true relationships of financial and sexual depend-ence in his society. Several characters in the novella, drawn as Kasda's antagonists, have in common their ability to recognize such social change and to act accordingly.

The plot of *Spiel im Morgengrauen* may be quickly summarized. On the first day, which corresponds to the first half of the novella, Kasda is awakened early in the morning to receive a former colleague, Otto Bogner, who was forced to resign his commission because of gambling debts. Bogner asks Kasda for a loan of 960 guilders, the amount he has embezzled from his office to help take care of his family. Kasda, though annoyed, agrees to help him, but since his means are limited, he can only offer to wager his remaining cash, 130 guilders, in a game of chance that he will join later that day. After spending the afternoon in the company of a family with whom he is casually acquainted, Kasda proceeds to the restaurant where he regularly gambles. The group that he plays with is a mixture of civilians and fellow officers, but the dominant personality is one Consul Schnabel, who, more frequently than not, provides the bank for the others, who tend to keep their wagers small. Kasda is drawn casually but inexorably into the action, wins enough to pay Bogner, and leaves the table to return to his acquaintances. Coincidentally, they are not home, so he returns to the game; this time he wins not only enough to pay Bogner but also enough for himself to buy a new uniform and accessories. When he gets up to leave, he dallies just long enough to miss the last train back to Vienna, so he returns to the table. This time, after initial success that puts him more than 4000 guilders ahead, he begins to lose. The game becomes a personal duel between Kasda and Consul Schnabel; as Kasda continues to lose, the consul offers him money so that he can continue playing. At the end of this disastrous sequence, Kasda owes Schnabel 11,000 guilders, between three and four years' salary. Kasda returns to Vienna in the consul's private coach, and, failing to convince him to relax the terms of repayment, realizes that he must raise the amount he owes within thirty-six hours or lose his honor, that is, be declared *satisfaktionsunfähig,* the consequences of which are either resignation from the officers' corps or suicide.

The second day (part) recounts Kasda's attempts to raise the money to pay off his debt to Schnabel. First he goes to his maternal uncle, Robert Wilram, who, until recently, had provided him with a regular allowance. Kasda finds, to his surprise, that his previously well-to-do uncle is not only a newlywed but also financially dependent on his wife, and thus unable to loan Kasda the money. During the course of their conversation, Kasda realizes that the woman Wilram has married is none other than Leopoldine Lebus, a former lover of Kasda's, who at that time was a prostitute. Buoyed by new hope, Kasda finds her at her place of business, a professional office. Although she says that her money is tied up in other investments, she leaves him with a small measure of hope, saying that she will consult with her lawyer and send news to him at his barracks. After whiling away the afternoon in deluxe fashion, spending more money that he does not have, Kasda returns to his barracks. When Leopoldine comes personally to deliver the news, he interprets it as a sign that she will indeed grant him the loan. They have dinner and sleep together. The next morning, as Leopoldine appears ready to go, Kasda finally dispenses with any pretense to military bearing and asks her where the money is. She produces a thousand-guilder note and thanks him for his services of the previous night; this gesture mirrors, with roles reversed, the end of their encounter years before, in which Kasda had left her ten guilders to ease his conscience. She specifically says that this payment has nothing to do with the loan. Kasda interprets her action as his death sentence, sends the thousand guilders to Bogner, and takes his own life.

Schnitzler succeeds in characterizing the conflicting and multiple impulses that prevent Kasda from reaching insight. Instead of proceeding in total denial to revelatory moments, Kasda displays periodic insight that is *not* broadened by experience; the surest proof that insight does not prevail is his ultimate self-destructive act. Schnitzler bases his depiction of Kasda on the multiple layers of the individual personality; the lieutenant pursues his instinctive needs through play and sex, sanctioned by a social code that mediates his experience of these drives and allows him to indulge them.

The story is told primarily from Kasda's point of view, through sequences of narrated monologue and stream of consciousness, and partly from a more omniscient perspective, but the reader is thrust into the thought processes of a mind that is unable to comprehend such manifestations of modernity as advanced market capitalism and emancipated women. The figural perspective generates a confrontation between a military ethos that props up a tired tradition (and, indeed, provides the cover for destructive behavior), and a modernist, materialistic ethic that dispenses with such tradition or manipulates it for its own ends.

Kasda's two principal antagonists, Schnabel and Leopoldine, have more in common than may first meet the eye: both have come to terms with a new social order by recognizing its mores, prejudices, and, especially, the primacy of money, without falling prey to any of them. Both have overcome shady pasts and socially inferior status to assume positions of power and financial independence. Because they are not beholden to a particular group, and by extension, tradition, they are able to master their changing circumstances in a way that is impossible for Kasda. The latter remains a prisoner of the honor code because of his inability to develop criteria of independent judgment; instead, he displays a pattern of self-deception brought about by the uncritical adoption of behavioral norms that are no longer socially relevant.

The martial discourse of the honor code prevents Kasda from acknowledging his antagonists' experience, worthiness as social partners, or interest in his own fate; rather, he projects his own lack of empathy onto them. It is the honor code that provides him with the justification for self-destructive behavior and a willful misapprehension of social reality. His antagonists, meanwhile, embrace an ethic of individual responsibility, which demystifies indebtedness to outmoded traditions; by over-coming the prejudice of others through discipline and self-knowledge, then translating this knowledge into activity, they provide a model for democratic practice.

One key to interpreting the novella is the way Kasda relates to others in his circle, particularly the three central civilians: former Lieutenant-Colonel Bogner, Consul Schnabel, and Leopoldine Lebus. They form, with Kasda, a complex web of sexual and financial dependence; what Kasda represses in his relationship with each is instrumental in his down-fall. All three represent, to varying degrees, successful integration into the modern world, since they have overcome obstacles to attain respect-able positions in Viennese society. Kasda, on the other hand, has a frac-tured relationship to his own social circumstances; although he admits that he does not have the means to sustain his lifestyle, it does not occur to him that his obedience to an outmoded code, which bestows privilege and prestige automatically, actually constitutes his financial and moral poverty. The respect that Schnabel and Leopoldine receive is indicated at the level of the physical gestures and demeanor of those who serve them, but Kasda, in spite of his uniform, only receives respect when he leaves a large sum of money.

The richness of the novella lies in its depiction of various social groups in turn-of-the-century Vienna, the impact of real and perceived status on individual behavior, the thin veneer of civilization that masks primal urges and actions, and finally, the way ritualized modes of experience inform decision-making. Embedded within this constellation is the metaphor of the game, with its qualities of ritualizing coincidence and chaos. The action is told, in varying degrees, from Kasda's perspective, yet it is often difficult to distinguish the voice of the authorial narrator from the descrip-tion of Kasda's thoughts or from the relatively unmediated rendering of the thoughts themselves. As is the case with much of Schnitzler's social and cultural criticism, it is generated from such a figural perspective, that is, from the thoughts and experiences of individuals who are beholden to the language and traditions of social convention, prejudice, and profes-sional institutions, so there is no authorial reflection on the socially con-structed nature of reality. Such a construction of reality is evident in the aggression that Kasda exhibits toward those whom he perceives to be beneath him in social status, and correspondingly represses toward those on whom he is financially dependent or must answer to in the military hierarchy, and is indicative of his psychological distress.

As early as the first scene, Schnitzler introduces a personality that de-rives primary meaning from appropriating external convention. Kasda's interaction with the first two people he encounters is conditioned by where he perceives them in relation to himself in the social hierarchy, so it inhibits any empathic exchange among equals. There is indeed evidence that, for Kasda, adherence to the military honor code is not accompanied by an understanding of its underlying ethical basis. Rather, it provides him with a cover to indulge his aggressive, violent tendencies and his gambling addiction.

Schnitzler ironically shades the first encounter between Kasda and Bogner through the narrative technique of doubling. The reader becomes aware of the similarities between the two characters at the same time that Kasda insists on his own superiority, given his status as an officer. Bogner's actions foreshadow, to a striking degree, what Kasda will go through himself. Bogner, like Kasda, is a compulsive gambler whose actions endanger his status; he appeals (through Kasda) to the latter's uncle, a civilian, for money. Both rationalize their embezzlement and gambling, respectively, by attributing them to the needs and wishes of another, in Bogner's case financing a family and sick child, and in Kasda's, now, the opportunity to help out his former comrade. In the sequence of narrated monologue immediately following their encounter, Kasda does not acknowledge any parallels, instead chastising Bogner for losing all control: "Ein Offizier mußte doch am Ende wissen, bis wohin er gehen dürfte. Er selbst zum Beispiel war vor drei Wochen, als ihn das Unglück beständig verfolgte, einfach vom Tisch aufgestanden . . . Er hatte überhaupt immer gewußt, Versuchungen zu widerstehen."[39] Bogner's fate appears to Kasda in a negative light because it is so close to his own; he is more upset that Bogner accumulated gambling debts, thereby being forced to resign his commission, than he is by the embezzlement committed by a civilian. Kasda's self-satisfied air prevents him from recognizing that Bogner's request has provided him with the perfect rationalization for giving free reign to his own psychotic potential.

There is an additional psychological rift that characterizes Kasda's apprehension of the world: the inability to fully acknowledge that his lifestyle is beyond his means. Thus, though he admits to himself that he is not satisfied with the condition of his uniform and equipment, and fantasizes about mundane necessities when he wins at cards, he never draws the conclusion that his lifestyle is untenable.

Schnitzler establishes this state of mind clearly in the second episode of the novella, at the Kessner family's home in Baden. Kasda has made the most of a casually extended invitation to join the family and has become a regular guest for meals on the weekends. As he approaches their house, he ruminates on the sad state of his material existence:

> Niemals noch war ihm die Enge seiner Verhältnisse so deutlich zum
> Bewußtsein gekommen als heute — an diesem wunderschönen Früh-
> lingstag, da er in einem leider nicht mehr funkelnden Waffenrock, in
> drappen Beinkleidern, die an den Knien ein wenig zu glänzen anfingen,
> und mit einer Kappe, die erheblich niedriger war, als die neueste Offi-
> ziersmode vorschrieb, durch die duftenden Parkanlagen den Weg zu
> dem Landhaus nahm, in dem die Familie Keßner wohnte — wenn es
> nicht gar ihr Besitz war. Zum erstenmal auch geschah es ihm heute,
> daß er die Hoffnung auf eine Einladung zum Mittagessen oder viel-
> mehr den Umstand, daß ihm diese Erwartung eine Hoffnung bedeu-
> tete, als beschämend empfand.[40]

Such admissions show Kasda to be entirely capable of assessing his own
financial situation, yet he willfully chooses to obey the prescribed lifestyle
of the officer instead of reaching a rational decision about becoming part
of civil society.

The narrative is structured so that the reader sees intimations on
Kasda's part that he recognizes the need to find other sources of income
and that his existence as an officer cannot be maintained, since he no
longer receives his uncle's allowance and has already used up the small
inheritance left by his mother. Thus, Kasda idly speculates about the
possibility of a financially advantageous marriage to Fräulein Kessner at
the same time he assumes that he will win the money for Bogner.[41]
Kasda's awareness of his financial status does not translate into concrete
actions to correct it. Rather, he is content to exhibit the outward appearance of a member of the officers' class. His inability to reconcile the real
conditions of his existence with his inflated self-image, derived from the
world of appearance, is the necessary condition for his upcoming crisis. In
fact, when Kasda enumerates all the areas where he has had to cut back
("Kaffeehausbesuch," "Neuanschaffungen," "Zigaretten," "Weiber") it
reads like a catalogue of the perquisites and privileges of the officer class.[42]

The battle between obedience to convention and acknowledgment
of its inability to explain the reality of his situation is fought at the level
of Kasda's *Mittelbewusstsein*. While the honor code provides the pretext
to join the game, it also allows Kasda to rationalize his own gambling
neurosis. Given this juxtaposition, it is not surprising that Kasda keeps
returning to the gambling table, even though the reader knows that he
is at times capable of a dispassionate analysis of his finances. For Kasda,
social expectation and wish fulfillment complement each other to form
a dangerous combination; that this mindset endangers him is clear, but
it is also clear that he is capable of acting responsibly. At this stage, what
appears in his thoughts, as rendered in the text, as a string of coinci-

dences is actually an exercise in wish fulfillment, one that is encouraged by the institution to which he pledges allegiance, and one of whose consequences he is but dimly aware.

Kasda joins the baccarat game at the Café Schöpf just as it is getting started. The gambling party consists of four civilians and four officers: the other officers include Regimental Doctor Tugut, Lieutenant-Colonel Wimmer, and Lieutenant Greising, and the civilians are Consul Schnabel, the actor Elrief (who shares with Schnabel the affections of Fräulein Rihoscheck, a frequent visitor to the games), the theater secretary Weiss, and the lawyer Flegmann. Of these, Greising and Schnabel are characterized at some length: Greising is suffering from venereal disease, but this fact does not stop him from bragging about having seduced a young woman the night before;[43] Schnabel remains somewhat of an enigma to the others, for he is described as a merchant and the representative of the interests of a South American country, but they do not know the details of his life.[44] Schnabel is the focal point of the games; he sets the stakes, decides when the games will be over, and indicates his likes and dislikes by gesture, thus implying that he has the others' attention at all times. The most important thing he brings to the table is money, so the others treat him with appropriate deference, respect, and fear. The narrator notes that the officers, who would under normal circumstances have made fun of Schnabel's loss of Fräulein Rihoscheck to Elrief, instead refrain from such taunting. The only exception is a remark by Greising made on a previous occasion, in which he made generally disparaging remarks about representatives of uncharted countries, to which Schnabel replies "Warum frozzeln Sie mich, Herr Leutnant? Haben Sie sich schon erkundigt, ob ich satisfaktionsfähig bin?"[45] This implicit challenge is met by silence: "Bedenkliche Stille war nach dieser Erwiderung eingetreten . . . und man entschloß sich ohne Verabredung, aber einmütig, nur zu einem vorsichtigeren Benehmen ihm gegenüber."[46]

Within the gambling party, then, the dictates of the honor code are suspended, since Schnabel is the primary source of money, so the power is determined by who is materially strongest, not by any received notion of social status. By all objective measures, then, the other officers, but particularly Kasda, should not sit down at the table with Schnabel. The latter reinforces such a notion when, in a general discussion of gambling between games, he characterizes as fraudulent the act of sitting down to gamble when one knows that it is possible to lose more than one can pay.[47] On the other hand, economic reality dictates that the officers find people with enough money to help them maintain their chosen lifestyle. Seen as a microcosm of social relations, the game itself becomes a ritual of escape for the officers, the consequences of which are most acute in Kasda's case, since he is both the poorest participant and a compulsive gambler.

The last chance for Kasda to avert disaster is lost when he misses his train back to Vienna. Although Schnabel has offered him the use of his carriage to take him to the station, Kasda dallies too long at the Kessners' table (that they show up there is but one of many coincidences that move the plot). As he approaches their table, the way that status informs his self-definition becomes apparent: "Ein fescher, junger Offizier, in behaglichen Umständen . . . und in diesem Augenblick ohne Konkurrenten, angenehm montiert."[48] This seemingly innocuous sequence of narrated monologue shows Kasda at the height of his self-idealization. Gone are the doubts about the condition of his uniform, his repressed concern about other male suitors at the Kessners', and his worry about his finances. In their place are feelings of superiority, if not infallibility. His status as officer, in this particular fantasy, will match the material conditions of his existence. Schnabel's coachman destroys the fantasy immediately when he shows Kasda little respect on the trip to the train station.

Paradoxically, his status as an officer is what sanctions the indulgence of denial and compulsion that marks Kasda's downfall. After he misses his train and before he returns to the game, he has a few minutes to reflect on his situation. This sequence shows him once again to be entirely capable of sober analysis: "Ah welche Wonne, nicht mehr genötigt sein, jeden Gulden zweimal umzudrehen, ehe man sich entschließen dürfte ihn auszugeben. Vorsicht, Willi, Vorsicht, sagte er sich, und er nahm sich fest vor, keineswegs den ganzen Spielgewinn zu riskieren, sondern höchstens die Hälfte."[49] What brings Kasda back to the table is the protection of the honor code; just as it allows Greising to infect and thereby harm another person, it provides the framework for Kasda to indulge his self-destructive tendencies.

This recourse to the honor code helps explain Kasda's inability to break out of the dream-like trance that takes hold of him during his final losing streak. Since money is only useful to him insofar as it can solidify his status as an officer, it is not tangibly real in and of itself. The fantasies of ultimate power that Kasda has are no more indicators of a rational engagement with money than the denial that characterizes his losing streak. When he wins, "das bedeutete: neuer Waffenrock, neues Portepee, neue Wäsche, Lackschuhe, Zigaretten, Nachtmähler zu zweit, dritt, Fahrten in den Wienerwald, zwei Monate Urlaub," and then: "Monte Carlo zum Beispiel, unten am Meeresstrand, — mit köstlichen Weibern aus Paris."[50] The amounts that Kasda wins and loses bear little relationship to what he earns for a living as an officer; they are qualitatively different.

It is as though Kasda's conscious concern for money, evidenced by his repeated reflections about his own poverty, is suspended in favor of the free reign of his desires, in whose scheme money is something entirely different. Since money at the gambling table no longer conforms to his conscious conception, Kasda suspends, in his own mind, the laws that traditionally govern its earning and trade. In the fifteen minutes it takes him to lose three to four years' salary, his reasoning faculty is inoperative; he can no longer distinguish the amounts on the bills, and even the sound of his own voice seems alien to him.[51] Reality is not completely suspended, though; by rendering Kasda's thought processes during his losing streak, Schnitzler shows that he retains the potential for self-control, but, as with his two missed opportunities to leave the game, he conflates the role of coincidence from his playing and non-playing moments. Kasda, in effect, suspends his own free will, even though he admits to himself that he knows better; "Tausend verloren, brummte es in Willis Hirn. Aber ich gewinn' sie zurück. Und wenn nicht, ist es ja doch egal. Ich kann tausend grad so wenig zurückzahlen wie zweitausend."[52]

During Kasda's losing streak, the other players do not actively intervene to stop him. Schnabel, who seizes upon the opportunity that Kasda's psychological discomfort presents, offers him money when all around him know that repayment will be impossible. Schnabel has no reason to stop playing, and, given the power relationships within the group that have been established, no one asks him to. This sequence shows, among other things, that Kasda is even willing to break rank if it interferes with the game. When Lieutenant-Colonel Wimmer, first calmly, then more urgently, admonishes Kasda to stop, the latter disobeys: "Ich bin ja nicht im Dienst, dachte Willi, kann außerdienstlich mit meinem Geld und mit meinem Leben anfangen, was ich will."[53] Such an admission invalidates any invocation of the honor code by Kasda to justify his behavior, including, finally, his suicide. In this way Schnitzler shows that the honor code serves not just as a cover for potentially murderous (Greising) or psychotic (Kasda) behavior, but that those who invoke it do so in partial, if not full, awareness of their own opportunism. The officers in the gambling party, Wimmer's protestations notwithstanding, are powerless to stop Kasda because they too are beholden to the same behavioral clichés; they are also acting opportunistically by consorting with Schnabel in the first place, since he is a convenient source of money and embodies the society that allows them to perpetuate their lifestyle. Schnabel symbolizes their own financial dependence, but since he is not *satisfaktionsfähig*, they can maintain a feeling of superiority in the face of a more objective assessment of the relationship's reality.

During their ride back to Vienna, Schnabel proves to be a telling analyst of Kasda's plight, in particular, and of the honor code in general.[54] He reveals contempt for the officer class, a byproduct of his own service as a non-commissioned member of the army and his more sober assessment of the social relations that prevail between officers and civilians. The dynamic of their conversation is charged by Kasda's desire to ease the terms of his debt repayment, while Schnabel assumes a didactic tone, offering Kasda nuggets of wisdom gleaned from his experiences. By setting up their conversation in this way, Schnitzler leaves unclear how much of the consul's recommendations Kasda retains. The change in narrative perspective subtly underscores a new and different Schnabel; during their trip the consul is in a sense demystified, since the two engage in a dialogue, whereas during the game he was seen as if through the eyes of the officers as a figure to be treated with contempt, but on whom they were dependent.

After they decide on the terms of the repayment schedule (to Kasda's dismay, Schnabel does not seem to be interested in relaxing them), Kasda casually remarks that he knows of similar cases in which the officer in question resigned his commission (as had been the case with Bogner). Schnabel's thoughtful reply does not cast this choice in a negative light, somewhat surprising if one assumes that his interests are purely financial: "Sie [the officers who resign] sind, vielmehr sie kommen sich lächerlicherweise deklassiert vor . . . Hingegen unsereiner — ich meine: Menschen, die durch keinerlei Vorurteile der Geburt, des Standes oder — sonstige behindert sind."[55] Schnabel actually presents the possibility of Kasda's resignation in terms of liberation from the dictates of the honor code, which he subsumes under the general heading of class prejudice. The use of the term "lächerlicherweise" in this context implies that the former officer's loss of status is ephemeral, that is, meaningful only if he puts external factors above intrinsic worth. The narrative perspective accounts for the consul's attempts to enlighten Kasda, but simultaneously evokes the latter's inability to understand, since he remains primarily interested in getting the terms of his debt repayment relaxed; at no point does he seriously consider resigning.

A pivotal point in the trip is reached when they pass a prison in a suburb of Vienna. Schnabel appears to recognize it, and Kasda interprets his reaction to mean that he is a former prisoner; Kasda recognizes, however, that this fact does not in and of itself absolve him from paying the debt. Schnabel's subsequent remark puts Kasda's adherence to the honor code to the test: "'Und Subjekte, wie zum Beispiel diesen Leutnant Greising,' sagte der Konsul, wie zum Beschluß eines inneren Gedankengangs, 'läßt man frei herumlaufen.'"[56] Such an insult to a fellow officer, under normal circumstances, would require Kasda to challenge Schnabel. When Kasda offers only token objection, however, Schnabel proceeds to point out the hypocrisy of the honor code: "Eigentlich merkwürdig . . . wie die Herren, die so streng auf ihre Standesehre halten, einen Menschen in ihrer Mitte dulden dürfen, der mit vollem Bewußtsein die Gesundheit eines anderen Menschen, eines dummen, unerfahrenen Mädels zum Beispiel, in Gefahr bringt, so ein Geschöpf krank macht, möglicherweise tötet —."[57] Schnabel implies that Kasda is similar to Greising in this respect, since the honor code provides him with a sanction to indulge his own gambling urge, which of course itself can lead to death.

Kasda is in no position to understand the thrust of Schnabel's comments, since he is still struggling to find the magic words to convince him to be merciful. Kasda projects his own feelings of desperation and self-pity onto the few people he sees on the streets at that early hour, endowing them with happy, unworried existences. Given his previous pattern of behavior toward those perceived to be socially inferior, it is surprising to find him envious of such lowly subjects.[58] When a schoolmaster looks at Schnabel and Kasda with respect, the latter comes close to admitting that maybe it would be better not to be an officer: "Willi hätte nie geahnt, daß er einen Moment erleben sollte, in dem sogar ein armer Schullehrer ihm als beneidenswertes Geschöpf vorkommen würde."[59] As was the case with the assessment of his financial situation, Kasda almost acknowledges that being an officer is untenable, but he does not draw any conclusions that translate into concrete actions to change his status.

Schnabel is in a sense taking on the roles of father and teacher by trying to show Kasda the emptiness of social convention and its dictates. During the game, Schnabel's gaze followed Kasda to the door, while the others did not look at him, especially after he lost. This gaze sets him apart from the others in Kasda's mind, a position that Schnabel uses to try to penetrate Kasda's psychic defense mechanisms and promote a clean break with the honor code. Schnitzler emphasizes this facet through the terms in which Schnabel's final admonition is couched: "'Ich rate Ihnen,' meinte er in fast väterlichem Ton, 'nehmen Sie die Angelegenheit nicht leicht, wenn Sie Wert darauf legen . . . Offizier zu bleiben'" [ellipsis in text].[60] Schnabel subtly emphasizes the subordinate clause, so the logical choice is clear: Kasda should resign his commission. Since legally this move would no longer obligate Kasda to repay him, Schnabel's suggestion amounts to a large financial sacrifice in the interest of pushing Kasda toward insight.

Kasda, having failed to effect a relaxation of the terms, promises Schnabel that he will pay the money at the appointed time. Upon returning to his barracks, he has a brief daydream that is perhaps a more valid indicator of his psychic state than the cool demeanor he presented to the consul. In it he fantasizes about challenging the consul to a duel, but his adherence to the honor code proves so strong that it intrudes on his dream when he acknowledges the impossibility of dueling, since Schnabel is not *satisfaktionsfähig*. Kasda displays symptoms of addiction, fantasizing about killing the one person who tries to intervene in his downward cycle; instead, by acting according to the letter of the honor code, he implicitly declares his solidarity with those who abandoned him to indulge his psychosis.

The second half of the novella chronicles Kasda's attempts to raise the money to pay his debt. At no point does he reflect on the possibility of resigning his commission (as Bogner had done), so evidently he has not interpreted Schnabel's remarks in the spirit that they were intended. This dismissal is revealed in Kasda's behavior when he returns to his barracks; he quickly resumes the expected behavior of the officer, casually saluting a company marching by and inquiring of the last cadet "Wohin Wieseltier?"[61] The arrogance that Kasda shows toward the cadet and Josef, his servant, indicates that he is back in his element; the arrogance permeates his thoughts and reduces the existential crisis of the previous hours to a trifle. In this frame of mind, the loan becomes a fait accompli, with an additional stab at Bogner for risking money: "Vor neun kann ich unmöglich zu Onkel Robert, dachte er. Ich werde ihn für alle Fälle gleich um zwölftausend bitten, kriegt der Bogner auch seine tausend, wenn er sich nicht inzwischen totgeschossen hat. Übrigens, wer weiß, veilleicht hat er wirklich beim Rennen gewonnen und ist sogar imstande, mich herauszureißen."[62] Kasda dismisses Bogner's efforts as hopeless and inferior to his own, even when he himself has just gambled away more than three years' salary. In such reveries Kasda displays a penchant for self-deception and denial that eventually allows him to believe that others will be grateful for the opportunity to grant an officer like himself a loan.

Yet, when Kasda asks his uncle Robert for help, he drops Bogner's suit and requests only the amount he needs for himself, justifying this action by invoking superstition. This omission is further indication that his actions on Bogner's behalf were merely the pretext he needed to suspend all self-control. If Bogner was to be believed (and there is no evidence in the text to think otherwise), his case had a broader human dimension than Kasda's, since Bogner is trying to take care of his family while Kasda is merely trying to raise money to support an untenable lifestyle. Symptomatic of Kasda's authoritarian tendencies is his inability to empathize with others; since his experience is mediated by the honor code, he is unable to grasp immediate emotional responses, be it his own or anyone else's. Thus when he encounters Bogner on his way to his uncle's apartment, he states the truth about his financial situation — "Du bist verrückt, Bogner. Ich werd' die elftausend so wenig kriegen, als ich zwölf kriegen tät"[63] — which stands in direct contrast to his self-satisfied reverie of moments ago. This admission once again shows Kasda capable of a reasonable assessment of his material affairs, yet it does not stop him from contradicting it by his actions. The more the role Kasda plays in society deviates from the objective reality of his situation, the less coherent his thoughts and actions become. This point is brought out at various stages in the story when Kasda appears alienated from his own self, especially as it manifests itself in his voice or appearance — these are the moments when his idealized self-image does not match up with reality.

The aspect of role-playing is especially evident in the two episodes when Kasda asks Wilram, then Leopoldine, for money. He is alternately described as an officer on duty,[64] a child,[65] a husband,[66] and a disappointed lover,[67] when he makes his requests. When he assumes these identities he is unable or unwilling to come to a meaningful understanding with those whom he encounters. As was the case with Consul Schnabel, Wilram and Leopoldine necessarily remain mysterious to Kasda, since he has not developed the capability to identify with the fates of others. His growing urgency and panic prevent him from comprehending their motivations, so he misses crucial opportunities that might otherwise have prevented his ultimate act.

Kasda's uncle, Wilram, is not in a position to help him, since his assets have been frozen as part of his prenuptial agreement. In what the narrator describes by using the military term *Ansturm*, Kasda tries repeatedly to persuade him to loan him the money. After his initial, neutrally phrased request is denied, Kasda resorts to empathy as an argument: "Du mußt dich nun in meine Lage versetzen, Onkel. Alles, alles steht für mich auf dem Spiel, nicht nur meine Existenz als Offizier. Was soll ich, was kann ich dann anders anfangen? Ich hab' ja nichts gelernt, ich versteh ja nichts weiter. Und ich kann doch überhaupt nicht als weggejagter Offizier — ."[68] He cannot finish this thought, so far is it from appearing as a real possibility. What is striking in Kasda's request is the honesty of his self-assessment; in a perverse turnabout, Kasda makes an appeal based on honesty and empathy, precisely the qualities that he lacks in his social relations. He admits that he does not understand the world beyond his limited horizon, implicitly denouncing the officers' corps and the honor code, since they have allowed him to perpetuate such an existence.

Kasda cannot comprehend why Wilram is not able to help him, given that the external trappings of the latter's comfortable bourgeois life appear the same as before, when he had provided him with a regular allowance. His final appeal to Wilram takes the form of an invocation of his mother's memory, as he adopts an abject pose. Wilram is unmoved but sees the situation quite clearly, given his response: "Und, meiner Ansicht nach, kann man immer noch ein ganz anständiger Mensch sein — und werden, auch in Zivil. Die *Ehre* verliert man auf andere Weise" [emphasis in text].[69] Wilram, like Schnabel, suggests that the possibility of Kasda's resignation from the officers' corps is a distinct, potentially even honorable, option. By emphasizing personal growth (hence the correction "und werden"), he encourages Kasda to examine the external and internal influences that have contributed to his crisis. He challenges Kasda's received notion of honor, stressing a more personal ethic of responsibility. However, by acknowledging Kasda's inability to comprehend, Wilram inadvertently condones his institutionally sanctioned flight from responsibility.

Kasda, as if to emphasize his lack of understanding, quickly turns to leave. Wilram calls him back to explain more fully the nature of his marriage. As Kasda grasps that his uncle's wife is Leopoldine Lebus, a woman with whom he had had a liaison on the night of their introduction, he is filled with new hope. In his memory, she appears — "wenn Willi auch diesen Namen längst wieder vergessen hatte"[70] — at first as one of his many conquests. Somehow, though, this memory allows him to accept as fact that she will lend him the money.[71] Since it is in Kasda's financial interest to keep their liaison a secret from his uncle, he begins to spin an elaborate account of a seemingly unrelated, though hardly trivial, matter involving a case of marital infidelity that he has read about in the newspapers. Such evasion is not psychologically convincing; indeed, it seems unintentionally designed to arouse suspicion. In any case, the reader shares in Kasda's perception of Wilram's enigmatic response to his request for help: "Willi sprach sehr lebhaft, als interessiere ihn diese Angelegenheit plötzlich mehr als seine eigene, und es kam ein Augenblick, in dem Robert Wilram einigermaßen befremdet zu ihm aufsah."[72] That he is more emotionally involved with a situation other than his own rather acute one is further evidence that he has not grasped its implications. Kasda displays the characteristics of the impressionist personality common to many of Schnitzler's leading characters: by denying the immediacy of his own experience, but instead wallowing sentimentally in the experiences of others or an idealized version of his own past, he fails to recognize the consequences of his actions in the present. Such a constellation is particularly dangerous for Kasda; the reader recognizes by now through the figural narrative perspective that his psyche is prone to the mechanisms of denial and evasion, to which the honor code is the perfect complement, since it allows him to ignore the consequences of his own actions as long as he abides by its external manifestations.

There are several indications that Kasda is repressing crucial details of his previous experience with Leopoldine. On the way to her office to ask her for the loan, his memories begin to take on a more distinct shape. In this initial version, the reasons he offers for not having seen her again are financial: "Sie hatte ihm so gut gefallen, daß er sich beim Abschied entschlossen glaubte, sie wiederzusehen; es traf sich aber zufällig, daß gerade damals ein anderes weibliches Wesen ältere Rechte an ihn hatte, die ihm als die ausgehaltene Geliebte eines Bankiers keinen Kreuzer kostete, was bei seinen Verhältnissen immerhin in Betracht kam."[73] Kasda, in the throes of his desperation, does not appreciate the inherent contradiction of asking for money from someone whom he left for financial reasons.

Kasda views their tryst as one of many in a string of purely sexual encounters. This position is convenient, since it absolves him of any responsibility that might arise were he to recall them as unique experiences. So a problem arises for him now if he is to invest their relationship with transcendent meaning, the assumption he makes when he asks for a loan based on its memory. By constructing the relationship through Kasda's recollections, Schnitzler shows him to be repressing Leopoldine's love; he cannot face its implications, so he rationalizes it by investing it with only stereotypical meaning. His parting gesture, leaving a ten-guilder note, returns the relationship to the conventional financial transaction for sex; when so doing, he repressed the inconvenience of her emotional commitment. Since he did — and does — not admit to returning her love in kind, he is in effect using her commitment as part of a financial calculation. Ironically, then, he appropriates the role of the prostitute from Leopoldine by objectifying himself.

When Kasda re-introduces himself to Leopoldine, he has trouble recognizing her. Indeed, in the course of the final scenes of the novella she becomes a protean presence, first appearing as a prim businesswoman,[74] then as the lover of two years before,[75] and subsequently as an upstanding middle-class woman;[76] she is also compared to a lawyer, doctor,[77] and general.[78] She no longer fits the stereotypical *süßes Mädl* of Kasda's memories, but presents him with a specific challenge to his self-justification, since she has achieved social status in spite of the obstacles of a paternalistic culture and has adapted successfully to changing circumstances. She underscores her power and mystery by modulating her form of address toward Kasda; at once intimate and business-like, she is the model of freedom from the dictates of social expectation. Kasda interprets her change to the familiar form of address as proof that he will be saved, but, analogous to his suspension of reason in the card game, he bases this assumption on the half-repressed memory of the power that he had over her previously. Leopoldine reinforces Kasda's optimism by not categorically denying his request, instead promising to consult her lawyer and send word to him in his barracks that evening.

The short intervening scene between Kasda's meeting with Leopoldine and their evening tryst is instructive because it shows Kasda alone with his own thoughts. Unlike the dialogues with his principal antagonists, in which appearance and financial dependence influenced his speech and actions, here Kasda gives free reign to his idealized self-image and megalomania. As he walks through the streets of Vienna with several hours to kill before receiving her answer, Kasda's fantasies take on an Oedipal tone: "Dieses Gefühl wirkte so stark in Willi nach, daß er sich, im Geist eine lange Frist überspringend, plötzlich als Gatten der verwitweten Frau Leopoldine Wilram, nunmehriger Frau Majorin Kasda, zu erblicken glaubte."[79] Kasda promotes himself and pushes his uncle out of the way in one stroke; his reverie is built upon assumptions that do not correspond to evidence in the text and that Kasda himself contradicts — as when, for instance, he admits to Leopoldine later on that his chances for promotion are slim.[80]

Kasda, like Gustl, luxuriates in his last hours, since he does not fully grasp the seriousness of his circumstances. He enjoys an expensive meal, smokes, and affects the outward appearance of a well-to-do man about town. Kasda's experience of the baccarat game, in which money lost all meaningful relationship to social reality, reaches its apotheosis on his walk through the city; rather than pursuing other possibilities for raising the money (as he had promised Wilram) he indulges in conspicuous consumption, the functional equivalent of gambling for someone of such limited means. Characteristically, he modulates his confrontation with reality by invoking a self-serving memory: "Und er erinnerte sich eines Abends, einer halben Nacht, die er vor zwei Jahren mit einem Kameraden verbracht hatte, der am nächsten Morgen auf Pistolen antreten sollte . . . daß die Sache damals gut ausgegangen war, erschien Willi wie eine günstige Vorbedeutung."[81] The comparison with the duel, which was also prohibited by civilian law while tolerated by the military, suggests another conventional yardstick of personal honor. The irony lies in what he remembers: he engaged his comrade in a lengthy philosophical discussion, presumably about the merits of dueling.[82] This memory may be productively contrasted with the present, when Kasda, who has been given three chances (Schnabel, Wilram, Leopoldine) to come to a more objective understanding of the honor code's damaging effects, has willfully ignored the didactic overtures of his antagonists, consumed as he is with raising the money to pay his debt. The good outcome of the duel he remembers, which he attributes in part, by implication, to its principal's introspection, cannot apply to his own case, since it is precisely this quality that he lacks. Kasda's walk through the streets of Vienna — described as "ziellos"[83] — becomes a symbol of both his lack of moral development and his habit of abdicating responsibility for his actions, under the guise of allowing fate to decide.

Kasda's final meeting with Leopoldine takes place in his barracks later that evening. When she arrives, he has been sleeping. A section of interior monologue renders Kasda's semi-conscious thoughts upon seeing her: "Wie lang mag sie schon dastehen, dachte Willi, und was ist denn das für eine Stimme? Und wie sieht sie aus? Das ist doch eine ganz andere als die von Vormittag. Sicher hat sie das Geld mitgebracht."[84] Her appearance and voice are puzzling to him, but this confusion does not prevent him from assuming that she has brought the money. In this regard, his experience mirrors the reader's, since the narrative provides little information about Leopoldine's biography, particularly how she has processed the memory of her relationship with Kasda. Since the narrative is generated from the figural perspective of Kasda, all his antagonists emerge as mysterious figures who do not conform to expectations; by adapting to their surroundings (hence the frequent changes of appearance) they confound conventional wisdom and expectation.

During their evening together Kasda is indeed curious about Leopoldine's life, but cannot find the right words to prompt her to talk about herself. At the same time, he is increasingly tormented by her circumspection regarding the status of his loan. Leopoldine underscores her own independence when Kasda asks her if she is happy: "Ich glaub' schon . . . Vor allem bin ich ein freier Mensch, das hab' ich mir immer am meisten gewünscht, bin von niemandem abhängig, wie — ein Mann."[85] The importance of her statement is emphasized in the text by setting it off between two long paragraphs. In the two years since their first meeting, then, Kasda still exists on the edge of poverty, while she has transformed herself into a successful businesswoman. Her declaration puts her in Schnabel's company; they are both autonomous actors who have overcome outsider status to reach positions of social prestige. She also implicitly presents herself as a model of liberation from social expectation, since she has transcended the stereotype of the *süßes Mädl*. In addition, her remarks put an ironic cast on the seduction/transaction that is taking place, since it signals a role-reversal in which she purchases the sexual favors. Kasda does not comprehend any of this, as his reply shows.[86] Thus, Kasda glides into the game of seduction without receiving an answer to the question that constantly inhabits his thoughts, namely, where is the money?

The answer that he receives the next morning is the culmination of a series of surprises. When he wakes up, Leopoldine is preparing to leave; seemingly as an afterthought, she place a thousand-guilder note on Kasda's night table, with the stipulation that it is not connected with the loan, but is payment for his services. Only now, after initial panic and shock at such impertinence, is Kasda able to remember their previous tryst in detail; at that time the roles were completely reversed. He perceives his own actions against the backdrop of her total emotional commitment to him: "All dies Vergessene, nun wußte er es wieder."[87] With this knowledge he is confronted with his own violation of her commitment implicit in the act of leaving money when he left. Kasda tries to convince her that he could not have known of her love, but is reduced to silence by her simple reply: "Hätt'st schon . . . war nicht so schwer."[88]

Leopoldine's turning of the tables has been interpreted as an act of gratuitous cruelty in the critical literature.[89] Such a position ignores Kasda's complicity in the episode, given that, at the level of the *Mittelbewusstsein*, he was steering toward just such a transaction when he repressed the experience of her love, turning it instead into a commodity to insure that she would lend him the money. In addition, after his initial reaction of aggression toward Leopoldine,[90] he admits that he was indeed prepared to sell himself to anyone if they could help him out of his financial trouble. Kasda experiences a deeper recognition of his own cruelty, but the narrative evokes a reflexive qualification of this position: "Er blickte auf, er sah rings um sich, es war ihm, als erwache er aus einem wirren Traum."[91] Leopoldine has left the room, but the last glimpse Kasda has of her is instructive: "Der Posten salutierte wie vor einer Respektsperson."[92] This emblematic gesture (which mirrors a similar one by Josef, Kasda's servant) reinforces the idea that she has won respect based on merit, while Kasda is plagued by a lack of respect in spite of his office.

Kasda's subsequent suicide is an act dictated by the military code of honor, but against the explicit or implicit suggestions of Schnabel, Wilram, and Leopoldine to quit his commission, which also would have been acceptable under military law. Rather than bowing to their suggestions, Kasda acts with Bogner's negative example in mind; their parallel, yet ultimately divergent, fates are revealed when Kasda turns up his collar as Bogner had done, and chooses his divan as the place of death, which is where Bogner had sat when he made the request that precipitated the action. When Kasda looks at himself in the mirror before his final act, he is disgusted by what he sees,[93] but particularly that he is not in uniform. When he is found by Tugut and Bogner, his uniform covers up a tattered and dirty shirt, an apt metaphor for what the honor code has obscured.

Schnitzler's criticism of the military honor code in these three no-vellas reflects a more global examination of the indebtedness of the individual to antiquated social organizations and normative codes of conduct. Gustl and Kasda's fates are paradigmatic, in that they freely choose complete allegiance to the honor code even when, in Kasda's case most clearly, it conflicts with his own better judgment and his antago-nists' pedagogical efforts. Faith in the martial values of the officers' corps frees them from socially responsible action, even if such action is defined narrowly as self-improvement, as Schnitzler implies in many of his apho-risms. The primary characters' adversaries suggest a successful integration into an acquisitive, capitalist, modern society, one that does not recog-nize received notions of personal worth through status, but one that rewards knowledge and its active application. They act with manifest self-interest, but that is not inconsistent with Schnitzler's position that Aus-trian society would only become more just when its institutions accom-modated such initiative. Schnitzler's turn to narrative forms coincided with an examination of what might be called political identity forma-tion.[94] Such political identity is the sum of external influences and indi-vidual predisposition that prevented the establishment of more honest and democratic social organization in the Austrian context.

Notes

[1] Arthur Schnitzler, *Tagebuch 1909–1912,* ed. Werner Welzig (Vienna: Österreichi-sche Akademie der Wissenschaften, 1981), 411.

[2] *Der Weg ins Freie* in ES I, 635–959; *Therese: Chronik eines Frauenlebens* in ES II, 625–882; *Sterben* in ES I, 98–175.

[3] See Konstanze Fliedl, *Arthur Schnitzler: Poetik der Erinnerung* (Vienna: Böhlau, 1997); Wolfram Kiwit, *"Sehnsucht nach meinem Roman": Arthur Schnitzler als Roman-cier* (Bochum: Winkler, 1991); Michaela Perlmann, *Der Traum in der literarischen Moderne: Untersuchungen zum Werk Arthur Schnitzlers* (Munich: Fink, 1987); and Horst Thomé, *Autonomes Ich und Inneres Ausland: Studien über Realismus, Tiefenpsy-chologie und Psychiatrie in deutschen Erzähltexten 1848–1918* (Tübingen: Niemeyer, 1993).

[4] This observation is put nicely by Kiwit, 208: "Schnitzler fügt das Zeitcharakteristische elliptisch in den auf die Konstitution des Ich konzentrierten Text, um auf der Folie der historischen Bedingtheit des Individuums den Inhalt des Ich in seinen divergierenden Einzelelmenten darzustellen. Der Ehrenkodex in der Offiziersgesellschaft der Donaumonarchie oder die gültige Moral der zeigenössisch patriarchalen Gesellschaft werden primär aus dem Figurenbewußtsein eintwickelt, so daß die zeitverhaftete Konstitution des Ich die Kontextualität des Erzählens generiert, ohne den Zeitbezug ausdrücklich hervorzuheben."

[5] *Jugend in Wien. Eine Autobiographie,* ed. Therese Nickl and Heinrich Schnitzler (Vienna, Munich, Zurich: Molden, 1968; Frankfurt: Fischer, 1968).

[6] *Casanovas Heimfahrt* in ES II, 231–323; *Die Frau des Richters* in ES II, 382–433.

[7] *Spiel im Morgengrauen* in ES II, 505–81.

[8] On Schnitzler's understanding of psychology and his development of the concept of the *Mittelbewußtsein,* see Horst Thomé, "Kernlosigkeit und Pose. Zur Rekonstruktion von Schnitzlers Psychologie," in *Fin de Siècle,* ed. Klause Bohnen (Copenhagen: Fink, 1984), 62–84.

[9] First published in Arthur Schnitzler, "Über Psychoanalyse," *Protokolle* 11/2 (1976): 283. Textual evidence suggests that these comments were written shortly after the publication of Freud's *Traumdeutung* in 1900. See also Fliedl, 28–30.

[10] See A. Clive Roberts, *Arthur Schnitzler and Politics* (Riverside: Ariadne Press, 1989): "Schnitzler's technique of combining psychological studies with political themes makes the political realm accessible to the reader. He demonstrated that the average person is involved in the political process, even though that person may not have realized it."

[11] For a discussion of Schnitzler's use of narrated monologue to describe individual consciousness, see Dorrit Cohn, *Transparent Minds* (Princeton: Princeton UP, 1978), 99–140.

[12] Breaks in such discipline thus become notable from a compositional standpoint: an example is the scene in *Der Weg ins Freie* between Berthold Stauber and his father — a scene where Baron von Wergenthin is not present, unusual in the novel — in which the two discuss the role of anti-Semitism in Austrian public life with a frankness unlikely to have the same poignant tone if the baron were present.

[13] Such narrative discipline is one of many aspects of Stanley Kubrick's *Eyes Wide Shut* (Warner Bros. 1999) that remains true to the spirit of its literary antecedent, Schnitzler's *Traumnovelle* (1926). One productive analogy when discussing Schnitzler's narrative technique is his use of what one might call cinematic effects, including the use, for instance, of point-of-view shots or the subjective camera.

[14] The term public sphere is used here in the sense developed by Jürgen Habermas, *Structural Transformation of the Public Sphere,* trans. Thomas Bürger (Cambridge, MA: MIT Press, 1989), 27: "The bourgeois public sphere may be conceived above all as the sphere of private people come together as a public; they soon claimed the public sphere regulated from above against the public authorities themselves, to engage them in a debate over the general rules governing relations the basically privatized but publicly relevant sphere of commodity exchange and social labor."

[15] See Rolf Allerdissen, *Arthur Schnitzler: Impressionistisches Rollenspiel und skeptischer Realismus in seinen Erzählungen* (Bonn: Grundmann, 1985).

[16] Horst Thomé, "Sozialgeschichtliche Perspektiven der neueren Schnitzler-Forschung" *Internationales Archiv für Sozialgeschichte der deutschen Literatur* 13 (1988): 160–61.

[17] For a survey of the extensive critical literature on *Leutnant Gustl*, see Michaela Perlmann, *Arthur Schnitzler* (Stuttgart: Metzler, 1987), 142–47.

[18] See Otto P. Schinnerer, "Schnitzler and the Military Censorship. Unpublished Correspondence," *Germanic Review* 5/3 (1930): 241–42.

[19] *Leutnant Gustl*, 338–39.

[20] *Leutnant Gustl*, 347.

[21] Hartmut Scheible, *Arthur Schnitzler in Selbstzeugnissen und Bilddokumenten* (Reinbek: Rowohlt, 1976), 83: "Nachdem durch den ökonomischen Niedergang des Kleinbürgertums auch die väterliche Autorität gebrochen ist . . . findet der Kleinbürger Gustl alles, worauf er sonst verzichten muss, in der militärischen Hierarchie: die Sicherheit eines definierbaren gesellschaftlichen Standorts und ein vages Gemeinschaftsgefühl."

[22] Arthur Schnitzler, *Aphorismen und Betrachtungen,* ed. Robert O. Weiss (Frankfurt: Fischer, 1967), 51.

[23] The secondary literature on *Casanovas Heimfahrt* is quite diverse, with several studies focusing on Schnitzler's reception of the historical Casanova or comparing the novella to his Casanova play. William Rey's structural analysis of the novella, in spite of its many insights, optimistically posits Casanova as the *uomo universale,* thereby missing much of Schnitzler's exposure of the adventurer's egocentricity, cruelty, and the political implications of his behavior: *Arthur Schnitzler: Die späte Prosa als Gipfel seines Schaffens* (Berlin: E. Schmidt, 1968), 28–48. More recent studies have begun to delve into the socially critical aspects of the work. See, for instance, Fritjof Stock, "Casanova als Don Juan: Bemerkungen über Arthur Schnitzlers Novelle *Casanovas Heimfahrt* und sein Lustspiel *Die Schwestern oder Casanova in Spa*," *Arcadia* Sonderheft (1978): 56–65; Martha Bodwich Alden, "Schnitzler's Repudiated Debt to Casanova," *Modern Austrian Literature* 13/3 (1980): 25–32; Albert Glaser, "Masken der Libertinage: Überlegungen zu Schnitzlers Erzählung Casanovas Heimfahrt," *Text + Kritik* 10/2 (1982): 355–64; Susan C. Anderson, "Shattered Illusions: Gambling in Arthur Schnitzler's Prose Works," *Modern Austrian Literature* 25/3–4 (1992): 248–51. An outstanding analysis may be found in Michaela Perlmann's chapter on the novella: *Der Traum in der literarischen Moderne: Untersuchungen zum Werk Arthur Schnitzlers* (Munich: Fink, 1987), 156–64.

[24] *Casanovas Heimfahrt,* 268.

[25] *Casanovas Heimfahrt,* 252.

[26] *Casanovas Heimfahrt,* 253.

[27] *Casanovas Heimfahrt,* 253.

[28] *Casanovas Heimfahrt,* 262.

[29] *Casanovas Heimfahrt,* 320–21.

[30] *Casanovas Heimfahrt,* 287–88.

[31] *Casanovas Heimfahrt,* 319.

[32] *Casanovas Heimfahrt,* 286.

[33] *Casanovas Heimfahrt,* 302.

[34] *Casanovas Heimfahrt,* 297.

[35] *Casanovas Heimfahrt,* 311.

[36] *Casanovas Heimfahrt,* 289.

[37] *Aphorismen und Betrachtungen,* 48.

[38] Two studies of *Spiel im Morgengrauen* distinguish themselves by a thorough analysis of the relationship between Schnitzler's narrative strategies and the depiction of social reality and psychological depth: Maria-Regina Kecht, "Analyse der sozialen Realität in Schnitzlers 'Spiel im Morgengrauen,'" *Modern Austrian Literature* 25/3–4 (1992): 181–97; and Horst Thomé, in his *Autonomes Ich und Inneres Ausland: Studien über Realismus, Tiefenpsychologie und Psychiatrie in deutschen Erzähltexten (1848–1918)* (Tübingen: Max Niemeyer, 1993), 670–93. See also Brenda Keiser, *Deadly Dishonor: The Duel and the Honor Code in the Works of Arthur Schnitzler* (New York: Peter Lang, 1990), 121–48; Michaela Perlmann, *Arthur Schnitzler* (Stuttgart: Metzler, 1987), 163–66; Allerdissen, 55–80; Klaus Laermann, "Spiel im Morgengrauen," in *Akten des internationalen Symposiums "Arthur Schnitzler und seine Zeit,"* ed. Giuseppe Farese (Bern: Peter Lang, 1985), 182–200; Nils Ekfelt, "Arthur Schnitzler's 'Spiel im Morgengrauen': Free Will, Fate, and Chaos," *German Quarterly* 51 (1978): 170–81; Hans-Ulrich Lindken, *Arthur Schnitzler — Erzählungen* (Munich: Oldenburg, 1970); William H. Rey, *Arthur Schnitzler: Die späte Prosa als Gipfel seines Schaffens* (Berlin: Erich Schmidt, 1968), 126–54.

[39] *Spiel im Morgengrauen,* 513.

[40] *Spiel im Morgengrauen,* 513.

[41] *Spiel im Morgengrauen,* 515.

[42] *Spiel im Morgengrauen,* 513.

[43] *Spiel im Morgengrauen,* 516.

[44] *Spiel im Morgengrauen,* 518.

[45] *Spiel im Morgengrauen,* 519.

[46] *Spiel im Morgengrauen,* 519.

[47] *Spiel im Morgengrauen,* 23.

[48] *Spiel im Morgengrauen,* 524.

[49] *Spiel im Morgengrauen,* 525.

[50] *Spiel im Morgengrauen,* 527.

[51] *Spiel im Morgengrauen,* 532, 528.

[52] *Spiel im Morgengrauen,* 530.

[53] *Spiel im Morgengrauen,* 531.

[54] The critical literature has emphasized Schnabel's demonic nature and negative qualities: for Perlmann, "[E]ine undurchschaubare mephistohafte Kunstfigur," 164; Rey calls him "einen Abgesandten der Hölle," 139; Allerdissen ascribes to him "a-personalen Haß auf das Offizierskorps," 64, to which "Willi als Person mehr oder

weniger zufällig zum Opfer fällt," 65; to Laermann, "Er verhält sich . . . nicht gerade nobel," 191. It is somewhat difficult to understand the critical consensus on this point; as Thomé points out, Schnabel suggests stopping the game when Kasda is still ahead and subsequently tries to educate him about the honor code (678).

[55] *Spiel im Morgengrauen,* 536.

[56] *Spiel im Morgengrauen,* 539.

[57] *Spiel im Morgengrauen,* 539.

[58] *Spiel im Morgengrauen,* 538, 540.

[59] *Spiel im Morgengrauen,* 542.

[60] *Spiel im Morgengrauen,* 549.

[61] *Spiel im Morgengrauen,* 549.

[62] *Spiel im Morgengrauen,* 550.

[63] *Spiel im Morgengrauen,* 549.

[64] *Spiel im Morgengrauen,* 550.

[65] *Spiel im Morgengrauen,* 551.

[66] *Spiel im Morgengrauen,* 564.

[67] *Spiel im Morgengrauen,* 569.

[68] *Spiel im Morgengrauen,* 552.

[69] *Spiel im Morgengrauen,* 554.

[70] *Spiel im Morgengrauen,* 557.

[71] *Spiel im Morgengrauen,* 558.

[72] *Spiel im Morgengrauen,* 558.

[73] *Spiel im Morgengrauen,* 558.

[74] *Spiel im Morgengrauen,* 560.

[75] *Spiel im Morgengrauen,* 560.

[76] *Spiel im Morgengrauen,* 566.

[77] *Spiel im Morgengrauen,* 560.

[78] *Spiel im Morgengrauen,* 570.

[79] *Spiel im Morgengrauen,* 564.

[80] *Spiel im Morgengrauen,* 567.

[81] *Spiel im Morgengrauen,* 564–65.

[82] *Spiel im Morgengrauen,* 564.

[83] *Spiel im Morgengrauen,* 564.

[84] *Spiel im Morgengrauen,* 560.

[85] *Spiel im Morgengrauen,* 571.

[86] *Spiel im Morgengrauen,* 570.

[87] *Spiel im Morgengrauen,* 574.

[88] *Spiel im Morgengrauen,* 573.

[89] To Allerdissen, she is characterized by a "mythische Feindschaft der Frau gegen den Mann," 70, and "unmenschliche Bösartigkeit," 72; to Lindken, she is "diabolisch" and prone to "Geschlechterhaß," 46. As with the critical reception of Schnabel, the moralistic tone does not match the textual evidence. After all, both act with honesty and productivity in the face of a society that treats them as outsiders; perhaps there is a perception of cynicism inhabiting their actions that drives the critical speculation.

[90] *Spiel im Morgengrauen,* 574.

[91] *Spiel im Morgengrauen,* 575.

[92] *Spiel im Morgengrauen,* 575.

[93] *Spiel im Morgengrauen,* 575.

[94] For a more thorough explanation of this argument, see Felix W. Tweraser, *Political Dimensions of Arthur Schnitzler's Late Fiction* (Columbia, SC: Camden House, 1998), and A. Clive Roberts's *Arthur Schnitzler and Politics* cited above.

A Century of Intrigue:
The Dramatic Works of Arthur Schnitzler

Elizabeth G. Ametsbichler

THE WORKS OF Arthur Schnitzler continue to capture the imagination of the viewing and reading public, as demonstrated by the continued presence of his plays in German-speaking theater repertoires, the abundance of literary criticism still dealing with him and his canon, and adaptations of his works into contemporary plays, including English-language versions. *Das weite Land* (1911) was adapted by Tom Stoppard as *Undiscovered Country* (1980),[1] and *Reigen* (1903) was adapted by David Hare as *The Blue Room*.[2] In 1999 *Traumnovelle* (1926) was made into the movie *Eyes Wide Shut* by Stanley Kubrick.[3] While Schnitzler considered himself to be the most vilified dramatist of his time,[4] by 1914 he was also the most frequently performed author in the Burgtheater.[5] This apparent contradiction reflects what seems to be an Austrian phenomenon, seen also in later playwrights such as Thomas Bernhard, Elfriede Jelinek, and Werner Schwab, all of whom have been immensely popular — and often performed — and regularly vilified. This discrepancy between an author's own assessment of his or her place in the world of theater and the reality of his or her success underscores the intensity and complexity of the relationships among author, text, critic, and audience, a particularly precarious and problematic but intriguing dynamic in the case of Arthur Schnitzler.

Intrigue has many significations. It implies fascination with someone or something; it can insinuate arousing curiosity by using new, unusual, or compelling devices and practices; it signifies underhanded plotting or machinations; it is used to describe illicit or secret love affairs; and in the literary world, it also means the series of complications that form the plot of a play. All of these various connotations of "intrigue" apply to Schnitzler's dramatic works. For a century, audiences have been captivated by the ways in which these different meanings and levels of "intrigue" are so thoroughly interconnected in his dramas. The fascination with Schnitzler derives from the plays themselves (themes, plot, dialogue), but it also has to do with the controversial reception of his work: involving, on the one hand, the scandals surrounding some of his plays, and on the other hand, his personality and the success he enjoyed as a playwright.

In the course of the last century, critics and scholars have written about every one of Schnitzler's plays and on almost every facet of his work. Intrigue, which is a component of the socio-historical context out of which Schnitzler's plays emerged, provides an underlying perspective with which to examine Schnitzler's dramas and their critical reception.

The Plays

Fin-de-siècle Vienna provided ample material for Schnitzler's works. It was the frivolous time of the Viennese waltz, of rendezvous at the Prater, and of carriage rides around the Ringstrasse. Yet, within the walls of the baroque imperial city, architectural, artistic, literary, philosophical, and scientific experimentation was thriving, which made Vienna one of the intellectual centers of *fin-de-siècle* modernity.[6] This "Golden Age" still continues to shape Vienna's image and tantalize audiences and readers. Both frivolity and intellectual activity are frequent focal points in studies of this era and of Schnitzler's plays. At the same time, the squalor of the underprivileged classes and the ethnic unrest plaguing the multicultural Danube monarchy also shaped turn-of-the-century Vienna and Schnitzler's work. Though he rarely offers a direct portrayal of the misery, it nonetheless lurks beneath the surface of his writing, insinuated by the social conditions that allowed prostitution to thrive and encouraged the objectification of *süße Mädel* — the "sweet," accessible girls of the lower classes — by upper-crust gentlemen. The multiethnic military often seen in Schnitzler's works offers additional examples of poverty and the ensuing corruption of large parts of the population. These circumstances stand in stark contrast to the apparent superficiality of many of his characters.

Schnitzler's lifetime (1862–1931), however, encompasses more than just *fin-de-siècle* Vienna; his life spans the founding of the Austro-Hungarian Empire (including the expansion of the Ringstrasse and the subsequent dismantling of much of the fortress wall around the city), its demise, the First World War, and the beginning of the First Republic and Austria's fledgling efforts at democracy. Schnitzler's works document the variety and range of Viennese society of this entire period. They reveal the glitter and sophistication, artistic and intellectual developments, and social and class-related issues. Within the larger context of this historical setting, Schnitzler's works must be understood as a quasi-clinical report about a society as it was observed through the eyes of a medical doctor. Because it was undergoing such rapid political and economic changes, this society and its people were subject to a fundamental structural transformation.[7]

Themes and motifs in Schnitzler's plays are indicative of this societal transformation. They add to the intrigue surrounding Schnitzler, epitomizing the controversies that arose out of the rapid social change that was altering the face of the Habsburg Empire. Familiar themes include love and death; double standards; moral issues, sexual relationships, and more specifically, faithfulness and infidelity; social conditions; the artist in society; illusion and reality; religion (being a Jew, being a Christian, anti-Semitism); politics; the military (the duel); war and peace; and language and its usage. Interest in Schnitzler remains strong because, through these themes, he addressed controversial and delicate issues, many foreshadowing later, painful events of the twentieth century. Other themes arouse interest because they appear charmingly antiquated.

While Schnitzler is entirely conscious about language and its usage, he regards both with profound skepticism, as did others of his contemporaries associated with the literary movement *Jung Wien*. Language skepticism also formed the basis of the work of the caustic critic and satirist Karl Kraus and the philosopher Ludwig Wittgenstein. The titles of Schnitzler's later series of one-act plays, *Komödie der Worte* (1915), and the title of his posthumously published drama fragment *Das Wort* (begun 1907, published 1966), reflect similar skepticism involving the paradox that words are nothing, yet "we have nothing but words."[8] Schnitzler's distrust of words is apparent from his first play, *Anatol* (1893), to his late plays, and though treated in various ways in different settings and with diverse motifs, language is a main thematic thread that connects all of his dramas.[9] Indeed, in an ironic twist, which is shared with other language skeptics of the time, Schnitzler uses language and irony as a weapon to combat and confront the unreliability and inadequacy of words.

Dialogue and action are the elements that constitute a drama. However, a relative lack of action as well as an emphasis on dialogue and words are characteristic of Schnitzler's plays. At the same time, however, it becomes apparent just how inadequate words are for true communication. Characters seemingly talk to one another, but in reality this connection is an illusion. They consistently "talk past" each other: "sie reden aneinander vorbei." *Reigen* is a well-known example of this focus on dialogue, revealed by the notable change between the pre- and post-coital conversations of the partners. Although physically and seemingly emotionally intimate, the characters do not really listen to each other, which is painfully clear in their easy dismissals of each other after the

sexual act. The motif of noncommunication or the failure to communicate is a feature shared by almost all of Schnitzler's plays. In *Der grüne
Kakadu* (1899), for example, words are purposely misused to create an
illusion. Yet, the boundaries of this intentionally created illusion are
crossed when the historical reality of the French Revolution breaks into
the make-believe world of the pub, and the real jealousy felt by the actor
Henri compels him to kill Emile, Duke of Cadignan, his wife's lover. *Das
Märchen* (1894) also illustrates the emptiness of mere words: Fedor
Denner voices liberal understanding about the sexual rights of women,
thus giving the actress Fanny Theren false hopes about his ability to love
her even though she has had a previous lover. When Fedor's actions
contradict his words, Fanny leaves Vienna for an acting engagement in
Russia. In this case, Fedor's inherent contradiction accelerates Fanny's
emancipation, and she pursues a career and her own self-fulfillment. The
illusions that words create in these works have little to do with a person's
character or with reality.

The dramatic conflict between reality and illusion and between "Sein
und Schein" is a recurrent motif in Schnitzler's plays, but is particularly
well illustrated by *Paracelsus* (1899).[10] In this play the murkiness of
boundaries between appearance and reality evoked by hypnosis calls into
question the very concept of reality and even confuses Paracelsus, who
ostensibly has had control of the situation. Everyone becomes alarmed
by the unknown that lurks beneath the surface. This situation illuminates
yet another point: the crisis of language is linked to the crisis of identity.[11] When Paracelsus, viewed by some as a healer and by others as a
quack, hypnotizes Justina to expose her self-possessed husband, Cyprian,
as well as Justina's repressed feelings for Paracelsus, this act ultimately
calls into question the self-understanding and identity not only of
Cyprian and Justina but also of the celebrated manipulator himself.

The question of control and manipulation is an integral and intriguing aspect of Schnitzler's dramas, as the three one-act plays of *Marionetten* (1906) — which include *Der Puppenspieler, Der tapfere Cassian,* and
Zum großen Wurstel — exemplify.[12] In the first playlet, the puppeteer
(Georg) had thought for years that because he had manipulated a first
encounter between "his puppets" Anna and Eduard that he also had
manipulated their lives. Yet, years later he finds out that the two have
long been happily married. *Der tapfere Cassian is* in fact a puppet play,
demonstrating quite literally the implications of manipulation, of controlling the strings. Also in this case the "characters" lose control of their
play-acting. In the third playlet, a burlesque, the fantastical chaos of a
play within a play satirizes the roles played by audience, actors, and

THE DRAMATIC WORKS OF ARTHUR SCHNITZLER   ◆   191

author, as well as the interaction of the three parties involved. Who is in charge? Who controls the situation? Schnitzler is carrying on a tradition in German-language theater that Heinrich von Kleist had also addressed in "Über das Marionettentheater" (1810). The language skepticism implied in and symbolized by such puppet theater, as well as the issues of questioning and manipulating reality, constitutes a tradition perpetuated in the works of late-twentieth-century Austrian dramatists such as Peter Handke and Thomas Bernhard.

In other plays the role of puppeteer is less obvious, but nevertheless crucial. For example, the factory owner Friedrich Hofreiter in *Das weite Land* "directs" and manipulates the actions of the other characters, most obviously his wife's. Hofreiter has carried on many extramarital affairs with the knowledge of his wife, Gena. Yet, when he blames her for the suicide of a family friend because she declined to have an affair with him and opted instead to stay faithful to her unloved and adulterous husband, she subsequently does have an affair with her next suitor, the young family friend Otto von Aigner. This affair ends in Aigner's tragic death because Hofreiter kills him in a duel — not out of jealousy, but out of a need and desire to manipulate. At the same time, this action also reflects Hofreiter's desire to challenge and defeat his younger rival as well as his adherence to a false code of honor.

On another level, the secrets that intrigue family members in several plays presuppose the drive to control as much as they denote dysfunctional families and relationships in conjunction with the attempt to circumvent normative social behavior. In this sense, secrets are an inherent component of dramatic intrigue. The artist Julian Fichtner in *Der einsame Weg* (1904), for example, feels compelled to divulge the secret that he is the biological father of Felix, the son of Professor Wegrat and his wife, Gabriele.[13] He had abandoned Gabriele, had never taken any responsibility for her or Felix, and had pursued the life of a confirmed bachelor. Now all of a sudden, after Gabriele has died, the aging Fichtner wants to claim his presumed right of fatherhood. No one had known the secret except for Gabriele, Reumann (her doctor), Fichtner, and his friend Stephan von Sala. By telling Felix, Fichtner attempts to gain control over the youth and to force filial affection from him. The dysfunctional family dynamics are made transparent by the lack of communication among all parties and are further complicated when the Wegrats' daughter, Johanna, commits suicide without anyone having noticed that she was emotionally disturbed.

Such lack of awareness within the family is particularly pronounced, if with a much lighter, even amusing tone, in *Komtesse Mizzi oder der Fami-*

lientag (1908).[14] Prince Egon visits his old friend Count Arpad Pazmandy in order to introduce him to the son that no one knew the prince had. When the count leaves the room, the audience discovers in a sudden turn of conversation that the mother, who according to the prince was of lower-class origins and deceased, is actually alive and is none other than the count's daughter Mizzi. *Fink und Fliederbusch* (1917) takes the plot point of manipulation and secret lives to an outrageous extreme when Fliederbusch, journalist for the newspaper *Die Gegenwart,* takes a second job for the weekly *Die elegante Welt* and, masquerading as a reporter named Fink, ends up writing against his other self.[15] In the end, he loses his sense of identity and is forced to call for a duel, unbeknownst to the others, against himself. Though this play takes a humorous twist, it none-theless moves the notion of manipulation to an absurd level while at the same time underscoring the meaninglessness of words. Fink espouses one idea, Fliederbusch another — yet they are the same character.

Language is the basis for communication ("we have nothing but words"), but the converse is inherently also the case. Miscommunication is the key element in the dialogues in one of Schnitzler's last published plays, *Der Gang zum Weiher* (1926).[16] When the protagonist, Albrecht Baron of Mayenau, misunderstands his daughter Leonilda's words, it is in part be-cause of his expectations, dictated by his station in life, and in part because of Leonilda's becoming an adult and her subsequent assertion of her own identity. The inadequacy of words limits the communication, in this case particularly between generations, but also between genders. The baron does not understand his daughter, but he does understand the youthful passion and lack of experience on the part of the marshal's son Konrad, who arrives with the news of impending war, and whose unquestioned patriotism pre-cludes any thoughtful reaction to the border conflicts that are precipitating war. The baron takes advantage of the lack of communication between the generations to expound on politics, on the state, and on war and peace, thereby assuming the role of mouthpiece for Schnitzler.

Studies of Schnitzler's plays frequently concentrate on the themes of social and moral double standards, *das süße Mädel,* and flirtations (*Liebe-leien*) that can take a deadly end, as seen in the play *Liebelei* (1896).[17] In this drama not only is the protagonist, Fritz, killed in a duel for his illicit affair with a married woman, but the *süße Mädel* Christine, who has taken Fritz's flirtatious overtures seriously, apparently commits suicide as a result of her disappointment. As tragic as her death is the implied commentary about the status of such young women, who represent little more than a plaything, an ultimately disposable commodity, for aristo-cratic gentlemen.

A few years after *Liebelei*, Schnitzler allowed one of his young gentleman characters to fall in love with his sweet young girl. In *Das Vermächtnis* (1899),[18] Hugo Losatti does love Toni Weber, with whom he has a child. Convention, however, forces him to keep his illegitimate family hidden from his parents until he is fatally wounded in an accident. On his deathbed, he elicits a promise from his family to take care of the woman he loves and his son, Franzi, despite the social disgrace this acknowledgment will invoke. The family reluctantly upholds the promise made to Hugo as long as Franzi is alive. However, after the boy falls ill and dies, the family turns its back on Toni, unable to tolerate such a "disreputable" woman in its midst, and the play again ends with the implied suicide of another repudiated *süßes Mädel*.

Das Märchen is the quintessential Schnitzler play about double standards. There is no deadly, tragic end, yet Fedor is unable to incorporate the principles he espouses into his life, which clearly exposes the degree to which social convention trumps personal conviction and permeates society. Fedor mouths liberal, tolerant words and advocates emancipation and equality for women, but his inability to live up to his alleged ideals underscores how deeply imprisoned he is by normative social standards and, more generally, how deeply rooted double standards are in this society. With this work, the language skeptic Schnitzler again demonstrates just how empty and inadequate words can be.

Schnitzler has often been described as a chronicler of *fin-de-siècle* Vienna. Indeed, his works are primarily discussed in terms of social criticism or are credited with capturing the atmosphere of his time and place. Yet, Schnitzler is also the author of several historical plays, including *Paracelsus, Der grüne Kakadu, Der Schleier der Beatrice* (1901), *Der Ruf des Lebens* (1906), *Der junge Medardus* (1910), *Die Schwestern oder Casanova in Spa* (1919), and *Der Gang zum Weiher.*[19] By setting a play in a particular historical time and place, Schnitzler explores the relationship between various levels of history and fiction. These settings also allow him to present new or different perspectives of past events or historic personalities. Yet, even his historical plays are often analyzed as commentaries on *fin-de-siècle* Vienna. This approach results in a narrow interpretation of these plays as well as of Schnitzler's intent. Besides serving as a political commentary or social critique of the author's time, these historical plays constitute a dialogue with past events. As literary works they make specific themes universal while showing that there are few reliable "facts"; rather, they suggest that any presentation of history is a matter of interpretation.

Der grüne Kakadu offers a case study of Schnitzler's historical method. Set in Paris on the evening of July 14, 1789, this play is most obviously concerned with the French Revolution. The title is derived from the name of Prospere's basement pub/theater, where the action takes place. This setting itself is a metaphor for one way of looking at the Revolution, namely, from below.[20] However, many other perspectives are explored as well. The characters cover a wide spectrum of Parisian society, from the aristocrats who make up the audience to bourgeois guests, and from actors who play at being criminals, to actual criminals. Prospere's theater consists of having actors mingle with the upper-class audience and relate the gruesome deeds they allegedly have committed. Through the interaction between audience and actors, different aspects of the Revolution and its causes come to light. The characters in the play relate to what happens both in and outside of Prospere's pub according to their needs and desires.[21] The different interpretations underscore the idea that there are no stable facts, but rather only interpretations and analyses of the Revolution as an historical event. As Marianna Squercina observes, the play "simultaneously questions the objectivity of such an analysis."[22]

The intermingling of illusion and reality, of theater (within a play) and audience, of "Sein und Schein," of history and fiction all serve to question the alleged objectivity of history. The character of Albin Chevalier de la Tremouille, a young provincial aristocrat visiting Paris and the pub for the first time, is introduced in order to reveal the blending of "Sein und Schein." He takes the words and actions of Prospere's actors at face value and thinks that the actresses are actual prostitutes and that the actors' stories about their petty thievery is real. He has to be reassured repeatedly by his friend François Vicomte von Nogeant that what he is seeing and hearing is *only* play-acting. But is it? Albin's misunderstanding and misinterpretation of the situation reflect Schnitzler's pervasive skepticism and show the relativity of truth.

The drama climaxes in the ultimate confusion of illusion — play-acting — and reality when the best actor in Prospere's troupe, Henri, relates how he has just killed the Duke of Cadignan because the duke had slept with Henri's wife, Leocadie, who is also an actress but in a different theater. Henri and Leocadie are newlyweds, and Henri is convinced that both of them will soon give up acting and move to the country. He is extremely jealous and wants to make certain that he has his wife to himself. Even though Henri's story is "just theater," Prospere, for one, believes the story because he has evidence that the duke really is Leocadie's lover. Prospere's reactions, in turn, convince Henri that what he took for fiction is at least partially true. When the duke finally walks through the door, the guests and actors are in a state of confusion, and Henri does kill his rival right before their eyes. At this point, acting becomes the truth.

Simultaneously, the Revolution taking place outside spills into the pub, so that Henri's revenge on the duke is celebrated as an act of insurrection and liberation. The least conscious of the characters/actors becomes the people's hero, providing additional evidence of the subjectivity of historical "fact" and the relativity of truth. Henri's act also reflects the brutality that marked the French Revolution. The murder highlights the extreme and often gratuitous violence associated with the Revolution while also questioning its very meaning and the values it espoused.

As a prose writer, Schnitzler is often credited with developing stream of consciousness as a narrative technique — even before James Joyce — in his novella *Leutnant Gustl* (1900).[23] Similarly, his dramas are innovative from a theatric point of view. They reveal a distinctive concept of language and emphasize dialogue over action. Even if characters do not truly communicate, they do talk. This strategy epitomizes as well as satirizes the very function and purpose of dialogue and calls for further examination of language usage. Moreover, Schnitzler's plays are largely situational, that is, situations prevail over plot development. *Reigen,* for example, consists of a series of ten dialogues, and while each sexual act implies action, it is only insinuated and not shown on stage. Thus the spoken interaction remains in the foreground. Indeed, Schnitzler himself was skeptical about a play so dominated by dialogue; in a January 1897 letter to his friend and patron Otto Brahm, Schnitzler questioned whether or not the colorful scenes of *Reigen* could actually be performed. And a little later, he commented in a letter to his friend Olga Waissnix that although he considered them unprintable and not worth much from a literary point of view, the dialogues could, if uncovered a hundred years later, provide insights into the culture of the *fin-de-siècle.*[24] This comment suggests that he had misgivings about the focus and the dramatic form of *Reigen* but was aware of its cultural and historic value. His remarks also reveal his sensitivity about the ways in which his plays and their intrigues are received by critics and audiences.

Reception

As often noted, Schnitzler has enjoyed a kind of critical renaissance in the last part of the twentieth century. Although during his lifetime (as his diaries substantiate[25]) he often felt attacked and misunderstood by critics (especially in the Viennese press), by the public, and even by author/journalist friends who wrote critical reviews of his work, he nonetheless was a successful playwright who was regularly performed throughout Germany, Austria, and Central Europe. There are many reasons for the contradictions in Schnitzler's reception, ranging from anti-Semitism, which subjected him to the anti-Jewish sentiments of many critics, to the explicit or implied sexual themes in his plays. Other controversial issues included his political stance; his critical position with regard to the military, which proved to be a source of much hostility; and also, as he perceived it, jealousy on the part of less successful friends.[26]

The success of *Liebelei* propelled Schnitzler into the world of German-speaking theater and literary history.[27] However, this triumph came with its downside, since he continued to be associated first and foremost with this play, even when his repertoire reached far beyond the themes presented in *Liebelei:* love and death and the trademark figure of the *süßes Mädel.* After the First World War, an even more turbulent time set in for Schnitzler, marked by scandals, protests, animosity, and rejection, while at the same time he enjoyed new successes with his fiction and even in the new medium of motion pictures.[28] Much negative criticism was based on the perception that he portrayed only *fin-de-siècle* Vienna and worn-out themes, and consequently the public and critics failed to assess his later plays in their own context and for their own merit, but rather, evaluated them according to their expectations.

From 1938 until 1945, the anti-Semitism with which Schnitzler was all too familiar and had pilloried on the stage officially eradicated his works from German literary studies and theater. After the collapse of the Nazi regime, Schnitzler's plays once again appeared in some Vienna theaters, a fact that must be viewed as a reflection of the effort by a segment of the cultural establishment to "reconnect" with pre-1938 Austrian culture. Yet, in his study on Schnitzler's reception after 1945, Johann Sonnleitner points out that despite widespread consensus that Schnitzler should again be part of the canon, that was not the case. Sonnleitner further maintains that in the effort to reclaim Schnitzler and his central place in literature, his works were in actuality misused as documents of great Austrian culture, while the anti-Semitism and hostility targeting him and his works were completely ignored.[29] Thus, while Schnitzler seemingly was being reintegrated into the literary canon — and his plays were once again being staged — something was amiss. Sonnleitner underscores his assertion by pointing out that besides a few dissertations, German Studies in Austria showed little interest in Schnitzler until the early 1960s.[30]

Despite the alleged desire to rehabilitate Schnitzler after his ejection from the literary scene during the Nazi years, the post-war reception returned to the ambivalent criticism and attitudes that had dominated while Schnitzler was still alive. He continued to be associated solely with the *fin-de-siècle*. The negative criticism also revealed persistent latent anti-Semitism and prudishness. Sonnleitner's remarks further illustrate that these perceptions continued to influence the general reception of his works and that any real efforts to "reclaim" him did not take hold until the "Schnitzler renaissance" of the 1960s. That he, by now, has definitively "arrived" is documented by W. E. Yates in his study, *Theatre in Vienna. A Critical History, 1776–1995* (1996). When discussing the repertoires of contemporary theater, he mentions Schnitzler as an Austrian "classic" along with Ferdinand Jakob Raimund (1790–1836), Johann Nestroy (1801–1862), and Franz Grillparzer (1791–1872).[31] The scandal-ridden playwright so often identified with his work and associated with the narrow time-frame of turn-of-the-century Vienna is thus one of few representatives of an earlier period still performed in German-speaking theaters. He is an author who continues to hold the attention of scholars and critics. In other words, the intrigue persists.

Reinhard Urbach asserts that Schnitzler made an effort to focus the public's attention on his work and to keep himself and his personal life in the background; he avoided the limelight. Although he was fairly successful at this endeavor, his reclusive behavior only added to the Schnitzler intrigue and resulted in the audience filling in the gaps by identifying Schnitzler with the characters in his work. Urbach further contends that the fact that Schnitzler did not seek to promote audience understanding of his works, as Hugo von Hofmannsthal or Thomas Mann did for theirs, often led to misunderstandings of his intentions. Schnitzler was of the opinion that his works were self-explanatory, and if not, then they were deficient.[32]

The gap between Schnitzler's intention and the viewing or reading public's interpretation of any given work has to do with the expectations of both public and author. The overall effect of the play arises from the tension between the two. The reception process is further complicated by the simultaneous presence of multiple layers of history. An initial level would be the location and time that Schnitzler chose for any given play: various milieus of his era or from history. Locating a play in an historical setting allows Schnitzler to open up a dialogue with the past and in so doing, explore his present, making his themes and his theatrics universal. Another level concerns the historical time of audience viewing. First, there is the issue of Schnitzler's contemporary audience interpreting his historical plays as well as the plays set in their present. Second, there are later audiences — including those of the twenty-first century — who attempt to come to terms with Schnitzler's works and who bring to them their own understanding of history. The latter is by necessity based on new context and is shaped in part by history, by the history of reception, and by contemporary values and experiences.

In Schnitzler's case, reception started with his peers, who generated a certain image of author and work that dominated Schnitzler criticism for a long time to come. For example, besides their perception that he was affixed to turn-of-the-century Vienna, his contemporaries also often assessed his works as a general diagnosis and analysis of the human condition. Overall, however, Schnitzler was seen as being apolitical. His friend, the author Felix Salten, for instance, wrote in an obituary of Schnitzler for the *Neue Freie Presse* that the deceased had lived a life apart from politics.[33] This type of assessment by friends and colleagues came to dominate public opinion of Schnitzler, indeed to "plague" the critical view of his works. Anton Pelinka, re-assessing Schnitzler's life and works fifty years later, vehemently disagrees with Salten's assessment and counters that the image of Schnitzler as an apolitical dramatist limited to diagnosing the condition of the human soul and who is therefore unaware of social conflicts and politics is not only a traditional but also an incorrect perception.[34] Pelinka further argues that referring to Schnitzler as "apolitical" is only possible by reading his works on the surface without regard to the social realities of his time, and he emphasizes that this attitude toward Schnitzler extends far beyond Salten.[35] Pelinka's remarks are important because they illustrate the contradictory nature of critical reception surrounding Schnitzler.

A brief overview of the reception of *Professor Bernhardi* (1912) from its premiere in 1912 until the present offers a case study of how context, historical events, and reception do indeed shape audience understanding of a work.[36] Peter Blickle, for example, in his essay on the scandal surrounding the play, shows which preconditions existed that allowed the subversive potential of the drama to spark virulent political scandals. In other works, the study examines the elements that caused the reading or viewing audience to react positively or negatively to the transgressive energy of the play.[37] Indeed, the Viennese censorship of the drama and the scandal involving the play have been thoroughly documented.[38]

To summarize, *Professor Bernhardi* did not pass Viennese censorship in fall 1912 because of what the bureaucrats considered its offensive portrayal of Catholic church politics. Yet, the work premiered in Victor Barnowsky's *Kleines Theater* in Berlin on November 28, 1912, contrary to the opinion voiced by Brahm that the play should first be performed in Vienna because of its specifically Austrian, Catholic-Jewish theme — an opinion shared by many.[39] Hans-Peter Bayerdörfer's article *"Professor Bernhardi* auf Berliner Bühnen" (1996)[40] summarizes how reviewers in Berlin reacted. The content of the play was primarily regarded as an

Austrian affair. The censorship situation in Austria had politicized the play and polarized the reception, with one side supporting Schnitzler and the other condemning him. Ultimately in both Vienna and Berlin, the critical reaction was determined by a culture-specific understanding of the socio-political and religious context. The Austrian audience was likely to read into the play observations and insinuations on Schnitzler's part aimed at the machinations of the Habsburg bureaucracy. They were also likely to recognize the blatant attitudes of anti-Semitism presented. A Berlin audience would have had a similar interpretation of the play even though they would not necessarily have understood the workings of the Habsburg government. Yet, because Berlin audiences did view the play as exemplifying an Austrian dilemma, they did not regard it as an indictment of their own anti-Semitism. Hence they were able to feel comfortable about their own acceptance of assimilated Jews.[41]

Finally, after the First World War and the collapse of the monarchy, *Professor Bernhardi* was performed in Vienna (December 1918). Still, the earlier censorship was justified by Austrian bureaucrats because of the way that Schnitzler had portrayed society as lacking in moral rigor, as being driven by social climbing, hypocrisy, and idiocy — in short, as a society whose unscrupulous representatives were given to unmitigated corruption. Meanwhile, however, the same bureaucrats had determined that *Professor Bernhardi* now could be performed because a negative portrayal of imperial Austria was no longer a topical issue.[42] Obviously these critics dismissed the past a little too soon — as subsequent historical events have proven.

In contrast to earlier audiences, the viewing public after Austro-Fascism and the collapse of the Third Reich could not help but view *Professor Bernhardi* with visions of Holocaust victims in mind. New interpretations of the work recognized that the Berlin critics had been short-sighted in their smugness and acknowledged that the seeds of the Nazi atrocities had already been sown in Berlin and in Vienna. Indeed, any post-1945 audience had to read *Professor Bernhardi* in a new light.

Professor Bernhardi is one of Schnitzler's dramas that is still frequently staged. A look at the program from a 1999 performance at the Burgtheater reveals that the awareness of the past shapes the contemporary audience's understanding of the play. Selected documentation on the censorship affair and selected essays and excerpts of texts by Schnitzler's contemporaries and current Austrian writers underscore that the play is taken to be a foreshadowing of the events that transpired under the auspices of the Third Reich as well as a diagnosis of the anti-Semitism and xenophobia that still permeate parts of Austrian society. By all appearances Schnitzler's work continues to have topical relevance.

Over the years, many of Schnitzler's works were subject to censorship and anti-Semitic coverage by the conservative press. They were also widely misunderstood and misinterpreted. The most notorious scandal, of course, involved *Reigen,* documented in thorough studies by Gerd Schneider and Alfred Pfoser.[43] Eventually Schnitzler himself "censored" the play and banned it from the stage. Meanwhile *Reigen* has become his best-known play, even more closely associated with his name than *Liebelei.* While on the one hand, scandals did typify the reception of Schnitzler's works, on the other, it must be remembered that Schnitzler was nonetheless one of the most frequently performed playwrights of his time as well as the present. The various adaptations of his works by contemporary playwrights for the stage as well as movie adaptations are evidence of his continued success. And, during Schnitzler's lifetime, *Liebelei,* for instance, took the theaters by storm; *Das weite Land* premiered in eight German-speaking theaters at once;[44] and *Der junge Medardus* received approximately thirty curtain calls at its premiere.[45] Schnitzler enjoyed greater and more lasting success than most of his peers, and he certainly is one of the most intriguing Austrian "classics."

Conclusion

Schnitzler's contemporaries were content to assess him as a controversial chronicler of their own times, the observer of a soon-to-be archaic world. Now, entering a new millennium, scholars are reassessing Schnitzler's life, his works, and his influence, all of which are interwoven. His appeal to the world of theater endures because of the wide range of provocative issues that his works cover — in direct contradiction to the often-perpetuated view that his dramas had become passé even while he was still alive. His medley of themes clearly demonstrates Schnitzler's artistic creativity as well as his medical, scientific training. Both his clinical eye and his literary talent enabled him to capture the essence of human nature and the confused condition of the human soul in his works, which ultimately represent a dramatic analysis of society.

The settings of Schnitzler's plays may be turn-of-the-century or historical, yet upon re-reading and re-enacting, they succeed in shedding light on societal values and perceptions of both the past and present. Attitudes and ideas may have changed, but the question remains as to how much and to what degree. Could Schnitzler hold an audience's imagination today if he had not somehow established a connection between this and the last *fin-de-siècle*? Each of his plays is a self-contained drama and intrigue in itself. At the same time, however, his dramatic works taken as a whole reveal just how deeply he delves into the conflicts that continue to plague and preoccupy the human psyche. He is particularly adept at presenting the intricacies of interpersonal and male-female relations, which, despite their romantic overtones, are characterized by unfulfilled or false love, or are vexed by infidelity and betrayal. These relationships are often based on empty words, deceptive premises, or hollow social codes, and are lacking in honesty but are therefore a reflection of social reality.

Schnitzler's works continue to provide intrigue and inspiration for the stage and movies, as recent theater and motion-picture adaptations of some of his works attest. Stanley Kubrick's adaptation of *Traumnovelle* into the movie *Eyes Wide Shut,* for example, transports the husband-wife relationship of Fridolin and Albertine, set originally in the Vienna of Schnitzler's day, into present-day New York City through the characters Bill and Alice. Both couples, though decades apart, are caught in a problematic deciphering of dream/illusion and reality, and Kubrick's version presents as disturbing and compelling a story today as when *Traumnovelle* was originally published in 1926. In a critique of Kubrick and the movie in the *London Review of Books,* Michael Wood states: "If you are expecting a masterpiece, you're in for a disappointment, but there is a weird success in the way the film stays afloat in spite of everything that might sink it. The chief reasons for this success are the plot and premise borrowed from Schnitzler, and shifted slightly but in interesting ways."[46] Schnitzler's ability to "tell a story"[47] is the force that convinced Kubrick of the adaptability of the novella. It is also the force that still draws contemporary authors and audiences to Schnitzler.

Another example of Schnitzler's contemporary appeal, also for the English-speaking world, is David Hare's adaptation of *Reigen* as *The Blue Room.* Hare has reset the round dance of sexual scenes into the present day. He revamps Schnitzler's perceptions of the gender gap, sex, and social class and incorporates the older playwright's observations about the nature of projection and desire into his own insightful version of male-female relations that is completely up-to-date.

Another revision of *Reigen* is Werner Schwab's *Der reizende Reigen nach dem Reigen des reizenden Herrn Arthur Schnitzler,* published in 1996.[48] The setting is still Vienna, and although some of the *fin-de-siècle* characters have been "updated," Schwab captures differences and contemporary versions of the character types portrayed by Schnitzler. Schwab's highly provocative play illustrates that transformations in audience expectation and tolerance have occurred; for instance, the detachable genitalia of his characters demonstrate that the notion of "provocative" has changed in the hundred years between the two *Reigen* versions, yet the basic premise underlying both continues to hold the attention of the audience.

These contemporary examples of adaptations of Schnitzler's works demonstrate convincingly the lasting vitality and appeal of his canon. Schnitzler's innovative use of theatrical devices and language, together with his insightful social criticism and observations about the psychology of sexuality, continue to challenge, fascinate, and intrigue the modern reader and viewer as they did the audiences of Schnitzler's times.

Notes

[1] Tom Stoppard, *Undiscovered Country* (Boston and London: Faber & Faber, 1980).

[2] David Hare, *The Blue Room* (London: Faber & Faber, 1999).

[3] *Eyes Wide Shut*, dir. Stanley Kubrick (New York: Warner Brothers, 1999); *Das weite Land* in DW II, 217–320; *Reigen* in DW I, 327–90; *Traumnovelle* in ES II, 434–504.

[4] See Ellen Butzko, *Arthur Schnitzler und die zeitgenössische Theaterkritik* (Frankfurt: Peter Lang, 1991), 2.

[5] Werner Wilhelm Schnabel writes that with 200 performances by 1914, Schnitzler was by far the most often performed author at the Burgtheater. Schnabel, "*Professor Bernhardi* und die Wiener Zensur," *Jahrbuch der deutschen Schillergesellschaft* 29 (1984), 358. See also Viktor Žmegač, "Die Wiener Moderne," *Geschichte der deutschen Literatur vom 18. Jahrhundert bis zur Gegenwart*, vol. II/2, ed. Viktor Žmegač (Königstein/Ts.: Athenäum, 1980), 264.

[6] See for example Wolfgang Lange, "Wien um 1900. Phantasmagorie einer Metropole," *Deutschunterricht* 47, no. 5 (1995), 30–44, particularly 30.

[7] See Walter Zettl, "Der politische und soziale Hintergrund für das Werk Arthur Schnitzlers," in *Studia Schnitzleriana*, ed. Fausto Cerciganani (Allessandria: Orso, 1991), 107–20, particularly 107.

[8] *Komödie der Worte* in DW II, 465–528; *Das Wort. Tragikomödie in fünf Akten. Fragment*, ed. Kurt Bergel (Frankfurt: Fischer, 1966). Gerhard Kluge, "Arthur Schnitzlers Einakterzyklus *Komödie der Worte*," in *Drama und Theater im 20. Jahrhundert, Festschrift für Walter Hinck*, eds. Hans Dietrich Irmscher and Werner Keller (Göttingen: Vandenhoeck & Ruprecht, 1983), 79.

[9] *Anatol* in DW I, 28–104.

[10] *Paracelsus* in DW I, 465–98.

[11] See Andreas Huyssen, "The Disturbance of Vision in Vienna Modernism," *Modernisms/Modernity* 5/3 (1998): 34: "While the crisis of language has often been understood as a trigger for, or part of, a crisis of identity and its overcoming . . ., the contemporary discourse about subjectivity, language, and visuality has opened up a new space for more precise theoretical readings of that link between the crisis of language and identity crisis."

[12] *Marionetten* in DW I, 838–70.

[13] *Der einsame Weg* in DW I, 759–837.

[14] *Komtesse Mizzi* in DW I, 1029–63.

[15] *Fink und Fliederbusch* in DW II, 555–650.

[16] *Der Gang zum Weiher* in DW II, 739–844.

[17] *Liebelei* in DW I, 215–64.

[18] *Das Vermächtnis* in DW I, 391–464.

[19] *Der Ruf des Lebens* in DW I, 963–1028; *Der junge Medardus* in DW II, 27–216; *Die Schwestern oder Casanova in Spa* in DW II, 651–738.

[20] See Franz Norbert Mennemeier, "Die Revolution, von unten gesehen. Zu Arthur Schnitzlers "Der grüne Kakadu," in *Deutsche Dichtung um 1890. Beiträge zu einer Literatur im Umbruch,* eds. Robert Leroy and Eckart Pastor (Bern: Peter Lang, 1991), 391–97.

[21] Marianna Squercina, "History and Fiction in a Drama on Revolution: Arthur Schnitzler's *Der grüne Kakadu*," *New German Review* 5–6 (1989–1990): 107.

[22] Squercina, 101.

[23] *Leutnant Gustl* in ES I, 337–66. See for example, Huyssen, 34.

[24] For these remarks, see Heinz Ludwig Arnold, "Der falsch gewonnene Prozeß. Das Verfahren gegen Arthur Schnitzlers *Reigen*," *Text + Kritik* 138/139 (1998): 115.

[25] For a summary of his skeptical reaction to critics, see, in addition to Schnitzler's *Tagebücher*, Butzko's study, *Arthur Schnitzler und die zeitgenössische Theaterkritik.*

[26] See Butzko, chapter 2.

[27] Reinhard Urbach, *Schnitzler Kommentar. Zu den erzählenden Schriften und dramatischen Werken* (Munich: Winkler, 1974), 22.

[28] Urbach, 22.

[29] Johann Sonnleitner, "Die Rezeption der Wiener Moderne in Österreich. Schnitzler und Hofmannsthal nach 1945," in *Die einen raus, die anderen rein. Kanon und Literatur. Vorüberlegungen. Zu einer Literaturgeschichte Österreichs,* eds. Wendelin Schmidt-Dengler, Johann Sonnleitner, and Klaus Zeyringer (Berlin: Schmidt, 1994), 158–59.

[30] Sonnleitner, 158.

[31] W. E. Yates, *Theatre in Vienna. A Critical History, 1776–1995* (Cambridge: Cambridge UP, 1996). See chapter 9 ("The Second Republic"), part 2 ("The Present"), 237–45, particularly 240, 241, and 242.

[32] Urbach, 29.

[33] *Neue Freie Presse* (October 22, 1931): 2. Quoted in Anton Pelinka, "Die Struktur und die Probleme der Gesellschaft zur Zeit Arthur Schnitzlers," *Literatur und Kritik* 163/164 (1982): 59–66. Salten's quote, p. 59.

[34] Pelinka, 59.

[35] Pelinka writes: "Die These vom 'unpolitischen' Schnitzler reicht weit über Felix Salten hinaus. So attestiert Hartmut Scheible Schnitzler eine 'vehement unpolitische Haltung'" (59). His reference is to Hartmut Scheible, *Arthur Schnitzler in Selbstzeugnissen und Bilddokumenten* (Reinbek bei Hamburg: Rowohlt, 1976), 95.

[36] *Professor Bernhardi* in DW II, 337–464.

[37] Peter Blickle, "Die Einlösung subversiven Wirkungspotentials: Die Theaterskandale um Arthur Schnitzlers *Professor Bernhardi* und Rolf Hochhuths *Stellvertreter*," *New German Review* 10 (1994): 103.

[38] See for example, Schnabel; Blickle (103–18); W. E. Yates, *Schnitzler, Hofmannsthal, and the Austrian Theatre* (New Haven: Yale UP, 1992), chapter 3 (66–114); and Hans-Peter Bayerdörfer, "Österreichische Verhältnisse'? — Arthur Schnitzlers *Professor Bernhardi* auf Berliner Bühnen 1912–1931," in *Von Franzos zu Canetti. Jüdische Autoren aus Österreich. Neue Studien,* eds. Mark H. Gelber, Hans Otto Horch, and Sigurd Paul Scheichl (Tübingen: Max Niemeyer, 1996), 211–24. Also see Butzko, 57–64.

[39] Brahm's comment was noted by Schnitzler in a diary entry (May 8, 1912). Quoted in Bayerdörfer, 211.

[40] Bayerdörfer, 211–24.

[41] See, for example, Bayerdörfer, 215: "Die Herablassung gegenüber Österreich könnte nicht deutlicher sein, die Aburteilung erfolgt aus einer Position, in der das deutsche Judentum seinen assimilatorischen Prämissen treu bleiben kann, da es deren Verteidigung offensichtlich nicht nötig zu haben glaubt."

[42] Schnabel, 268. Schnabel refers in his article to Karl Glossy, *Vierzig Jahre Deutsches Volkstheater. Ein Beitrag zur deutschen Theatergeschichte* (Vienna: Deutsches Volkstheater, 1929), 223.

[43] See Gerd K. Schneider, *Die Rezeption von Arthur Schnitzlers Reigen 1897–1994. Text, Aufführungen, Verfilmungen; Pressespiegel und andere zeitgenössische Kommentare* (Riverside: Ariadne, 1995); Alfred Pfoser, Kristina Pfoser-Schweig, and Gerhard Renner, eds. *Schnitzlers "Reigen,"* vol. I: *Der Skandal: Analysen und Dokumente;* vol. II: *Die Prozesse: Analyse und Dokumente* (Frankfurt: Fischer, 1993).

[44] Anton Mayer, *Theater in Wien um 1900. Der Dichterkreis Jung Wien* (Vienna: Böhlau, 1997), 28.

[45] Butzko, 57.

[46] Michael Wood, "Quite a Night!" *London Review of Books* (September 20, 1999), 52.

[47] Kubrick told his screenplay writer, Frederic Raphael, to "[t]rack Arthur. He knows how to tell a story" (Wood, 52).

[48] Werner Schwab, *Der Reizende Reigen nach dem Reigen des reizenden Herrn Arthur Schnitzler* (Graz: Literaturverlag Droschl, 1996).

Arthur Schnitzler's Puppet Plays

G. J. Weinberger

WHEN ARTHUR SCHNITZLER created his puppet plays — *Zum gro-ßen Wurstel* (1905), *Der tapfere Cassian* (1904), *Die Verwandlung des Pierrot* (1908), and *Der Schleier der Pierrette* (1910) — over a span of nine years, from his first version of *Zum großen Wurstel* in 1901 to the appearance of *Der Schleier der Pierrette* in 1910, he participated in a body of literary and theatrical traditions reaching back, in one instance, to ancient Greece or earlier and enjoying a revival around the turn of the century.[1] Moreover, a look beyond these plays to those featuring humans as puppeteers, such as *Paracelsus* (1899) and *Zug der Schatten* (1970), which remained incomplete at his death, reveals that Schnitzler's interest in the broad area of the "Puppenspiel" was one that occupied him during most of his literary career.[2]

Specifically, these traditions, which tend to appear in various overlapping configurations, include: the *commedia dell'arte*, essentially a Renaissance form, but one with parallels, if not actual roots in antiquity and medieval times; the marionette or puppet-play, a genre of great and enduring popularity to this day, and one that may be partly or wholly pantomimic; and the anti-illusionist play, in which actors fall out of their roles to address or interact with the audience (or more than one audience).

Schnitzler's interest in puppets, whether humans or marionettes, and in their puppet-masters is one aspect of his lifelong concern with the element in human nature that seeks to control the other, be it for the satisfaction of some drive for power or to do something for another person's "good."[3] There is, of course, a degree of arrogance implied in behavior of this sort, but human nature being what it is, it should come as no surprise to find an individual wanting to play God on occasion.[4] In fact, Schnitzler's puppet-masters go far beyond the early Anatol's "head games" with his several lovers. The actual "Puppenspieler" actively manipulates, or tries to manipulate, another person's life, most often without the latter's knowledge. Merklin, the title character of Schnitzler's one-act play *Der Puppenspieler* (1903), for example, plays God with the Jagisches, who remain ignorant of his determining influence on their

lives until years after the fact, just as the supposedly human characters in
Zum großen Wurstel remain unaware until the very end that they are
puppets as well. Only the "real" puppets in the latter play "know" that
someone is pulling their strings.

The question of the origins of the *commedia dell'arte* has resulted in
considerable speculation and controversy. Ruth E. Peabody, among others, lists Greek and Atellan farces and medieval mystery plays as possible
sources.[5] The term "commedia dell'arte" first appeared in Italy in the
eighteenth century, although actors as far back as the sixteenth century
referred to themselves as *comici dell'arte*.[6] According to John Rudlin,
"*Commedia dell'arte* was born, some time around the middle of the sixteenth century, in the market place where a crowd was to be attracted,
interested and then held if a living is to be made."[7] This living was not,
however, necessarily made simply by the *zanni* (comic actors) entertaining
audiences with their *lazzi* (physical comedy). The performance involved
mountebanks, often medicinal quacks or magician-illusionists assisted by
jesters who would, after sufficient sales had been made, entertain with a
commedia performance,[8] one that often led to a wrathful reaction on the
part of the legal and religious authorities,[9] of the sort manifested by Copus's response to Paracelsus's performance in Basel and by Cyprian's threat
to have Paracelsus charged with witchcraft and thrown in the deepest of
dungeons.[10]

The inveterate English traveler Thomas Coryat recorded such a performance in 1611: "In the meane time while the musicke playes, the prin-
cipall Mountebanke which is the Captaine and ring-leader of all the rest,
opens his trunke, and sets abroach his wares: after the musicke has ceased,
he maketh an oration to the audience of half an houre long, or almost an
houre. Wherein he doth most hyperbolically extoll the vertue of his drugs
and confections. . . . "[11] This is not to say, however, that the *commedia*
could not also be performed as "respectable" entertainment. Indeed, its
spreading to the German-speaking lands from its origins in Italy was aided
when a *commedia* troupe was invited to perform at the 1568 wedding of
Ludwig V of Bavaria.[12] In Austria, the Emperor Matthias called the Italian
troupe of the Cecchini to Vienna in 1614, and the first opera performance
with *commedia dell'arte* types took place in Vienna in 1625.

The most important stock characters of the *commedia* include Pierrot,
"the love-struck simpleton and victim of life"; Columbine, "the light-
minded sex object"; and Harlequin, "the brutal and cynical trickster."[13] In
a typical play involving this triad, Alain-René Lesage's *Harlequin Orphée fils*
(1718), Harlequin marries Columbine and Pierrot ends up killing himself,[14]
a turn of events not unlike that of Schnitzler's *Der Schleier der Pierrette*.

Pierrot — originally Pedrolino, a valet character from the *commedia* — is given his French name by Molière in *Dom Juan, ou le festin de Pierre* (1665),[15] and has survived to the present in spite of changing fashions. One reason may well be that merry characters are always manifestations of a certain aspect of a national character, which explains the hardiness ("Zählebigkeit") of this comic type.[16] Moreover, the defining gesture that Pierrot, like all the *commedia* characters, received from his Italian beginning assured his continued attractiveness to modern sensibilities: "Pierrot, der Melancholiker in dem weiten fließenden Gewand, hat es wohl nicht zuletzt seiner träumerischen Gebärde zu verdanken, daß ihn die Romantiker . . . zu ihrer Lieblingsfigur machten," with his "getragene, traurige Gestus, Ausdruck eines Weltschmerzes, in dem sich alte Romantiker und junge Existentialisten zusammenfanden."[17] Still, Pierrot undergoes change. From his beginning as a "cringing zany," he begins over time to expand his range considerably, taking on a variety of different roles, such as that of a cobbler, grocer, photographer, or gardener,[18] much as he does in Schnitzler's *Die Verwandlung des Pierrot*.

In a similar manner, Harlequin underwent changes as well. By the eighteenth century he had become "a rather strict, neurotic patriarchal type"[19] who, like his descendants in *Die Verwandlung des Pierrot* and *Zum großen Wurstel,* may also be the "deceived father of an eager virgin."[20] Less subject to change over the centuries are the characters of the Dottore — usually a satire on lawyers and learned men, represented in Schnitzler most clearly by Copus in *Paracelsus* — and the Capitano. The latter, originally a lover, was gradually transformed into the familiar *miles gloriosus* of antiquity, given to hyperbolic language, vain about his looks, and confident of his ability to conquer women.[21] He typically appears sporting a big mustache and wearing a flamboyant outfit, including a plumed hat and large sword, creating "terror for a moment, swaggering, parading, blustering, threatening, bragging of his feats in love and war," much like Schnitzler's Cassian but, when all is said and done, a coward after all.[22]

The connection between the *commedia* and the marionette theater has been recognized by many students;[23] according to Pierre Louis Ducharte, it is in marionette shows that last vestiges of *commedia* are to be seen.[24] The precise time and place of the origin of puppets and puppet plays have also been subjects of much debate;[25] but whether they arose in Asia or in ancient Greece, there is agreement as to their antiquity and to their universal popularity.

Among the great English Jacobean dramatists, for example, there are references to puppet shows in Francis Beaumont's *Knight of the Burning Pestle* (1613) and in Ben Jonson's *Bartholomew Fair* (1614). In German-

speaking lands the marionette theaters appear toward the end of the sixteenth and beginning of the seventeenth centuries. Their increasing popularity in the Renaissance may well have been the result of the breakdown
of the orderly medieval world, as Luzia Glanz suggests: only when the
world began to seem "sinnlos" did the symbolism of the marionette become relevant.[26] In turn, its popularity waned again during the Enlightenment of the eighteenth century, especially after Johann Christoph
Gottsched's rationalist "reforms," when the notion of a puppet being
controlled or having its strings pulled by an unknown force lost its relevance.[27] In Vienna, where the well-documented family Hilversing is known
to have presented marionette plays on the Neuer Markt and the Juden-
platz in the later seventeenth century,[28] all puppet theaters were forced into
the suburbs in 1716 and 1717 and then banned altogether in 1728.[29]

However, as was the case with Pierrot and his companions, popular
forms of entertainment cannot be suppressed for long. Literary marionette
plays, acted by human beings rather than by puppets, began to appear in
the 1760s and 1770s. They enjoyed a flowering of sorts in the Romantic
period, attracting the attention of figures such as Heinrich von Kleist and
E. T. A. Hoffmann as well as Ludwig Tieck, who found marionettes particularly suited to the interplay of illusion and reality which he clearly
favored.[30] In fact, the alternation between conventional and marionette
performances was not uncommon. While literary marionette plays were
often performed by actors, some troupes did it both ways, especially for
budgetary reasons: a family troupe could put on a performance with puppets if financial constraints did not permit the hiring of outside actors.[31]

In Vienna, the direction taken by the traditions under consideration —
the *commedia,* Pierrot and his analogues, the puppet play, and the pantomime — was influenced most strongly by Franz Stranitzky, the creator of
Hanswurst, and his followers. The ancestor of this typically Viennese figure
appears to be Pickelhäring, a stock figure of the English traveling troupes
common on the Continent in the late sixteenth and early seventeenth
centuries, who is first recorded in a collection of English plays, titled *Enge-
lische Comedien und Tragedien,* published in 1620,[32] and was soon taken
over in the German theater. When Pickelhäring's popularity began to fade,
Stranitzky revived the character and turned it, as Hanswurst, into a fixture
of Viennese folk comedy. However, like the marionette theaters, the folk-
theaters and their stock characters were put under pressure by eighteenth-
century "reform." With the Enlightenment, improvisations and "Hanswur-
stiaden" were either banned from the royal stages or subjected to fines.
Hence Joseph Johann La Roche, who eventually transformed Hanswurst
into Kaspar Larifari, had to perform in the suburbs.

The figure of Kaspar — who, like so many of his Italian, French, English and German forebears, is also originally a servant — held sway in Vienna for forty years before becoming a stock character in the mario-nette-theater of the entire German sphere.[33] In creating Kaspar, La Roche saved "das barocke Erbe eines vom Mimus und vom Impetus des szenischen Augenblicks abhängigen Theaters," and paved the way for the later folk-theater of Adolf Bäuerle, Johann Nestroy, and Ferdinand Raimund. The enduring popularity of the Kaspar figure in Vienna is attested to by the appearance of Mozart's 1788 *Kanon* ("Gehn ma in'n Prater, / Gehn ma in d'Hötz / Gehn wir zu'n Kasperl, zu'n Kasperl, zu'n Kasperl"); Joachim Perinet's *Kaspar, der Fagottist* (1791), which became as popular as Mozart's *Zauberflöte;* and a variety of "Volksmärchen" featuring Kaspar — dating from the 1790s, such as Karl Friedrich Hensler's "Donauweibchen" (1798), which was praised by Tieck,[34] to the twentieth century, such as Walter Benjamin's "Radaun um Kasper" (1932), Max Kommerell's "Das verbesserte Biribi" (1948), and Hans Carl Artmann's "die liebe fee pocahontas oder kasper als schildwache" (1961).

Coexistent with the *commedia* and with folk-theater, whether performed with marionettes or human actors, is the pantomime. Thus, for instance, Rommel notes the performance in Vienna of the pantomimes "Arlequin. Ein Neben Buhler seines Herrn" in 1746[35] and "Harlequin auf dem Paradebette oder: Nach dem Schlimmen folgt das Gute" (at the Leopoldstheater) in 1790.[36] An extremely ancient form, having enjoyed a flowering as early as the Imperial Rome era,[37] pantomime gained popularity in seventeenth-century France, especially after mainstream theatrical companies pressured the authorities to ban dialogue from street performances.[38] It was readily adopted by Stranitzky, who sought to present experience through gesture and mimicry. By the 1740s Hanswurst became a "Verwandlungskünstler" who would appear in such varied disguises as a beggar, astrologer, chimney-sweep statue, four-year-old child, or alchemist. In the late nineteenth century, the pantomime enjoyed a revival: among Schnitzler's contemporaries and friends, Hermann Bahr, Hugo von Hofmannsthal, and Richard Beer-Hoffmann all experimented with pantomimes.[39]

Of the traditions in question, the anti-illusionist theater is, curiously, at once the most ancient, dating back to Aristophanes, and the most modern, as may be seen in several works by Luigi Pirandello. It is common in Renaissance English and, later, in German Romantic theater; indeed, the breaking of convention, of the illusion that something "real" is taking place upon a stage, itself becomes a sort of convention, one that may be elaborated in many ways.

Theatrical illusions are readily broken by self-referential interpolations, what Friedrich von Schlegel, speaking of Tieck's *Der Gestiefelte Kater* (1797), refers to as "Die Selbstreflexion des Theaters, die Unterbrechungen der dichterische Illusion und die Satire,"[40] well illustrated also in Tieck's *Prinz Zerbino* (1799). In the latter work, Hanswurst and the Old King both remark on characters' being subject to the whim of their creators[41] and, in the play-within-the-play, one puppet begs Jeremias, the puppet-master, "O gütiges Geschick, laß mich doch wenigstens meine Rolle zu Ende spielen."[42] Later in the same play, Zerbino, unhappy with the plot, says to Nestor, "Wollen Sie mich nicht aus dem Stücke heraus lassen, so will ich wenigstens dem Verfasser eine solche Ohrfeige reichen, daß er Zeit seines Lebens an mich denken soll."[43] The illusions may also be broken by characters' apparent departure from the script: when Peter Squentz forgets some of his lines he apologizes to the King in the audience.[44]

Among the most amusing and enduring devices in the anti-illusionist repertory is the anachronism, evident, for example, in the anonymous *Doktor Johannes Faust,* with Kasperl, and the *Ulmer Puppenspiel* of *Doktor Johann Faust,* with Pickelhäring, two plays Goethe admits had a stimulating effect on him.[45] In the latter, Pickelhäring makes extemporaneous references to events of the day,[46] a common element in both Pickelhäring and Kaspar plays, and one that survives, for example, in Frosch's comments in Strauss's *Die Fledermaus* (1874).

Common as well is characters' interaction with an audience, be it one on stage, with no illusion that they are anything other than actors, or one with whom interaction requires crossing the invisible line between stage and orchestra/audience, either by addressing the audience directly or in some other way.[47] In Aristophanes's *Clouds,* the chorus (of "Clouds"), addressing the audience in matters not related to the plot, says to the audience that if they — that is, the play — should win the palm, people's fields will be watered and so on; if not, "Not a single grape" will grow nor "olives bud."[48] A similar threat is issued at the beginning of the third act of Tieck's *Prinz Zerbino.* The hunter warns the audience to approve of the play lest they be punished as he has been: he was in the audience of a better play than this one but was fashionably negative toward it; as soon as the play ended, the gods showed their anger, and "Sie legten mir zur schweren Strafe auf / Als Chorus durch dies lange Stück zu wandeln."[49]

In Renaissance England, Jonson's *Bartholomew Fair* begins with an "Induction" in which, among other things, the "Scrivener" draws up a contract between the audience and the author concerning the audience's behavior. Later, the puppet-master Leatherhead has to break the illusion to explain things to the foolish Cokes, such as to assure him that the puppet striking him has not hurt and to warn him, "Aye, peace, sir, they'll be angry, if they hear you eavesdropping" (V, iv). In the following scene, the puppet Dionysius defeats the character Zeal-of-the-Land Busy in debate. Beaumont's *Knight of the Burning Pestle* is anti-illusionist from the outset, when the Citizen, a grocer by trade, interrupts the Prologue and complains about plays insulting good citizens.[50] He insists that there be a part for a grocer in the play, which, it turns out, will be played by his apprentice, Rafe, who will appear as "The Knight of the Burning Pestle," since there is no such thing as a "grocer errant."[51] This introduction of a member of the audience on to the stage to take a role looks ahead to Tieck's *Verkehrte Welt* (1799) as well as to Schnitzler's *Zum großen Wurstel;* and what follows, amid the grocer's and his wife's constant interruptions, is a crisscrossing of the intended plot and Rafe's performance, a mixture of genres that looks ahead to Hofmannsthal's *Ariadne auf Naxos* (1912).[52] A further crossing of the line between stage and audience takes place in the last scene of Christian Dietrich Grabbe's *Scherz, Satire, Ironie und tiefere Bedeutung* (1827), when the characters Mordax and Wernthal, in their "real" identities as Schauspieler X and Y, escape the punishment for their misdeed within the plot by escaping into the pit, shortly before Grabbe himself appears carrying a lantern and bringing the play to its conclusion.[53]

In the twentieth century, although *Six Characters in Search of an Author* (1921) is probably the best-known anti-illusionist play, Pirandello is not the only one to make use of the available devices. For example, in Kommerell's "Das verbesserte Biribi" (1948), Kasper speaks to Biribi and then turns to the audience: "Jetzt tu' ich mir was Schwarzes um, daß ihr's alle wißt! Aber nicht dem Biribi sagen."[54] At the beginning of the second scene of Hans Carl Artmann's "die liebe fee pocahontas oder kasper als schildwache," Kasper wakes up and asks, "wo bin ich, lieber spezi?" to which the "waldhornist," also transported, replies, "im zweiten aufzug, mister, auf, auf!!"[55]

Among Schnitzler's puppet plays, *Der tapfere Cassian* and *Der Schleier der Pierrette* adhere most closely to the *commedia* tradition. That is, they present several conventional types and plots while merely acknowledging, by dint of their being marionette plays, the existence of a puppet-master, without implying any relationship of cosmic dimensions between him and his puppets.

Der tapfere Cassian, with its original subtitle, "Burleske in einem Akt,"[56] replaced by "Puppenspiel in einem Akt,"[57] was first published in 1904. Beyond its designation as a "Puppenspiel," what distinguishes this play is the straightforward, transparent, marionette-like presentation, most evident toward the end when Sophie leaps out the window: Cassian leaps after her and catches her in mid-air and they both land safely on the street below.[58] But even beyond this scene, the décor, clothing, and food are all subject to exaggerations beyond the usual Capitano conventions; and, while one man's being untrue to his lady is as commonplace in literature as in life, Sophie's attempting to cling to Martin and to dissuade him from leaving her is as reminiscent of the pleading Columbine of the *commedia* as of the rejected woman of the Hanswurst play. At the same time, Martin, like his *commedia* ancestors, will never win the woman of his desires, the dancer Eleonora Lambriani.[59] The latter, thanks to Cassian's summary of her past —

> Die einmal schwor, neunundneunzig Nächte lang jede Nacht einen andern Liebhaber zu beglücken, von denen keiner was Geringeres sein durfte als ein Fürst. . . . Es könnte sein, daß du sie für einen Groschen kriegst; — es ist aber auch möglich, daß sie zehntausend Dukaten fordert für einen Kuß auf die Fingerspitzen. . . .[60]

— appears as a variation of Schnitzler's "dämonische Frau" turned into a *commedia* character. All men who see her become "toll von Entzücken," and Martin cannot even speak of her without getting dizzy.[61]

Most closely related to the *commedia* in this play is the *miles gloriosus*/Capitano element, present from the beginning, when Sophie's worrying about Martin's possibly enlisting in the army raises the subject of his cousin, Cassian: "Der tapfere Cassian. . . . Der schlug schon, als er dreizehn Jahr alt war, zwei Raüber tot. . . . Das ist ein Held! Ich wette, über kurz oder lang wird er Oberst, General."[62] This portrayal is enhanced when Cassian, in reply to Martin's asking where he has been, reports, among other things:

> Ich komme aus einer Schlacht, wo mir zwei Pferde unterm Leib und drei Mützen vom Schädel weggeschossen wurden. . . . Ferner vom Richtplatz, wo sieben an meiner Seite füsiliert und ich mit ihnen für tot in eine Grube geworfen wurde. . . . Ferner aus den Krallen eines Geiers, der mich für Aas hielt . . . und der mich aus Bergeshöhe auf die Erde herunterfallen ließ — glücklicherweise auf einen Heuschober.[63]

Cassian's penchant for exaggeration is obvious from his appearance, *"in phantastischer Uniform,"*[64] and, after noticing the changes in his cousin, from his fantastic inquiry:

> Hast du dem Schah von Persien die Krone vom Nachttisch gestohlen? . . . fährst du morgen in einem vergoldeten Gespann mit sechs weißen Pferden nach Hinterindien? . . . hast du den Erzbischof von Bamberg vergiftet und ist man dir auf der Spur?[65]

Sophie, influenced by Martin's bragging about his cousin, is smitten with Cassian from the moment he appears, in a manner similar to Agnes's being smitten by the new Duke Karl Eberhard in Schnitzler's later story *Die Frau des Richters* (1925).[66] Sophie is only too eager to provide a far better dinner than what she suggested fetching for Martin just moments before and to put on a new bonnet for Cassian.[67] Later, she abruptly asks Cassian to take her along on his way back to his regiment,[68] much as Agnes asks Karl Eberhard to make her one of his "Gartenmagdelein."[69]

A similar serious or tragic conclusion is to be found in *Der Schleier der Pierrette,* featuring Pierrot, Columbine (appearing as Pierrette), and, most notably, Harlequin or Arlecchino. In his earlier incarnations, he is the one who loses his girlfriend, Columbine, to an older man and wants to die,[70] but by the eighteenth century, especially in Carlo Goldoni's works, he "often becomes a typical honest and good-hearted old burgher."[71] By the time he appears in Schnitzler's *Der Schleier der Pierrette* he has become the older man. In fact, Schnitzler's Arlecchino has some of the characteristics of the traditional Pantalone, the middle-aged or older man courting younger women (a type going back in English literature at least as far as Chaucer) who would either scoff at him or trick him.[72]

Der Schleier der Pierrette is the one pantomime-puppet play of Schnitzler's most closely following (and limiting itself to) the *commedia* tradition. Subtitled "Pantomime in drei Bildern"[73] and written as a libretto for Ernst von Dohnányi, it brings together themes from Schnitzler's earlier drama *Der Schleier der Beatrice* (1901) with his most extensive use of *commedia* motifs and a touch of the Viennese *Volkspiel*.[74] The initial indication of this mixture is Pierrot's costume: *"ein Gemisch des traditionellen Pierrot-und des Altwiener Kostüms",*[75] later, Pierrette appears dressed in *"Altwiener Brautkleid mit Nuancen des Pierrettekostüms,"*[76] and Arlecchino in *"Altwiener Kostüm."* Arlecchino is also Pantalone-like, *"groß, hager, nicht mehr jung . . . düster,"* and vengeful. When Pierrette cannot be found, he threatens, "Ich werde fürchterliche Rache nehmen. Ich werde das Haus anzünden. Ich werde all umbringen." Then, *"rasend vor Wut,"* he trashes the buffet and destroys the musicians' instruments.[77]

The dramatic situation is familiar *commedia* stuff. Pierrot, although attractive to women — Annette and Alumette are charmed by the sleeping Pierrot, and the latter wishes to kiss him[78] — has been abandoned by his beloved, Pierrette (née Columbine) for an older, wealthier man, Arlecchino. It is the day of the wedding, and Pierrot, inconsolable, refuses to go out with his friends. Pierrette comes to see him, says she will stay with him, produces a vial with poison, and proposes their mutual suicide. Pierrot suggests they run away together, but when Pierrette points out they have no money, he drinks the poison. She does not and flees after he dies. Back at the reception, Pierrot's ghost appears several times while Pierrette is dancing with Arlecchino, but as in *Die Verwandlung des Pierrot*, he is visible only to her. The last time he appears he is holding her veil. She pursues him, accompanied by Arlecchino, who will not let go of her hand.[79] Arriving at Pierrot's apartment, Arlecchino mocks the dead man as well as Pierrette, then locks her in the room and leaves. She dances, goes mad, collapses, and dies just as Pierrot's returning friends knock on the door. The four enter and dance until they discover the dead couple, "*fassen, was geschehen ist, und weichen entsetzt zurück.*"[80]

Die Verwandlung des Pierrot — subtitled "Pantomime in einem Vorspiel und sechs Bildern" — also brings together aspects of the *commedia* and the *Volksspiel*: Pierrot, the temporarily deserted Columbine who eventually wins him back, and the woman he seems to desire but who is destined for another man, are placed in the context of the Prater, where they play their roles amid typically Viennese merrymakers and amusements. The play is significantly different from *Der tapfere Cassian* and *Der Schleier der Pierrette*, however, in also making use of a "Puppenspieler" element not present in the other two plays.

In his pursuit of Katharina at the various Prater venues, adopting a different disguise on each occasion, Pierrot is, in effect, playing with Katharina, leading her to question her own sense of reality and, ultimately, driving her almost to suicide. In the end, having barely kept her from leaping into the Danube, and caught up with by Anna (his Columbine) and his other *Wurstelprater* colleagues, Pierrot, like Paracelsus and others among Schnitzler's "Puppenspieler" before him, realizes that he has lost control of the situation: he can do little more than shrug his shoulders and ask Anna, in words one can readily imagine Herbot addressing to Sophie, "Du wirst mir doch nicht böse sein?" Immediately thereafter, he avoids everyone's demands for an explanation of his behavior by inviting them back to the Prater, where he will treat them in celebration of his engagement to Anna.[81]

Die Verwandlungen des Pierrot is different from other "Puppenspieler" plays or from those featuring a return to something akin to the status quo, such as *Die große Szene* (1915) or *Im Spiel der Sommerlüfte* (1930).[82] Its being a marionette play adds a level of complexity not found in these other works. Pierrot, given his history and the context in which Schnitzler places him, is not only an actor — controlling others, tempting them to adventure or blurring their sense of reality — but also, simultaneously, a marionette. While this detail may not be readily apparent on the printed page, one must recall, besides the subtitle of the play, that on stage all the action is in pantomime, including the occasional unlikely movement to emphasize that the characters are, in fact, marionettes.[83] Indeed, one of the principal "Verwandlungen" accomplished by Schnitzler is his taking Pierrot, a stock figure from the *commedia dell'arte,* and converting him into a "Puppenspieler" who toys with humans. In other words, Schnitzler has created a character who is conventionally played with by an outside force, literally, by having his strings pulled, and made him into one who, if only for a while, controls the actions of others.[84]

But the question then arises, who or what is manipulating him? Is he somehow controlled by his promises to Anna, by his obligations to his colleagues, or by Katharina's repeated escapes? Why is Pierrot "not free," as Martin Swales says? Simply put, one must assume that because he is a "pierrot" — that is, a type of marionette — there must be *someone* pulling *his* strings. As in *Zum großen Wurstel,* the fact that one or more characters who consider themselves "real" are toying with others does not obviate the existence of an "über"-manipulator who may himself not occupy the top spot on his particular chain of being. What audiences are left with, then, is a play within a play, much like *Der grüne Kakadu* (1899), performed for an easily satisfied audience that is unable always to distinguish between illusion and reality,[85] and in which, when all is said and done, the nature and identity of whoever is in charge must remain a mystery. Thus, *Die Verwandlungen des Pierrot* illustrates the *theatrum mundi* motif and, as such, serves as a critique of the world, in both its "real" and "puppet" manifestations. As Swales puts it, "The rapid, jerky movements, the bewildering pace of the 'Wirtshauskomödie,' the violent passions which last only a matter of seconds, all these features belong as much to the world of Katharina and Eduard, to the respectable bourgeois world, as to the world of Harlequin and Columbine."[86]

Zum großen Wurstel, originally titled "Marionetten," was first produced on March 8, 1901 at Hans Paul von Wolzogen's *Überbrettl* in Berlin.[87] It was later reworked into its present form, subtitled "Burleske in einem Akt," and published in 1905. More than the other marionette plays, *Zum großen Wurstel* represents an elaboration of the *theatrum mundi* motif thanks to its setting, the *Wurstelprater,* to its use of marionettes in a play-within-a-play, and, most important, to the appearance of the "Unbekannte" at the end, his cutting the puppets' strings, and the resumption of the performance from its beginning.

In keeping with the lack of sophistication suggested by the setting (the *Wurstelprater* not being associated with high culture), Schnitzler lulls his audiences — on stage, in the theater, or reading the play — with an almost farce-like comedy before obliging them to face an extremely serious issue, one that may result in a good deal of discomfort for all of them. The Director hints at this shift when he says to the Author, "Ich hab's Ihnen g'sagt: Wenn der Schluß ernst wird, hilft's Ihnen nicht mehr, daß der Anfang ein Blödsinn war"; this immediately prior to his attempting to calm his restive audience by reminding them that the stage is only a mirror of real life: "Alsdann, wenn sich das Wesen . . . daß die Bühne das Abbild des Erdentreibens, auch Spiegel der Welt genannt . . . die Belustigung hat."[88]

Indeed, to emphasize the relationship of stage to reality, of *theatrum* to *mundi,* Schnitzler presents his audience with three stages (or four, including the larger, actual theater): the stage itself, a large Marionettentheater, and a smaller Wursteltheater. The latter, being of "alter Konstruktion," emphasizes the timelessness of both theme and situation. Indeed, one of the things that makes the "Naïve Man" naïve is his thinking there is a new show playing at the *Wurstelprater*[89] when, in fact, the underlying message is very old. Moreover, the timelessness of the theme and its implications are made clear by Schnitzler's pointing to the ever-recurring nature of the human dilemma. This concept is most obvious in the "Reigen"-like structure of the play, in which the ending replicates the beginning, but it is also the reason for his placing on stage a partially visible carousel. In addition, immediately prior to being revealed as a "Hanswurst" himself — that is, as just another puppet, and a foolish one at that — the character of Death refers directly to the "Reigen," as well as to the underlying seriousness of an apparently humorous puppet show:

> Lacht sich heut im eignen Haus
> Publikum und Dichter aus,
> Mag sich zum Beschluß im Reigen
> Ehrlich auch der Tod erzeigen.[90]

This particular "Death," however, while reminiscent of his forebears in medieval morality plays — the overweening fool destined to be overcome by a benevolent deity — fails to understand the eternal nature of the "Reigen," is powerless to stop it in any event, and can neither offer nor imply the existence of any transcendent reality. Consequently, the "Herr im Parkett" is absolutely right in feeling he is being cheated out of a conclusion.[91] Thus, although the Author declares "Das Spiel ist aus" after losing control of the scene, the puppets assert their "independence" and carry on their never-ending comedy with the words, "Laßt uns unser Spiel beginnen."[92] Of course, the "real" puppets are no more in control of their actions than the human ones. The only one with any measure of control, limited as it turns out to be, is the mysterious "Unbekannte" who appears almost at the end of the play and cuts all the puppets' strings just prior to the action resuming from the beginning.

Although several critics have proposed suggestions regarding the identity of the "Unbekannte,"[93] his "real" identity must ultimately remain unknowable, although he is related to the "Unsichtbarer Geist" in the story *Die dreifache Warnung* (1911).[94] His name certainly points to the unknowable nature of popular divinity, but whether the chain of being culminates with him or with some still more powerful force must remain a mystery, although a higher power is suggested by his revealing, "Seit manchem Erdentag / Bin ich verdammt, ein Rätsel mir und andern, / Die Welt nach allen Winden zu durchwandern."[95] Still, as far as the puppets (on all levels) are concerned, the "Unbekannte" may as well be the only divinity, albeit one unsure of his own identity ("Was ich bedeuten mag — / Ich weiß es nicht") and lacking any foreknowledge concerning who is and is not a puppet. When everyone on stage, including the Author, falls before his sword, he can only exclaim, "Auch ihr? . . . Auch du? . . . Mir graut vor meiner Macht!"[96]

As the only character without strings, the "Unbekannte" must also be viewed as the principal puppeteer, or "Puppenspieler." Typically, the "Puppenspieler" negates his victims' humanity.[97] Put another way, the "Puppenspieler" imposes upon them "theater," the mirror of real life, where all manner of illusion is conventionally acceptable, to take the place of genuine real life (or what passes as such). And if that individual, that puppeteer, is of a cosmic dimension, such as a god, then humans are left with no free will at all and are subject to the crassest determinism.[98] In other words, those who operate under an illusory reality generated by an outside agent become, in effect, puppets. In *Zum großen Wurstel*, the play's resuming from the beginning immediately after the "Unbekannte" cuts the strings signifies that the presumably false reality of the puppet play in its broadest sense — including its author, director and different audiences — is the only reality.

This does not mean that the "Unbekannte" has any more real control over the other characters than Schnitzler's eponymous "Puppenspieler," Georg Merklin, has over Eduard and Anna Jagisch; and his confusion ("Bin ich ein Gott? . . . ein Narr?") is not unlike that experienced by Paracelsus when he feels he is losing control of his magic:

> Schlägt mir überm Haupt
> Des eignen Zaubers Schwall mit Hohn zusammen?
> Und wirren sich die Grenzen selbst für mich — ?[99]

Zum Großen Wurstel, then, ultimately presents a particularly modern, gloomy (some might add, "realistic") interpretation of the *theatrum mundi* theme. Schnitzler's theater of the world turns out to be a "Wurstelspiel"[100] under the putative control of a director who is a puppet, using the flawed script of an author who is also a puppet, presumably to entertain an audience of puppets by means of "real" puppets who are the only ones who "know" that they are puppets. And over it all there looms an Unknown who can only cut the puppets' strings, but not permanently, who is helpless to keep the "Reigen" of the play within a play within a play from starting all over again, and who may or may not be under the control of an absent and none-too-caring god.[101]

Clearly, the notion of an unseen puppet-master, a destiny-controlling force of some form or another, provides a ready vehicle for Schnitzler's skepticism. Obviously, the appearance (actual or implied) of such a puppet-master changes the questions about person-to-person interaction, elevating them, as it were, to a cosmic dimension — indeed, to the basic questions human beings ask of the cosmos: Who, if anyone, is in charge? If so, what *is* the nature of the ultimate "Puppenspieler"? Do we have free will or are we merely fated to believe we have free will?

All this touches on two issues that have occupied scholars and critics over the years: Schnitzler's views on religion and, more to the point, on determinism. Beyond being recognized as a skeptic, Schnitzler was seen from early on as having little use for religion.[102] And it is true that the plots of the majority of his works, both dramatic and in prose, tend to play out in a secular, post-Enlightenment world that, for better or worse, is free of scripture-based morality and other traditional religious markers. As to whether or not Schnitzler was a determinist, the answer to this question must be the same as to many others regarding what appears at times to be his position (such as, "Wir spielen immer") — yes and no. It is probably true of any thinking human being that he or she, while insisting on (or admitting to) having free will, does at least occasionally think or feel that this or that event was fated. Indeed, like Konrad in *Der Gang zum Weiher* (1926), people are all too prone to attribute necessity to any course of events taking place, else how could it have come to pass? But the Baron in that play insists humans have free will; and, of course, in *Das Weite Land* (1911), Aigner gives voice to yet another view: "Das Natürliche . . . ist das Chaos."[103] In effect, the puppet plays emphasize the difficulty in answering the question in that they suggest the existence of an invisible and/or unknowable *possible* puppet master. Hence, it can be answered only subjectively, depending on the individual's mood or spiritual state, as it were, of the moment.

In the end, as the audience assesses the marionettes' (or their own) relationship to the unseen puppet-master posited by Schnitzler, it may be instructive to consider the view presented by Kleist in his 1810 essay, "Über das Marionettentheater." Perhaps the most striking aspect of the essay is the sympathetic and benevolent relationship between puppet-master and puppet. In reply to the narrator's question, "ob er glaubte, daß der Maschinist, der diese Puppen regierte, selbst ein Tänzer sein oder wenigstens einen Begriff vom Schönen im Tanz haben müsse," his interlocutor, the first dancer at the local opera, replies, "daß, wenn ein Geschäft, von seiner mechanischen Seite, leicht sei, daraus noch nicht folge, daß es ganz ohne Empfindung betrieben werden könne." That Kleist is not speaking of marionettes, at least not exclusively, becomes clear when he states that the mysterious "Linie" extending from the puppet-master to the marionette is nothing other than "der Weg der Seele des Tänzers," by means of which the "Maschinist" transports himself into the marionette's center of gravity ("Schwerpunkt") — that is, dances along.[104]

Curiously, though, Kleist does not stress only the puppet-master's divine qualities. He is also concerned with establishing "the parallel between the puppet and God."[105] Nevertheless, according to Günter Blöcker, the essay represents Kleist's

Apotheose des Unbewußten. . . . Das göttliche Bewußtsein ist allumfassend, es kennt keine Fesselung durch das Einzelne. Die Marionette ist Apparat, hat selber kein Bewußtsein, überläßt sich aber widerstandslos einem höheren Willen, der über sie verfügt. Die Unfehlbarkeit ihrer Bewegungen wird durch eine außerhalb ihrer waltende Kraft verbürgt, die sich gnadenvoll in den Schwerpunkt eben dieser Bewegungen versetzt. Der Spieler läßt die Puppe tanzen, indem er selber in ihr tanzt. Innen und Außen, Person und Schicksal, Ich und Gott sind im Gliederspiel der gehorsamen Kunstfigur eines.[106]

As interesting as Kleist's essay may be to the reader of Schnitzler's puppet plays, the differences in worldview between the former, writing in 1810, and the latter at the turn of the twentieth century will be readily apparent. There are precious few among Schnitzler's characters who enjoy an existence unmolested by their consciousness; and if they stand "widerstandlos" before their puppet-masters, they do so out of hopelessness or helplessness, or because they are unaware that a puppet-master is pulling their strings; and in any case, there is not much of the "gnadenvoll" to be seen in the relationship.

Notes

[1] *Zum großen Wurstel* in DW I, 871–962; *Der tapfere; Cassian* in DW I, 855–70; *Die Verwandlung des Pierrot* in DW I, 1063–78; *Der Schleier der Pierrette* in DW II, 321–36.

[2] Arthur Schnitzler, *Zug der Schatten. Drama in neun Bildern. Aus dem Nachlaß* (Frankfurt: Fischer, 1970). *Paracelsus* in DW I, 465–98.

[3] Cf. the ultimately failed attempt on the part of Karl Bern in *Zug der Schatten*.

[4] This tendency is not to be mistaken for an individual's attempting to control or manipulate matters in order to protect someone: Weiring in *Liebelei* (1896), Gräsler in *Doktor Gräsler, Badearzt* (1917), and the Baron in *Der Gang zum Weiher* (1926) are not "Puppenspieler."

[5] Ruth E. Peabody, *Commedia Works* (n.p.: Amos Press, 1984), 24. Kenneth Richard names these as well as Turkish puppet theater, carnival plays, and mountebank performances, even as he acknowledges the difficulty of making definitive statements regarding possible sources (*The Commedia dell'Arte: A Documentary History* [Oxford: Blackwell, 1990], 11–31), a notion seconded by John Rudlin (*Commedia dell'Arte: An Actor's Handbook* [London and New York: Routledge, 1994], 2), and by Douglas Radcliffe-Umstead, who agrees that "documentation does not exist to support the theory of an unbroken tradition of popular buffoonery" ("The Erudite Comic Tradition of the *commedia dell'arte*," in *The Science of Buffoonery: Theory and History of the Commedia dell'Arte*, ed. Domenico Pietropaolo [Toronto: Dovehouse, 1989], 33).

[6] Robert Erenstein, "The Rise and Fall of Commedia dell'Arte," in *500 Years of Theatre History*, eds. Michael Bigelow Dixon and Val Smith (Lyme, NH: Smith and Kraus, 2000), 3.

[7] Rudlin, 23.

[8] Rudlin, 24, 27–28.

[9] Michael Anderson, "Making Room: Commedia and the Privatisation of the Theatre," in *The Commedia dell'Arte from the Renaissance to Dario Fo*, ed. Christopher Cairns (Lewiston: Edwin Mellen P, 1988), 77.

[10] *Paracelsus*, 467–68, 488.

[11] Cited in Anderson, 79.

[12] Karl Günter Simon, *Pantomime. Ursprung, Wesen, Möglichkeiten* (Munich: Nymphenburger Verlagshandlung, 1960), 25.

[13] Martin Green and John Swan, *The Triumph of Pierrot. The Commedia dell'Arte and the Modern Imagination* (New York: Macmillan, 1986), 3.

[14] Green, 4–5.

[15] In fact, he appears only in Act Two, a simple and courageous peasant and the insufficiently loved fiancé of Charlotte, whom he has to protect from Don Juan's seductive wiles immediately after having saved the latter from drowning (*Don Juan*, transl. Christopher Hampton [London: Faber, 1974] 33ff.).

[16] Otto Rommel, *Die alt-wiener Volkskomödie. Ihre Geschichte vom Barocken Welt-Theater bis zum Tode Nestroys* (Vienna: Anton Schroll, 1952), 158. Rommel's work has been particularly important in my research, and much of what follows reflects my debt.

[17] Simon, 21.

[18] A. G. Lehmann, "Pierrot and Fin de Siècle," in *Romantic Mythologies,* ed. Ian Fletcher (New York: Barnes & Noble, 1967), 212.

[19] Peabody, 14.

[20] David Madden, *Harlequin's Stick, Charlie's Cane: A Comparative Study of Commedia dell'Arte and Silent Slapstick Comedy* (Bowling Green: U Popular P, 1975), 4.

[21] Giacomo Oreglia, *The Commedia dell'Arte,* transl. Lovett F. Edwards (New York: Hill & Wang, 1968), 103.

[22] Madden, 8.

[23] For example, Green, 19; and Dario Fo, *The Tricks of the Trade,* transl. Joe Farrell (New York: Routledge, 1991), 24.

[24] Pierre Louis Ducharte, *The Italian Comedy* [1929] (New York: Dover, 1966), 120.

[25] See Hans R. Purschke, *Die Anfänge der Puppenspielformen und ihre vermutlichen Ursprünge* (Bochum: Deutsches Institut für Puppenspiel e. V., 1979), 1–10.

[26] Luzia Glanz, *Das Puppenspiel und sein Publikum* (Berlin: Junker & Dünnhaupt, 1941), 16–18.

[27] Glanz, 64.

[28] Rommel, 199.

[29] Glanz, 64.

[30] A puppet play has an important function in Tiecks's *Prinz Zerbino.* The popularity of the genre is attested to by the appearance in 1806 of a collection of plays called "Das Marionettentheater," presumably by August Mahlmann, which uses a Harlequin figure alongside Hanswurst (Glanz, 67–68). Others who wrote puppet plays include Achim von Arnim (*Die Appelmänner,* 1813) and Joseph Freiherr von Eichendorff (*Das Incognito,* 1841).

[31] Günther Mahal, ed. *Doktor Johannes Faust, Puppenspiel in vier Aufzügen* hergestellt von Karl Simrock [1846] (Stuttgart: Reclam, 1991), 120.

[32] Helen Watanabe-O'Kelly, "The Early Modern Period (1450–1720)," in *The Cambridge History of German Literature,* ed. Helen Watanabe-O'Kelly (Cambridge: Cambridge UP, 1997), 109.

[33] See Rommel, 430.

[34] See Norbert Miller and Karl Riha, eds. *Kasperltheater für Erwachsene* (Frankfurt am Main: Insel, 1978), 17–18, 39–40.

[35] Rommel, 313n.

[36] Rommel, 723.

[37] Simon, 13.

[38] Peabody, 39–40.

[39] Donald G. Daviau, *Hermann Bahr* (Boston: Twayne, 1985), 76. Bahr, whose interest in pantomime dates back to 1891, when he wrote a review of the pantomime

L'enfant prodigue by Michel Carrès, and who was influenced by Japanese theater, where "actors learn to move as living puppets," urged the adoption of the panto-mime as a counter to what he perceived to be the "overemphasis on naturalism." Bahr himself wrote three pantomimes — *Pantomime vom braven Manne* (1901), *Der Minister* (1902), and *Der liebe Augustin* (1902) — none of which was ever performed (Daviau, 76–77). On the revival of marionette theatres, see Glanz, 79–81.

[40] Cited in Karl Pestalozzi, "Tieck-Der gestiefelte Kater," in *Die deutsche Komödie vom Mittelalter bis zur Gegenwart,* ed. Walter Hinck (Düsseldorf: August Bagel, 1977), 110–26.

[41] Ludwig Tieck, *Prinz Zerbino oder die Reise nach dem guten Geschmack,* in vol. 10 of his *Schriften* (Berlin: de Gruyter, 1966), 148.

[42] Tieck, 207.

[43] Tieck, 337.

[44] Andreas Gryphius, *Absurda Comica oder Herr Peter Squentz,* ed. Herbert Cysarz (Stuttgart: Reclam, 1954), 30. Aside from anti-illusionist comments and improvisations, this play also includes typical *commedia lazzi,* physical humor. Piramus curses the wall; the fellow playing the wall takes offense ("Ei, Pickelhering, das ist wider Her' und Redlichkeit, es stehet auch in dem Spiel nicht"); at which Piramus strikes the actor who, in turn, hits Piramus on the head with the "wall" (35). Later, the actors portraying the Moon and the Lion have an argument and fight (43–44).

[45] Johann Wolfgang von Goethe, *Aus meinem Leben: Dichtung und Wahrheit* (1811–1813), ed. Liselotte Blumenthal, with commentary by Erich Trunz, 14 vols. (Munich: Deutscher Taschenbuch Verlag, 1991), vol. 3: 438–67; vol. 9: 413, 782.

[46] Mahal, ed. *Doktor Johannes Faust,* 119.

[47] Actually, audience participation is a common element in the *commedia* as well (Peabody 64, 71); and, as Miller and Riha state, "In den Jahrhunderten ihrer europäischen Wirksamkeit hatte die italienische Stegreifbühne das sinnverwirrende Spiel mit Traum und Wirklichkeit, mit Illusion und Illusionsaufhebung, mit der erdschweren Drastik von Sprache und Geste einmal und mit der fast abstrakten Kunstfertigkeit, ja Künstlichkeit der Maske, auf eine heute kaum noch vorstellbare Höhe gebracht" (24–25).

[48] Aristophanes, *Clouds,* trans. Robert Henning Webb (Charlottesville: U Virginia P, 1960), 86–87.

[49] Tieck, 96–97.

[50] Francis Beaumont, *The Knight of the Burning Pestle,* ed. John Doebler (Lincoln: U Nebraska P, 1967), 7.

[51] Beaumont, 24.

[52] It is also reminiscent of Gryphius's *Herr Peter Squentz* in which, because the townsfolk putting on the performance cannot really act, the tragic fate of Piramus and Thisbe becomes a comedy or parody.

[53] Christian Dietrich Grabbe, *Scherz, Satire, Ironie und tiefere Bedeutung* [1827] (Stuttgart: Reclam, 1970), 61, 65. Diethelm Brüggemann notes Grabbe's "romantischen Effekte . . . die Dichterauftritte, Schauspieler-Demaskierung und Publikumsansprechen" (131) as well as his "Tendenz zur Zerstörung der Handlungsstruktur" ("Grabbe —

Scherz, Satire, Ironie und tiefere Bedeutung," in *Die deutsche Komödie vom Mittelalter bis zur Gegenwart,* ed. Walter Hinck [Düsseldorf: August Bagel, 1977], 131, 133).

[54] Miller and Riha, 382.

[55] Miller and Riha, 409.

[56] Reinhard Urbach, *Schnitzler Kommentar zu den erzählenden Schriften und dramatischen Werken* (Munich: Winkler, 1974), 178.

[57] The *Singspiel* version written in verse for the composer Oskar Straus was first performed and published in 1909 (Urbach, 69).

[58] *Der tapfere Cassian,* 870.

[59] Martin also embodies another Schnitzler type, the user; that is, the individual who uses another for his or her own purpose, such as in *Literatur* (1902) or *Die Frau mit dem Dolche* (1902). Moreover, he also resembles Willi Kasda (*Spiel im Morgengrauen,* 1927), in his fantasizing about winning a woman who is actually beyond his reach and in his thinking he can control fate — that is, never lose at dice (*Der tapfere Cassian,* 863).

[60] *Der tapfere Cassian,* 862.

[61] *Der tapfere Cassian,* 858, 862.

[62] *Der tapfere Cassian,* 866–67.

[63] *Der tapfere Cassian,* 866–67. There is an element of the Austrian fairy tale play in the reference to the Emperor of China (*Der tapfere Cassian,* 863).

[64] *Der tapfere Cassian,* 860.

[65] *Der tapfere Cassian,* 861.

[66] *Die Frau des Richters* in ES II, 382–433.

[67] *Der tapfere Cassian,* 864–65.

[68] *Der tapfere Cassian,* 867.

[69] Ending as it does with the death of one of the principal characters, *Der tapfere Cassian* appears to move beyond the traditional *commedia* play. However, as comical as these tend to be, they need not end comically: as noted earlier, many a *harlequinade* ends with the death of a jilted lover.

[70] Peabody, 10.

[71] Oreglia, 81.

[72] Peabody, 12.

[73] Lest there be any mistake, Schnitzler provides a clarifying footnote: "Auch was im Text dialogartig gebracht ist, wird selbstverständlich nur pantomimisch ausgedrückt" (*Der Schleier der Pierrette,* 323).

[74] Nevertheless, even if it is more *commedia*-like than *Die Verwandlung des Pierrot,* for example, the play does, as Martin Swales has pointed out, embody several elements familiar in Schnitzler's work: it "gives drastic expression to the violent fluctuations of mood, feeling, and intention which plague so many of Schnitzler's characters. In a matter of seconds love turns to hatred, despair to frenetic gaiety, sanity to madness" (Martin Swales, *Arthur Schnitzler. A Critical Study* [Oxford: Oxford UP, 1971], 265).

[75] *Der Schleier der Pierrette,* 322.

[76] *Der Schleier der Pierrette,* 326.

[77] *Der Schleier der Pierrette,* 330–32.

[78] *Der Schleier der Pierrette,* 323.

[79] *Der Schleier der Pierrette,* 333–34.

[80] *Der Schleier der Pierrette,* 336.

[81] *Die Verwandlung des Pierrot,* 1077.

[82] *Die große Szene* in DW II, 491–528; *Im Spiel der Sommerlüfte* in DW II, 975–1034.

[83] For instance, Pierrot "*nimmt den Clown beim Kragen, dreht ihn etliche Male in der Luft herum*" (*Die Verwandlung des Pierrot,* 1069).

[84] Although Swales argues that Pierrot differs from the conventional actor because the latter "may to a large extent be in control of his own performance" whereas Pierrot "is very largely manipulated by events"(263), I find that he plays his roles of his own volition (notwithstanding for the moment the matter of his being a puppet), losing control only when his ploys are revealed, when the illusions he created are destroyed; that is, when he is brought back to earth by Anna's reappearance. Indeed, most of Schnitzler's actors have to face reality eventually, be they "real" (i.e. professional) actors or, like Casanova, a man who spends his life trying to play his chosen role until he is overtaken by poverty and old age.

[85] *Der grüne Kakadu* in DW I, 515–52. This allows Swales to say, "*Die Verwandlungen des Pierrot* creates a pantomime play within a pantomime play" (264). On the subject of easily satisfied *Wurstelprater* audiences, as well as a brief survey of its attractions (fortunetellers, puppet shows incorporating a degree of violence, etc.) see Felix Salten, *Wurstelprater* (Vienna: Goldmann, 1981).

[86] Swales, 264.

[87] Urbach, 178.

[88] *Zum großen Wurstel,* 891.

[89] *Zum großen Wurstel,* 873.

[90] *Zum großen Wurstel,* 892.

[91] *Zum großen Wurstel,* 892.

[92] *Zum großen Wurstel,* 893.

[93] See, for example, Hans-Peter Bayerdörfer, "Vom Konversationsstück zur Wurstelkomödie. Zu Arthur Schnitzlers Einaktern," *Jahrbuch der deutschen Schillergesellschaft* 16 (1972): 569–70 and "Eindringlinge, Marionetten, Automaten. Symbolistische Dramatik und die Anfänge des modernen Theaters," in *Deutsche Literatur der Jahrhundertwende,* ed. Viktor Žmegač (Königstein: Verlagsgruppe Athenäum et al., 1981), 203; Christa Melchinger, *Illusion und Wirklichkeit im dramatischen Werk Arthur Schnitzlers* (Heidelberg: Carl Winter, 1968), 128; Gunter Selling, *Die Einakter und Einakterzyklen Arthur Schnitzlers* (Amsterdam: Rodopi, 1975), 156–59; and Heinz Politzer, "Arthur Schnitzler: The Poetry of Psychology," *Modern Language Notes* 78 (1963): 366.

[94] *Die dreifache Warnung* in ES II, 7–10. In the short parable, the "Geist" reveals itself to the young man about to die as another manifestation of the "Unbekannte":

Erkannt hat mich kein Sterblicher noch, der Namen hab' ich viele. Be-
stimmung nennen mich die Abergläubischen, die Toren Zufall und die
Frommen Gott. Denen aber, die sich die Weisen dünken, bin ich die Kraft,
die am Anfang aller Tage war und weiter wirkt unaufhaltsam in die Ewigkeit durch alles Geschehen.

When the young man curses the unknown force, calls it "Hohn über allem
Hohn," and asks it why, if his destiny was predetermined, must he now, in his dying
moment, whimper forth his powerless "Why," the only reply he receives, from the
invisible edge of the heavens, is "ein unbegreifliches Lachen hin."

[95] *Zum großen Wurstel,* 894. The existence of a power higher than the "Unbekannte"
is also suggested by one of Schnitzler's aphorisms:

> Ihr sagt: Ein Übermensch. Verzeiht, ich merkte nichts.
> Was mir erschien an heil'ger Bühnenstätte —
> *Wenn auch mit einer Maske menschlichen Gesichts —*
> War doch nur eine Übermarionette.

> (Arthur Schnitzler, *Aphorismen und Betrachtungen,* ed. Robert
> O. Weiss. [Frankfurt am Main: S. Fischer, 1967], 14)

[96] *Zum großen Wurstel,* 894.

[97] Carol S. Starrels, "The Problem of the "Puppenspieler" in the Works of Arthur
Schnitzler" (Ph.D. diss., University of Pennsylvania, 1973), 78.

[98] Seen in this context, the confusion that leads to characters' abandoning their roles
illuminates more than the illusion vs. reality motif alone. Thus, for instance, the
"Bissige" man demands of the "Wohlwollende," "Sind Sie der Bissige oder ich?"
(DW I, 881), because he can never ask anything else at that particular point, any
more than Pirandello's characters in *Six Characters in Search of an Author* can act or
speak differently than they do.

[99] *Paracelsus,* 490.

[100] Bayerdörfer, 574.

[101] The portrayals of deity in *Zum großen Wurstel* and *Die dreifache Warnung* may
represent Schnitzler's sharing the view, if only temporarily, of the Marcionists who
flourished in Prague between 1890 and 1930, and who, following Marcion (ca. 85–ca.
155 A.D.), held that "the Creator God of the Jews was an evil demiurge, whose
Creation had trapped men until Christ came to deliver them" (William Johnston, *The
Austrian Mind* [Berkeley: U of California P, 1983], 270). While Johnston finds that
the writers of Young Vienna did not formulate a corresponding cosmology, the factors
he presents as leading to Marcionism's flourishing in Prague apply to Schnitzler as
well:

> Germans and especially Jews in Prague struggled against mounting odds to
> preserve their culture. Theirs was a siege mentality: Marcionism expressed
> the desperation of a beleaguered minority that yearned to silence its tor-
> mentor. (273)

[102] Frida Ilmer, referring specifically to *Die dreifache Warnung* and *Zum großen Wurstel*, alludes to Schnitzler's "affirmation of the essential injustice of the power which we call divine" ("Schnitzler's Attitudes with Regard to the Transcendental," *Germanic Review* 10 [1935]: 118).

[103] *Das weite Land*, DW II, 217–320. Here, 281.

[104] Heinrich von Kleist, "Über das Marionettentheater" (1810) in *Heinrich von Kleist, Sämtliche Werke*, ed. Erwin Laaths (Munich and Zurich: Droemersche Verlagsanstalt, 1959), 826.

[105] Curt Hohoff, *Heinrich von Kleist 1777/1977* (Bonn: Inter Nationes, 1977), 129. Regarding the puppets' gracefulness ("Anmut"), Kleist finds, "daß es dem Menschen schlechthin unmöglich wäre, den Gliedermann darin auch nur zu erreichen. Nur ein Gott könne sich, auf diesem Felde, mit der Materie messen; und hier sei der Punkt, wo die beiden Enden der ringförmigen Welt ineinandergriffen" (828).

[106] Günter Blöcker, *Heinrich von Kleist oder das absolute Ich* (Berlin: Argon, 1960), 189.

"Medizin ist eine Weltanschauung": On Schnitzler's Medical Writings

Hillary Hope Herzog

SINCE THE PUBLICATION in 1988 of his collected medical writings in one volume, little attention has been devoted to the relationship between Arthur Schnitzler's training and career in medicine and his literary work.[1] In fact, the writer's relationship to medicine has been relatively neglected in Schnitzler scholarship. While one may encounter many references to his astute diagnosis of the Viennese bourgeoisie, the implication is frequently limited to the notion that Schnitzler's medical background sharpened his eye as a keen observer when he turned to literary endeavors.

Many scholars seem to adhere to the underlying assumption that Schnitzler was dragged reluctantly into a medical career in order to maintain a family tradition and never applied himself to his medical studies or practice. Schnitzler is often thought to have been merely biding his time during the many years of his engagement with medicine, until his father's death freed him from this undesired career. By the beginning of the twentieth century, so this story goes, his medical career was definitively over, and he was able to devote himself to literature, cast in this line of argument as his "true calling." This point of view is expressed, for example, in an article that appeared in the journal of the Virchow-Pirquet Medical Society in 1979, bluntly titled "Physicians who Abandoned Medicine for Literature."[2] While this article is especially dismissive of Schnitzler's relationship to medicine, its author is nevertheless fairly typical in concluding that Schnitzler "never attained any expertise in his medical practice, partly because, as he says in his memoirs, he felt the onus of being the son of a successful and prominent physician and partly because he was drawn so strongly to writing and literature."[3]

Those critics who do discuss the relationship between Schnitzler's medical and literary work tend to cast medicine and writing as two successive careers, establishing a distinct end point to Schnitzler's work in medicine but allowing for some influence from this first period of his professional life to the second. Several scholars refer to his highly developed powers of observation, his "ärztlicher" or "klinischer Blick." His works have been variously described as penetrating diagnoses of his society or as psychological studies.[4]

There is a smaller body of literature offering a productive examination of the "ärztliche Elemente" in Schnitzler's work. This scholarship generally falls into three broad categories: a focus on Schnitzler's representations of the psychological, especially analyses of his relationship to Sigmund Freud, following Freud's oft-cited reference to Schnitzler as his doppelgänger; examinations of the figure of the physician in Schnitzler's works; and a small number of studies devoted to his treatment of a particular disease or medical condition in the literary works.[5]

Additionally, a handful of scholars have undertaken a more extensive consideration of Schnitzler's medical work, making important advances in evaluating Schnitzler's relationship to medicine and the meaning of this relationship for his literature.[6] These critics see the early medical writing as foundational for Schnitzler's later literary explorations of illness and the individual.

Schnitzler's medical training exerted a crucial and lifelong influence on his way of looking at, imagining, and writing about the world. His involvement with medicine is significant in two respects. First, the early medical writings he produced represent a still under-utilized resource in Schnitzler scholarship. They are valuable because he introduced in them many of the themes and techniques to which he returned throughout his literary career. An analysis of Schnitzler's early medical publications demonstrates the ways in which Schnitzler first formulated his conception of the individual psyche, a model that he transformed into a literary vein at the end of his career.

Second, as reflections of an extensive engagement with the medical science of the era, the medical writings may also be seen as a contribution to the history of Viennese medicine. Schnitzler has perhaps not been adequately considered as a figure who possessed the skills and qualifications, as well as the forum, to comment on the state of the profession in Vienna at the turn of the century. While always overshadowed by his famous father, Schnitzler was certainly respected by his physician contemporaries as a medical journalist, his reviews providing a valuable resource for doctors unable to afford the time and expense of staying abreast of current research. An examination of themes Schnitzler discussed in his medical journalistic writings points toward further areas of investigation not only for Schnitzler scholars, but also for those interested more broadly in the history of medical culture in Europe at the turn of the century.

Although as a young man Schnitzler often expressed doubts about his suitability for the medical profession, his later statements attest to the significant and sustained influence of the study of medicine on his intellectual development. A comment attributed to him by his wife, Olga, has become quite well known: "Wer je Mediziner war, kann nie aufhören, es zu sein. Denn Medizin ist eine Weltanschauung."[7] Writing on the nineteenth-century novel, Lawrence Rothfield similarly describes medicine as a way of looking at the world: "To see with a medical eye means invoking, however tacitly, a complicated system of techniques, conceptual configurations, presuppositions, and protocols of interpretation that enable one to take signs as symptoms and thereby to impose a particular order on reality."[8] Schnitzler also draws on this language in the medical writings, describing the physician's training as learning to see in a new way. Through his training Schnitzler learned to see with a medical eye and to use this vision to order reality within and beyond the practice of medicine. Medicine served Schnitzler as the primary system of knowledge informing his view of the individual within the social world, and it remained the source of authority with which he supported this view throughout his life.

Schnitzler was a product of the famous Vienna School of Medicine, one of the most important sites of medical training in Europe at the time. He began his studies at the University of Vienna on completion of his secondary education in 1879 and shared several prominent professors with Sigmund Freud, who was also a student there from 1873 to 1881 — teachers such as Ernst Brücke in physiology and Theodor Meynert in psychology. Schnitzler assisted in Meynert's clinic at the *Allgemeines Krankenhaus,* trained at the hospital from 1885 to 1888, then moved to the private *Poliklinik* that had been founded by Johann Schnitzler and a group of other physicians; at the clinic, he assisted his father in laryngology (1888–1893). After his father's death, he left the clinic and established a private practice. He never developed an extensive pool of patients but continued to see patients into the 1920s. When Schnitzler writes about the practice of medicine and comments on the social, ethical, and political dimensions of the profession, this particular institution — medicine as it was conceived of, taught, and practiced in Vienna from the 1880s through the first decades of the twentieth century — is his primary referent.

Schnitzler's primary contribution to the *fin-de-siècle* medical world is the journalistic texts he wrote in the late 1880s and early 1890s as editor and contributor to the medical press, collected in *Medizinische Schriften* (1988). Schnitzler wrote extensively for the journals for practicing physicians published by his father, first the *Wiener medizinische*

Presse and then its successor, the *Internationale klinische Rundschau,* in which he reviewed the latest scholarship by leading researchers in medicine and psychology. He was also active as a correspondent, reporting on several important international conferences. In addition, Schnitzler made at least one significant independent contribution to medical science when he published his own research on aphonia, or hysterical voicelessness, in 1889, capping several years of collaboration with his father, an internationally renowned laryngologist.

In Schnitzler's reviews of new publications, he presents concise characterizations of the significant medical debates of the period. Four reviews of monographs on syphilis, for example, attest to the high degree of anxiety within the medical community over this disease as a threat to public health.[9] These reviews, written in 1887, 1891, and 1892, center around the transmission of the disease, discussing contagion, the issue of heredity, and the important debates surrounding the existence of a syphilis microbe.

Significant attention is also devoted in the medical writings to mental and nervous illnesses.[10] This attention not only reflects Schnitzler's deep personal interest in these subjects, but also captures an important moment in Viennese medicine, a period of intense debate surrounding the interpretation and treatment of those conditions for which a locatable source is not readily apparent in or on the body of the patient. These reviews address both the materialist position emphasizing diagnosis through objective observation and several newly emerging approaches that did not rely primarily on physiological evidence in the interpretation of diseases or symptoms. Through Schnitzler's discussion of these texts, the problems in identifying clear classifications in such cases become evident.

The reviews address the practice of medicine in Vienna, one of the most important sites of that profession in central Europe and the training ground for physicians from throughout the Habsburg Empire. Schnitzler comments on the state of medical education in the city, for example, and addresses the need for reform in his discussion of the state of Viennese hospitals. Alongside these specific issues, the essays include broader reflections on the state of medical practice. Schnitzler begins to articulate his own conception of the professional ethos of the physician, which is a recurring theme in the literary works, and to elaborate his critique of the profession as practiced in Vienna.

Two early reports covering international medical conferences preserve Schnitzler's first impressions of the medical profession as a trained physician.[11] Both reports reflect his clear excitement at the collegiality and energy of the professional gathering. In these articles Schnitzler is charged with the task of describing the conference proceedings, but also with providing an account of the experience of participating in these international events. He seeks to present this experience vividly for those physicians in Vienna too busy or too poorly paid to attend, giving his impression of the participants, the atmosphere at the conferences, and the host cities. His further aim is to spark greater interest in such events at home. In each report Schnitzler draws distinctions between Viennese physicians and his colleagues abroad. He laments the lack of Austrian participation and notes that this absence seems to reflect a more general lack of enthusiasm for new work stemming from abroad and resentment toward new developments, even from within Austria. He describes a far better atmosphere among his German colleagues, contrasting their shared sense of purpose and commitment to higher ideals with the Viennese preoccupation with petty jealousies and insecurities.

In these writings Schnitzler begins to establish a professional model in which the physician is highly active, engaged with his colleagues, and interested in expanding the body of medical knowledge. What begins to emerge as his conception of a professional ethos becomes more distinct when Schnitzler turns to a critique of the Viennese medical world, as he highlights what he perceives to be lacking in the lived experience of medicine at home.

The central text in Schnitzler's critique of the medical profession is the melancholic "Silvesterbetrachtungen," dated New Year's Eve, 1888. The holiday provides Schnitzler the occasion to examine the progress of medical science over the past year and assess the state of the profession. He does not, however, advance a scientific critique of medicine at the end of the 1880s; rather, the substance of his claims is moral and ethical. The essay is underscored by Schnitzler's deep sense of disappointment that the profession has failed to realize its full potential, figured explicitly as a failure to recognize the humanizing capacity of the medical world.

More specifically, Schnitzler charges the medical community with a lack of tolerance, a quality that he sees as central to the profession. By virtue of his special training and intimate knowledge of the human being, the physician sees the world from an unusual vantage point, based, the article implies, on the recognition of the fundamental similarity of all people. The particular knowledge of the physician gives rise to a certain responsibility vis-à-vis those who lack this knowledge, requiring a commitment to the truth. The prejudice and blindness that is to be expected from other strands of the population is anathema to the physician. The prejudice to which he refers is anti-Semitism, cast in this text as a pathology, in biological language reminiscent of another noted physician and writer, Max Nordau (1849–1923).

Schnitzler does not seek to explain the phenomenon of anti-Semitism (in this work or elsewhere); nor does he present a concrete proposal for the reform of the medical profession to combat the lack of tolerance that he laments. Rather, although he identifies anti-Semitism as a universal problem of the era, he favors an individual over any social or political response. Schnitzler continues his exploration of this theme in his novel *Der Weg ins Freie* (1908), in which he casts anti-Semitism as a pathology encompassing the social world but rejects all collective responses as inadequate. In his drama *Professor Bernhardi* (1912) he examines one such individual response.[12] In *Professor Bernhardi*, as in "Silvesterbetrachtungen," Schnitzler appeals to the individual physician to offset the ethical failures of the medical community. In the medical writings, as in the later literary work, Schnitzler holds up a professional ethical code as an appropriate response to the ethical and moral failings of the medical community as a whole.

Like his literary writings, Schnitzler's medical writings thus not only provide a nuanced account of the most significant medical discourse of the period, but also afford access to those issues that extended beyond medicine into other aspects of cultural life. The texts can therefore be seen as part of a continuum in which the doctor and writer Arthur Schnitzler sought to examine and intervene in what he considered to be the crucial ethical and social issues of his time. Throughout his career, Schnitzler ascribes to the physician a special role in his literary works, broadly transforming medical authority into moral and ethical terms, so that the physician's role is often to point the way to greater tolerance and understanding. Aside from these meditations on the physician's professional ethos, Schnitzler's medical writings also demonstrate the diagnostic abilities that later reappear in the literary writings. His work on aphonia and experimentation with hypnosis, for example, represent a crucial first formulation of his view of the self. In these works Schnitzler first begins to elaborate a conception of the individual, reflecting on the relationship between role-playing and identity.

During the second half of the 1880s, the Viennese medical community engaged in a prolonged and sometimes heated debate over the therapeutic value of hypnosis. Interest was sparked by the pioneering research on hysteria emerging from France, principally written by Jean-Martin Charcot and Hyppolite Bernheim. While the response of the Viennese medical community to the French research on hysteria has often been characterized as uniformly negative, Schnitzler's account of the debate in the medical press, his reviews of new scholarship and discussion of its reception, reveal the complexity of the various responses of his colleagues.[13] As hypnosis emerged rather suddenly on the local scene as an object of psychological-physiological research through the work in hysteria, this experimentation posed immediate challenges to the fundamental materialist basis of Viennese medicine, as well as to the self-conception of the profession. The debates surrounding hypnosis posed several thorny, high-stakes questions, such as the issue of how to understand psychic symptoms that do not reveal themselves in physical or neurological examination (and, more broadly, the nature of nervous illnesses); the scientific legitimacy of hypnosis in medical practice, as it became a key issue around which certain professional anxieties of the period crystallized; and the implications of hypnotic experiments for contemporary understanding of the psyche and the boundaries of the self. This latter arena perhaps contains the most significant aspect of Schnitzler's involvement.

Schnitzler was an active participant in these debates in his many reviews of monographs on hypnosis and hysteria research, as well as in his own research on the application of hypnosis in the treatment of aphonia. In addition, he explored the literary possibilities of hypnotic experimentation in his early fictional writing, for example *Der Empfindsame* (1895), and in the early drama *Paracelsus* (1899).[14]

In 1889, Schnitzler described a highly charged atmosphere in Vienna surrounding the issue of hypnosis, splitting the community into two opposing camps: those who viewed hypnotic practice as one of the most valuable therapeutic developments of the century, and those who saw it as degrading to the human race. For Schnitzler, hypnosis was not only a divisive issue in clinical practice; he also saw it as a litmus test for the profession, arguing that the local debates were driven by secondary, political concerns rather than rational judgment. His criticism implies a lack of professionalism, as he saw his colleagues allowing themselves to be swayed by widely held opinions and misconceptions in lieu of undertaking an objective review of the new research.

Schnitzler's enthusiasm for Bernheim's work on hypnosis is perhaps greater than for any other text he reviewed in his extensive writing for the medical press. Not only did he count Freud's translation of Bernheim among the required reading for all physicians, he also twice offered support for Bernheim's conclusions with observations from his own experience with hypnosis.[15] In the years that followed, Schnitzler continued to react strongly to what he perceived as the overly hasty dismissal of hypnosis by his colleagues. In 1892, for example, he took his prominent former professor, the anatomist Meynert, to task for the superficiality of his remarks on hypnosis.[16]

Schnitzler thus emerges in his reviews for the medical press as a strong proponent of hypnotic experimentation, exhorting his readers to view this new area of research as serious science, with the potential for significant therapeutic breakthroughs. His own publication on the topic appears in the middle of this longer discussion, and he clearly places himself within the trajectory of researchers on hypnosis. In 1889, as an assistant at the *Poliklinik*, Schnitzler published his only independent medical research paper, "Über funktionelle Aphonie und deren Behandlung durch Hypnose und Suggestion."[17]

In this text Schnitzler presents the case histories of six women between the ages of sixteen and thirty-six, suffering from functional aphonia. In each case presentation Schnitzler follows a similar pattern, beginning with a brief summary of the patient's medical history and family background. He also conducts a physical examination, describing in detail the results of the laryngoscopy. The emphasis throughout, however, lies on the therapeutic course pursued through hypnosis. Schnitzler describes the course of treatment, in which he employs Bernheim's method to induce hypnotic sleep and delivers the hypnotic suggestion that the patient will awaken with a fully restored voice. During hypnosis, he conducts several minor neurological experiments and tests various types of suggestion and post-hypnotic suggestion, as for example when he suggests a temporary paralysis of the right arm along with the restoration of the voice.

By Schnitzler's account, he was generally successful in restoring the patient's voice through hypnosis, although he only rarely achieved permanent results. The article concludes with a strong recommendation for the adoption of hypnosis in treating aphonia, as well as a broader, if less emphatic, suggestion that the practice might be of therapeutic value in treating all manner of neurotic conditions.

Perhaps the primary reason for Schnitzler's deep and sustained interest in hypnosis lay in the fact that it yielded a closer look at the psyche of the hypnotic subject and invited reflection on the boundaries that constitute the individual self. Laura Otis, in *Membranes: Metaphors of Invasion in Nineteenth-Century Literature, Science, and Politics* (1999), has suggested a model for Schnitzler's understanding of the individual, rooted in his medical experience and indebted to his work in hypnosis. She sees his notion of the self not as a stable and fixed entity, but rather as determined by the permeability of its boundaries. She writes: "Schnitzler's own consciousness of infectious diseases shaped the way he conceived of the individual: a mind and a body without barriers, forever open to suggestion in a system of free circulation."[18] This characterization of a Schnitzlerian model of the psyche as an essentially open system represents an important insight, but the argument needs to be qualified in light of a re-examination of Schnitzler's work with hypnosis. Otis rightly sees Schnitzler's early work in hypnosis as significant for the development of his thoughts on the constitution of the individual. She has suggested that Schnitzler's interest in hysteria and its treatment through hypnosis is grounded in its theatrical dimensions, in the role-playing enacted by the hypnotic subject. Precisely this aspect of the practice was objectionable to those who saw the openness to suggestion in terms of an improper invasion of the psyche, flouting the traditional notions of free will and of the boundaries of the individual.[19]

In "The Language of Infection: Disease and Identity in Schnitzler's *Reigen*" (1995), Otis characterizes Schnitzler's defense of hypnosis as grounded in the idea that the role-playing produced by hypnotic suggestion represents no departure from the norm. She observes that "for Schnitzler, hypnosis as a medical treatment merely intensified the suggestion and role-playing already occurring in everyday life."[20] Otis argues that Schnitzler saw suggestion as the "normal course of life" and cites a passage from the aphonia case studies in which he enumerates examples of suggestion in daily life, from pedagogy to religious teaching to politics. However, Schnitzler goes on to draw distinctions between various practices of persuasion or command in daily life and hypnotic suggestion, which ultimately indicates that such analogies go too far:

> Jedenfalls aber ist die Phrase von der Suggestion neuerdings etwas wohlfeil geworden, und gar so selbstverständlich, als sie manche gerne darstellen möchten, ist die Lehre von der Übertragung des eigenen Willens auf eine fremde Person noch lange nicht.[21]

In light of Schnitzler's cautionary remarks, it would seem that Otis's reading of the text places too much emphasis on role-playing in Schnitzler's view of the individual. If hypnotic practice, in which the subject is conditioned to adopt a role suggested by an extrinsic source, is merely an intensification of the normal course of life, then the identity of the individual is nothing more than the ongoing, constantly changing assumption of various roles. Role-playing thus becomes identity itself. Otis rightly demonstrates Schnitzler's interest in extrinsic effects (suggestion) on the constitution of the self. Yet, the equation of role-playing and identity has the effect of emptying out the category of identity, essentially casting the individual as a repository of external — psychological, biological, and social — influences in tension with each other. Schnitzler's experimentation with hypnosis presents a different and more complex picture. Alongside his moderate successes in restoring the voices of his patients, he catalogs several minor failures with hypnosis — specific suggestions not followed, patients resistant to hypnosis, and an inability to achieve permanent results. These failures show the limits of the psyche's openness to suggestion. Identity, then, is not strictly an equilibrium existing between various forces, but rather approaches a dialogue between inside and outside.

In a review of Bernheim, Schnitzler asserts a limit to the individual's openness to suggestion. He cites Bernheim's argument that in all of the role-playing enacted during hypnosis, the unique character of the individual comes to the fore, as each subject brings to the role the various qualities and abilities he or she possesses.[22] Schnitzler's own clinical experience testifies to the psyche of the patient asserting itself within the hypnotic experiment. He describes a failed attempt to transform a timid girl into an adventurous North Pole explorer; when Schnitzler told her that a polar bear was approaching, the girl seized his arm and pleaded that they run away. A subsequent attempt to induce the same subject to take on the role of a queen facing revolt by her subjects was successful, which Schnitzler attributes to the girl's familiarity with such roles from the theater. Hypnosis, he argues, reveals the "Fähigkeit zur Pose" and not a process of "Heraustreten aus dem eigenen Charakter."[23] Even under hypnosis, the individual personality is not entirely eclipsed by the role the subject is assuming or by the suggestions the hypnotist imparts.

This examination of Schnitzler's early thinking on the psyche gives rise to the interesting question of the relationship between his medical understanding of the constitution of the individual and his treatment of this issue as a writer of fiction. What light can the medical writings shed on his later psychological explorations in the literary realm? How does Schnitzler use his medical knowledge, and to what end? The literary works include a broad range of psychological portraits, close examinations of the biological and social forces operating within the concept of selfhood, reflecting a lifelong interest in the questions he first began to investigate as a physician. Schnitzler's exploration of the fragility of the individual psyche, which he began early in his career, culminates in the novel *Flucht in die Finsternis* (1931).[24] In this late work he presents his protagonist, Robert, at the brink of mental collapse and deftly reveals Robert's awareness of his fragile mental state, drawing the reader into that character's experience of the dissolution of his stable sense of self.

The novel exemplifies Schnitzler's concern with what Otis has characterized as "the tragic and sometimes violent interplay between outside forces and the sensitive self in the making."[25] Schnitzler's narrative depicts the tensions between the fragile individual and the external forces whose value and authority he has internalized, but whose demands he cannot meet. The role-playing prescribed by bourgeois society is depicted not as a source of identity, but as an excessive burden on the psyche of the individual. In this respect, Schnitzler returns to an important feature of his early experimentation with hypnosis. For like the hypnotic subject who surrenders her will to the hypnotist yet somehow refrains from carrying out his every command, the very process by which the central character's self dissolves contains an element of resistance to external pressures. In his descent into mental illness, Robert continues to exhibit a measure of autonomy, providing glimpses into a reserve of personal and individual identity not subject to social expectations — a kernel of autonomy, of non-suggestibility.

This resistance takes several different forms. Most dramatically, paranoia itself becomes a way to resist social expectations. Robert's anxieties about the masculine roles he is called upon to play in bourgeois society serve to distinguish him as an individual and provoke non-conformist behavior. He adopts a pattern of absenteeism from work, finding in the status of the chronically ill (or at least chronically nervous) worker a way of escaping from responsibility without suffering negative consequences. Having lost his wife to illness as a young man, Robert now leads the bachelor's life, living in a hotel and keeping odd hours, resisting the pressure from family and friends to settle down. Instead, he pursues relationships with two different women in the course of the novel, the stark contrast between them signaling the extent to which his desires conflict with the social codes governing relations between the sexes. In different ways, each relationship represents an attempt to preserve his autonomy and salvage a coherent sense of self.

The first is a purely sexual encounter with a woman who is poor, hungry, and lonely; this brief encounter is set in opposition to his engagement to an educated, middle-class woman. The first liaison represents an attempt to assert his independence in relation to women. He has sex with a stranger in defiance of the social expectations that he will find a woman within his own social class, remarry, and settle down. The second relationship is in apparent harmony with the standards of bourgeois respectability. Yet, in choosing a woman whose family is embroiled in scandal and of whom his brother disapproves, Robert again — even in his desire to conform — flouts social expectations.

Robert's resistance to these social norms becomes more evident in contrast to his physician brother, Otto. For Robert, Otto is the embodiment of bourgeois success. Otto appears to exhibit a complete congruity between his personal identity and the social roles — physician, husband, father, head of household — he occupies. Robert idealizes his brother's position and sees him as the standard against which he can never measure up.

However, while Robert's perspective is an important strand of the narrative structure of the novel, it is not the only one presented. Schnitzler adopts a multiple-perspective strategy, presenting layers of commentary alongside Robert's own experience of his breakdown. Seen from a different point of view, Otto's individuality seems to be entirely eclipsed by the prescribed roles he fulfills; and indeed, these societal demands seem to require a loss of self as a condition of their fulfillment. This requirement of the suppression of one's individuality, which Otto seems to have accepted and internalized as natural, is precisely the "unbearable idea" that Robert, in his descent into madness, seeks a means to resist.[26]

This literary text from the end of Schnitzler's career may thus be seen as a further reflection on the constitution of the individual psyche. In both his medical research and this late fictional case study, Schnitzler was engaged in a process of experimentation with the effects of external pressures on the fragile self. The fictional case presented in *Flucht in die Finsternis* exhibits greater complexity than the six medical cases he presented in the aphonia research, indicating that Schnitzler continued to develop his techniques of medical observation long after he allegedly "abandoned medicine for literature." By locating his protagonist at the brink of mental collapse, Schnitzler presents a powerful portrait of Robert's attempt to maintain control of the collapsing borders of his psyche.

Of course, despite the care with which he depicts Robert's moments of resistance and attempts to achieve and sustain autonomy — the kernel of non-suggestibility evident in the hypnotic experiments of the 1890s — Robert's attempts at self-preservation ultimately fail. The story is one of the complete dissolution of the self. The protagonist's breakdown is mirrored in the fractured conclusion to the narrative. As the novel ends, Robert's friend Doctor Leinbach attempts to write his case history, to explain his illness within the accepted psychiatric discourse of the day. The attempt is unsuccessful; Leinbach is unable to contain Robert's case within the form of the *Krankengeschichte*, to view it from the distanced vantage point of the physician, for he finds himself confronted with a reflection on his own professional identity. Schnitzler's novel is also a confrontation with his own professional identity, with his role as a writer of case histories, both medical and literary. Leinbach's language breaks down, and his synopsis of the case breaks off short of a conclusion, as he is unable to find a way to integrate the multiple perspectives and valuations called forth by Robert's case. In his novel Schnitzler attempts to write a case history that does justice to the full range of implications of this individual case, ultimately avoiding the "Flucht ins System" that Leinbach' s closing remarks lament, not explaining and thereby containing the case. Schnitzler's multiple-perspective and constantly shifting narrative structure attempts not only to evoke the destabilizing, disruptive force of mental illness itself, but also to point to the ways in which Robert's breakdown serves to destabilize and disrupt the "normal" order of the world.

Rather than presenting a closed-off case history of mental illness in this work, Schnitzler instead insists on the complexity of this individual case. The fractured narrative denies the possibility of fully containing and explaining the case. Thus, what at first appears to be the story of an individual who suffered a mental breakdown by failing to maintain a healthy equilibrium between the various internal and external forces acting on his psyche instead becomes a critical reflection on his culture's reliance on those external forces to define the individual. Just as he does in the aphonia research, Schnitzler again distinguishes between role-playing and identity. Thus in the last publication of his lifetime, Schnitzler returns — indeed one cannot properly say returns, as he never left — to the concerns he first explored in his medical writings of the 1880s and 1890s.

Notes

[1] Arthur Schnitzler, *Medizinische Schriften,* ed. Horst Thomé (Frankfurt: Fischer, 1991).

[2] Oscar Bodansky, "Physicians Who Abandoned Medicine for Literature: John Keats, Arthur Conan Doyle, Arthur Schnitzler, Somerset Maugham," *Proceedings of the Virchow-Pirquet Medical Society* 33 (June 1979).

[3] Bodansky, 6.

[4] See, for example, Heinz Politzer, "Diagnose und Dichtung. Zum Werk Arthur Schnitzlers," in *Das Schweigen der Sirenen. Studien zur deutschen und österreichischen Literatur* (Stuttgart: Metzler, 1968), 110–47; and Rolf-Peter Janz and Klaus Laermann, *Arthur Schnitzler: Zur Diagnose des Wiener Bürgertums im Fin de Siècle* (Stuttgart: Metzler, 1977).

[5] On Freud and Schnitzler, see Mark Luprecht, *What People Call Pessimism: Sigmund Freud, Arthur Schnitzler, and Nineteenth-Century Controversy at the University of Vienna Medical School* (Riverside: Ariadne, 1991), and Wolfgang Nehring, "Schnitzler, Freud's Alter Ego?" *Modern Austrian Literature* 10/3–4 (1977), 179–94. Works dealing with Schnitzler's treatment of the physician include Maria Pospischill Alter, *The Concept of the Physician in the Writings of Hans Carossa and Arthur Schnitzler* (Frankfurt: Herbert Lang, 1971), and Walter Müller-Seidel, *Arztbilder im Wandel. Zum literarischen Werk Arthur Schnitzlers* (Munich: Bayerischer Akademie der

Wissenschaften, 1997). On particular illnesses in the literary works, see Thomas Freeman, "*Leutnant Gustl:* A Case of Male Hysteria?" *Modern Austrian Literature* 25/3–4 (1992); Robert O. Weiss, "The Psychoses in the Works of Arthur Schnitzler," *German Quarterly* 41/3 (1968): 377–400; and Theodor W. Alexander, "The Author's Debt to the Physician: Aphonia in the Works of Arthur Schnitzler," *Journal of the International Arthur Schnitzler Research Association* 4/4 (1965): 4–15.

[6] The first to approach this topic rigorously was Horst Thomé, who edited and wrote a preface to the 1988 edition of Schnitzler's medical writings. See also his "Kernlosigkeit und Pose: Zur Rekonstruktion von Schnitzlers Psychologie," *Text und Kontext* 20 (1984): 62–87. See also Laura Otis, *Membranes: Metaphors of Invasion in Nineteenth-Century Literature, Science, and Politics* (Baltimore: Johns Hopkins UP, 1999), and Dirk von Boetticher, *Meine Werke sind lauter Diagnosen. Über die ärztliche Dimension im Werk Arthur Schnitzlers* (Heidelberg: Winter, 1999).

[7] Olga Schnitzler, *Spiegelbild der Freundschaft* (Salzburg: Residenz, 1962), 53.

[8] Lawrence Rothfield, *Vital Signs: Medical Realism in Nineteenth Century Fiction* (Princeton: Princeton UP, 1992), 175.

[9] See in *Medizinische Schriften,* "Rez. zu Rumpf, *Die syphilitischen Erkrankungen des Nervensystems,*" 121–27; "Rez. zu Fülles, *Über Mikroorganismen bei Syphilis,*" 138–40; "Rez. zu Schuster, *Die Syphilis, deren Wesen, Verlauf und Bedeutung,*" 248–50; and "Rez. zu Fournier, *Die Vererbung der Syphilis,*" 268–70.

[10] In *Medizinische Schriften,* see Schnitzler's reviews of works by Jean-Martin Charcot (82, 90–93, 291–92), Weir Mitchell (93–100), Adolf Seeligmüller (145–47), Ottomar Rosenbach (225–27), Theodor Meynert (241–42), Léon Bouveret (309–10), and Valentin Magnan (323–24), as well as the many discussions of hysteria and hypnosis research.

[11] "Von Amsterdam nach Ymuiden" (1879), *Medizinische Schriften,* 63–67, and "Versammlung deutscher Naturforscher und Ärzte in Wiesbaden, 19. September 1887," *Medizinische Schriften,* 132–38. Schnitzler wrote the former piece just after completing his secondary education, accompanying his father on a trip that was clearly intended to spark his interest in a medical career; Johann Schnitzler withheld the name of his correspondent because of his youth.

[12] *Der Weg ins Freie* in ES I, 635–958; *Professor Bernhardi,* DW II, 337–464.

[13] Thomé, in his preface to Schnitzler's medical writings, assigns this common view to the realm of the "psychoanalytischen Legenden" (*Medizinische Schriften,* 35). For a representative view of the Viennese response, see Frank J. Sulloway, *Freud: Biologist of the Mind* (New York: Basic Books, 1979), 35–69.

[14] *Der Empfindsame* in ES I, 255–61; *Paracelsus* in DW I, 465–98.

[15] See Schnitzler, rev. of *Die Suggestion und ihre Heilwirkung,* H. Bernheim, *Internationale klinische Rundschau* 3 (1880), *Medizinische Schriften,* 213.

[16] Schnitzler, rev. of *Sammlung von populär-wissenschaftlichen Vorträgen über den Bau und Leistungen des Gehirns,* Theodor Meynert, *Internationale klinische Rundschau* 6 (1892), *Medizinische Schriften,* 270–71.

[17] Schnitzler, "Über funktionelle Aphonie und deren Behandlung durch Hypnose und Suggestion," *Internationale klinische Rundschau* 3 (1889), *Medizinische Schriften*, 176–209.

[18] Otis, *Membranes*, 147.

[19] Recall the near circus atmosphere of Charcot's public lectures, in which his hysterics performed their symptoms for a large audience in response to his suggestions.

[20] Otis, "The Language of Infection," *Germanic Review* 70/2 (1995), 66.

[21] Schnitzler, "Über funktionelle Aphonie," 180.

[22] *Medizinische Schriften*, 213.

[23] *Medizinische Schriften*, 213 n.

[24] *Flucht in die Finsternis* in ES II, 902–85.

[25] Otis, *Membranes*, 128.

[26] The phrase is from Freud, who argued in 1894 that unbearable ideas could produce psychoses through the repetition of the idea in hallucinations as wish-fulfillment. See Sander Gilman, *Disease and Representation* (Ithaca: Cornell UP, 1988), 212.

Schnitzler and the Discourse of Gender in *Fin-de-siècle* Vienna

Katherine Arens

ARTHUR SCHNITZLER'S WORKS are taken as evidence for stereotypes of the female and of gender relations in *fin-de-siècle* Vienna. His women, from young widows through *das süße Mädl,* the shop girls who may seek love but only get sex, emerge as what Bram Dijkstra has called "idols of perversity," or as *Nervenkunst.*[1] Traditionally, Schnitzler is seen as a "klassische[s] Beispiel eines unpolitischen Dichters."[2] However, more recently, a small number of critics agrees that "Schnitzler emphasizes the means by which the political suffuses daily life and individual consciousness."[3] Thus Egon Schwarz, in his article "Milieu oder Mythos?: Wien in den Werken Arthur Schnitzlers" (1984), can call "the Viennese Bourgeoisie" Schnitzler's real milieu.[4]

Eva Klingenstein, in *Die Frau mit Eigenschaften* (1997), has taken the political relevance of Schnitzler's work to heart in attacking the narrowness of the gender stereotypes attributed to the end of the century.[5] She documents a much broader picture of what was at stake in the discourse on women in Vienna 1900, ranging from liberal to conservative and across class lines, including issues such as motherhood, the role of wives, child-rearing, *Wohnkultur,* and professions. Klingenstein argues that the traditional images of sex relations at the turn of the century were from the first nostalgic artifacts, established in no small measure by Stefan Zweig's oft-quoted *Die Welt von Gestern* (1944).[6] In her estimation, Zweig's (and the modern reader's) dominant vision about the woman of 1900 most closely resembles those of liberalism "in den Zeitschriften der bürgerlichen Frauenbewegung."[7]

Schnitzler's assumptions about gender and class — not just about women — may be seen as a product of the liberal political and social inheritance of the day.[8] Several of Schnitzler's most prickly novellas — *Frau Berta Garlan* (1901), *Der Mörder* (1911), *Frau Beate und ihr Sohn* (1913), *Doktor Gräsler, Badearzt* (1917), and *Therese: Chronik eines Frauenlebens* (1928) — figure as extremely political diagnoses of Vienna's gendered and class-based economic and social expectation.[9] In this reading, Schnitzler emerges as a writer with a much broader vision of Viennese and Austrian society than he is often given credit for,[10] writing from within a distinct class position to offer a critique of a class that suffered deeply from a disappointment of its hopes and focus. The liberal Vienna that came into being the 1860s fell after the collapse (*Krach*) of the Viennese stock market, on May 9, 1873; the public's faith in free-market capitalism and in liberalism evaporated, as the state was forced for financial means to limit access to the public amenities that had brought the class to its zenith: "the Parliament, the Rathaus, and the University."[11]

Over the second half of the nineteenth century, the hope of Austro-Hungary as a meritocracy gradually gave way to the reality of a nation whose *arrivistes* no longer wanted to finance general social capital. *Die Jungen,* to contemporary ears, was a political term from the era of the *Krach,* from the 1873 elections that had split liberals across generational lines. In that election, local liberal parties began to challenge central parliamentarianism, asserting their privilege to join in setting policy, but losing their reforming zeal: "The *Jungen* were outsiders who wanted to become insiders. They were local activists, lawyers, journalists, and schoolteachers with substantial local associational experience, who sought election to the city councils, provincial diets, and the *Reichsrat.*"[12] *Fin-de-siècle* Vienna thus had inherited the core of an educated, socially aware populace fragmented politically across class, regional, and ethnic lines, but then was forced into the kind of economic turmoil that could not sustain the expansion necessary to capitalize on the hopes held by the members of its unique "imagined community," to use Benedict Anderson's term. The name of *Jung Wien,* the literary generation to which Schnitzler belonged, associates it with this political shift.

And on the streets of Schnitzler's Vienna, the world as the liberals imagined it — not necessarily how it was — was beginning to come apart. The actual living conditions of the mass of Austro-Hungarians were different than those of the bourgeois liberals whose lifestyle has come to symbolize Vienna for scholars today. For instance, Reinhard Sieder documents the real class rifts within the purportedly monolithic working class. Families weathered the shifting economic times by taking in boarders (sometimes multiple boarders, leading to six or eight people living in two rooms) when their wage-earners were ill. And even further down the hierarchy, employees lived in workers' barracks established by government in an era without rent or lease protections until 1917.[13] The city held far too many blue-collar, service-industry, and manual laborers who were underpaid, underfed, and underhoused.[14] The newly risen classes — or their children — thus saw persistent images of how their rise might easily be rolled back, given that their advance depended on state prosperity.

No wonder, then, that there was in Schnitzler's Vienna a high incidence of family violence, prostitution, and public-health problems (especially venereal disease).[15] Aside from sexually transmitted diseases, lung diseases such as tuberculosis were prevalent in this overcrowded, undernourished population, as well. The tuberculosis mortality rate was 390 per 100,000 cases in 1890, with higher rates in poor districts.[16] Jan Tabor concludes that the "decadent" faces familiar from Oskar Kokoshka's, Egon Schiele's, and Anton Romako's paintings show colorations characteristic of tubercular or syphilitic constitutions.[17] These purportedly decadent faces of *fin-de-siècle* Vienna are thus those of victims of economic circumstance, not the perpetrators of a decadent culture.

And Schnitzler, as a physician inheriting liberal traditions from his father, held a mirror up to his generation to ask it how it was going to cope with these changes.

Schnitzler's Women and Their *Doppelgänger*

The women in Schnitzler's stories follow these realities; they are neither *femmes fatales* nor *femmes fragiles*. The female protagonists (like their male counterparts) in Schnitzler's works often reflect lifestyles of the liberal classes who learned in the 1860s and 1870s to make their way upward in Austro-Hungarian society, yet whose rise came under threat by social and economic changes. This precise sociological marking of the characters, however, has not been fully appreciated by many critics, who state more generally that Schnitzler drew on people he knew to create many of his most famous characters.[18] Yet Schnitzler's work shows the costs of individuals' self-proclaimed class positions; his often unreliable narrators seek to define themselves within the values of liberal Vienna.

One of the most indicative of such stories is *Frau Berta Garlan*, begun on January 1, 1900, under the original title "Jugendliebe" but published in 1901 as a serial.[19] In it, Schnitzler revises a passing *amour* he had in 1899 with a young woman named Franziska Reich, for whom he played the role of Emil Lindbach. Critics underscore the social stereotyping of the female role:[20] Berta Garlan is a young widow with a small son, living in a town along the Danube, two hours from Vienna. Schnitzler first shows her walking between a river and a cemetery — suspended, as it were, between life and death, disengaged from her surroundings, and clueless about what those surroundings might really mean. Yet Schnitzler has also built a more complex narrative point of view into the story, including at least one doppelgänger whose motivation emerges only to readers. Through the naïve and petit bourgeois eyes of Berta Garlan, we also see the story of Frau Anna Rupius, a woman situated higher in society than Berta (she is always "Frau Rupius" and has money).

Berta had been raised at the heart of the liberal bourgeoisie, the world of self-made professionals. Her ideals, however, remained thoroughly romantic, leading her to reject suitors who did not live up to her dreams because they were ugly or lived in a *Provinzstadt*. She attended the conservatory in Vienna to study piano until her father pulled her out, presumably because she was in love with a violinist-Lothario ("in einer Aufwallung seiner bürgerlichen Anschauungen").[21] Berta remembers her goals as high: she wanted to be a virtuoso, or at least be married to one. These dreams ended when she was twenty-six, with her father's bankruptcy. Her sole remaining suitor was a "distant relation" of Berta's mother, a simple man who worked for an insurance company and who had moved from a rural town, no longer thinking that he would ever marry. When her parents died a week apart, Garlan helped her settle the estate and her future; she married him out of need "mit dem Gefühl der tiefsten Dankbarkeit . . . Schon in den ersten Tagen merkte sie freilich selbst, daß sie keine Liebe für ihn fühlte."[22] Garlan gave her a son and then died, three years into their marriage. This woman is left in straitened circumstances in the company (almost the custody) of her in-laws in a provincial town, two hours away from Vienna; these relations arrange for her to give piano lessons under the pretense that she is doing them a favor. As a reasonably young single widow, she is propositioned by all the men in town, from the local Lothario who flunked out of medical school through her nephew and her brother-in-law.

Berta's doppelgänger in the town is Frau Anna Rupius, wife of a forty-two-year-old wheelchair-bound cripple and subject of much gossip. Rupius and his wife had decided to move out of Vienna when he was crippled and retired from his job at an unnamed Ministry: "Wer weiß, in Wien wäre es schon ganz zu Ende."[23] It is unlikely that he really believes she shops so frequently in Vienna, since he has a rehearsed cover story for her: "es klang, als wenn er sich vorgenommen, diese Dinge jedem zu erzählen, der heute ins Zimmer träte."[24] Quite unexpectedly, Berta is invited to visit Anna's dressmaker in Vienna with her, a trip that reveals that her one-time crush, the violin virtuoso Emil Lindbach, is giving a concert. Her dreams are triggered:

> sie begriff es mit einemmal nicht mehr, wie leicht sie damals ihre eige-
> nen Hoffnungen, ihre künstlerische Zukunft und den Geliebten aufge-
> geben, um ein sonnenloses Dasein zu führen und in der Menge zu
> verschwinden . . . die Witwe eines unansehnlichen Menschen, die in ei-
> ner kleinen Stadt lebte, sich mit Klavierlektionen fortbrachte und lang-
> sam das Alter herankommen sah.[25]

From this point on, she is hell-bent on changing her life. Unwittingly,
Berta has already changed her life, at least in the public mind. Back in her
small town, everyone knows she has been in Vienna and asks about her
adventures, hoping for some gossip about Anna Rupius: "[Frau Martin]
wollte durchaus herausbekommen, ob Berta nicht irgend etwas bemerkt
hätte."[26] And she begins to fill their expectations, as she writes Emil to
arrange a visit, an offer he takes up immediately. She lies to her students
and family about another proposed visit to her cousin, but her real goal
is clear: "Sie fährt nur nach Wien, um seine Geliebte zu werden und
nachher, wenn's sein muß, zu sterben."[27]

Emil flirts with her and intimates that there are other men in her life;[28]
they arrange a secret evening meeting in a modest, out-of-the-way restaurant. Thereafter, he takes her not to his apartment, but to a rented room
with a painting of "eine nackte Frauengestalt";[29] he takes her off to bed
after he makes her play for him. Late that night, as they part in the street,
he puts her off, preferring to see her next time she comes to Vienna. In
anguish, she has long inner monologues about how she has sinned: "daß
sie kaum mehr eine Mutter ist, . . . nein, nichts als seine Geliebte,"[30] one
of the many women who have affairs and lovers. But Berta also feels proud
of her affair. In a subsequent exchange of letters, she offers to move to
Vienna and be Emil's mistress, but he suggests instead that she could
come visit him once every six weeks or so, which enrages her.

Unsure, Berta feels compelled to confess, and she naturally chooses
Anna, who reciprocates:

> Sie erzählte von ihrem Vater, der Offizier im Generalstab gewesen, von
> ihrer Mutter, die als ganz junge Frau gestorben war, von dem kleinen
> Haus mit Garten, in dem sie als Kind gespielt hatte. Jetzt erst erfuhr
> Berta, daß Frau Rupius ihren Mann schon als Knaben kennen gelernt,
> daß er mit den Seinen im angrenzenden Haus gewohnt und daß sie
> sich schon als Kinder verlobt hatten. Es war für Berta, das wenn die
> ganze Jugend dieser Frau wie sonnenbestrahlt auftauchte, eine Jugend
> voll Glück und voll Hoffnung . . .[31]

The Rupius couple forces Berta to rethink her own life. For instance,
Anna had commented that she envies Berta, particularly her child: "So

einen Buben zu haben, das muß ein großes Glück sein."[32] The situation
becomes more complicated when Rupius confides that his wife wants to
leave him, although she had actually only said: "ich will auf einige Wochen an einen See . . ."[33] But he is convinced she wants to leave the
cripple, that he owes her for sacrificing her youth for him. Anna ends up
not going: "Aus der langen Reise wird nichts, ich habe mich . . . zu
etwas anderem entschließen müssen."[34]

When Berta confesses her affair to Anna, the two stories converge in
discussions about women's fates. Anna laughs that Berta does not know
that her sister-in-law has had an affair. Berta naively asserts that her brother-
in-law did not throw his wife out, to which Anna rejoins: "Aus Bequem-
lichkeit hat er ihr verzeihen — und hauptsächlich, weil er dann selber tun
konnte, was er wollte. Sie sehen ja, wie er sie behandelt. Sie ist doch nichts
viel Besseres als sein Dienstmädchen."[35] Later, Berta hears that a doctor has
been called to the Rupius home. When Berta visits, the maid reports that
the wife has "eine Entzündung," then "Blutvergiftung."[36] Following her
most romantic instincts, Berta thinks it has been a suicide attempt. On a
later visit, "diese Sache ist entschieden."[37] She overhears the wife's last
words to her husband: "indem sie sich vergeblich aufzurichten trachtete:
'Nur dich, nur dich . . . glaub' mir, nur dich hab' ich . . .' Das letzte Wort
war nicht zu verstehen, aber Berta erriet es."[38] The readers realize what she
does not understand as one physician informs another: "In jedem andern
Falle hätte' ich die Anzeige erstattet, aber da die Sache so ausgeht . . .
Überdies wär' es ein entsetzlicher Skandal, und der arme Rupius litte am
meisten darunter."[39] To Berta, he covers up the situation: "Blutvergiftung . . . manchmal schneidet man sich in den Finger und stirbt daran; die
Verletzung ist nicht immer zu entdecken."[40] In case readers missed it,
Schnitzler visits Rupius in his moment of agony: "Warum nur hat sie's
getan? hat sie *das* getan? . . . Es war nicht notwendig — heiliger Himmel,
es war nicht notwendig! Was gehen mich die anderen Menschen an —
nicht wahr? . . . Ich hätt' es aufgezogen, aufgezogen wie mein eigenes
Kind."[41] Finally, belatedly, Berta may understand that Anna had had an
abortion, instead of being able to go away and have the child anonymously.

Berta fleetingly realizes that she, too, might have gotten pregnant in
her own one-night stand: "der Tod Annas war eine Vorbedeutung, ein
Fingerzeig Gottes."[42] She had wanted a child with Emil twelve years earlier, but not now. Thus she falls at the foot of Anna's deathbed and prays:
"Plötzlich flimmerte es ihr vor den Augen, eine wohlbekannte plötzliche
Schwäche kam über sie, ein Schwindel, der sich gleich verlor."[43] And the
reader knows that she had earlier felt "ermattet," worn out. Her attack of
false Christian piety leads her to recast the disaster as a legal matter:

mußte sie an den Unbekannten denken, für den sie [Anna] hatte sterben müssen und der straflos und wohl auch reuelos draußen in der
großen Stadt herumgehen und weiterleben durfte . . . Und sie ahnte
das ungeheure Unrecht in der Welt, daß die Sehnsucht nach Wonne
ebenso in die Frau gelegt ward, als in den Mann; und daß es bei den
Frauen Sünde wird und Sühne fordert, wenn die Sehnsucht nach Wonne nicht zugleich die Sehnsucht nach dem Kinde ist.[44]

She decides that her pain makes her able to understand Rupius, who had
told her to leave; her final gesture is telling: she sits down beside him.

The two stories emerge as grisly parallels. Both women are nominally
involved in situations that call love and lust into question, but love is
clearly not the core of the story. Rather, it is a morality fable about the
lot of women, with clear social implications. Two women married men
they had known since childhood; Anna had married up (her husband was
in the Ministry, while her family's house was small), while Berta married
down (because her dowry had been lost). Both, however, remain utterly
unable to deal openly with their environments. Their "adventures" are
just as much about unfulfilled dreams as they are about sex — neither
one had a real choice about moving out of Vienna and into a small town;
neither one had a family or circle of her own, but lived only through her
husband's modest circle. Both are trapped in a small-town world with a
double standard. So the novella is not about sexual mores, per se, but
rather about the social games associated with them.

Maybe even more significantly, in that final passage about the "Sehnsucht nach Wonne" the verb form is biblical: "ward," not "wurde."[45] And
Berta also called her own acts "sins" and Anna's death a sign of the "hand
of God." These women are utterly without the ability to resist such negative judgments because they seem unaware that they are playing social
games. Rendered decorative and useless as wives and mistresses, mothers
and lovers, they remain passive, stuck between the graveyard and the river.
They have no purpose as adults, once their children are gone. And there
is always an Emil to exploit them. They are held in a world of appearances
with no substance, dead in the midst of what should be life. In this sense,
Anna has opened a new life for Berta, at the side of Herr Rupius, gazing
at engravings of the paintings he will never again see. Berta, however, may
have learned that she has, finally, found a man she has power over.

Frau Berta Garlan is not alone among Schnitzler's stories in having
women imagine themselves in terms of sexual transgression, covering the
actual causes of their misery. *Frau Beate und ihr Sohn,*[46] for example,
again tells the story of a young widow who married down. Beate, however, has sufficient means and opportunity to indulge herself. She is

possibly even more self-centered and unpleasant than Berta Garlan,[47] leading critics to dismiss her story for everything from "Lüsternheit und Ernüchterung" through "blutschändischerische Brunst."[48] Yet ultimately, Beate seeks only to hold onto her class position and respectability, even as she begins to indulge her sexual fantasies with a friend of her seventeen-year-old son Hugo. Her situation is doubled, as was Berta Garlan's: Beate fears that her "little boy" has been seduced by an actress, just as she seduces the other youth. Beate makes the final decision to "save" them both, and they jump out of a boat together into the dark waters of their small resort town: "Beate zog den Geliebten, den Sohn, den Todgeweihten, an ihre Brust."[49] This closing scene is almost a pietà, a sacrifice based on Christian morals and prevailing social forms gone mad. In this work, as in *Frau Berta Garlan,* a woman recognizes the power of outward appearances and that there is no role for a woman in this world, outside that of wife, mother, aging old maid, or mistress.

Therese: Chronik eines Frauenlebens goes even further in this vein, as a daughter of an impoverished army officer and a would-be romance novelist abandons her teaching certificate to pursue an independent "career" in Vienna. She finds only penury, abuse inflicted by her upper-middle-class employers, seduction, and, ultimately, death at the hands of an illegitimate son whom she cannot keep in the class in which he expects to move.

These women — Anna, Berta, Beate, and Therese — play out variants of the same game, moving from powerlessness to the minor empowerment of choice. They are, first and foremost, constrained in their choices by the fact that they are all social climbers who live at the sufferance of their husbands, those husbands' sets and families. They have no backup systems of their own, no relatives, and no skills, having abandoned (or having been forced to abandon) whatever they had hoped to undertake when they were young. More seriously, they do not understand how their expectations were colored by romantic, social, or religious notions of female subjectivity. Even Anna Rupius, seemingly more worldly, ultimately will fall back into that pattern of trusting appearances rather than the reality of her relationships — or else she knows that her husband is actually no better than other men over the long run.

One is tempted now to move to an old-school feminist conclusion about the double standard, that the social scripts presented to the women are virgin or whore, *femme fatale* or *femme fragile,* mother or non-entity. However, Schnitzler tells stories of males who are in many ways as naïve as Berta Garlan and Beate Heinold, a fact that thwarts any too-simple feminist interpretation and forces readers to consider that class expectations, not just gender identity, appears as the real oppressive force in Schnitzler's Austria.

Schnitzler's Men

Like Schnitzler's women characters, the eponymous "hero" of *Doktor Gräsler, Badearzt*[50] lives a life characterized by one critic as full of "shabby betrayals."[51] Yet his life is not that simple, if readers again factor in a narrator's point of view and become aware of how gendered these critical perspectives have been. While critics admit that Gräsler is obnoxious, they have not dared to ask the more interesting question: why women are "attracted" to this non-entity who floats through marginal jobs — or why he thinks they are. Schnitzler has built the answer to that question into his story. Through Gräsler's uncomprehending eyes, Schnitzler presents a nuanced picture of the women in his life, women who span Austrian society and live lives of quiet despair. The result is not only Gräsler's story, but also that of the women in his life. At the same time, however, Gräsler himself emerges as a victim to the social order, different in kind but not necessarily in degree from the women he hopes to romance.

The first woman is his elder sister, Friederike, who is named only on the third page of the story; the first page introduces Gräsler in mourning for her after she has committed suicide in their shared house on the resort island of Lanzerote, where he is the spa doctor. His employment seems not to be going particularly well overall, because the director is sending Gräsler off condescendingly. The director's tone toward Gräsler is crucial evidence of how little professional clout Gräsler has at his age of forty-eight.[52] He is told to bring a wife back with him, which surprises him, but nonetheless tempts him, as he recalls a picture-book wife "mit einem rotbäckigem Puppengesicht."[53] Clearly, Gräsler has a thoroughly romanticized vision of what his life is and should be.

Yet Schnitzler has again plotted the tale to intertwine the fates of Friederike and Gräsler as doppelgängers. His nightmare is hers, as they enter their late middle age. One day, he fell asleep over his medical journals after lunch. When he roused himself and went home, he found her not looking out the window, as he had thought, but hanging from a noose. His observation both tells readers how little he knows and establishes her as his double:

> Im Anfang mühte er sich vergeblich, eine Erklärung für diesen Selbstmord zu finden. Daß das ernste, in Würde alternde Mädchen, mit dem er sich noch während des letzten Mittagsmahls in harmloser Weise über die bevorstende Abreise unterhalten hatte, mit einem Male verrückt geworden sein sollte, war nicht wahrscheinlich.[54]

Much later the story hints that he had probably spoken to her about his need to marry for professional reasons.

Gräsler only discovers the truth of his sister's life much later, and reluctantly. He had not seen his elder sister for years during the time he was a ship's doctor for Lloyd's. Then, fifteen years before the novel opens, when she was well over thirty, she had taken up with him after their parents died, "um ihm als Haushälterin in seine verschiedenen Aufenthaltsorte zu folgen."[55] He remembers reproachful looks from her, what Schnitzler called "das Bewußtsein eines verlorenen Lebens,"[56] but he had assumed she would still find a suitor. With overwhelming egotism he took her suicide as a personal abandonment:

> Den ahnungslosen Bruder hatte sie hierdurch freilich in die Notwendigkeit versetzt, sich in einer Lebensperiode, die neuen Gewöhnungen im allgemeinen abbhold zu sein pflegt, um Angelegenheiten des Haushaltes und der Wirtschaft zu kümmern, was ihm bisher durch Frederikens Fürsorge erspart geblieben war . . .[57]

Gräsler to the end does not see his sister as a full person. The final act of his sister's story reveals itself only after two of his own subsequent affairs. After he returns home, he finds out that his sister had redecorated his (their) apartment almost sumptuously, including electric light. In the attic he finds that she had many opulent possessions that he does not recognize, along with a pile of love-letters reaching back thirty years.

His first revelation is that his sister and his friend and legal adviser, the lawyer Robert Böhlinger, had intended to marry, until Böhlinger had found out she had "a past":

> daß seine Schwester vor mehr als zwangig Jahren, also schon als ziemlich reifes Mädchen, mit Böhlinger im geheimen verlobt gewesen war, daß dieser mit Rücksicht auf irgendeine früher vorgefallene Herzensgeschichte Friederikens die Heirat hinausgezögert, daß Friederike ihn dann mit irgend jemandem aus Ungeduld, Laune oder Rache betrogen, und daß sie endlich eine Versöhnung angestrebt, welche Versuche Böhlinger nur mit Ausbrüchen des Hohns und der Verachtung beantwortet hatte.[58]

Gräsler's attention is rapidly drawn off to other letters that confirm that she had been seducing his patients, even a terminally ill nineteen-year-old whom she probably helped into the grave.[59] His reaction is typical, utterly egotistical, as he wants to be absolved of all responsibility for her. He has turned into a voyeur of his sister's life, regretting what he had not known or shared: "doch fand er sich nicht so tief ergriffen, als er eigentlich gefürchtet hatte."[60] He does not see the key that readers must, once they realize that she has left a considerable inheritance. She had probably amassed whatever fortune she did as a mistress, driven by the fact that she and her brother had no inheritance from her parents. And there is a point not noted by the critics: that her career built a better future than his had. She had used her brother as cover, until the day when he threatened to bring a wife into their *ménage*. From that moment on, Friederike truly had no future, in her old age and without the apartment she had thought to command in comfort.

Was Gräsler in a more respectable profession than she was? Grasler's second "love," Sabine Schleheim, calls that assumption into question. When he returns to Europe, he makes rounds to do publicity in Berlin, "wo er sich bei einer Anzahl klinischer Professoren für die beginnende Kurzeit in Erinnerung brachte,"[61] and he revisits a spa where he used to work during the summers. There in the country, he feels all is still well, as it had been when his sister was there — except that he has to pour his own coffee. When he gets actually called out on a case, he is annoyed: "Der Doktor war hiervon wenig erfreut, wie er überhaupt für ortsansässige Kranke, deren Behandlung weder viel Ruhm, noch viel Gewinn zu bringen pflegte, keinerlei Vorliebe hegte."[62] The mother of the captivating Sabine, "eine junge Dame,"[63] is diagnosed with an upset stomach and complains that the spa is a fraud, bottling doctored water and selling it as therapeutic. That claim offends Gräsler, "so daß Doktor Gräsler, der sich stets an dem Rufe der Badeorte, in denen er gerade praktizierte, mitbeteiligt und für Erfolge and Mißerfolge mitverantwortlich fühlte, eine gewisse Verletztheit nicht völlig unterdrücken konnte."[64] The innuendo is also inevitable: there is not much medicine being practiced at such health spas. Sabine's father even notes that the spa owners hire actors to play sick — as only the year-round inhabitants would note.[65]

Sabine is a double to Gräsler's sister. She is twenty-seven, but her eyes and blond braids make her look younger. Her parents, her fifteen-year-old brother, and she had moved to the country more than seven years earlier. The father is now ill and old ("schon zweiundfünfzig Jahre alt"),[66] and he had to give up a career as a singer because of his health. Before this unilateral decision, Sabine traveled to the various small cities in which he played (only on mid-size stages). Sabine had originally been sent to study to be an actress, but gave it up because she had fallen in love with a singer who dumped her. She then enrolled in a nursing course — perhaps because the stage was not the profession for her, as she states later, or perhaps because she became engaged to a young doctor who died before they were married. Gräsler takes this information at its face value and does not realize that Sabine has chosen to embrace a different kind of respectability.

That Sabine knows medicine makes Gräsler momentarily ambitious, professionally: "Er fühlte sich als Mann von Welt und nahm sich flüchtig vor, im nächsten Sommer doch wieder in einem größeren Badeort seine Praxis auszuüben."[67] He meditates that he is not the physician he had once hoped to be, that he has not cared about his patients. Then he convinces himself that he loves her (afternoons with her are much more pleasant than those with his sister had been), while she suggests that the dying spa could be made profitable. After all, she notes, any doctor would like to be permanently attached to a *Heilsanstalt* where therapeutic methods could be tested and where relationships to patients could develop. With such chances at a new life, Gräsler tries to study his medical journals, to make himself worthy of her. Nonetheless, he hesitates, worried by a sense that she might be better than he, and from a reluctance to take his own profession quite this seriously.

As autumn draws near, and the time for Gräsler's departure, nothing is resolved, although it is clear that the family is hoping for something. Gräsler finds out why the old director wants to sell the sanitarium: "in möglichster Entfernung von wirklichen und eingebildeten Kranken zu verbringen und sich von den hunderttausend Lügen zu erholen wünschte, zu denen ihn sein Beruf zeitlebens gezwungen hätte."[68] Gräsler decides to buy it and present it to Sabine "als seiner Gefährtin und Frau gleichsam."[69] But that decision never is acted upon, and he bolts, purportedly to put his sister's affairs in order. Sabine writes him a long letter that she hopes will not be considered "unweiblich,"[70] and asks to be not his wife, but the manager of the spa: "Hausverwalterin . . . eine solche Oberaufsicht von gewissermaßen gesellschaftlichen Charakter, die der Anstalt im Laufe der letzten Jahre vor allem gefehlt habe."[71] Sabine, it turns out, has had her eye on the situation for a long time and has decided to accept only nervous patients, not any with real mental diseases.[72] She would even happily run it *in absentia,* so as not to ruin Gräsler's lifestyle. Or, if he insists, she would even marry him, although she does not love him.

This four-page letter (which he does not answer) is not mentioned by the critics. They prefer to take his point of view that he has no confidence,[73] or believe that she is his romantic fantasy. But the sheer calculation in the letter suggests rather that she has him scared; he fears that she would always be watching him, waiting for him to disappoint her: "Immer auf der Hut sein, gewissermaßen Komödie spielen, was in seinem Alter nichts sonderlich Leichtes war."[74] Sabine remains his obsession for the rest of the story, although their moment — his fantasy — has definitely passed. Sabine is honest where Gräsler is not, focused and hard-working where he is lazy, desirous of upward mobility where he is content to remain at the periphery of the genteel world. Much later, Gräsler tries to buy the sanitarium and to propose marriage to Sabine by letter. Yet the sanitarium is no longer for sale — the seller will run it himself. The clear implication is that she has made the deal that Gräsler would not.

The third woman in Gräsler's life is a shop girl who picks him up on a tram in the city as he runs from Sabine. Katharina, pale and simply dressed, is unmarried and lives with her parents. She is happy to find out he is single and agrees to go out with him, first to the theater. When he takes her to his apartment, his housekeeper gets pushy and asks for some of his sister's things, so he fires her. The shawl he seeks for the girl, however, leads him to find out about his sister, to find her letters. When he is called to a neighbor's sick child, Katharina puts herself to bed to wait for him. She shows up the next day with her suitcase, to take her vacation with him, having told her parents that she was going to the country to visit a friend: "Gräsler aber war danach von einer gesteigerten Zärtlichkeit für Katharina erfüllt, die sich wie als Hausfrau auch gesellschaftlich so vollkommen zu bewähren wußte."[75] That is, he is pleased to have a woman he thinks he recognizes. Yet Gräsler has underestimated his shop girl. Anything but retiring, Katharina gossips with the neighbors, making herself known (the widow cheerfully asks about "his little friend").[76] Gräsler, still pining for Sabine, is not so far gone as to lose his head for this "Ladenmamsell."[77] Katharina will get presents, and he has decided to treat her like a lady, but they both know the arrangement is temporary. Yet after he breaks with Sabine, Gräsler decides that Katharina is the girl for him: "Keine so reine Seele als Sie, mein Fräulein, aber dafür auch keine so kalte! Nicht so stolz, aber gütig. Nicht so keusch, aber süß!"[78]

Schnitzler characterizes Gräsler's prejudices carefully. When Gräsler cannot find Katharina at work, he assumes that she has already gone off with another, a tramp.[79] How could he have wanted to make her "Frau Doktor" and bring her to Lanzerote? He goes to her house in a final attempt to find her and discovers that her parents know who he is: "So genau nahm man es wohl nicht in einer Familie, wo das Fräulein Tochter mit doppelt soviel Gepäck vom Lande zurückkam, als sie abgereist war."[80] Katharina is in bed with scarlet fever, and so he tends her, even when her parents let him know that her "trip" had exhausted their funds. He sits with her all night, but Katharina dies of the fever he had probably brought home with him from the bedside of his neighbor's — Frau Sommer's — sick child. He feels that his future has disappeared, alternately scared about losing his job and realizing he does not need it because of his sister's legacy. To ease his own mind, he goes to Böhlinger and confesses the whole awful truth about all four women in his life; Frau Sommer tends him, and they go to Katharina's funeral together.

The ruin of Katharina leads Gräsler to his third affair, to take up with Frau Sommer, the fourth woman in his life. Frau Sommer plays the game well. She had originally asked for his help with her sick child, because she purportedly did not trust doctors, since she had lost a child three years earlier: "Und wenn irgendeiner, das fühle sie, sei er imstande, ihr das geliebte Kind zu retten."[81] And when he is in grief, she steps in to help:

> Von nun an nahm sich Frau Sommer des vereinsamten Junggesellen mit unaufdringlicher Güte an; er verbrachte viele Stunden, insbesondere jeden Abend in ihrer Wohnung und brachte der Kleinen, die er immer zärtlicher liebgewann, allerlei Spielzug mit . . . Frau Sommer aber zeigte sich in Wort und Blick von Tag zu Tag dankbarer für all das Liebe, das der Doktor ihrem vaterlosen Kinde erwies.[82]

This passage ends with the dashes that also end each scene in *Reigen*. Gräsler and Frau Sommer marry within a month after Katharina's death, and the final scene of the novella shows them being greeted by the director of the island resort at which the story had opened. But in this last scene, Gräsler appears to find the fifth female in his life:

> voran der Direktor und die junge Frau im lebhaften Gespräch, hinter ihnen Doktor Gräsler und die kleine Fanny in einem etwas zerdrückten weißen Leinenkleid . . . Gräsler hielt ihre weiche Kinderhand in der seinen und sagte: "Siehst du dort das kleine weiße Haus, wo alle Fenster offen stehen? Da wirst du wohnen . . . " So redete er weiter, immer die weiche Kinderhand in der seinen, deren Druck ihn beglückte, wie nie eine andere Berührung ihn beglückt hatte. Die Kleine, neugierig zu ihm aufblickend, horchte ihn zu.[83]

Note that the passage has the "soft child's hand" twice — signs that another girl may well be sacrificed to the ego of her father.

Schnitzler has told a set of compelling women's tales in Gräsler's four adult women, but it is difficult to argue them as his victims, since they clearly use him. Gräsler is thus himself a sort of victim, a man without social ties, an important commodity in this world of women who cannot move on their own. Schnitzler builds a telling set of details into the story that confirm how clueless Gräsler is about his own role in his game. Early on, he had meditated on all the women who ran away from him: an *Ingenieurswitwe* from Rio who had been traveling with him, but who then jumped ship; an *Advokatentochter* from Nancy, who dumped him in St. Blasien, after they had gotten engaged; Fräulein Lizzie from his student time in Berlin, who shot herself "a little" for his sake ("das sich seinetwegen soger ein wenig angeschossen");[84] Henriette with the nice apartment in Hamburg over the Alster; and "die Dame mit dem Puppengesicht" whom he wooed on a ship.[85] To call this a list like Casanova's is a gross understatement, since there is no evidence that he seduced them. In fact, Gräsler has probably been used by each of them, perhaps at the price of sex; he has no family ties, and great freedom of motion — the perfect cover for the women's own motivations, a key to their ability to manipulate the appearances of society and end up where they wish to. Sabine will be the mistress of the sanitarium for an absentee landlord; Friederike had the chance to travel and arrange a household of her own, at the price of indulging a foolish brother; Katharina has gotten gifts and a vacation; and Frau Sommer has gotten out of her small back apartment and into the world.

That this reading of Dr. Gräsler's situation is not overblown can be confirmed in comparison with another story about an unattached man, Alfred, in *Der Mörder*.[86] The hero is a more urbane, younger version of Gräsler, who believes he can marry an heiress, but instead ends up murdering his mistress and losing everything. Such a plot comes full circle with the question of who is victim and who is perpetrator. These men arguably are stuck in precisely the same situations as Berta Garlan and Beate Heinold, stressing artificial respectability. To be sure, they are not judged as husbands and fathers while the women are judged as women and "good daughters," but they are judged as professionals — they are expected to be something, to be educated and live up to their professions, no matter how little appeal they really hold. Still, it would be an overstatement to say that they live such different lives than the women — they all trade sex for other advantages.

Even Therese falls out of her class position because of that combination of circumstance and belief in society.[87] She chooses love over her teaching credential, herself the daughter of a mother who writes romance novels and a father who has invested his identity in a job he can no longer do. The result is the birth of her son, who will literally be the agent of her death, just as he kills her inner life, her love life, and any hopes at social standing. The parallels between Therese and these men are indeed striking.

Conclusion

Critics still generally prefer to look at the libidinous inner lives of Schnitzler's characters rather than to consider the more detailed "case histories." And in this light, his women seem to be more shocking than the men, given the seemingly more overt description of their power

258   ◆   THE DISCOURSE OF GENDER IN FIN-DE-SIÈCLE VIENNA

defined by external role-playing, with values of respectability, religion, goodness, and duty. Yet Schnitzler offers a detailed diagnosis of the lives of "his" class, of the supposedly liberal bourgeoisie who abuse their legacies, or who perhaps have been duped as to the impact and import of such a legacy.

All his characters seem to be the children of his own father's generation, believing the promise of the monarchy that children could be educated and move into new roles in the society of the Dual Monarchy. At the same time, those parents have often failed: they are financially ruined, or isolated from any extended family structures, or strong to the point of egotism. Their children are all carefully placed between the true upper bourgeoisie of long standing and the upper end of the working classes — they are, by reason of inheritance, connections, or disposition, ultimately outside the oligarchy, outside the traditional power centers of government, military, and economics. Many of them are educated (and that education is gendered), but that education is taken as something romantic or fine, leading them to see professional credentials almost as entitlements. They playact their professions; they are not real people, in the sense of contributing to a community. Too many of them have the *Puppengesichter* that Gräsler identifies as ideal on a woman. They are thus easily preyed upon by those closer to the inside: the barons who call one out for duels, the concert-giving heartthrobs, the actors, and the bank directors and lawyers.

More significantly, Schnitzler's women conceive of their roles as mothers not as angels of the house, nor in terms of Johann Jakob Bachofen's *Mutterrecht* (1861), but as professions that cease when their children grow up, and that are replaced by no others (as caregivers, or matriarchs, or society patronesses) because they are so removed from their society.[88] They are actually not much more marginalized than the Dr. Gräslers and Alfreds, who leave no marks of their passing, unnoted except by the truly unfortunate or predatory who hope to profit from them. Moreover, the women are every bit as arrogant as the men are: when they have means, they too can destroy others. Most women are in greater need of protection or advocacy than their male counterparts, yet they also may have the greater chance of successfully jumping class boundaries, if the circumstances allow it.

If there is a "discourse of gender" in Schnitzler's Austro-Hungary, it lies mainly in the fact that women have greater costs to pay for sexuality than men do, that the "double standard" is at play for the consequences of sex. Men and women both rely on the social games that the astute can play with prescribed social norms for ethics, religion, and personal or social destiny. In this sense, Schnitzler's stories do not simply personalize or aestheticize politics; they show the personal costs of not realizing the prevailing politics of society and law as mutually reinforcing systems. These are the true victims of society, not the acknowledged victims of the lower classes (such as Katharina, who knows the costs and benefits of her life), nor those who will fit into the ruling classes (including the Emil Lindbachs, Ferdinand Heinolds, and Fortunatas, who profit from those truly in power). But the characters in these stories have no dowries, no inheritance, a certain amount of knowledge, but not enough savvy or energy to leave a trace.

The story of gendered discourses in Schnitzler's Austro-Hungary is thus much crueler, much less personal than has been assumed. Art and education are not meant to be speculation, they are meant to be in service of the state, in its teachers, its advocates and judges, its bank directors, and architects who shape the social fabric as they shape their own lives. The characters in these stories, however, have another catechism: to save face while they live small lives and ruin their children. Schnitzler is thus much less the doppelgänger of Freud or a romance novelist than an astute observer of Austro-Hungary's social and political scenes.

Schnitzler is the novelist of people between classes, who fear falling back into disease, overcrowding, and poverty because they lack (or eschew) family and group ties. In this view, Schnitzler is less anti-liberal than despairing of the class politics of his peers. If the story had played out in the German Democratic Republic, one might have called it an *Ankunftsliteratur,* the literature that documents the fate of a success, not the proverbial "world of yesterday" or *versunkene Welt* that critics insist on.

Notes

[1] For examples of decadent and psychologizing approaches to Schnitzler, see Bram Dijkstra, *Idols of Perversity: Fantasies of Feminine Evil in fin-de-siècle Culture* (New York: Oxford UP), 1986; Wolfgang Nehring, "Schnitzler, Freud's Alter Ego?" *Modern Austrian Literature* 10/3–4 (1977): 179–94; and Friedrich Hacker, "Im falschen Leben gibt es kein Richtiges," in *Literatur und Kritik* 163/164 (1982): 36–44. They can take Schnitzler and Freud as alter egos. And even Andreas Huyssen in "The Disturbance of Vision in Vienna Modernism," *Modernisms/Modernity* 5/3 (1998): 33–47 can still take Schnitzler as a typical modernist who privileges the visual gaze that objectifies women.

[2] See Robert A. Kann, "Die historische Situation und die entscheidenden politischen Ereignisse zur Zeit und im Leben Arthur Schnitzlers," *Literatur und Kritik* 161/62 (1982): 19.

[3] Felix W. Tweraser, *Political Dimensions of Arthur Schnitzler's Late Fiction* (Columbia, SC: Camden House, 1998), 27; see also Anton Pelinka, "Die Struktur und die

Probleme der Gesellschaft zur Zeit Arthur Schnitzlers," *Literatur und Kritik,* 163/164 (1982): 59. Elizabeth G. Ametsbichler's "Der Reiz des Reigens': Reigen Works by Arthur Schnitzler and Werner Schwab," *Modern Austrian Literature* 31/3–4 (1998): 288–300, is typical in new claims that Schnitzler was less interested in psychological symbolism and perhaps more realistic.

[4] Egon Schwarz, "Milieu oder Mythos?: Wien in den Werken Arthur Schnitzlers," *Literatur und Kritik* 163/164 (1982): 29; Ernst L. Offermann, *Arthur Schnitzler: Das Komödienwerk als Kritik des Impressionismus* (Munich: Fink, 1973), 57. G. J. Weinberger, in *Arthur Schnitzler's Late Plays: A Critical Study* (New York: Peter Lang, 1997), makes a point of refuting Offermann's, Brigitte L. Schneider-Halvorson's, and A. C. Roberts's approaches to Schnitzler's politics, as his "Introduction" provides a succinct overview of the generations of Schnitzler criticism, a useful starting point for any later discussion. Trend-setting because of his use of materials not published at the time, Roberts makes a special point of using the diaries to work out Schnitzler's attitudes to the political issues of the day, including dueling, the military, and the First World War.

[5] Eva Klingenstein, *Die Frau mit Eigenschaften: Literatur und Gesellschaft in der Wiener Frauenpresse um 1900* (Cologne: Böhlau, 1997).

[6] Klingenstein, 286. The English version of Zweig's text (in a translation by Benjamin W. Huelsch and Helmut Ripperger) appeared first, as *World of Yesterday: An Autobiography* (New York: Viking Press; London: Cassell, 1943), with the German *Die Welt von Gestern: Erinnerungen eines Europäers* (London: Hamilton; Stockholm: Vermann-Fischer, 1944) later. That discrepancy between "autobiography" and "memoirs" characterizes the text: it tells Zweig's own story as if it were *the* story of Vienna and its Jews.

[7] Klingenstein, 289.

[8] Pieter M. Judson's *Exclusive Revolutionaries: Liberal Politics, Social Experience, and National Identity in the Austrian Empire, 1848–1914* (Ann Arbor: U of Michigan P, 1996) is the primary source for descriptions of liberal politics. For more information on the living and social conditions of Vienna 1900, see particularly Gernot Ehalt, Hubert Ch. Heiß, and Hannes Stekl, eds. *Glücklich ist, wer vergisst?: Das andere Wien um 1900* (Vienna: Böhlau, 1986). Gary B. Cohen's *Education and Middle-Class Society Imperial Austria 1848–1918* (West Lafayette, IN: Purdue UP, 1996) has described the dynamics of class-bound education. John W. Boyer in *Culture and Political Crisis in Vienna: Christian Socialism in Power, 1897–1918* (Chicago: U of Chicago P, 1995) and *Political Radicalism in Late Imperial Vienna: Origins of the Christian Social Movement 1848–1897* (Chicago: U of Chicago P, 1981) has offered the standard accounts of the political rise of the conservatives in two massive books.

[9] *Frau Berta Garlan* in ES I, 390–513; *Doktor Gräsler, Badearzt* in ES II, 113–205; *Frau Beate und ihr Sohn* in ES II, 42–112; *Der Mörder* in ES I, 992–1010; *Therese: Chronik eines Frauenlebens* in ES II, 625–881.

[10] Horst Thomé, "Sozialgeschichtliche Perspektiven der neueren Schnitztler-Forschung," *Internationales Archiv für Sozialgeschichte der Deutschen Literatur* 13 (1988): 184. Thomé points out that there are few studies that take Schnitzler's career as a writer seriously, as part of the "Literaturbetrieb." And Herbert Seidler in "Die

Forschung zu Arthur Schnitzler seit 1945," *Zeitschrift für Deutsche Philologie* 95/4 (1976): 580, underscores Thomé's points by noting that Urbach is one of the few scholars who have undertaken detailed text analyses.

[11] Carl E. Schorske, *Thinking with History: Explorations in the Passage to Modernism* (Princeton: Princeton UP, 1998), 114.

[12] Judson, 168.

[13] Reinhard Sieder, "'Vata, derf i aufstehn?': Kindheitserfahrungen in Wiener Arbeiterfamilienum 1900," in *Glücklich ist, wer vergisst?: Das andere Wien um 1900*, eds. Gernot Ehalt, Hubert Ch. Heiß, and Hannes Stekl (Vienna: Böhlau, 1986), 77.

[14] See Josef Ehmer, "Wiener Arbeitswelten um 1900," in Ehalt et al., eds., *Glücklich ist*, 195–214.

[15] See Sabina Kolleth, "Gewalt in Ehe und Intimpartnerschaft," in Ehalt et al., eds., *Glücklich ist*, 145–71. Prostitution was legalized in 1873. Inge Pronay-Strasser, "Von Ornithologen und Grashupgerinnen: Bemerkungen zur Sexualität um 1900," in Ehalt et al., eds., *Glücklich ist*, 128.

[16] Jan Tabor, "An dieser Blume gehst Du zugrunde: Bleich, purpurot, weiß — Krankheit als Inspiration," in Ehalt et al., eds., *Glücklich ist*, 222.

[17] *Glücklich ist*, 225–30.

[18] Elsbeth Dangel, "Vergeblichkeit und Zweideutigkeit: *Therese, Chronik eines Frauenlebens*," in *Arthur Schnitzler in neuer Sicht*, ed. Hartmut Scheible (Munich: Fink, 1981), 164–65. Dangel argues that *Therese* moves beyond Schnitzler's own milieu, and that the "Nichtigkeit und Ziellosigkeit dieser Gesellschaft" (184) makes the work "durch und durch sozialhistorisch" (165). Ruth K. Angress, "Schnitzler's 'Frauenroman' *Therese*," *Modern Austrian Literature* 10/3–4 (1977): 275, does a good job enumerating the people and stages in Therese's life, but does not see her pretensions. One notable contribution to the literature on *Frau Berta Garlan* is by Silvia Jud, "Arthur Schnitzler: Frau Berta Garlan (1901)," in *Erzählkunst der Vormoderne*, eds. Rolf Tarot and Gabriela Scherer (Bern: Peter Lang, 1996), 417–74. Jud presents a narratological analysis that aims at specifying the slippery narrative perspective of the story. However, her conclusions differ radically from mine.

[19] Renate Wagner, *Arthur Schnitzler: Eine Biographie* (Vienna: Fritz Molden, 1981), 113; Reinhard Urbach, *Schnitzler Kommentar zu den erzählenden Schriften und dramatischen Werken* (Munich: Winkler-Verlag, 1974), 109.

[20] See Elsbeth Dangel, "Augenblicke Schnitzlerscher Frauen," *Sprache und Literatur in Wissenschaft und Unterricht* 67 (1991): 107.

[21] *Frau Berta Garlan*, 392.

[22] *Frau Berta Garlan*, 394.

[23] *Frau Berta Garlan*, 407.

[24] *Frau Berta Garlan*, 407.

[25] *Frau Berta Garlan*, 421.

[26] *Frau Berta Garlan*, 431.

[27] *Frau Berta Garlan*, 446.

[28] *Frau Berta Garlan*, 458.

[29] *Frau Berta Garlan,* 473.

[30] *Frau Berta Garlan,* 478.

[31] *Frau Berta Garlan,* 438.

[32] *Frau Berta Garlan,* 437.

[33] *Frau Berta Garlan,* 447.

[34] *Frau Berta Garlan,* 494.

[35] *Frau Berta Garlan,* 497.

[36] *Frau Berta Garlan,* 505.

[37] *Frau Berta Garlan,* 508.

[38] *Frau Berta Garlan,* 510.

[39] *Frau Berta Garlan,* 510.

[40] *Frau Berta Garlan,* 511.

[41] *Frau Berta Garlan,* 511–12.

[42] *Frau Berta Garlan,* 512.

[43] *Frau Berta Garlan,* 512.

[44] *Frau Berta Garlan,* 513.

[45] *Frau Berta Garlan,* 513.

[46] Its working title was "Mutter und Sohn," based on sketches from 1906 and 1909; the final version was begun on April 3, 1911, but finished in 1912; it was published in early 1913 in *Neue Rundschau* (Urbach, 126). Schnitzler's friends questioned it ethically (Wagner, 265).

[47] "Nun gehört 'Frau Beate' zu jenen Werken, die auch ausgesprochenen Schnitzler-Freunden zuwider sein können. Manchmal, so scheint es, ist seine schonungslose Ehrlichkeit der Mitwelt peinlich, manchmal will sie gar nicht so genau wissen, was in Menschenseelen alles Platz hat. Unter der schönen Fassade der Frau Beate geht ja wirklich viel Abgründiges vor" (Wagner, 265).

[48] Richard Specht, *Arthur Schnitzler: Der Dichter und sein Werk* (Berlin: Fischer, 1922), cited by Wagner, *Arthur Schnitzler,* 266.

[49] *Frau Beate und ihr Sohn,* 111–12.

[50] Schnitzler started working at Gräsler's story in 1911, although it was not published until 1917 (Urbach, 127). Notes for the story went back to 1908, based on two real stories that he was told by a friend; one turns into the Katharina story, and the other Sabine (see Urbach, 127–28). C. E. J. Brinson, "Searching for Happiness: Towards an Interpretation of Arthur Schnitzler's *Doktor Gräsler, Badearzt,*" *Modern Austrian Literature* 16/2 (1983): 47–63 is a good discussion of Gräsler. In another vein, Ernest H. von Nardroff, in "*Doktor Gräsler, Badearzt*: Weather as an Aspect of Schnitzler's Symbolism," *Germanic Review* 43/2 (March 1968): 109–19, tries a close analysis of the text, to prove the text is a well-wrought urn. Nonetheless, he reports details from the male point of view, differently than I am doing here.

[51] Martin Swales, *Arthur Schnitzler: A Critical Study* (Clarendon. Oxford, 1971), 283.

[52] Brinson argues the contrary: "Professional activity . . . is not open to Friederike, whose role it is merely to run her brother's household, thereby facilitating for him the exercise of *his* profession" (51).

[53] *Doktor Gräsler, Badearzt*, 114.

[54] *Doktor Gräsler, Badearzt*, 115.

[55] *Doktor Gräsler, Badearzt*, 115.

[56] *Doktor Gräsler, Badearzt*, 116.

[57] *Doktor Gräsler, Badearzt*, 116.

[58] *Doktor Gräsler, Badearzt*, 180–81.

[59] *Doktor Gräsler, Badearzt*, 181.

[60] *Doktor Gräsler, Badearzt*, 117.

[61] *Doktor Gräsler, Badearzt*, 117.

[62] *Doktor Gräsler, Badearzt*, 117.

[63] *Doktor Gräsler, Badearzt*, 117.

[64] *Doktor Gräsler, Badearzt*, 120.

[65] *Doktor Gräsler, Badearzt*, 147.

[66] *Doktor Gräsler, Badearzt*, 125.

[67] *Doktor Gräsler, Badearzt*, 127.

[68] *Doktor Gräsler, Badearzt*, 140.

[69] *Doktor Gräsler, Badearzt*, 140.

[70] *Doktor Gräsler, Badearzt*, 143.

[71] *Doktor Gräsler, Badearzt*, 141.

[72] *Doktor Gräsler, Badearzt*, 156.

[73] Brinson, 53.

[74] *Doktor Gräsler, Badearzt*, 147.

[75] *Doktor Gräsler, Badearzt*, 175.

[76] *Doktor Gräsler, Badearzt*, 176.

[77] *Doktor Gräsler, Badearzt*, 177.

[78] *Doktor Gräsler, Badearzt*, 192.

[79] *Doktor Gräsler, Badearzt*, 193.

[80] *Doktor Gräsler, Badearzt*, 194.

[81] *Doktor Gräsler, Badearzt*, 172.

[82] *Doktor Gräsler, Badearzt*, 204.

[83] *Doktor Gräsler, Badearzt*, 205.

[84] *Doktor Gräsler, Badearzt*, 122.

[85] *Doktor Gräsler, Badearzt*, 190.

[86] The first sketch dates to 1897; it appeared in 1911 (Urbach, 125). It was translated as "The Murderer" by O. F. Theis in *The Shepherd's Pipe and Other Stories* (New York: Brown, 1922), 81–120, and reprinted in various collections.

[87] *Therese* has received what is closest to a modern feminist reading among all the Schnitzler novellas. See particularly Ulrike Weinhold, "Arthur Schnitzler und der weibliche Diskurs: Zur Problematik des Frauenbilds der Jahrhundertwende," in *Jahrbuch für Internationale Germanistik* 19/1 (1987): 110–45, who concludes that Schnitzler exploits female stereotypes; and Konstanze Fliedel, "Verspätungen: Schnitzlers *Therese* als Anti-Trivialroman," in *Jahrbuch der Deutschen Schiller-Gesellschaft* 33 (1989): 323–47, who discusses the genre conventions of the work.

[88] Johann Jakob Bachofen, *Das Mutterrecht: Eine Untersuchung über die Gynaikokratie der alten Welt nach ihrer religiösen und rechtlichen Natur* (Stuttgart: Krais und Hoffman, 1861).

The Overaged Adolescents of Schnitzler's *Der Weg ins Freie*

John Neubauer

I. The Vanishing World of the Fathers

GEORG VON WERGENTHIN is dining alone in the opening scene of Schnitzler's novel *Der Weg ins Freie* (1908).[1] His father died two months ago, his mother nine years ago, and his older brother, Felician, has resumed his habit of eating at his club with his male aristocratic friends. The twenty-seven-year-old Georg finds that his imposing home is becoming friendly again, but when his glance passes the sunlit empty chair at the upper end of the table, his dead father reappears to him as vividly as if he had sat there just an hour ago.[2] Old von Wergenthin had earned a doctorate in philosophy but devoted himself to botanical studies, first as an amateur, later as a professional. He even became the honorary president of the Botanical Society, an honor, the narrator adds, he did not achieve merely because he belonged to the nobility.

In the rest of the novel readers encounter old von Wergenthin only in passing,[3] but his life and achievements represent a silent foil to his son's story, and the image of the empty seat at the head of the dining table may be taken as an emblem of his generation's absent presence in the life of the next one. Several other fathers are still alive, but in a figural sense they too are empty chairs. The young people should define themselves in response to their father's worldview and their mode of life; but the generational conflict is not played out as a confrontation between youth and patriarchal tyranny, because the ideals, values, and successes of the old generation have lost their power and become outmoded or discredited. The narrative correlate to the empty chair is a novel by the fictional writer Edmund Nürnberger about the all-but-bygone age ("halbvergangene Zeit") of the fathers. "Über jene lügendumpfen Welt, in der erwachsene Menschen für reif, altgewordene für erfahren und Leute, die sich gegen kein geschriebenes Gesetz vergingen als rechtlich; in der Freiheitsliebe, Humanität und Patriotismus schlechtweg als Tugenden galten, auch wenn sie dem faulen Boden der Gedankenlosigkeit oder der Feigheit entsproßt waren, hatte Nürnberger grimmige Leuchten angezündet," Nürnberger explains.[4] Nürnberger's "tätiger und braver" hero is carried to the top of his social world by the "wohlfeilen Phrasen der Epoche," but having reached there he recognizes those slogans for what they are and tumbles into "das Leere . . ., aus dem er gekommen war."[5]

Schnitzler's narrator compresses this summary into a single-sentence, free, indirect discourse that presents Georg von Wergenthin's reaction to the novel he just read. The ambiguous merging of the narrator's and the protagonist's voices disappears in the subsequent sentences, which are unequivocally focused through Georg's mind: he used to wonder why, after writing a strong novel, Nürnberger wrote only casual and mocking marginal notes on his times. When Heinrich Bermann, another Jewish writer-friend, tells him that anger may be productive, but disgust is not, Georg realizes that Nürnberger is burned out.[6]

The multiple perspectives in this short passage offer rich information. Readers learn that Nürnberger's relationship to the "halbvergangene Zeit" of the fathers is as problematic as Georg's is, though in a different way. Nürnberger is unable to climb because he cannot muster that faith in humanism and patriotism that his paternal figure lost only at the top. Still worse, having written his angry young work, he is now incapable of the ire that would engender other significant books. Neither his father's world nor his own can offer him creative impulses. Having written a work of adolescent rebellion, he cannot find his mature identity and voice.

Nürnberger's failure to grow up both attracts and repulses Georg, who has his own problems with professional and sexual maturity. His aristocratic and well-to-do father neither climbed like Nürnberg's fictional hero nor fell like him. Georg's aristocratic world is milder and more pastel-colored; no angry rebellion is necessary or possible. And yet, the father's successful amateurism is a troublesome legacy, for it remains unclear even at the end of the novel whether Georg will eventually make the transition from amateur to professional musicianship.

The fate of old Bermann, Heinrich's father, resembles that of Nürnberger's hero. He was a patriot, an enthusiastic supporter of the emperor,[7] and a member of the parliament who made a name for himself with a speech against the introduction of Czech in certain Bohemian districts,[8] but he was forced out of his party because of his Jewishness and is now hospitalized with deep depression.[9] Heinrich wants to commemorate him but cannot find the appropriate mode. Lacking Nürnberger's adolescent anger, he can write only in a less productive satiric mode, and he is not even sure as to the correct subgenre. He wants to present his father as a tragicomic hero in a political drama, because Jews who fervently love their country and their emperor are necessarily tragicomic.[10] But he is uncertain about this genre positioning, because he adds that such Jews were tragicomic only in the 1870s and 1880s, when even clever people were seduced by the fashionable liberal slogans. From a present perspective they are merely ridiculous.[11] Tragicomic and ridiculous thus define a perspectival difference between the fathers and the sons. Once more, the father can neither be followed nor rejected outright. Once more, the legacy inhibits Heinrich's growth and artistic productivity. A comic monument is an oxymoron.

The surviving fathers are uncomfortable in the Vienna of the early 1900s. Dr. Stauber, one of the most attractive figures, looks with great suspicion at his son's attempt to enter politics, and he is happy when the latter decides to return to his "real" profession, medical research, for Stauber had always considered his son a guest in the parliament.[12] He recognizes that his views are old-fashioned, and he wistfully remembers his youth, when he could hope that the Jews would one day be at home in the parliament. The features of his nostalgically evoked world of yesterday are by now familiar: ideals were then irrevocably established; everybody knew that one was a scoundrel if one did not honor one's parents; true love came only once in a lifetime; it was a pleasure to die for one's fatherland; and every decent person held high a banner, or had at least something on his banner. Listening to this depiction, Georg is suddenly seized by guilt with respect to his own father.[13]

The other Jewish fathers have an even more difficult time than Stauber. Salomon Ehrenberg, who earned his fortune by manufacturing munitions,[14] is so unhappy with his wife's pretentious soirées that he dreams of showing up one day in a caftan and with orthodox Jewish side curls.[15] While he has a certain admiration for Zionism, he does not join it. Visiting Palestine, he is disappointed by the landscape, sees hardly any of the new Jewish settlements, and concludes that he is too old to emigrate.[16] Old Golowski, Leo's father, who went bankrupt some five years ago, is unable to eke out a living for his family by being a broker in sundry matters. His wife has to complement his income by knitting, and they must move to simpler quarters.[17] When Georg finally meets him, old Golowski appears to him like an aging comedian from the provinces, not "patriarchalisch, graubärtig und ehrwürdig, sondern glattrasiert und mit breit verschlagenen Mienen."[18] In contrast, old Eißler, a monocled giant with a long, gray beard, resembles a Hungarian magnate rather than a Jewish patriarch. This imposing figure, once one of Vienna's most famous boxers, is a composer of pleasant waltzes

268 ◆ THE OVERAGED ADOLESCENTS OF SCHNITZLER'S *DER WEG INS FREIE*

and an expert collector of art and archaeological objects.[19] His son, Willy, is incapable of resolving the cultural ambiguity in his father's character: he assiduously works at his image as a gentile cavalier; although he does not deny his Jewishness and makes no attempt at assimilation, he is defensive about his real social standing.[20] And finally there is the insignificant and powerless father Rosner, head of a lower-middle-class Gentile family,[21] who impotently watches as his daughter Anna becomes Georg's mistress and his no-good son joins the extreme right-wing. When Rosner's wife makes him talk to Georg about Anna's pregnancy, he can utter only dejected fragments: "im übrigen kann ich Ihnen nicht schildern, Herr Baron, wie schwer getroffen . . . wie, ich möchte sagen . . . wie aus allen Himmeln gerissen . . . nie, nie hätte ich geglaubt."[22]

The afterglow of the vanishing paternal world is like a gentle sunset. The young people must break away from it, as the title suggests, but this move gets only Oskar Ehrenberg into an Oedipal conflict. The source of the conflict is his desire to escape from the Jewish identity that his father ostentatiously displays. While his sister Else demonstratively shows in public her affection for her father, Oskar is embarrassed at him, for he does not meet his high standards. When the elder Ehrenberg sees that Oskar crosses himself passing a Catholic church, he slaps his son in public; Oskar attempts to kill himself, survives, and goes on to lead an aimless life.

In all other cases, the fathers have no authority and offer no model to follow or to reject, and this absence is one reason why the young people cannot find their own identity. *Der Weg ins Freie* is populated with over-aged adolescents: Else Ehrenberg is twenty-four, Leo Golowski twenty-five, Georg von Wergenthin twenty-seven, and Demeter Stanzides thirty-seven. As Georg Lukács brilliantly recognized in an early Hungarian review of the novel, the major theme of *Der Weg ins Freie* is not just a general identity crisis, as Janz would have it,[23] but extended adolescence. The characters of the novel reincarnate Schnitzler's earlier figures, for example "Anatol" (1893; tr. 1917); Frita, Theodor, and Christine in "Liebelei" (1896; *Light-o'-love,* 1912), and Gustl in *Leutnant Gustl* (1900; *None But the Brave,* 1926). However, now they are at the threshold of an adulthood they should have reached some time ago. They are aging Anatols, aesthetes of life, anarchists of mood still playing with everything even though life is slipping out of their hands. They are yearning to belong somewhere and to have obligations; but when the opportunity comes, they back away, and once they missed it they cry about its loss.[24] Indeed, none of Schnitzler's overaged adolescents finds a judicious way toward domestic and professional engagement.

II. Diffusely Focalized Adolescence

Lukács, in *Der Weg ins Freie*, objected not only to Schnitzler's interest in aimless characters (thus anticipating his later demand for positive heroes) but also, and primarily, to the alleged formlessness of the novel. He approvingly quotes Alfred Kerr's remark that Schnitzler did not portray confusion but portrayed the world in a confusing manner, and he concludes with the generalization that the "absolute formlessness" of the age kills even the "healthy sense for form, adequate expression, construction, and proportion" that great writers possess.[25] Lukács was not alone in making this criticism. Many early as well as recent articles on *Der Weg ins Freie* find it troublesome that Schnitzler's novel resists categorization. According to Josef Hofmiller, it is not a "novel of Vienna," for it is too much preoccupied with the Jews;[26] according to Ruth Klüger, it is not a "Jewish novel," for its key figure is an aristocrat;[27] according to Carl Busse and Erich Schmidt, it is not a love story, because it includes endless Jewish self-analyses;[28] and according to a great many critics, it is not a novel of ideas, because its love story is maudlin. Hermann Bahr criticized Schnitzler for singling out the Jews at the expense of other groups of class and ethnicity.[29]

The notion of delayed adolescence is no panacea for the problem of form in *Der Weg ins Freie*, but it allows readers to see the central issues of sexuality and Jewishness as aspects of the broader category of identity. It does offer an answer to reviewers such as Hermann Kinzel,[30] who saw no connection between Georg's love affair and his socialization with Jews. These are arguably interrelated on the thematic as well as on the narrative level.

On the thematic level, the novel presents both gender and Jewishness as problems of identity for characters who are well into the third decade of their lives. Perhaps because of this characteristic delay or extension of the portrayed adolescence, *Der Weg ins Freie* explores sexual identity in exclusively heterosexual terms — in contrast, for instance, to Thomas Mann's *Tonio Kröger* (1903) and Robert Musil's *Die Verwirrungen des Zöglings Törleß* (1906), which include early, pubescent phases of adolescent homoeroticism. Nevertheless, Schnitzler's concern with gender (as opposed to merely sexual) identity does go beyond heterosexuality, for it gives a central role to male homosocial ties. Indeed, one of the key elements linking the love story to the Jewish Question is that Georg is simultaneously but differently attracted to Anna Rosner on the hand and to the Jewish intellectuals and writers Bermann, Nürnberger, and Golowski on the other. Critics seem to have overlooked this tension between Georg's heterosexual and homosocial attractions, because the latter appears in the first instance as a problematic philo-Semitism. Georg has apparently only weak ties to his brother, to his Gentile friends, and to his club. Yet Georg's desire to be with Bermann, Nürnberger, and Golowski is surely not because of a need to discuss "the Jewish Question"; rather, he wants male companionship, and this need repeatedly clashes with his heterosexual desires. It may even be argued that the real competitor to (and final victor over) the heterosexual commitment to Anna is not Georg's musical profession (which would require the same kind of serious commitment as a permanent relationship with Anna), but rather the free-floating and uncommitted homosocial engagement that Georg maintains with his Jewish friends (and with them only). What he shares with them are a *disponibilité* and detachment that can be easily transferred to other males in Detmold.

Der Weg ins Freie looks at the identity of women and Jews through a male aristocrat that faces his own problems of identity because he is torn between them. Narrative theory would designate Georg as the "reflector figure" or main focalizer of the novel.[31] But these visual metaphors are somewhat misleading. Georg filters rather than "reflects," and he does not focalize if one defines this term as focusing in on something. He functions not like a fixed lens but like an eye that constantly readjusts its focus and image. Georg's perception of women and Jews (as well as of other objects, of himself, and of his relations to others) is diffuse, unstable, and continually changing according to the situation and his mood — most appropriate would perhaps be the untranslatable German term *verwackelt*, which designates a photo that became vague because of the movement of the camera at the moment of taking the picture. This instability is evident in the frequent shifts readers observe in him while he is in the company of Anna or his Jewish friends. The composite image produced by his eye is so diffuse that one may say it disperses rather than focuses. Why this quality occurs may be answered in terms of psychology or narrative function. In psychological terms, Georg's diffuse images of others are a result of his own emotional and intellectual instability; more persuasively, in narrative terms, this diffuseness is related to Schnitzler's modernist narrative disposition.

How does the narrative mode of the novel connect to Georg's relations to women and Jews? Schnitzler pioneered the internal monologue in *Leutnant Gustl* (1900), and he was a master of theatrical dialogues.[32] *Der Weg ins Freie* employs, of course, both internal monologues and dialogues, but these are not the dominant modes of the novel. Schnitzler did not aim in this novel at a "vanishing narrator" by employing either techniques from the theater (which would yield a novel of almost pure dialogue, such as Henry James's *The Awkward Age* [1899]) or internal monologues, as in some of his short narratives. Georg is not even a rigorously employed reflector figure, like K. in Franz Kafka's novels. Nevertheless, the novel is overwhelmingly filtered through Georg's perspective. Readers get to know the women and the Jews in his company and through their conversations with him, — with three important exceptions: Else Ehrenberg's dialogue with her mother,[33] Berthold Stauber's discussion with his father,[34] and the brief paragraph that describes how, lying in bed, Anna has happy visions of a future with Georg.[35] In the rest of the book, Georg is present; and, equally important, the conversations reveal his mind, not those of his partners. Readers learn his secret reactions to them but are hardly ever privy to their thoughts about him.[36] While it is true that the book mediates several different views to the reader, Heidi Gidion exaggerates this feature by calling the novel polyperspectival[37] The perspectives in *Der Weg ins Freie* are all mediated and filtered through Georg's mind, whereas true polyperspectivism would be unmediated.

The images of women and Jews in *Der Weg ins Freie* are thus co-produced by Georg. Readers cannot see these persons directly; like Heinrich von Kleist's (1777–1811) famous green glasses, the "Wergenthin lens" colors everything. Moreover, Georg adjusts his mode of focusing to the nature of his conversational partners and his relations to them. Georg's homosocial relation to male Jews appears to be intellectual but freewheeling, whereas his tie to Anna is an unstable sexual drive, even if he claims that she is on his intellectual level.[38] This contrast manifests itself on the textual level in the distinction that Georg's Jewish friends incessantly talk to him, while Anna is mostly silent, especially in the last part of the novel, when she suffers most. Whereas in the case of the Jewish men the narrator compensates for the inaccessibility of their minds by giving them freedom to speak aloud, Anna is given no such compensation. The brief glimpse of her mind and her occasional contributions to the dialogues tell readers little about her. She is a black hole, a thing in itself, as Busse has complained.[39]

Georg is then torn between heterosexual commitment and freewheeling, casual homosocial camaraderie. But why should his homosocial contacts be almost exclusively limited to male Jews? Why is he distinctly less interested in aristocrats? He has only three short conversations with his brother Felician;[40] he meets the other aristocrat, Demeter Stanzides, only sporadically and accidentally;[41] and although he feels comfortable in his Gentile club, he meets only twice with its members.[42] The answer may again be given in terms of either psychology (psychoanalysis) or narrative theory. Instead of guessing what psychological mechanisms may engender questionable philo-Semitic sentiments in Georg, a more plausible approach might be to look for its narrative function. Georg is useful as a lens for looking at women and Jews, that is, social groups of which he is not a member; he is considerably less useful and revealing in looking from inside at his own male aristocratic circles.

Does the lens adjust itself as it is directed toward different members of the Jewish male society? How different is Georg in his relations to Bermann, Nürnberger, and Golowski? The bond with Golowski is the strongest, suggesting occasionally even touches of homoeroticism. In any case, conversations with Golowski do not lead to the kind of irritated anti-Semitic thoughts that frequently characterize Georg's reactions to Bermann and Nürnberger. Indeed, he seems to have an admiration for Golowski's Zionism, not because the idea itself appeals to him but rather because it shows (together with Golowski's duel) that he is a decisive and active person who forges new ideals to replace the outdated ones: Golowski has the determination and commitment that Georg is lacking. The conversations with Bermann and Nürnberger differ, in part because they frequently focus on writing and creativity. The extension of Georg's adolescence is related to his ambition of becoming a composer. As Mann's *Tonio Kröger* and several other early-twentieth-century stories show, financial as well as social factors delayed and destabilized modernist artistic careers.

If Georg's dialogues with male Jews are dominated by the latter, he is dominating the conversations with Anna, and her reactions are, with few exceptions, subordinate and complementary. As in the case of the Jews, readers do not know her mind, for they see her (with the one noted exception) only in Georg's company, and in his presence they always see her through him. But since the relationship with her is emotional and intense rather than intellectual and loose, the inaccessibility of her mind and heart is more decisive, as the last two dramatic and heart-wrenching encounters between Georg and Anna show.[43] Their baby had died after birth; Georg received a position at the provincial opera of Detmold, and in the first of these final meetings he hesitatingly tries to cut himself loose. He still invites her to a performance of *Tristan und Isolde* and for a holiday to be spent on his way to Detmold,[44] but she rejects the former and seems uninterested in the latter. Georg is forced to fill the conversational vacuum with trivial items that he has already reported in his letters. When she suddenly and harshly remarks that his letters, for all their detail, said nothing, Georg understands her hidden meaning, even though she is as reticent about it as ever.[45] What follows is a litany of her unvoiced reproaches, which Georg, who was vaguely aware of them, now silently recites in his mind. He concludes with her rhetorical question about what it means that he always left her alone, even when she conceived and carried their child that was destined to grow up with strangers, if it had lived. Georg silently admits that the reproach is justified; but unable to say so aloud, he continues to speak trivialities and lies. Departing, he is moved by reading in her eyes "a tired but no longer painful disappointment," the meaning of which does not escape him: "Alle die Worte, die er zu ihr gesprochen, nichts, weniger als nichts hatten sie ihr zu bedeuten gehabt, da das einzige, das kaum mehr erwartete und immer wieder ersehnte doch nicht gekommen war."[46]

During his last visit, Georg is taken aback by Anna's cool and distanced reactions, but he continues to paper over his embarrassment with talk, until she ironically remarks, as if speaking to a child: "Nein, wie er sich an- strengt."[47] She thus lets him know that his chatter is a vain replacement for explanation and then falls silent, except for a few short remarks. The re- mainder of the scene is focused through Georg by means of the narratorial remarks "he knew," "he felt," "it appeared to him." He lucidly knows that she is waiting for the redeeming statement that she belongs to him and he wants to live with her in marriage. He is on the verge of uttering these words but refrains, and he concludes that he wants to be free.[48]

Schnitzler's manner of presenting their farewell thus climaxes a nar- ration that had minimized Anna's voice throughout. This muting could be seen as a patriarchal narratorial decision to silence a suffering and weak female — especially since there is an asymmetry with respect to the homosocial partners, who are at least given ample space to talk, even if their minds are not transparent. However, Schnitzler's indirect repre- sentation may instead be viewed as a form of narrative alienation, familiar to readers from a great many modernist narratives, as well as from the writings of the Russian formalists. Indirection does not necessarily di- minish the value of what is represented. Looking at the final scenes of the lovers in *Der Weg ins Freie,* one may remark, to begin with, that Anna's composure reveals an admirable strength, one that is precisely lacking in Georg. On the textual level, an emotional outburst on her part could easily slide into melodrama. By letting Georg recite her reproaches (read- ers may be reasonably certain that he is on this occasion a reliable narra- tor of her mind) Schnitzler tempers the melodramatic element. The real gain, however, is in what this method reveals of Georg. By inserting into the voiced dialogue a second, internal and unvoiced conversation in Georg's mind between Georg and Anna, Schnitzler created a double monologue. The strength of the scene lies in the discrepancy between

Georg's spoken and silent thoughts. It would be different if, out of simplicity or stupidity, he had no notion what Anna thinks and feels. At issue, however, is not his lack of understanding, but his cowardice and duplicity in speaking internally with insight and externally as if he did not know. The polyphony of the novel consists not of the multiplicity of voices in the world but of the heteroglossia in the voice and mind of its central male character.

Der Weg ins Freie, often maligned for its alleged formlessness, has both a formal and a thematic structure, and furthermore, these structures are interrelated. The indirect dialogues in Georg's heterosexual love affair, and the direct ("mimetic") dialogues in Georg's homosocial fellowship with Jewish intellectuals and writers, are facets of a broad portrayal of overaged adolescents at a historically and culturally unique moment.

To what extent these features are present in Schnitzler's other works should be explored further. Studies of his works tend to focus either on the formal-narrative innovations of *Leutnant Gustl* and his other shorter works, or on the social-sexual thematics of his fiction. Bringing together the formal and thematic concerns, or more specifically, showing how the narrative mode implies a certain vision of the themes, can be a rewarding approach. Such a linkage is by no means self-evident: some believe that each narrative mode has an inherent ideology, while others are highly skeptical about the connection between formal and thematic concerns. That the focalizer of *Der Weg ins Freie* is largely but not exclusively Georg has distinctive implications for the social panorama of this novel that will not allow easy generalizations about inherent ideology in form. The same narrative mode may acquire a different meaning and function in Schnitzler's others works, and in the fiction of other writers. The methodology will be useful if its application to Schnitzler's other works yields divergent conclusions.

Notes

1. *Der Weg ins Freie* in ES I, 635–958.
2. *Der Weg ins Freie,* 635.
3. *Der Weg ins Freie,* 679, 830, 872, 876.
4. *Der Weg ins Freie,* 826.
5. *Der Weg ins Freie,* 826.
6. *Der Weg ins Freie,* 826.
7. *Der Weg ins Freie,* 708, 830.
8. *Der Weg ins Freie,* 847.

[9] *Der Weg ins Freie*, 679, 709.

[10] *Der Weg ins Freie*, 831.

[11] *Der Weg ins Freie*, 831.

[12] *Der Weg ins Freie*, 660, "im Parlament nur wie zu Gaste sitzt . . ."

[13] *Der Weg ins Freie*, 775–76.

[14] *Der Weg ins Freie*, 644.

[15] *Der Weg ins Freie*, 642.

[16] *Der Weg ins Freie*, 741.

[17] *Der Weg ins Freie*, 725.

[18] *Der Weg ins Freie*, 935.

[19] *Der Weg ins Freie*, 643.

[20] *Der Weg ins Freie*, 643.

[21] *Der Weg ins Freie*, 648.

[22] *Der Weg ins Freie*, 766–67.

[23] Rolf-Peter Janz and Klaus Laermann, *Arthur Schnitzler: Zur Diagnose des Wiener Bürgertums im Fin de siècle* (Stuttgart: Metzler, 1977); Georg Lukács, "'Der Weg ins Freie.' (Arthur Schnitzler regénye)," *Nyugat* 1 (1908): 222–24. Rpt. Lukács, *Ifjúkori művek (1902–1918)* (Budapest: Magvetö, 1977), 174–78.

[24] Janz and Laermann, 175.

[25] Lukács, 178.

[26] Quoted in Andrea Willi, *Der Weg ins Freie. Eine Untersuchung zur Tageskritik und ihren Zeitgenössischen Bezügen* (Heidelberg: Winter, 1989), 271.

[27] Ruth Klüger, "Die Ödnis des entlarvten Landes — Antisemitismus im Werk jüdisch-österreichischer Autoren," in *Katastrophen. Über deutsche Literatur* (Göttingen: Wallerstein, 1994), 65–70.

[28] Quoted in Willi, 278, 297.

[29] Willi, 284–85.

[30] Willi, 73–274.

[31] Shlomith Rimmon-Kennan, *Narrative Fiction: Contemporary Poetics* (London: Methuen, 1983), 71–85.

[32] *Leutnant Gustl* in ES I, 337–66.

[33] *Der Weg ins Freie*, 684–87.

[34] *Der Weg ins Freie*, 903–9.

[35] *Der Weg ins Freie*, 711.

[36] I am deeply grateful to Dorrit Cohn for calling my attention to further inconsistencies in Schnitzler's focalization. There are additional instances in which Georg is not the central viewpoint or where readers get brief insights into another character's mind: (1) during his first portrayed visit to the Rosners he accompanies Anna on the piano while the narrator follows the conversation in the Rosner family and the appearance of Berthold Stauber, and in the subsequent conversation readers get a glimpse of Berthold Stauber's feelings and thoughts about Anna; (2) at the Ehrenberg party, after Else's

conversation with her mother, Georg is present, but the party scenes are not always viewed through him; (3) during the bicycle tour there are moments when Heinrich's feelings are directly portrayed; and (4) in a conversation between Heinrich and Georg in chapter 6 readers catch Heinrich's irritated thoughts.

[37] Heidi Gidion, "Haupt-und Nebensache in Arthur Schnitzlers Roman '*Der Weg ins Freie*,'" *Text + Kritik* 138/139 (April 1998): 47–60.

[38] *Der Weg ins Freie*, 782.

[39] Quoted in Willi, 277.

[40] *Der Weg ins Freie*, 681–84, 777–82, 897–98.

[41] *Der Weg ins Freie*, 801, 812f, 926.

[42] *Der Weg ins Freie*, 710–11, 922–26.

[43] *Der Weg ins Freie*, 914–17, 946–52.

[44] *Der Weg ins Freie*, 915.

[45] *Der Weg ins Freie*, 917.

[46] *Der Weg ins Freie*, 917.

[47] *Der Weg ins Freie*, 948.

[48] *Der Weg ins Freie*, 950.

"Thou Shalt Not Make Unto Thee Any Graven Image": Crises of Masculinity in Schnitzler's *Die Fremde*

Imke Meyer

I N THE SPRING of 1902, Arthur Schnitzler completed an eight-page story now known under the title *Die Fremde* (1902).[1] While this story, during the one hundred years that have passed since its first publication, has received comparatively little critical attention, the concerns about issues of gender and class raised in *Die Fremde* are in fact of a piece with those addressed in Schnitzler's better-known narratives, such as *Fräulein Else* (1924) or *Traumnovelle* (1926). Like Schnitzler's firmly canonized narratives, *Die Fremde* uses a complex web of narrative discourses and allusions and an intricate interplay of form and content to articulate a critique of bourgeois morality and gender stereotypes. Thus, *Die Fremde* can be understood as representative of the concerns addressed in Schnitzler's narrative fiction in general. In particular, *Die Fremde* focuses critically on crises of masculinity at the turn of the last century.

I.

Originally, while working on the story, Schnitzler had referred to it as "Theoderich."[2] This working title directs attention not to either of the human protagonists, Albert and Katharina, but rather to a statue of Theodoric the Great at which both Katharina and Albert gaze in Innsbruck's *Hofkirche*. The statue, which literally is a "graven image" (Exodus 20:4), sets in motion the dynamics that dominate the last part of Schnitzler's narrative. Gazing and processes of image-making figure prominently in the text.

The story line of *Die Fremde* unfolds as follows: Alfred has recently married Katharina, a woman whom he views as a rather mysterious human being. On the fourteenth day of their honeymoon, Katharina abandons Albert, leaving behind only a brief note of farewell. The events that led up to this point are recapitulated from Albert's perspective, until the chronology of the flashback narrative reaches the fictional present. Albert then leaves the hotel in order to commit suicide, but on his way to a suitable location for this act he sees Katharina on the street and follows her into the Innsbruck *Hofkirche,* where she gazes at Theodoric's statue for a prolonged period of time. Albert observes Katharina in secret, later orders a copy of the statue to be placed in the garden of a house he purchased for her in Vienna, and then walks to a secluded area, where he shoots himself. The last paragraph is related by an omniscient narrator: Katharina arrives at her house in Vienna, gazes at the statue that has, in the meantime, been placed in the garden, and then writes a letter to an Italian man "von dem sie ein Kind unter dem Herzen trug";[3] Katharina never receives an answer to her letter.

When Schnitzler's narrative was first published in May of 1902 in the *Neue Freie Presse,* it was titled *Dämmerseele.* Schnitzler changed the title to *Die Fremde* in 1907, when he included the story in a collection titled *Dämmerseelen* (1907).[4] Besides *Die Fremde,* the collection included *Das Schicksal des Freiherrn von Leisenbohg* (1904); *Die Weissagung* (1905); *Das neue Lied* (1905); and *Andreas Thameyers letzter Brief* (1902).[5] The story title of *Dämmerseele* would, at first sight, seem to refer to the female protagonist, Katharina, a figure who is described as dreamy and withdrawn. But a different light is shed on this title when one considers that Schnitzler chose its plural form, *Dämmerseelen,* as the title for a collection in which the focal points are male characters and crises of masculinity. *Das Schicksal des Freiherrn von Leisenbohg* treats a man's continually frustrated desire for an opera singer and his eventual death. *Die Weissagung* focuses on a male protagonist's thwarted need for control. *Das neue Lied* centers on the consequences of a male protagonist's emotional dishonesty. Finally, *Andreas Thameyers letzter Brief* is the fictional letter written by a white man whose white wife has given birth to a black baby, a fact the letter writer endeavors to explain with the help of the concept of "das Versehen der Frauen."[6] The latter concept implies that when pregnant women look intensely at someone or are shocked by a particular vision, their offspring — because women are supposedly so impressionable that they can easily be penetrated not only by direct physical means but also by sights — will bear the features of this vision.[7] Schnitzler's story makes clear that this pseudo-scientific concept serves to combat men's fears and anxieties surrounding fatherhood and the preservation of the blood line: Thameyer uses the concept of "das Versehen der Frauen" to convince himself that his wife did not have intercourse with a black man, but that she was instead shocked by the sight of a black man she saw while taking a walk.

Given the context provided by the other narratives in the *Dämmerseelen* collection, it would indeed be curious if *Die Fremde* treated something other than a crisis of masculinity. The earlier title, *Dämmer-*

seele, can therefore be read as referring to the male protagonist, Albert, and need not be understood simply as a reference to Katharina. Albert is indeed a character who leads his life in a realm that is suspended between the real and the imaginary — in other words, he can be understood as a "Dämmerseele." The eventual title *Die Fremde* describes not Katharina's actual nature, but the nature of Albert's projections onto Katharina. This hypothesis can also be supported by the fact that the dominant narrative perspective is not an omniscient one, but rather third-person, Albert's viewpoint.

The crisis of masculinity, then, that is played out in *Die Fremde* is a crisis of the male gaze, which has lost its power to penetrate. Albert is unable to gain access to, or an understanding of, his object of desire, Katharina; she cannot be possessed. The less accessible she is, the more obsessed with her Albert becomes. For Albert, this obsession entails a progressive loss of power not just over his object of desire, but also over himself. He tries to counter this loss of power with various attempts to contain Katharina in images. However, since these are not images of Katharina's actual being — a being Albert has failed to penetrate — but rather images of his own making, that is, projections, Albert ends up not containing Katharina, but rather himself: he falls victim to his own projections. By fashioning Katharina as the quintessential Other who becomes ever more "foreign" to him, Albert cuts off all access routes to his object of desire, at the same time that Katharina's status as Other only heightens Albert's longing for her. Thus confronted with the prospect of a complete loss of control, Albert attempts, in an effort to save face, to reinterpret the history of his relationship with Katharina as a story not of his own design, but rather of fate.

A close reading of *Die Fremde,* then, shows that this story, much like its companion pieces in the *Dämmerseelen* collection, presents the reader with a diagnosis and critical analysis of *fin-de-siècle* crises of masculinity and male identity.[8]

II.

To date, only scant critical attention has been paid to *Die Fremde*. In his 1968 discussion of the story, Gottfried Just claimed that Albert turns into an "Opfer dessen, was ihn als faszinierendes Dämmerleben anmutet."[9] Just also writes:

> Da der Erzähler sich auf die Perspektive Alberts beschränkt, erscheint dessen Auslegung der Dinge auch in ironischer Objektivation im Erzählbild, doch dadurch, daß sie nicht als sein Reflex deutlich und sichtbar gemacht werden, mit einem über seine Gestalt scheinbar hinausweisenden Anspruch.[10]

Arguably, the fact that the bulk of the narrated events is presented not by an omniscient narrator, but rather from a third-person figural narrative perspective aligned with Albert's character, is "deutlich and sichtbar" for the reader. The usage of free indirect discourse in the opening paragraphs of Schnitzler's story and tags such as "er dachte" and "er erinnerte sich" eliminate any doubt regarding the narrative perspective. Only if the reader fails to identify these obvious clues will she read *Die Fremde* as a tale of the victimization of a male protagonist at the hands of a woman. Identifying the narrative perspective correctly will lead to a different conclusion, namely, that Albert ultimately falls victim to his own projections and attempts to turn into an Other his female object of desire. Just further notes, with regard to the ending of the story:

> Die Kontinuität des Textes, in ihrer als solche nicht klar gemachten Beschränkung auf die Sicht des Helden schon doppeldeutig, setzt sich, da der Wechsel der Erzählerperspektive ohne Erklärung bleibt, in einen verknappenden Schlußsatz fort, dessen verdeutlichende Verbindungsglieder fehlen und der in seiner Gedrängtheit einen formalen Gegensatz bildet zu der episch referierenden Weise des bisherigen Berichts.[11]

Just reads the change in narrative perspective at the end of the text — the events described in the last paragraph are related by an omniscient narrator — not as a break in the text, but rather as a continuity. He arrives at this interpretation by constructing a parallel between what he sees as a deliberately obscured usage of a figural narrative perspective throughout the text and an equally obscure, that is, unexplained switch to an omniscient perspective in the last paragraph. Just argues that the text ultimately betrays its readers because it fails to fulfill its promise of an "Aufklärung" (119) of the depicted events, and he claims that Schnitzler "erleidet die schriftstellerische Ironie des Scheiterns," because "der Erzähler [überfordert] seine Möglichkeiten."[12]

It may be argued, in contrast to Just, that the switch to an omniscient narrative perspective in the last paragraph of the story finds its logical explanation in Albert's death. Once Albert commits suicide at the end of the second-to-last paragraph, his consciousness is extinguished, and the narrator has to abandon Albert's perspective. The content of the story remains obscure only to the extent that Albert hides from himself the true motives for his own actions. The figural narrative perspective that dominates the text leaves a vacuum of critical analysis: an interpretation or evaluation of the depicted events by the reliable voice of an omniscient narrator is, for the most part, not suggested to the reader. The story thus calls upon the reader to fill this critical vacuum. This call to critical analysis is enhanced by the fact that the last paragraph of the story presents a perspective different from Albert's: the reader is once again made aware that Albert's worldview is an utterly subjective one.

In 1972, Elisabeth Lebensaft analyzed the structure of *Die Fremde* and concluded that Albert's perspective is the one that dominates the narrative.[13] Lebensaft also identifies Albert's death as the reason for the shift in narrative perspective in the last paragraph of Schnitzler's story. Lebensaft states that, given the fact that Alfred's viewpoint is the one with which the reader is mainly confronted in the story, "eine letzte Unsicherheit und Unbeantwortbarkeit bleibt" with regard to Katharina's character and that "ihre Gestalt [ist] nie eindeutig zu analysieren."[14] The point of presenting Katharina mainly from Albert's perspective, I argue, is precisely to give the reader insight into the ways in which Albert constructs an image of Katharina — ways that cannot but obscure Katharina's character. Schnitzler's narrative does not aim to depict Katharina's character; rather, the goal is to analyze the origins and developments of a crisis of masculinity produced by none other than Albert himself.

In 1978, Barbara Gutt wrote that Katharina has "ein gebrochene[s] Verhältnis . . . zur Realität" and accused Katharina of a "schuldhaftes Versagen im Sozialen" which "ihren Gatten in den Selbstmord treibt."[15] However, Albert's evaluation of Katharina — an evaluation to which Gutt implicitly seems to subscribe — needs to be seen in a different context. In fact, Albert's reflections on Katharina tend to make it difficult for the reader to gain reliable insight into her character, but a close reading of Albert's thoughts about Katharina can reveal some of the mechanisms Albert employs in fashioning an image of his object of desire. The image Albert eventually creates is that of an exotic other. Analysis of Albert's reflections allows one to trace the outlines of the crisis of masculinity in which Albert is engulfed.

III.

Throughout Schnitzler's narrative, Katharina's voice is not heard. The only utterance of Katharina's that is not filtered through Albert's thoughts is placed prominently at the end of the first paragraph of the text. During the honeymoon, Albert awakes early in the morning to find the bed next to him empty. On Katharina's night stand, he discovers a note that reads: "Mein lieber Freund, ich bin früher aufgewacht als du. Adieu. Ich gehe fort. Ob ich zurückkommen werde, weiß ich nicht. Leb wohl. Katharina."[16]

Katharina clearly claims responsibility for the content of the note by signing it. In the preceding lines of the paragraph, a third-person figural narrative perspective with Albert as the reflector figure is established. In these lines, it seems as though Albert implicitly wants to contest Katharina's ownership of her written utterance: the text does not refer to the note as, say, a letter from Katharina, but rather calls it "ein beschriebener Zettel."[17] The words on the "Zettel" are not identified as Katharina's, but rather simply as "folgende Worte."[18] It is as though Albert had to counteract Katharina's emphatic claim to the ownership of her words by attempting to erase authorship as much as possible: the "Zettel" is simply "beschrieben," and reference to an origin of the writing is not made outside the note itself. Katharina's voice is not heard at all in the remainder of the text. Rather, Albert makes an attempt to assert complete control over the shaping of her image — an attempt that actually leads to a progressive loss of control on Albert's part.

Albert designates Katharina's note as the endpoint of his own history. He claims to have known that Katharina would leave him sooner or later and that when it occurred his life would lose all meaning. Hence, he intends to commit suicide. However, prior to this act, he recounts to himself the story of his relationship with Katharina. In the fashion of an amateur Hegelian, he endows the history of his life with meaning by surveying this history from its end. Albert wants to view his life as a chain of events that unfolded in accordance with the laws of an inner necessity. Just as the endpoint of his personal history is arbitrarily chosen, the meaning Albert claims his life to have when viewed from this arbitrary vantage point is an entirely constructed one.

Albert tries to banish any thought of arbitrariness from his life by referring repeatedly to fate. Intending to stand by his decision to commit suicide, he begins his musings about his relationship with Katharina:

> [Albert] war sehr weh ums Herz. Er dachte, wie doch alle *Voraussicht* und selbst ein *vorgefaßter Entschluß* ein *schweres Geschick* nicht leichter, sondern nur mit besserer Haltung tragen ließen. Er zögerte eine Weile. Aber was sollte er jetzt noch abwarten? War es nicht das beste, gleich ein *Ende* zu *machen*? War nicht schon die Neugier, die ihn quälte, ein *Verrat* an seinen *Vorsätzen*? *Sein Los mußte sich erfüllen. Entschieden war es doch schon gewesen,* als er vor zwei Jahren beim Tanze das erstemal den kühlen Hauch der geheimnisvollen Lippen seine Wange streifen fühlte.[19]

Albert's use of the term "Voraussicht" implies that personal history is a continuum that stretches into the future and is clearly surveyable for all who care to see it. However, the fact that such a view of history is nothing but a construction, as well as the fact that Albert is implicitly aware that it is nothing but a construction, is made apparent by Albert's use of the words "vorgefaßter Entschluß." If "Entschlüsse" can be "vorgefaßt," that is, made prior to and regardless of any actual events that might follow and might sensibly demand altering a "vorgefaßter Entschluß," history cannot be a force that moves forward regardless of human actions, tantamount to a preordained fate. That Albert indeed helps create his history, rather than being subject to its impersonal workings, is made clear when he wonders whether it would not be best "gleich ein Ende zu *machen*": the "making" of an end is a purposeful production of history, not a helpless subjugation to its supposedly unalterable course. But Albert needs to deny his personal responsibility for his life — rather attributing responsibility to a "schweres Geschick" and to "[s]ein Los" — in order to endow his existence with a meaning beyond the realm of his personal decisions. Thus, Albert is able to conceal from himself the solipsism and self-referentiality of his life, viewing himself instead as part of fate's grand plan for humankind. Already Albert appears to be the "Dämmerseele"; Katharina is "früher aufgewacht als [Albert]," whereas Albert continues to live in a self-constructed dream world ruled by fabricated notions of fate and destiny.

Albert begins his reminiscences by asserting that "es" — that is, his supposed fate — was "doch schon" "entschieden" when he danced with Katharina for the first time. The use of the word "doch" betrays some possible doubt about whether things really were already "entschieden" at this point, as "doch" is a particle used to counter a negative assertion, such as "es war nicht entschieden." There is further evidence that Albert may not believe so much in fate as in the possibility of its construction for the purpose of creating meaning. As Albert recalls, after meeting Katharina for the first time at the "Weiße [. . .] Kreuz-Ball," his friend Vincenz presents him with an account of several episodes in Katharina's life. Vincenz's narrative is then recounted by Albert and related to the reader by the narrator of the text. Katharina's image, in other words, is not presented directly, but rather is refracted through the lenses of several other observers.

Vincenz tells Albert that Katharina's family has suffered financial losses because her father, a military officer, was killed by an insurgent in Bosnia, and because her brother gambled away a good part of the family's fortune and later committed suicide. Katharina's fiancée, Baron Maassburg, soon withdrew his engagement — not simply because of the family's "nunmehr erklärt ärmliche . . . Verhältnisse . . ."[20] but, rumor has it, also because Katharina cried at her brother's funeral in the arms of a man with whom she was not previously acquainted. According to Vincenz, Katharina was then gripped by a "heftige [. . .] Schwärmerei"[21] for a famous organ player by the name of Banetti, whom she had never met. At some point, Katharina supposedly dreamt of Banetti's death. Soon thereafter, Banetti committed suicide by jumping from a church tower. After this incident, "Anzeichen einer Gemütskrankheit" are said to have manifested themselves in the young woman. Katharina's mother prevented her daughter from being checked into an "Anstalt,"[22] and by the time Albert meets Katharina, she is "aus ihrem Trübsinn [erwacht]"[23] and is socializing again. Albert now recalls that when he met Katharina, "war sie [Albert] von einer solchen Ruhe des Gemütes erschienen, daß er den *Erzählungen* seines Freundes auf dem Heimweg nur zweifelnd zu folgen vermochte."[24]

Vincenz's tales are just that: "Erzählungen," not reports of confirmed facts. Rather, Vincenz presents Albert with a collection of rumors about Katharina. But Albert ultimately chooses to let these rumors redefine his first image of Katharina as a person characterized by a "Ruhe des Gemütes." Vincenz's tales retrospectively are adorned with a "zarte Ton früher Warnung"[25] and cancel out Albert's original impression. Albert locates the moment in which his "Geschick" was "entschieden" in his first encounter with Katharina, which took place prior to his exposure to Vincenz's "Erzählungen." Now, instead of appearing in Albert's recollection as a person of exceptional "Ruhe des Gemütes," Katharina does not appear as a complete person at all; rather, fragmented body parts are the focus of Albert's memory: Katharina is retroactively objectified as an exotic Other with "geheimnisvolle [. . .] Lippen."[26]

However, other moments in which Albert's "Geschick" is supposedly "entschieden" continue to appear in the text. It seems as though Albert needs to convince himself that his fate is not only one that was decided from the beginning but also one that continues to be decided, always toward the same outcome. For instance, when rumor has it that Katharina is engaged to a certain Graf Rummingshaus, Albert reacts by thinking that he "wußte . . ., daß der Tag, an dem Katharina einem andern die Hand zur Ehe reichte, der letzte seines Lebens sein würde."[27] In this passage, it seems as though Albert thinks that his "Geschick" is not already "entschieden," but rather will be decided if Katharina marries somebody other than Albert. Later, after Katharina accepts Albert's marriage proposal, the text reads:

> Und wie [Albert] so durch den Sonntag spazierte, von Straße zu Straße, durch Gärten und Alleen, den Frühjahrshimmel über sich, an manchen fröhlichen und unbekümmerten Menschen vorbei, *da* fühlte er, daß er *von nun an* nicht mehr zu diesen gehörte, und daß über ihm *ein Geschick* anderer und besonderer Art *zu walten begann.*[28]

It now seems that Albert views his fate as sealed not from the first moment in which he met Katharina, but rather once she accepts his proposal. Albert thus ironically considers his "Geschick" as "entschieden" regardless of whether Katharina accepts his hand in marriage or not; Katharina's marrying somebody else would, Albert claims, have spelled the end of his life, but Katharina marrying Albert likewise seals his supposedly preordained fate.

It seems that Albert is primarily interested in not being an average "fröhlich [. . .] und unbekümmert" person, but rather someone "ander[s]" and "besonder[s]." Yet he epitomizes the virtues of the bourgeoisie. He works as a civil servant and

> hatte sein anständiges Auskommen und konnte als Junggeselle ein recht behagliches Leben führen, aber Reichtum hatte er von keiner Seite zu erwarten. Eine sichere, aber gewiß nicht bedeutende Laufbahn stand ihm bevor. Er kleidete sich mit großer Sorgfalt, ohne jemals wirklich elegant auszusehen, er redete nicht ohne Gewandtheit, hatte aber niemals irgend etwas Besonderes zu sagen, und er war stets gerne gesehen, ohne jemals aufzufallen.[29]

Albert wants to depart from the average path on which he has walked prior to meeting Katharina. However, he feels himself to be so average that he is apparently unable to change anything about his own persona that would effect a departure from this stifling regime. He needs to locate the non-average outside of himself. Thus, he proceeds to project onto Katharina all that is exotic and "fremd." That way, he can, he hopes, possess that which is "anders" and "besonders" without having to take responsibility for violating or deviating from any bourgeois norms. Rather, he can lay the responsibility for the course he hopes his life will take at the feet of a "Geschick" that "zu walten begann" after Katharina accepts his marriage proposal.

Thus, Albert needs to preserve Katharina's status as "*Die Fremde*," as an Other utterly foreign to the world of bourgeois order. This goal is best achieved if true communication with her does not take place. Here lies the crux of Albert's problem: if Katharina's status as Other is to be preserved, he cannot be interested in truly knowing her — rather, she needs to function as a projection screen for Albert's desires. On the other hand, by using Katharina in this fashion, Albert prevents himself from gaining any significant access to her — thus, he can never really possess his object of desire. Albert's self-made "Geschick" — a crisis of meaning and of identification with bourgeois virtues — relies on the construction of woman as Other and cannot but ultimately result in the frustration of male desire.

In his attempt to construct Katharina as a desirable Other, Albert has to obscure the true power relations between himself and Katharina. Instead of acknowledging that, as a man, he has the opportunity to earn a living for himself and, in contrast to a woman, does not have to rely on a financially stable suitor to secure his economic survival, the text states that "[v]on seiner Nichtigkeit Katherinen gegenüber war [Albert] völlig durchdrungen."[30] In his narrative of their relationship, Albert thus reverses the actual power relations: Katharina is painted as a queen-like creature — with, for instance, her "einzige, ja königliche Weise, das Haupt zu neigen, wenn sie jemandem zuhörte"[31] — of whom Albert is not necessarily worthy. In reality, Katharina, because of the financial situation of her family, is utterly dependent on the attention and mercy of a male suitor such as Albert. By painting an image of Katharina as an exotic and "geheimnisvoll" Other, Albert ascribes seductive powers to her. However, in order to preserve Katharina's status as "königlich," as well as his own saint-like self image, Albert cannot openly hold the "Fremde" responsible for his fate; rather, he needs to leave Katharina on the pedestal he constructed for her and to attribute the supposed necessity of his suicide to an impersonal "Geschick." Thus, Albert continues to construct a communicative hierarchy between himself and Katharina:

> Und so fühlte er, daß ein Wesen, geheimnisvoll und gleichsam aus einer andern Welt wie Katharina, sich tief zu ihm herablassen müßte, wenn er sie *gewinnen* wollte, und daß sie jedenfalls von ihm verlangen durfte, ein *unverdientes* Glück *teuer zu bezahlen*. Da er sich aber zu jedem Opfer bereit wußte, schien er sich auch allmählich ihrer würdig zu werden.[32]

In this passage, Albert tries to hide the true power dynamic behind a façade of emotional heroism: Albert will become worthy of the "[geheimnisvolles] Wesen" because he is "zu jedem Opfer bereit." The language repeatedly hints at the economic realities underlying Albert's fictitious narrative: Albert can "gewinnen" Katharina if he is ready to pay a high price for the exotic commodity — he has "teuer zu bezahlen" for what he chooses to interpret as "ein unverdientes Glück," but what turns out literally to be an "unearned fortune." After his engagement to Katharina, Albert starts to live far beyond his means, buying extravagant presents for her and purchasing the house in Vienna. When Albert asks for Katharina's hand in marriage, she is

> nicht so erstaunt über [Alberts] Besuch, als er eigentlich erwartete. Sie hörte ihm freundlich zu und nahm seinen Antrag an, kaum in größerer Bewegung, als wenn er die Einladung zu einem Ball überbracht hätte.[33]

Since Albert has not made any real efforts to get to know Katharina, he is quick to chalk up her reaction to his proposal to her supposedly cool and withdrawn personality. He does not pause to wonder whether Katharina's lack of surprise could indicate that the feelings Albert has for her are, in fact, requited. Most likely, however, Katharina was aware of Albert's feelings and accepts his proposal regardless of her own feelings for him, simply because economic necessity forces her to do so. Albert himself does not come up with this interpretation, though, since such a reading of Katharina's behavior would endanger his narrative of her as a "Wesen" "gleichsam aus einer andern Welt" — a creature entirely unconcerned with mundane bourgeois issues such as financial security.

Albert nevertheless seems to sense that financial issues are indeed of import to Katharina. By showering her with presents, Albert can create the impression that he is actually rather wealthy and that it would therefore make little sense for her to abandon him in favor of other potential suitors. In this manner, Albert can cement his powerful position vis-à-vis Katharina, but in his narrative he is able to pass off his behavior as the selfless and generous gift-giving of a man hopelessly in love.

> Gewiß hielt [Katharina Albert] für reicher, als er war. Im Anfang hatte er natürlich daran gedacht, auch über seine Vermögensverhältnisse mit ihr zu reden. Er schob es von Tag zu Tag hinaus, da ihm die Worte versagten; aber endlich kam es dahin, daß er jede Aussprache über dergleichen Dinge für überflüssig hielt. Denn wenn sie über ihre Zukunft redete, so tat sie das nicht wie jemand, dem ein vorgezeichneter Weg ins Weite weist; vielmehr schienen ihr alle Möglichkeiten nach wie vor offen zu stehen, und nichts in ihrem Verhalten deutete auf innere oder äußere Gebundenheit.[34]

Albert's reasoning appears flawed and seems designed to conceal a different insight. If Katharina displays a lack of "Gebundenheit," Albert feels he needs to counter this assumed lack of commitment by leaving undisturbed the impression Katharina has formed of Albert's financial situation — as long as she believes him to be rich, he can exercise power over her. These economic issues and power relations are once again hidden behind the veil of a man's devotion to an ethereal Other who cannot be bothered with conversations about economic realities. If Albert were to enlighten Katharina about the state of his accounts, the real and tangible basis for his relationship to her — economic necessities, rather than the necessities dictated by an assumed fate — would be revealed and would render it impossible for Albert to uphold his narrative of fate and love. Worse yet, if Albert were to disclose his finances to Katharina, the relationship itself might collapse.

Yet, at no point does Albert seem willing to transform his relationship to Katharina from a largely imaginary one, in which the terms are implicitly dictated by him, into a real one. Albert refuses to discuss the realities of his life with Katharina, yet complains that she does not act like someone "dem ein vorgezeichneter Weg ins Weite weist." Without any knowledge of the parameters that would define their life together, Katharina can hardly be expected to have much of an inkling of what her future with Albert might look like. However, since sharing such knowledge might not only entail a loss of power for Albert but would also drag Katharina down to the level of that which is neither "anders" nor "besonders," thus endangering her status as exotic Other, Albert chooses to keep all information about his finances to himself.

On the other hand, since Albert believes that "alle Möglichkeiten" seem "nach wie vor offen" to Katharina, he can shape these possibilities for her. He can define her image in such a way that he is able to insert her without difficulty into the narrative of his own personal history. In this manner, Albert is able to interpret Katharina as the catalyst for the creation of meaning in his life. He therefore has another reason to keep from Katharina any details about his financial situation; if this information were available to Katharina, she might stop acting in a way that Albert can interpret as he wishes in order to maintain his narrative. In keeping the truth about his finances hidden, Albert is not selfless but rather selfish in his desire to cement his power over Katharina. Of course, Albert needs to conceal from himself the true motives for his actions in order to be able to uphold a martyred image of himself.

Albert's actual financial situation and his tendency to use money to exercise power over Katharina complicate Gutt's interpretation of Albert's suicide as a consequence of a "schuldhaftes Versagen im Sozialen" on the part of Katharina "das ihren Gatten in den Selbstmord treibt."[35] Rather, Albert's decision to commit suicide may be a consequence of the dire financial straits in which he finds himself at the point of Katharina's departure from the hotel. Toward the beginning of his reminiscences about Katharina, Albert had remembered her brother, who had taken his own life when he became unable to pay his gambling debts. By recalling not just this suicide but also its motives, Albert establishes a connection not simply to his own planned suicide but also to its underlying motives.

When Albert's reminiscences reach the point of the narrative present again, his musings about his current situation betray the real reasons for his intended suicide:

[Albert] wußte nichts und brauchte nicht mehr zu wissen, als daß [Katharina] ihm nicht mehr gehörte. Vielleicht war es sogar gut, daß *das Unvermeidliche* so früh gekommen war. *Sein Vermögen war durch den Kauf des Hauses auf das Geringste zusammengeschmolzen, und von seinem kleinen Gehalt konnten sie beide nicht leben.* Mit [Katharina] von Einschränkungen und von den *gewöhnlichen* Sorgen des Alltags zu reden, wäre ihm *in jedem Fall unmöglich* gewesen. Einen Moment fuhr es ihm durch den Sinn, von ihr Abschied zu nehmen. Sein Blick fiel auf die Bettdecke, wo der beschriebene Zettel lag. Der flüchtige Einfall kam ihm, *auf die weiße Seite ein kurzes Wort der Erklärung hinzuschreiben.* Aber in der *deutlichen Empfindung,* daß ein solches Wort *für Katharina* nicht das geringste Interesse haben könnte, stand er wieder davon ab.[36]

When Albert thinks of "das Unvermeidliche," he means to depict his having to commit suicide as a consequence of Katharina's departure. However, as becomes evident from the thoughts that immediately follow, Albert's suicide appears necessitated more by his financial situation than by anything else: he has spent most of his money and does not feel able to support a family with his civil servant's salary. Rather than forcing him to face this difficult situation, the unwritten bourgeois moral code allows Albert an out: he can kill himself, just like Katharina's brother.

Even if Albert were to admit to himself the real motives for his suicide, he would be able to portray it as an act designed to spare Katharina shame. However, since economics were crucial to Albert's efforts to secure Katharina, he needs to continue to gloss over his actual motivations in planning to take his life; only in this manner is he able to uphold his narrative of love and devotion. He needs to prevent the intrusion of mundane necessities into his story, so that he may instead be able to read his relationship with Katharina as a story written by fate, a story for whose outcome he bears no personal responsibility.

Similarly, Albert cannot speak to Katharina about "gewöhnliche [. . .] Sorgen" as doing so would overturn his view of his relationship with her. But, based on what he terms a "deutliche Empfindung" — a rather oxymoronic expression — Albert shifts onto Katharina the responsibility for his not leaving an explanation. Not coincidentally, Katharina's name appears in combination with the preposition "für": hidden behind the use of this preposition is Albert's desire to see himself as a man who does something "for" the supposedly cool and cruel woman. But the preposition "für" also puts Katharina's name in the accusative case: Albert implicitly accuses her of driving him to commit suicide, when in fact the situation in which he finds himself is entirely of his own making. However, rather than taking responsibility for his actions, Albert overtly holds fate responsible for his actions and covertly resents Katharina as an agent of this supposed fate.

The passage also illustrates that the character in Schnitzler's narrative who exhibits a desire for remaining "unreadable" is not Katharina but Albert. Katharina leaves a written note that can be read and interpreted by Albert. In contrast, Albert decides to leave blank the "weiße Seite" of the piece of paper on which Katharina has written her note. While Albert is interested in only allowing a reading of Katharina he has authorized, he does not want to open up the possibility of a reading of his own person that cannot be controlled by himself. If he were to leave a note, he would have no power over its interpretation by others. Rather than relinquish control over his narrative, he will take his life without "ein kurzes Wort der Erklärung."[37]

During Albert's reminiscences, it becomes clear that Katharina not only literally woke up earlier than Albert, as she states in her note, but possibly also metaphorically. By leaving him, she implicitly refuses to continue playing the role Albert has assigned her in his narrative. Katharina wakes up and takes cognizance of her situation, while Albert continues his existence as a "Dämmerseele" by hiding from himself the true motives of his actions.

Having reached the end of his reminiscences, Albert decides not to postpone his suicide any further. He intends "irgendwo hinaus vor die Stadt zu wandern, um dort *mit Anstand,* und ohne jemanden zu stören, seine Tat zu verüben."[38] Once again, this passage shows that Albert has thoroughly internalized bourgeois norms: even an extreme act such as suicide is not one during which bourgeois decorum can be abandoned; rather, "Anstand" is of paramount importance. Albert is so thoroughly a creature of his societal surroundings that a repressed desire for the non-bourgeois can only manifest itself in his projections onto somebody other than himself, namely Katharina. By possessing that which is "fremd," in marriage, Albert can reintegrate the non-bourgeois into his life in a socially sanctioned manner. Of course, Albert never truly possessed Katharina, but rather only the image he had constructed of her. This image, as well as his self-image — the bourgeois man who turns himself into someone who is not "gewöhnlich" through his heroic and selfless behavior in a relationship with a "Fremde" — must not be endangered by his suicide. Rather, it must be cemented by means of weaving the suicide seamlessly into a narrative of fate: the bourgeois proves his inner greatness and nobility of spirit one last time by showing "Anstand" even under the most extreme of circumstances. Never mind that, in reality, the suicide only proves that Albert is nothing but a quite "gewöhnlich" specimen of the bourgeois male.

Shortly after leaving the hotel, Albert catches sight of Katharina in the streets of Innsbruck:

> Die erste Regung Alberts war, in eine andere Straße abzubiegen; aber *eine Macht, die heftiger war als alle seine Vorsätze und Überlegungen,* drängte ihn, ihr zu folgen, um sich nun doch die Gewißheit zu verschaffen, der er vor einer Minute noch mit Gleichgültigkeit gegenüberzustehen geglaubt hatte. *Er bekam sogar einige Angst, daß [Katharina] sich umwenden und ihn entdecken könnte.*[39]

It becomes clear that Albert cannot be as sure of his "deutliche Empfindungen" and the judgments and decisions he derives from them as he would like to be. Once again, he does not simply take responsibility for changing his mind but rather attributes the cause for his departure from his planned course of action to an impersonal power. This "Macht" is not characterized as curiosity or desire; it is simply "heftiger als alle seine Vorsätze und Überlegungen." The "Macht" turns Albert into a voyeur — he wants to re-establish control over Katharina by observing her without her knowledge.

Katharina eventually enters the *Hofkirche.* Albert hides "im tiefsten Schatten" close to the church entrance while Katharina "langsam durch das Mittelschiff zwischen den dunklen Bildsäulen der Helden und Königinnen hindurchschritt."[40] The description of Katharina is again from Albert's viewpoint, in this instance even literally so, as his eyes follow her movements. It is therefore telling that the "Bildsäulen" are characterized as those of "Helden und Königinnen": Albert sees the relationship he attempted to construct between himself and Katharina reflected in the interior of the church. Albert wants to fashion himself as a "Held" who wooed a "Königin," or at least a creature to whom he attributes a "königliche Weise, das Haupt zu neigen."[41] The *Hofkirche,* a church explicitly linked to the court rather than to commoners, provides the perfect ambience for Albert's self-made narrative of noble worship. When Katharina suddenly stops walking, Albert sneaks "in einem weiten Bogen hinter das Grabmal des Kaisers Maximilian, das gewaltig in der Mitte der Kirche ragte."[42] From this position, he can continue to observe his wife while hiding himself from her view:

> Katharina stand *regungslos* vor der Statue des Theoderich. Die Linke auf den Degen gestützt, blickte der *erzene Held wie aus ewigen Augen* vor sich hin. *Seine Haltung war von erhabener Müdigkeit, als sei er sich zugleich der Größe und der Zwecklosigkeit seiner Taten bewußt, und als*

ginge sein ganzer Stolz in Schwermut unter. Katharina stand vor der Bildsäule und starrte dem Gotenkönig ins Antlitz. Albert blieb einige Zeit in der Verborgenheit, *dann wagte er sich vor.* Sie hätte die Schritte hören müssen, aber sie wandte sich nicht um; *wie gebannt* blieb sie auf derselben Stelle.[43]

Although Albert tries to reproduce the direction of Katharina's gaze at the statue by changing his viewing position, he does, of course, see the statue through his own eyes rather than hers. This fact is emphasized especially in the description of Theodoric's statue: Albert seems to see in the "erzene Held" a copy of himself. Albert attributes "Größe und . . . Zwecklosigkeit" to his own actions and sees his "Stolz" drowned by "Schwermut." Albert projects the identity he would like to possess onto Theodoric's statue. The statue, though it is three-dimensional, presents nothing but surface to the viewer — a surface that, for Albert, becomes a perfect projection screen. Unaware of his own projections, though, Albert attributes something resembling interiority to the statue: he finds the statue gazing "wie aus ewigen Augen." Hiding his own interior behind a façade of what he deems "Anstand" and about to extinguish his own gaze by committing suicide, Albert seems especially taken with the "ewige Augen." An eternal gaze might be able to exercise control eternally.

Katharina, whom Albert had long ago turned into a "graven image" of his own making, now seems to turn into a statue herself: she is described as "regungslos," standing "wie gebannt" in front of the statue. Later, she is even characterized as "in ihrer Bewegungslosigkeit selber einer Bildsäule gleich."[44] Katharina's transformation into a living fetish in and by Albert's eyes becomes most strikingly apparent in this passage. Albert conflates the direction of Katharina's gaze with its content: he seems to think that, since he views the statue from the same direction as Katharina, their respective interpretations of the statue must also be the same. Identifying himself with the statue, Albert apparently thinks that Katharina identifies him with the statue as well. Therefore, he seems to want to interpret Katharina's behavior in front of the statue as a sign of devotion to him. He thus "wagte . . . sich vor."[45]

Thinking that a connection between him and Katharina might be established after all, he is no longer afraid of detection. However, Albert has so thoroughly turned Katharina into a "Bildsäule" — into pure surface, into nothing but a screen for his own projections — that he now literally fails to enter her consciousness: "[s]ie hätte die Schritte hören müssen, aber sie wandte sich nicht um." Albert undertakes no further effort to make Katharina aware of his presence, as it is actually preferable that a connection between them remain in the realm of the imaginary, after all. If there turned out to be a real connection, their relationship might become "gewöhnlich." Moreover, if the constructed reasons for Albert's suicide — the reasons in his narrative of fate and noble devotion — were to disappear because of a newly established connection, Albert would still have to face suicide because of his adverse financial circumstances. Therefore, rather than risk the transformation of his tale of suicide for noble reasons into a quite ordinary story of economic necessity, Albert decides simply to leave the church.

Katharina continues to look at the statue. It is relevant that of all the statues at which she could gaze in the *Hofkirche,* she chooses the one of Theodoric, especially given the fact that Schnitzler had originally given his narrative the working title "Theoderich."[46] While Theodoric was decidedly tolerant of Christianity, he also exhibited a clear interest in the survival of his own Arian belief system, an interest that is not necessarily made obvious by the context in which his statue is placed in the *Hofkirche*. Rather, Theodoric is appropriated as part of a generalized Germanic heritage and history, and his actual history is drained of its specificity: his statue, along with twenty-seven others, is part of the tomb Emperor Maximilian I had constructed for himself in the *Hofkirche*.[47] Furthermore, the *Hofkirche* epitomizes a violation of the very Judeo-Christian conventions it supposedly represents and upholds; the interior of the *Hofkirche* violates the *Bilderverbot,* since it is filled with "graven images": the Second Commandment has at various times been understood to place a taboo on the making of any graven images, not just images of God.[48]

Theodoric's story thus appears to resemble Katharina's in several ways. Just like Theodoric, Katharina was turned into a "graven image," and this image was inserted into a history of somebody else's making. Albert has made Katharina into "*Die Fremde,*" into an exotic Other. By leaving Albert, Katharina reclaims her "foreignness" for herself — like Theodoric, she retrospectively seems to find meaning in a prohibition of marriage between people whose beliefs are foreign to each other.

The *Hofkirche* violation of the taboo associated with representation, in contrast, can be paralleled with Albert's behavior: although his carefully groomed exterior represents bourgeois "Anstand," his desires are fixated on the exotic Other. Lacking such an actual Other, he fashions an image of it that is to his own liking. Of course, bourgeois convention discourages the transgression of norms. However, just as the *Hofkirche* is not the only Christian church that violates the representational taboos (although it is an especially striking example), Albert is certainly not the only person who ever tried to transgress the norms of the bourgeoisie by fixating on the creation of an exotic Other. To the contrary, the taboo the Old Testament placed on representation is actually violated in almost every Christian church with the tacit understanding that, to a certain degree, the continued existence of the church actually depends on a violation of this taboo, as it is splendid representations that can make believers stand before the altar "wie gebannt." Similarly, the successful repression of non-bourgeois elements in the façade of bourgeois life depends on the existence of hidden outlets where a desire for an "other" can be pursued. Just like the church, the bourgeoisie hypocritically depends on the tacit and paradoxical understanding that norms can be violated as long as this violation is necessary for the ultimate survival of the norms. Thus, Albert behaves as any good bourgeois would: he keeps the façade intact by projecting his desires for the non-bourgeois onto a woman whom he turns into an Other.

Before Albert steps out of the church, he turns around one more time; "da sah er, wie Katharina nahe an die Statue herangetreten war und mit ihren Lippen den erzenen Fuß berührte."[49] Katharina's gesture evokes the Pygmalion myth, although with a twist: Katharina could want to awaken the statue not because of her own desires as they relate to the statue; rather, she could want to set Theodoric free by awakening him and releasing him to his own history, no longer beholden to the images others have made of him. Similarly, Katharina's decision to leave Albert indicates her desire to leave the prison of the image he has constructed for her. The capacity for empathy Katharina demonstrates with regard to Theodoric's statue parallels the reactions she had earlier in the narrative to music and to painting. In a dream, Katharina anticipated the death of the organ player Banetti, whom she admired; and, after viewing a landscape painting in Albert's company, she talked about the place depicted as if she had really visited it. Albert reacts with a "schmerzliches Grauen"[50] to this latter incident. It is entirely possible, though, that Katharina simply has a rather emotional way of reacting to musical and visual art. It seems as though she finds articulated in these works of art things she herself has trouble expressing: Albert recalls, for instance, that Katharina sings "mit einer angenehmen Stimme, aber beinahe völlig ausdruckslos."[51]

After turning around on the steps of the church and observing Katharina as she kisses the foot of Theodoric's statue, Albert has an "Einfall." He tells himself that now "hatte er noch etwas für die Geliebte zu tun, bevor er dahinging": he tries to obtain a bronze copy of Theodoric's statue "in natürlicher Größe."[52] Luck would have it that an art dealership nearby has just such a copy available. The price of the statue "entsprach ungefähr dem Rest [von Alberts] Vermögen."[53] Albert buys the statue and orders it to be placed in the garden of the house he bought for Katharina. Afterward, he shoots himself in a "Wäldchen" outside of the city.

By ordering a copy of the statue (with which he identifies), Albert symbolically places an image of himself in Katharina's future dwellings: "wie aus ewigen Augen" the statue can look on as Katharina conducts her life as a widow. Thus, Albert is not really doing something "für die Geliebte," but rather for his own benefit. However, the "eternal gaze" can only be sustained with the help of multiple mediations: the figure in the garden is neither the statue of Theodoric, nor is it a statue of Albert. Rather, it is the copy of a representation of Theodoric that itself has been mediated by almost a thousand years of distance between the historical subject Theodoric and the creation of his bronze image. The "natürliche Größe" of the statue cannot erase the fact that its "eternal gaze" is a highly artificial construct.

Albert's turning around on the church steps also evokes the story of Sodom and Gomorrah: by turning again to gaze upon what is really a scene of destruction — namely, the destruction of his marriage, a relationship that was built on perverse mechanisms — Albert turns into a pillar, albeit not a pillar of salt. Rather, he willingly turns himself into a bronze statue whose dead eyes, contrary to what Albert wants to believe, will not be able to exercise control over Katharina. Rather, the eyes of the beholder, namely Katharina's, will exercise control over the interpretation of the statue's copy.

When Katharina returns to Vienna and discovers the copy of the statue in her garden, she gazes at it for "eine geraume Weile" and afterward

> begab sie sich in ihr Zimmer und schrieb einen längeren Brief nach Verona postlagernd an Andrea Geraldini. So hatte sich nämlich ein Herr genannt, der ihr von der Hofkirche aus gefolgt war, als sie Theoderich den Großen verlassen hatte, und von dem sie ein Kind unter dem Herzen trug. Ob das auch der richtige Name des Herrn war, erfuhr sie nie; denn sie erhielt keine Antwort.[54]

These concluding sentences reveal that, contrary to Albert's intentions, Katharina might not necessarily assume that the statue was placed in the garden by Albert. More likely, she believes that the statue was sent by the man who had called himself Andrea Geraldini, since she is aware that this man had observed her in the *Hofkirche*. She is not, however, aware that Albert also observed her. Thus, instead of having ensured his continued presence in Katharina's life even after his death, Albert might have unwittingly aided his own erasure from Katharina's life by ordering the statue, since Katharina is likely to associate someone other than Albert with it.

In a further twist of irony, the woman who was turned by Albert into "*Die Fremde*" felt herself attracted to an exotic Other, namely to a man with an Italian name. She promptly betrayed Albert with this man. Albert has thus lost control over his bloodline: the offspring that will be raised in Albert's name is not his. Rather, this offspring is a "fake," like the statue in the garden.

The narrative that had opened with the quotation of a note written by Katharina also closes with her composing a letter. Though the man who called himself Andrea Geraldini usurps the legacy Albert had intended to leave, Katharina's experience with the Italian is at least in one way no different than the experience she had with Albert. Just as Albert had left blank the "weiße Seite" of the "Zettel" on which Katharina had written her note, so is her letter to Geraldini answered only with silence. Neither Albert nor Geraldini is ultimately willing to take responsibility for his actions toward Katharina; they are, in this respect, mirror images of each other. The "other" that Katharina may have sought in Geraldini really turns out to be no other at all.

IV.

Schnitzler's narrative can be understood as a searing indictment of the double standards underlying bourgeois morality, and especially of turn-of-the-century bourgeois men's attempts to address their crises of masculine identity by turning women into the Other. *Die Fremde* highlights the destructive consequences of Albert's attempts to imprison Katharina in an image of otherness, not just for Katharina but ultimately also for Albert himself. Albert's actions are permeated by a capitalist logic of exchange: Katharina can be bought with the offer of economic security. In keeping with this logic, the truth is exchanged for an imaginary narrative of fate and noble devotion, which Albert purchases in the form of expensive presents for Katharina. These actions soon undermine the very economic basis that had made it possible for Albert to seek a desirable Other in the first place. Thus, the logic of exchange ultimately collapses under its own weight and buries Albert as well as his self-constructed narrative of fate.

Albert's attempts to turn Katharina into an Other eventually distance him from his object of desire to such an extent that he loses control of her. The more Albert turns Katharina into an image of otherness, the more he turns her into a screen for his own projections, a surface he is soon unable to penetrate. The invented qualities that made Katharina desirable in Albert's eyes in the first place, namely her status as Other, ultimately also make it impossible for Albert to possess this Other: the imaginary distance between them has become too great to be overcome.

Die Fremde subtly analyzes bourgeois morals and crises of masculinity, and thus not only forms an integral part of Schnitzler's *Dämmerseelen* collection but also exhibits many of the same feminist concerns that are familiar to readers from Schnitzler's more canonized narratives. *Die Fremde* can thus be read as a text that is paradigmatic for the issues Schnitzler seeks to raise in his prose oeuvre.[55]

Notes

[1] *Die Fremde* in ES I, 551–59.

[2] Theodoric, king of the Ostrogoths, was sent to Italy in A.D. 488 by the Byzantine emperor to fight Odoacer, who had become too powerful a ruler. After defeating Odoacer, Theodoric left in place the Roman political institutions and ruled Italy peacefully. He granted Christians the right to practice their religion, in spite of the fact that his Arian beliefs were in conflict with those of the Christians. Romans could fill political offices, while the Gothic troops guaranteed Italy's military security. Theodoric did, however, put in place a marriage prohibition that was supposed to prevent a mixing between the Germanic peoples and the Catholic Romans. He had striven for a union of all Germanic tribes, but his plans failed when Chlodwig, king of the Franks, converted to Christianity.

[3] ES I, 559.

[4] The publication history of the text is described in detail in Reinhard Urbach, *Schnitzler-Kommentar zu den erzählenden Schriften und dramatischen Werken* (Munich: Winkler, 1974), 114.

[5] *Das Schicksal des Freiherrn von Leisenbohg* in ES I, 580–97; *Die Weissagung* in ES I, 598–619; *Das neue Lied* in ES I, 620–34; *Andreas Thameyers letzter Brief* in ES I, 514–20. See Hugo von Hofmannsthal and Arthur Schnitzler, *Briefwechsel*, ed. Therese Nickl and Heinrich Schnitzler (Frankfurt: Fischer, 1964), 375.

[6] *Andreas Thameyers letzter Brief*, 515.

[7] The pseudo-scientific concept of "das Versehen der Frauen" was most infamously popularized by Otto Weininger in his 1903 anti-Semitic and anti-feminist tract *Geschlecht und Charakter*. Schnitzler's "Thameyer" narrative was written in 1900, prior to the publication of Weininger's tract, and Schnitzler used as a source Gerhard von Welsenburg's 1899 history of the concept of "das Versehen der Frauen." For additional sources for Schnitzler's text, see Urbach, 111.

[8] An excellent account of identity crises in Viennese Modernism is offered by Jacques Le Rider, *Das Ende der Illusion. Die Wiener Moderne und die Krisen der Identität* (Vienna: Österreichischer Bundesverlag, 1990).

[9] Gottfried Just, *Ironie und Sentimentalität in den erzählenden Dichtungen Arthur Schnitzlers* (Berlin: Erich Schmidt, 1968), 116.

[10] Just, 116.

[11] Just, 118.

[12] Just, 127.

[13] Elisabeth Lebensaft, *Anordnung und Funktion zentraler Aufbauelemente in den Erzählungen Arthur Schnitzlers* (Vienna: Notring, 1972), 20–22.

[14] Lebensaft 22.

[15] Barbara Gutt, *Emanzipation bei Arthur Schnitzler* (Berlin: Spiess, 1978), 68, 70.

[16] ES I, 551.

[17] ES I, 551.

[18] ES I, 551.

[19] ES I, 551 (my emphasis).

[20] ES I, 552.

[21] ES I, 552

[22] ES I, 552.

[23] ES I, 552

[24] ES I, 552 (my emphasis).

[25] ES I, 551.

[26] ES I, 551.

[27] ES I, 553.

[28] ES I, 554 (my emphasis).

[29] ES I, 553.

[30] ES I, 553.

[31] ES I, 553.

[32] ES I, 553 (my emphases).

[33] ES I, 554.

[34] ES I, 556.

[35] Gutt, 70.

[36] ES I, 557 (my emphases).

[37] ES I, 557.

[38] ES I, 557 (my emphasis).

[39] ES I, 557–58 (my emphases).

[40] ES I, 558.

[41] ES I, 553.

[42] ES I, 558.

[43] ES I, 558 (my emphases).

[44] ES I, 558.

[45] ES I, 558.

[46] The Innsbruck *Hofkirche,* built between 1553 and 1563, contains, in addition to many other art works, twenty-eight different sixteenth-century bronze statues.

[47] The tomb consists of twenty-eight bronze statues that depict historical figures whom Maximilian I wanted to be associated with his own lineage. Theodoric's statue was cast in 1513 by Peter Vischer the Elder and later placed in the *Hofkirche*. The cast is based on sketches by Albrecht Dürer. On the construction of the tomb, see Vinzenz Oberhammer, *Die Bronzestandbilder des Maximiliangrabmales in der Hofkirche zu Innsbruck* (Innsbruck: Tyrolia Verlag, 1935).

[48] The early Christian church respected the Old Testament taboo on representation, expressed in the Second Commandment, rather strictly. Approximately during the middle of the third century, adherence to this taboo started to slip. In A.D. 717, the so-called *Bilderstreit* broke out: critics saw Christian art as a practice suborning superstition, thus watering down Christian beliefs. The continuing influence of eastern Christian sects, Judaism, and Islam — which all adhered to the taboo on representation — contributed to a critical view of visual representations within the Christian church. Pope Gregor III condemned the *Bilderstürmer*, though, and eventually, after a synod held in 843, the practice of placing representations in churches was finally officially declared to be legitimate. The Old Testament's original Second Commandment was dropped; instead, the Tenth Commandment was split into two separate commandments, so that the original number of ten would remain. Not until the Reformation was the original Second Commandment taken seriously again: followers of Huldrych Zwingli and John Calvin started a *Bildersturm*, removing religious images from churches. The Reformed Church reintegrated the Old Testament Second Commandment into the decalogue, whereas the original remains excluded from the Catholic and the Lutheran decalogue. See, for instance, Ruggerio Romano and Alberto Tenenti, *Die Grundlegung der modernen Welt: Spätmittelalter, Renaissance, Reformation* (Frankfurt: Fischer, 1984), 220–87; Hermann Kinder and Werner Hilgemann, *dtv-Atlas zur Weltgeschichte* (Munich: Deutscher Taschenbuch Verlag, 1981), vol. 1; Günter Lange, "Zum Umgang mit Bildern der Kunst im Religionsunterricht," February 10, 2002 <http://www.uni-leipzig.de/ru/lange/rukunst>; and Hartwig Weber, *Lexikon Religion* (Reinbek bei Hamburg: Rowohlt Taschenbuch Verlag, 2001). In its entirety, the Old Testament Second Commandment reads: "Thou shalt not make unto thee any graven image, or any likeness of anything that is in heaven above, or that is in the earth beneath, or that is in the water under the earth." Interpretations as to whether the Second Commandment places a taboo on all representation, or merely a taboo on the making of idols, have varied. Theodor W. Adorno, in *Ästhetische Theorie* (Frankfurt: Suhrkamp Verlag, 1973), suggests a literal reading of Exodus 20:4: "Das alttestamentarische Bilderverbot hat neben seiner theologischen Seite eine ästhetische. Daß man sich kein Bild, nämlich keines von etwas machen soll, sagt zugleich, kein solches Bild sei möglich" (106). An excellent elaboration of the implication of the Second Commandment with regard to the impossibility of representation can be found in Lisa Saltzman, *Anselm Kiefer and Art After Auschwitz* (Cambridge: Cambridge UP, 1999), 17–47. Saltzman sides with Adorno: "[T]he Second Commandment [. . .] proposes a world without images, a world in which not only God, but no other thing, be it from the earth, the sea, or the sky, may be represented. Further, the Second Commandment does not simply proscribe that God *should* not be portrayed. What the Second Commandment implies is that God *cannot* be portrayed. God is beyond the knowable or perceptible. God is thus unrepresentable. [. . .] [T]he Second Commandment determines a representational impossibility a priori" (19).

[49] ES I, 558.
[50] ES I, 555.
[51] ES I, 554.
[52] ES I, 558.
[53] ES I, 559.
[54] ES I, 559.
[55] I owe thanks to Jens Rieckmann and Heidi Schlipphacke for their helpful comments on earlier versions of this essay.

In the Loge, *1879; Mary Cassatt, American (1844–1926).*
Oil on canvas. The Hayden Collection.
Courtesy and © 2000 Museum of Fine Arts, Boston.
Reproduced with permission. All Rights Reserved.

The Power of the Gaze: Visual Metaphors in Schnitzler's Prose Works and Dramas

Susan C. Anderson

VISUAL METAPHORS, ranging from blindness to dreams to voyeurism, abound in the work of Arthur Schnitzler. These visual metaphors are used to question *fin-de-siècle* gender norms and to offer a more differentiated idea of shifting gender roles. As literary and cultural scholar Andreas Huyssen has shown, these tropes connect Schnitzler's texts to other modernist attempts, such as those by Hugo von Hofmannsthal (1874–1929) and Robert Musil (1880–1942), to express an increasing sense of disorientation and even paranoia in the close and crowded confines of urban Europe.[1] Schnitzler wrote during a period of high bourgeois anxiety over changing ideas about identity, social relations (the "self" in flux, the body under threat by invisible germs, socialist and nationalist movements), and gender roles (women's suffrage, women entering the workforce, new views of marriage). These changes entailed new ways of occupying public and private spheres, especially within middle-class circles. Bourgeois women, for example, assumed a greater public presence by attending universities, working, or becoming politically active. Such public involvement also placed them under the scrutiny of anonymous viewers. Indeed, making one's way through the city in general implied putting oneself on display and entering into an economy of glances and stares. This sense of being watched helped enforce social and gender norms.[2] The blurring of gender roles, which Schnitzler shows through different ways of seeing, parallels other challenges to concepts of gender at the time — in the work of Mary Cassatt (1844–1926), for example. Karl Kraus (1874–1936), Otto Weininger (1880–1903), August Strindberg (1849–1912), and Edgar Degas (1834–1917), on the other hand, wrote or painted in ways that tried to "fix" the meaning of masculinity and femininity. Schnitzler experimented with a variety of notions of masculinity and femininity, and he connected these notions to ways of looking and being looked at. The end of *Traumnovelle* (1926; *Rhapsody: A Dream Novel*, 1927) suggests a way out of fixed gender concepts and set ways of seeing. Already in *Paracelsus* (1899; tr. 1913), *Leutnant Gustl* (1900; *None But the Brave,* 1926), and *Fräulein Else* (1924; tr. 1925), works in which male figures could at times appear "feminine" and vice versa,[3] Schnitzler was questioning conventional ideas of gender and established ways of seeing. His solution to the problem of stereotyping is different from Cassatt's, who stressed the woman as the one who views, but both of them try to conceive of seeing as something other than merely mastery over a feminized "other."

As art historian Griselda Pollock notes, "The significant spaces of modernity are neither simply those of masculinity, nor are they those of femininity. . . . They are . . . the marginal or interstitial spaces where the fields of the masculine and feminine intersect and structure sexuality within a classed order."[4] And this order gave preference to an objectifying, "masculine" way of looking.[5] Pollock cites cultural critic Walter Benjamin's *flâneur* as exemplary of modernist man, one whose gaze "articulates and produces a masculine sexuality which in the modern sexual economy enjoys the freedom to look, appraise and possess, in deed or in fantasy."[6] She posits an alternative feminist gaze that interacts rather than judges, one that crosses gender divisions that are based on an economy of seeing and being seen, as evident, for example, in the paintings of Cassatt and Berthe Morisot (1841–1895).

Defining the gaze as masculine or feminine lends it a stability that theorists such as Jonathan Crary have shown to be inadequate. In his studies of the observer in nineteenth-century Europe, Crary documents the change from an early modern concept of a stable subject of observation — one who reflects with detachment on an object perceived through the medium of transparent eyes — to a modern idea of an unreliable observer. Nineteenth-century discoveries in physiology and optics identified the body as the site of vision; such phenomena as afterimages and binocular vision showed the relation between eyes and perception to be complex and fluid.[7] This shifting in turn implied a blurring of interior and exterior spheres of experience. Together with German scientist and philosopher Hermann von Helmholtz's (1821–1894) and Austrian physicist and philosopher Ernst Mach's (1838–1916) treatises on attentiveness and sight, such ideas also stimulated attempts to redefine the relation between perception and cognition.[8]

These efforts suggested a need to rethink how self and identity are formed. And questions of modern identity are tied to concepts of gender and sexual difference. Consequently, as Lisa Tickner asserts, "The battle of the sexes (for pro- and antifeminists, especially men) and the exploration of a modern, self-determined identity (particularly by women) is *the* modern subject matter, even where talk of speed, electricity, cars, planes, and war dominates the manifest content of a work."[9] Schnitzler's prose and drama are interesting in this regard because they use tropes of watching, being watched, eluding observation, voyeurism, and the hypnotic gaze to explore ideas about sexual difference, subjectivity, voice, and the social roles of men and women in early twentieth-century Vienna. Schnitzler uses what Huyssen calls "disturbances of vision" aesthetically to criticize a persisting hierarchy of "masculine" observer to "feminine" observed and replace it with a fluid exchange of shifting gazes and positionalities.

The hypnotist is the most extreme case of an objectifying viewer who strives for mastery over another's body and mind, often in a public setting. Such influence also affects the hypnotized figure's ability to speak. The spectacular quality of hypnotism emphasizes its isolating factor, for the hypnotized individual is immobilized and separated from others. In this sense, the hypnotic gaze functions to manage the otherwise uncontrollable impulses of the human psyche.[10] Physicians such as Jean-Martin Charcot (1825–1893) and Hippolyte Bernheim (1840–1919) at first used the process in attempts to cure their patients, but it became associated with loss of subjectivity and rational thought processes and fell out of favor by the early twentieth century.[11] Late twentieth-century theorists and philosophers like Jean-Luc Nancy or François Roustang, however, have regarded hypnotism as potentially liberating, as enabling the ostensibly passive subject to attain another state of wakefulness and thereby resist authority.[12] Schnitzler, who exhibited an avid interest in hypnotism, described his experience with it in his medical treatises, later collected in *Medizinische Schriften* (1988), and played with its contradictions in his literary texts. As Horst Thomé describes, Schnitzler published almost all of his medical essays between the time he received his medical degree in 1885 and the death of his father in 1893. He worked as a *Sekundararzt* in Vienna's *Allgemeines Krankenhaus* from 1885 to 1888 and then in his father's clinic from 1888 to 1893.[13]

Schnitzler's writings demonstrate the reconnection of the verbal with the visual in the hypnotized subject. For instance, he documents in *Medizinische Schriften* several cases from the 1880s of loss of voice, or aphonia, which he attempts to cure with hypnotism. It is important to note that his patients are usually women, and that his experiments are carried out in the presence of other (male) doctors.[14] He includes doctors as spectators to legitimate his results, for many of his colleagues regarded hypnotism with skepticism.[15] His descriptions of how he hypnotized a series of women, each time witnessed by staring men, are emblematic of a way of seeing that aims to take possession of its object. For instance, in addition to suggesting to his aphonic patients that they would be able to speak upon awakening, he also conducted experiments without the patients' knowledge, such as telling a woman under hypnosis her right arm was lame; she had trouble moving her arm afterward.[16] The women who feared hypnosis or did not fall completely under the spell of the hypnotist's eyes had the most problems regaining their voices.[17] A woman's ability to speak appeared related to the degree of her submission to a controlling male look and to her desire to yield to this look. Schnitzler's role as paternal healer thus vacillated between success and failure with the different responses to his stare.

Likewise, figures under observation in Schnitzler's fictional world shift their positions, and the relation between speaking and looking or being observed also changes. In *Paracelsus,* for example, the trope of hypnosis reveals how illusory the "detached" observer's power can be, for his influence depends on the stability of his object. Yet, while hypnosis immobilizes the main female character into a spectacle, it also releases a free play of desires, which weakens the hypnotist's visual power over her. It allows impulses from what Schnitzler called the half-conscious to be voiced and thereby enter consciousness.[18] These half-conscious urges complicate the observer/observed role, moving the hypnotized woman into a subject position.

Paracelsus appears to present femininity primarily as the inability to resist the objectifying gaze. The main figure, the matron Justina, succumbs twice to the hypnotic powers of her former love, Dr. Paracelsus, which expose her body and mind to the curious eyes of her husband, Cyprian, as well. Yet, the pairing of another female "patient," Cäcilia, Cyprian's young sister, with a different male doctor, Copus, calls the power of the controlling male gaze into question. The discrepancy between conventional and modern forms of observation emerges in the contrast between how Paracelsus and Copus treat Cäcilia after she returns with a headache from a trip to town. Cäcilia is suffering from a disease of perception that debilitates her both physically and mentally, and this handicap is connected to her forays into public space, that is, into sixteenth-century Basel. Her independent stroll through the city allows her, like the later *flâneur,* to take in sights without communicating, to consume the views around her; but unlike the *flâneur'*s experiences, the results disorient her — "mich schwindelt noch," she avers to Justina.[19] The urban world outside her home exceeds her visual command. Copus, who is more like a nineteenth-century Viennese physician but blind to Cäcilia's psychological response to external stimuli, looks only at her tongue and feels her pulse.[20] He is a type of doctor figure whose "psychic abandonment of the patient" Schnitzler criticizes throughout his work.[21] Cäcilia, however, can at least direct Copus's "objective" attention to her surface symptoms, while she would lose her psychological integrity if she were to allow Paracelsus to mesmerize her. Secure within the limits of her home, she successfully repels "seiner Augen Macht,"[22] in keeping with theories about the inability to hypnotize a resisting subject.[23] Cäcilia rejects the docile, "feminine" position of the hypnotized by voicing her wishes about her treatment, even though she depends on male figures such as Copus for assistance.

Schnitzler uses Cäcilia and Justina to suggest a fluctuating relation between gender and the viewing subject. In contrast to Cäcilia, Justina, who has not ventured outside the private sphere, enacts the role of feminine object; but appearances deceive. Her potential to become a subject is already evident in her interactions with Junker Anselm, whose propositions tempt her, but only slightly. While Anselm strives to fix her as an object of his sexual desire, Justina's unacknowledged attraction to him entices her both to occupy the role into which he pushes her and to make of him an object of her own erotic urges. However, by speaking from a position of bourgeois morality, she can resist Anselm's glances. She counters, for example, his probing looks by announcing to him, "Eure Blicke kränken meine Würde."[24] Such words enable her to elude his optic power because they force him to explain himself, to reveal openly his wish for a kiss from her, that is, the thought behind his looks. At hearing his sentiments, she is able to regain the composure she lost while he was eyeing her and to rebuff his proposition by threatening to laugh at him.

This precursor to the scenes with Paracelsus shows a contest of subjectivities, neither character willing to accept the role of object. They uphold through speech the conventions of willpower and morality as antidote to temptation. Yet, the recourse to moralizing speech shows that Justina's subjectivity cannot assert itself merely through the force of her look. Her ambivalent feelings for Anselm threaten to slide her into an object position because his attentions also attract her, as she confesses later. This subject/object ambivalence reaches across genders, for Anselm also experiences similar conflicts with Paracelsus. Anselm becomes susceptible to Paracelsus's glare and must leave in order to avoid being hypnotized like a woman. "Nicht länger konnt' ich diesen Blick ertragen,"[25] he explains. His fear of hypnosis implies an unacknowledged male desire to submit to Paracelsus's visual control, a desire that is similar to the "feminine."

When Justina becomes the focal point of the doubled male gaze, she becomes almost aphonic. Her susceptibility to suggestion becomes evident when Paracelsus, whom she loved years ago, and Cyprian both focus their attention on her. The two male characters then vie over their perceived knowledge of her, united in their efforts to maintain their sense of masculine superiority.[26] In contrast to the different types of resistance to the hypnotic gaze embodied by Cäcilia and Anselm, Justina seems the perfect construct to prove the superiority of Paracelsus's fixed manner of observation.

> CYPRIAN: Sieh, wie sie rot wird
>
> PARACELSUS: Und so verwirrt, als wäre Schönheit Schuld!
>
> JUSTINA *fast in Tränen:*   ch bitt' Euch sehr . . .
>
> CYPRIAN *zu Paracelsus:* Ihr seht, sie ist wie einst.
>
> PARACELSUS *mit Bedeutung:* Ich seh's.[27]

They dispute over her affections in her presence, speaking of her in the third person as if she were not in the room. And indeed she has lost presence by becoming a spectacle and losing her voice. Her earlier utterances not withstanding, she appears to exist only in exterior form and becomes completely objectified while they discuss her.

The "cure" for her "illness" is hypnosis, although, as Michaela Perlmann asserts, Paracelsus is more interested in dominance than healing.[28] The hypnotist first visually overwhelms the feminized object of his efforts in order to penetrate the psyche and learn its "true" thoughts. He can then manipulate these at will, confusing memories and wishes so that only the present state of mind — under his influence — matters. When Paracelsus exclaims "Der Augenblick regiert!" his avowal is also literal, for the objectifying look rules over the psyches of those who let themselves be caught in its trajectory, and Justina is caught in Paracelsus's hypnotic stare.[29] As in so many modernist texts, however, the feminized object can also elude control.[30]

The public nature of the hypnotic process, according to Crary, "provided a set of powerful images of a hypnotic experience that defined it as an event or object from which a truth could be extracted objectively, from the outside."[31] However, the presentation of a collective search for truth allows Justina to gain the upper hand and present her own verity. Instructed to tell the "truth" to whoever asks, Justina's articulation of her half-conscious thoughts reveals surprising information. While she asserts her loyalty to Cyprian, she confesses how easily she would have betrayed him with Paracelsus: "Du [Cyprian] dachtest, war ich dir erst angetraut, / So war dir meine Zärtlichkeit gewiß. / Und doch! in mancher Nacht, hättst du gefühlt, / Wie fern ich dir war — wahrlich! minder stolz / Wärst du der Frau gewesen, dir im Arm!"[32] The power of her words spoken from such an ostensibly unassailable source of probity astounds the others into silence. Beginning with Anselm, who withdraws from her look and turns his gaze to Cäcilia, the other characters react to the strength of Justina's heartfelt stance and allow themselves to learn from her. The result is new and unsettling knowledge, for they understand that there are invisible aspects of her persona beyond constraint, aspects that change continually.

However, Justina is unable to maintain her subject position. Her gaze, speech, and subjectivity converge only for a moment. Similarly, after Anselm asserts his dominance by staring at Cäcilia, the latter's own position of strength wavers. Being a subject is bound to independent sight and speech, but those elements depend in turn on unstable, semiconscious desires. Thus the male gazer and female object are merely stages along a mutating spectrum of dominance and submission. Cyprian's statement, "Ein Sturmwind kam, der hat auf Augenblicke / Die Tore unsrer Seelen aufgerissen, / Wir haben einen Blick hineingetan,"[33] ascribes to Justina's apparent truth-telling the opening of all their eyes. Yet Justina's role as teacher was limited to a few hours; her superior stance was achieved under the careful watch of her husband and admirers. She returns at the end to her role as chaste wife and upholder of bourgeois virtue, as a speaker of superficial proprieties. Nevertheless, the knowledge that her unconscious erotic urges cannot be completely satisfied within the confines of her marriage is an unsettling truth from which the male characters prefer to avert their eyes. Yet, they are also fascinated by this "empowered feminine."[34]

Paracelsus's penetrating perception thus stirs up a sexual dynamic beneath the static bourgeois world he encounters and, in the end, disorients them all.[35] As Thomé explains in his foreword to Schnitzler's *Medizinische Schriften*, "Der sexuelle Wunsch und die Phantasie von der eigenen Omnipotenz sind, so wird man folgern dürfen, stets präsente Störfaktoren eines ärztlichen Handelns, das sich auf die psychotherapeutische Kur eingelassen hat."[36] The shifting roles of hypnotist and hypnotized performed in *Paracelsus* reveal an ambivalence toward the efficacy of hypnotism as psychotherapy. The half-conscious thoughts and wishes of both doctor and "patient" deflect and scatter the power of the penetrating look. Hypnotism also becomes in this theater piece a metaphor for the disorienting effects of modernization, which, like Paracelsus himself, intrude into the private sphere and upset conventions of seeing.

The shock to the presumably stable position of the male gaze recurs with more nuance (and with more complications) almost thirty years later in *Traumnovelle*, with a much different outcome. That outcome is presaged in Schnitzler's two celebrated stream-of-consciousness narratives *Leutnant Gustl* and *Fräulein Else*, which offer further perspectives on the fluctuating intersection of gaze, voice, and subjectivity.

Leutnant Gustl marks a weakening of the masculine gaze within a highly regimented social context. As Gustl's gaze fails, so do his words and sense of self-worth. And as he loses control over his gaze, he becomes more engrossed in his own disjointed thoughts, unable to interact with those around him or to voice his anxieties. Only after he regains an illusory sense of manly subjectivity through the unexpected death of his rival can he ignore the looks of others and reassert his own privileged position as watcher or as dominant player in what Klaus Laermann describes as a phallic "Machtkampf durch Blicke."[37] This interior-monologue novella reveals continual slippages between positions of control and viewing.

Misdirected sight and inarticulateness show from the start how tenuous Gustl's hold on his middle-class, masculine status is. For instance, the lieutenant hesitates to check his watch during an oratorio at which a fellow officer's sister is singing because others might observe him and deduce that he is not appreciative of the music — that is, not a member of the *Bildungsbürgertum*. He thus places himself in the position of the observed, subordinate to the disciplining looks of the anonymous members of the audience. His justification for his decision to look at his watch after all is telling, for it connects class with attentiveness. He muses, "Aber, wer sieht's denn? Wenn's einer sieht, so paßt er gerade so wenig auf, wie ich, und vor dem brauch' ich mich nicht zu genieren."[38] Inattentiveness also means viewing in a random, impulsive fashion, as he does by glancing at others and his watch, or not looking at all. This wandering gaze expresses his incoherent sense of identity.[39] Indeed, as Gustl struggles psychologically to maintain his "identity" as a man of honor, he also battles to focus his attention and his sight.

This initial scene at the opera house is a literary manifestation of a common theme in the paintings of the time, many of which portrayed theater audiences as spectacles for the viewer.[40] A different approach to this topos is Cassatt's painting *In the Loge* (1879), which can help place Gustl's problems at the oratorio in context.[41] One of several Cassatt paintings of women at the opera or theater, *In the Loge* shows a well- but soberly dressed woman sitting in a loge and peering into the interior of an auditorium through opera glasses. Her studied posture implies an absorption with the object of her gaze, so much so that she neglects to use the closed fan clasped in her lap as a shield from the probing eyes of others. This position is an example of an outwardly directed gaze, of a figure oblivious to her effect on others, such as the man in another loge who is peering directly at her through his opera glasses. In contrast to her composed sitting posture, he seems on the edge of his seat, avidly attempting to capture her in his focus. Yet, the perspective of the person viewing the painting is drawn from the woman back to the man, turning, as it were, his gaze back onto itself.[42] Nevertheless, both figures prop their right elbow on the edge of the balcony in front of them, which lends them a degree of similarity, for both have the role of subject while looking. The woman's indifference to the fact that she is also the object of the man's ogling suggests the strength of her subjectivity. There is no sideways glance to assess her allure. The fact that she dominates the foreground, taking up much more space on the canvas than the tiny male figure in the background, shows a self-confident attentiveness to the exterior world as more powerful than the projection of desire emanating from the male figure. She appears to both extend the man's look but also to rework it into a calm scrutiny of something in the distance. She thus maintains her role as a subject because her position as feminized object is beyond her field of vision and therefore inconceivable to her. Gustl, in contrast, perceives subjectivity only as the power to objectify, and his experience in the opera house staring at others, including a woman in a loge, is Schnitzler's first step in putting this notion to the test.

Gustl's efforts to assert his masculinity by looking at women in the audience combine with images of himself as a visual object, such as when he muses, "Das Mädel drüben in der Loge ist sehr hübsch. Sieht sie mich an oder den Herrn dort mit dem blonden Vollbart?"[43] This comment and others also show a desire to see that is thwarted by his distance from the objects he wishes to discern, thereby emphasizing his isolation. The woman he glimpses in the loge and his friend Kopetzky's sister in the choir are beyond his full visual grasp, which leaves him coveting another patron's opera glasses but too embarrassed to ask to borrow them. The whole scene during the concert is one of obstructed vision, in part because Gustl himself feels exposed to the more educated and wealthy members of the audience with their opera glasses. Their focused binocular vision can capture him without his being aware of it. Like Cassatt's spectators, their possession of visual aids appears a privilege that a man of his social standing does not have. This lack further emasculates him. Yet, even if he did possess opera glasses or a lorgnette, his poor visual memory and deficient attention would prevent him from recognizing all he might see.

This first scene sets the stage for further hindrances to clear sight. As the subsequent exchange with the *Bäckermeister* shows, Gustl's lack of visual acuity parallels a more general lack of empathy for others, in part out of fear of being exposed as a social interloper. At the same time, he craves looks of admiration, especially from young women. For instance, "Die da ist nett . . . Wie sie mich anschaut! . . . O ja, mein Fräulein, ich möchte schon!"[44] Of course, the baker's gripping Gustl's sword and threatening to pull it out of its sheath and break it are an obvious menace to his sense of manhood. The exchange between the two occurs immediately after he sees the woman from the loge meet another man. She then laughs over at Gustl, wounding his masculine pride. His aggressive words to the *Bäckermeister* at the coat checkout suggest an inarticulateness that is in keeping with his objectification in the eyes of the laughing woman. As an object, he loses his facility to communicate effectively and vents his frustration over his inability to dominate through looking.

The baker's threat reinforces Gustl's own qualms about the weakness of his gaze. As soon as the baker leaves, the lieutenant feels even more exposed, thinking, "Wie schau ich denn aus — Merkt man mir was an?"[45] This confirmation of his feminine position, as a figuratively castrated spectacle, is what drives him to consider suicide. It also detracts from everything but his imagined fears. Indeed, he becomes, in a figurative sense, doubly castrated, through the woman's laughing glance and the baker's grip on his sword.[46] If, as John Berger argues, "A man's presence is dependent upon the promise of power which he embodies," and that presence derives from an impression that one is capable of acting,[47] then Gustl's paralysis before the baker demonstrates an absence of the masculinity that he so desperately pretends to inhabit. Like Berger's assertion about modern, Western women, Gustl defines himself according to how others regard him.[48]

A break with the exterior world is connected to loss of voice and ability to direct one's gaze, which recalls the effects of hypnosis. In this case, however, Gustl is in the thrall of his self-observation, which diffuses his gaze. In the words of Evelyne Polt-Heinzl, "Der Wortzerfall ist ein Anzeichen des Wirklichkeitsverlustes."[49] Gustl's psychological disorientation manifests itself in visual confusion: "Was, bin ich schon auf der Straße? Wie bin ich denn da herausgekommen?"[50] he wonders. His subsequent panic-stricken thoughts about his death accompany increasingly paranoid suspicions that others are looking at him and seeing his shame — shame at his loss of manhood and social standing. These scenes of humiliation occur in public, before the eyes of countless Viennese, any one of whom could have overheard his argument with the baker. Gustl's crisis is intimately bound up with the cityscape that exposes him to the view of anonymous urbanites. Only after he withdraws into a café and learns of the baker's sudden death does he regain his ability to speak, and with it his aggression and sense of masculine privilege. His questions to the waiter about the baker's fate express, on the one hand, his most selfish need to know, but they also exhibit an effort to interact with another, to emerge from his internal exile. His regained sense of confidence that he can pass himself off as the man he desires to be, that he can assume his mask of officer and gentleman, is evident in his self-congratulation: "Das hab' ich jetzt famos gesagt — kein Mensch könnt mir was anmerken."[51] And this time he recognizes someone else, the customer to whom the waiter is talking. His nearsightedness has improved a bit as he reorients himself in his position as officer, lover, and potential winner of a duel.

Thus visual metaphors in this narrative evoke an illusion of control or lack of it over one's sense of self. Insufficient restraint is coded as social inferiority or femininity, and readers trace Gustl's journey along the spectrum from unstable masculinity, to feminized spectacle, to a shored-up sense of manhood, yet still susceptible to blocked vision. External conditions have improved his sight only superficially. What Gustl cannot perceive is that he is still a spectacle, still at the mercy of social forces beyond his control, such as class structures, the honor code, and gender distinctions — forces that can disrupt his vision and sense of self again at any time. Instead of expressing an unvoiced desire to submit to another's gaze or the triumph of temporarily suppressing disloyal thoughts, as in *Paracelsus,* this narrative depicts an example of an inability to become the subject of one's gaze and the frustrations inherent in this situation.[52] Gustl cannot gain agency through speaking because he is disconnected from his half-conscious desires — anger rather than moral indignation result. Indeed, the phrases and slogans he employs hinder any individualizing tendencies. Bettina Matthias contends, "Sobald sich Individualität oder Persönlichkeit, vor allem in Form von Schwäche, ausdrücken, greifen vorgegebene Sprachmuster und holen den Monolog wieder zurück in die geordneten Bahnen fast endlos fortsetzbarer Phrasen."[53] Gustl regains dialogic speech and visual attention to those around him only when conditions allow the illusion of being a subject to recur. He perceives as little at the end of the narrative as at the beginning. In this respect, he remains mute and blind, in ironic contradiction to the healing of the blind Saul in Felix Mendelssohn Bartoldy's (1809–1847) oratorio *Paulus* (1836), which Gustl attends at the beginning of the narrative.[54]

Schnitzler reworks this problem of vision and control much later in *Fräulein Else* as a question of voyeurism. A voyeur is someone who tries to gain mastery over another through observing the other's naked body, usually in secret, and is usually ascribed a male role.[55] According to Dorothy Kelly, who refers to Sigmund Freud's theories of voyeurism, the voyeur looks to assuage fears of effeminate passivity by checking whether the observed woman's body is different from his own, but he also looks because of a secret desire to be feminine, a desire he denies by seeking confirmation of his masculinity. Thus his scoptophilic instinct is a product of gender uncertainty.[56] In Schnitzler's novella, the voyeuristic object is complicit in her own "feminization." Else is also a victim of social forces, locked in an interior monologue. However, she attains more insight than Gustl and also achieves a sense of agency in an impossible situation — that is, when the only way she can obtain money to repay her father's debts is to pose naked for her father's acquaintance, Herr Dorsday.

Similar to Gustl, Else embodies both the observing subject and the observed, but the struggle is different. While Gustl strove to assert his role as subject of the gaze, Else looks at others only to check if her visual effect on them corresponds to that of her internalized, objectifying eye.[57] They serve her as mirrors. She uses others to confirm her own status as object. As the unmarried daughter in an assimilated Jewish bourgeois family, she takes pains to appear desirable and to keep her Jewish heritage unnoticeable.[58]

She and Dorsday share voyeuristic tendencies. He desires to watch her unclothed, while she constantly observes how others react to her. Her every move and word appear calculated to achieve an effect, to mask her unease at being someone who needs a good match in order to maintain her standard of living. Dorsday's voyeurism also discloses his shaky position as observer. He can assert his "male" controlling look only covertly. He is also caught up in a struggle over visual effect. As an assimilated Jew, he still occupies a feminized position in Viennese culture, where, as Sander Gilman has documented, circumcision was regarded as making Jewish men like women and where theories that Jewish men spoke in high voices were used to further question their virility.[59] Dorsday's lack of success at disguising his Jewish heritage implies that he does not monitor his appearance as Else does hers. Viewed against the background of such prejudices against the Jews and anxieties over changing gender roles in Viennese society, Dorsday's recourse to voyeurism fits the stereotype of a man uncertain of his own sexuality, staring secretly at a woman in order to reassure himself of his masculinity.[60]

While Else surveys herself in relation to her surroundings, she still operates under the illusion that she can manipulate her objectification to achieve a kind of passive control over those gazing at her, for she can see her beauty confirmed only in the appreciative glances of men whom she finds attractive.[61] However, when placed in the dilemma of having to expose herself to Dorsday, whose affectations repel her, in order to obtain a loan for her father, who is in dire financial straits, Else risks losing her sense of control. In this situation, Dorsday, not Else, would be the one setting the stage for her display of beauty. In addition, Dorsday's proposition does not correspond to her romantic ideas of passion. His gaze would parody the image of desirability she strives to create, as Naomi Segal asserts.[62] Yet Dorsday's eyes have an "almost hypnotic effect" on her, and she experiences an erotic thrill at her impending self-exposure.[63] Because she is unable to express verbally her conflicting emotions and desires, she feels her only recourse to self-expression is in the visual realm by publicly exposing herself. As Lorna Martens argues, "Else's psychological conflicts center on her femaleness, hence her body."[64] Ironically, her strongest act is to make herself a passive object of visual titillation. By fainting after she bares her body, she displays her mute feminine position and blinds herself from registering the reactions of others. Her de-animated body merely reflects the stares of the onlookers.[65]

Else's decision to deprive Dorsday of his private viewing yet to fulfill his request to "see" her anyway is her way of managing her status as beautiful spectacle. What she does not perceive, however, is that she is caught up in a social structure that prevents her from breaking out of her role as voyeuristic object. Unlike Cassatt's woman in the loge, she cannot even conceive of alternative ways of seeing. Only when she lies dying with her eyes closed, completely exposed to others, does she sense the futility of her "revolt." Her act of agency has made her an object of scandal and pity. And her doubled objectification, through her own eyes and through society's, implies a total lack of subjectivity. In contrast to Justina and Cäcilia, she cannot voice her indignation. Her inability to communicate shows, in the words of Ulrike Weinhold, "daß Else realiter in der Rolle der Schweigenden steckenbleibt."[66] This silence opens her up to probing glances that nevertheless cannot penetrate beneath the skin. While the reader sees the tensions arising from the double exposure of Else's body and thoughts, the figure herself attempts to elude all gazes, including her own internalized one, by neither speaking nor looking. If her eyes are closed then she cannot see, and, according to her logic, she cannot really be seen. Thus her death is her own act to leave behind the visual field in which she is trapped.[67] It is the logical consequence of "her status as object of vision, power, and possession."[68]

Traumnovelle reweaves themes from Schnitzler's previous works to offer a glimpse of feminized figures who go even further to achieve a voice and a gaze of their own. The dangers inherent in this attainment and the damage it does to the male psyche almost destroy the main characters. Yet, this later narrative also offers glimpses of a different kind of perception that does not trap figures in the hierarchy of observer and observed. The desire and release of desire intimately bound to these roles complicate the loosening of their grip on the mindset of the characters, especially on Fridolin, the threatened husband.

While Fridolin is astounded that his wife, Albertine, expresses sexual desire for other men (for a Danish officer, for example), just as Cyprian was with Justina, he is the one who increasingly becomes a spectacle as he withdraws into himself and plays over in his mind imagined scenes of Albertine and the officer in bed. As his masculine self-identity falters, images of dying men or men in danger increase, as do those of mysterious female figures of all ages and social classes. Fridolin projects his loss of a sense of controlling masculinity onto the figures he encounters. The different stages on his journey to rediscover his identity all revolve around sight and looking.

The problem of the gaze appears in the first paragraph, as Fridolin and Albertine's daughter reads a fairy tale about a prince alone under the night sky. She falls asleep just as she reads the words "und sein Blick — ,"[69] but when her father closes her book, "Das Kind sah auf wie ertappt,"[70] thus coming to consciousness under the power of the male gaze.[71] Yet, the mother is also watching them both, and her presence draws the father's attention back to her, "und mit zärtlichem Lächeln, das nun nicht mehr dem Kinde allein galt, begegneten sich ihre Blicke."[72] The motifs of sleeping and waking combine with that of looking to introduce the recasting in the novella of the viewer/viewed duality as related to being awake or conscious. Through visual metaphors the novella shows how the male figure is awakened from his complacent position of authority and forced to acknowledge the real strength of the woman character's position and subjectivity.

The male and female positions appear at first on an equal level, for both parents exchange glances with each other. Both seem at first to be self-aware, but as the narrative progresses, Fridolin is the one whose gaze needs to be readjusted. Only after Albertine's and his confessions that each has lusted after someone else does the conventional hierarchy of their position as watcher or watched come into view. Albertine shows that like a man she too surveys others for their sexual desirability. Specifically, while on vacation with her husband she saw a Danish officer, who became the object of her fantasies and of her furtive, admiring glances, without apparent knowledge of her desire. Fridolin's shock at his wife's heretofore unexpressed sexual longings cannot be assuaged by his own confession about a fifteen-year-old Danish girl he found appealing during a morning walk. The sudden interrupting announcement that a male patient of Fridolin has just suffered a heart attack and needs urgent care parallels Fridolin's wounded pride and need to "cure" himself of his slipping status at the top of the male/female hierarchy of libidinous control.

The attempts to regain his lost sense of male superiority push him further into a subordinate role. Significantly, the women Fridolin encounters become increasingly powerful, although often childlike, a reflection of his own childlike psychological position. Marianne, the daughter of the heart-attack victim, for example, cannot engage him in any meaningful looks and maintains a submissive posture. Yet, her obvious longing for him exerts an attraction that makes it difficult to leave her. The prostitute Mizzi is more self-confident, yet still playing the role of erotic object by undressing before him. This encounter happens after he has met and then yielded to the gaze of a fraternity student who bumped into him, causing him to wonder whether he is a coward, or in other words, whether he is still manly. His initial diffidence toward Mizzi, his refusal to play his role of erotic gazer, causes her to stop her game, dress, and converse with him. His subsequent attempt to seduce her fails because he has allowed himself to exchange looks and words with her. Once again, speech interferes with illusion and interrupts the erotic power of the objectifying gaze.

The eyes of his old friend Nachtigall, which bore into him after he enters a café, stress the role reversal he has undergone, for he is now the object of penetrating looks. His eagerness to participate in the erotic, secretive meeting that Nachtigall describes is a chance to regain his male role, for Nachtigall informs him that naked women will be present — women who are offering themselves to the power of the voyeuristic gaze. His ensuing adventure at the costume shop, under the stare of the owner's mentally disturbed, sexually precocious daughter, arouses and frightens him, but also makes him feel protective of the girl. He experiences both a renewed sense of control and a fear of losing it.

However, the climactic masked ball stages Fridolin's complete objectification. He is the object of men's and women's voyeuristic stares and speaks only in response to their questions. He is powerless yet also excited in his weak position. The masked woman whom he admires appears to know more about him than can be explained. Indeed, the whole society appears to know him and judge him harshly. The paranoid atmosphere of this secret meeting hints at danger. That danger is psychological, for it threatens to destroy completely his attempts to regain his position as subject of the penetrating gaze. Fridolin at this point still measures masculine value in terms of dominating the feminine. In Eric Santner's words, "What makes Fridolin so unsuited for this game is his impulse to possess in an absolute way the woman he desires."[73] This sterile, erotic adventure, which involved only looking, no action, pales in comparison to Albertine's later dream of having sex with the Dane and watching Fridolin be crucified for his loyalty. While she can articulate her desires to him and thus integrate them into her consciousness, he remains mute about his, still in their thrall.[74]

As a doctor, he is used to making decisions based on observation, but empirical knowledge is of little help here, as it also did little for Dr. Copus in *Paracelsus*. Fridolin has become like the young women and girls he gazed upon. Albertine is the one who exercises authority in her questions to him and in her forgiving look at him. Yet, he fears her unfathomable wishes because they are not under his control; they are not meant to attract his looks. Albertine observes him while knowing things that he does not, just as the masked ball participants did. He is the object of her "voyeuristic" gaze. After his attempts to revoke this role reversal fail, his leave-taking from the corpse of the figure he believes to be the masked woman from the ball becomes an adieu to his previous objectifying gaze.[75] He seeks atonement from her dead eyes and from his own paralysis at not being able to articulate his fears and desires, in not being able to see beyond his misconceptions. And he discovers that in all the unknown faces he observed, "ununterbrochen seine Gattin als die Frau vor Augen geschwebt war."[76] Only after he has been able to tell everything to Albertine does he begin to see again,[77] but the conclusion implies this resolution is only temporary. The woman observer, Albertine, turns out to be the one most in control of her speech and field of vision. Fridolin regains his speech and redirects his sight from a strict focus on possession to an exchange of looks, with Albertine as his model. However, as with many of Schnitzler's tales, this reciprocity is under threat from half-conscious impulses that can cloud vision and silence speech, that can make for a "gefährliche Dynamisierung der Beziehung."[78]

These four examples reveal recurring attempts in Schnitzler's work to grasp the uncertainties of modern subjectivity as a problem of vision and voice. Speech as "true" expression of half-conscious desires allows for a subject stance that may or may not be coded as masculine or feminine. Paracelsus is forced to recognize the physicality and thus instability of the objects in his field of vision after Justina speaks up, Cäcilie rejects him, and Anselm flees. As their roles change, so must his. Gustl, on the other hand, remains trapped within his illusion of masculine bravado, unable to perceive how anachronistic his way of seeing has become and how much his position has shifted toward the feminine he strives to objectify. By having Else become mute and blind as self-punishment for her brief revolt against her visual commodification, the narrative stresses the isolating effect of the "feminine" manner of observation inculcated in her. On a more utopian note, Fridolin learns from Albertine to express himself and to accept that each of them has aspects that elude the other's purview. He is compelled to abandon his domineering gaze for one like hers, at least for a while.

Different ways of seeing, then, show a clash between idealized notions of stability and shifting experiences of the gendered self. Gender also affects sight. There is a tension between looking as an emancipating act, watching in order to control, and observing oneself as a strategy of conformity. The narratives reveal an increasing insecurity about masculine gender roles combined with an inability to act — thus the need for an illusion of acting to preserve a semblance of masculine control. However, the weakening of the male observer does not mean that the female observer fills his vacant role. Nor is the female position necessarily objectified. Rather, the positions of the observer and observed alternate between each other and within themselves, thereby exceeding notions of a purely masculine or a feminine gaze. These literary selections thus evince the complexity of Schnitzler's engagement with questions of gender and subjectivity and link his ideas to other explorations of modern visual culture in the arts, philosophy, and science of his time.

Notes

[1] See Andreas Huyssen, "The Disturbance of Vision in Vienna Modernism," in *Modernisms/Modernity* 5/3 (1998): 33–47 for more on Schnitzler within the context of *fin-de-siècle* Viennese visual culture. Huyssen also analyzes Hofmannsthal's "Brief der Lord Chandos" ("Letter to Lord Chandos," 1902) and "Das Märchen der 672. Nacht" ("The Tale of the 672nd Night," 1895) as well as Musil's essay "Triëdere" ("Binoculars," 1926).

[2] See John Berger, "Ralph Fasanella and the Experience of the City," in *About Looking,* by Berger (New York: Pantheon, 1980), 46–47.

[3] *Paracelsus* in DW I, 465–98; *Leutnant Gustl* in ES I, 337–66; *Fräulein Else* and *Traumnovelle* in ES II, 324–81, 434–504.

[4] Griselda Pollock, *Vision and Difference: Femininity, Feminism, and Histories of Art* (New York: Routledge, 1988), 70.

[5] See Pollock; John Berger, *Ways of Seeing* (London: BBC and Penguin, 1988), 36–64.

[6] *Ways of Seeing,* 79.

[7] Jonathan Crary, *Techniques of the Observer: On Vision and Modernity in the Nineteenth Century* (Cambridge, MA: MIT Press, 1992), 127–32; see also Dagmar Lorenz, *Wiener Moderne* (Stuttgart: Metzler, 1995), 103–7.

[8] Crary, 215–21.

[9] Lisa Tickner, "Men's Work? Masculinity and Modernism," in *Visual Culture: Images and Interpretations,* ed. Norman Bryson, Michael Ann Holly, and Keith Moxey (Hanover, NH: Wesleyan UP, 1994), 44.

[10] Jonathan Crary, *Suspensions of Perception: Attention, Spectacle, and Modern Culture* (Cambridge, MA: MIT Press, 1999), 74–75.

[11] Crary, *Suspensions,* 69.

[12] See Crary, *Suspensions,* 235; François Roustang, *Influence* (Paris: Editions de Minuit, 1990), 84; Jean-Luc Nancy, *The Birth to Presence,* trans. Brian Holmes (Stanford: Stanford UP, 1993), 15–23.

[13] See Horst Thomé, "Vorwort," in Schnitzler, *Medizinische Schriften,* ed. Thomé (Vienna: Paul Zsolnay Verlag, 1988), 11–59.

[14] Schnitzler, *Medizinische Schriften,* 184, 208. Schnitzler's work on the treatment of aphonia through hypnosis originally appeared as "Über funktionelle Aphonie und deren Behandlung durch Hypnose und Suggestion" in *Internationale Klinische Rundschau* 3 (1889).

[15] *Medizinische Schriften,* 184.

[16] *Medizinische Schriften,* 200, 208.

[17] *Medizinische Schriften,* 199, 206.

[18] For more on Schnitzler's concept of the half-conscious, see Laura Otis, "The Language of Infection: Disease and Identity in Schnitzler's *Reigen,*" *Germanic Review* 70/2 (1995): 73, and *Membranes: Metaphors of Invasion in Nineteenth-Century Literature, Science, and Politics* (Baltimore: Johns Hopkins UP, 1999), 146. Likewise see Walter Müller-Seidel, *Arztbilder im Wandel: Zum literarischen Werk Arthur Schnitzlers* (Munich: Verlag der Bayerischen Akademie der Wissenschaften, 1997), 39, and Claudio Magris, "Arthur Schnitzler und das Karussell der Triebe," in *Arthur Schnitzler in neuer Sicht,* ed. Hartmut Scheible (Munich: Fink, 1981), 74.

[19] DW I, 467.

[20] See Gunter Selling, *"Paracelsus,"* in *Die Einakter und Einakterzyklen Arthur Schnitzlers* (Amsterdam: Rodopi, 1975), 42.

[21] Felix W. Tweraser, *Political Dimensions of Arthur Schnitzler's Late Fiction* (Columbia, SC: Camden House, 1998), 103.

[22] DW I, 480.

[23] See Otis, *Membranes,* 123–24. As Laura Otis explains, such theories include French physician Hippolyte Bernheim's (1840–1919) assertions that unwilling subjects

could not be hypnotized unless convinced "they were in the hands of a superior power"; Swiss psychiatrist August Forel's (1848–1931) idea that a resisting subject could not be hypnotized unless "taken by surprise"; or American physician John Kearsley Mitchell's (1798–1858) and Spanish neurohistologist Santiago Ramon y Cajal's (1852–1934) views that a strong will was "a defense mechanism against pernicious suggestions from without" (123–24).

[24] DW I, 473.

[25] DW I, 476.

[26] See also Jenneke A. Oosterhoff, *Die Männer sind infam, solang sie Männer sind: Konstruktionen der Männlichkeit in den Werken Arthur Schnitzlers* (Tübingen: Stauffenburg, 2000), 231.

[27] DW I, 477.

[28] Michaela L. Perlmann, *Arthur Schnitzler* (Stuttgart: Metzler, 1987), 45.

[29] DW I, 481.

[30] See Marianne Dekoven, "Modernism and Gender," in *The Cambridge Companion to Modernism,* ed. Michael Levenson (Cambridge: Cambridge UP, 1999), 174–93.

[31] Crary, *Suspensions,* 236.

[32] DW I, 495.

[33] DW I, 498.

[34] Dekoven, 183.

[35] See also Herbert Lederer, "Afterword," in Schnitzler, *Paracelsus and Other One-Act Plays,* trans. G. J. Weinberger (Riverside: Ariadne, 1995), 218; Franz Baumer, *Arthur Schnitzler* (Berlin: Colloquium, 1992), 65. On the disorienting effects of the modern city, see John Tagg, "The Discontinuous City: Picturing and the Discursive Field," in *Visual Culture,* 83–103. As Schnitzler's early modern Basel resembles modern Vienna, it is important to note Tagg's assertion that the modern city was the privileged site of a "new economy of sexual difference" (84).

[36] Thomé, 50–51.

[37] Laermann means that Gustl uses the force of his look to compete with other men for power over women and in society. Klaus Laermann, "Leutnant Gustl," in *Arthur Schnitzler: Zur Diagnose des Wiener Bürgertums im Fin de siècle,* ed. Rolf-Peter Janz and Laermann (Stuttgart: Metzler, 1977), 122.

[38] ES I, 339.

[39] See also Crary, *Suspensions,* 4, 65.

[40] See Susan Fillin Yeh, "Mary Cassatt's Images of Women," *Art Journal* 35/4 (1976): 359–63; see also Gustav Klimt's painting *Zuschauerraum im alten Burgtheater* (1888). Bram Dijkstra emphasizes that there was an intense exchange of imagery between *fin-de-siècle* writers and painters. Dijkstra, *Idols of Perversity: Fantasies of Feminine Evil in Fin-de-Siècle Culture* (New York: Oxford UP, 1986), 150.

[41] Cassatt painted several theater scenes, including *In the Box* (1879), *Woman with a Pearl Necklace in a Loge* (1879), *At the Theatre* (1879), and *The Loge* (1882), depicting, in the words of Yeh, "a new type of female, the one who participates in cultural events" (360), or showing, as Pollock wrote in *Mary Cassatt: Painter of*

Modern Women (New York: Thames & Hudson, 1998), "self-confident New Women at the matinée" (145). Linda Nochlin writes in *Representing Women* (New York: Thames & Hudson, 1999) about the woman in black's "assertive visual thrust into space" in *In the Loge* (194).

[42] See also Kaja Silverman, "Fassbinder and Lacan: A Reconsideration of Gaze, Look, and Image," in *Visual Culture*, 272–302. Silverman claims about a scene from German director Rainer Werner Fassbinder's motion picture *Warnung vor einer heiligen Nutte* (*Beware of a Holy Whore*, 1971) that "The turning back of the look upon itself — the mimicry on the part of the camera of a scopic drive made suddenly to go 'backward' — also suggests its inability both to reach and to subjugate its object and so inverts the usual scopic paradigm" (278).

[43] ES I, 337.

[44] ES I, 342.

[45] ES I, 344.

[46] See also Oosterhoff, 62–63; Laermann, 114, 119.

[47] Berger, *Ways*, 45–47.

[48] Berger, *Ways*, 47; see also Otis, "Language," 131–34.

[49] Evelyne Polt-Heinzl, *Erläuterungen und Dokumente: Arthur Schnitzler: Leutnant Gustl* (Stuttgart: Reclam, 2000), 84.

[50] ES I, 345.

[51] ES I, 365.

[52] See Katherine Arens, "Schnitzler and Characterology: From Empire to Third Reich," *Modern Austrian Literature* 19/3–4 (1986): 97–127.

[53] Bettina Matthias, *Masken des Lebens, Gesichter des Todes: Zum Verhältnis von Tod und Darstellung im erzählerischen Werk Arthur Schnitzlers* (Würzburg: Königshausen & Neumann, 1999), 119.

[54] Erich Kaiser, *Arthur Schnitzler: Leutnant Gustl und andere Erzählungen* (Munich: Oldenbourg, 1997), 52.

[55] Dorothy Kelly, *Telling Glances: Voyeurism and the French Novel* (New Brunswick, NJ: Rutgers UP, 1992), 7–11 and 34–36.

[56] Kelly, 37–39. Kelly explains: "The voyeur's scenario negotiates conflict: it represents both the male desire to be feminine (the pleasure of his femininity is repeated in the voyeuristic act) along with his fear of being feminine and his desire not to be feminine (he puts the female victim in her place and feels the pleasure of reasserting his masculinity in his active viewing and mastering of the unsuspecting female)" (39).

[57] See also Rolf Allerdissen, *Arthur Schnitzler: Impressionistisches Rollenspiel und skeptischer Moralismus in seinen Erzählungen* (Bonn: Grundmann, 1985).

[58] See Andrew Barker, "Race, Sex, and Character in Schnitzler's *Fräulein Else*," *German Life and Letters* 54/1 (2001): 1–9.

[59] Sander L. Gilman, *Sexuality: An Illustrated History Representing the Sexual in Medicine and Culture from the Middle Ages to the Age of AIDS* (New York: John Wiley, 1989). "According to European anti-Semitism, as has been discussed, Jews show their inherent difference through their damaged sexuality, and the sign of that

is, in the popular mind, the fact that their males menstruate" (265), Gilman writes. With regard to the gender ambivalence attributed to Jews he maintains: "For the late nineteenth-century view associated the act of religious circumcision with the act of castration, the unmanning, the feminizing of the Jew in the act of making him a Jew" (265). Finally, he notes that "male Jews are feminized and signal this feminization through their discourse. . . . With the use of the cracked voice of the Jew, Jewish thinkers may indicate the force that the persecution of the Jew had in forming the Jew's sexual identity" (267).

[60] Kelly, 39.

[61] See also Siew Lian Yeo, "'Entweder oder': Dualism in Schnitzler's Fräulein Else," *Modern Austrian Literature* 32/2 (1999): 19.

[62] Naomi Segal, "Style indirect libre to Stream-of-Consciousness: Flaubert, Joyce, Schnitzler, Woolf," in *Modernism and the European Unconscious,* eds. Peter Collier and Judy Davies (Cambridge: Polity Press, 1990), 104.

[63] Eva Kuttenberg, "The Tropes of Suicide in Arthur Schnitzler's Prose" (Ph.D. diss., New York University, 1998), 201.

[64] Lorna Martens, "Naked Bodies in Schnitzler's Late Prose Fiction," in *Die Seele . . . ist ein weites Land: Kritische Beiträge zum Werk Arthur Schnitzlers,* ed. Joseph P. Strelka (New York: Peter Lang, 1996), 124.

[65] Andrea Allerkamp, "' . . . Ich schreibe ja keine Memoiren': Über die ars memoriae als Spiel zwischen Bild und Text in Schnitzlers *Fräulein Else,*" *Cahiers d'Etudes Germaniques* 29 (1995): 106.

[66] Ulrike Weinhold, "Arthur Schnitzler und der weibliche Diskurs: Zur Problematik des Frauenbildes der Jahrhundertwende," *Jahrbuch für Internationale Germanistik* 19/1 (1987): 122.

[67] See Susan Anderson, "Seeing Blindly: Voyeurism in Schnitzler's *Fräulein Else* and Andreas-Salomé's *Fenitschka,*" in *Die Seele . . . ist ein weites Land,* 13–27.

[68] Elisabeth Bronfen, "Rigor has Set in — the Wasted Bride," in *Over Her Dead Body: Death, Femininity, and the Aesthetic,* by Bronfen (New York: Routledge, 1992), 285.

[69] ES II, 434.

[70] ES II, 434.

[71] W. G. Sebald, "Das Schrecknis der Liebe: Zu Schnitzlers *Traumnovelle,*" in *Die Beschreibung des Unglücks: Zur Österreichischen Literatur von Stifter bis Handke,* by Sebald (Vienna: Residenz, 1985), 42.

[72] ES II, 434.

[73] Eric L. Santner, "Of Masters, Slaves, and Other Seducers: Arthur Schnitzler's *Traumnovelle,*" *Modern Austrian Literature* 19/3–4 (1986): 39. See also Frederic Raphael, who interprets Fridolin's insecurities as typical of the way Austrian Jews felt at the time and as evidence that he is Jewish, even though this is not stated in the narrative. Raphael sees Fridolin's eviction from the masked ball as connected to his monk costume, which "means that, in disguise, he has chosen to cross the line between Jews and Catholics" (xv). Raphael claims the masked woman, in rescuing Fridolin, "becomes in a sense, more manly than he is allowed, or dares to be" (xiv).

Raphael, "Introduction," *Dream Story* by Arthur Schnitzler, trans. J. M. Q. Davies (New York: Penguin, 1999), v–xvii.

[74] See also Guiseppe Farese, *Arthur Schnitzler: Ein Leben in Wien 1862–1931,* trans. Karin Krieger (Munich: Beck, 1999), 267–68.

[75] See also Michael Scheffel, *Formen selbstreflexiven Erzählens: Eine Typologie und sechs exemplarische Analysen* (Tübingen: Niemeyer, 1997), 45.

[76] ES II, 497.

[77] Scheffel, 191–92.

[78] Wolfgang Lukas, *Das Selbst und das Fremde: Epochale Lebenskrisen und ihre Lösungen im Werk Arthur Schnitzlers* (Munich: Fink, 1996), 211.

Suicide as Performance in Dr. Schnitzler's Prose

Eva Kuttenberg

> *Auch der Selbstmord wird eine*
> *sinnlose Sache, wenn man keinem*
> *Menschen mehr dadurch einen*
> *Schmerz bereitet. Dies erst heißt*
> *sich völlig ins Nichts stürzen.*[1]

I DON'T WANT TO DIE. I WANT NOT TO BE,"[2] wrote the Russian poet Marina Tsvetaeva, who voluntarily ended her life in 1941. Her statement most succinctly describes the mindset of select Arthur Schnitzler characters who are torn between an intensified wish to live and the simultaneous impossibility of doing so.

By definition, the study of suicidal phenomena — suicidology — is an interdisciplinary field of inquiry drawing on sociology, medicine, psychology, and literature, as well as other sources. Despite lively scholarly debates in psychiatry, psychoanalysis, and psychology, suicide remains an enigma. Sigmund Freud's cautious yet inconclusive understanding of suicide as a multidimensional phenomenon still holds true.[3] His contemporary, Schnitzler — physician by training and writer by passion, equally well versed in human anatomy, psyche, and language — endows suicide with new meaning by reading the willful absence from life as an act of performance ending an ill-balanced process of self-construction. Additionally, he challenges the prevailing late-nineteenth-century myth, created in fiction, that primarily women committed suicide to escape a bourgeois social order; he designs several countermodels, male characters of all walks of life who deliberately opt for self-murder. In the 1960s, the suicide researchers Norman Farberow and Edwin Shneidman practiced psychological autopsy[4] as a method to differentiate suicide, murder, accident, and natural death; Schnitzler had already adopted this technique as an aesthetic strategy to design an impressively broad spectrum of suicide plots. Typically, his suicidal characters are social drifters who consciously or subconsciously act as if they were living corpses, given their social, ethnic, financial, professional, or artistic status, and they often seek a way out of abusive relationships.

Although suicide is a key motif in Schnitzler's works, neither the distinguished Viennese Psychoanalytic Society nor suicidologists (except for Erwin Ringel) have read his literary works to broaden their perspectives, traditionally based on specific case studies. Similarly, literary critics only sporadically explore suicide as an aesthetic strategy, which is somewhat surprising, at least for Margaret Higonnet, who argues that voluntary death invites immediate interpretation;[5] however, the inevitable blurring of fact and fiction tempts the reader to mistake the latter for the former. Jean Améry sees Schnitzler's sophisticated blend as a major asset of his fictional suicide scenarios.[6]

In contrast to existing cultural readings of suicide as a symbolic act in the context of gender, ethnicity, nationality, or a historical period, Schnitzler prefers an all-encompassing larger perspective that invites multiple interpretations.[7] The approach that stands out as his most provocative and sophisticated is that of plotting suicide as performance — a strategy he rehearsed throughout his work and brought to completion in his posthumously published drama *Zug der Schatten* (1970) when the actress Franzi Friesel seamlessly makes her suicide part of a dramatic scene on stage.[8] The drama reads like a shorthand version of his aesthetic program for suicide plots: first settling the question of genre — drama or prose; then fleshing out theoretical concepts. Characters metaphorically announce their intent; sketch a quick self-portrait in the mirror; add drama with accessories such as letters, flowers, and music; swiftly change from body to corpse; and are finally attacked for their lack of discipline as they challenged systems of authority by committing suicide.

In prose works his aesthetic scheme follows a three-part structure that consists of an audition, rehearsals, and an opening night arranged as public, semiprivate, and private affairs. Auditions take place in a variety of public spaces and casually introduce characters who quickly engage in verbal or visual rehearsals for their meticulously planned opening night. Suicide as a performance relies on a script that for Schnitzler is either the female body or a suicide note, typically written by a male author. Anticipating clinical observations of two British psychoanalysts, the contemporary Freudians Peter Fonagy and Mary Target, Schnitzler's female characters (unlike Fonagy's male patients) use their bodies to stage the mental drama[9] and their narrative voices to eloquently articulate disintegration. Schnitzler adds sophisticated stage instructions in reference to postures, gestures, or fashion for flamboyant acts of self-presentation. Performance also requires a cast and an audience, and thus splits self-conscious actors into simultaneous spectators and commentators who excel at role-playing and escape social-moral taboos by living out their fantasies. Characters continuously assume and reject socially assigned personae, which become arbitrary images of themselves. By doing so, however, they mistake a narrowing set of possibilities for a myriad of opportunities and fail to realize that their temporary survival strategies are actually fatal traps. Every effort to stage their grand entrance only brings them closer to staging their grand finale. Their impressive inventory of self-defense mechanisms helps them postpone but not avoid the inevitable. Eric L. Santner aptly reads Schnitzler's characters as devoted "hunger artists" who re-engineer their miseries without ever breaking free.[10] Voluntary death marks the end of their performance that traps them in a tightly woven cocoon.

Although suicide is ubiquitous in Schnitzler's plays, prose fiction, diaries, aphorisms, biography, and letters, which immediately dismisses the idea that he preferred a specific literary genre for the topic, there is no clear evidence, short of a detailed examination of his letters and dream diary, that he sought refuge in aesthetics to redirect his own suicidal thoughts. Undoubtedly, he was genuinely interested in secularizing the taboo act, mapping its paradoxical ambiguity, and making its duplicity transparent. Historically, Western societies have regarded suicide as a crime from a legal perspective and a sin from a moral perspective, and as an act of great defiance, primarily in the Jewish and Christian traditions. As opposed to philosophy and ethics that grant suicide victims a continuous presence in abstract debates, Schnitzler at times pragmatically includes self-destruction in a fictional murder plot. Without advocating a particular psychoanalytic school or intending to create his own, he cautions against a typology of suicide by not arranging character traits like symptoms and avoiding predictable narrative patterns, such as either ending or beginning his plots on the note of suicide. On the contrary, the act can occur at any given moment in the text, and is performed without witnesses yet in close proximity to an audience. He continuously revised his theories, which forces the critic not only to carefully examine every scenario but also to compare it against countermodels. The inversion of *Fräulein Else* is the depiction of the male love slave in *Spiel im Morgengrauen* (1927), whereas *Der Letzte Brief eines Literaten* is a reversal of the situation in *Der Empfindsame* (1932), a novella in which a female singer gets involved with a young man to regain artistic acclaim. The lover functions as a kind of prescription drug, and once his services are no longer needed, the singer leaves him and embarks on her career.

For Schnitzler suicide is not an act of heroism, martyrdom, morbid celebration of utmost creativity, or a spectacle. His literary imagination

lags behind theatrical scenarios of prominent Viennese artists and intellectuals, as in the case of the twenty-five-year-old painter Richard Gerstl,
who, in 1908, "first set fire to most of the contents of his studio, then
put a noose around his neck, and, in front of the mirror he had used for
his self-portraits, plunged a butcher knife into his heart."[11] The philosopher and psychologist Otto Weininger (1880–1903) proceeded in a
similar dramatic fashion, renting a room in the house where Ludwig van
Beethoven had died and then shooting himself. Equally prominent yet
less spectacular were the suicides of three of Ludwig Wittgenstein's
brothers; the physicist Ludwig Boltzmann (1844–1906); Georg Trakl
(1887–1914); the poet Ferdinand von Saar (1833–1906); Colonel Alfred Redl (1864–1913); Crown Prince Rudolf (1858–1889); and Baron-
ess Maria Vetsera (1871–1889), to name but a few.[12] As Ringel points
out, this Viennese reality found its echo in literary works and inspired
Marie von Ebner-Eschenbach's (1830–1916) suicide plots in *Das tägli-
che Leben* (1910) and *Der Vorzugsschüler* (1900); Jakob Wassermann's
(1873–1934) in *Laudin und die Seinen* (1925); and Friedrich Torberg's
(1908–1979) in *Der Schüler Gerber* (1930).[13]

Besides these prominent and fictional cases, hundreds of ordinary
citizens of all ages, social classes, and educational backgrounds took their
lives. According to reports in the *Neue Freie Presse,* the suicide rate in
Vienna climbed from 330 cases in 1892 to 452 in 1904. In July 1895,
the liberal newspaper even spoke of a "Hochsaison der Donauleichen"
and announced financial rewards for pulling corpses out of the Danube.
On a daily basis it briefly listed suicide attempts and suicides, without
shying away from moral judgments. The paper actually used expressions
such as "rueful suicide" when a person survived an attempt. One cannot
help noticing striking parallels with Schnitzler's plots. Reading his work
as straight reportage or as a coping mechanism for personal crisis, however, would fall short of actually understanding suicide as process instead
of mere content in his fiction. What drives his plots is a meticulous description of the mindset of the individual deliberately and desperately
announcing, and thereby simultaneously delaying, the symbolic act.

A note in Schnitzler's autobiography in 1884 confirms how much
the taboo act had become a fact of turn-of-the-century life. In a coffeehouse discussion, he vehemently argued for man's fundamental right to
end his life at any given moment without taking into consideration the
concerns of others, only to quickly and apologetically add that he might
have merely spoken for the sake of argument.[14] When brought into
historical perspective, however, his spontaneously shared and daring take
on suicide dates back to audacious European thinkers of the sixteenth

through the eighteenth centuries. Among them, David Hume and his essay "Of Suicide" (1757) may be best known.[15]

Linguistic and intellectual kinship with the secular humanist Georg Christoph Lichtenberg (1742–1799), whose ideas experienced a revival among *fin-de-siècle* intellectuals, also confirms Schnitzler's affinity with Enlightenment thought. Though Schnitzler does not explicitly refer to works of this highly original thinker, whom he mentions in his diary,[16] the eighteenth-century professor of natural philosophy expresses thoughts similar to Schnitzler's when he writes what may seem almost commonplace and claims that "Krankheiten der Seele können den Tod nach sich ziehen, und das kann Selbstmord werden."[17] Besides their dual interest in the sciences and humanities and their fascination with ironic and deceptive language, they shared nonjudgmental views on suicide that for both were as much a necessary aesthetic strategy as an attitude toward life. They emphasize its essential incomprehensibility and tie their arguments to universal figures who are notorious drifters between extremes. When Lichtenberg's tragicomic character Harlequin, for instance, sketched in *Sudelbücher,* weighs his options for how to kill himself, he deems tickling himself to death the only feasible one.[18] His hysterical laughter echoes in Schnitzler's *Fräulein Else* immediately after Else's public exposure.

Both authors deem suicide a fundamentally private act made public. Lichtenberg's witty aphorism, *Rede eines Selbstmörders,* poignantly renders the unsayable.[19] Delivering a suicide speech, as such, is impossible, because it forces the audience to instantly prevent the victim from carrying out the plan. Lichtenberg's title thus mocks speech as silence and anticipates Schnitzler's technique of interior monologue, in which seemingly unedited speech disguises carefully edited thought and restricts outside intervention to the character's imagination.

For both intellectuals, suicide is an act of speech, using body and language as preeminent tools to stage a performance. Moreover, Lichtenberg wonders about possible consequences if suicide victims could describe their motives rather than having them modified by survivors. Schnitzler instantly takes up his idea when subtly juxtaposing motive and subsequent interpretation by a survivor in *Der Letzte Brief eines Literaten.* Reviving Enlightenment thought in late-nineteenth- and early-twentieth-century fictional suicide scenarios is particularly important as, according to the suicide researcher Georges Minois, only in the Enlightenment did suicide slowly emerge from the ghetto of taboos and unnatural acts.[20] In doing so, Schnitzler moves beyond the mind-body split of Enlightenment thought and elaborates on issues of gender in reference to male and female self-fabrication and subsequent self-effacement.

Schnitzler's most productive years coincided with the beginning of systematic suicide research, spearheaded by Freud and by Emile Durkheim's seminal *Le Suicide* (1897).[21] Although Schnitzler quickly raised controversy as a writer, it was not until 1982 that he found national and international recognition as a suicidologist. While David Lester in *Suicide: A Guide to Information Sources*[22] still omits his name, Joanne Trautmann, author of *Literature and Medicine: An Annotated Bibliography,*[23] corrects this oversight and lists four of Schnitzler's works under the keyword "suicide," which is a modest yet promising beginning. In the same year, Ringel, the renowned Austrian postwar suicide expert and founder of the International Society for Suicide Prevention, finally grants Schnitzler a preeminent position in suicide research in his essay "Das Selbstmordproblem bei Schnitzler."[24] He compares Schnitzler's accomplishments in suicide analysis to Freud's in psychoanalysis, based on Schnitzler's thorough understanding of the presuicidal phenomenon and his ability to link suicide with language. Ringel argues that a failed or ill-fated conversation precedes every suicide, which makes sensitivity to every word imperative in suicide research. In a similar vein, two cultural critics and experts on the late nineteenth and early twentieth centuries, Allan Janik and Stephen Toulmin, deem the problem of communication the overarching theme in both Schnitzler's texts and Viennese society.[25]

Contrary to Anne Sexton's lines "suicides have a special language / Like carpenters they want to know *which* tools / They never ask *why* build,"[26] for Schnitzler, understanding the contingencies of voluntary death takes priority over selecting specific methods. The latter, nonetheless, are usually divided by gender, and a simple list illustrates the prominence of suicide in Schnitzler's prose fiction. His female characters opt for Veronal (*Fräulein Else*); leap from a staircase (Maria Ladenbauer in *Das neue Lied* [1905]); die of implied yet unconfirmed suicide (Mathilde Samodeski in *Die griechische Tänzerin* [1902]); hang themselves (Friederike in *Doktor Gräsler, Badearzt* [1917]); or drown (Frau Beate in *Frau Beate und Ihr Sohn* [1913] and Heinrich Bermann's lover in *Der Weg ins Freie* [1908]). His male victims also leap to their deaths (Martin Brand in *Mein Freund Ypsilon* [1889] and, most spectacularly, the organ player Banetti in *Die Fremde* [1902], who jumps from a church tower in such a way that his body lands, dramatically, next to a cross in the church cemetery) or hang themselves (Friedrich Roland in *Der Ehrentag* [1897]). Most frequently, however, male characters die of self-inflicted gunshot wounds (Fritz Platen in *Der Empfindsame,* Lieutenant Willi Kasda in *Das Spiel im Morgengrauen,* and Albert in *Die Fremde*). Fewer female than male victims die of unknown methods, such as Andreas Thameyer in *Andreas Thameyers Letzter Brief*

(1902), Gabriel in *Der tote Gabriel* (1907), Labinski in *Der Weg ins Freie*, Richard in *Therese. Chronik eines Frauenlebens* (1928), Anselmo Rigardi in *Abenteurernovelle* (1937), and Robert in *Flucht in die Finsternis* (1931). Traditionally suicides choose whatever is readily available to them: ropes, high places, rivers, guns, or pharmaceuticals.[27]

Schnitzler's fiction takes on a premonitory aspect when readers recall that on July 26, 1928, his beloved eighteen-year-old daughter, Lili, fatally shot herself in the chest with her husband's gun. Not even the master-mind of countless suicide plots could escape the stigma associated with this taboo act; he preferred Lili's suicide to be camouflaged in the media as an accident. Testimony to his grief beyond words is his aphorism that deems suicide meaningless if it does not inflict pain on survivors. Since this tragic loss occurred toward the end of Schnitzler's career as a writer, it did not affect the vast majority of his works, but it draws attention to a striking omission: the process of mourning a suicide victim. Thus his diary adds to an interesting continuum throughout his work when suicide is read as a process of self-construction and mourning as one of recon-struction. For Schnitzler, both are intimately bound to reading and writ-ing. His wordy diary entries on July 29, 30, and 31, 1928 not only unabashedly reveal his adversarial attitude toward funerals as rituals de-void of true meaning but also showcase his technique of using language for anesthetic purposes. Repetitious one-word utterances, typical in his prose fiction, such as Frau Beate's "Fort, fort, fort," echo in "Lili, Lili, Lili!"[28] At a superficial first glance, these mechanical repetitions are simply a cover-up for the emotion that paralyzes the survivor who is condemned to live. Looked at more closely, however, this technique mirrors the rehearsals and re-enactments in his fictional suicide scenarios.

The broken father systematically re-establishes Lili's presence by re-cording his dreams of postmortem imaginary encounters with her in addition to carefully organizing, reading, and commenting on her dia-ries, the passionate letters to her husband, Arnoldo Cappellini, and books from her library.[29] He complements this spiritual bond with a materialis-tic one by turning her room into a sanctuary and decorating it with memorabilia that previously appeared in dream passages of his prose fiction.[30] Lili's last photograph in a bathing suit evokes uncanny parallels to Else's suicide fantasy, in which the guests at her wake wear the same outfit. Schnitzler never judges his daughter for what she has done, but he desperately looks for hints as to her intent. Unmistakably, the father realizes his much-needed presence in the silent scream, "Warum war ich nicht da!"[31] The more Lili's suicide becomes an event of the past, the more his diary implies that he should not have mistaken her pathological blurring of fact and fiction for the capricious attitudes of a teenager. Her final words, *"Vorrei morir,"* leave no room for ambiguity.[32]

Suicide in Schnitzler's Literary Imagination

Schnitzler approaches suicide as a diagnostician who is less concerned with providing a cure than with transferring his skills to the critical reader, who gradually becomes a lay suicidologist sensitive to fatal traps that characters encounter when negotiating the self. In *Fräulein Else* and *Der Letzte Brief eines Literaten,* suicide is intimately linked to experiences of loss, abuse, and rejection. Traditional psychoanalysis argues that narcissism and possible identification with the lost or rejecting person heighten potential suicides' feelings of ambivalence, which they are no longer able to synthesize cohesively.

Positive narcissism enabling self-cohesion and negative narcissism working against it, distinctions drawn by the psychoanalyst André Green,[33] play an important role in Schnitzler's dramaturgy of self-effacement. Initially, his characters audition for their final performance, that is, suicide, in lobbies, on staircases, in dining rooms of grand hotels, or on dance floors of lavish ballrooms. Private and semiprivate rehearsals follow, such as suicide fantasies, daydreams, narcissistic encounters with mirror images, or self-critical evaluations of social or artistic success. Characters continuously create fictions of themselves and for that purpose resort to behavior patterns, dress styles, or creative ambitions; these are inhibiting instead of liberating, and accompanied by fears of mediocrity or failure. The rehearsals, in turn, lead to even more conflicting perceptions of their social, gendered, and artistic positions and eventually foreclose possible compromise. Else vehemently rejects the position assigned to her by the Viennese bourgeoisie, whereas the unnamed playwright in *Der Letzte Brief eines Literaten* can only conceive of the masterwork. Both scripts, that of Else's body and that of the writer, are made public.

Fräulein Else: Nobody's Body is No-Body

This dramatic prose fiction tells the story of young and beautiful Else, who is vacationing in a glamorous grand hotel in the Italian mountains when suddenly a fateful telegram from her mother urges her to save her family from bankruptcy. As instructed, she turns to the wealthy art dealer Dorsday, who offers financial compensation in exchange for contemplating her naked body, either in the privacy of his room or divinely clothed in moonlight. Torn between the prospect of being married off to the highest bidder or selling her body as a prop for a private spectacle, Else takes matters into her own hands and establishes her autonomy by killing herself. Denied her sexual fantasies of uniting with a thousand lovers, she in turn denies Dorsday his exclusive gaze and instead exposes herself in the crowded music room, then breaks down. Once she is taken to her room, she swallows a presumably lethal dose of Veronal.

Two feminist scholars, Elisabeth Bronfen and Astrid Lange-Kirchheim, have added new insights into *Fräulein Else*. Bronfen's essay "Rigor Has Set In — The Wasted Bride"[34] offers a theoretically informed feminist reading of the semiotics of Else's body. Most important, it raises the question of whether Dorsday's demand serves as merely a pretext or as the actual cause of Else's suicide, and thus inspires a new look at her existential crisis. She was born into impoverished privilege, and her family desperately tried to maintain a bourgeois lifestyle — an effort doomed to failure. From the outset, Else is the fifth wheel in terms of her sexual, class, and professional identity. In the midst of a casual tennis match where Schnitzler peculiarly enough has three people playing, Else suddenly decides to stop playing and applauds herself for her successful exit. She becomes painfully aware of her role as a chaperone when Dorsday suggests that a tennis racket may also be carried as a mere accessory. Her presence at the tennis match helps to cover up the illicit affair between her cousin Paul, a shy gynecologist, and his acquaintance Cissy, a wife and mother. While the structure of this particular tennis match illustrates Else's marginal position, it also functions as Schnitzler's most favored rhetorical strategy, that of casually staging the catastrophe as an aesthetic construct of deliberate randomness.

Undoubtedly, this opening scene functions as a rehearsal for Else's irrevocable decision that frees her from parental abuse and the rigid social codes of turn-of-the-century Viennese society. This freedom-seeker perceives wedlock as deadlock, and although she is ill prepared for an independent lifestyle, she resents marrying an older gentleman merely to ensure financial stability. She prefers suicide. In "Adoleszenz, Hysterie und Autorschaft in Arthur Schnitzler's Novelle *Fräulein Else*," Lange-Kirchheim[35] draws on Bronfen and similarly argues that Else's primary dilemma originates in the impossibility of femininity in a patriarchal social order; yet she continues to focus on the abusive father-daughter relationship as the catalyst for Else's actions. However, Else's mother is the one who is willing to auction off her daughter. Else perceives herself primarily as a performer — a characteristic she has witnessed all along in her mother, whom she endearingly calls a true artist when preparing lavish dinner parties despite serious financial constraints.

Fully aware of her parents' implications and Dorsday's expectations, Else repeatedly speaks of murder and is asked not only to commit the crime but also to provide the murder weapon, all without any witnesses. Her predisposition to self-murder partly originates in her love-hate relationship with her mother. Unable to escape her mother's demands yet painfully aware of her family's parasitic existence, the obedient bourgeois daughter and soon-to-be prostitute also is confused about the ravenous adversary within herself as she is simultaneously embarrassed and excited about displaying her body. After satisfying a corrupt moral order and demimonde desires, she instantly seeks self-punishment: suicide. Her hated mother also patiently endures being a betrayed wife, a position Else doubly rejects. She radically ruptures the gender continuum and breaks away from the prescribed feminine roles of wife, mother, or lover. In Else's eyes, her acquaintance Cissy embodies the ideal new female as wife, mother, *and* lover.

The mother-daughter relationship, however, is only one of several threats to Else's existence. Lange-Kirchheim explains part of her emotional distress as premenstrual syndrome (PMS). Although it is practically a household word now, PMS and its impact on the female psyche were largely ignored by the medical profession until the 1980s, when reports confirm what Schnitzler anticipated: its correlation with suicidal thoughts.[36] For Else, both PMS and menstruation mean a temporary loss of control over her body. Therefore, she quickly resorts to pharmaceuticals, such as Veronal, to regain stability. The text is rather explicit. Else refers to her period, the aches in her legs, etc. Overdoses with fatal consequences were far from unusual once this barbiturate was introduced around the turn of the century. As this natural process in her body has already made her unsteady, her pending display throws her completely off balance. She consolidates her efforts to regain control over her body by performing what is in effect an abortion: killing off a part of the self while allowing another part of the self to continue. At least three interpretations of this act are possible; all appear equally plausible and entail her outlook for the future, assessment of her present situation, and attempt to cope with a past that continues to haunt her. In terms of future prospects, Else unambiguously rejects traditional gender expectations and thus performs an imaginary abortion of children she is expected to have as a wife or fastidiously avoid as a lover. To solve her current dilemma, she rids herself of a body that is the object of aesthetic, erotic, and economic speculation and leaves behind an empty shell to be readily viewed at Dorsday's convenience. In an effort to break with her past, she radically distances herself from her intrusive and domineering mother.

Else's self-understanding and body image are also those of an assimilated Jew, which according to Lange-Kirchheim magnifies her suicidal inclination to a genetically determined trauma within the Jewish tradition. Although Schnitzler has Else mention that her father's youngest brother killed himself at the age of fifteen, the writer was skeptical about a genetic predisposition to self-destruction. Considering suicide as innate behavior would invite another minor biographical footnote and make his daughter's voluntary death a hereditary necessity, as Schnitzler's uncle Julius died from a self-inflicted gunshot wound. Ethnicity, however, is closely tied to Else's perceptions of her body and to mocking identity. The behavior and appearance of the assimilated Jew Dorsday bring her own self-hatred to the surface; she tries to compensate with narcissistic self-love and reassurance that she is strawberry blonde and pretty. This strategy inadvertently increases her vulnerability and reminds her of her marginal existence.

The psychoanalysts Fonagy and Target argue that suicidal patients perceive their bodies as troublesome and their psyches as unreliable in conceptualizing a coherent self.[37] Thus, the mind-body split, a relic of the Enlightenment tradition, becomes magnified to a life-death split. Else, seemingly enchanted with her own beauty and perfectly happy with her physical self as long as she dictates the rules for her exhibitionistic performances, splits her body into an actress and a material stage for her spectacle, a hysteric self-display that corresponds to an autobiographical play with herself as the protagonist. This public performance also brings her most intimate sexual fantasies to the surface. In the first act, a pantomime, she is on the verge of consciously becoming a commodity when posing against an imaginary canvas. She compares the request of her display to the pleasures of looking at a Peter Paul Rubens painting. In the second act she poses as a nude model in plain view of a large audience in the doorway of the music room and practices for a definite transition from body to corpse. In her final pose, Else re-enacts a previous private regression during which she speculated about her future as the wife of a rich American with a villa on the ocean. She imagines resting — this time divinely clothed in sunlight — on a marble staircase descending into the ocean, and thus simultaneously alludes to the universal image of death as the crossing of a river and subsequently to the possibility of rebirth.

While preparing for her final performance, she engages in thought experiments that work like booster shots, keeping her alive when she repeatedly reports herself as dead. The arrival of her mother's letter, her death sentence, terrifies her to the extent that she instantly envisions herself as a corpse. She prefers to open the letter while sitting on the windowsill, mentally preparing herself for the leap. The first thought that crosses her mind is that her parents may have committed suicide. Before reading the letter entirely, she snaps into her first suicide fantasy, which includes a fictional media report camouflaging her deadly fall as a "tragic accident." As socially acceptable motives she lists unrequited love and unwanted pregnancy, both of which are intimately linked to rejection and female biology that becomes destiny. Else's fragmentary report leaves the actual word "suicide" to the imagination of the reader, only hinting at it with punctuation marks. Interestingly, in an earlier passage punctuation marks allude to sexual encounters. Schnitzler not only links suicide and sexuality in reference to the psyche of the suicide victim but also reinforces the connection rhetorically.

In the letter, Else's mother bluntly lays out the financial crisis and without further hesitation assigns her daughter the role of a prostitute to immediately resolve the problem. Fully aware of the impending scandal, Else romanticizes suicide until she receives yet another telegram that throws her into a state of shock. Rhetorically, the mother blackmails her daughter and plays her against her father by implying the possibility of his suicide. Else, in turn, quickly adopts this strategy to distance herself from Dorsday by suggesting, "Bilden Sie sich nicht ein, daß Sie, elender Kerl, mich in den Tod getrieben haben."[38] Without this threat being made public and shared with the potential perpetrator, however, it remains ineffective. Nonetheless, her imaginary line of reasoning develops as follows: because Dorsday causes her trauma, he ought to endure the trauma of her suicide, then finally also terminate his life because his request has resulted in her death. This strategy allows Else to at least temporarily regain control of the stressful situation. Without the slightest bit of remorse, she speculates about her wake, exemplifying Schnitzler's take on suicide as an act of human freedom.

While leaping from a cliff is restricted to her personal suicide fantasy, she envisions a self-inflicted gunshot wound or hanging as adequate modes of self-destruction for her father. Once the fantasy crystallizes to clear intent, Else opts for Veronal as the most accessible method that will allow her to preserve an intact body. Incapable of tolerating disfigurement, she sees freezing to death in solitude or her body decaying beyond recognition and reduced to a skeleton as complete erasure. She is giving up her position as the bourgeois daughter; it is imperative for her to at least reclaim her body.

Immediately after she has chosen a method and verified its availability, she imagines her rebirth. As final preparation for this transition, she deposits her fading self-image in the mirror and seals her narcissistic union with a kiss. Her mirror image provides self-cohesion, which her mental state does not, and turns her narcissism into a defense strategy. Therefore she experiences Cissy's reflection in the mirror as intrusive and ignorant of her imaginary "No trespassing" sign. Else spends her final hours in an exuberant mood and eagerly anticipates fusing her surviving self with a split-off idealized part. According to clinical observations, select suicide patients believe that a part of the self will survive.[39] They merely wish to discard irreconcilable or terrifying parts of themselves and merge with ideal or idealized qualities — in Else's case, a femininity unattainable for her once she meets Dorsday's request, as she is then no longer a desirable bride. Her suicide simply erases the contingencies of the Dorsday episode, and she can reclaim her surviving self from her mirror to strive toward a new femininity. The body she uses for her public display is merely a cast, and completes the ego split into body and object. Thus, Else's suicide constitutes, as Higonnet astutely observes, "a metaphoric transition between two lives when the dying heroine yields to her double."[40]

Schnitzler implicitly criticizes the mid-nineteenth-century medical practice of clinical restraint as a cure for "scandalous behavior" when Else's aunt urges hospitalization after the public display requested by her parents. What society finds shocking is Else's disrobing in public, not the suicide she ponders in her fantasies.

Der Letzte Brief eines Literaten: Curtain Call for the Final Comedy *Murderers Are Among Us*

In the lengthy suicide note of *Der Letzte Brief eines Literaten,* an anonymous yet well-known, moderately successful Viennese playwright carefully prepares his final literary statement along with his suicide. While it is not uncommon to leave a note either for immediate family or for the world at large, this suicide's unusual addressee is a physician attending the author's dying lover Maria. Such a missive does not traditionally elicit a response; however, the suicide's former acquaintance, Dr. Anton Vollbringer, actually replies. These two accounts amount to distorted, narcissistic mirror images of the authors' artistic, professional, and personal ambitions and shortcomings. Technically speaking, the suicide note provides a plot, whereas the physician in the addendum explains how the suicide was actually carried out, speculates on the particulars of the last night, and criticizes the playwright's morals and creative talent (or lack thereof). While the *Literat* supplies the medical information, the physician acts as a literary critic. An unknown third reader, providing two perspectives on the same incident and blending professional worlds and private affairs, has posthumously edited both letters.

Reading *Fräulein Else* in tandem with *Der Letzte Brief eines Literaten* evokes parallels between the strained relationship of mother and daughter in the former and of male scientist and artist in the latter, along with the parasitic existence of abusive parents and their daughter and the play-wright's love affair with Maria. Perhaps the most striking difference lies in the framing devices of their final performances: Else prefers an optical frame, while the *Literat* creates a textual one; this difference leads to reading Else's suicide as visual and visionary and that of the *Literat* as verbal and terminal. Moreover, both plots invite interpretations of suicide as an act of self-punishment and autonomy that frees the author from the chore of adequately mourning the death of his partner by writing a masterpiece. Does it, however, also imply an outlook for the future? If so, is it tied to a new masculinity, to a new self-understanding of the writer, or to new aesthetic expressions?

Among the pioneering discussions of this relatively ignored prose fiction, Maja D. Reid's essay *"Andreas Thameyers Letzter Brief and Der Letzte Brief eines Literaten:* Two Neglected Schnitzler Stories," deserves special mention.[41] Reid points to the autobiographical dimension in the second story à la Franz Kafka's posthumously published *Brief an den Vater* (1952) and reads the physician as a father figure disapproving of the son's lifestyle. Egon Schwarz's claim that "Schnitzlers sonderbarste Marotte vom Judentum stammend, ist die Idee, daß ein Jude keine rechten Dramen schreiben, ja vielleicht überhaupt kein vollgültiger Dichter sein könne"[42] supports Reid's autobiographical interpretation. Finally, the date of the suicide of the *Literat,* October 11, 1887, coincides with Schnitzler's dilemma to decide between medicine and literature; he had just assumed his duties as a resident and was simultaneously writing book reviews for the *Internationale Klinische Rundschau.* Despite Martin Swales's sophisticated reading in his major study on Schnitzler and G. J. Weinberger's follow-up,[43] feminist readings and those exploring the suicide constellation are still missing.

The self-centered narrative reveals the poet's egotistical motives for becoming involved with a beautiful, terminally ill young woman, Maria, and exploiting her disease to experience sensations of pain and grief that will enhance his writing. Thus, the dying female body on the verge of turning into a corpse is endowed with new meaning as the poet's muse. The seemingly two-dimensional physical gamble uniting invincible virility and tender frailty is initially planned as a one-sided, artistic endeavor to legitimize ruthless behavior. Under extraordinary circumstances, that is, in light of Maria's pending death, the *Literat* hopes to produce works beyond the ordinary. After realizing the inevitable failure of his highly calculated strategy, he imposes his own death sentence, reinforced by a suicide fantasy, the imaginary fatal leap from a cliff. Mere embarrassment, should Maria eventually learn about his reckless behavior, keeps him from immediately implementing his plan.

This plot, once again, serves as a cover-up for a more complex existential crisis that is bound to intellect and to the status of the writer. Drafting the suicide note, for the playwright, means "meinen Brief abzufassen, eine Beichte abzulegen, vielleicht auch nur eine letze Komödie zu spielen, was weiß ich" (ES II, 209).[44] The written medium is the most logical vehicle of dramatic self-articulation, and ultimately also of self-destruction. Not unlike Lichtenberg's Harlequin, he writes himself to death with deliberate poor style and inflated language and ultimately compares his suicide to a comedy, that is, a performance. His final comedy then merely re-enacts what he previously practiced — ironically mourning the deaths of loved ones by writing witty comedies. Inevitably, the process of writing allows him to rethink his options, not unlike Else's reiterations of her public and private image repertoires. Peter Brooks attributes the emergence of narrative plot to the larger process of secularization gaining force during the Enlightenment and suggests that the plotting of the individual life story "takes on new urgency when one no longer can look to a sacred masterplot that organizes and explains the world."[45]

Calmly — in fact, so calmly that he is caught by surprise — the poet acknowledges that he is not pressured by society, by any given honor code, or by mental illness but simply is determined to end his life. Moral labels are attached posthumously to the act of free will. When the poet admires Maria's wonderfully free attitude despite her pending death, it underscores his own longing for freedom. Swales points out that the playwright understands his suicide as part of his mission as an artist, which demands this union with his partner.[46] The egocentric *Literat,* however, hardly envisions such a noble endeavor of following her in death. On the contrary, Maria plays a peripheral role in the playwright's existential crisis. The ego-split of the poet into essence and performance of poetic speech takes place when he burns his most recent manuscript shortly after meeting Maria, which links his suicide to a body of literary works. He figuratively decides to plunge from life to death by pursuing her after their random encounter in the ballroom, fully aware of her condition. She is no more than a surrogate to carry out his plan, and not unlike Dorsday for Else, her illness serves as a welcome pretext to leave his desk for good. Suicide for the playwright means formally bidding goodbye to his not-too-successful academic career as a medical student, the preeminent reader and interpreter of symptoms; to his current dilemma of artistic crisis; and to the future pressure to re-create the world in words. Subsequently it puts a sudden end to his crisis of representation. In terms of future prospects it pushes for new aesthetic forms, for alternatives to respond to the First World War, and for adequate expression of pain and sorrow without silencing the scream with hysterical laughter.

Since the symbolic act is "eine Form, nicht mehr"[47] and re-enacts a previously staged exit, the *Literat*'s final words, "Ich lösche mich aus, eh ich mich vollende. Darum habe ich mich entschlossen —"[48] are an empty gesture perfectly disguising the eloquence one would expect from a playwright. His suicide note makes his most intimate trauma, that of being a second- or third-rate writer, public.

Higonnet suggests that "Language becomes action; action becomes and yet requires language."[49] In this particular prose fiction, Schnitzler inscribes action in the characters' names. "Vollbringer" implies action and accomplishment and grammatically refers to the agent responsible for carrying out a set plan, that is, the physician. The playwright's anonymity alludes to his failure to build a literary legacy. Without a masterpiece, he will quickly vanish from the literary landscape; however, that is inevitable for him anyway, as according to the physician, a person of no virtue and low morals will never become a true genius. The name "Maria" supposedly signifies redemption and purity, which is ironic as she opts for sexual pleasure that will inevitably shorten her life. She elopes without getting her mother too upset, as the mother's vanity keeps her from objecting too strongly to her daughter's love affair, although she is fully aware of the fatal consequences of such an adventure. Finally, the most revealing name is that of the poet's former lover, "Syringe," actually Fräulein Josefine, who seems capable of endangering his intent and infusing the poet with too much of a desire to live.

What Higonnet suggests for female characters who yield to their double is epitomized in the poet who indeed yields to his other, the physician — the double is everything but an idealized image of himself.

The Dramaturgy of Suicide: Singing the Body and Mind Electric

Both texts operate with a master narrative voice reminiscent of Lichtenberg's *"Rede eines Selbstmörders."* Else's impressive voice ensemble draws primarily on interior monologue, interspersed with occasional dialogue, dreams, or brief notes, similar to the playwright's monologue that is annotated with rhetorical questions, requests to the addressee, and the physician's commentary. Clearly, the suicide victim plays the solo part in the pastiche of texts. The histrionic female voice and the meticulously crafted male one are literally active up until their last breath. Gender determines their respective communication media: the female body

functions as Else's testament, the letter as the playwright's. Her performance and his suicide note each have an addressee yet require their
authors' bodies as the final word. Female body and written text serve as
depositories of fantasies and secrets, respectively; they not only offer
storage space but also need to be safely stored away to be reclaimed later.
Thus, Else deposits her body in the mirror, and the *Literat* leaves his
suicide note to the physician, who in turn keeps it for an editor.

Schnitzler's previously sketched distinction between female and male
modes of self-destruction comes full circle when Else reaches for Veronal
and the playwright reaches for the gun. Equally gender-driven is their
distinct transition to permanent states of silence. Else's verbal cascades,
although paradoxically unspoken as she is supposedly unconscious, are
the map of her precarious mind. She eloquently articulates her self-
effacement as her speech deteriorates from logical units to isolated words
and finally to particles. The *Literat*'s wordy elegy mirrors his desired self-
composed posture, undercut only by his pathos.

Whereas Else postpones suicide by staging her body, the poet does
so through writing. She can only envision transferring authorship when
all that is at stake is her dead body; while the author of fiction claims
authorship of his life, his plan goes awry as the physician in his response
takes over authorship of the *Literat*'s death. Consequently, female self-
love rests on conflicting erotic and sexual desires, while male narcissistic
self-love is driven by professional and intellectual ambition.

As a structuring principle and narrative device, suicide gives definite
shape to the plot. In reference to character constellation, Schnitzler
typically works with triadic structures of suicide victim, pretext, and
actual perpetrator. Similarly, the ego-split, which is necessary to actually
commit suicide, has three components; Else steps out of her body and
contemplates herself as a spectacle, assuming the role of simultaneous
actress, stage, and audience. Likewise, the playwright blurs the boundary
between narrative voice, narrator, and narrated event and seamlessly steps
into and out of his narrative frame.

Schnitzler shifts between extremes, between radical change and continuity, making suicide as much an act of resistance to the status quo as
a reconciliatory act, a feasible solution to a dilemma. Suicide enables Else
to escape her mother's efforts of creating a replica of herself and grants
her the utopian wish of idealized reinscription modeled after Cissy. Yet
it is a successful inscription on bourgeois hypocrisy, which now has to
bury an actual corpse. Moreover, the suicide victim becomes a perpetrator — a fact that the social order completely denies. In *Der Letzte Brief
eines Literaten* the poet has failed to inscribe himself in the literary canon

but succeeded in inscribing himself on the physician, who in turn continues the writing process.

In both works, Schnitzler orchestrates suicide as performance in the style of a Gesamtkunstwerk, with musical and visual scores. Else's requiem is Robert Schumann's piano cycle "Carnaval" (1834/1835), and its implied *carne vale* is a radical inversion of "Here Comes the Bride." The poet's requiem is a *danse macabre* first performed in a festive ballroom where a scene of infinite bliss suddenly shifts to one of horror; love at first sight meets death at first sight, and the potential bridal chamber quickly changes to a morgue. Maria seems a ghostly apparition of a deceased lover returned to snatch her bridegroom. A variation is re-enacted in Schnitzler's communication short-circuits between suicide victim and survivor when the physician knowingly writes to a corpse and keeps both letters so that they can be readily found and made public.

The astute observer of human behavior is also a gifted painter evoking allegorical imagery. In *Frau Beate und Ihr Sohn,* for instance, mother and son drown in a fatal embrace reminiscent of Egon Schiele's many maternal allegories. Schnitzler also excels in landscape, portraits, and deceptive still-lives. The poet begins writing his letter against the backdrop of a lake and dark mountains soaring into the sky, and he even mentions lighting instructions. Among Schnitzler's masterworks, however, are scenes for which he tried to freeze the most dramatic action in a snapshot. Window and door frames create thresholds arbitrarily blurring the boundaries between inside and outside worlds, providing opportunities for "accidentally" terminating one's life or reconnecting with the outside world. Behind their deceptive stabilizing quality lurks pronounced polarized thinking. After all, the door frame marks the crossroads where the male voyeur meets the female exhibitionist. Once again, pictorial elements are at stake in the transition from body to corpse. In *Fräulein Else* and also in *Doktor Gräsler, Badearzt,* imaginary dolls make the suicides seem surreal or magical, and most definitely nonviolent.

Schnitzler's Hidden Agenda: Why Not Live?

Vienna's coexisting rich aesthetics and atmosphere of crisis did not entice Schnitzler to aestheticize or trivialize suicide but rather to embed psychoanalytic insights in literary plots — without, however, sparking a major public debate. Despite several inconsistencies, perhaps reflecting the paradoxes of Viennese society, Schnitzler's prose fiction provides rich terrain for exploring the poetics of suicide. The inconsistencies are clearest in the prominence of suicide in Schnitzler's works and the absence of discussion in secondary sources; the fact that the Viennese Medical School dismissed the doctor whom it trained and instantly lost interest in him as a poet; and the persistent stubbornness with which Ringel's essay has been met: although published in an academic journal for literary critics, it has so far failed to inspire significant studies on Schnitzler and suicide.

As a suicidologist Schnitzler did not merely describe the phenomenon but also contributed to its prevention; *Fräulein Else* and *Der Letzte Brief eines Literaten* easily meet criteria for an antisuicide campaign. They function as passionate pleas for life rather than celebrating fatal morbidity. Schnitzler grants his characters the benefit of the doubt and suggests, "You may as well live!" — issuing a proactive, moral order without ever taking a moralistic view of the act itself.

Notes

[1] Arthur Schnitzler, *Aphorismen und Betrachtungen,* ed. Robert O. Weiss (Frankfurt am Main: Fischer, 1967).

[2] Quoted from Toril Moi, ed., *The Kristeva Reader* (New York: Columbia UP, 1986), 158.

[3] For more, see Robert Litman, "Sigmund Freud on Suicide," in *Essential Papers on Suicide,* ed. John T. Maltsberger and Mark Goldblatt (New York: New York UP, 1996), 200–220.

[4] Antoon A. Leenaars, ed., *Suicidology: Essays in Honor of Edwin S. Shneidman* (Northvale, NJ: Aronson, 1993), 207.

[5] Margaret R. Higonnet, "Speaking Silences: Women's Suicide," in *The Female Body in Western Culture: Contemporary Perspectives,* ed. Susan Rubin Suleiman (Cambridge, MA: Harvard UP, 1986), 68–83.

[6] Jean Améry, *Diskurs über den Freitod. Hand an sich legen* (Stuttgart: Klett-Cotta, 1976).

[7] For other approaches, see Janet Hadda, *Passionate Women, Passive Men: Suicide in Yiddish Literature* (Albany: State U of New York P, 1988); Peter von Haselberg, "Psychologie oder Konstellationen? Am Beispiel von *Dr. Gräsler, Badearzt,*" in *Arthur Schnitzler in neuer Sicht,* ed. Sigurd Paul Scheible (Munich: Wilhelm Fink, 1981), 188–99; Alan Stephen Wolfe, *Suicidal Narrative in Modern Japan: The Case of Dazai Osamu* (Princeton, NJ: Princeton UP, 1990); Barbara Gates, *Victorian Suicides: Mad Crimes and Sad Histories* (Princeton, NJ: Princeton UP, 1988); and Irina Paperno, *Suicide as a Cultural Institution in Dostoevsky's Russia* (Ithaca: Cornell UP, 1997).

[8] Schnitzler, *Zug der Schatten. Drama in 9 Bildern* (Frankfurt: Fischer, 1970).

[9] For more, see Peter Fonagy and Mary Target, "Towards Understanding Violence: The Use of the Body and the Role of the Father," in *Psychoanalytic Understanding of Violence and Suicide,* ed. Rosine Jozef Perelberg (New York: Routledge, 1999), 51–72.

[10] Eric L. Santner, "Of Masters, Slaves, and Other Seducers: Arthur Schnitzler's *Traumnovelle,*" *Modern Austrian Literature* 19/ 3–4 (1986): 35.

[11] For more, see Alexandra Comini, "Through a Viennese Looking Glass Darkly: Images of Arnold Schoenberg and His Circle," *Arts Magazine* 58/59 (1984): 107–19.

[12] For more, see William Johnston, *The Austrian Mind: An Intellectual and Social History 1848–1938* (Berkeley: U of California P, 1983), 174–80. Also see Allan Janik and Stephen Toulmin, *Wittgenstein's Vienna* (New York: Simon and Schuster, 1973), 64–65.

[13] For more, see Erwin Ringel, *Das Leben Wegwerfen? Reflexionen über den Selbstmord* (Vienna: Herder, 1978).

[14] Arthur Schnitzler, *Jugend in Wien. Eine Autobiographie* (Vienna: Fritz Molden, 1968), 184.

[15] For more, see Georges Minois, *History of Suicide: Voluntary Death in the Western World,* trans. Lydia G. Cochrane (Baltimore: Johns Hopkins UP, 1999).

[16] Schnitzler made three diary entries mentioning the name Georg Christoph Lichtenberg: July 8, 1896; August 29, 1896; and July 1, 1909.

[17] Georg Christoph Lichtenberg, *Lichtenbergs Werke in einem Band,* ed. Hans Friederici (Berlin, Weimar: Aufbau-Verlag: 1982), 98.

[18] Lichtenberg, *Sudelbücher II, Materialhefte, Tagebücher,* ed. Wolfgang Romies (Munich: Carl Hanser Verlag, 1971), 163.

[19] Lichtenberg, *Lichtenbergs Werke in einem Band,* 19, 20.

[20] Minois, 314.

[21] Emile Durkheim, *Le Suicide: étude de sociologie* (Paris: F. Alcan, 1897).

[22] David Lester, Betty H. Sell, and Kenneth D. Sell, *Suicide: A Guide to Information Sources* (Detroit, Mich.: Gale Research, 1980).

[23] Joanne Trautmann and Carol Pollard, *Literature and Medicine: An Annotated Bibliography* (Pittsburgh: U of Pittsburgh P, 1982).

[24] Ringel, "Das Selbstmordproblem bei Schnitzler," *Literatur und Kritik* 161–62 (1982): 33–51.

[25] Janik and Toulmin, 63.

[26] These lines are taken from Anne Sexton's poem, "Wanting to Die," which appears in the collection *Live or Die* (Boston: Houghton Mifflin, 1974). Sexton wrote the poem on February 3, 1964, about a year after Sylvia Plath's suicide.

[27] *Das neue Lied* in ES I, 620–34; *Die griechische Tänzerin* in ES I, 569–79; *Doktor Gräsler, Badearzt* in ES II, 113–205; *Frau Beate und Ihr Sohn* in ES II, 42–112; *Der Weg ins Freie* in ES I, 635–958; *Mein Freund Ypsilon* in ES I, 28–39; *Die Fremde* in ES I, 551–59; *Der Ehrentag* in ES I, 278–95; *Der Empfindsame* in ES I, 255–61; *Das Spiel im Morgengrauen* in ES II, 505–81; *Andreas Thameyers Letzter Brief* in ES I, 514–20; *Der tote Gabriel* in ES I, 973–84; *Therese. Chronik eines Frauenlebens* in ES II, 625–881; *Abenteurernovelle* in ES II, 582–624; *Flucht in die Finsternis* in ES II, 902–85.

[28] Arthur Schnitzler, *Tagebuch,* ed. Werner Welzig (Vienna: Verlag der Österreichischen Akademie der Wissenschaften, 1981–2000), 176 (July 31, 1928).

[29] Particularly Schnitzler's choice of Hamsun's *Landstreicher* (*Tagebuch,* 186 [August 30, 1928]) from Lili's library is interesting, as Hamsun's *Das letzte Kapitel* has a character called suicide.

[30] *Tagebuch,* 225 (February 4, 1929).

[31] *Tagebuch,* 181 (August 15, 1928).

[32] This statement is the last sentence in Lili's diary, as Schnitzler notes in his own diary (*Tagebuch,* 182 [August 16, 1928]).

[33] Quoted by Perelberg in "Psychoanalytic Understanding of Violence and Suicide: A Review of the Literature and Some New Formulations," in *Psychoanalytic Understanding of Violence and Suicide,* ed. Rosine Jozef Perelberg (New York: Routledge, 1999), 36.

[34] Elisabeth Bronfen, "Rigor Has Set in — The Wasted Bride," in *Over Her Dead Body: Death, Femininity and the Aesthetic* (New York: Routledge, 1992), 269–90.

[35] Astrid Lange-Kirchheim, "Adoleszenz, Hysterie und Autorschaft in Arthur Schnitzler's Novelle *Fräulein Else," Jahrbuch der Deutschen Schillergesellschaft* 42 (1998): 265–300.

[36] For more, see Lange-Kirchheim, 268, note 9. It is also interesting to note that Richard Freiherr von Krafft-Ebing (1840–1902) published a monograph in 1902, *Psychosis menstrualis,* according to Erna Lesky in *The Vienna Medical School of the 19th Century* (Baltimore: Johns Hopkins UP, 1976), 346.

[37] Fonagy and Target, 51–72.

[38] *Fräulein Else,* 368.

[39] Perelberg, 6.

[40] Higonnet, "Suicide as Self-Construction," in *Germaine de Stael: Crossing the Borders,* ed. Madelyn Gutwirth, Avriel Goldberger, and Karyna Szmurlo (New Brunswick, NJ: Rutgers UP, 1991), 71.

[41] Maja D. Reid, *"Andreas Thameyers letzter Brief* and *Der letzte Brief eines Literaten:* Two Neglected Schnitzler Stories," *German Quarterly* 45 (1972): 443–60.

[42] Egon Schwarz, "Arthur Schnitzler und das Judentum," in *Im Zeichen Hiobs: Jüdische Schriftsteller und deutsche Literatur im 20. Jahrhundert,* ed. Gunter E. Grimm and Hans-Peter Bayerdörfer (Königstein: Athenäum, 1985), 67–83.

[43] Martin Swales, *Arthur Schnitzler. A Critical Study* (Oxford: Oxford UP, 1971); G. J. Weinberger, "Arthur Schnitzler's 'Der letzte Brief eines Literaten,'" *Michigan Germanic Studies* 22/2 (Fall 1996): 162–71.

[44] *Der letzte Brief eines Literaten,* 209.

[45] Peter Brooks, *Reading for the Plot: Design and Intention in Narrative* (New York: Knopf, 1984), 6.

[46] Swales, 89.

[47] *Der letzte Brief eines Literaten,* 227.

[48] *Der letzte Brief eines Literaten,* 228.

[49] Higonnet, "Speaking Silences," 69.

The Legacy

The Difficult Rebirth of Cosmopolitanism: Schnitzler and Contemporary Austrian Literature

Matthias Konzett

IF THE PRESENT European Union can be seen as an attempt at cosmopolitan governance by accommodating the ever-increasing erosion of national boundaries through economic market forces and transnational patterns of migration and cultural exchange, the question of what constitutes a cosmopolitan identity on a cultural level cannot be ignored. As David Held points out, "Globalization, far from creating a sense of common human purpose, interest and value, has arguably served to reinforce the sense of significance of identity and difference, further stimulating the 'nationalization' of politics."[1] The political trends in Europe at the turn of the millennium reflect this growing tendency toward nationalism. They point to an increasing insecurity with multiculturalism and its potential to open up new possibilities for cultural self-definition. Instead, multiculturalism is understood by the general public more as a polemic force dividing mainstream society into the entrenched camps of reactionary nationalists and liberal pluralists. While the former still believe in the ontogenetic constitution of a people and remain hostile to cultural diversity, the latter indiscriminately preach cultural diversity, though rarely with the serious vision toward true integration of so-called foreign residents into the mainstream middle-class structure of society. Cultural minorities are instead patronized as economically and linguistically deficient groups requiring the protective care of the native-born liberal.

The challenge in turning to Viennese Jewish culture at the *fin-de-siècle* lies in the distinct position that this community occupied as a cultural minority. To a large extent, this community possessed solid middle- and upper-class status and therefore does not resemble the stereotypical economic migrants of the present era. From a Marxist and other social critical perspectives, authors such as Schnitzler, Hugo von Hofmannsthal, or Karl Kraus enjoyed the class privileges of the high bourgeois and would therefore have to be considered politically conservative, if not with regard to their literary message, at least in their social status. Present criticism often divides the roles between German Jewish and Turkish minorities without seeing their internal connection, specifically with regards to the present issue of citizenship. In this framework, German Jewish writers of the past and present are more suitable for melancholy ruminations on the Holocaust and its legacy of the unspeakable, thus removing cultural debate from a politics of citizenship to a quasi-theological level.

However, an examination of the issue of cosmopolitan citizenship in Schnitzler and the recent example of the Austrian Jewish writer Robert Schindel, who was born in 1944, challenges the perception that contemporary European culture can do entirely without the ambivalent legacy of bourgeois culture that consisted not only of class privilege but also paradoxically of a cosmopolitan outlook largely absent in the increasingly provincial perspectives of contemporary Europe.

Schnitzler's works reflect the gains of Jewish emancipation and assimilation by allowing him to speak comfortably from the center rather than the margin of society. In his reflections on his youth, Schnitzler writes:

> Damals, es war in der Spätblütezeit des Liberalismus, existierte der Antisemitismus zwar, wie seit jeher, als Gefühlsregung in zahlreichen, dazu disponierten Seelen und als höchst entwicklungsfähige Idee; aber weder als politischer noch als sozialer Faktor spielte er eine bedeutende Rolle. Nicht einmal das Wort war geprägt.[2]

Schnitzler's distinction between a pervasive cultural prejudice and an institutionalized politics of anti-Semitism is highly important in understanding the liberal climate that persisted until the anti-Semitic Karl Lueger took office as mayor of Vienna in 1897.[3] This impression is also confirmed by Stefan Zweig in his frequently cited *Die Welt von Gestern* (1942). He viewed Vienna before the political onset of anti-Semitism as a center of cosmopolitan culture: "Wer dort lebte und wirkte, fühlte sich frei von Enge und Vorurteil. Nirgends war es leichter, Europäer zu sein."[4] Curiously, one finds a parallel in present Austria to Schnitzler's late liberal era. In spite of the growing popularity of Jörg Haider during the late 1980s and early 1990s, an observer would not necessarily call this era a reactionary one in Austrian culture. Even Kurt Waldheim's election to president in 1986, while indicating a disturbing shift in voting behavior, did not fundamentally challenge the then-ruling Socialist government and its legislative power. Artists and writers could still rely heavily on subsidies and state support regardless of their political message. However, with Haider's Freedom Party joining Austria's government in February of 2000, the cultural climate drastically changed by legitimating prejudice on an institutional level. Critical artistic voices were conveniently silenced through a *Sparprogramm* cutting back on their state support. Xenophobic messages have become an integral part of the political culture. Politicians' remarks and statements as part of their official function show a strong tendency toward xenophobia. Because such statements are now supported by their status of official government communications, they have ceased to be prejudices of a subjective nature. In the context of Nazi legislation beginning in 1933, Saul Friedlander points out how quickly racial policies become facts of life and give citizens the official excuse to act on their prejudices.[5]

It is important to bear in mind this functional difference between subjective prejudice and officially or objectively sanctioned prejudice so as not to depict anti-Semitism in turn-of-the-century Vienna in an undifferentiated manner. Recent criticism on this era in Vienna's history, it appears, has shifted from its former idealistic and apolitical assessment of its aesthetic achievement to a wholesale condemnation of its anti-Semitic ambience, leaving little room for a more nuanced perception. Sander Gilman, for example, delineates the career of Karl Kraus in the following terms:

> The complex case of the *fin-de-siècle* Viennese cultural critic and writer Karl Kraus is an excellent example of the means by which individuals, labeled as Jews, internalized and projected the qualities of differences attributed to themselves onto other subgroups. Kraus's case is of interest because it illustrates the formation of a fictive personality within the world of words, within the culture of writing during a time of an extraordinary public manifestation of anti-Semitism in Austria in the earliest stages of his career and the success of Nazism in Germany at the close of his career.[6]

In Gilman's framing of Kraus's career, anti-Semitism appears as an expanding historical, and therefore quasi-teleological, force rather than a political threat that was checked and challenged at various points in history. Jews are accused of having enabled or at least facilitated the rise of fascism because of their attitude of self-hatred produced by their internalization of the prevailing anti-Jewish biases. Likewise Michael P. Sternberg's compelling study of Hofmannsthal's nationalist cosmopolitanism, one paradigmatically displayed in the Salzburg Festival, makes it appear as if most Jewish cultural representatives in Austria had willingly embraced *völkisch* ideologies and capitulated to their enemies.[7]

However, in assessing Schnitzler's career as a writer and the careers of other writers at the turn of the century, it is important not to treat them wholesale in view of the pressures of anti-Semitism. According to

Schnitzler's own comments, these pressures increased significantly around 1900, when Lueger had taken charge fully in Vienna's public and political life. These pressures are duly reflected in Schnitzler works such as *Leutnant Gustl* (1901), *Der Weg in Freie* (1908), and *Professor Bernhardi* (1912), written during the period in which Lueger occupied the mayor's office in Vienna. Yet, while Lueger helped make anti-Semitism acceptable on the municipal level, he could not seriously interfere with Austria's national politics still opposed to an intensified politics of anti-Semitism. Although Habsburg Austria was vulnerable to anti-Semitic prejudice and practiced anti-Semitic policies of exclusion in areas of the civil service, it did not institutionally increase its discriminatory practices after Lueger took office. In 1902, in the midst of a scandal ensuing from Gustav Klimt's display of his university murals, derided as possessing a *gout juif,* Sigmund Freud received his long awaited promotion as a professor. In spite of the uproar following the performance of *Liebelei* (1896), the revocation of Schnitzler's officer rank in the wake of *Leutnant Gustl,* and the hostile reaction to the publication of *Reigen* (1903), the majority of his plays were continually performed at the Burgtheater, Austria's national theater. Notable exceptions such as *Reigen* (withheld by the author) and *Professor Bernhardi* (censored and performed in Berlin; performed in Austria after the First World War) cannot conceal the fact that the author had consistent access to a theater representing Austria's most prestigious and esteemed forum of culture. While admittedly Schnitzler's relations with the Burgtheater were temporarily strained, the situation improved under Baron Alfred von Berger (1910–1912) and his successors. Vienna's most famous actors, including Adolf Ritter von Sonnenthal, Adele Sandrock, and Joseph Kainz, appeared in Schnitzler's plays that were also performed at other important Viennese theaters such as the Theater in der Josefstadt and the Volkstheater.[8]

If the Vienna of the 1880s and 1890s offered a less burdened climate of cosmopolitan culture than in the following decade under the anti-Semitic mayor Karl Lueger, how can it be traced in the early works of Schnitzler, who does not seem to address cosmopolitanism explicitly? An examination of the persona of the dandy and its transformation in Schnitzler's career reveals that his cosmopolitanism can be traced as a literary stance stemming from the legacy of liberalism; this stance is eventually refined into the plurivocal depiction of Habsburg Austria in *Der Weg ins Freie,* a form that is re-appropriated in Schindel's novel *Gebürtig* (1992) for Austria's contemporary cultural setting.[9] Particularly the notion of cultural irony demonstrates Schnitzler's evolving political and cosmopolitan sensibility. The notion of mainstream and marginal cultures in relation to Schnitzler's work is also significant in this context: to what extent did Vienna's cosmopolitanism allow Schnitzler to speak not as a marginal but a central voice of culture? In early twenty-first-century Austrian culture there is a remaining paradox in its so-called enlightened postwar political atmosphere: why is it that in spite of the promotion of multiculturalism, minority cultures rarely, if ever, are granted any central role in the liberal institutions of Austria's cultural life? Discussion of these issues not only sheds light on easily identifiable reactionary stances in cultural politics but also questions the complacent premises of liberal culture with its continuing patronization of minorities.

Schnitzler's favored persona in his early writings, including the *Anatol* cycle (1893), *Liebelei,* and *Reigen,* is the careless and witty dandy-womanizer, a representative of decadent bourgeois culture. Schnitzler claims that his own generation differed from a previous generation "durch ein Mehr an Witz und die . . . Neigung zur Selbstironie."[10] The dandy adopts a cynical attitude toward society by placing his social and cultural inheritance at risk in a life of consciously cultivated irresponsibility and hedonism.[11] As Jean-Paul Sartre comments skeptically on the political significance of the dandy in the case of Charles Baudelaire: "He applies his will to the negation of established order, but at the same time preserves this order."[12] This persona was by no means ill received among the Viennese public as long as it stayed within the confines of the apolitical nature of the social enfant terrible. It is seen, for example, in the popularity of the Viennese "bohemian" writer Peter Altenberg. Paradoxically, this persona also reflects the liberal climate of the 1890s, which did not yet subject Jewish writers to moral stances required of model minorities but permitted an amorality enjoyed by the general public. Schnitzler's early dramas enjoyed success with the Viennese public, since they were not viewed suspiciously in anti-Semitic terms of Jewish corruption and degeneracy. Schnitzler's *Reigen,* by violating the appearance of political innocence, triggered for the first time hostile responses with undertones of anti-Semitism.[13] While the work was frequently misunderstood as pornographic, it also managed to implicate an entire social order in practices of perceived immorality. Rather than being a harmless social satire, the work possesses a quality of conscious contamination, of vocal public dissent found today commonly in the writings of Thomas Bernhard or Elfriede Jelinek.

Indeed, the critical reception of *Reigen* alerts readers to the fact that Schnitzler's earlier dandy-personae may not have been entirely innocent and playful creations of bourgeois boredom and spleen. Instead, they reflect a subversive spirit of non-orthodoxy in the realms of politics, nation, and religion. This persona, depicted variously in figures such as Anatol and Max (*Anatol*), Fritz and Theodor (*Liebelei*), and der junge Herr and der Dichter (*Reigen*), ultimately reflects Schnitzler's own stance as a writer. He treats his literary heritage with the same flippancy and frequently has a laugh at the expense of poets, literary figures, or serious literary topoi. *Anatol,* for example, offers an episodic carnivalization of interpersonal relationships marked by the will to domination rather than love. Unlike Johann Wolfgang von Goethe's *Die Wahlverwandtschaften* (1809), in which spiritual betrayal (by Eduard and Charlotte) leads to concrete physical tragedy, betrayal becomes the daily fare of Anatol's life and is humorously redeemed by ingenuity of deception and verbal battle. In *Liebelei* the pathos of a *Liebestod* in the manner of *Tristan and Isolde* or *Romeo and Juliet* is deflated and shown to be the consequence of repetition rather than unique love, as Richard Alewyn suggests.[14] The young lovers Fritz and Christine die futile deaths for petty and outmoded bourgeois ideals of culture and respectability. Finally, in *Reigen* the figure of the poet is infatuated with his *nom de plume* and is taken by surprise when he finds out that his fame does not extend beyond the Burgtheater. Art is thus questioned both on the level of subject matter in its deflation of Romantic pathos to banality and in the variously comedic depictions of the artist's persona.

Schnitzler's tragicomedy *Das weite Land* (1911), which he started to write as early as 1901, underscores this sobered evaluation of art in the suicide of the Russian pianist Korsakov. He is assumed to have killed himself because of criticism that his renditions of Johann Sebastian Bach and Ludwig van Beethoven are inferior to his interpretations of Frédéric Chopin and Robert Schumann. Dr. Mauer, the physician and thinly disguised mouthpiece of Schnitzler, receives the sad news with scorn rather than sympathy:

> Ich bitt' dich, ein Künstler! Die sind alle mehr oder weniger anormal. Schon daß sie sich so wichtig nehmen. Der Ehrgeiz an und für sich ist ja eine Geistesstörung. Dieses Spekulieren auf die Unsterblichkeit! Und die reproduzierenden Künstler, die haben's gar schlecht. Sie mögen so groß sein, wie sie wollen, es bleibt doch nichts übrig als der Name und nichts von dem, was sie geleistet haben.

Elsewhere in the play, the poet's exclusive access to the sublime is dismissed with derision, ridiculing the presumed originality of art: "die Seele ist ein weites Land, wie ein Dichter es einmal ausdrückte. . . . Es kann übrigens auch ein Hoteldirektor gewesen sein." Schnitzler's artist personae are not spared the oncoming reality of a growing culture industry in which individuals (women and artists) are turned into interchangeable and ultimately dispensable commodities. Apart from this social-realistic ironization of the artist, a certain iconoclastic and postnational attitude is associated with Schnitzler's *flâneur* attitude toward his art. Unlike the works of the Weimar sages Goethe and Friedrich Schiller that have been elevated to national icons of German language and culture, Schnitzler's ironic depictions of art and artists do not allow for such national idolization. The writer's cultivated irreverence betrays a deassimilative gesture beneath the appearance of cultural assimilation. The cosmopolitanism in Schnitzler results not so much from an international perspective than a critical national one. As Kraus once remarked: "Am Chauvinismus ist nicht so sehr die Abneigung gegen die fremden Nationen als die Liebe zur eigenen unsympathisch."[15] This critical self-relativization of one's cultural status, ethnicity, and nationality cannot be ignored as a key ingredient of a cosmopolitan outlook. What Schnitzler may have called in somewhat questionable terms "die *rasseneigentümliche* Neigung zur Selbstironie" can be understood as the competence of a diaspora culture to look at itself critically from the outside. This critical double vision is rarely found in monocultural formations of invented indigenous or native cultures. The critical spirit found in Schnitzler, Kraus, Freud, and Ludwig Wittgenstein is more indicative of cosmopolitan attitudes than the sentimental clichés of the Viennese coffeehouse, theater, and opera, to which Vienna is often reduced. While these spheres played a vital part in the increased democratic dissemination of thought and culture, they were also frequented, as a 1999 study by Brigitte Hamann has shown, by society's reactionary elements.[16]

These factors point to a strongly subjective element of self-criticism on the part of Schnitzler and make it appear that subjects can easily transcend the institutionalized norms of identity in a culture. Schnitzler emerges in his early years as the apolitical bohemian such as described by Sartre and Walter Benjamin in their respective studies of Baudelaire. In contrast to Sartre, however, Benjamin describes Baudelaire as an heir of the French Revolution who in his own seemingly apolitical manner carries on the legacy of social revolt: "Allenfalls hätte er Flauberts Wort 'Von der ganzen Politik verstehe ich nur ein Ding: die Revolte' zu seinem eigenen machen können."[17] While critical of bourgeois culture, Benjamin also acknowledges it as the true heir of the French Revolution: "Der Protest gegen die bürgerlichen Begriffe von Ordnung und Ehrbarkeit war nach der Niederlage des Proletariats im Junikampf bei den Herrschenden besser aufgehoben als bei den Unterdrückten."[18] This type of post-revolutionary bohemian intervention characterizes the early work of Schnitzler. Its politics is less strategic than provocative, less systematic than idiosyncratic in its dissent. Schnitzler's play *Der grüne Kakadu* (1899), which takes place on the eve of the French Revolution and is set in the suburbs of Paris with its bohemian elements gathering in the inns of wine merchants, offers a direct link between Schnitzler and the tradition of the "bohemian" or "Gelegenheitsverschwörer," as Karl Marx described this new class of the disenchanted bourgeois.[19] Schnitzler's politics in a new key indebted to the tradition of French bohemianism, however, baffled the Austrian authorities, who could not decide whether to censor the play. As Hartmut Scheible notes: "Erst allmählich dämmerte es den Hofkreisen, daß es mit diesem Historienstück wohl eine eigene Bewandtnis habe, ohne daß man der Parallelität von Gegenwart und Geschichte ganz habhaft zu werden vermochte: deshalb das Taktieren der Behörden, die zwar weitere Aufführungen verhindern, nicht jedoch zu einem Verbot sich durchringen wollten."[20]

Der grüne Kakadu complicates the apparent historicism of its setting, Paris, July 14, 1789, by re-enacting, alongside the developing revolution, the social ambience that may have given rise to that revolution. In an inn on the outskirts of Paris, the nobility gathers to watch a spectacle staged by actors impersonating society's marginal elements such as murderers, criminals, pimps, and prostitutes. In its naivety, the nobility is amused by the spectacle of staged resentment and revolt, only to be awakened from its slumber when a jealousy plot turns into real murder and when news of the revolution is finally reaching the inn. Schnitzler's complicated staging of an inextricable interplay between illusion and reality may at first rob the play of any concrete political message. However, in its suggestion of an acute self-deception on the part of the nobility enjoying the spectacle of society's misery, it challenges the narcissistic complacency of the audience that attends the play in a similar fashion. As such the play calls the very institution of theater into question and anticipates Bertolt Brecht's critique of bourgeois theater and its delight in theatrical illusion. The innkeeper's remark about his delight in provoking his unknowing public is to be taken literally for the play as well: "Es macht mir Vergnügen genug, den Kerlen meine Meinung ins Gesicht sagen zu können und sie zu beschimpfen nach Herzenslust — während sie es für einen Scherz halten." Illusionary action, as the play shows, can quickly and unexpectedly turn into real action. Similar to Hofmannsthal's "Ein Brief" (1902), in which language carries its own seeds of destruction, Schnitzler deconstructs bourgeois theater and its complacent construction of spectatorship from within its conventions.

In this context, it is also interesting to recall the function of the Burgtheater for Jewish and other migrant communities in Vienna seeking cultural guidance in the process of acculturation and assimilation. As Edward Timms points out, the Burgtheater exerted a significant formative influence on the speech and bearing of its audience:

> The elevated status of actors was enhanced by an idealized mode of performance which predominated in Burgtheater performances of the nineteenth century. It seems to have served as a model for social decorum for a bourgeois audience with aspirations to be accepted into polite society. . . . Elias Canetti records that for his parents, living in a small town of Bulgaria, the experience of its productions was so memorable that they spoke together a "secret language" based on the diction of the Burgtheater.[21]

The Burgtheater, as Timms notes, was not the exclusive domain of the aristocracy, but served as an educational institution for the aspiring bourgeois class. Seen in this light, Schnitzler's highly ironic plays take on a much more visible political function than the author himself would let one surmise by his many disparaging remarks about politics. By questioning bourgeois society at heart, namely in its use of culture as social ornament, Schnitzler's plays make it difficult for the audience to leave the theater with a validation of their sense of bourgeois ideology. In Theodor W. Adorno's sense of the avant-garde, his plays rather refuse to become instrumentalized within bourgeois ideology. Schnitzler's ironic treatment of art and its naïve consumers makes it difficult for the audience to attain the self-assurance projected in conventional plays. Particularly, the assimilative process of taking on cultural capital and decorum in exchange for an increased sense of belonging appears to have been prevented in Schnitzler's consciously diffuse, skeptical, and tacitly self-parodying dramaturgy.

With the demise of liberalism and the rise of Lueger and the Christian Social Party at the beginning of the new century, the cultural climate of Vienna shifted on the local level radically from a cosmopolitan to a more nationally oriented one. Anti-Semitism, much like present-day xenophobia in Austria, attempted to reverse the cultural assimilation of Jews that had already occurred. These years, as Hamann has shown, became the years of apprenticeship for the young Adolf Hitler, who initially adored Richard Wagner performances given by Gustav Mahler and staged by Alfred Roller.[22] Racial prejudice, which had never ceased to exist, took on a more systematic nature in Vienna's politics as quotas were being debated and set for Jewish participation in the university and public affairs. In this climate, Schnitzler could no longer continue with his dandy de-

meanor risking alienation from Jewish audiences looking for some affirmation of their embattled identity. The ethical turn in Schnitzler's work
seen clearly in *Der Weg ins Freie, Das weite Land,* and *Professor Bernhardi*
can already be detected in *Leutnant Gustl,* which offers an interior view
of the social resentment beginning to ferment among Vienna's lower-
middle class, a class to whom Lueger particularly appealed. Fearing for its
social descent, this class as personified by Leutnant Gustl feels threatened
in paranoid fashion by almost any segment of society expressing any sense
of independence such as the Jews, the prosperous bourgeois class, and the
increasingly self-aware women. Burdened by his volatile class status between desired bourgeois ascent and feared proletarian descent, Gustl
resorts to collective stereotyping and prejudice. Much like the duels that
he incurs through his own provocations, he is at the same time dueling
with the phantoms of his own social paranoia, prompting frequent disparaging remarks of social groups that resemble in their vulnerability his own
precarious social status. It is not coincidental that Gustl lashes out against
the presence of Jews in a cultural arena such as the opera, where he feels
out of place and is reminded of his déclassé status. Rather than giving
readers the self-hating Jew, Schnitzler presents them with the dangerously
other-hating Austrian that is afraid of not being able to live up to imagined norms of belonging and respectability and descends into pathological
resentment and racism.

Schnitzler's concern about the rise of anti-Semitism, Ruth Kluger
notes, remains ultimately peripheral to his works: "Schnitzler never gave
the 'Jewish problem' or anti-Semitism, a central place in any of his
works. . . . While anti-Semitism is a recurrent theme in his autobiography,
it never becomes dominant, and there is some evidence that Schnitzler
thought the problem would ultimately take care of itself."[23] While this
assessment is correct with regard to the explicit themes of the work, it does
not fully explain why Schnitzler chose to treat the problem in a peripheral
manner. Kluger's observation that "Schnitzler has given us a picture of
Jewish life in Vienna at a time when anti-Semitism was on the rise but Jews
also had opportunities to make a good living and contributed importantly
to the city's intellectual productivity" gives readers an indication of what
may have been at stake.[24] Kluger describes Schnitzler's position as a writer
of Vienna's mainstream, unwilling to retreat into the voice of a minority.
In spite of his increasingly challenged position as a Jew, Schnitzler refuses
to resort to ethnic essentialism but confidently asserts his cosmopolitan
perspective. However, Schnitzler is not entirely unaffected by the rise of
anti-Semitism and shifts the accent of his work toward a more ethical
treatment of society. The irreverent laughter of the dandy undergoes a

transformation to make room for a deeper socio-psychological analysis of society's regression into nationalism and provincialism.

The transformation of the dandy in Schnitzler's work announces itself in plays such as *Der einsame Weg* (1904), originally titled "Die Egoisten," with its critique of a hedonist and egocentric culture unable to show empathy in the face of human tragedy. *Zwischenspiel* (1906) exposes the fake liberal spirit of its protagonist practicing an open marriage that eventually runs afoul of deep-seated and conventional bourgeois jealousy. In these plays, Schnitzler distances himself from the social irresponsibility associated with the "leichtlebige Mensch" or dandy. Nevertheless he retains the deeper subversive spirit of the dandy as an authorial stance that can be identified with that of what Gilles Deleuze and Felix Guattari call a minor literature written from within major literature to subvert established icons of power.[25] *Der Ruf des Lebens* (1906) shows this iconoclastic trait with its heroine, Maria, who gets away with the murder of her tyrannic father who had kept her in unreasonable emotional dependence at his sickbed, while exposing the military sacrifice of its male protagonists as well as the suicide of honor by Max as entirely useless and founded on empty myths of male and patriotic chauvinism. Jack Zipes, who has invoked the term of minor literature for promoting a new generation of German Jewish writers, in his good intentions stretches and distorts the concept of minor writing by extending it to minority literature. Minor literature, however, has to work from within major national institutions so as not to become a mere marginal phenomenon: "A minor literature," as Deleuze and Guattari put it in linguistic terms, "doesn't come from a minor language; it is rather that which a minority constructs within a major language." Writers such as Rafael Seligmann, Katja Behrens, and Esther Dischereit, cited by Zipes, unfortunately do not occupy center stage, as is perhaps the case with the better-suited example of George Tabori.[26] In fact, Schnitzler fits the prototype of the minor writer even better than Deleuze and Guattari's exemplary Franz Kafka, whose subversions remained exclusively on the level of language and barely drew any public attention during his lifetime nor managed to intervene in public cultural institutions. Schnitzler, an early favorite with Vienna's public, increasingly deflates the icons of nation, art, and culture in his work and thereby pushes his seeming cultural assimilation into the reverse direction, and along with it challenges his audience and readers to do likewise.

His work reflects this shift in its increased focus on Viennese Jewish culture and its constructive civic importance. Meanwhile, the role of the decadent dandy is displaced onto the Austrian aristocrat or parvenu bourgeois (Wergenthin, Hofreiter, Hochroitzpointner). As this shift occurs, Schnitzler speaks for the first time from the margin rather than the center of society. Nevertheless, his works remain, in spite of controversy, at the center of Vienna's culture and are not yet forced to speak in the diminished sense of a minority. More like the works of Thomas Bernhard that raised frequent debate in the public, Schnitzler's works still retain their sense of addressing a mainstream audience and speak with the inclusiveness of a lingua franca. They are not yet marked by the insiderism that reduces a minority often to a lingo or patois. This emphasis on not relinquishing one's territory to the encroaching enemy explains why Schnitzler does not treat anti-Semitism as the exclusive topic in his works. For example, after *Leutnant Gustl,* his portrayal of the prototypical anti-Semite, Schnitzler makes sure not to become reductive in his analysis of society by placing his own position as artist beyond reproach. In a series of subsequent plays, art is thus questioned in its ability to provide answers and solutions for society's everyday problems.

Harking back to his earlier critical perspective on art, *Der einsame Weg* looks at the failure of artists to cope with the most common human situations that demand solidarity, such as birth, marriage, and death. The bohemianism of the painter Julian Fichtner merely serves as an excuse to forego his parental duties and to exhaust his artistic energies in aimless wandering. Meanwhile, the professionalism of the state-sponsored painter Professor Wegrat, the director of the academy of art, produces likewise a disingenuous form of life marked by a conventional marriage and artistic mediocrity. Finally, the writer Stephan von Sala is indirectly responsible for the suicide of Wegrat's daughter by proposing marriage to her on the eve of his own imminent death. Thus the play provides ultimately no correct ethical position, since even commitment as shown by Sala leads to tragedy and death. The existential drama retreats from social satire and aims to highlight a condition shared by all the characters who must pursue the lonely path of life. As a transitional play, this work can be understood as a critique of the artist (dandy, professional, or committed) as society's single redemptive figure, calling instead for a greater degree of social empathy and solidarity, as personified in Felix's attention to his widowed stepfather. Yet, with its inevitable tragedies, it also stresses the inability to provide an ethical map through life.

It is interesting to note how often Schnitzler changes the tone and emphasis of his work so as to keep his readers and audience in a constant state of surprise. As a master in avoiding a reductive agenda for art, he retreats from and re-enters the arena of politics in unpredictable fashion, thereby securing the openness for his artistic discourse. The existential play

Der einsame Weg is followed by the comedy *Zwischenspiel,* only to give way to his more serious novel *Der Weg ins Freie,* followed by the tragicomedy *Das weite Land,* countered by the highly political comedy *Professor Bernhardi,* and retreating again to the self-reflective satire *Komödie der Wort* (1915). As with his contemporary Mahler, who consciously mismatches musical passages with inappropriate instruments, demanding high notes from instruments such as the tuba and low notes from the flute, Schnitzler's genre markings of comedy and tragedy are often misleading and appear purposely misassigned. Mahler amends his symphonies with iconoclastic markings such as "im Tempo eines gemächlichen Ländlers. Etwas täppisch und sehr derb,"[27] thereby creating an ambivalent tone. A similar carnivalization of genre is at work in Schnitzler when he denotes the serious subject matter of *Professor Bernhardi* as comedy or settles for the ambivalent tone of tragicomedy in *Das weite Land.*

Adorno, commenting on the ambivalent use of tone in Mahler, states: "Mahler's major-minor manner has its function. It sabotages the established language of music with dialect."[28] Like Schnitzler, Mahler places modern art in question but does so through the medium of art. Both Schnitzler and Mahler provide the link between traditional art solidly rooted in society's mainstream culture and a more radical avant-garde, dismantling art entirely as a futile bourgeois practice. Schnitzler and Mahler, while venturing into the territory of doubt, resist this final dogmatic rejection of art and opt instead to have the public engage with the doubt surrounding modern art. While Mahler's art is "inimical to art," Adorno notes, it "needs art in order to manifest itself."[29] In the same spirit Schnitzler asserts a complex aesthetics of subversion that can be reduced neither to an ideology of social progress nor to an affirmation of tradition.

Professor Bernhardi exploits the ambivalent tone of comedy in the face of the serious subject matter of anti-Semitism. This tone would have to be considered objectionable if one approached the play from a purely political position. However, aesthetically the play imparts unease to its viewers and thereby manages to implicate them as active participants in social and cultural conflicts rather than allowing them to be passive spectators. In its inability to discern the right moment of laughter, the audience is forced to enter the author's perspective and take on a more globally ironic attitude toward a politics of cultural identity exploited to promote self-interest rather than social communication. The play, as Allan Janik and Stephen Toulmin rightly note, "is a morphology not only of anti-Semitism, but of all the destructive and dehumanizing forces at work in society," particularly an inability to communicate and an adherence to "social roles which satisfy . . . immediate desires."[30] As

Professor Bernhardi prevents a Catholic priest from administering the final rites to a dying yet drug-induced euphorically alive patient, he triggers a "comic" series of events that expose a ruthless politics of self-interest masked by appeals to higher morality. In order to make good for his affront to the Catholic Church, he is offered a bargain to appoint a mediocre candidate over the much more deserving Jewish candidate Wenger. Reluctant to do so, Bernhardi is indicted in parliament, forced to resign from his institute, and eventually jailed for two months for "Religionsstörung." Upon his release he is celebrated by his students and appointed to become the private physician of Prince Konstantin and thereby fully reinstated.

The play can be read as a comment on the Lueger era that came to an end in 1910 with the mayor's death. Bernhardi, a temporary political hostage, is finally released from the powers of anti-Semitic and Christian Social ideology that provided a pretext for career opportunism (Hochroitzpointner, Flint) and racial discrimination (Ebenwald, Filitz). The ending of the play offers the conventional, though historically realistic, solution whereby the Habsburg monarchy protects Jews against anti-Semitic ideologies and recognizes them as vital to their interests of a multinational dynasty. The notion of social intrigue so readily associated with Vienna's court society is extended to the bourgeois sphere that had been encouraged by Lueger to act upon self-serving prejudices and sectarianism rather than an inclusive cosmopolitan spirit.

The play was censored because of its purported distortion of the political situation in Austria, particularly what was deemed its parody of parliamentary procedures. Not performed in Vienna until 1920, when Vienna's mayor Jakob Reumann was for the first time a Socialist, while the nation was in the hands of Catholic clerical power and the Christian Social party, Schnitzler's play encountered a reversed political situation with Vienna going left and the nation turning right. Because of the delay in performance, the play had lost some of its immediate political impact and appeared anachronistic with regards to the demise of the Habsburg Empire that had served as a protective power for Jews. Nevertheless, the play manages to expose stereotypes as calculated strategic dismissal of minorities for the promotion of mono-ethnic interests. It provides an important link between ethnicity and economic struggle that had heretofore been solely understood in terms of class struggle. In a more complicated revision of Marx's view, it alerts audiences that social injustice at any class level of society endangers the stability and equilibrium of a society. While mainstream culture is often derided as conforming to the status quo, its ethnic composition is itself an indicator of society's adherence to a fair multicultural representation and its affirmation of social mobility for all ethnic groups.

In *Der Weg ins Freie,* published still during the Lueger era, the cosmopolitan vision of Schnitzler remains unchanged but is expressed with a more intensified and impending sense of social disaster. The earlier microcosm of personal conflict (*Liebelei, Der einsame Weg, Zwischenspiel*) is now combined with the macrocosm of society (*Der grüne Kakadu, Reigen, Der Ruf des Lebens*), erecting a complex maze of competing discourses and conflicting claims of identity. The novel opens with the death of Georg von Wergenthin's father, whose papers the son orders in the manner of Adalbert Stifter's *Die Mappe meines Urgroßvaters* (1841; 1847). However, unlike the unfolding of the plot in Stifter's story, no legacy is remembered or excavated by Georg, although his father's death pressures the son finally to strike out on his own. The legacy of the family is instead preserved biologically, as Georg begins to take a serious interest in Anna Rosner, a young woman from a Christian family. Georg's relationship with the Jewish Else Ehrenberg, with whom he shares childhood experiences and a considerable degree of personal compatibility, must now come to an end as he is eager to establish himself in the blood line of his Christian ancestry. In fact, to the Rosner family, whose son has turned into an anti-Semite, Georg belittles his contacts with the Ehrenbergs: "Ich stehe ja in keinerlei näheren Verbindungen mit dem Hause Ehrenberg, so gern ich mit den beiden Damen zu plaudern pflege."[31] This betrayal on the part of Georg shows how unreliable Christian-Jewish relations are when put to the test. Betrayal reappears throughout the novel as a central theme but is best embodied by Georg in various forms of personal and social non-commitment. Afflicted by the malaise of the already arrived social insider, he neither bothers to promote his musical career nor to honor commitment in affairs with women. Whereas Oskar Ehrenberg provides for an abandoned mistress financially, Georg simply drops his mistress without any recompense. With Anna carrying his child, he cannot bring himself to marry her and indirectly causes the stillbirth of his own child.

Alongside Georg, a young Jewish generation is also shown to betray the cosmopolitan legacy of their fathers, engaging increasingly in fundamentalist politics (Therese and Leo Golowski) or assimilationist endeavors (Oskar Ehrenberg). The novel's mood conveys sense of closure of horizon in a society marked by opportunism, self-promotion and lack of civic solidarity. The once-thriving salon culture of the Ehrenbergs is no longer a preferred meeting point for intercultural encounter. As Steven Beller notes: "Non-Jews go off and become antisemitic German nation-

alist, that is insiders, while it is the Jews who have to seek a 'way out.'"[32]
Particularly Georg represents the increasing loss of solidarity among non-
Jewish Austrians and their former allies and fellow citizens, leading to the
eventual marginalization and persecution of Jewish culture in Austria.
Yet in spite of the apparent asymmetry in this cultural conflict, Schnitzler
preserves a self-critical attitude in showing that the Jewish community
itself is torn between nationalist and cosmopolitan perspectives, between
Zionism and supranational dynastic allegiances. Schnitzler, like Kraus,
reserves the right to criticize the Jewish community as an insider. In
doing so, he cannot be accused of being a "self-hating Jew," a figure
Schnitzler parodies in the extreme assimilationist Oskar Ehrenberg.
Schnitzler never conflates Zionism and anti-Semitism as identical forms
of ethno-nationalism, as may be the case with Kraus. Moreover, the
various diffuse prejudices held by Jews against Jews in the debate between assimilation and de-assimilation (Berman, Ehrenberg) are seen as
misguided subjective prejudices. They do not, as Robert Wistrich has
similarly pointed out in the case of Kraus, "translate into political action
against the civil rights of the Jewish minority."[33]

Schnitzler's novel can be considered one of his greatest achievements
in expressing a cosmopolitan perspective. The plurivocal structure of the
novel makes sure that a wide range of political opinions and ideologies,
ranging from liberalism, Socialism, Zionism, and atheism to pan-
Germanic nationalism and moderate Christian-Catholicism, are heard
and placed into conflict with one another. In addition, the overlapping
of private and public interests, as seen for example in Georg's search for
German-Christian roots after the death of his father, demonstrates that
political views are not entirely built on rational decisions. Similarly, the
feud between Oskar (assimilationist) and his father, Salomon Ehrenberg
(Zionist), bears also the mark of a struggle for identity with a son trying
to face up to his overpowering father. This private dimension of politics
calls the political beliefs themselves into question and exposes them as
commodities for identity formation. A further complication of the novel
is presented by the enduring friendship between Bermann and Georg in
spite of the latter's growing detachment from the Jewish community.
Both characters struggle in the aftermath of their fathers' deaths with
legacies that they are unable to confront or project with any resolution
into the future. As such, they share a sense of dissociation from their
respective cultural backgrounds and embody the spirit of a modernism
deprived of a supporting ancestral history. Their common project of an
opera, while evoking the collaborative efforts of Richard Strauss and

Hofmannsthal, ends ultimately in failure and bodes ominously for the productive co-existence of Austrian and Jewish culture.

Far from diffusing political questions through private concerns, Schnitzler equally recoils from pat political answers. His community of characters evolves in relation to one another and presents political views as part of a greater need to find an adequate form of life. Salomon Ehrenberg's search for a Zionist homeland ends with his reluctant acknowledgment that Palestine remains a thoroughly underdeveloped country and cannot accommodate the lifestyle of a Viennese bourgeois. His public humiliation of his son in front of a Catholic church leads to the latter's tragicomic suicide attempt and exposes, not unlike in the case of Georg, desperate attempts to achieve a form of cultural belonging. The cosmopolitanism of the novel is once again underscored in parodying creeds and dogmatic belief systems of any kind, including that of art as society's redemptive power. All artists in the novel bear the stamp of second-rate accomplishment. Georg, as a procrastinating composer and aspiring conductor, ends up in the remote and provincial opera of Detmold. Else and Anna, trained as singers, possess only weak voices and do not qualify for serious careers. Nürnberger, the novelist, has stopped writing ever since his first novel gained him wide acclaim. Eissler, a gifted composer of waltz melodies, lacks the musical skills to put his compositions to paper. Rapp and Gleissner appear as second-rate embodiments of Kraus, the acerbic critic, and Altenberg, the decadent poet of the Kaffeehaus. Finally, Bermann proposes a grand opera but is unable to complete it, with the result that his own characters desert him in "in schattenhafter Verwirrung, höhnisch, ohne Abschied und ohne das Versprechen, wiederzukommen." Robert Schindel's novel *Gebürtig* responds to *Der Weg ins Freie* in a postwar and post-Shoah culture of Austria with its various encounters of Jewish and non-Jewish Austrians. In mirror reversal to its precursor, the novel reconstructs the Austrian-Jewish dialogue that had shown growing signs of disintegration in *Der Weg ins Freie*. At the outset, the novel depicts patterns of interaction typical of Austria's amnesiac society: "Er betonte seine jüdische Herkunft, sie sagte, damit könne sie nichts anfangen, sie interessiere sich nicht für Politik." Nevertheless, Schindel's sympathetic novel shows most of his characters struggling for more viable forms of cultural identity in which difference and commonality can co-exist. While the past is acknowledged, it is not necessarily the single determining avenue to Jewish identity: "Dürfen unsere Juden gelegentlich ein bißchen tot sein oder müssen sie auch als Knochenmehl ständig gespitzt bleiben?" The work further highlights generational conflicts between survivors and their descendants, such as Emmanuel Katz, who becomes the indirect victim of his mother's traumatic memory, or Susanne Ressel, who questions her father's fond memories of communist activism and comradeship during the Spanish Civil War. In the end, however, the novel presents more positive transformations in the public outing of a repressed Jewish identity (Katz, Adel) and a hidden Nazi past (Konrad Sachs). The commitment to confront once again a traumatic past as a witness in a Nazi trial (Gebirtig) is paralleled by the ending, which culminates in the main characters' approximation of the Shoah experience, albeit highly ironized, as stand-ins on a Holocaust movie set. Also, in contrast to Schnitzler, many of the characters take up writing and art and thereby gain a reflective distance from their various traumatic pasts.

Schindel's conciliatory work further highlights the assimilative potential that Vienna harbored once beneath its diasporic identity that allowed, apart from cultural tension, for hybridities and mutually enriched cultural contexts. This transregional and cosmopolitan confidence is also reflected in the constant shifting of scenery in the novel between Vienna, Venice, Hamburg, Munich, Frankfurt, and New York, all distinctive cities with equally distinctive traditions. Schindel's cosmopolitan perspective, critically grounded in distinct regional settings, does not attempt to make global or universal its theme of various cultural encounters between Jews and non-Jews. Indeed, each of the encounters in the novel produces a unique negotiation of Jewish identity from within individually interpreted cultural settings. Renewing the significance of Jewish identity and its public visibility, Schindel ultimately manages to avoid a facile pluralism and a dogmatic politics of identity obliging every Jew to be Jewish in the same manner. Since Jewishness, as Schindel realizes, overlaps with other private and public identities, it recedes or presses into the foreground in accordance with changing subject positions influenced by age, gender, generation, community, region, and language. Its visibility, while desirable in Austria's all-too-homogeneous cultural landscape, cannot be reduced to any single strategy or form of public disclosure.

The positive reception and resonance of Schindel's novel, along with the political changes of the early 1990s, might lead one to believe that the specter of fascism was finally duly confronted in Austria's amnesiac society. However, even Schindel's novel, with its stereotypical portrayal of its only Turkish character as a sexual predator (during a party he makes undue advances and after a fight is asked to leave), shows a lapse of judgment commonly seen in present Austrian xenophobia. While Jewish and non-Jewish character receive in Schindel a plurivocal treatment similar to that of Schnitzler's *Der Weg ins Freie*, the Turkish representative stands isolated and alone and is forced to represent his culture in the form of a collective stereotype.[34] Thus, by not linking historical accountability to the present issue of citizenship, the novel allows Austrian readers to show remorse toward the past while remaining xenophobic in the present. The belated and repeated apologies of Austria's populist leader Jörg Haider to the Jewish community come easy, as this community is demographically (though not culturally and historically) insignificant in present Austria. It is rather his strategic attempt to reverse a trend of immigration and integration that gives rise to worry. At a time when Austria's economy is stable, when children of immigrants have achieved acculturation and can no longer be distinguished on account of linguistic differences, ideologies of race, class, and nationality remain the only criteria to hamper their economic rise to middle-class status.

One wonders whether the current xenophobic environment in Austria does not in part also stem from weak liberal stances viewing minorities rarely in the central role that Schnitzler and the Viennese Jewish community once were permitted to assume for a short time. Cosmopolitanism, in the context of Schnitzler's Vienna, is less characterized by internationalism than the ability to maintain an ironic distance toward one's cultural legacy in the spirit of the self-mocking bohemian or dandy. Deflating the cultural significance of one's own community, particularly when it occupies the position of a majority culture, may help to create the much-needed cosmopolitan space within the regional. In present Austria, this space is not yet made available by a bourgeois culture that lacks cosmopolitan irony, be it on the spectrum of the political right or the left. These positions should not be conflated entirely, since the liberals have made an attempt to change the existing laws of citizenship, probably more radically in Germany than in Austria. Jürgen Habermas's demand that "national-understanding . . . is no longer [to be] based on ethnicity but [to be] founded on citizenship" is a first and important step in creating the legal conditions for an integrated and multicultural society.[35] However, laws create only a basic denominator on a structural level of society and say little about cultural recognition and practices of intercultural understanding. Zafer Senocak's essay "Ein Türke geht nicht in die Oper" comes to mind when one considers the continuing reluctance in Germany and Austria to view cultural minorities other than in their marginal and collectively framed position.[36] The excuse that Austria produces no significant ethnic literature at present can be dismissed on account of the existing German body of ethnic literatures. While Austria was eager to import literature from the former East Germany and study it devotedly as part of an expanding tradition of German literature, no similar effort is made with regard to Germany's well-known migrant literatures. Only as such a diverse body of literature is once again permitted to take on a central role in

Austria's mainstream cultural discourses will there be a type of cosmopolitanism reminiscent of Schnitzler's Vienna.

Notes

[1] David Held, *Democracy and the Global Order: From the Modern State to Cosmopolitan Governance* (Stanford: Stanford UP, 1995), 94.

[2] Arthur Schnitzler, *Jugend in Wien: Eine Autobiographie,* eds. Therese Nickl and Heinrich Schnitzler (Frankfurt: Fischer, 1996), 77. The term "anti-Semitism" was coined by Wilhlem Marr in his *Der Sieg des Judenthums über das Germanenthum,* published in 1879.

[3] Lueger, as Carl Schorske points out, sat on the *Reichsrat* as a liberal Democrat from 1882 to 1887 before transforming into an anti-Semitic populist leader. Lueger, who won the municipal elections in 1895, was barred by the Emperor from taking office until 1897. See Carl E. Schorske, *Fin-de-Siècle Vienna: Politics and Culture* (New York: Vintage, 1980), 139–45.

[4] Stefan Zweig, *Die Welt von gestern: Erinnerungen eines Europäers* (Frankfurt: Fischer, 1998), 40.

[5] Saul Friedländer, *Nazi Germany and the Jews: The Years of Persecution, 1933–1939* (New York: HarperCollins, 1997) 10–40.

[6] Sander L. Gilman, "Karl Kraus's Oscar Wilde," in *Vienna 1900: From Altenberg to Wittgenstein,* eds. Edward Timms and Ritchie Robertson (Edinburgh: Edinburgh UP, 1990), 12.

[7] Michael P. Steinberg, *Austria as Theater and Ideology: The Meaning of the Salzburg Festival* (Ithaca: Cornell UP, 2000). See particularly chapter 3 on nationalist cosmopolitanism. Unfortunately, this chapter does not mention any critical counter-traditions such as represented by Schnitzler, Kraus, or Joseph Roth, thereby giving an uneven impression of the cultural forces shaping the Habsburg and post-Habsburg era.

[8] Michaela L. Perlmann, *Arthur Schnitzler* (Stuttgart: J. B. Metzler, 1987), 32–33.

[9] Robert Schindel, *Gebürtig* (Frankfurt: Suhrkamp, 1992).

[10] *Jugend in Wien,* 17.

[11] See, for example, Alfred Fritsche, *Dekadenz im Werk Arthur Schnitzlers* (Frankfurt: Peter Lang, 1974). This study makes a strong case for the importance of the dandy in Schnitzler's work. However, in its defense of Schnitzler against charges of decadence, it fails to acknowledge fully the use of the dandy as a strategic pose or consciously adopted persona in Schnitzler's work.

[12] Jean-Paul Sartre, *Baudelaire,* trans. Martin Turnell (New York: New Directions, 1950), 71.

[13] Gerd K. Schneider, *Die Rezeption von Arthur Schnitzlers Reigen 1897–1994* (Riverside: Ariadne, 1995), 50–52.

[14] Richard Alewyn, "Nachwort," *Reigen. Liebelei* (Frankfurt: Fischer, 1986), 171–76.

[15] Karl Kraus, *Karl Kraus für Gestreßte: Aphorismen,* ed. Christian Wagenknecht (Frankfurt: Suhrkamp, 1997), 30.

[16] Brigitte Hamann, *Hitlers Wien: Lehrjahre eines Diktators* (Munich: Piper, 1999), 42–52.

[17] Walter Benjamin, "Das Paris des Second Empire bei Baudelaire," *Charles Baudelaire. Ein Lyriker des Hochkapitalismus,* ed. *Rolf Tiedemann (Frankfurt: Suhrkamp, 1992), 11.*

[18] Benjamin, 21.

[19] Karl Marx, quoted in Benjamin, 9.

[20] Hartmut Scheible, *Schnitzler* (Hamburg: Rowohlt, 1976), 74.

[21] Edward Timms, *Karl Kraus, Apocalyptic Satirist: Culture and Catastrophe in Habsburg Vienna* (New Haven: Yale UP, 1986), 24.

[22] Hamann, 93–95.

[23] Ruth Kluger, "The Theme of Anti-Semitism in the Work of Austrian Jews," *Anti-Semitism in Times of Crisis,* eds. Sander L. Gilman and Steven T. Katz (New York: New York UP, 1991), 177.

[24] Kluger, 178.

[25] Gilles Deleuze and Felix Guattari, *Kafka: Toward a Minor Literature,* trans. Dana Polan (Minneapolis: U of Minnesota P, 1986), 16.

[26] Jack Zipes, "The Contemporary German Fascination for Things Jewish: Toward a Minor Jewish Culture," in *Reemerging Jewish Cultures in Germany,* eds. Sander L. Gilman and Karen Remmler (New York: New York UP, 1994), 15–45.

[27] Gustav Mahler, *Symphonie No. 9,* 1911.

[28] See Theodor Adorno, *Mahler: A Musical Physiognomy* (Chicago: U of Chicago P, 1991), 23. Adorno's essay on Mahler, published originally in 1971, spells out the idea of a subversive music similar to the minor literature as defined by Deleuze and Guattari in their work on Kafka (published in 1973).

[29] Adorno, 6.

[30] Allan Janik and Stephen Toulmin, *Wittgensteins Vienna* (New York: Touchstone, 1973), 63.

[31] *Der Weg ins Freie* in ES I, 635–958.

[32] Steven Beller, *Vienna and the Jews 1867–1938: A Cultural History* (Cambridge: Cambridge UP, 1989), 217.

[33] Robert Wistrich, *The Jews of Vienna in the Age of Franz Joseph* (Oxford: Oxford UP, 1990), 509. Here lies the significant difference between ethnic self-hatred and an instituted politics of systematic discrimination and exclusion that escapes critics such as Gilman, who view Viennese Jewish intellectual culture as mostly complicit with anti-Semitism. See, for example, Gilman, "Karl Kraus's Oscar Wilde," 12–26.

[34] Doron Rabinovici's novel *Suche nach M.* (Frankfurt: Suhrkamp, 1997) treats a similar episode of a Turkish blood vendetta with more ironic distance by pointing to its stereotypical nature. The judge at the trial calls the whole event a "türkische G'schicht." In doing so, the novel presents the stereotype as stereotype but nevertheless shows a tendency to imagine Turkish culture in Austria in a problematic exotic and criminal light.

[35] Jürgen Habermas, "Struggles for Recognition in the Democratic Constitutional State," in *Multiculturalism: Examining the Politics of Recognition,* ed. Amy Gutman (Princeton: Princeton UP, 1994), 148.

[36] Zafer Senocak, "Ein Türke geht nicht in die Oper," in *Atlas des tropischen Deutschland* (Berlin: Babel, 1993), 20–30.

Contributors

ELIZABETH G. AMETSBICHLER is Associate Professor of German at the University of Montana. Her research and publications are on nineteenth-century women authors and turn-of-the-century literature, particularly drama. She is the author of "Else Lasker-Schüler (1869–1945) Germany/Israel" (1998) and "'Der Reiz des Reigens': Reigen Works by Arthur Schnitzler and Werner Schwab" (1998). She is co-editor, with Elke Frederiksen, of *Women Writers in German-Speaking Countries. A Bio-Bibliographical Critical Sourcebook* (1998).

SUSAN C. ANDERSON is Professor of German at the University of Oregon in Eugene. Her areas of specialization are twentieth and seventeenth-century German literature and publications with emphases on *fin-de-siècle* Austrian and postwar German literature and culture, multiculturalism, and literary and narrative theory. She is the co-editor, together with Bruce Tabb, of *Water, Leisure and Culture: European Historical Perspectives* (2002) and *Water, Culture, and Politics in Germany and the American West* (2001).

KATHERINE ARENS is Professor of Germanic Studies and Comparative Literature at the University of Texas at Austin. Specializing in eighteenth to twentieth century comparative literature, culture and civilization, and theory and history of the humanities, she has published widely on topics in Austrian and German intellectual, cultural and literary history since 1750. Her recent publications are *Austria and Other Margins* (1996) and *Empire in Decline: Fritz Mauthner's Critique of Wilhelminian Germany* (2001). Together with Jorun Johns she coedited *Elfriede Jelinek: Framed by Language* (1994).

IRIS BRUCE is Assistant Professor of German and Comparative Literature at McMaster University, Hamilton, Ontario, Canada. Her areas of research and publication are German-Jewish Studies, Yiddish literature, and Franz Kafka. She is the author of "Kafka and Jewish Folklore" (2002), "Kafka and Popular Culture" (2002), "'A Frosty Hall of Mirrors': *Father Knows Best* in Franz Kafka and Nadine Gordimer" (2002), "Mysterious Illnesses of Human Commodities in Woody Allen and Franz Kafka" (1998), "Seductive Myths and Midrashic Games in Franz Kafka's Parables and Paradoxes" (1997), and "*Der Process* in Yiddish, or 'The Importance of Being Humorous'" (1994).

EVELYN DEUTSCH-SCHREINER is Professor for Dramaturgy, History of Literature and Theater at the University of Music and Dramatic Arts in Graz, Austria. She specializes in theater of the twentieth century, particularly Austrian theater, women in theater, and the avant-garde. Recent publications include *Theater im Wiederaufbau. Zur Kulturpolitik im Parteien-und Verbändestaat* (2001), "Katholisches aus Polen. Polnische Dramatik im Lichte des Kalten Kriegs" (2000), "Theaterland Österreich. Die Rolle des Theaters zur Konstituierung von Identität in der Nachkriegszeit" (2001), and "Impulse aus Wien für die Theater-Avantgarde" (2001).

HILLARY HOPE HERZOG is Assistant Professor of German Studies at the University of Kentucky, and is the author of *Männerkrankheiten: Medicine and Masculinity in the Works of Arthur Schnitzler* (2001). She specializes in Austrian Jewish writing at the turn of the two centuries and early twentieth-century German literature.

MATTHIAS KONZETT is Associate Professor of Germanic Languages and Literatures, Yale University. He is the author of *The Rhetoric of National Dissent in Thomas Bernhard, Peter Handke and Elfriede Jelinek* (2000) as well as of numerous essays on modern and contemporary German and Austrian literature. He is also the editor of *Encyclopedia of German Literature* (2000) and *The Companion to the Works of Thomas Bernhard* (2002).

EVA KUTTENBERG is Assistant Professor of German at Albion College. Her research interests focus on suicide as a narrative and aesthetic strategy in turn-of-the-century Viennese authors, Thomas Bernhard's prose, and Margarethe von Trotta's films. She is updating her manuscript "The Tropes of Suicide in Arthur Schnitzler's Prose" (1998).

ELIZABETH LOENTZ is Assistant Professor of Germanic Studies at the University of Illinois at Chicago. She is the author of *Negotiating Identity: Bertha Pappenheim (Anna O.) as German-Jewish Feminist, Social Worker, Activist, and Author* (1999). Her research interests lie in nineteenth- and twentieth-century Central European literature and culture, including German-Jewish Studies, Yiddish language and literature, Minority Literatures, the First German Women's Movement, and secular Yiddish schools in Chicago.

DAGMAR C. G. LORENZ is Professor of German at the University of Illinois-Chicago and Editor of *The German Quarterly*. She focuses in her research on Austrian and German Jewish literary and cultural issues and

Holocaust Studies with an emphasis on history and social thought, aesthetics, and minority discourses. Recent book publications include *Keepers of the Motherland: German Texts by Jewish Women Writers* (1997), and *Verfolgung bis zum Massenmord. Diskurse zum Holocaust in deutscher Sprache* (1992). Edited volumes include *Contemporary Jewish Writing in Austria* (1999); *Transforming the Center, Eroding the Margins: Essays on Ethnic and Cultural Boundaries in German-Speaking Countries*, co-editor: Renate S. Posthofen (1998); *Insiders and Outsiders. Jewish and Gentile Culture in Germany and Austria* (1994).

IMKE MEYER is Associate Professor of German and Chair of the Department of German at Bryn Mawr College. She has published on topics in nineteenth- and twentieth-century German and Austrian literature and culture. She is the author of *Jenseits der Spiegel kein Land: Ich-Fiktionen in Texten von Franz Kafka und Ingeborg Bachmann* (2001), as well as a number of articles and essays such as "The Trouble with Elfriede: Jelinek and Autobiography" (1999), "Hugo von Hofmannsthals Weltgeheimnis: Ein Spiel mit dem Unaussprechlichen" (1996), "'Ein Schandgesetz erkennt man, nach dem alles angerichtet ist': Täter-Opfer-Konstellationen in Ingeborg Bachmanns Erzählung 'Unter Mördern und Irren'" (1998).

JOHN NEUBAUER is Professor of Comparative Literature at the University of Amsterdam, Netherlands. His publications include *Symbolismus und symbolische Logik* (1978), *The Emancipation of Music from Language* (1986), *The Fin-de-Siècle Culture of Adolescence* (1992), as well as contributions to the Munich Edition of Goethe's works (1986–). He is a corresponding member of the British Academy, editor of the comparatist journal *Arcadia,* and is presently editing a four-volume collaborative history of literary cultures in East-Central Europe.

GERD K. SCHNEIDER is Professor of German at Syracuse University, specializing in early twentieth-century literature and contemporary Austrian and German authors, including Tankred Dorst, Anna Mitgutsch, Felix Mauthner, Felix Mitterer, Peter Turrini, and Johannes Mario Simmel. He also published on the history of Jewish settlements in New York City. His publications include "'I Wept while I Was Dreaming': How to Survive the Holocaust after the Holocaust in Jon Marans' Play Old Wicked Songs" (2000), "Die Verwandlung von Arthur Schnitzlers Reigen bei Max Ophuls und in amerikanischen Filmversionen" (1998), "'Und dennoch sagt der viel der Heimat sagt': Turrinis Ansichten über Österreich und die österreichische Seele" (1996), and "Die Verwandlung oder der Altersprozess als Entfremdung bei Jean Améry" (1995). His book *Die Rezeption von Arthur Schnitzlers Reigen, 1897–1994: Aufführ-*

rungen, Verfilmungen, Pressespiegel und andere zeitgenössische Kommenta-re (1995) is the authoritative study on the topic of *Reigen* reception.

FELIX TWERASER is Assistant Professor of German, Utah State University. His publications include *Political Dimensions of Arthur Schnitzler's Late Fiction* (1998), *The Dawn of an Old Age: Arthur Schnitzler's Critique of Monarchical Ideology and Institutions in First Republic Austria* (1996), and he edited *Imagining the Holocaust: The Problems and Promise of Representation* (1999).

G. J. WEINBERGER has been a member of the English Department at Central Connecticut State University since 1967, currently holding the title of Professor Emeritus. He is the author of numerous Schnitzler translations, including *The Final Plays* (1996), *Paracelsus and Other One-Act Plays* (1995), *Professor Bernhardi and Other Plays* (1993), *Three Late Plays* (1992), and of the critical study *Arthur Schnitzler's Late Plays* (1997).

Works Cited

Works by Arthur Schnitzler

Standard Edition

Gesammelte Werke. [*Die Erzählenden Schriften* I and II; *Die Dramatischen Werke* I and II]. Frankfurt: Fischer, 1961–62. Cited as: DW=*Die Dramatischen Werke*; ES=*Die Erzählenden Schriften.*

Autobiography and Diaries

Jugend in Wien. Eine Autobiographie. Ed. Therese Nickl and Heinrich Schnitzler. Vienna, Munich, Zurich: Fritz Molden, 1968; Frankfurt: Fischer, 1984, 1996.

Tagebuch. 10 vols. Vienna: Österreichischen Akademie der Wissenschaften, 1981 ff.

Correspondence

Briefe. 2 vols. Frankfurt: Fischer, 1982–1984. [Vol I: *Briefe 1875–1912.* Eds. Therese Nickl & Heinrich Schnitzler. Frankfurt: Fischer, 1981]; [Vol. II: *Briefe 1913–1931.* Eds. P. M. Braunwarth, R. Miklin, S. Pertlik & H. Schnitzler. Frankfurt: Fischer, 1984]. Cited as Briefe I and II.

Hofmannsthal, Hugo von, and Arthur Schnitzler. *Briefwechsel.* Ed. Therese Nickl and Heinrich Schnitzler. Frankfurt: Fischer, 1964.

Collections and Anthologies

Buch der Sprüche und Bedenken: Aphorismen und Fragmente. Vienna: Phaidon, 1927.

Aphorismen und Betrachtungen. Ed. Robert O. Weiss. Frankfurt: Fischer, 1967.

Entworfenes und Verworfenes: Aus dem Nachlaß. Ed. Reinhard Urbach. Frankfurt: Fischer, 1977.

Medizinische Schriften. Ed. Horst Thomé. Frankfurt: Fischer, 1991; Vienna: Paul Zsolnay, 1988.

Über Kunst und Kritik Vol. 3. "Aphorismen und Betrachtungen." Frankfurt: Fischer, 1993.

Publications in Journals

"Über Psychoanalyse." *Protokolle* 11/2 (1976): 283.

Critical Literature

Adorno, Theodor W. *Ästhetische Theorie*. Frankfurt: Suhrkamp Verlag, 1973.

———. *Mahler: A Musical Physiognom*. Chicago, U of Chicago P, 1991.

Alden, Martha Bodwich. "Schnitzler's Repudiated Debt to Casanova." *Modern Austrian Literature* 13/3 (1980): 25–32

Alewyn, Richard. "Nachwort." *Reigen. Liebelei*. Frankfurt: Fischer, 1986. 171–76.

Alexander, Theodor W. "The Author's Debt to the Physician: Aphonia in the Works of Arthur Schnitzler." *Journal of the International Arthur Schnitzler Research Association* 4/4 (1965).

Allerdissen, Rolf. *Arthur Schnitzler: Impressionistisches Rollenspiel und skeptischer Moralismus in seinen Erzählungen*. Bonn: Grundmann, 1985.

Allerkamp, Andrea. "'. . . Ich schreibe ja keine Memoiren:' Über die ars memoriae als Spiel zwischen Bild und Text in Schnitzlers *Fräulein Else*." *Cahiers d'Etudes Germaniques* 29 (1995): 95–108.

Alter, Maria Pospischil. *The Concept of the Physician in the Writings of Hans Carossa and Arthur Schnitzler*. Frankfurt: Herbert Lang, 1971.

Améry, Jean. *Diskurs über den Freitod. Hand an sich legen*. Stuttgart: Klett-Cotta, 1976.

Ametsbichler, Elizabeth G. "'Der Reiz des Reigens': *Reigen* Works by Arthur Schnitzler and Werner Schwab." *Modern Austrian Literature* 31/3–4 (1998): 288–300.

Anderson, Susan C. "Profile of a Gambler: Willi Kasda in *Spiel im Morgengrauen*." In Tax and Lawson eds., *Arthur Schnitzler and his Age. Intellectual and Artistic Currents*.

———. "Seeing Blindly: Voyeurism in Schnitzler's *Fräulein Else* and Andreas-Salomé's *Fenitschka*." In *Die Seele . . . ist ein weites Land: Kritische Beiträge zum Werk Arthur Schnitzlers*. Ed. Joseph P. Strelka. NY: Lang, 1996. 13–27.

———. "Shattered Illusions: Gambling in Arthur Schnitzler's Prose Works," *Modern Austrian Literature* 25/3–4 (1992): 248–51.

Anderson, Michael. "Making Room: Commedia and the Privatisation of the Theatre." In *The Commedia dell'Arte from the Renaissance to Dario Fo*. Ed. Christopher Cairns. Lewiston: Edwin Mellen P, 1988.

Angress, Ruth K. "Schnitzler's 'Frauenroman' Therese." *Modern Austrian Literature* 10/3–4 (1977): 265–82.

Arendt, Hannah. *The Jew as Pariah: Jewish Identity and Politics in the Modern Age.* New York: Grove Press, 1978.

———. *Rahel Varnhagen: Lebensgeschichte einer deutschen Jüdin aus der Romantik.* Munich: Piper, 1962.

Arens, Detlev. *Untersuchungen zu Arthur Schnitzlers Roman "Der Weg ins Freie."* Frankfurt: Peter Lang, 1981.

Arens, Katherine. "Schnitzler and Characterology: From Empire to Third Reich." *Modern Austrian Literature* 19/3–4 (1986): 97–127.

Aristophanes. *Clouds.* Trans. Robert Henning Webb. Charlottesville: U Virginia P, 1960.

Arnold, Heinz Ludwig. "Der falsch gewonnene Prozeß. Das Verfahren gegen Arthur Schnitzlers *Reigen.*" *Text + Kritik* 138/139 (1998).

Bachofen, Johann Jakob. *Das Mutterrecht; eine Untersuchung über die Gynaikokratie der alten Welt nach ihrer religiösen und rechtlichen Natur.* Stuttgart: Krais und Hoffman, 1861.

Barker, Andrew. "Race, Sex, and Character in Schnitzler's *Fräulein Else.*" *German Life and Letters* 54/1 (2001): 1–9.

Baumer, Franz. *Arthur Schnitzler.* Berlin: Colloquium, 1992.

Bayerdörfer, Hans-Peter. "Eindringlinge, Marionetten, Automaten. Symbolistische Dramatik und die Anfänge des modernen Theaters." In *Deutsche Literatur der Jahrhundertwende.* Ed. Viktor Žmegač. Königstein: Verlagsgruppe Athenäum et al., 1981.

———. "'Österreichische Verhältnisse'? — Arthur Schnitzlers *Professor Bernhardi* auf Berliner Bühnen 1912–1931." In *Von Franzos zu Canetti. Jüdische Autoren aus Österreich. Neue Studien.* Eds. Mark H. Gelber, Hans Otto Horch, Sigurd Paul Scheichl. Tübingen: Max Niemeyer, 1996. 211–24.

———. "Vom Konversationsstück zur Wurstelkomödie. Zu Arthur Schnitzlers Einaktern." *Jahrbuch der deutschen Schillergesellschaft* 16 (1972).

Beaumont, Francis. *The Knight of the Burning Pestle.* Ed. John Doebler. Lincoln: U Nebraska P, 1967.

Beckermann, Ruth. "Jean Améry and Austria." In Lorenz and Weinberger, eds., *Insiders and Outsiders. Jewish and Gentile Culture in Germany and Austria.* 73–88.

———. *Die Mazzesinsel. Juden in der Wiener Leopoldstadt.* Vienna: Löcker, 1984.

———. *Unzugehörig: Österreicher und Juden nach 1945.* Vienna: Löcker, 1989.

Beller, Steven. *Vienna and the Jews 1867–1938: A Cultural History.* Cambridge: Cambridge UP, 1989.

Beniston, Judith. *"Welttheater": Hofmannsthal, Richard von Kralik and the Revival of Catholic Drama in Austria 1890–1934.* London: W.S. Manley & Son Ltd, 1998.

Benjamin, Walter. *Charles Baudelaire Ein Lyriker des Hochkapitalismus.* Ed. Rolf Tiedemann. Frankfurt: Suhrkamp, 1992.

Benthien, Claudia. "Masken der Verführung — Intimität und Anonymität in Schnitzlers *Reigen.*" *Germanic Review* 72/2 (1997): 130–41.

Berchtold, Klaus, ed. "Das Linzer Programm der Deutschnationalen, 1882." *Österreichische Parteiprogramme* 1868–1966. Munich: R. Oldenbourg, 1967. 198–203.

——. "Das Salzburger Programm der Großdeutschen Volkspartei, 1920." *Österreichische Parteiprogramme* 1868–1966. Munich: R. Oldenbourg, 1967. 439–82.

Berger, John. "Ralph Fasanella and the Experience of the City." In *About Looking.* New York: Pantheon, 1980. 96–102.

——. *Ways of Seeing.* London: BBC and Penguin, 1988.

Berlin, Jeffrey B. "Arthur Schnitzler: A Bibliography of Criticism, 1965–1971." *Modern Austrian Literature* 4/4 (1971): 7–20.

Berkley, George E. *Vienna and Its Jews: The Tragedy of Success, 1880s–1980s.* Cambridge, MA: Abt, 1988.

Bertha Pappenheim zum Gedächtnis. Blätter des Jüdischen Frauenbundes 12 (1936).

Bettelheim, Bruno. *Freud's Vienna and Other Essays.* New York: Alfred A. Knopf, 1990.

Billroth, Theodor. *Über das Lehren und Lernen der medicinischen Wissenschaften an den Universitäten der deutschen Nation nebst allgemeinen Bemerkungen über Universitäten. Eine culturhistorische Studie.* Vienna: Carl Gerold's Sohn, 1876.

Binder, Hartmut, ed. *Kafka Handbuch. Bd. 1: Der Mensch und seine Zeit.* Stuttgart: Alfred Kröner Verlag, 1979.

Blaha, Paul. "Heinrich Schnitzler — oder Die Arbeit mit dem Schauspieler." *Maske und Kothurn. Vierteljahresschrift für Theaterwissenschaft* 8 (1962): 182.

Blickle, Peter. "Die Einlösung subversiven Wirkungspotentials: Die Theaterskandale um Arthur Schnitzlers *Professor Bernhardi* und Rolf Hochhuths *Stellvertreter.*" *New German Review* 10 (1994): 103–18.

Blöcker, Günter. *Heinrich von Kleist oder das absolute Ich.* Berlin: Argon, 1960.

Bodansky, Oscar. "Physicians Who Abandoned Medicine for Literature: John Keats, Arthur Conan Doyle, Arthur Schnitzler, Somerset Maugham." *Proceedings of the Virchow-Pirquet Medical Society* 33 (June 1979).

Boetticher, Dirk von. *Meine Werke sind lauter Diagnosen. Über die ärztliche Dimension im Werk Arthur Schnitzlers.* Heidelberg: Universitätsverlag Carl Winter, 1999.

Boyarin, Daniel. *Unheroic Conduct. The Rise of Heterosexuality and the Invention of the Jewish Man.* Berkeley: U of California P, 1997.

Boyer, John W. *Culture and Political Crisis in Vienna: Christian Socialism in Power, 1897–1918.* Chicago: U of Chicago P, 1995.

———. *Political Radicalism in Late Imperial Vienna: Origins of the Christian Social Movement 1848–1897.* Chicago: U of Chicago P, 1981.

Breuer, Josef, and Sigmund Freud. *Studien über Hysterie.* Frankfurt: Fischer, 1996. [Original 1895].

Brinson, C. E. J. "Searching for Happiness: Towards an Interpretation of Arthur Schnitzler's *Doktor Gräsler, Badearzt.*" *Modern Austrian Literature* 16/2 (1983): 47–63.

Brod, Max. *Jüdinnen.* Berlin: A. Juncker, 1911.

Bronfen, Elisabeth. *Over Her Dead Body: Death, Femininity, and the Aesthetic.* New York: Routledge, 1992.

Brooks, Peter. *Reading for the Plot: Design and Intention in Narrative.* New York: Knopf, 1984.

Brüggemann, Diethelm. "Grabbe—Scherz, Satire, Ironie und tiefere Bedeutung." In *Die deutsche Komödie vom Mittelalter bis zur Gegenwart.* Ed. Walter Hinck. Dusseldorf: August Bagel, 1977.

Buber, Martin. *Der Jude und sein Judentum: Gesammelte Aufsätze und Reden.* Cologne: Joseph Melzer Verlag, 1963.

Bunzl, John. *Klassenkampf in der Diaspora: Zur Geschichte der jüdischen Arbeiterbewegung.* Vienna: Europaverlag, 1975.

Bunzl, John, and Bernd Marin. *Antisemitismus in Österreich: Sozialhistorische und soziologische Studien.* Innsbruck: Inn Verlag, 1983.

Bunzl, Matti. "From Kreisky to Waldheim. Another Jewish Youth in Vienna." In *Contemporary Jewish Writing in Austria.* Ed. Dagmar C. G. Lorenz. Lincoln and London: U of Nebraska P, 1999. 346–58.

Butzko, Ellen. *Arthur Schnitzler und die zeitgenössische Theaterkritik.* Frankfurt: Peter Lang, 1991.

Campbell, Donald. "The Role of the Father in a Pre-Suicide State." In *Psychoanalytic Understanding of Violence and Suicide.* Ed. Rosine Jozef Perelberg. London, New York: Routledge, 1999. 73–86.

Chamberlain, Houston Stewart. *Die Grundlagen des neunzehnten Jahrhunderts.* Munich: Bruckmann, 1944.

Cohen, Gary B. *Education and Middle-Class Society in Imperial Austria 1848– 1918.* West Lafayette, IN: Purdue UP, 1996.

Cohn, Dorrit. *Transparent Minds.* Princeton: Princeton UP, 1978.

Comini, Alexandra. "Through a Viennese Looking Glass Darkly: Images of Arnold Schoenberg and His Circle." *Arts Magazine* 58/9 (1984): 107–19.

Crary, Jonathan. *Suspensions of Perception: Attention, Spectacle, and Modern Culture.* Cambridge, MA: MIT Press, 1999.

———. *Techniques of the Observer: On Vision and Modernity in the Nineteenth Century.* Cambridge, MA: MIT Press, 1992.

Dangel, Elsbeth. "Augenblicke Schnitzlerscher Frauen." *Sprache und Literatur in Wissenschaft und Unterricht* 67 (1991): 100–110.

———. "Vergeblichkeit und Zweideutigkeit: *Therese, Chronik eines Frauenlebens.*" In Hartmut Scheible, ed. *Arthur Schnitzler in neuer Sicht,* 164–87.

Daviau, Donald G. *Hermann Bahr.* Boston: Twayne, 1985.

Dekoven, Marianne. "Modernism and Gender." In *The Cambridge Companion to Modernism.* Cambridge: Cambridge UP, 1999. 174–93.

Deleuze, Gilles, and Felix Guattari. *Kafka: Toward a Minor Literature.* Trans. Dana Polan. Minneapolis: U of Minnesota P, 1986.

Delius, Annete. "[Arthur] Schnitzlers *Reigen* und der *Reigen*-Prozeß. Verständliche und manipulierbare Mißverständnisse in der Rezeption." *Der Deutschunterricht* 28/2 (1976): 98–115.

Dessau, Bettina. *Nathans Rückkehr. Studien zur Rezeptionsgeschichte seit 1945.* Frankfurt, Peter Lang, 1986.

Deutsch-Schreiner, Evelyn. "Die Opfer schützen die Täter. Jüdische Figuren in der österreichischen Bühnenpraxis nach dem Holocaust." *Theatralia Judaica 2: Nach der Shoah. Israelisch-deutsche Theaterbeziehungen seit 1949.* Ed. Hans-Peter Bayerdörfer. Tübingen: Niemeyer, 1996. 100–114.

———. *Theater im Wiederaufbau. Zur Kulturpolitik im Parteien-und Verbändestaat.* Vienna: Sonderzahl, 2001.

Dieterle, Bernard. "Keineswegs kann ich weiterleben. Figurationen des Schreibens bei Arthur Schnitzler." *Modern Austrian Literature* 30/1 (1997): 20–38.

Doppler, Alfred. "Der Wandel der Darstellungsperspektive in den Dichtungen Arthur Schnitzlers. Mann und Frau als sozialpsychologisches Problem." In *Akten des Internationalen Symposions "Arthur Schnitzler und seine Zeit."* Ed. Giuseppe Farese. Bern: Peter Lang, 1985. 41–59.

Ducharte, Pierre Louis. *The Italian Comedy.* New York: Dover, 1966.

Durkheim, Emile. *Le Suicide: étude de sociologie.* Paris: Presses universitaires de France, 1930.

Ehalt, Hubert Ch., Gernot Heiß, and Hannes Stekl, eds. *Glücklich ist, wer vergisst?: Das andere Wien um 1900.* Vienna: Böhlau, 1986.

Ehalt, Silvia. "Wiener Theater um 1900." In Ehalt et al., eds. *Glücklich ist, wer vergisst.* 325–42.

Ehmer, Josef. "Wiener Arbeitswelten um 1900." In Ehalt et al., eds. *Glücklich ist, wer vergisst,* 195–214.

Ekfelt, Nils. "Arthur Schnitzler's 'Spiel im Morgengrauen:' Free Will, Fate, and Chaos." *German Quarterly* 51 (1978): 170–81.

Englisch, Paul. *Geschichte der erotischen Literatur.* Stuttgart: Julius Püttmann, 1927. 273.

Erenstein, Robert. "The Rise and Fall of Commedia dell'Arte." In *500 Years of Theatre History.* Eds. Michael Bigelow Dixon and Val Smith. Lyme, NH: Smith and Kraus, 2000.

Farese, Guiseppe, ed. *Akten des Internationalen Symposions "Arthur Schnitzler und seine Zeit."* Bern: Peter Lang, 1985.

———. *Arthur Schnitzler: Ein Leben in Wien 1862–1931.* Trans. Karin Krieger. Munich: Beck, 1999.

Feuchtwanger, Lion. *Die Geschwister Oppenheim.* Amsterdam: Querido: 1934.

Fliedl, Konstanze. *Arthur Schnitzler: Poetik der Erinnerung.* Vienna: Böhlau, 1997.

———. "Verspätungen: Schnitzlers *Therese* als Anti-Trivialroman." *Jahrbuch der Deutschen Schiller-Gesellschaft* 33 (1989): 323–47.

Fonagy, Peter and Mary Target. "Towards Understanding Violence: The Use of the Body and the Role of the Father." *Psychoanalytic Understanding of Violence and Suicide.* Ed. Rosine Jozef Perelberg. London, New York: Routledge, 1999. 51–72.

Forchheimer, Stephanie. "Wiener Erinnerungen." *Bertha Pappenheim zum Gedächtnis. Blätter des Jüdischen Frauenbundes* 12 (1936): 27–28.

Freeman, Thomas. "*Leutnant Gustl:* A Case of Male Hysteria?" *Modern Austrian Literature* 25/3–4 (1992).

Freud, Sigmund. *Briefe, 1879–1939.* Eds. Ernst and Lucie Freud. Frankfurt: Fischer, 1960.

———. *Das Unbehagen in der Kultur.* Vienna: Internationaler Psychoanalytischer Verlag, 1930.

Frey, Philipp. "Schnitzlers *Reigen.*" *Die Wage* 6/17 (April 18, 1903): 532–33.

Friedländer, Saul. *Nazi Germany and the Jews: The Years of Persecution, 1933–1939.* New York: Harper/Collins, 1997.

Friend. "Arthur Schnitzler: 'Ich habe Heimatgefühl, aber keinen Patriotismus.'" *Literatur und Kritik* 269/270 (November 1992): 55–62.

Fritsche, Alfred. *Dekadenz im Werk Arthur Schnitzlers.* Frankfurt: Peter Lang, 1974.

Fuchs, Eduard. *Die Juden in der Karikatur.* Munich: Verlag Albert Langen, 1921.

Gates, Barbara. *Victorian Suicides: Mad Crimes and Sad Histories.* Princeton, NJ: Princeton UP, 1988.

Gay, Peter. *Schnitzler's Century: The Making of Middle-Class Culture, 1815–1914.* New York: Norton, 2001.

Gidion, Heidi. "Haupt-und Nebensache in Arthur Schnitzlers Roman *Der Weg ins Freie.*" *Text + Kritik* 138/39 (1998): 47–60. (Special volume on Arthur Schnitzler, ed. H. L. Arnold).

Gilman, Sander. *Disease and Representation.* Ithaca: Cornell UP, 1988.

———. *The Jew's Body.* New York: New York UP, 1991.

———. "Karl Kraus's Oscar Wilde." In *Vienna 1900: From Altenberg to Wittgenstein.* Eds. Edward Timms and Ritchie Robertson. Edinburgh: Edinburgh UP, 1990. 12–26.

Gilman, Sander, and Jack Zipes, eds. *Yale Companion to Jewish Writing and Thought in German Culture 1096–1996.* New Haven and London: Yale UP, 1997.

Glanz, Luzia. *Das Puppenspiel und sein Publikum.* Berlin: Junker & Dünnhaupt, 1941.

Glaser, Albert. "Masken der Libertinage: Überlegungen zu Schnitzlers Erzählung Casanovas Heimfahrt." *Text + Kritik* 10/2 (1982): 355–64.

Glossy, Karl. *Vierzig Jahre Deutsches Volkstheater. Ein Beitrag zur deutschen Theatergeschichte.* Vienna: Deutsches Volkstheater, 1929.

Gölter, Waltraud. "Weg ins Freie oder Flucht in die Finsternis — Ambivalenz bei Arthur Schnitzler." In Scheible, ed. *Arthur Schnitzler in neuer Sicht,* 241–91.

Gordon, Mel. *Voluptuous Panic. The Erotic World of Weimar and Berlin.* Los Angeles: Feral House, 2000.

Grabbe, Christian Dietrich. *Scherz, Satire, Ironie und tiefere Bedeutung.* Stuttgart: Reclam, 1970.

Grimstad, Kari. *Masks of the Prophet. The Theatrical World of Karl Kraus.* Toronto: U of Toronto P, 1982.

Green, Martin, and John Swan. *The Triumph of Pierrot. The Commedia dell'Arte and the Modern Imagination.* New York: Macmillan, 1986.

Gruber, Helmut. *Red Vienna: Experiment in Working-Class Culture 1919–1934.* New York: Oxford UP, 1991.

Grunberger. Richard. *Germany 1918–1945.* Philadelphia: Dufour Editions, 1964.

Gryphius, Andreas. *Absurda Comica oder Herr Peter Squentz.* Ed. Herbert Cysarz. Stuttgart: Reclam, 1954.

Günther, Klaus. "'Es ist wirklich, wie wenn die Leute wahnsinnig wären': Bemerkungen zu Arthur Schnitzler und Ernst Mach." *Arthur Schnitzler in neuer Sicht.* Ed. Hartmut Scheible. Munich: Fink, 1981. 99–116.

Gutt, Barbara. *Emanzipation bei Arthur Schnitzler.* Berlin: Spiess, 1978.

Habermas, Jürgen. *Structural Transformation of the Public Sphere.* Trans. Thomas Bürger. Cambridge: MIT Press, 1989.

———. "Struggles for Recognition in the Democratic Constitutional State." In *Multiculturalism: Examining the Politics of Recognition.* Ed. Amy Gutman. Princeton: Princeton UP, 1994.

Hacker, Friedrich. "Im falschen Leben gibt es kein Richtiges." *Literatur und Kritik* 163/164 (1982): 36–44.

Hadda, Janet. *Passionate Women, Passive Men: Suicide in Yiddish Literature.* Albany: State U of New York P, 1988.

Hamann, Brigitte. *Hitlers Wien: Lehrjahre eines Diktators.* Munich: Piper, 1999.

Hare, David. *The Blue Room.* London: Faber and Faber, 1999.

Haselberg, Peter von. "Psychologie oder Konstellationen?: Am Beispiel von Dr. Gräsler, Badearzt." In Hartmut Scheible, ed. *Arthur Schnitzler in neuer Sicht,* 188–99.

Hasuner, Henry H. "Die Beziehungen zwischen Arthur Schnitzler und Sigmund Freud." *Modern Austrian Literature* 3/2 (1970): 48–61.

Heine, Wolfgang, ed. *Der Kampf um den Reigen. Vollständiger Bericht über die sechstägige Verhandlung gegen Direktion und Darsteller des Kleinen Schauspielhauses Berlin.* Berlin: Ernst Rowohlt, 1922.

Held, David. *Democracy and the Global Order: From the Modern State to Cosmopolitan Governance.* Stanford: Stanford UP, 1995.

Heller, Peter. "Freud as a Phenomenon in the Fin de Siècle." In Tax and Lawson eds., *Arthur Schnitzler and his Age. Intellectual and Artistic Currents.* 2–28.

Hermand, Jost. "The Wandering Jew's Rhine Journey: Heine's Lorelei." In Lorenz and Weinberger, eds., *Insiders and Outsiders. Jewish and Gentile Culture in Germany and Austria.* 39–46.

Higonnet, Margret R. "Speaking Silences: Women's Suicide." In *The Female Body in Western Culture.* Ed. Susan Rubin Suleiman. Cambridge, MA: Harvard UP, 1986.

———. "Suicide as Self-Construction." *Germaine de Stael: Crossing the Borders.* Eds. Madelyn Gutwirth, Avriel Goldberger, and Karyna Szmurlo. New Brunswick: Rutgers UP, 1991. 69–81.

Hirschmüller, Albrecht. *The Life and Work of Josef Breuer: Physiology and Psycho-analysis.* New York: New York UP, 1978.

Hitler, Adolf. *Mein Kampf.* Munich: F. Eher nachf., 1935.

———. *Mein Kampf.* Trans. Ralph Manheim. Boston/New York: Houghton Mifflin, 1999.

Hohoff, Curt. *Heinrich von Kleist 1777/1977.* Bonn: Inter Nationes, 1977.

Huizinga, Johan. *Homo ludens.* Boston: Beacon Press, 1955.

Huyssen, Andreas. "The Disturbance of Vision in Vienna Modernism." *Modernism/Modernity* 5/3 (1998): 33–47.

Iggers, Wilma Abeles. *Karl Kraus. A Viennese Critic of the Twentieth Century.* The Hague: Martinus Nijhoff, 1967.

Ilmer, Frida. "Schnitzler's Attitudes with Regard to the Transcendental." *Germanic Review* 10 (1935).

Janik, Allen, and Stephen Toulmin. *Wittgenstein's Vienna.* New York: Simon and Schuster/Touchstone, 1973.

Janz, Rolf-Peter. "Professor Bernhardi — 'Eine Art medizinischer Dreyfus'? Die Darstellung des Antisemitusmus bei Arthur Schnitzler." In *Akten des Internationalen Symposiums: "Arthur Schnitzler und seine Zeit."* Ed. Giuseppe Farese. Bern: Peter Lang, 1985. 108–17.

Janz, Rolf-Peter, and Klaus Laermann. *Arthur Schnitzler: Zur Diagnose des Wiener Bürgertums im Fin de siècle.* Stuttgart: Metzler, 1977.

Jensen, Ellen M. *Streifzüge durch das Leben von Anna O./Bertha Pappenheim: Ein Fall für die Psychiatrie — Ein Leben für die Philanthropie.* Frankfurt: dtv, 1984.

John, Michael. "Obdachlosigkeit — Massenerscheinung und Unruheherd im Wien der Spätgründerzeit." In Ehalt et al., eds., *Glücklich ist, wer vergisst.* 173–94.

Johnston, William M. *The Austrian Mind. An Intellectual and Social History 1848–1938.* Berkeley: U of California P, 1983.

———. "Death as Refuge: Suicides by Austrian Intellectuals." In *The Austrian Mind.* 1983.

Jud, Silvia. "Arthur Schnitzler: Frau Berta Garlan (1901)." In *Erzählkunst der Vormoderne.* Eds. Rolf Tarot and Gabriela Scherer. Bern: Peter Lang, 1996. 417–47.

Judson, Pieter M. *Exclusive Revolutionaries: Liberal Politics, Social Experience, and National Identity in the Austrian Empire, 1848–1914.* Ann Arbor: U of Michigan P, 1996.

Just, Gottfried. *Ironie und Sentimentalität in den erzählenden Dichtungen Arthur Schnitzlers.* Berlin: Erich Schmidt, 1968.

Kaes, Anton, ed. *Weimarer Republik. Manifeste und Dokumente zur deutschen Literatur 1918–1933.* Stuttgart: Metzler, 1983.

Kafka, Franz. *Tagebücher in der Fassung der Handschrift.* Eds. Hans-Gerd Koch, Michael Müller, and Malcolm Pasley. Frankfurt: Fischer, 1990. [Kritische Ausgabe].

Kaiser, Erich. *Arthur Schnitzler: Leutnant Gustl und andere Erzählungen.* Munich: Oldenbourg, 1997.

Kann, Robert A. "Die historische Situation und die entscheidenden politischen Ereignisse zur Zeit und im Leben Arthur Schnitzlers." *Literatur und Kritik* 161/62 (1982): 19–25.

Kaulen, Heinrich. "Antisemitismus und Aufklärung: Zum Verständnis von Arthur Schnitzlers Professor Bernhardi." *Zeitschrift für Deutsche Philologie* 102/2 (1981): 177–98.

Kecht, Maria-Regina. "Analyse der sozialen Realität in Schnitzlers 'Spiel im Morgengrauen.'" *Modern Austrian Literature* 25/3–4 (1992): 181–97.

Kelly, Dorothy. *Telling Glances: Voyeurism and the French Novel.* New Brunswick, NJ: Rutgers UP, 1992.

Keiser, Brenda. *Deadly Dishonor: The Duel and the Honor Code in the Works of Arthur Schnitzler.* New York: Peter Lang, 1990.

Kinder, Hermann, and Werner Hilgemann. *dtv-Atlas zur Weltgeschichte.* Munich: Deutscher Taschenbuch Verlag, 1981.

Kleist, Heinrich von. *Sämtliche Werke.* Ed. Erwin Laaths. Munich and Zurich: Droemersche Verlagsanstalt, 1959.

Klieneberger, H. R. "Arthur Schnitzler and the Jewish Question." *Forum for Modern Language Studies* 19/3 (1983): 261–73.

Kiwit, Wolfram. '*Sehnsucht nach meinem Roman.' Arthur Schnitzler als Romancier.* Bochum: Verlag Dr. Dieter Winkler, 1991.

Klingenstein, Eva. *Die Frau mit Eigenschaften: Literatur und Gesellschaft in der Wiener Frauenpresse um 1900.* Cologne: Böhlau, 1997.

Kolleth, Sabina. "Gewalt in Ehe und Intimpartnerschaft." In Ehalt et al., eds., *Glücklich ist, wer vergisst.* 145–71.

Kluge, Gerhard. "Arthur Schnitzlers Einakterzyklus *Komödie der Worte.*" *Drama und Theater im 20. Jahrhundert. Festschrift für Walter Hinck.* Eds. Hans Dietrich Irmscher and Werner Keller. Göttingen: Vandenhoeck & Ruprecht, 1983.

Kluger, Ruth. "Die Ödnis des entlarvten Landes — Antisemitismus im Werk jüdisch-österreichischer Autoren." In *Katastrophen. Über deutsche Literatur.* Göttingen: Wallstein, 1994. 65–70.

———. "The Theme of Anti-Semitism in the Work of Austrian Jews." In *Anti-Semitism in Times of Crisis.* Eds. Sander L. Gilman and Steven T. Katz. New York: New York UP, 1991.

Körner, Josef. *Arthur Schnitzlers Gestalten und Probleme.* Zurich: Amalthea, 1921.

Kracauer, Siegfried. *From Caligari to Hitler. A Psychological History of the German Film*. Princeton, NJ: Princeton UP, 1947.

Kraus, Karl. *Die Fackel* 87 (December 7, 1901): 12–23.

———. *Karl Kraus für Gestreßte: Aphorismen*. Ed. Christian Wagenknecht. Frankfurt: Suhrkamp, 1997.

Kreissler, Felix. "Österreichische Nation und Kultur im Theater des Exils. Ein fragmentarischer Essay." In *Zeit der Befreiung. Wiener Theater nach 1945*. Eds. Hilde Haider-Pregler and Peter Roessler. Vienna: Picus, 1997. 12–39.

Kristeva, Julia. *The Kristeva Reader*. Ed. Toril Moi. New York: Columbia UP, 1986.

Kuttenberg, Eva. *The Tropes of Suicide in Arthur Schnitzler's Prose*. Ph.D. diss., New York University, 1998.

Laermann, Klaus. *"Leutnant Gustl." Arthur Schnitzler: Zur Diagnose des Wiener Bürgertums im Fin de siècle*. Ed. Rolf-Peter Janz and Klaus Laermann. Stuttgart: Metzler, 1977.

———. "Spiel im Morgengrauen." In *Akten des internationalen Symposiums "Arthur Schnitzler und seine Zeit."* Ed. Giuseppe Farese. Bern: Peter Lang, 1985. 182–200.

Lange, Wolfgang. "Wien um 1900. Phantasmagorie einer Metropole." *Deutschunterricht* 47.5 (1995): 30–44.

Lange-Kirchheim, Astrid. "Adoleszenz, Hysterie und Autorschaft in Arthur Schnitzlers Novelle *Fräulein Else*." *Jahrbuch der Deutschen Schillergesellschaft* 42 (1998): 265–300.

Lebensaft, Elisabeth. *Anordnung und Funktion zentraler Aufbauelemente in den Erzählungen Arthur Schnitzlers*. Vienna: Notring, 1972.

Lederer, Herbert. "Afterword." *Paracelsus and Other One-Act Plays by Arthur Schnitzler*. Trans. G. J. Weinberger. Riverside: Ariadne, 1995. 207–20.

Leenaars, Antoon A. "Psychological Perspectives on Suicide." In *Current Concepts of Suicide*. Ed. David Lester. Philadelphia: Charles Press, 1990. 159–67.

Leenaars, Antoon A., ed. *Suicidology: Essays in Honor of Edwin S. Shneidman*. Northvale, NJ: Aronson, 1993.

Le Rider, Jacques. *Das Ende der Illusion. Die Wiener Moderne und die Krisen der Identität*. Trans. Robert Fleck. Vienna: Österreichischer Bundesverlag, 1990.

Lesky, Erna. *The Vienna Medical School of the 19th Century*. Baltimore, London: The Johns Hopkins UP, 1976.

Lester, David, Betty H. Sell, and Kenneth D. Sell. *Suicide: A Guide to Information Sources*. Detroit, MI: Gale Research, 1980.

Lehmann, A. G. "Pierrot and Fin de Siècle." *Romantic Mythologies*. Ed. Ian Fletcher. New York: Barnes & Noble, 1967.

Lichtenberg, Georg Christoph. *Lichtenbergs Werke in einem Band.* Ed. Hans Friederici. Berlin, Weimar: Aufbau-Verlag: 1982.

———. *Sudelbücher II, Materialhefte, Tagebücher.* Munich: Carl Hanser Verlag, 1971.

Lindken, Hans-Ulrich. *Arthur Schnitzler Aspekte und Akzente: Materialien zu Leben und Werk.* Frankfurt: Peter Lang, 1984.

———. *Arthur Schnitzler-Erzählungen.* Munich: Oldenburg, 1970.

Liptzin, Sol. *Arthur Schnitzler.* New York: Prentice Hall, 1931.

Litman, Robert. "Sigmund Freud on Suicide." In *Essential Papers on Suicide.* Eds. John T. Maltsberger and Mark Goldblatt. New York: New York UP, 1996.

Lorenz, Dagmar. *Wiener Moderne.* Stuttgart: Metzler, 1995.

Lorenz, Dagmar C. G., and Gabriele Weinberger, eds. *Insiders and Outsiders. Jewish and Gentile Culture in Germany and Austria.* Detroit: Wayne State UP, 1994.

Lukács, Georg. "'Der Weg ins Freie.' (Arthur Schnitzler regénye)." *Nyugat* 1 (1908): 222–24. Rpt. Lukács, *Ifjúkori müvek (1902–1918).* Budapest: Magvetö, 1977. 174–78.

Lukas, Wolfgang. *Das Selbst und das Fremde: Epochale Lebenskrisen und ihre Lösungen im Werk Arthur Schnitzlers.* Munich: Fink, 1996.

Luprecht, Mark. *"What People Call Pessimism": Sigmund Freud, Arthur Schnitzler, and Nineteenth-Century Controversy at the University of Vienna Medical School.* Riverside: Ariadne Press, 1991.

Madden, David. *Harlequin's Stick Charlie's Cane.* Bowling Green U Popular P, 1975.

Maderthaner, Wolfgang, and Lutz Musner. *Die Anarchie der Vorstadt. Das andere Wien um 1900.* Frankfurt/New York: Campus Verlag, 1999.

Magris, Claudio. "Arthur Schnitzler und das Karussell der Triebe." In *Arthur Schnitzler in neuer Sicht.* Ed. Hartmut Scheible. Munich: Fink, 1981. 71–80.

Mahal, Günther, ed. *Doktor Johannes Faust, Puppenspiel in vier Aufzügen.* Stuttgart: Reclam, 1991.

Mann, Thomas. *Die Briefe Thomas Manns. Regesten und Register. Band II. Die Briefe von 1934 bis 1943.* Eds. Hans Bürgin and Hans-Otto Mayer. Frankfurt: S. Fischer, 1980.

Marcuse, Ludwig. "Berlin 1920: Sex, Politik und Kunst im *Reigen.*" In *L.M. Obszön. Geschichte einer Entrüstung.* Munich: Paul List, 1962. 207–63;

———. "Berlin 1920: Sex, Politik und Kunst im *Reigen.*" *Der Monat* 14/168 (September 1962): 48–55 and 14/169 (Oktober 1962): 34–46.

Marr, Wilhelm. *Der Sieg des Judenthums über das Germanenthum.* Bern: Rudolph Costenoble, 1879.

Matt, Peter von. *Liebesverrat. Die Treulosen in der Literatur*. Munich: Deutscher Taschenbuchverlag, 1991.

Martens, Lorna. "Naked Bodies in Schnitzler's Late Prose Fiction." In *Die Seele … ist ein weites Land: Kritische Beiträge zum Werk Arthur Schnitzlers*. Ed. Joseph P. Strelka. NY: Peter Lang, 1996. 107–29.

Matthias, Bettina. *Masken des Lebens, Gesichter des Todes: Zum Verhältnis von Tod und Darstellung im erzählerischen Werk Arthur Schnitzlers*. Würzburg: Königshausen & Neumann, 1999.

Mayer, Anton. *Theater in Wien um 1900. Der Dichterkreis Jung Wien*. Vienna: Böhlau, 1997.

Melchinger, Christa. *Illusion und Wirklichkeit im dramatischen Werk Arthur Schnitzlers*. Heidelberg: Carl Winter, 1968.

Mendelssohn, Peter de. "Zur Geschichte des *Reigen*. Aus dem Briefwechsel zwischen Arthur Schnitzler und S. Fischer." *Almanach. Das sechsundsiebzigste Jahr*. Frankfurt: S. Fischer Verlag, 1962. 18–35.

Mennemeier, Franz Norbert. "Die Revolution, von unten gesehen. Zu Arthur Schnitzlers "Der grüne Kakadu." In *Deutsche Dichtung um 1890. Beiträge zu einer Literatur im Umbruch*. Eds. Robert Leroy and Eckart Pastor. Bern: Peter Lang, 1991. 391–97.

Merz, Carl, and Helmut Qualtinger. *Der Herr Karl und andere Texte fürs Theater*. Vienna: Deuticke, 1995.

Middell, Eike. *Literatur zweier Kaiserreiche. Deutsche und österreichische Literatur der Jahrhundertwende*. Salzburg: Akademie Verlag, 1993.

Miklin, Richard. "Heimatliebe und Patriotismus: Arthur Schnitzlers Einstellung zu Österreich-Ungarn im Ersten Weltkrieg." *Modern Austrian Literature* 19/3–4 (1986): 197–212.

Miller, Norbert, and Karl Riha, eds. *Kasperltheater für Erwachsene*. Frankfurt: Insel, 1978.

Minois, Georges. *History of Suicide: Voluntary Death in the Western World*. Trans. Lydia G. Cochrane. Baltimore and London: The Johns Hopkins UP, 1999.

Möhrmann, Renate. "Schnitzlers Frauen und Mädchen. Zwischen Sachlickeit und Sentiment." In *Akten des Internationalen Symposions "Arthur Schnitzler und seine Zeit."* Ed. Giuseppe Farese. Bern: Peter Lang, 1985. 93–107.

Morris, Craig. "Der vollständige inner Monolog: Eine erzählerlose Erzählung? Eine Untersuchung am Beispiel von *Leutnant Gustl* und *Fräulein Else*." *Modern Austrian Literature* 31/2 (1998): 30–51.

Müller-Seidel, Walter. *Arztbilder im Wandel: Zum literarischen Werk Arthur Schnitzlers*. Munich: Verlag der Bayerischen Akademie der Wissenschaften, 1997.

———. "Moderne Literatur und Medizin. Zum literarischen Werk Arthur Schnitzlers." *Akten des Internationalen Symposiums "Arthur Schnitzler und seine Zeit."* Ed. Giuseppe Farese. Frankfurt: Peter Lang, 1985.

Muerdel Dormer, Lore. "Felix Salten." In *Major Figures of Turn-Of-The-Century Austrian Literature.* Ed. Donald G. Daviau. Riverside: Ariadne Press, 1991. 405–40.

Nancy, Jean-Luc. *The Birth to Presence.* Trans. Brian Holmes. Stanford: Stanford UP, 1993.

Nardroff, Ernest H. von. "*Doktor Gräsler, Badearzt:* Weather as an Aspect of Schnitzler's Symbolism." *Germanic Review* 43/2 (1968): 109–19.

Nehring, Wolfgang. "Schnitzler, Freud's Alter Ego?" *Modern Austrian Literature* 10/3–4 (1977): 179–94.

———. "Zwischen Indentifikation und Distanz: Zur Darstellung der jüdischen Charaktere in Arthur Schnitzlers Der Weg ins Freie." In *Kontroversen, alte und neue, V: Auseinandersetzungen um jiddische Sprache und Literatur; Jüdische Komponente in der deutschen Literatur — die Assimilationskontroverse.* Eds. Schöne, Albrecht et al. Tübingen: Niemeyer, 1986. 162–70.

Niewyk. Donald L. *The Jews in Weimar Germany.* Baton Rouge: Louisiana State UP, 1980.

Oberhammer, Vinzenz. *Die Bronzestandbilder des Maximiliangrabmales in der Hofkirche zu Innsbruck.* Innsbruck: Tyrolia Verlag, 1935.

Offermann, Ernst L. *Arthur Schnitzler: Das Komödienwerk als Kritik des Impressionismus.* Munich: Fink, 1973.

Oosterhoff, Jenneke A. *Die Männer sind infam, solang sie Männer sind: Konstruktionen der Männlichkeit in den Werken Arthur Schnitzlers.* Tübingen: Stauffenburg, 2000.

Oreglia, Giacomo. *The Commedia dell'Arte.* Trans. Lovett F. Edwards. New York: Hill & Wang, 1968.

Otis, Laura. "Arthur Schnitzler: The Open Self." *Membranes: Metaphors of Invasion in Nineteenth-Century Literature, Science, and Politics.* Baltimore: Johns Hopkins UP, 1999. 119–47.

———. "The Language of Infection: Disease and Identity in Schnitzler's *Reigen.*" *Germanic Review* 70/2 (1995).

Oxaal, Ivar, Michael Pollak, and Gerhard Botz, eds. *Jews, Antisemitism and Culture in Vienna.* London and New York: Routledge/Kegan Paul, 1987.

Paperno, Irina. *Suicide as a Cultural Institution in Dostoevsky's Russia.* Ithaca: Cornell UP, 1997.

Pappenheim, Bertha. "Der echte Ring." *Frankfurter Israelitisches Gemeindeblatt* 14/10 (1936): 393–94.

————. "Der Einzelne und die Gemeinschaft." *Blätter des jüdischen Frauenbundes* 9/6 (1933): 1.

————. "Die Erbschaft." *Frankfurter Israelitisches Gemeindeblatt* 11 (1933): 277–8.

————. "Die jüdische Frau." In *Bertha Pappenheim: Leben und Schriften*. Ed. Dora Edinger. Frankfurt: Ner Tamid Verlag, 1963.

————. "Jüdische Mütter: Pogrom 1905." Ms. Leo Baeck Institute Archives, New York.

————. *Kämpfe: Sechs Erzählungen*. Frankfurt: J. Kauffmann, 1916.

————. *Sisyphus-Arbeit: Reiseberichte aus den Jahren* 1911–1912. Leipzig: Paul Linder, 1924.

————. "Die sozialen Grundlagen der Sittlichkeitsfrage." *Die Frau* 9/3 (December 1901). 129–38.

————. *Zur Lage der jüdischen Bevölkerung in Galizien: Reise-Eindrücke und Vorschläge zur Besserung der Verhältnisse*. Frankfurt: Neuer Frankfurter Verlag, 1903.

————. "Zur Sittlichkeitsfrage." 2. Delegiertentage des Jüdischen Frauenbundes. Frankfurt am Main. October 2–3, 1907.

Peabody, Ruth E. *Commedia Works*. n.p.: Amos Press, 1984.

Pelinka, Anton. "Die Struktur und die Probleme der Gesellschaft zur Zeit Arthur Schnitzlers." *Literatur und Kritik* 163/164 (1982): 59–66.

Perlmann, Michaela L. *Arthur Schnitzler*. Stuttgart: J. B. Metzler, 1987.

Pestalozzi, Karl. "Tieck-Der gestiefelte Kater." In *Die deutsche Komödie vom Mittelalter bis zur Gegenwart*. Ed. Walter Hinck. Düsseldorf: August Bagel, 1977.

Pfoser, Alfred. *Literatur und Austromarxismus*. Vienna: Löcker, 1980.

Pfoser, Alfred, Kristina Pfoser-Schweig, and Gerhard Renner, eds. *Schnitzlers "Reigen." Zehn Dialoge und ihre Skandalgeschichte*. Vol. I: *Der Skandal: Analysen und Dokumente*. Vol. II: *Die Prozesse: Analyse und Dokumente*. Frankfurt: Fischer, 1993.

Pinson, Koppel S. *Modern Germany. Its History and Civilization*. New York: The Macmillan Company, 1954.

Politzer, Heinz. "Arthur Schnitzler: The Poetry of Psychology." *Modern Language Notes* 78 (1963).

————. "Nachwort" to *Leutnant Gustl. By Arthur Schnitzler*. Berlin: Fischer, 1962. 40–50

————. *Das Schweigen der Sirenen. Studien zur deutschen und österreichischen Literatur*. Stuttgart: Metzler, 1968.

Pollock, Griselda. *Vision and Difference: Femininity, Feminism, and Histories of Art.* New York: Routledge, 1988.

Polt-Heinzl, Evelyne. *Erläuterungen und Dokumente: Arthur Schnitzler: Leutnant Gustl.* Stuttgart: Reclam, 2000.

Pronay-Strasser, Inge. "Von Ornithologen und Grashupgerinnen: Bemerkungen zur Sexualität um 1900." In Ehalt et al., eds., *Glücklich ist, wer vergisst,* 113–32.

Purschke, Hans R. *Die Anfänge der Puppenspielformen und ihre vermutlichen Ursprünge.* Bochum: Deutsches Institut für Puppenspiel e. V., 1979.

Qualtinger, Helmut. "Reigen 51." In *Der Herr Karl und andere Texte fürs Theater.* Vol. I. Ed. Traugott Krischke. Vienna: Deuticke, 1995. 75–161.

Rabinovici, Doron, *Suche nach M.* Frankfurt: Suhrkamp, 1997.

Radcliffe-Umstead, Douglas. "The Erudite Comic Tradition of the commedia dell'arte." In *The Science of Buffoonery: Theory and History of the Commedia dell'Arte.* Ed. Domenico Pietropaolo. Toronto: Dovehouse, 1989.

Raphael, Frederic. "Introduction." *Dream Story. By Arthur Schnitzler.* Trans. J.M.Q. Davies. New York: Penguin, 1999. v–xvii.

Raymond, Cathy. "Masked in Music: Hidden Meaning in Schnitzler's *Fräulein Else.*" *Monatshefte* 85 (1993): 170–88.

Rey, William H. *Arthur Schnitzler: Die späte Prosa als Gipfel seines Schaffens.* Berlin: Erich Schmidt, 1968.

Reid, Maja D. "Andreas Thameyers letzter Brief" and "Der letzte Brief eines Literaten": Two Neglected Schnitzler Stories." *German Quarterly* 45 (1972): 443–60.

Richard, Kenneth. *The Commedia dell'Arte: A Documentary History.* Oxford: Blackwell, 1990. 11–31.

Rimmon-Kenan, Shlomith. *Narrative Fiction: Contemporary Poetics.* London: Methuen, 1983.

Ringel, Erwin. *Das Leben Wegwerfen? Reflexionen über den Selbstmord.* Vienna: Herder, 1978.

———. "Das Selbstmordproblem bei Schnitzler." *Literatur und Kritik.* 161–2 (1982): 33–51.

Roberts, Adrian Clive. *Arthur Schnitzler and Politics.* Riverside: Ariadne, 1989.

Rohling, August. *Der Talmudjude: zur Beherzigung für Juden und Christen aller Stände* Münster: Adolph Russell's Verlag, 1872.

Rohrwasser, Michael. "Arthur Schnitzler's Erzählung 'Die Weissagung': Asthetizismus, Antisemitismus und Psychoanalyse." *Zeitschrift für deutsche Philologie* 118 (1999 Supplement): 60–79.

Rommel, Otto. *Die alt-wiener Volkskomödie. Ihre Geschichte vom Barocken Welt-Theater bis zum Tode Nestroys.* Vienna: Anton Schroll, 1952.

Rothfield, Lawrence. *Vital Signs: Medical Realism in Nineteenth-Century Fiction*. Princeton: Princeton UP, 1992.

Rozenblit, Marsha. *The Jews of Vienna, 1867–1914: Assimilation and Identity*. Albany: State U of New York P, 1983.

Rudlin, John. *Commedia dell'Arte: An Actor's Handbook*. London and New York: Routledge, 1994.

Ryan, Judith. "Arthur Schnitzler." In *The Vanishing Subject. Early Psychology and Literary Modernism*. Chicago and London: U of Chicago P, 1991. 127–37.

Sabler, Wolfgang. "Moderne und Boulvardtheater." *Text + Kritik* 4 (1998): 89–101.

Salten, Felix. *Bambi. Eine Lebensgeschichte aus dem Walde*. Berlin/Vienna/Leipzig: Paul Zsolnay Verlag, 1928.

———. *Bambis Kinder. Eine Familie im Walde*. Zurich: Albert Müller Verlag, 1940.

———. *Freunde aus aller Welt. Roman eines zoologischen Gartens*. Berlin/Vienna/Leipzig: Paul Zsolnay Verlag, 1931.

———. *Neue Menschen auf alter Erde. Eine Palästinareise*. Berlin/Vienna/Leipzig: Paul Zsolnay Verlag, 1925.

Saltzman, Lisa. *Anselm Kiefer and Art After Auschwitz*. Cambridge: Cambridge UP, 1999.

Santner, Eric L. "Of Masters, Slaves and Other Seducers: Arthur Schnitzler's Traumnovelle." *Modern Austrian Literature* 19/3–4 (1986): 33–48.

Sartre, Jean-Paul. *Baudelaire*. Trans. Martin Turnell. New York: New Directions, 1950.

Scheffel, Michael. *Formen selbstreflexiven Erzählens: Eine Typologie und sechs exemplarische Analysen*. Tübingen: Niemeyer, 1997.

———. "'Ich will dir alles erzählen': Von der 'Märchenhaftigkeit des Alltäglichen' in Arthur Schnitzlers *Traumnovelle*." *Arthur Schnitzler: Text + Kritik* 138/139 (1998): 123–37.

Scheible, Hartmut. *Arthur Schnitzler in Selbstzeugnissen und Bilddokumenten*. Reinbek bei Hamburg: Rowohlt, 1976.

———. *Liebe und Liberalismus: Über Arthur Schnitzler*. Bielefeld: Aisthesis Verlag, 1996.

Scheible, Hartmut, ed. *Arthur Schnitzler in neuer Sicht*. Munich: Wilhelm Fink, 1981.

Scheichl, Sigurd Paul. "Juden, die keine Juden sind: Die Figuren in Schnitzler's Fink und Fliederbusch." In *Von Franzos zu Canetti: Jüdische Autoren aus Österreich, Neue Studien*. Eds. Mark H. Gelber, Hans Otto Horch, Sigurd Paul Scheichl. *Conditio Judaica* 14. Tübingen: Max Niemeyer, 1996. 225–38.

Schindel, Robert. *Gebürtig.* Frankfurt: Suhrkamp, 1992.

Schinnerer, Otto P. "Schnitzler and the Military Censorship. Unpublished Correspondence." *Germanic Review* 5/3 (1930): 241–42.

Schnabel, Werner Wilhelm. "Professor Bernhardi und die Wiener Zensur: Zur Rezeptionsgeschichte der Schnitzlerschen Komödie." *Jahrbuch der Deutschen Schillergesellschaft* 28 (1984): 349–83.

Schnabl, Katja Sturm. "Soziales Engagement und symbolistische Stilmittel bei Ivan Cankar. Das Wien der Jahrhundertwende aus der Jahrhunderwende eines europäisch-slowenischen Autors." *Trans: Internet-Zeitschrift für Kulturwissenschaften* 7 (September 1999): 1–6.

Schneider, Gerd K. "The Reception of Arthur Schnitzler's Reigen in the Old Country and the New World: A Study in Cultural Differences." *Modern Austrian Literature* 19/3–4 (1986): 75–90.

———. *Die Rezeption von Arthur Schnitzlers Reigen 1897–1994. Text, Aufführungen, Verfilmungen; Pressespiegel und andere zeitgenössische Kommentare.* Riverside: Ariadne Press, 1995.

Schneider-Halvorson, Brigitte L. *The Late Dramatic Works of Arthur Schnitzler.* New York: Peter Lang, 1983.

Schnitzler, Heinrich, Christian Brandstätter, and Reinhard Urbach, eds. *Arthur Schnitzler. Sein Leben. Sein Werk. Seine Zeit.* Frankfurt: Fischer, 1981.

Schnitzler, Olga. *Spiegelbild der Freundschaft.* Salzburg: Residenz, 1962.

Schorske, Carl E. *Fin-de-Siècle Vienna. Politics and Culture.* New York: Vintage Books/A Division of Random House, 1981.

———. "Politics and the Psyche." In Schorske, *Fin-de-Siècle Vienna. Politics and Culture.* New York: Vintage Books, 1981. 1–23.

———. *Thinking with History. Explorations in the Passage to Modernism.* Princeton: Princeton UP, 1999.

Schwab, Werner. *Der Reizende Reigen nach dem Reigen des reizenden Herrn Arthur Schnitzler.* Graz: Literaturverlag Droschl, 1996.

Schwarz, Egon. "Arthur Schnitzler und das Judentum." In *Im Zeichen Hiobs: Jüdische Schriftsteller und deutsche Literatur im 20. Jahrhundert.* Eds. Gunter E. Grimm and Hans-Peter Bayerdörfer. Königstein: Athenäum, 1985. 67–83.

———. "Jews and Anti-Semitism in Fin-de-Siècle Vienna." In Lorenz and Weinberger, eds., *Insiders and Outsiders.* 47–65.

———. "Milieu oder Mythos?: Wien in den Werken Arthur Schnitzlers." *Literatur und Kritik* 163/164 (1982): 22–35.

———. "1921. The Staging of Arthur Schnitzler's Play Reigen Creates a Public Uproar That Draws Involvement by the Press, the Police, the Viennese City Administration, and the Austrian Parliament." In *Yale Companion to Jewish Writing and Thought in German Culture 1096–1996*. Eds. Sander L. Gilman and Jack Zipes. New Haven and London: Yale UP, 1997. 412–19.

Schwartz Seller, Maxine. *Ethnic Theatre in the United States*. Greenwood, CT and London: Greenwood Press, 1983.

Sebald, W. G. "Das Schrecknis der Liebe: Zu Schnitzlers *Traumnovelle*." In *Die Beschreibung des Unglücks: Zur österreichischen Literatur von Stifter bis Handke*. Vienna: Residenz, 1985.

Segal, Naomi. "Style indirect libre to Stream-of-Consciousness: Flaubert, Joyce, Schnitzler, Woolf." In *Modernism and the European Unconscious*. Ed. Peter Collier and Judy Davies. Cambridge: Polity Press, 1990. 94–126.

Segar, Kenneth. "Determinism and Character: Arthur Schnitzler's *Traumnovelle* and his Unpublished Critique of Psychoanalysis." *Oxford Germanic Studies* 8 (1973): 114–27.

Seidler, Herbert. "Die Forschung zu Arthur Schnitzler seit 1945." *Zeitschrift für Deutsche Philologie* 95/4 (1976): 567–95.

Selling, Gunter. *Die Einakter und Einakterzyklen Arthur Schnitzlers*. Amsterdam: Rodopi, 1975.

Senocak, Zafer. "Ein Türke geht nicht in die Oper." In *Atlas des tropischen Deutschland*. Berlin: Babel Verlag, 1993.

Sexton, Anne. *The Death Notebooks*. Boston: Houghton Mifflin, 1974.

———. *Live or Die*. Boston: Houghton Mifflin, 1974.

Sherman, Murray H. "Reik, Schnitzler, Freud, and 'The Murderer.'" *Modern Austrian Literature* 10/3–4 (1977): 163–67.

Sichrovsky, Peter. *Wir wissen nicht was morgen wird, wir wissen wohl was gestern war: Junge Juden in Deutschland und Österreich*. Cologne: Kiepenheuer und Witsch, 1985.

Sieder, Reinhard. "'Vata, derf i aufstehn?': Kindheitserfahrungen in Wiener Arbeiterfamilienum 1900." In Ehalt et al., eds., *Glücklich ist, wer vergisst*. 38–39.

Simon, Karl Günter. *Pantomime. Ursprung, Wesen, Möglichkeiten*. Munich: Nymphenburger Verlagshandlung, 1960.

Sonnleitner, Johann. "Die Rezeption der Wiener Moderne in Österreich. Schnitzler und Hofmannsthal nach 1945." In *Die einen raus, die anderen rein. Kanon und Literatur. Vorüberlegungen. Zu einer Literaturgeschichte Österreichs*. Eds. Wendelin Schmidt-Dengler, Johann Sonnleitner, and Klaus Zeyringer. Berlin: Schmidt, 1994. 158–59.

Sontheimer, Kurt. *Antidemokratisches Denken in der Weimarer Republik*. Munich: Deutscher Taschenbuch Verlag, 1992.

Specht, Richard. *Arthur Schnitzler. Der Dichter und sein Werk.* Berlin: Fischer, 1922.

Spiel, Hilde. "Im Abgrund der Triebwelt oder Kein Zugang zum Fest. Zu Schnitzlers 'Traumnovelle.'" In *Akten des Internationalen Symposions "Arthur Schnitzler und seine Zeit."* Ed. Guiseppe Farese. Bern: Peter Lang, 1985. 164–71.

Squercina, Marianna. "History and Fiction in a Drama on Revolution: Arthur Schnitzler's *Der grüne Kakadu.*" *New German Review* 5/6 (1989–90).

Starrels, Carol S. *The Problem of the "Puppenspieler" in the Works of Arthur Schnitzler.* Ph.D. diss., University of Pennsylvania, 1973.

Steinberg, Michael P. *Austria as Theater and Ideology: The Meaning of the Salzburg Festival.* Ithaca: Cornell UP, 2000.

Stock, Fritjof. "Casanova als Don Juan: Bemerkungen über Arthur Schnitzlers Novelle Casanovas Heimfahrt und sein Lustspiel Die Schwestern oder Casanova in Spa." *Arcadia* (1978): 56–65.

Stoppard, Tom. *Undiscovered Country.* Boston and London: Faber & Faber, 1980.

Strelka, Joseph P., ed. *Die Seele . . . ist ein weites Land: Kritische Beiträge zum Werk Arthur Schnitzlers.* Bern: Peter Lang, 1996.

Sulloway, Frank J. *Freud: Biologist of the Mind.* New York: Basic Books, 1979.

Swales, Martin. *Arthur Schnitzler. A Critical Study.* Oxford: Clarendon Press, 1971.

Tagg, John. "The Discontinuous City: Picturing and the Discursive Field," In *Visual Culture: Images and Interpretations.* Ed. Norman Bryson, Michael Ann Holly, and Keith Moxey. Hanover, NH: Wesleyan UP, 1994. 83–103.

Trautmann, Joanne, and Carol Pollard. *Literature and Medicine: An Annotated Bibliography.* Pittsburgh: U of Pittsburgh P, 1982.

———. "Schnitzler als Realist." *Literatur und Kritik* 161/162 (1982): 52–61.

Tabor, Jan. "An dieser Blume gehst Du zugrunde: Bleich, purpurot, weiß — Krankheit als Inspiration." In Ehalt et al., eds., *Glücklich ist, wer vergisst.* 235–43.

Talos, Emmerich, and Wolfgang Neugebauer. *Austrofaschismus. Beiträge über Politik, Ökonomie und Kultur 1934–1938.* Vienna: Verlag für Gesellschaftskritik, 1988.

Tax, Petrus W., and Richard H. Lawson, eds. *Arthur Schnitzler and his Age. Intellectual and Artistic Currents.* Bonn: Bouvier, 1984.

Tenenti, Alberto. *Die Grundlegung der modernen Welt: Spätmittelalter, Renaissance, Reformation.* Frankfurt: Fischer, 1984.

Thomé, Horst. *Autonomes Ich und Inneres Ausland: Studien über Realismus, Tiefenpsychologie und Psychiatrie in deutschen Erzähltexten 1848–1918.* Tübingen: Niemeyer, 1993.

———. "Kernlosigkeit und Pose: Zur Rekonstruktion von Schnitzlers Psychologie." *Text-und-Kontext* 20 (1984): 62–87. Also in *Fin de Siècle*. Ed. Klause Bohnen. Copenhagen: Fink, 1984. 62–84.

———. Preface. *Medizinische Schriften*. Ed. Horst Thomé. Frankfurt: Fischer, 1991.

———. "Sozialgeschichtliche Perspektiven der neueren Schnitzler-Forschung." In *Internationales Archiv für Sozialgeschichte der Deutschen Literatur* 13 (1988): 158–87.

Thompson, Bruce. "Politics and the Jewish Question." In *Schnitzler's Vienna. Image of a Society*. London and New York: Routledge, 1990. 160–76.

Tickner, Lisa. "Men's Work? Masculinity and Modernism." In *Visual Culture: Images and Interpretations*. Ed. Norman Bryson, Michael Ann Holly, and Keith Moxey. Hanover, NH: Wesleyan UP; UP of New England, 1994. 42–82.

Tieck, Ludwig. *Prinz Zerbino oder die Reise nach dem guten Geschmack*. In Vol. 10 of *Schriften*. Berlin: de Gruyter, 1966.

Timms, Edward. *Karl Kraus Apocalyptic Satirist: Culture and Catastrophe in Habsburg Vienna*. New Haven: Yale UP, 1986.

Törnsee, Fr[iedrich]. "Bücherschau: Arthur Schnitzlers *Reigen*." *Neue Bahnen* 3/4 (May 1, 1903): 245.

Tucholsky, Kurt [Ignaz Wrobel, pseud.]. "Brunner im Amt." *Die Weltbühne* 18/36 (September 1922): 266–67.

Tweraser, Felix W. *Political Dimensions of Arthur Schnitzler's Late Fiction*. Columbia, SC: Camden House, 1998.

Urbach, Reinhard. *Arthur Schnitzler*. Velber bei Hannover: Friedrich, 1968.

———. *Schnitzler-Kommentar zu den erzählenden Schriften und dramatischen Werken*. Munich: Winkler, 1974.

Urban, Bernd. "Arthur Schnitzler und Sigmund Freud: Aus den Anfängen des Doppelgängers. Zur Differenzierung dichterischer Intuition und Umgebung der frühen Hysterieforschung." *Germanisch-Romanische Monatschrift* 24 (1974): 193–223.

———. John Menzies, and Peter Nutting. "Schnitzler and Freud as Doubles: Poetic Intuition and Early Research on Hysteria." *Psychoanalytic Review* 65 (1978): 131–65.

Volkelt, Johannes. "Ueber Schnitzlers *Reigen*." *Voralberger Tagblatt* (February 15, 1921): 1–2.

Völker, Klaus. *Fritz Kortner. Schauspieler und Regisseur*. Berlin: Hentrich, 1987

Völpel, Annegret. "1928." In *Yale Companion to Jewish Writing and Thought in German Culture 1096–1996*. Eds. Sander L. Gilman and Jack Zipes. New Haven and London: Yale UP, 1997. 485–91.

Wagner, Renate. *Arthur Schnitzler: Eine Biographie.* Vienna: Fritz Molden, 1981.

Wagner, Renate, and Brigitte Vacha. *Wiener Schnitzler-Aufführungen 1891–1970.* Munich: Prestel Verlag, 1971.

Wassermann, Jakob. *Mein Weg als Deutscher und Jude.* Berlin: Fischer, 1921.

Watanabe-O'Kelly, Helen. "The early modern period (1450–1720)." In *The Cambridge History of German Literature.* Ed. Helen Watanabe-O'Kelly. Cambridge: Cambridge UP, 1997.

Weber, Hartwig. *Lexikon Religion.* Reinbek bei Hamburg: Rowohlt Taschenbuch Verlag, 2001.

Weigel, Hans, ed. *Olga Waissnix. Liebe, die starb vor der Zeit. Ein Briefwechsel.* Vienna: Fritz Molden, 1970.

Weinberger, G. J. *Arthur Schnitzler's Late Plays: A Critical Study.* Peter Lang. New York, 1997.

———. "'Sicherheit ist nirgends': Arthur Schnitzler's *Paracelsus* Revisited." *Neophilologus* 77 (1993): 249–59.

Weinhold, Ulrike. "Arthur Schnitzler und der weibliche Diskurs: Zur Problematik des Frauenbildes der Jahrhundertwende." *Jahrbuch für Internationale Germanistik* 19/1 (1987): 110–45.

Weininger, Otto. *Geschlecht und Charakter. Eine prinzipielle Untersuchung.* Vienna: Braumüller, 1903; 1906.

Weinzierl, Ulrich. *Arthur Schnitzler. Lieben, Träumen, Sterben.* Frankfurt: Fischer, 1994.

Weiss, Robert O. "The Psychoses in the Works of Arthur Schnitzler." *German Quarterly* 41/3 (1968): 377–400.

———. "A Study of the Psychiatric Elements in Schnitzler's *Flucht in die Finsternis.*" *Germanic Review* 33/4 (1958): 189–275.

Weitzmann, Walter R. "The Politics of the Viennese Jewish Community, 1890–1914." *Jews, Antisemitism and Culture in Vienna.* Eds. Ivar Oxaal et al. London and New York: Routledge/Kegan Paul, 1987. 121–51.

Wiesmayr, Elisabeth. "Patt der Herzen: Inszenierungen der Liebe im fin de siècle." In Ehalt et al., eds., *Glücklich ist, wer vergisst.* 133–44.

Willi, Andrea. *Arthur Schnitzlers Roman 'Der Weg ins Freie.' Eine Untersuchung zur Tageskritik und ihren zeitgenössischen Bezügen.* Heidelberg: Carl Winter, 1989.

Wistrich, Robert. *The Jews of Vienna in the Age of Franz Joseph.* Oxford: Oxford UP, 1990.

Wolf, Friedrich. *Professor Mamlock.* Berlin: Volk und Wissen, 1957.

Wolfe, Alan Stephen. *Suicidal Narrative in Modern Japan: The Case of Dazai Osamu.* Princeton, NJ: Princeton UP, 1990.

Wolff, Lutz-W. "'Bürger der Endzeit': Schnitzler in socialistischer Sicht." In Hartmut Scheible, ed., *Arthur Schnitzler in neuer Sicht*, 330–59.

Wood, Michael. "Quite a Night!" *London Review of Books* (September 20, 1999): 52.

Worbs, Michael. *Nervenkunst: Literatur und Psychoanalyse in Wien der Jahrhundertwende*. Frankfurt am Main: Athenäum, 1983.

Yates, W. E. "The Tendentious Reception of Professor Bernhardi: Documentation in Schnitzler's Collection of Press-Cuttings." In *Vienna 1900: From Altenberg to Wittgenstein*. Austrian Studies 1. Eds. Edward Timms and Ritchie Robertson. Edinburgh: Edinburgh UP, 1990. 108–25.

———. *Theatre in Vienna. A Critical History, 1776–1995*. Cambridge: Cambridge UP, 1996.

Yeo, Siew Lian. "'Entweder oder': Dualism in Schnitzler's *Fräulein Else*." *Modern Austrian Literature* 32/2 (1999): 15–26.

Zettl, Walter. "Der politische und soziale Hintergrund für das Werk Arthur Schnitzlers." In *Studia Schnitzleriana*. Ed. Fausto Cerciganani. Allessandria: Orso, 1991. 107–20.

Zipes, Jack. "The Contemporary German Fascination for Things Jewish: Toward a Minor Jewish Culture." In *Reemerging Jewish Cultures in Germany*. Eds. Sander L. Gilman and Karen Remmler. New York: New York UP, 1994. 15–45.

Žmegač, Viktor. "Die Wiener Moderne." In *Geschichte der deutschen Literatur vom 18. Jahrhundert bis zur Gegenwart*. Vol. II/2. Ed. Viktor Žmegač. Königstein/Ts: Athenäum, 1980.

Zweig, Stefan. *Die Welt von gestern: Erinnerungen eines Europäers*. Frankfurt: Fischer, 1998.

Index